W9-BDL-652

EXHIBIT 1-9 Financial Statements of Cookie Lapp Travel Design, Inc.

COOKIE LAPP TRAVEL DESIGN, INC.
Income Statement
Month Ended April 30, 2008

Revenue:		
Service revenue		$8,500
Expenses:		
Salary expense	$1,200	
Rent expense, office	1,100	
Rent expense, computer	600	
Utilities expense	400	
Total expenses		3,300
Net income		$5,200

1

COOKIE LAPP TRAVEL DESIGN, INC.
Statement of Retained Earnings
Month Ended April 30, 2008

Retained earnings, April 1, 2008	$ 0
Add: Net income for the month	5,200
	5,200
Less: Dividends	(2,000)
Retained earnings, April 30, 2008	$3,200

2

COOKIE LAPP TRAVEL DESIGN, INC.
Balance Sheet
April 30, 2008

Assets		Liabilities	
Cash	$19,900	Accounts payable	$ 200
Accounts receivable	2,000	**Stockholders' Equity**	
Office supplies	500	Common stock	30,000
Land	11,000	Retained earnings	3,200
		Total stockholders' equity	33,200
Total assets	$33,400	Total liabilities and stockholders' equity	$33,400

3

COOKIE LAPP TRAVEL DESIGN, INC.
Statement of Cash Flows*
Month Ended April 30, 2008

Cash flows from operating activities:		
Receipts:		
Collections from customers ($5,500 + $1,000)		$ 6,500
Payments:		
To suppliers ($600 + $1,100 + $400 + $300)	$ (2,400)	
To employees	(1,200)	(3,600)
Net cash provided by operating activities		2,900
Cash flows from investing activities:		
Acquisition of land	$(20,000)	
Sale of land	9,000	
Net cash used for investing activities		(11,000)
Cash flows from financing activities:		
Issuance of stock	$ 30,000	
Dividends	(2,000)	
Net cash provided by financing activities		28,000
Net increase in cash		19,900
Cash balance, April 1, 2008		0
Cash balance, April 30, 2008		$19,900

*Chapter 16 shows how to prepare this statement.

Color-Coded Accounting Equation

This color-coded accounting equation is a tool you will use throughout your first accounting course. This tool is so important that we have to put it here for quick reference. You may find this helpful when preparing your homework assignments. Each financial statement is identified by a unique color. You will see these colors throughout the chapters when we present a financial statement.

1 The **income statement**, enclosed in the red box, provides the details of revenues earned and expenses incurred.

2 The revenue and expense transactions are then condensed into one number—net income—that becomes part of the **statement of retained earnings**, which appears in the yellow box.

3 Information from the statement of retained earnings flows into the **balance sheet**, shown in the blue box.

4 The **statement of cash flows**, as indicated by the green box, provides details of how a company got its cash and how it spent cash during the accounting period.

Financial and Managerial Accounting

Chapters 1–13

1e

Charles T. Horngren Series in Accounting

Auditing and Assurance Services: An Integrated Approach, 11th ed.
Arens/Elder/Beasley

Governmental and Nonprofit Accounting: Theory and Practice, 8th ed.
Freeman/Shoulders

Financial Accounting, 6th ed.
Harrison/Horngren

Cases in Financial Reporting, 5th ed.
Hirst/McAnally

Cost Accounting: A Managerial Emphasis, 12th ed.
Horngren/Datar/Foster

Accounting, 7th ed.
Horngren/Harrison

Introduction to Financial Accounting, 9th ed.
Horngren/Sundem/Elliott

Introduction to Management Accounting, 13th ed.
Horngren/Sundem/Stratton

Financial and Managerial Accounting
Chapters 1–13

Charles T. Horngren
Stanford University

Walter T. Harrison Jr.
Baylor University

Upper Saddle River, New Jersey 07458

Library of Congress Cataloging-in-Publication Data
Horngren, Charles T.
Financial and managerial accounting / Charles T. Horgren, Walter T. Harrison
p. cm.
Includes index.
ISBN 978-0-13-156877-8
1. Accounting. 2. Managerial accounting. I. Harrison, Walter T. II. Title.
HF5636.H67 2007
657—dc22 2006103241

Executive Editor: Jodi McPherson
Editorial Director: Jeff Shelstad
Developmental Editors: Claire Hunter, Ralph Moore
Product Development Manager, Media: Nancy Welcher
Executive Marketing Manager: Sharon Koch
Associate Director, Production Editorial: Judy Leale
Permissions Supervisor: Charles Morris
Manufacturing Manager: Arnold Vila
Creative Director: Maria Lange
Cover Design: Solid State Graphics
Illustrator (Interior): BookMasters, Inc.
Director, Image Resource Center: Melinda Patelli
Manager, Rights and Permissions: Zina Arabia
Manager, Visual Research: Beth Brenzel
Manager, Cover Visual Research & Permissions: Karen Sanatar
Image Permission Coordinator: Nancy Seise
Photo Researcher: Diane Austin
Composition/Full-Service Project Management: BookMasters, Inc.
Printer/Binder: RR Donnelley–Willard
Typeface: 10/12 Sabon

Credits and acknowledgments borrowed from other sources and reproduced, with permission, in this textbook appear on appropriate page within text.

Pearson Education LTD.
Pearson Education Singapore, Pte. Ltd
Pearson Education, Canada, Ltd
Pearson Education–Japan
Pearson Education Australia PTY, Limited
Pearson Education North Asia Ltd
Pearson Educación de Mexico, S.A. de C.V.
Pearson Education Malaysia, Pte. Ltd

10 9 8 7 6 5 4 3 2
ISBN-13: 978-0-13-614301-7
ISBN-10: 0-13-614301-6

Brief Contents

Contents

2 Recording Business Transactions 60

6 Merchandise Inventory 314

7 Internal Control and Cash 356

11 Corporations: Paid-In Capital and the Balance Sheet 544

To Billie Harrison, who taught me excellence

The *Financial and Managerial Accounting, 1e,* Demo Doc System:
For professors whose greatest joy is hearing students say "I get it!"

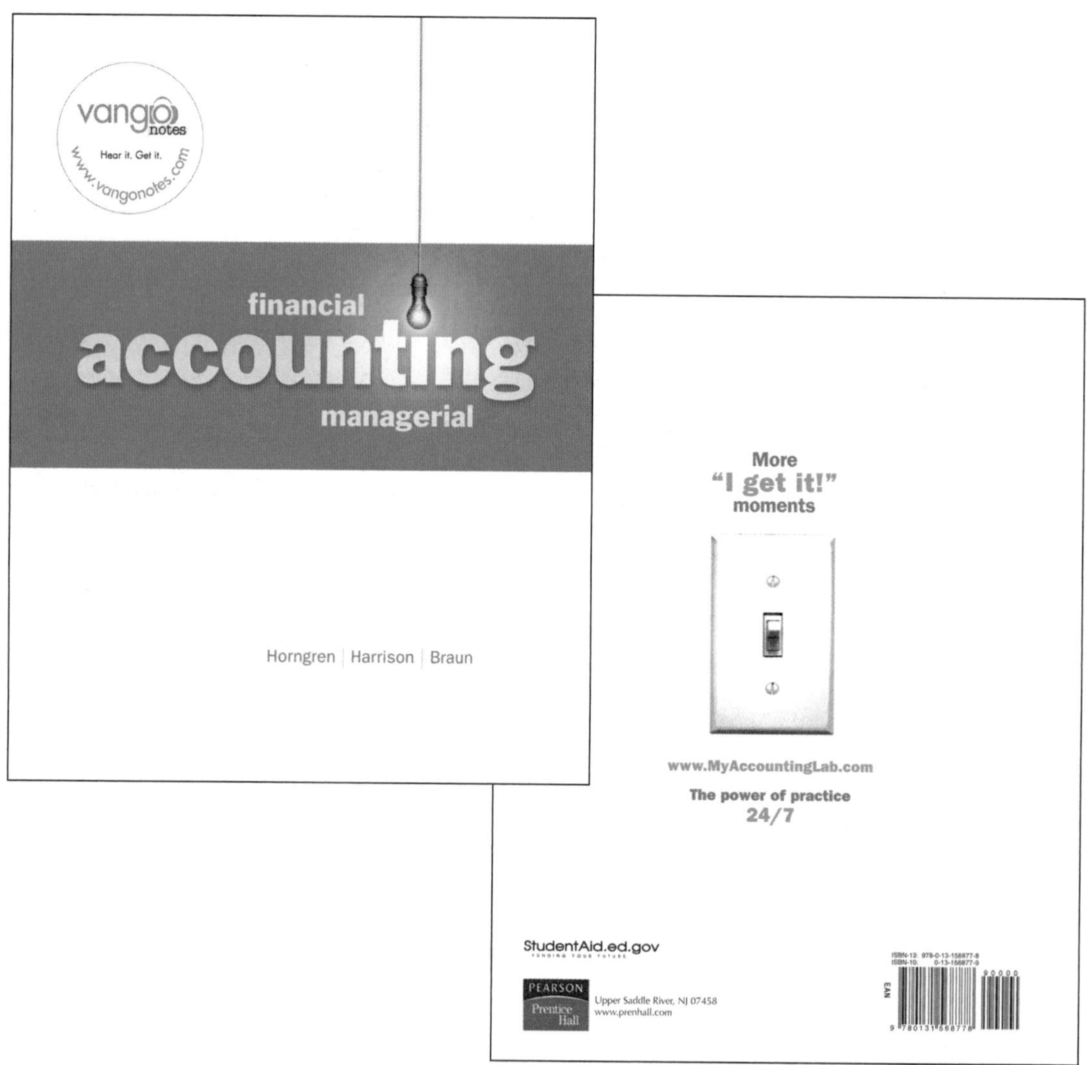

Help your students achieve "I get it!" moments when you're with them AND when you're NOT.

When you're there demonstrating how to solve a problem in class, students "get it." When you're not there, they get stuck—it's only natural.

You deliver the best "I get it!" moments, so our system is designed to support you in the classroom. (Instructor's Edition, Instructor Demo Docs)

But it's the really tricky moments, the ones no one else has zeroed in on—the 2 A.M. outside-of-class moments, when you're not there—that present the greatest challenge.

That's where we come in, at these "they have the book, but they don't have you" moments. The ability of the *Financial and Managerial Accounting, 1e,* Demo Doc System will help in those critical times. That's what makes this package different from all other textbooks.

The *Financial and Managerial Accounting, 1e,* Demo Doc System provides the vehicle for you and your students to have more "I get it!" moments inside and outside of class.

The *Financial and Managerial* Accounting, Demo Doc System

Duplicate the classroom experience anytime, anywhere with Horngren and Harrison's *Financial and Managerial Accounting.*

How The System Works

- The Demo Docs are entire problems worked through step-by-step, from start to finish, with the kind of comments around them that YOU would say in class. They exist in the first four chapters of this text to support the critical accounting cycle chapters, in the Study Guide both in print and in Flash versions, and as a part of the instructor package for instructors to use in class.
- The authors have created a "no clutter" layout so that critical content is clear and easily referenced.
- Consistency is stressed across all mediums: text, student, and instructor supplements.
- MyAccountingLab is an online homework system that combines "I get it!" moments with the power of practice.

The System's Backbone

Demo Docs in the Text, the Study Guide, and MyAccountingLab.

► ***NEW*** **DEMO DOCS** – Introductory accounting students consistently tell us, "When doing homework, I get stuck trying to solve problems the way they were demonstrated in class." Instructors consistently tell us, "I have so much to cover in so little time; I can't afford to go backward and review homework in class." Those challenges inspired us to develop Demo Docs. Demo Docs are comprehensive worked-through problems, available for nearly every chapter of our introductory accounting text, to help students when they are trying to solve exercises and problems on their own. The idea is to help students duplicate the classroom experience outside of class. Entire problems that mirror end-of-chapter material are shown solved and annotated with explanations written in a conversational style, essentially imitating what an instructor might say if standing over a student's shoulder. All Demo Docs will be available online in Flash and in print so students can easily refer to them when and where they need them.

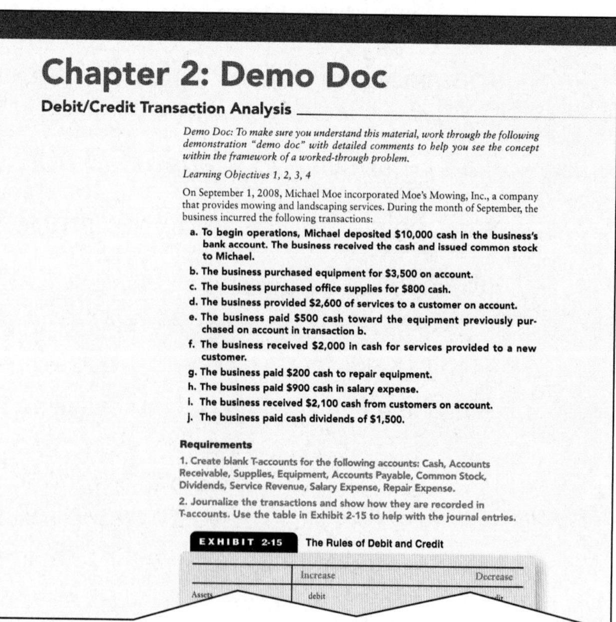

Chapter 2: Demo Doc

Debit/Credit Transaction Analysis

Demo Doc: To make sure you understand this material, work through the following demonstration "demo doc" with detailed comments to help you see the concept within the framework of a worked-through problem.

Learning Objectives 1, 2, 3, 4

On September 1, 2008, Michael Moe incorporated Moe's Mowing, Inc., a company that provides mowing and landscaping services. During the month of September, the business incurred the following transactions:

a. **To begin operations, Michael deposited $10,000 cash in the business's bank account. The business received the cash and issued common stock to Michael.**
b. **The business purchased equipment for $3,500 on account.**
c. **The business purchased office supplies for $800 cash.**
d. **The business provided $2,600 of services to a customer on account.**
e. **The business paid $500 cash toward the equipment previously purchased on account in transaction b.**
f. **The business received $2,000 in cash for services provided to a new customer.**
g. **The business paid $200 cash to repair equipment.**
h. **The business paid $900 cash in salary expense.**
i. **The business received $2,100 cash from customers on account.**
j. **The business paid cash dividends of $1,500.**

Requirements

1. Create blank T-accounts for the following accounts: Cash, Accounts Receivable, Supplies, Equipment, Accounts Payable, Common Stock, Dividends, Service Revenue, Salary Expense, Repair Expense.
2. Journalize the transactions and show how they are recorded in T-accounts. Use the table in Exhibit 2-15 to help with the journal entries.

EXHIBIT 2-15 The Rules of Debit and Credit

	Increase	Decrease
Assets	debit	[illegible]

MyAccountingLab – This online homework and assessment tool supports the same theme as the text and resources by providing "I get it!" moments inside and outside of class. It is in MyAccountingLab where "I get it!" moments meet the power of practice. MyAccountingLab is about helping students at their teachable moment, whether that is 1 P.M. or 1 A.M. MyAccountingLab is packed with algorithmic problems because practice makes perfect. It is also packed with the exact same end-of-chapter material in the text that you are used to assigning for homework. MyAccountingLab features the same look and feel for exercises and problems in journal entries and financial statements so that students are familiar and comfortable working in it. Because it includes a Demo Doc for each of the end-of-chapter exercises and problems that students can refer to as they work through the question, it extends The System just one step further by providing students with the help they need to succeed when you are not with them.

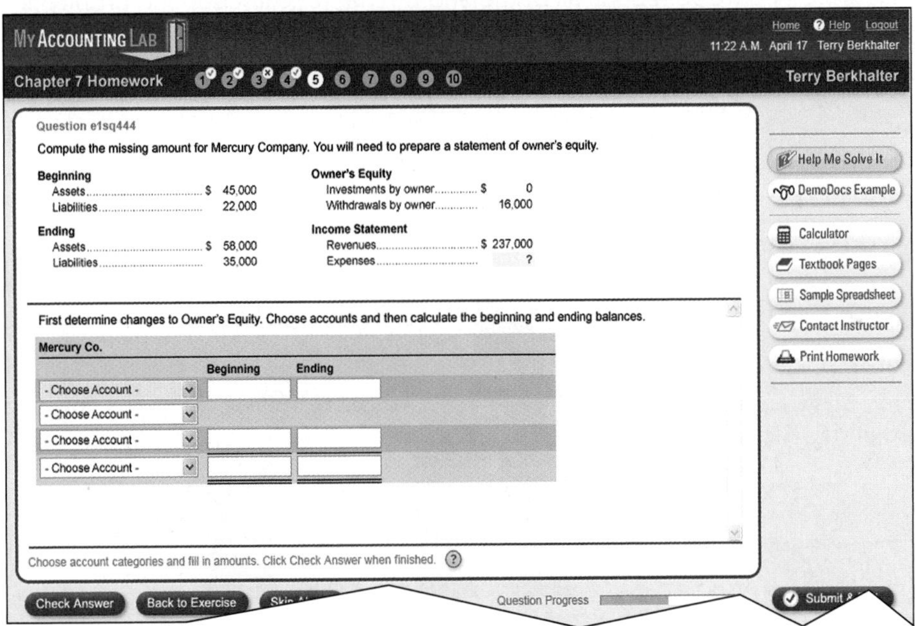

The System's Details

CHAPTERS 1–4 – We know it's critical that students have a solid understanding of the fundamentals and language surrounding the accounting cycle before they can move to practice. To that end, we're spending extra time developing the accounting cycle chapters (Chs 1–4) to make sure they will help students succeed. We're adding extra visuals, additional comprehensive problems, and a Demo Doc per chapter to give students additional support to move on through the material successfully. You'll be able to stay on schedule in the syllabus because students understand the accounting cycle.

CONSISTENCY – The entire package matters. Consistency in terminology and problem set-ups from one medium to another—test bank to study guide to MyAccountingLab—is critical to your success in the classroom. So when students ask "Where do the numbers come from?," they can go to our text ***or*** go online and see what to do. If it's worded one way in the text, you can count on it being worded the same way in the supplements.

CLUTTER-FREE – This edition is built on the premise of "Less is More." Extraneous boxes and features, non-essential bells and whistles—they are all gone. The authors know that excess crowds out what really matters—the concepts, the problems, and the learning objectives. Instructors asked for fewer "features" in favor of less clutter and better cross-referencing, and Horngren/Harrison, *Financial and Managerial Accounting, 1e,* is delivering on that wish. And we've redone all of the end-of-chapter exercises and problems with a renewed focus on the critical core concepts.

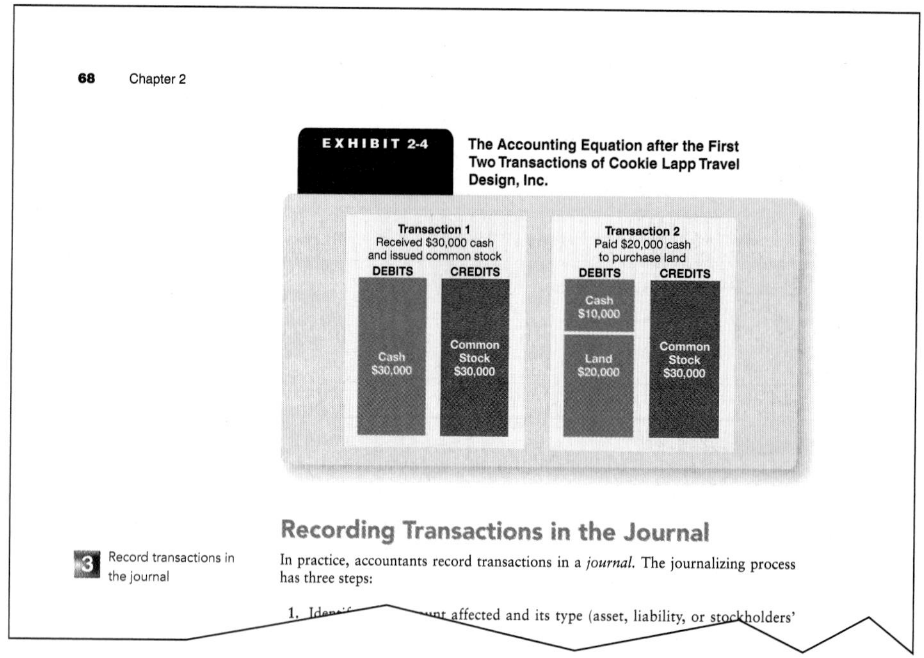

68 Chapter 2
EXHIBIT 2-4
The Accounting Equation after the First Two Transactions of Cookie Lapp Travel Design, Inc.
Transaction 1
Received $30,000 cash and issued common stock
DEBITS
CREDITS
Cash $30,000
Common Stock $30,000
Transaction 2
Paid $20,000 cash to purchase land
DEBITS
CREDITS
Cash $10,000
Land $20,000
Common Stock $30,000
Recording Transactions in the Journal
3 Record transactions in the journal
In practice, accountants record transactions in a journal. The journalizing process has three steps:

INSTRUCTOR SUPPLEMENTS

Instructor's Edition Featuring *Instructor Demo Docs*

▶ The New Look of the Instructor's Edition

We've asked a lot of instructors how we can help them successfully implement new course-delivery methods (e.g. online) while maintaining their regular campus schedule of classes and academic responsibilities. In response, we developed a system of instruction for those of you who are long on commitment and expertise—but short on time and assistance.

The primary goal of the Instructor's Edition is **ease of implementation, using any delivery method**—traditional, self-paced, or online. That is, the Instructor's Edition quickly answers for you, the professor, the question "What must the student do?" Likewise, the Instructor's Edition quickly answers for the student "What must I do?," offers time-saving tips with "best of" categories for in class discussion, and strong examples to illustrate difficult concepts to a wide variety of students. The Instructor's Edition also offers a quick one-shot cross-reference at the exact point of importance with key additional teaching resources, so everything is in one place. The Instructor's Edition includes summaries and teaching tips, pitfalls for new students, and "best of" practices from instructors from across the world.

▶ The Instructor's Edition also includes *Instructor Demo Docs*

In ***Instructor Demo Docs***, we walk the students through how to solve a problem as if it were the first time they've seen it. There are no lengthy passages of text. Instead, bits of expository text are woven into the steps needed to solve the problem, in the exact sequence—for you to provide at the teachable ***"I get it!"*** moment. This is the point at which the student has a context within which he or she can understand the concept. We provide conversational text around each of the steps so the student stays engaged in solving the problem. We provide notes to the instructor for key teaching points around the Demo Docs, and "best of" practice tid-bits before each ***Instructor Demo Doc***.

The ***Instructor Demo Docs*** are written with all of your everyday classroom realities in mind—and trying to save your time in prepping new examples each time your book changes. Additionally, algorithmic versions of these Demo Docs are provided to students in their student guide. We keep the terminology consistent with the text, so there are no surprises for students as they try and work through a problem the first time.

Solutions Transparencies

These transparency masters are the **Solutions Manual** in an easy-to-use format for class lectures.

Instructor's Resource Center CD or www.prenhall.com/horngren

The password-protected site and resource CD includes the following:

- **The Instructor's Edition with *Instructor Demo Docs***
- **Problem Set C**

- **Solutions Manual with Interactive Excel Solutions**

  The Solutions Manual contains solutions to all end-of-chapter questions, multiple-choice questions, short exercises, exercise sets, problems sets, and Internet exercises. The Solutions Manual is available in Microsoft Excel, Microsoft Word, and in print. You can access the solutions in MS Excel and MS Word formats by visiting the Instructor's Resource Center on the Prentice Hall catalog site at www.prenhall.com/horngren or on the Instructor's CD. You will need a Pearson Educator username and password to retrieve materials from the Web site.

  Solutions to select end-of-chapter exercises and problems are available in **interactive MS Excel format** so that instructors can present material in dynamic, step-by-step sequences in class. The interactive solutions were prepared by Kathleen O'Donnell of the State University of New York, Onondaga Community College.

- **Test Bank**

The test item file includes more than 2,000 questions:

- Multiple Choice
- Matching
- True/False
- Computational Problems
- Essay

- **Test Bank** is formatted for use with WebCT, Blackboard, and Course Compass.
- **PowerPoints (instructor and student)** summarize and reinforce key text materials. They capture classroom attention with original problems and solved step-by-step exercises. These walk-throughs are designed to help facilitate classroom discussion and demonstrate where the numbers come from and what they mean to the concept at hand. There are approximately 35 slides per chapter. PowerPoints are available on the Instructor's CD and can be downloaded from www.prenhall.com/horngren.

New *MyAccountingLab* Online Homework and Assessment Manager

The **"I get it!"** moment meets ***the power of practice***. The power of repetition when you "get it" means learning happens. **MyAccountingLab** is about helping students at their teachable moments, whether it's 1 P.M. or 1A.M.

MyAccountingLab is an online homework and assessment tool, packed with algorithmic versions of every text problem, because practice makes perfect. It's also packed with the exact same end-of-chapter material that you're used to assigning for homework. Additionally, **MyAccountingLab** includes:

1. A **Demo Doc** for each of the end-of-chapter exercises and problems that students can refer to as they work through the questions.
2. A **Guided Solution** to the exact problem they are working on. It helps students when they're trying to solve a problem the way it was demonstrated in class.
3. A full **e-book** so the students can reference the book at the point of practice.
4. New **topic specific videos** that walk students through difficult concepts.

Companion Web Site–www.prenhall.com/horngren

The book's Web site at www.prenhall.com/horngren—contains the following:

- Self-study quizzes—interactive study guide for each chapter
- MS Excel templates that students can use to complete homework assignments for each chapter (e-working papers)
- Samples of the Flash Demo Docs for students to work through the accounting cycle

Online Courses with WebCT/BlackBoard/Course Compass

Prentice Hall offers a link to MyAccountingLab through the Bb and WebCT Course Management Systems.

Classroom Response Systems (CRS)

CRS is an exciting new wireless polling technology that makes large and small classrooms even more interactive, because it enables instructors to pose questions to their students, record results, and display those results instantly. Students can easily answer questions using compact remote-control–type transmitters. Prentice Hall has partnerships with leading classroom response-systems providers and can show you everything you need to know about setting up and using a CRS system. Prentice Hall will provide the classroom hardware, text-specific PowerPoint slides, software, and support.

Visit **www.prenhall.com/crs** to learn more.

STUDENT SUPPLEMENTS

Runners Corporation PT Lab Manual

Containing numerous simulated real-world examples, the **Runners Corporation** practice set is available complete with data files for Peachtree, QuickBooks, and PH General Ledger. Each practice set also includes business stationery for manual entry work.

A-1 Photography-Manual PT Lab Manual

Containing numerous simulated real-world examples, the **A-1 Photography** practice set is available complete with data files for Peachtree, QuickBooks, and PH General Ledger. Each set includes business stationery for manual entry work.

Study Guide including Demo Docs and e-Working Papers

Introductory accounting students consistently tell us, "When doing homework, I get stuck trying to solve problems the way they were demonstrated in class." Instructors consistently tell us, "I have so much to cover in so little time; I can't afford to go backwards and review homework in class." Those challenges inspired us to develop Demo Docs. Demo Docs are comprehensive worked-through problems available for nearly every chapter of our introductory accounting text to help students when they are trying to solve exercises and problems on their own. The idea is to help students duplicate the classroom experience outside of class. Entire problems that mirror end-of-chapter material are shown solved and annotated with explanations written in a conversational style, essentially imitating what an instructor might say if standing over a student's shoulder. All Demo Docs will be available in the Study Guide—in print and on CD in Flash, so students can easily refer to them when they need them. The Study Guide also includes a summary overview of key topics and multiple-choice and short-answer questions for students to test their knowledge. Free electronic working papers are included on the accompanying CD.

MyAccountingLab Online Homework and Assessment Manager

The **"I get it!"** moment meets ***power of practice***. The power of repetition when you "get it" means that learning happens. **MyAccountingLab** is about helping students at their teachable moment, whether that is 1 P.M. or 1A.M.

MyAccountingLab is an online homework and assessment tool, packed with algorithmic versions of every text problem because practice makes perfect. It's also packed with the exact same end-of-chapter that you're used to assigning for homework. Additionally, **MyAccountingLab** includes:

1. A **Demo Doc** for each of the end-of-chapter exercises and problems that students can refer to as they work through the question.
2. A **Guided Solution** to the exact problem they are working on. It helps students when they're trying to solve a problem the way it was demonstrated in class.
3. A full **e-book** so the students can reference the book at the point of practice.
4. New **topic specific videos** that walk students through difficult concepts.

PowerPoints

For student use as a study aide or note-taking guide, these PowerPoint slides may be downloaded at the companion Web site at www.prenhall.com/horngren.

Companion Web Site–www.prenhall.com/horngren

The book's Web site at www.prenhall.com/horngren—contains the following:

- Self-study quizzes—interactive study guide for each chapter
- MS Excel templates that students can use to complete homework assignments for each chapter (e-working papers)
- Samples of the Flash Demo Docs for students to work through the accounting cycle

Classroom Response Systems (CRS)

CRS is an exciting new wireless polling technology that makes large and small classrooms even more interactive because it enables instructors to pose questions to their students, record results, and display those results instantly. Students can easily answer questions using compact remote-control-type transmitters. Prentice Hall has partnerships with leading classroom response-systems providers and can show you everything you need to know about setting up and using a CRS system. Prentice Hall will provide the classroom hardware, text-specific PowerPoint slides, software, and support.

Visit **www.prenhall.com/crs** to learn more.

- **VangoNotes in MP3 Format**

  Students can study on the go with VangoNotes, chapter reviews in downloadable MP3 format that offer brief audio segments for each chapter:

  - Big Ideas: the vital ideas in each chapter
  - Practice Test: lets students know if they need to keep studying
  - Key Terms: audio "flashcards" that review key concepts and terms
  - Rapid Review: a quick drill session—helpful right before tests

  Students can learn more at **www.vangonotes.com**

Acknowledgments

We'd like to thank the following contributors:

Florence McGovern *Bergen Community College*
Sherry Mills *New Mexico State University*
Suzanne Oliver *Okaloosa Walton Junior College*
Helen Brubeck *San Jose State University*

We'd like to extend a special thank you to the following members of our advisory panel:

Jim Ellis *Bay State College, Boston*
Mary Ann Swindlehurst *Carroll Community College*
Andy Williams *Edmonds Community College*
Donnie Kristof-Nelson *Edmonds Community College*
Joan Cezair *Fayetteville State University*
David Baglia *Grove City College*
Anita Ellzey *Harford Community College*
Cheryl McKay *Monroe County Community College*
Todd Jackson *Northeastern State University*
Margaret Costello Lambert *Oakland Community College*
Al Fagan *University of Richmond*

We'd also like to thank the following reviewers:

Shi-Mu (Simon) Yang *Adelphi University*
Thomas Stolberg *Alfred State University*
Thomas Branton *Alvin Community College*
Maria Lehoczky *American Intercontinental University*
Suzanne Bradford *Angelina College*
Judy Lewis *Angelo State University*
Roy Carson Anne *Arundel Community College*
Paulette Ratliff-Miller *Arkansas State University*
Joseph Foley *Assumption College*
Jennifer Niece *Assumption College*
Bill Whitley *Athens State University*
Shelly Gardner *Augustana College*

Becky Jones *Baylor University*
Betsy Willis *Baylor University*
Michael Robinson *Baylor University*
Kay Walker-Hauser *Beaufort County Community College, Washington*
Joe Aubert *Bemidji State University*
Calvin Fink *Bethune Cookman College*
Michael Blue *Bloomsburg University*
Scott Wallace *Blue Mountain College*
Lloyd Carroll *Borough Manhattan Community College*
Ken Duffe *Brookdale Community College*
Chuck Heuser *Brookdale Community College*
Shafi Ullah *Broward Community College South*
Lois Slutsky *Broward Community College South*
Ken Koerber *Bucks County Community College*

Julie Browning *California Baptist University*
Richard Savich *California State University—San Bernardino*
David Bland *Cape Fear Community College*
Robert Porter *Cape Fear Community College*
Vickie Campbell *Cape Fear Community College*
Cynthia Thompson *Carl Sandburg College—Carthage*
Liz Ott *Casper College*
Joseph Adamo *Cazenovia College*
Julie Dailey *Central Virginia Community College*
Jeannie Folk *College of DuPage*
Lawrence Steiner *College of Marin*
Dennis Kovach *Community College Allegheny County—Allegheny*
Norma Montague *Central Carolina Community College*
Debbie Schmidt *Cerritos College*
Janet Grange *Chicago State University*
Bruce Leung *City College of San Francisco*
Pamela Legner *College of DuPage*
Bruce McMurrey *Community College of Denver*
Martin Sabo *Community College of Denver*
Jeffrey Jones *Community College of Southern Nevada*
Tom Nohl *Community College of Southern Nevada*
Christopher Kelly *Community College of Southern Nevada*
Patrick Rogan *Cosumnes River College*
Kimberly Smith *County College of Morris*

Jerold Braun *Daytona Beach Community College*
Greg Carlton *Davidson County Community College*
Irene Bembenista *Davenport University*
Thomas Szczurek *Delaware County Community College*
Charles Betts *Delaware Technical and Community College*
Patty Holmes *Des Moines Area Community College—Ankeny*
Tim Murphy *Diablo Valley College*

Phillipe Sammour *Eastern Michigan University*
Saturnino (Nino) Gonzales *El Paso Community College*
Lee Cannell *El Paso Community College*
John Eagan *Erie Community College*

Ron O'Brien *Fayetteville Technical Community College*
Patrick McNabb *Ferris State University*
John Stancil *Florida Southern College*
Lynn Clements *Florida Southern College*
Alice Sineath *Forsyth Technical Community College*
James Makofske *Fresno City College*
Marc Haskell *Fresno City College*
James Kelly *Ft. Lauderdale City College*

Christine Jonick *Gainesville State College*
Bruce Lindsey *Genesee Community College*
Constance Hylton *George Mason University*
Cody King *Georgia Southwestern State University*
Lolita Keck *Globe College*
Kay Carnes *Gonzaga University, Spokane*
Carol Pace *Grayson County College*
Rebecca Floor *Greenville Technical College*
Geoffrey Heriot *Greenville Technical College*
Jeffrey Patterson *Grove City College*
Lanny Nelms *Gwinnet Technical College*
Chris Cusatis *Gwynedd Mercy College*

Tim Griffin *Hillsborough Community College*
Clair Helms *Hinds Community College*
Michelle Powell *Holmes Community College*
Greg Bischoff *Houston Community College*
Donald Bond *Houston Community College*
Marina Grau *Houston Community College*
Carolyn Fitzmorris *Hutchinson Community College*

Susan Koepke *Illinois Valley Community College*
William Alexander *Indian Hills Community College—Ottumwa*
Dale Bolduc *Intercoast College*
Thomas Carr *International College of Naples*
Lecia Berven *Iowa Lakes Community College*
Nancy Schendel *Iowa Lakes Community College*
Michelle Cannon *Ivy Tech*
Vicki White *Ivy Tech*
Chuck Smith *Iowa Western Community College*

Stephen Christian *Jackson Community College*
DeeDee Daughtry *Johnston Community College*
Richard Bedwell *Jones County Junior College*

Ken Mark *Kansas City Kansas Community College*
Ken Snow *Kaplan Education Centers*
Charles Evans *Keiser College*
Bunney Schmidt *Keiser College*
Amy Haas *Kingsborough Community College*

Jim Racic *Lakeland Community College*
Doug Clouse *Lakeland Community College*
Patrick Haggerty *Lansing Community College*
Patricia Walczak *Lansing Community College*
Humberto M. Herrera *Laredo Community College*
Christie Comunale *Long Island University*
Ariel Markelevich *Long Island University*
Randy Kidd *Longview Community College*
Kathy Heltzel *Luzerne County Community College*
Lori Major *Luzerne County Community College*

Fred Jex *Macomb Community College*
Glenn Owen *Marymount College*
Behnaz Quigley *Marymount College*
Penny Hanes *Mercyhurst College, Erie*
John Miller *Metropolitan Community College*
Denise Leggett *Middle Tennessee State University*
William Huffman *Missouri Southern State College*
Ted Crosby *Montgomery County Community College*
Beth Engle *Montgomery County Community College*
David Candelaria *Mount San Jacinto College*
Linda Bolduc *Mount Wachusett Community College*

Barbara Gregorio *Nassau Community College*
James Hurat *National College of Business and Technology*
Denver Riffe *National College of Business and Technology*
Asokan Anandarajan *New Jersey Institute of Technology*
Robert Schoener *New Mexico State University*
Stanley Carroll *New York City Technical College of CUNY*
Audrey Agnello *Niagara County Community College*
Catherine Chiang *North Carolina Central University*
Karen Russom *North Harris College*
Dan Bayak *Northampton Community College*
Elizabeth Lynn Locke *Northern Virginia Community College*
Debra Prendergast *Northwestern Business College*
Nat Briscoe *Northwestern State University*
Tony Scott *Norwalk Community College*

Deborah Niemer *Oakland Community College*
John Boyd *Oklahoma City Community College*
Kathleen O'Donnell *Onondaga Community College*
J.T. Ryan *Onondaga Community College*

Toni Clegg *Palm Beach Atlantic College*
David Forsyth *Palomar College*
John Graves *PCDI*
Carla Rich *Pensacola Junior College*
Judy Grotrian *Peru State College*
Judy Daulton *Piedmont Technical College*
John Stone *Potomac State College*
Betty Habershon *Prince George's Community College*

Kathi Villani *Queensborough Community College*

William Black *Raritan Valley Community College*
Verne Ingram *Red Rocks Community College*
Paul Juriga *Richland Community College*
Patty Worsham *Riverside Community College*
Margaret Berezewski *Robert Morris College*
Phil Harder *Robert Morris College*
Shifei Chung *Rowan University of New Jersey*

Charles Fazzi *Saint Vincent College*
Lynnette Yerbuy *Salt Lake Community College*
Susan Blizzard *San Antonio College*
Hector Martinez *San Antonio College*
Audrey Voyles *San Diego Miramar College*
Margaret Black *San Jacinto College*
Merrily Hoffman *San Jacinto College*
Randall Whitmore *San Jacinto College*
Carroll Buck *San Jose State University*
Cynthia Coleman *Sandhills Community College*
Barbara Crouteau *Santa Rosa Junior College*
Pat Novak *Southeast Community College*
Susan Pallas *Southeast Community College*
Al Case *Southern Oregon University*
Gloria Worthy *Southwest Tennessee Community College*
Melody Ashenfelter *Southwestern Oklahoma State University*
Douglas Ward *Southwestern Community College*
Brandi Shay *Southwestern Community College*
John May *Southwestern Oklahoma State University*
Jeffrey Waybright *Spokane Community College*
Renee Goffinet *Spokane Community College*
Susan Anders *St. Bonaventure University*
John Olsavsky *SUNY at Fredonia*
Peter Van Brunt *SUNY College of Technology at Delhi*

David L. Davis *Tallahassee Community College*
Kathy Crusto-Way *Tarrant County Community College*
Sally Cook *Texas Lutheran University*
Bea Chiang *The College of New Jersey*
Matt Hightower *Three Rivers Community College*

Susan Pope *University of Akron*
Joe Woods *University of Arkansas*
Allen Blay *University of California, Riverside*
Barry Mishra *University of California, Riverside*
Laura Young *University of Central Arkansas*
Jane Calvert *University of Central Oklahoma*
Bambi Hora *University of Central Oklahoma*
Joan Stone *University of Central Oklahoma*
Kathy Terrell *University of Central Oklahoma*
Harlan Etheridge *University of Louisiana*
Pam Meyer *University of Louisiana*
Sandra Scheuermann *University of Louisiana*
Tom Wilson *University of Louisiana*
Lawrence Leaman *University of Michigan*
Larry Huus *University of Minnesota*
Brian Carpenter *University of Scranton*
Ashraf Khallaf *University of Southern Indiana*
Tony Zordan *University of St. Francis*
Gene Elrod *University of Texas, Arlington*
Cheryl Prachyl *University of Texas, El Paso*
Karl Putnam *University of Texas, El Paso*
Stephen Rockwell *University of Tulsa*
Chula King *University of West Florida*
Charles Baird *University of Wisconsin—Stout*

Mary Hollars *Vincennes University*
Lisa Nash *Vincennes University*
Elaine Dessouki *Virginia Wesleyan College*

Sueann Hely *West Kentucky Community and Technical College*
Darlene Pulliam *West Texas A&M University, Canyon*
Judy Beebe *Western Oregon University*
Michelle Maggio *Westfield State College*
Kathy Pellegrino *Westfield State College*
Nora McCarthy *Wharton County Junior College*
Sally Stokes *Wilmington College*
Maggie Houston *Wright State University*

Gerald Caton *Yavapai College*
Chris Crosby *York Technical College*
Harold Gellis *York College of CUNY*

About the Authors

Charles T. Horngren is the Edmund W. Littlefield Professor of Accounting, Emeritus, at Stanford University. A graduate of Marquette University, he received his M.B.A. from Harvard University and his Ph.D. from the University of Chicago. He is also the recipient of honorary doctorates from Marquette University and DePaul University.

A Certified Public Accountant, Horngren served on the Accounting Principles Board for six years, the Financial Accounting Standards Board Advisory Council for five years, and the Council of the American Institute of Certified Public Accountants for three years. For six years, he served as a trustee of the Financial Accounting Foundation, which oversees the Financial Accounting Standards Board and the Government Accounting Standards Board.

Horngren is a member of the Accounting Hall of Fame.

A member of the American Accounting Association, Horngren has been its President and its Director of Research. He received its first annual Outstanding Accounting Educator Award.

The California Certified Public Accountants Foundation gave Horngren its Faculty Excellence Award and its Distinguished Professor Award. He is the first person to have received both awards.

The American Institute of Certified Public Accountants presented its first Outstanding Educator Award to Horngren.

Horngren was named Accountant of the Year, Education, by the national professional accounting fraternity, Beta Alpha Psi.

Professor Horngren is also a member of the Institute of Management Accountants, from whom he has received its Distinguished Service Award. He was a member of the Institute's Board of Regents, which administers the Certified Management Accountant examinations.

Horngren is the author of other accounting books published by Prentice-Hall: *Cost Accounting: A Managerial Emphasis*, Twelfth Edition, 2006 (with Srikant Datar and George Foster); *Introduction to Financial Accounting*, Ninth Edition, 2006 (with Gary L. Sundem and John A. Elliott); *Introduction to Management Accounting*, Thirteenth Edition, 2005 (with Gary L. Sundem and William Stratton); *Financial Accounting*, Sixth Edition, 2006 (with Walter T. Harrison, Jr.).

Horngren is the Consulting Editor for Prentice-Hall's Charles T. Horngren Series in Accounting.

Walter T. Harrison, Jr. is Professor Emeritus of Accounting at the Hankamer School of Business, Baylor University. He received his B.B.A. degree from Baylor University, his M.S. from Oklahoma State University, and his Ph.D. from Michigan State University.

Professor Harrison, recipient of numerous teaching awards from student groups as well as from university administrators, has also taught at Cleveland State Community College, Michigan State University, the University of Texas, and Stanford University.

A member of the American Accounting Association and the American Institute of Certified Public Accountants, Professor Harrison has served as Chairman of the Financial Accounting Standards Committee of the American Accounting Association, on the Teaching/Curriculum Development Award Committee, on the Program Advisory

Committee for Accounting Education and Teaching, and on the Notable Contributions to Accounting Literature Committee.

Professor Harrison has lectured in several foreign countries and published articles in numerous journals, including *Journal of Accounting Research*, *Journal of Accountancy*, *Journal of Accounting and Public Policy*, *Economic Consequences of Financial Accounting Standards*, *Accounting Horizons*, *Issues in Accounting Education*, and *Journal of Law and Commerce*.

He is co-author of *Financial Accounting*, Sixth Edition, 2006 (with Charles T. Horngren), published by Prentice Hall. Professor Harrison has received scholarships, fellowships, and research grants or awards from PriceWaterhouse Coopers, Deloitte & Touche, the Ernst & Young Foundation, and the KPMG Foundation.

Financial and Managerial Accounting

Chapters 1–13

1e

1 Accounting and the Business Environment

Learning Objectives

1. Use accounting vocabulary
2. Apply accounting concepts and principles
3. Use the accounting equation
4. Analyze business transactions
5. Prepare the financial statements
6. Evaluate business performance

You may dream of running your own business. Where do you begin? How much money does it take? How will you measure success or failure?

Haig Sherman operated a lawn-service business while in college and graduated with thousands in the bank. Julie DeFilippo started a successful catering business. How did they do it? By following their dreams, treating people fairly, and having realistic expectations. It didn't hurt that Sherman majored in accounting. His accounting knowledge gave him a leg up on organizing the business and keeping track of important details. ■

We'll start with a small business such as Sherman Lawn Service or DeFilippo Catering. What role does accounting play for Sherman Lawn Service or DeFilippo Catering?

Accounting: The Language of Business

Accounting is the information system that measures business activity, processes the data into reports, and communicates the results to decision makers. Accounting is "the language of business." The better you understand the language, the better you can manage the business. For example, how will you decide whether to borrow money? You need to consider your income: The concept of income comes straight from accounting.

A key product of accounting is a set of documents called the financial statements. **Financial statements** report on a business in monetary terms. Is Sherman Lawn Service making a profit? Should DeFilippo Catering expand? Answering these questions requires the financial statements.

1 Use accounting vocabulary

Exhibit 1-1 illustrates the role of accounting in business. The process shows people making decisions.

EXHIBIT 1-1 How People Use Accounting Information

I need a loan.
Let's see your financial statements.
Here's my income statement.

Decision Makers: The Users of Accounting Information

Decision makers need information. The bigger the decision, the greater the need. Here are some of the ways people use accounting information.

Individuals

You use accounting information to manage your bank account, evaluate a new job, and decide whether you can afford a new car. Haig Sherman and Julie DeFilippo make the same decisions that you do.

Businesses

Business owners use accounting information to set goals. They evaluate progress toward those goals and take corrective action when needed. For example, Julie DeFilippo must decide how many heaters she'll need to keep food warm on a catering job. Accounting provides this information.

Investors

Outside investors often provide the money to get a business going. To decide whether to invest, a person predicts the amount of income to be earned on the investment. The investor analyzes the financial statements and keeps up with the company. For large public companies, log onto www.yahoo.com (click on Finance), www.hoovers.com (click on Companies), and the SEC's EDGAR database.

Creditors

Before lending money to Haig Sherman, a bank evaluates Sherman's ability to make the loan payments. This requires a report on Sherman's predicted income. To borrow money before striking it rich, Michael Dell, who founded Dell Inc., the computer company, probably had to document his income and financial position.

Taxing Authorities

Local, state, and federal governments levy taxes. Income tax is figured using accounting information. Sales tax depends upon a company's sales.

Financial Accounting and Management Accounting

Accounting can be divided into two fields—financial accounting and management accounting.

Financial accounting provides information for people outside the company. Outside investors and lenders are not part of day-to-day management. These outsiders use the company's financial statements. Chapters 2–15 of this book deal primarily with financial accounting.

Management accounting focuses on information for internal decision making by the company's managers. Chapters 16 through 25 cover management accounting. Exhibit 1-2 illustrates the difference between financial accounting and management accounting.

EXHIBIT 1-2 **Financial Accounting and Management Accounting**

Outside Investors:	DeFilippo Catering:	Creditors:
Should we invest in DeFilippo Catering? Is the business profitable? Investors use financial accounting information to measure profitability. →	Julie DeFilippo uses management accounting information to operate her business.	← Should we lend money to DeFilippo Catering? Can DeFilippo pay us back? Creditors use financial accounting information to decide whether to make a loan.

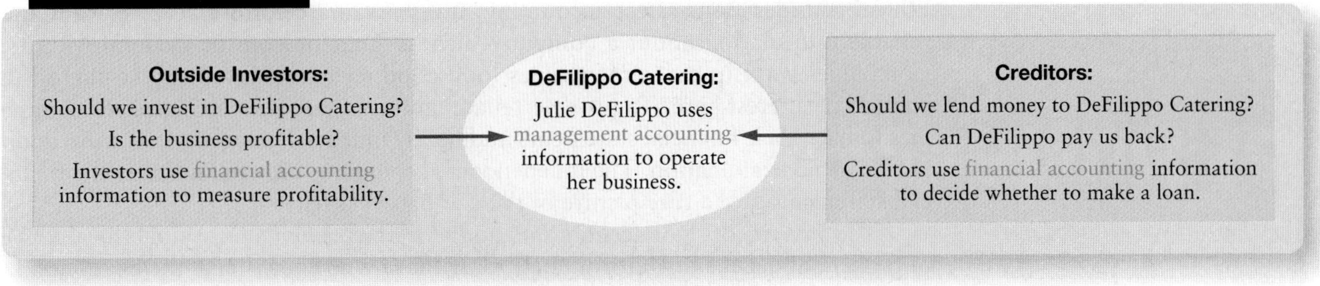

The Accounting Profession

There are several learned professions, including accounting, architecture, engineering, law, and medicine. To be certified in a profession, one must pass a qualifying exam, and professionals are paid quite well. For example, the starting salary for a college graduate with a bachelor's degree in accounting can range from $35,000 to $50,000. A graduate with a master's degree earns about $2,000 more to start. After five years you may be earning as much as $75,000.

Many accounting firms are organized as partnerships, and the partners are the owners. It usually takes 10 to 15 years to rise to the rank of partner. The partners of the large accounting firms earn from $150,000 to $500,000 per year. In private accounting, the top position is called the chief financial officer (CFO), and a CFO earns about as much as a partner in an accounting firm.

What do businesses such as Sherman Lawn Service, DeFilippo Catering, General Motors, and Coca-Cola have in common? They all need accountants! That's why accounting opens so many doors to a job upon graduation.

Accountants get to the top of organizations as often as anyone else. Why? Because the accountants must deal with everything in the company in order to account for all of its activities. Accountants often have the broadest view of what's going on in the company. People sometimes complain that the accountants control the purse strings, but they must admit that accountants often keep companies on the straight and narrow path to success.

As you move through this book, observe that you will learn to account for everything that affects the business—all the income, all the expenses, all the cash, all the inventory, and all the debts. Accounting requires you to consider everything, and that's why it's so valuable to an organization.

All professions have regulations. Let's see the organizations that govern the accounting profession.

Governing Organizations

In the United States the **Financial Accounting Standards Board (FASB)**, a private organization, formulates accounting standards. The FASB works with governmental agencies, the Securities and Exchange Commission (SEC) and the Public Companies Accounting Oversight Board (PCAOB), and private groups, the American Institute of Certified Public Accountants (AICPA) and the Institute of Management Accountants (IMA). **Certified public accountants**, or **CPAs**, are professional accountants who are licensed to serve the general public. **Certified management accountants**, or **CMAs**, are licensed professionals who work for a single company.

The rules for public information are called *generally accepted accounting principles (GAAP)*. Exhibit 1-3 diagrams the relationships among the various accounting organizations.

Ethics in Accounting and Business

Ethical considerations affect accounting. Investors and creditors need relevant and reliable information about a company such as Amazon.com or General Motors. Companies want to make themselves look good to attract investors, so there is a conflict of interest here. To provide reliable information, the SEC requires companies to have their financial statements audited by independent accountants. An **audit** is a financial examination. The independent accountants then tell whether the financial statements give a true picture of the company's situation.

The vast majority of accountants do their jobs professionally and ethically. We never hear about them. Unfortunately, only those who cheat make the headlines. In recent years we've seen more accounting scandals than at any time since the 1920s.

EXHIBIT 1-3 **Key Accounting Organizations**

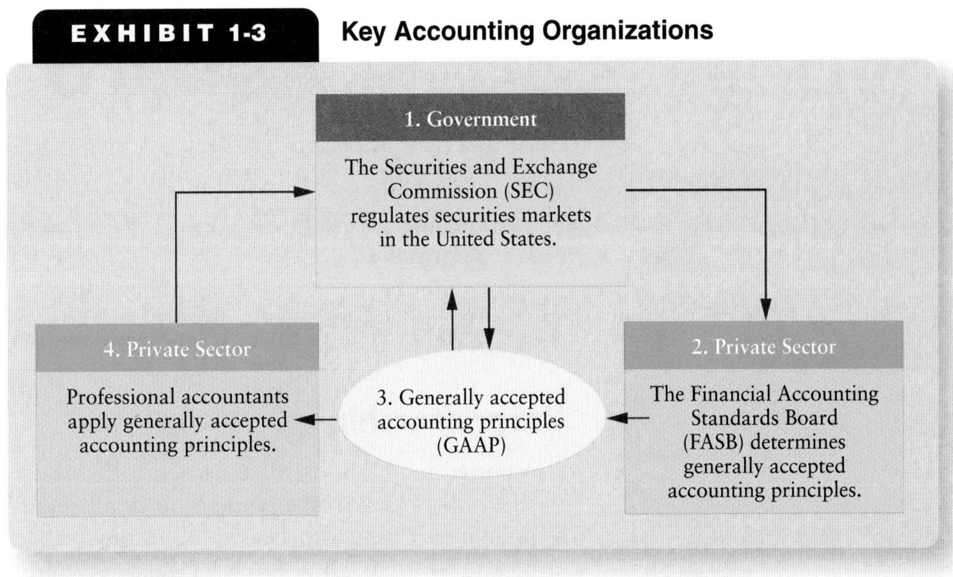
1. Government
The Securities and Exchange Commission (SEC) regulates securities markets in the United States.
2. Private Sector
The Financial Accounting Standards Board (FASB) determines generally accepted accounting principles.
3. Generally accepted accounting principles (GAAP)
4. Private Sector
Professional accountants apply generally accepted accounting principles.

Enron Corp., for example, was one of the largest companies in the United States before reporting misleading data. WorldCom, a major long-distance telephone provider, admitted accounting for expenses as though they were assets (resources). These and other scandals rocked the business community and hurt investor confidence. Innocent people lost their jobs, and the stock market suffered. The U.S. government took swift action. It passed the Sarbanes-Oxley Act that made it a criminal offense to falsify financial statements. It also created a new watchdog agency, the Public Companies Accounting Oversight Board, to monitor the work of accountants.

Standards of Professional Conduct

The AICPA's Code of Professional Conduct for Accountants provides guidance to CPAs in their work. Ethical standards are designed to produce relevant and reliable information for decision making. The preamble to the Code states:

> "[A] certified public accountant assumes an obligation of self-discipline above and beyond the requirements of laws and regulations . . . [and] an unswerving commitment to honorable behavior. . . ."

The opening paragraph of the Standards of Ethical Conduct of the Institute of Management Accountants (IMA) states:

> "Management accountants have an obligation to the organizations they serve, their profession, the public, and themselves to maintain the highest standards of ethical conduct."

Most companies also set standards of ethical conduct for employees. DeFilippo Catering must comply with state health standards in order to serve customers ethically. The Boeing Company, a leading manufacturer of aircraft, has a highly developed set of business conduct guidelines. A business's or an individual's reputation is fragile and can easily be lost. As one chief executive has stated, "Ethical practice is simply good business." Truth is always better than dishonesty—in accounting, in business, and in life.

Types of Business Organizations

A business can be organized as a:

- Proprietorship
- Partnership
- Corporation
- Limited-liability partnership (LLP) and limited-liability company (LLC)

You should understand the differences among the four.

Proprietorships

A **proprietorship** has a single owner, called the proprietor, who often manages the business. Proprietorships tend to be small retail stores or professional businesses, such as physicians, attorneys, and accountants. As to its accounting, each proprietorship is distinct from its owner: The accounting records of the proprietorship do *not* include the proprietor's personal records. However, from a legal perspective, the business *is* the proprietor. In this book, we start with a proprietorship because many students will organize their first business that way.

Partnerships

A **partnership** joins two or more individuals as co-owners. Each owner is a partner. Many retail stores and professional organizations of physicians, attorneys, and accountants are partnerships. Most partnerships are small or medium-sized, but some are gigantic, with 1,000 or more partners. As to its accounting the partnership is a separate organization, distinct from the partners. But from a legal perspective, a partnership *is* the partners in a manner similar to a proprietorship.

Corporations

A **corporation** is a business owned by **stockholders**, or **shareholders**. These are the people who own shares of ownership in the business. A business becomes a corporation when the state approves its articles of incorporation. Unlike a proprietorship and a partnership, a corporation is a legal entity distinct from its owners.

The largest businesses in the United States and in other countries are corporations. The Coca-Cola Company, for example, has billions of shares of stock owned by many stockholders. An investor with no personal relationship to Coca-Cola can become a stockholder by buying 50, 100, 5,000, or any number of shares of Coca-Cola stock.

Limited-Liability Partnerships (LLPs) and Limited-Liability Companies (LLCs)

A *limited-liability partnership* is one in which a wayward partner cannot create a large liability for the other partners. Each partner is liable only for his or her own actions and those under his or her control. And a proprietorship can be organized as a *limited-liability company*. In an LLC the business, and not the proprietor, is liable for the company's debts. Today most proprietorships and partnerships are organized as LLCs and LLPs. The limited-liability aspect gives these organizations one of the chief advantages of a corporation.

Exhibit 1-4 summarizes the differences among the four types of business organization.

EXHIBIT 1-4 Comparison of the Four Forms of Business Organization

	Proprietorship	Partnership	Corporation	LLC
1. Owner(s)	Proprietorship—only one owner	Partners—two or more owners	Stockholders—generally many owners	Members
2. Life of the organization	Limited by the owner's choice, or death	Limited by the owner's choice, or death	Indefinite	Indefinite
3. Personal liability of the owner(s) for the business's debts	Proprietor is personally liable	Partners are personally liable*	Stockholders are not personally liable	Members are not personally liable

*unless it's a limited-liability partnership (LLP)

Characteristics of a Corporation

We now look at the principal features of a corporation to distinguish corporations from proprietorships and partnerships.

Separate Legal Entity

A **corporation** is a business entity formed under state law. The state grants a **charter**, which is the document that gives the state's permission to form a corporation.

A corporation is a distinct entity from a legal perspective. It's like an artificial person that exists apart from its owners, the **stockholders** or **shareholders**. The corporation has many of the rights that a person has. For example, a corporation may buy, own, and sell property. Assets and liabilities in the business belong to the corporation and not to the stockholders individually. The corporation may enter into contracts, sue, and be sued.

The ownership interest of a corporation is divided into shares of **stock**. A person becomes a stockholder by purchasing the stock of the corporation. The corporate charter specifies how much stock the corporation can issue (sell) to the public.

Continuous Life and Transferability of Ownership

Corporations have continuous lives regardless of changes in the ownership of their stock. Stockholders may transfer stock as they wish. They may sell or trade the stock to another person, give it away, bequeath it in a will, or dispose of it in any way they desire. The transfer of the stock does not affect the continuity of the corporation. Proprietorships and partnerships, on the other hand, terminate when their ownership changes.

No Mutual Agency

Mutual agency of the owners is not present in a corporation as it is in a partnership. This means that the stockholder of a corporation cannot commit the corporation to a contract (unless he or she is also an officer in the business). For this reason, a stockholder need not exercise the care that partners must in selecting co-owners of the business.

Limited Liability of Stockholders

A stockholder has **limited liability** for the corporation's debts. Unlike proprietors and partners, a stockholder has no personal obligation for corporation liabilities. The most that a stockholder can lose on an investment in a corporation's stock is the cost of the investment. On the other hand, proprietors and partners are personally liable for the debts of their businesses.

The combination of limited liability and no mutual agency means that persons can invest limited amounts in a corporation without fear of losing all their personal wealth because of a business failure. This feature enables a corporation to raise more money than proprietorships and partnerships.

Separation of Ownership and Management

Stockholders own the business, but a board of directors—elected by the stockholders—appoints corporate officers to manage the business. Thus stockholders don't have to manage the business or disrupt their personal affairs.

This separation between owners—stockholders—and management may create problems. Corporate officers may decide to run the business for their own benefit and not to the stockholders' advantage. Stockholders may find it difficult to lodge an effective protest against management because of the distance between them and the top managers.

Corporate Taxation

Corporations are separate taxable entities. The pay a variety of taxes not borne by proprietorships or partnerships, including:

- Annual franchise tax levied by the state. The franchise tax is paid to keep the corporation charter in force and enables the corporation to continue in business.
- Federal and state income taxes. Corporate earnings are subject to **double taxation**.

First, corporations pay their own income tax on corporate income. Then, the stockholders pay personal income tax on the cash dividends that they receive from corporations. This is different from proprietorships and partnerships, which pay no business income tax. Instead, the tax falls solely on the owners.

Government Regulation

Government regulation is a disadvantage for corporations. Because stockholders have only limited liability for corporation debts, outsiders doing business with the corporation can look no further than the corporation itself for any claims that may arise against the business. To protect persons who loan money to a corporation or who invest in its stock, states monitor the affairs of corporations. This government regulation can be expensive.

Organization of a Corporation

Creation of a corporation begins when its organizers, called the **incorporators**, obtain a charter from the state. The charter includes the authorization for the corporation to issue a certain number of shares of stock, which represent the ownership in the corporation. The incorporators pay fees, sign the charter, and file the required documents with the state. Then the corporation comes into existence. The incorporators agree to a set of **bylaws**, which act as the constitution for governing the corporation.

The ultimate control of the corporation rests with the stockholders, who receive one vote for each share of stock they own. The stockholders elect the members of the **board of directors**, which sets policy for the corporation and appoints the

EXHIBIT 1-5 Structure of a Corporation

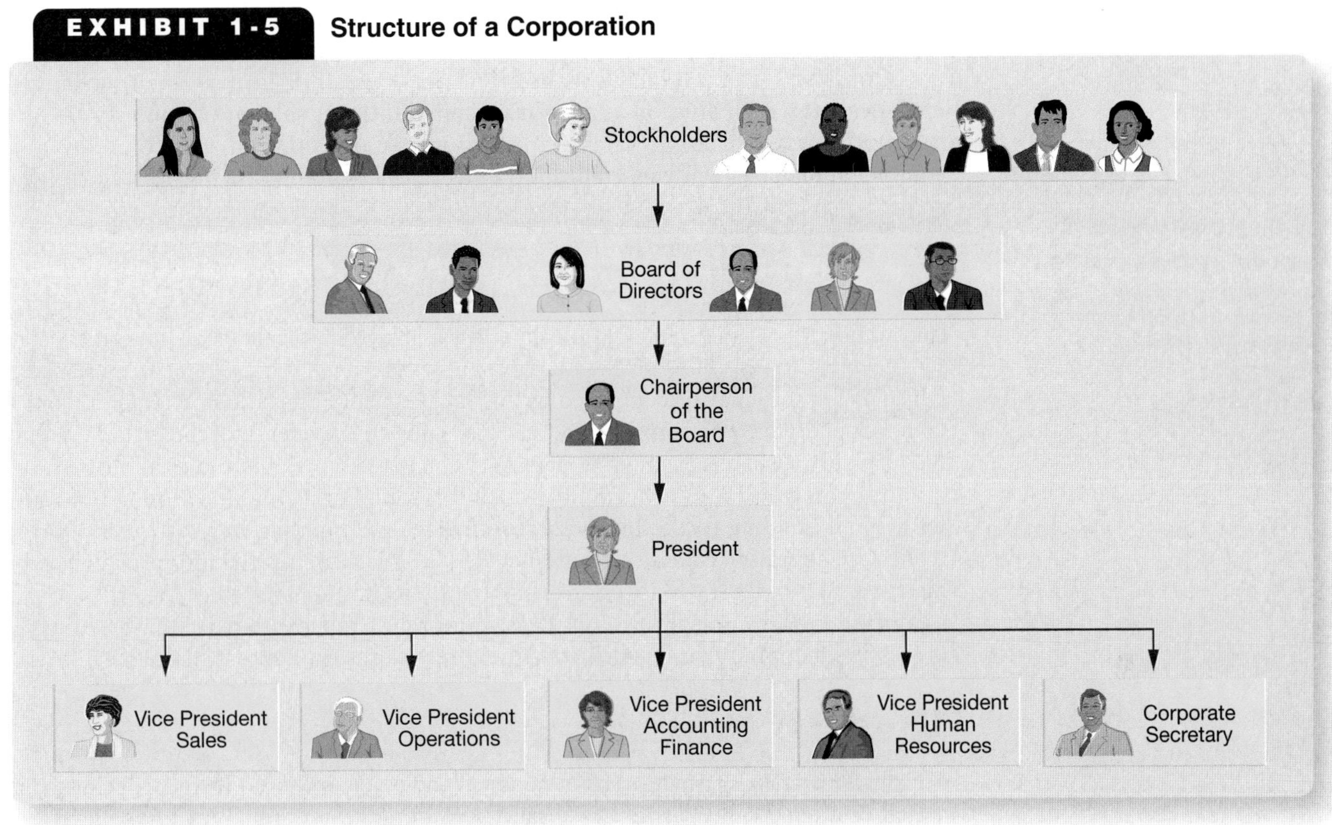

officers. The board elects a chairperson, who usually is the most powerful person in the corporation. The board also designates the president, who as chief operating officer manages day-to-day operations. Most corporations also have vice-presidents in charge of sales, operations, accounting and finance, and other key areas. Exhibit 1-5 shows the authority structure in a corporation.

Accounting Concepts and Principles

The rules that govern accounting fall under the heading **GAAP**, which stands for **generally accepted accounting principles**. GAAP rests on a conceptual framework.

> The primary objective of financial reporting is to provide information useful for making investment and lending decisions.

To be useful, information must be relevant, reliable, and comparable. We begin the discussion of GAAP by introducing basic accounting concepts and principles.

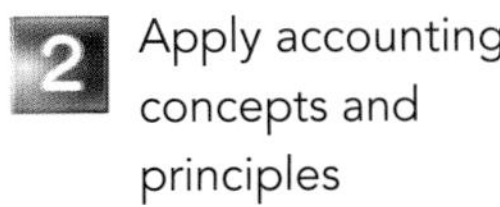
2 Apply accounting concepts and principles

The Entity Concept

The most basic concept in accounting is that of the **entity**. An accounting entity is an organization that stands apart as a separate economic unit. We draw boundaries around each entity so as not to confuse its affairs with those of other entities.

Consider Sherman Lawn Service. Assume Haig Sherman started the business with $500 obtained from a bank loan. Following the entity concept, Sherman would account for the $500 separately from his personal assets, such as his clothing and automobile. To mix the $500 of business cash with his personal assets would make it difficult to measure the success or failure of Sherman Lawn Service.

Consider Toyota, a huge organization with several divisions. Toyota management evaluates each division as a separate entity. If Lexus sales are dropping, Toyota can find out why. But if sales figures from all divisions of the company are combined, management can't tell that Lexus sales are going down. Thus, *the entity concept applies to any economic unit that needs to be evaluated separately.*

The Reliability (Objectivity) Principle

Accounting information is based on the most reliable data available. This guideline is the *reliability principle,* also called the *objectivity principle.* Reliable data are verifiable, which means they may be confirmed by any independent observer. For example, a bank loan is supported by a promissory note. This is objective evidence of the loan. Without the reliability principle, accounting data might be based on whims and opinions.

Suppose you want to open an electronics store. For a store location, you transfer a small building to the business. You believe the building is worth $50,000. A real estate appraiser values the building at $40,000. Which is the more reliable estimate of the building's value, your estimate of $50,000 or the $40,000 professional appraisal? The appraisal of $40,000 is more reliable because it is supported by a professional appraisal. The business should record the building at $40,000.

The Cost Principle

The *cost principle* states that acquired assets and services should be recorded at their actual cost (also called *historical cost*). Even though the purchaser may believe the price is a bargain, the item is recorded at the price actually paid and not at the "expected" cost. Suppose your electronics store purchases TV equipment from a supplier who is going out of business. Assume that you get a good deal and pay only $2,000 for equipment that would have cost you $3,000 elsewhere. The cost principle requires you to record the equipment at its actual cost of $2,000, not the $3,000 that you believe the equipment is worth.

The cost principle also holds that the accounting records should continue reporting the historical cost of an asset over its useful life. Why? Because cost is a reliable measure. Suppose your store holds the TV equipment for six months. During that time TV prices rise, and the equipment can be sold for $3,500. Should its accounting value—the figure on the books—be the actual cost of $2,000 or the current market value of $3,500? By the cost principle, the accounting value of the equipment remains at actual cost of $2,000.

The Going-Concern Concept

Another reason for measuring assets at historical cost is the *going-concern concept.* This concept assumes that the entity will remain in operation for the foreseeable future. Under the going-concern concept, accountants assume that the business will remain in operation long enough to use existing resources for their intended purpose.

To understand the going-concern concept better, consider the alternative—which is to go out of business. A store holding a going-out-of-business sale is trying to sell everything. In that case, the relevant measure is current market value. But going out of business is the exception rather than the rule.

The Stable-Monetary-Unit Concept

In the United States, we record transactions in dollars because the dollar is the medium of exchange. The value of a dollar changes over time, and a rise in the price level is called *inflation.* During inflation, a dollar will purchase less food and less gas for your car. But accountants assume that the dollar's purchasing power is stable.

The Accounting Equation

3 Use the accounting equation

The basic tool of accounting is the **accounting equation.** It measures the resources of a business and the claims to those resources.

Assets and Liabilities

Assets are economic resources that are expected to benefit the business in the future. Cash, merchandise inventory, furniture, and land are assets.

Claims to those assets come from two sources. **Liabilities** are debts payable to outsiders. These outside parties are called *creditors.* For example, a creditor who has loaned money to DeFilippo Catering has a claim to some of DeFilippo's assets until DeFilippo pays the debt. Many liabilities have the word *payable* in their titles. Examples include Accounts Payable, Notes Payable and Salary Payable.

The owners' claims to the assets of the business are called **owners' equity.** These insider claims begin when a stockholder, such as Julie DeFilippo, invests assets in the business and receives the corporation's stock.

The accounting equation shows how assets, liabilities, and owners' equity are related. Assets appear on the left side of the equation, and the liabilities and owners' equity appear on the right side. Exhibit 1-6 diagrams how the two sides must always be equal (amounts are assumed for this illustration):

(Economic Resources)		(Claims to Economic Resources)
ASSETS	=	LIABILITIES + OWNERS' EQUITY
\$5,000	=	\$2,000 + \$3,000

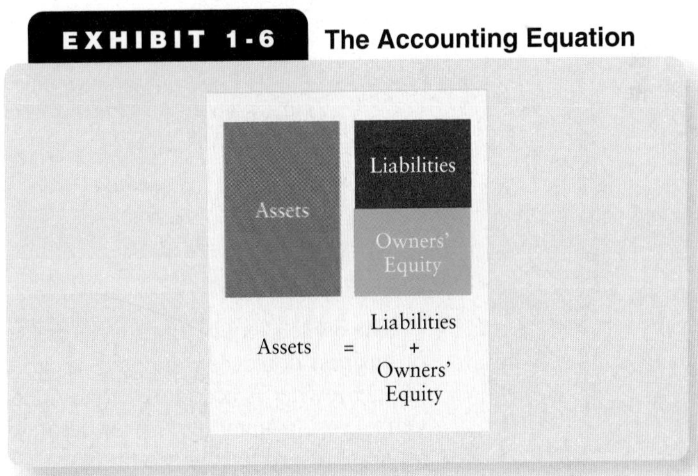

EXHIBIT 1-6 The Accounting Equation

Owners' Equity

The owners' equity of a corporation—called **stockholders' equity**—is divided into two main categories, paid-in capital and retained earnings. For a corporation the accounting equation can be written as

ASSETS = LIABILITIES + STOCKHOLDERS' EQUITY

ASSETS = LIABILITIES + PAID-IN CAPITAL + RETAINED EARNINGS

COMMON STOCK

- **Paid-in**, or **contributed, capital** is the amount invested in the corporation by its owners, the stockholders. The basic component of paid-in capital is common stock, which the corporation issues to the stockholders as evidence of their ownership. **Common stock** represents the basic ownership of every corporation.
- **Retained earnings** is the amount earned by income-producing activities and kept for use in the business. Two types of transactions that affect retained earnings are revenues and expenses. **Revenues** are increases in retained earnings from delivering goods or services to customers. For example, DeFilippo's receipt of cash from a customer for serving a banquet brings in revenue and increases the business's retained earnings. **Expenses** are the decreases in retained earnings that result from operations. For example, the wages that the catering business pays to servers is an expense and decreases retained earnings.

  Businesses strive for profitability. When revenues exceed expenses, the result of operations is a profit or net income. When expenses exceed revenues, the result is a net loss.

  After earning net income, the business may pay dividends, the third type of transaction that affects retained earnings. **Dividends** are distributions to stockholders of assets (usually cash) generated by net income. Dividends are not expenses. A corporation may or may not pay dividends. Exhibit 1-7 shows the components of retained earnings.

EXHIBIT 1-7 **Components of Retained Earnings**

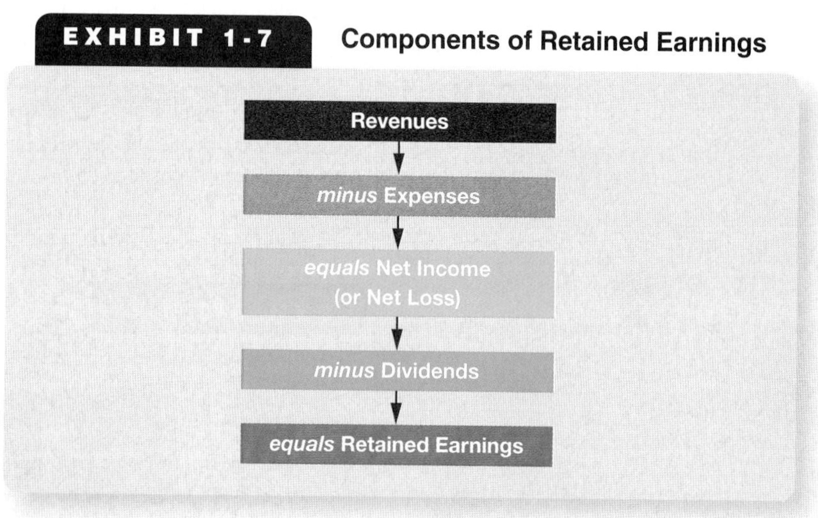

The owners' equity of proprietorships and of partnerships is different. These types of business don't separate paid-in capital from retained earnings. Instead, the equity of each owner is accounted for under the single heading of Capital—for example, Gary Lyon, Capital for a proprietorship. The partnership of Pratt and Nagle has a separate record for the capital of each partner: Pratt, Capital and Nagle, Capital.

There are relatively few types of revenue, including:

- **Sales revenue.** DeFilippo Catering earns sales revenue by selling food to customers.
- **Service revenue.** Sherman Lawn Service earns service revenue by mowing customers' lawns.
- **Interest revenue.** Interest revenue is earned on bank deposits and on money lent out to others.
- **Dividend revenue.** Dividend revenue is earned on investments in the stock of other corporations.

Exhibit 1-7 also shows expenses, which follow.

- **Expenses** decrease owners' equity by using up assets or increasing liabilities in order to deliver goods or services to customers. For example, DeFilippo Catering paid its chef a salary of $4,000, and that's an expense of the business. You can see that expenses are the opposite of revenues. Unfortunately, businesses have lots of expenses, including:
  - Rent expense
  - Salary expense for employees
  - Advertising expense
  - Utilities expense for water, electricity, and gas
  - Insurance expense
  - Supplies expense for supplies used up
  - Interest expense on loans payable
  - Property tax expense

Accounting for Business Transactions

Accounting is based on actual transactions, not opinions or desires. A **transaction** is any event that affects the financial position of the business *and* can be measured reliably. Many events affect a company, including economic booms and recessions. Accountants do not record the effects of those events because they can't be measured reliably. An accountant records only those events that can be measured reliably, such as the purchase of a building, a sale of merchandise, and the payment of rent. The dollar amounts of these events can be measured reliably, so accountants record these transactions.

What are some of your personal transactions? You may have bought a car. Your purchase was a transaction. If you are making payments on an auto loan, your payments are also transactions. You need to record all your business transactions just as DeFilippo catering does in order to manage your personal affairs.

To illustrate accounting for a business, let's use Cookie Lapp Travel Design, Inc., a travel agency organized as a corporation. Online customers can plan and pay for their trips through the business's Web site. The Web site is linked to airlines, hotels, and cruise lines, so clients can obtain the latest information 24/7. The Web site allows the agency to transact more business. Now let's account for the transactions of Cookie Lapp Travel Design, Inc.

4 Analyze business transactions

Transaction 1: Starting the Business

Cookie Lapp starts her *new business* as a corporation named Cookie Lapp Travel Design, Inc. The *Inc.* in the company name abbreviates *Incorporated*, which lets people know the business is a corporation. The travel agency receives Lapp's initial investment of $30,000 cash and issues common stock to Cookie Lapp. The effect of this transaction on the accounting equation of the business is:

Assets		Liabilities	+	Stockholders' Equity (SE)	Type of SE Transaction
Cash	=			Common Stock	
(1) +30,000				+30,000	*Issued stock*

For each transaction, the amount on the left side of the equation must equal the amount on the right side. The first transaction increases both the assets (in this case, Cash) and the stockholders' equity (Common Stock) of the business. To the right of the transaction, we write "Issued Stock" to keep track of the source of the equity.

VERY IMPORTANT TO START ON THE RIGHT TRACK—Keep in mind that we are doing the accounting for Cookie Lapp Travel Design, Inc., the business. We are *not* accounting for Cookie Lapp, the person.

View all transactions, and do all the accounting, from the perspective of the business—not from the viewpoint of its owners. This same idea applies throughout accounting.

Transaction 2: Purchase of Land

Lapp purchases land for an office location, paying cash of $20,000. This transaction affects the accounting equation of Cookie Lapp Travel Design, Inc., as follows:

	ASSETS				LIABILITIES +	STOCKHOLDERS' EQUITY
	Cash	+	Land			Common Stock
(1)	30,000			=		30,000
(2)	−20,000	+	20,000			
Bal.	10,000		20,000			30,000
	30,000					30,000

The cash purchase of land increases one asset, Land, and decreases another asset, Cash. After the transaction is completed, the travel agency has cash of $10,000, land of $20,000, no liabilities, and stockholders' equity of $30,000. Note that the total balances (abbreviated Bal.) on both sides of the equation must always be equal—in this case $30,000.

Transaction 3: Purchase of Office Supplies

The travel agency buys stationery and other office supplies, agreeing to pay $500 within 30 days. This transaction increases both the assets and the liabilities of the business, as follows:

	ASSETS						LIABILITIES	+	STOCKHOLDERS' EQUITY
	Cash	+	Office Supplies	+	Land		Accounts Payable	+	Common Stock
Bal.	10,000				20,000	=			30,000
(3)			+500				+500		
Bal.	10,000		500		20,000		500		30,000
			30,500					30,500	

Office Supplies is an asset, not an expense, because the supplies can be used in the future. The liability created by this transaction is an account payable. **A payable is always a liability.**

Transaction 4: Earning of Service Revenue

Cookie Lapp Travel Design earns service revenue by providing travel services for clients. Lapp earns $5,500 revenue and collects this amount in cash. The effect on the accounting equation is an increase in Cash and an increase in Retained Earnings, as follows:

	Assets				Liabilities +	Stockholders' Equity		Type of SE Transaction
	Cash +	Office Supplies +	Land		Accounts Payable +	Common Stock +	Retained Earnings	
Bal.	10,000	500	20,000	=	500	30,000		
(4)	+5,500	___	___		___	___	+5,500	*Service revenue*
Bal.	15,500	500	20,000		500	30,000	5,500	
	36,000				36,000			

A revenue transaction grows the business, as shown by the increases in assets and stockholders' equity (retained earnings).

Transaction 5: Earning of Service Revenue on Account

The travel agency performs service for clients who do not pay immediately. Lapp receives the clients' promises to pay $3,000 within one month. This promise is an asset, an account receivable, because Lapp expects to collect the cash in the future. In accounting, we say that Lapp performed this service *on account*. It's performing the service, not collecting the cash, that earns the revenue. Lapp records the earning of $3,000 of revenue on account, as follows:

	Assets					Liabilities +	Stockholders' Equity		Type of SE Transaction
	Cash +	Accounts Receivable +	Office Supplies +	Land		Accounts Payable +	Common Stock +	Retained Earnings	
Bal.	15,500		500	20,000	=	500	30,000	5,500	
(5)	___	+3,000	___	___		___	___	+3,000	*Service revenue*
Bal.	15,500	3,000	500	20,000		500	30,000	8,500	
	39,000					39,000			

Transaction 6: Payment of Expenses

During the month, Lapp pays $3,300 in cash expenses: rent expense on a computer, $600; office rent, $1,100; employee salary, $1,200; and utilities, $400. The effects on the accounting equation are:

	Assets					Liabilities +	Stockholders' Equity		Type of SE Transaction
	Cash +	Accounts Receivable +	Office Supplies +	Land		Accounts Payable +	Common Stock +	Retained Earnings	
Bal.	15,500	3,000	500	20,000		500	30,000	8,500	
(6)	−600							−600	*Rent expense, computer*
(6)	−1,100				=			−1,100	*Rent expense, office*
(6)	−1,200							−1,200	*Salary expense*
(6)	−400	___	___	___		___	___	−400	*Utilities expense*
Bal.	12,200	3,000	500	20,000		500	30,000	5,200	
	35,700					35,700			

Expenses have the opposite effect of revenues. Expenses shrink the business, as shown by the decreased balances of assets and stockholders' equity (retained earnings).

Each expense should be recorded separately. The expenses are listed together here for simplicity. We could record the cash payment in a single amount for the sum of the four expenses: $3,300 ($600 + $1,100 + $1,200 + $400). In all cases, the accounting equation must balance.

Transaction 7: Payment on Account

Cookie Lapp pays $300 to the store from which she purchased supplies in transaction 3. In accounting, we say that she pays $300 *on account.* The effect on the accounting equation is a decrease in Cash and a decrease in Accounts Payable, as shown here:

	ASSETS								LIABILITIES	+	STOCKHOLDERS' EQUITY		
	Cash	+	Accounts Receivable	+	Office Supplies	+	Land		Accounts Payable	+	Common Stock	+	Retained Earnings
Bal.	12,200				500		20,000	=	500		30,000		5,200
(7)	−300								−300				
Bal.	11,900		3,000		500		20,000		200		30,000		5,200
				35,400							35,400		

The payment of cash on account has no effect on office supplies or expenses. Lapp was paying off a liability, not an expense.

Transaction 8: Personal Transaction

Cookie Lapp remodels her home at a cost of $40,000, paying cash from personal funds. This event is *not* a transaction of Cookie Lapp Travel Design. It has no effect on the travel agency and, therefore, is not recorded by the business. It is a transaction of the Cookie Lapp *personal* entity, not the travel agency. This transaction illustrates the *entity concept.*

Transaction 9: Collection on Account

In transaction 5, Lapp performed services for a client on account. The business now collects $1,000 from the client. We say that Lapp collects the cash *on account.* She will record an increase in Cash. Should she also record an increase in service revenue? No, because she already recorded the revenue when she earned the revenue in transaction 5. The phrase "collect cash on account" means to record an increase in Cash and a decrease in Accounts Receivable. The effect on the accounting equation is:

	ASSETS								LIABILITIES	+	STOCKHOLDERS' EQUITY		
	Cash	+	Accounts Receivable	+	Office Supplies	+	Land		Accounts Payable	+	Common Stock	+	Retained Earnings
Bal.	11,900		3,000		500		20,000	=	200		30,000		5,200
(9)	+1,000		−1,000										
Bal.	12,900		2,000		500		20,000		200		30,000		5,200
				35,400							35,400		

Total assets are unchanged from the preceding total. Why? Because Lapp merely exchanged one asset for another.

Transaction 10: Sale of Land

Lapp sells some land owned by the travel agency. The sale price of $9,000 is equal to Lapp's cost of the land. The business receives $9,000 cash, and the effect on the accounting equation of the travel agency follows:

	Cash	+	Accounts Receivable	+	Office Supplies	+	Land		Accounts Payable	+	Common Stock	+	Retained Earnings
	ASSETS								**LIABILITIES + STOCKHOLDERS' EQUITY**				
Bal.	12,900		2,000		500		20,000	=	200		30,000		5,200
(10)	+9,000		—		—		−9,000		—		—		—
Bal.	21,900		2,000		500		11,000		200		30,000		5,200
	35,400								35,400				

Transaction 11: Payment of Cash Dividend

The business declares and pays Cookie Lapp a $2,000 cash dividend. The effect on the accounting equation is:

	Cash	+	Accounts Receivable	+	Office Supplies	+	Land		Accounts Payable	+	Common Stock	+	Retained Earnings	Type of SE Transaction
	ASSETS								**LIABILITIES + STOCKHOLDERS' EQUITY**					
Bal.	21,900		2,000		500		11,000	=	500		30,000		5,200	
(11)	−2,000		—		—		—		—		—		−2,000	*Dividends*
Bal.	19,900		2,000		500		11,000		200		30,000		3,200	
	33,400								33,400					

The dividend decreases the business's Cash and stockholders' equity (retained earnings). *Dividends do not represent an expense because they are not related to the earning of revenue. Therefore, dividends do not affect the business's net income or net loss.* The double underlines below each column indicate a final total after the last transaction.

Evaluating Business Transactions—The User Perspective of Accounting

We have now recorded Cookie Lapp Travel Design's transactions, and they are summarized in Exhibit 1-8. Note that every transaction maintains the equation

Assets = Liabilities + Stockholders' Equity

But a basic question remains: How will people actually use this information? The mass of data in Exhibit 1-8 won't tell a lender whether Cookie Lapp Travel Design can pay off a loan. The data in the exhibit don't tell whether the business is profitable.

To address these important questions, we need financial statements. The **financial statements** are business documents that report on a business in monetary terms. People use the financial statements to make business decisions, such as:

- Cookie Lapp wants to know whether her travel agency is profitable. Is the business earning a net income—is it profitable—or is it experiencing a net loss? The **income statement** answers this question by reporting the net income or net loss of the business.
- Suppose Lapp needs $200,000 to buy an office building. She calls her banker and requests a loan. The banker wants to know how much in assets the travel agency has and how much it already owes. The **balance sheet** answers this question by reporting

Continued on page 21

EXHIBIT 1-8 Analysis of Transactions, Cookie Lapp Travel Design, Inc.

PANEL A—Details of Transactions

1. The travel agency received $30,000 cash and issued common stock to the new stockholder.
2. Paid $20,000 cash for land.
3. Bought $500 of office supplies on account.
4. Received $5,500 cash from clients for service revenue earned.
5. Performed travel service for clients on account, $3,000.
6. Paid cash expenses: computer rent, $600; office rent, $1,100; employee salary, $1,200; utilities, $400.
7. Paid $300 on the account payable created in transaction 3.
8. Remodeled Lapp's personal residence. This is *not* a transaction of the business.
9. Collected $1,000 on the account receivable created in transaction 5.
10. Sold land for cash at its cost of $9,000.
11. Paid a cash dividend of $2,000.

PANEL B—Analysis of Transactions

	Assets					Liabilities +	Stockholders' Equity		Type of Stockholders' Equity Transaction
	Cash +	Accounts Receivable +	Office Supplies +	Land	=	Accounts Payable +	Common Stock +	Retained Earnings	
1.	+ 30,000						+ 30,000		*Issued stock*
Bal.	30,000						30,000		
2.	− 20,000			+ 20,000					
Bal.	10,000			20,000			30,000		
3.			+ 500			+ 500			
Bal.	10,000		500	20,000		500	30,000		
4.	+ 5,500							+ 5,500	*Service revenue*
Bal.	15,500		500	20,000		500	30,000	5,500	
5.		+ 3,000						+ 3,000	*Service revenue*
Bal.	15,500	3,000	500	20,000		500	30,000	8,500	
6.	− 600							− 600	*Rent expense, computer*
6.	− 1,100							− 1,100	*Rent expense, office*
6.	− 1,200							− 1,200	*Salary expense*
6.	− 400							− 400	*Utilities expense*
Bal.	12,200	3,000	500	20,000		500	30,000	5,200	
7.	− 300					− 300			
Bal.	11,900	3,000	500	20,000		200	30,000	5,200	
8.	Not a transaction of the business								
9.	+ 1,000	− 1,000							
Bal.	12,900	2,000	500	20,000		200	30,000	5,200	
10.	+ 9,000			− 9,000					
Bal.	21,900	2,000	500	11,000		200	30,000	5,200	
11.	− 2,000							− 2,000	*Dividends*
Bal.	19,900	2,000	500	11,000		200	30,000	3,200	
	33,400					33,400			

the business's assets and liabilities. The banker asks what Lapp did with any profits the business earned. Did the business pay large dividends, or did it keep the money in the travel agency? The **statement of retained earnings** answers this question.
- The banker wants to know if the travel agency generates enough cash to pay its bills. The **statement of cash flows** answers this question by reporting cash receipts and cash payments and whether cash increased or decreased.
- Outside investors also use financial statements. Cookie Lapp may need to issue more common stock to raise cash for an expansion. Suppose you are considering buying some stock in the travel agency. In making this decision, you would ask the same questions that Lapp and her banker have been asking.

Now let's examine the financial statements in detail.

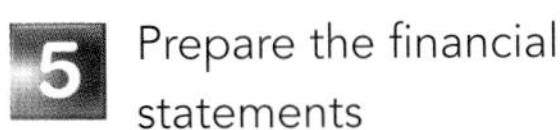
Prepare the financial statements

The Financial Statements

After analyzing transactions, we want to see the overall results. We look now at the financial statements discussed in the preceding section. The financial statements summarize the transaction data into a form that's useful for decision making. The financial statements are the:

- Income statement
- Statement of retained earnings
- Balance sheet
- Statement of cash flows

Income Statement

The **income statement** presents a summary of an entity's revenues and expenses for a period of time, such as a month or a year. The income statement, also called the **statement of earnings** or **statement of operations**, is like a video—a moving picture of operations during the period. The income statement holds one of the most important pieces of information about a business:

- ***Net income*** (total revenues greater than total expenses) or
- ***Net loss*** (total expenses greater than total revenues)

Net income is good news, and a net loss is bad news. What was the result of Cookie Lapp Travel Design's operations during April? Good news—the business earned net income (see the top part of Exhibit 1-9, page 22). The income statement is very important!

Statement of Retained Earnings

The **statement of retained earnings** shows the changes in *retained earnings* during a time period, such as a month or a year.

The only increase in retained earnings comes from:

- Net income (revenues exceed expenses)

Decreases in retained earnings result from two things:

- Dividends
- Net loss (expenses exceed revenues)

Balance Sheet

The *balance sheet* lists the entity's assets, liabilities, and stockholders' equity as of a specific date, usually the end of a month or a year. The balance sheet is like a snapshot of the entity. For this reason, it is also called the *statement of financial position* (see the middle of Exhibit 1-9, page 22). The balance sheet is very important!

EXHIBIT 1-9 Financial Statements of Cookie Lapp Travel Design

COOKIE LAPP TRAVEL DESIGN, INC. Income Statement Month Ended April 30, 2008		
Revenue:		
Service revenue		$8,500

Statement of Cash Flows

The **statement of cash flows** reports the cash coming in (cash receipts) and the cash going out (*cash payments*) during a period. Business activities result in a net cash inflow or a net cash outflow. The statement of cash flows reports the net increase or decrease in cash during the period and the ending cash balance.

In the first part of this book, we focus on the:

- Income statement
- Balance sheet
- Statement of retained earnings

The income statement and the balance sheet are more important than the statement of retained earnings. In Chapter 14 we cover the statement of cash flows in detail.

Financial Statement Headings

Each financial statement has a heading giving three pieces of data:

- Name of the business (such as Cookie Lapp Travel Design, Inc.)
- Name of the financial statement (income statement, balance sheet, and so on)
- Date or time period covered by the statement (April 30, 2008, for the balance sheet; month ended April 30, 2008, for the other statements)

An income statement (or a statement of retained earnings) that covers a year ended in December 2008 is dated "Year Ended December 31, 2008." A monthly income statement (or statement of retained earnings) for September 2008 shows "Month Ended September 30, 2008." Income must be identified with a particular time period.

Relationships Among the Financial Statements

6 Evaluate business performance

Exhibit 1-9 illustrates all four financial statements. Their data come from the transaction analysis in Exhibit 1-8 that covers the month of April 2008. Study the exhibit carefully. Then, observe the following in Exhibit 1-9:

1. The *income statement* for the month ended April 30, 2008:
   a. Reports April's revenues and expenses. Expenses are listed in decreasing order of their amount, with the largest expense first.
   b. Reports *net income* of the period if total revenues exceed total expenses. If total expenses exceed total revenues, a *net loss* is reported instead.
2. The *statement of retained earnings* for the month ended April 30, 2008:
   a. Opens with the retained earnings balance at the beginning of the period (zero for a new entity).
   b. Adds *net income* (or subtracts *net loss*, as the case may be). Net income or net loss come directly from the income statement (see arrow 1 in Exhibit 1-9).
   c. Subtracts *dividends*. Parentheses indicate a subtraction.
   d. Ends with the retained earnings balance at the end of the period.
3. The *balance sheet* at April 30, 2008:
   a. Reports all *assets*, all *liabilities*, and *stockholders' equity* at the end of the period.
      Assets are listed in the order of their liquidity (closeness to cash) with cash coming first because it is the most liquid asset.
      Liabilities are reported similarly. That is, list first the liability that must be paid first, usually Accounts Payable.
   b. Reports that total assets equal total liabilities plus total equity.
   c. Reports the ending retained earnings balance, taken directly from the statement of retained earnings (see arrow 2).

4. The *statement of cash flows* for the month ended April 30, 2008:
   a. Reports cash flows from three types of business activities (*operating, investing,* and *financing activities*) during the month. Each category of cash-flow activities includes both cash receipts (positive amounts), and cash payments (negative amounts denoted by parentheses).
   b. Reports a net increase in cash during the month and ends with the cash balance at April 30, 2008. This is the amount of cash to report on the balance sheet (see arrow 3).

As we conclude this chapter, we return to our opening question: Have you ever thought of having your own business? The Decision Guidelines feature on the next page shows how to make some of the decisions that you will face if you start a business. Decision Guidelines appear in each chapter.

Decision Guidelines

MAJOR BUSINESS DECISIONS

Suppose you open a business to take photos at parties at your college. You hire a professional photographer and line up suppliers for party favors and photo albums. Here are some factors you must consider if you expect to be profitable.

Decision	Guidelines
How to organize the business?	If a single owner—a *proprietorship*. If two or more owners, but not incorporated—a *partnership*. If the business issues stock to stockholders—a *corporation*.
What to account for?	Account for the business, a separate entity apart from its owner (*entity concept*). Account for transactions and events that affect the business and can be measured reliably.
How much to record for assets and liabilities?	Actual historical amount (*cost principle*).
How to analyze a transaction?	The accounting equation: **Assets = Liabilities + Stockholders' Equity**
How to measure profits and losses?	Income statement: **Revenues − Expenses = Net Income (or Net Loss)**
Did stockholders' equity increase or decrease?	Statement of retained earnings: **Beginning retained earnings** **+ Net income (or – Net loss)** **– Dividends** **= Ending retained earnings**
Where does the business stand financially?	Balance sheet (accounting equation): **Assets = Liabilities + Stockholders' Equity**

Summary Problem

Ron Smith opens an apartment-locator business near a college campus. The corporation will be named Campus Apartment Locators, Inc. During the first month of operations, July 2007, the business completes the following transactions:

a. Smith invest $35,000. The business receives $35,000 cash and issues common stock to Smith.

b. Purchases on account office supplies costing $350.

c. Pays cash of $30,000 to acquire a lot next to the campus. Smith intends to use the land as a future building site for the business office.

d. Locates apartments for clients and receives cash of $1,900.

e. Pays $100 on the account payable he created in transaction b.

f. Pays $2,000 of personal funds for a vacation.

g. Pays cash expenses for office rent, $400, and utilities, $100.

h. Sells office supplies to another business for its cost of $150.

i. Declares and pays a cash dividend of $1,200.

Requirements

1. Analyze the preceding transactions in terms of their effects on the accounting equation of Campus Apartment Locators, Inc. Use Exhibit 1-8 as a guide but show balances only after the last transaction.

2. Prepare the income statement, statement of retained earnings, and balance sheet of the business after recording the transactions. Use Exhibit 1-9 as a guide.

Solution

Requirement 1

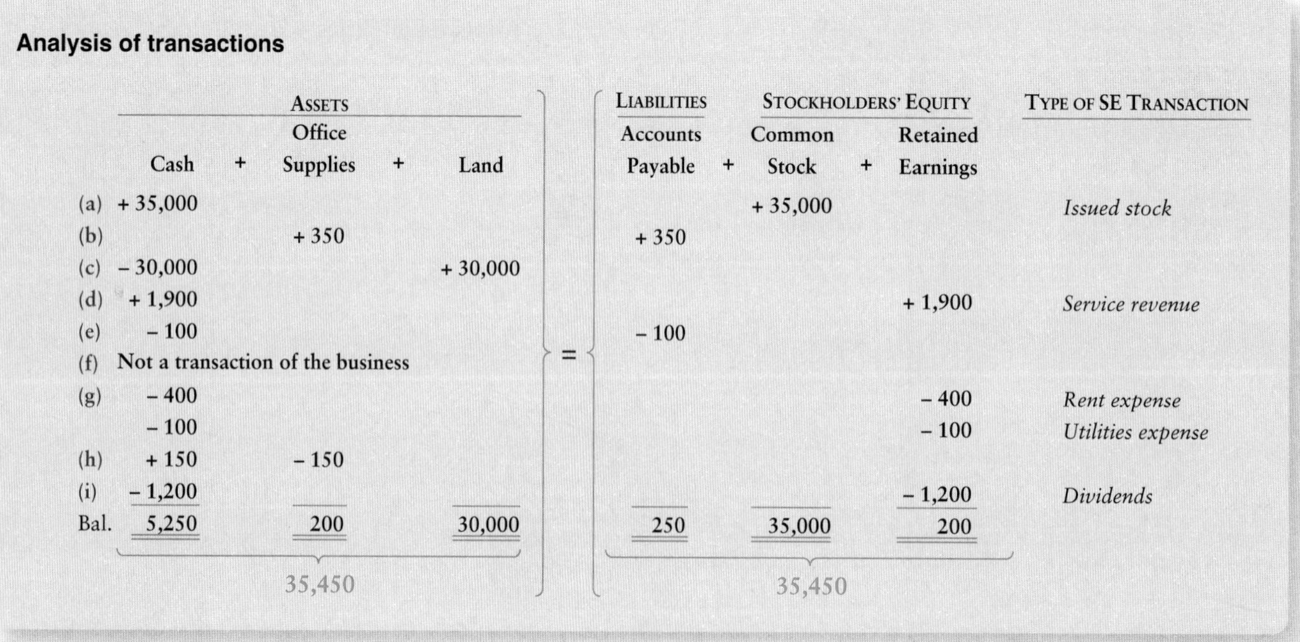

Analysis of transactions

	Assets				Liabilities	Stockholders' Equity		Type of SE Transaction
	Cash +	Office Supplies +	Land		Accounts Payable +	Common Stock +	Retained Earnings	
(a)	+ 35,000					+ 35,000		*Issued stock*
(b)		+ 350			+ 350			
(c)	– 30,000		+ 30,000					
(d)	+ 1,900						+ 1,900	*Service revenue*
(e)	– 100				– 100			
(f)	Not a transaction of the business			=				
(g)	– 400						– 400	*Rent expense*
	– 100						– 100	*Utilities expense*
(h)	+ 150	– 150						
(i)	– 1,200						– 1,200	*Dividends*
Bal.	5,250	200	30,000		250	35,000	200	
	35,450				35,450			

Requirement 2

Financial Statements of Campus Apartment Locators, Inc.

CAMPUS APARTMENT LOCATORS, INC. Income Statement Month Ended July 31, 2007		
Revenue:		
Service revenue		$1,900
Expenses:		
Rent expense	$400	
Utilities expense	100	
Total expenses		500
Net income		$1,400

CAMPUS APARTMENT LOCATORS, INC. Statement of Retained Earnings Month Ended July 31, 2007		
Retained earnings, July 1, 2007	$ 0	
Add: Net income for the month	1,400	
	1,400	
Less: Dividends	(1,200)	
Retained earnings, July 31, 2007	$ 200	

CAMPUS APARTMENT LOCATORS, INC. Balance Sheet July 31, 2007			
Assets		**Liabilities**	
Cash	$ 5,250	Accounts payable	$ 250
Office supplies	200		
Land	30,000	**Stockholders' Equity**	
		Common stock	35,000
		Retained earnings	200
		Total stockholders' equity	35,200
Total assets	$35,450	Total liabilities and stockholders' equity	$35,450

Accounting Vocabulary

Account Payable
A liability backed by the general reputation and credit standing of the debtor.

Account Receivable
A promise to receive cash from customers to whom the business has sold goods or for whom the business has performed services.

Accounting
The information system that measures business activities, processes that information into reports, and communicates the results to decision makers.

Accounting Equation
The basic tool of accounting, measuring the resources of the business and the claims to those resources: Assets = Liabilities + Owner's Equity

Asset
An economic resource that is expected to be of benefit in the future.

Audit
An examination of a company's financial situation.

Balance Sheet
An entity's assets, liabilities, and owners' equity as of a specific date. Also called the **statement of financial position**.

Certified Management Accountant (CMA)
A licensed accountant who works for a single company.

Certified Public Accountant (CPA)
A licensed accountant who serves the general public rather than one particular company.

Corporation
A business owned by stockholders; it begins when the state approves its articles of incorporation. A corporation is a legal entity, an "artificial person," in the eyes of the law.

Dividends
Distributions by a corporation to its stockholders.

Entity
An organization or a section of an organization that, for accounting purposes, stands apart from other organizations and individuals as a separate economic unit.

Equity
The claim of a corporation's owners to the assets of the business. Also called **shareholders' equity**.

Expense
Decrease in owners' equity that occurs from using assets or increasing liabilities in the course of delivering goods or services to customers.

Financial Accounting
The branch of accounting that focuses on information for people outside the firm.

Financial Accounting Standards Board (FASB)
The private organization that determines how accounting is practiced in the United States.

Financial Statements
Documents that report on a business in monetary amounts, providing information to help people make informed business decisions.

Generally Accepted Accounting Principles (GAAP)
Accounting guidelines, formulated by the Financial Accounting Standards Board, that govern how accountants measure, process, and communicate financial information.

Income Statement
Summary of an entity's revenues, expenses, and net income or net loss for a specific period. Also called the **statement of earnings** or the **statement of operations**.

Liability
An economic obligation (a debt) payable to an individual or an organization outside the business.

Management Accounting
The branch of accounting that focuses on information for internal decision makers of a business.

Net Income
Excess of total revenues over total expenses. Also called **net earnings** or **net profit**.

Net Loss
Excess of total expenses over total revenues.

Note Payable
A written promise of future payment.

Partnership
A business with two or more owners.

Proprietorship
A business with a single owner.

Revenue
Amounts earned by delivering goods or services to customers. Revenues increase owners' equity.

Shareholder
A person who owns stock in a corporation.

Statement of Cash Flows
Report of cash receipts and cash payments during a period.

Statement of Earnings
Summary of an entity's revenues, expenses, and net income or net loss for a specific period. Also called the **income statement** or the **statement of operations**.

Statement of Operations
Summary of an entity's revenues, expenses, and net income or net loss for a specific period. Also called the **income statement** or **statement of earnings**.

Statement of Retained Earnings
Summary of the changes in an entity's retained earnings during a specific period.

Stockholder
A person who owns stock in a corporation. Also called a **shareholder**.

Stockholders' Equity
The claim of a corporation's owners to the assets of the business. Also called **shareholders' equity**.

Transaction
An event that affects the financial position of a particular entity and can be recorded reliably.

Review Accounting and the Business Environment

Quick Check

1. Generally accepted accounting principles (GAAP) are formulated by the
   a. Institute of Management Accountants (IMA)
   b. American Institute of Certified Public Accountants (AICPA)
   c. Securities and Exchange Commission (SEC)
   d. Financial Accounting Standards Board (FASB)

2. Which type of business organization is owned by its stockholders?
   a. Corporation
   b. Partnership
   c. Proprietorship
   d. All the above are owned by stockholders

3. Which accounting concept or principle specifically states that we should record transactions at amounts that can be verified?
   a. Entity concept
   b. Going-concern concept
   c. Cost principle
   d. Reliability principle

4. Fossil is famous for fashion wristwatches and leather goods. At the end of a recent year, Fossil's total assets added up to $381 million, and stockholders' equity was $264 million. How much were Fossil's liabilities?
   a. Cannot determine from the data given
   b. $381 million
   c. $117 million
   d. $264 million

5. Assume that Fossil sold watches to a department store on account for $50,000. How would this transaction affect Fossil's accounting equation?
   a. Increase both liabilities and stockholders' equity by $50,000
   b. Increase both assets and liabilities by $50,000
   c. Increase both assets and stockholders' equity by $50,000
   d. No effect on the accounting equation because the effects cancel out

6. Which parts of the accounting equation does a sale on account affect?
   a. Accounts Receivable and Accounts Payable
   b. Accounts Receivable and Common Stock
   c. Accounts Payable and Retained Earnings
   d. Accounts Payable and Cash

7. Assume that Fossil paid expenses totaling $35,000. How does this transaction affect Fossil's accounting equation?
   a. Increases assets and decreases liabilities
   b. Increases both assets and stockholders' equity
   c. Decreases assets and increases liabilities
   d. Decreases both assets and stockholders' equity

8. Consider the overall effects of transactions 5 and 7 on Fossil. What is Fossil's net income or net loss?
   a. Net income of $15,000
   b. Net loss of $35,000
   c. Net income of $50,000
   d. Cannot determine from the data given

9. The balance sheet reports
   a. Results of operations on a specific date
   b. Financial position on a specific date
   c. Financial position for a specific period
   d. Results of operations for a specific period

10. The income statement reports
   a. Financial position on a specific date
   b. Results of operations on a specific date
   c. Results of operations for a specific period
   d. Financial position for a specific period

Answers are given after Apply Your Knowledge (p. 50).

Assess Your Progress

Short Exercises

Explaining revenues, expenses

S1-1 Sherman Lawn Service has been open for one year, and Haig Sherman, the owner, wants to know whether the business earned a net income or a net loss for the year. First, he must identify the revenues earned and the expenses incurred during the year. What are *revenues* and *expenses?* (pp. 13–15)

Explaining assets, liabilities, owners' equity

S1-2 Suppose you need a bank loan in order to purchase food-service equipment for DeFilippo Catering, Inc., which you manage. In evaluating your loan request, the banker asks about the assets and liabilities of your business. In particular, the banker wants to know the amount of the business's stockholders' equity. In your own words, explain the meanings of *assets, liabilities,* and *stockholders' equity.* Also show the relationship among assets, liabilities, and stockholders' equity. (pp. 13–15)

Applying accounting concepts and principles

S1-3 Suppose you are starting a business, T-Shirts Plus, to imprint logos on T-shirts. In organizing the business and setting up its accounting records, consider the following:

1. Should you combine your personal assets and personal liabilities with the assets and the liabilities of the business, or should you keep the two sets of records separate? Why? Which accounting concept or principle provides guidance? (pp. 11, 12)
2. In keeping the books of T-Shirts Plus, you must decide the amount to record for assets and liabilities. At what amount should you record assets and liabilities? Which accounting concept or principle provides guidance? (pp. 11, 12)

Applying accounting concepts and principles

S1-4 Claire Hunter owns and operates Claire Hunter Floral Designs. She proposes to account for flowers at current market value in order to have realistic amounts on the books if the business liquidates. Which accounting concept or principle is Hunter violating? How should Hunter account for the assets of the business? Which concept or principle governs this decision? (pp. 11, 12)

Using the accounting equation

S1-5 You begin A-1 Accounting Service by investing $2,000 of your own money in a business bank account. You receive the company's common stock. Then the business borrows $1,000 cash by signing a note payable to Summit Bank. Write the business's accounting equation after it has completed these transactions (Exhibit 1-6, page 13).

Using the accounting equation

S1-6 Wendy Craven owns a travel agency near the campus of Prince George's Community College. The business has cash of $2,000 and furniture that cost $8,000. Debts include accounts payable of $6,000. Using Craven's figures, write the accounting equation of the travel agency. There are no retained earnings yet. How much equity does Craven have in the business? (pp. 13–15)

Analyzing transactions

S1-7 Monte Jackson paid $20,000 cash to purchase land. To buy the land, Jackson was obligated to pay for it. Why, then, did Jackson record no liability in this transaction? (p. 16)

Analyzing transactions

S1-8 Air & Sea Travel recorded revenues of $3,000 earned on account by providing travel service for clients. How much are the business's cash and total assets after the transaction? Name the business's asset. (pp. 16, 17)

Analyzing transactions

S1-9 Brad Polson collected cash on account from a client for whom he had provided delivery services one month earlier. Why didn't Polson record revenue when he collected the cash on account? (p. 18)

Analyzing transactions

S1-10 Quail Creek Kennel, Inc., earns service revenue by caring for the pets of customers. Quail Creek's main expense is the salary paid to an employee. Write two accounting equations to show the effects of:

a. Receiving cash of $300 for service revenue earned

b. Payment of $200 for salary expense.

Show all appropriate headings, starting with the accounting equation. Also list the appropriate item under each heading. (pp. 14, 15)

Preparing the financial statements

S1-11 Examine Exhibit 1-8 on page 20. The exhibit summarizes the transactions of Cookie Lapp Travel Design for the month of April 2008. Suppose Cookie has completed only the first seven transactions and needs a bank loan on April 21. The vice president of the bank requires financial statements to support all loan requests. Prepare the balance sheet that Cookie Lapp would present to the banker *after completing the first seven transactions* on April 21, 2008. Exhibit 1-9, page 22, shows the format of the balance sheet.

Format of the income statement

S1-12 Cookie Lapp wishes to know how well her business performed during April. The income statement in Exhibit 1-9, page 22, helps answer this question. Write the formula for measuring net income or net loss on the income statement. (pp. 21–22)

Preparing the income statement
6

S1-13 Advanced Automotive Corporation has just completed operations for the year ended December 31, 2008. This is the third year of operations for the company. As the proprietor, you want to know how well the business performed during the year. To address this question, you have assembled the following data:

Insurance expense	$ 4,000	Salary expense	$42,000
Service revenue	90,000	Accounts payable	8,000
Supplies expense	1,000	Supplies	2,000
Rent expense	13,000	Dividends	16,000

Prepare the income statement of Advanced Automotive Corporation for the year ended December 31, 2008. Follow the format in Exhibit 1-9, page 22.

Exercises

Deciding on an investment

E1-14 Suppose you have saved some money and you are investing in eBay stock. What accounting information will you use to decide whether to invest in eBay? Which accounting principle do you hope eBay's accountants follow closely? Explain your answer. (pp. 4, 11)

Explaining the income statement and the balance sheet

E1-15 Terry Maness publishes a travel magazine. In need of cash, Maness asks Metro Bank for a loan. The bank requires borrowers to submit financial statements. With little knowledge of accounting, Maness doesn't know

continued . . .

how to proceed. Explain to him the information provided by the balance sheet and the income statement. Indicate why a lender would require this information. (pp. 4, 21)

Business transactions
2

E1-16 As the manager of a Wendy's restaurant, you must deal with a variety of business transactions. Give an example of a transaction that has each of the following effects on the accounting equation: (pp. 15–19)

a. Increase one asset and decrease another asset.
b. Decrease an asset and decrease stockholders' equity.
c. Decrease an asset and decrease a liability.
d. Increase an asset and increase stockholders' equity.
e. Increase an asset and increase a liability.

Transaction analysis
2

E1-17 Jake's Roasted Peanuts, a proprietorship, supplies snack foods. The business experienced the following events. State whether each event (1) increased, (2) decreased, or (3) had no effect on the *total assets* of the business. Identify any specific asset affected. (pp. 15–19)

a. Jake's Roasted Peanuts issued common stock after receiving cash from a stockholder.
b. Cash purchase of land for a building site.
c. Paid cash on accounts payable.
d. Purchased equipment; signed a note payable in payment.
e. Performed service for a customer on account.
f. Paid cash dividends.
g. Received cash from a customer on account receivable.
h. Borrowed money from the bank.

Accounting equation
3

E1-18 Compute the missing amount in the accounting equation for each entity: (p. 13)

	Assets	Liabilities	Stockholders' Equity
Pep Boys	$?	$60,000	$21,000
Eddie Bauer	72,000	?	40,000
Benbrook Exxon	100,000	79,000	?

Accounting equation
3

E1-19 Allison Landscaping started 2006 with total assets of $22,000 and total liabilities of $10,000. At the end of 2006, Allison's total assets stood at $30,000, and total liabilities were $14,000.

Requirements

1. Did the stockholders' equity of Allison Landscaping increase or decrease during 2006? By how much? (pp. 13–15)
2. Identify two possible reasons for the change in stockholders' equity during the year. (p. 22)

Accounting equation
3

E1-20 A-1 Rentals' balance sheet data at May 31, 2009, and June 30, 2009, follow.

	May 31, 2009	June 30, 2009
Total assets	$150,000	$195,000
Total liabilities	100,000	130,000

continued . . .

Requirements

Following are three situations about stockholders' investments and dividends of the business during June. For each situation, compute the amount of net income or net loss during June 2009.

1. The company issued $2,000 of common stock and paid no dividends.
2. The company issued no common stock. It paid dividends of $5,000.
3. The company issued $6,000 of common stock and paid dividends of $10,000.

Transaction analysis

E1-21 Indicate the effects of the following business transactions on the accounting equation of a Gangbuster Video location. Transaction (a) is answered as a guide. (pp. 15–19)

a. Received cash of $10,000 and issued common stock.
Answer: Increase asset (Cash)
Increase stockholders' equity (Common Stock)

b. Earned video rental revenue on account, $1,200.

c. Purchased office furniture on account, $600.

d. Received cash on account, $300.

e. Paid cash on account, $250.

f. Sold land for $12,000, which was the cost of the land.

g. Rented videos and received cash of $600.

h. Paid monthly office rent of $800.

i. Paid $100 cash to purchase supplies.

Transaction analysis; accounting equation

E1-22 Maria Lange opened a medical practice. During July, the first month of operation, the business, titled Maria Lange, M.D., P.C. (Professional Corporation), experienced the following events.

July 6	Lange invested $45,000 in the business by opening a bank account in the name of M. Lange, M.D., P.C. The corporation issued common stock to Lange.
9	Paid $35,000 cash for land.
12	Purchased medical supplies for $2,000 on account.
15	Officially opened for business.
15–31	During the rest of the month, Lange treated patients and earned service revenue of $7,000, receiving cash.
15–31	Paid cash expenses: employees' salaries, $1,700; office rent, $1,000; utilities, $300.
28	Sold supplies to another physician for the cost of those supplies, $500.
31	Paid $1,500 on account.

continued . . .

Requirement

Analyze the effects of these events on the accounting equation of the medical practice of M. Lange, M.D., P.C. Use a format similar to that of Exhibit 1-8 (p. 20), with headings for Cash; Medical Supplies; Land; Accounts Payable; Common Stock and Retained Earnings.

Business transactions and net income

E1-23 The analysis of Rountree TV Service's first eight transactions follows. Stockholders made only one investment to start the business and there were no dividend payments.

	Cash	+	Accounts Receivable	+	Equipment	=	Accounts Payable	+	Common Stock	Retained Earnings
1.	+25,000								+25,000	
2.			+2,400							+2,400
3.					+10,000		+10,000			
4.	+150		−150							
5.	−400				+400					
6.	−8,000						−8,000			
7.	+900									+900
8.	−2,000									−2,000

Requirements

1. Describe each transaction. (pp. 15–19)
2. If these transactions fully describe the operations of Rountree TV Service, Inc., during the month, what was the amount of net income or net loss? (p. 22)

Business organization, balance sheet

E1-24 The account balances of Allen Samuel Road Service, Inc., at November 30, 2009, follow.

Equipment	$15,500	Service revenue	$12,000
Supplies	500	Accounts receivable	6,000
Note payable	5,000	Accounts payable	3,500
Rent expense	800	Common stock	10,000
Cash	2,000	Salary expense	2,000
Retained earnings	?		

Requirements

1. Prepare the balance sheet of the business at November 30, 2009. (p. 22)
2. What does the balance sheet report—financial position or operating results? Which financial statement reports the other information? (p. 21)

Income Statement

5

E1-25 The assets, liabilities, stockholders' equity, revenues, and expenses of Ciliotta Design Studio, Inc., have the following balances at December 31, 2006, the end of its first year of operation. During the year, the business issued common stock for $15,000.

continued . . .

Note payable	$41,000	Office furniture	$ 45,000
Rent expense	24,000	Utilities expense	6,800
Cash	3,600	Accounts payable	3,300
Office supplies	4,800	Total stockholders' equity	27,100
Salary expense	60,000	Service revenue	158,100
Salaries payable	2,000	Accounts receivable	9,000
Property tax expense	1,200	Supplies expense	4,000

Requirements

1. Prepare the income statement of Ciliotta Design Studio, Inc. for the year ended December 31, 2006. What is the result of operations for 2006? (p. 22)
2. What was the amount of the company's dividend payments during the year? (p. 22)

Evaluating the performance of a real company

6

E1-26 In this exercise you will practice using the data of a well-known company with the amounts rounded. The 2004 annual report of UPS, the shipping company, reported revenue of $32 billion. Total expenses for the year were $29 billion. UPS ended the year with total assets of $33 billion, and it owed debts totaling $17 billion. At year-end 2003, UPS reported total assets of $30 billion and total liabilities of $17 billion.

Requirements

1. Compute UPS's net income for 2004. (p. 22)
2. Did UPS's stockholders' equity increase or decrease during 2004? By how much? (p. 22)
3. How would you rate UPS's performance for 2004—good or bad? Give your reason. (Challenge)

Using the financial statements

E1-27 Compute the missing amount for Jupiter Company. You will need to work through total stockholders' equity.

Jupiter Company	
Beginning:	
Assets	$ 50,000
Liabilities	20,000
Ending:	
Assets	$ 70,000
Liabilities	30,000
Stockholders' Equity:	
Issuance of stock	$ 0
Dividends	45,000
Income Statement:	
Revenues	$230,000
Expenses	?

Did Jupiter earn a net income or suffer a net loss for the year? Compute the amount. (pp. 13, 22)

Problems (Group A)

Entity concept, transaction analysis, accounting equation

P1-28A Abraham Woody practiced accounting with a partnership for five years. Recently he opened his own accounting firm, which he operates as a professional corporation. The name of the new entity is Abraham Woody, CPA, P.C. (Professional Corporation). Woody experienced the following events during the organizing phase of his new business and its first month of operations. Some of the events were personal and did not affect the business.

Feb. 4	Woody received $75,000 cash from former accounting partners.*
5	Woody deposited $60,000 cash in a new business bank account titled Abraham Woody, CPA, P.C. The business issued common stock to Woody.
6	Paid $300 cash for letterhead stationery for the new office.
7	Purchased office furniture for the office. The business will pay the account payable, $7,000, within 3 months.
10	Woody sold personal investment in Amazon.com stock, which he had owned for several years, receiving $50,000 cash.*
11	Woody deposited the $50,000 cash from sale of the Amazon.com stock in his personal bank account.*
12	A representative of a large company telephoned Woody and told him of the company's intention to transfer its accounting business to Woody.
18	Finished tax hearings on behalf of a client and submitted a bill for accounting services, $5,000. Woody expected to collect from this client within two weeks.
25	Paid office rent, $1,000.
28	Paid cash dividends of $3,000.

*Personal transaction of Abraham Woody.

Requirements

1. Analyze the effects of the events on the accounting equation of the proprietorship of Abraham Woody, CPA, PC. Use a format similar to Exhibit 1-8 on page 20.
2. At February 28, compute:
   a. Total assets (p. 20)
   b. Total liabilities (p. 20)
   c. Total stockholders' equity (p. 20)
   d. Net income or net loss for February (p. 22)

Transaction analysis, accounting equation, financial statements

P1-29A Marilyn Crone owns and operates a public relations firm called Best Foot Forward, Inc. The following amounts summarize her business on August 31, 2007:

	ASSETS								=	LIABILITIES + STOCKHOLDERS' EQUITY				
	Cash	+	Accounts Receivable	+	Supplies	+	Land		=	Accounts Payable	+	Common Stock	+	Retained Earnings
Bal.	2,200		1,500				12,000			8,000		5,000		2,700

continued . . .

During September 2007, the business completed these transactions.

a. Issued common stock and received cash of $20,000.
b. Performed service for a client and received cash of $700.
c. Paid off the beginning balance of accounts payable.
d. Purchased supplies on account, $1,000.
e. Collected cash from a customer on account, $1,000.
f. Received cash of $1,000 and issued common stock.
g. Consulted for a Senate candidate and billed the client for services rendered, $3,000.
h. Recorded the following business expenses for the month:
   1. Paid office rent, $900.
   2. Paid advertising, $100.
i. Sold supplies to another business for $100 cash, which was the cost of the supplies.
j. Paid cash dividends of $1,500.

Requirements

1. Analyze the effects of the preceding transactions on the accounting equation of Best Foot Forward, Inc. Adapt the format of Exhibit 1-8, page 20.
2. Prepare the income statement of Best Foot Forward, Inc., for the month ended September 30, 2007. List expenses in decreasing order by amount. (p. 22)
3. Prepare the entity's statement of retained earnings for the month ended September 30, 2007. (p. 22)
4. Prepare the balance sheet at September 30, 2007 (p. 22)

Business transactions and analysis

P1-30A Carolina Sports Consulting Corp. was recently formed as a corporation. The balance of each item in the company's accounting equation is shown for June 1 and for each of the following business days.

	Cash	Accounts Receivable	Supplies	Land	Accounts Payable	Common Stock	Retained Earnings
June 1	$ 4,000	$4,000	$1,000	$ 8,000	$4,000	$10,000	$3,000
4	13,000	4,000	1,000	8,000	4,000	19,000	3,000
9	6,000	4,000	1,000	15,000	4,000	19,000	3,000
13	6,000	4,000	3,000	15,000	6,000	19,000	3,000
16	5,000	4,000	3,000	15,000	5,000	19,000	3,000
19	7,000	2,000	3,000	15,000	5,000	19,000	3,000
22	15,000	2,000	3,000	15,000	5,000	27,000	3,000
25	12,000	2,000	3,000	15,000	2,000	27,000	3,000
27	11,000	2,000	4,000	15,000	2,000	27,000	3,000
30	9,000	2,000	4,000	15,000	2,000	27,000	1,000

Requirement

A single transaction took place on each day. Briefly describe the transaction that most likely occurred on each day, beginning with June 4. Indicate which accounts were increased or decreased and by what amounts. No revenue or expense transactions occurred on these dates. (pp. 15–19)

Preparing the financial statements—simple situation 5

P1-31A Accent Photography, Inc., works weddings and prom-type parties. The balance of retained earnings was $16,000 at December 31, 2006. At December 31, 2007, the business's accounting records show these balances:

Insurance expense	$ 2,000	Accounts receivable	$ 3,000
Cash	14,000	Note payable	35,000
Accounts payable	1,000	Retained earnings	?
Advertising expense	4,000	Salary expense	14,000
Service revenue	71,000	Equipment	80,000
Dividends	46,000	Common stock	40,000

Prepare the following financial statements for Accent Photography:

a. Income statement for the year ended December 31, 2007 (p. 22)

b. Statement of retained earnings for the year ended December 31, 2007 (p. 22)

c. Balance sheet at December 31, 2007 (p. 22)

Income statement, statement of retained earnings, balance sheet 5 6

P1-32A Presented here are (a) the assets and liabilities of Security Systems Corporation at December 31, 2007, and (b) the revenues and expenses of the company for the year ended on that date.

Land	$ 60,000	Common stock	$100,000
Note payable	35,000	Accounts payable	19,000
Property tax expense	4,000	Accounts receivable	12,000
Dividends	40,000	Advertising expense	13,000
Rent expense	23,000	Building	131,000
Salary expense	63,000	Cash	14,000
Salary payable	1,000	Equipment	20,000
Service revenue	189,000	Insurance expense	2,000
Supplies	3,000	Interest expense	9,000

The retained earnings balance was $50,000 one year ago, at December 31, 2006.

Requirements

1. Prepare Security Systems Corporation's income statement for the year ended December 31, 2007. (p. 22)
2. Prepare the statement of retained earnings for the year ended December 31, 2007. (p. 22)
3. Prepare the balance sheet at December 31, 2007. (p. 22)
4. Answer these questions about the company:
   a. Was the result of operations for the year a profit or a loss? How much? (p. 22)
   b. How much in total economic resources does the company have as it moves into the new year? How much does the company owe? What is the dollar amount of the stockholders' equity in the business at the end of the year? (p. 22)

Balance sheet, entity concept

P1-33A Jan Featherston is a realtor. She organized her business as a corporation, Jan Featherston, Realtor, P.C. (Professional Corporation), by investing $20,000 cash. The business issued common stock to her. Consider the following facts at November 30, 2006.

a. The business owes $55,000 on a note payable for land that the business acquired for a total price of $80,000.

b. The business spent $20,000 for a Coldwell Banker real estate franchise, which entitles Featherston to represent herself as a Coldwell Banker agent. This franchise is a business asset.

c. Featherston owes $60,000 on a personal mortgage for her personal residence, which she acquired in 2003 for a total price of $150,000.

d. Featherston has $4,000 in her personal bank account, and the business has $7,000 in its bank account.

e. Featherston owes $3,000 on a personal charge account with Nordstrom.

f. The office acquired business furniture for $14,000 on November 25. Of this amount, the business owes $5,000 on account at November 30.

g. Office supplies on hand at the real estate office total $1,000.

1. Prepare the balance sheet of the real estate business of Jan Featherston, Realtor, P.C. at November 30, 2006. (p. 22)
2. Identify the personal items that would not be reported on the balance sheet of the business. (pp. 11, 12, 22)

Correcting a balance sheet
5

P1-34A The bookkeeper of Lone Star Landscaping, Inc. prepared the company's balance sheet while the accountant was ill. The balance sheet contains numerous errors. In particular, the bookkeeper knew that the balance sheet should balance, so he plugged in the stockholders' equity amount needed to achieve this balance. The stockholders' equity is totally incorrect. All other amounts are accurate, but some are out of place.

LONE STAR LANDSCAPING, INC.
Balance Sheet
Month Ended July 31, 2008

Assets		Liabilities	
Cash	$ 4,000	Accounts receivable	$ 23,000
Office supplies	1,000	Common stock	34,000
Land	50,000	Service revenue	39,500
Salary expense	2,500	Property tax expense	800
Office furniture	16,000	Accounts payable	8,000
Note payable	36,000		
Rent expense	2,500	**Stockholders' Equity**	
		Retained earnings	6,700
Total assets	$112,000	Total liabilities	$112,000

Requirement

Prepare the correct balance sheet, and date it correctly. Compute total assets, total liabilities, and total stockholders' equity. (p. 22)

Problems (Group B)

Entity concept, transaction analysis, accounting equation

P1-35B Amy Fisk practiced law with a partnership for 10 years. Recently she opened her own law office, which she operates as a professional corporation. The name of the new entity is Amy Fisk, Attorney, P.C. (Professional Corporation). Fisk experienced the following events during the organizing phase of the new business and its first month of operation. Some of the events were personal and did not affect the law practice. Others were business transactions and should be accounted for by the business.

July 1	Fisk sold personal investment in eBay stock, which she had owned for several years, receiving $29,000 cash.*
2	Fisk deposited the $29,000 cash from sale of the eBay stock in her personal bank account.*
3	Fisk received $150,000 cash from former law partners.*
5	Fisk deposited $100,000 cash in a new business bank account titled Amy Fisk, Attorney, P.C. The business issued common stock to Fisk.
6	A representative of a large company telephoned Fisk and told her of the company's intention to transfer its legal business to Amy Fisk, Attorney.
7	Paid $500 cash for letterhead stationery for the new law office.
9	Purchased office furniture for the law office, agreeing to pay the account, $9,500, within 3 months.
23	Finished court hearings on behalf of a client and submitted a bill for legal services, $3,000, on account.
30	Paid office rent, $1,500.
31	Paid cash dividends of $500

* Personal transaction of Amy Fisk.

Requirements

1. Analyze the effects of the preceding events on the accounting equation of the proprietorship of Amy Fisk, Attorney, PC. Use a format similar to Exhibit 1-8, page 20.
2. At July 31, compute the business's
   a. Total assets (p. 20)
   b. Total liabilities (p. 20)
   c. Total stockholders' equity (p. 20)
   d. Net income or net loss for the month (p. 22)

Transaction analysis, accounting equation, financial statements

P1-36B Bob Grayson owns and operates an architectural firm called Grayson Architecture, Inc. The following amounts summarize his business on April 30, 2007.

	ASSETS								=	LIABILITIES	+	STOCKHOLDERS' EQUITY		
	Cash	+	Accounts Receivable	+	Supplies	+	Land		=	Accounts Payable	+	Common Stock	+	Retained Earnings
Bal.	1,720		3,240				24,100			5,400		10,000		13,660

continued . . .

During May 2007, the business completed these transactions:

a. Grayson received $12,000 as a gift and deposited the cash in the business bank account. The corporation issued common stock to Grayson.

b. Paid off the beginning balance of accounts payable.

c. Performed services for a client and received cash of $1,100.

d. Collected cash from a client on account, $750.

e. Purchased supplies on account, $720.

f. Consulted on the interior design of a building and billed the client for services rendered, $5,000 on account.

g. Received cash of $1,700 and issued common stock.

h. Recorded the following business expenses for the month:
   1. Paid office rent, $1,200.
   2. Paid advertising, $600.

i. Sold supplies to an interior designer for $80 cash, which was the cost of the supplies.

j. Paid cash dividends of $2,400.

Requirements

1. Analyze the effects of the preceding transactions on the accounting equation of Grayson Architecture, Inc. Adapt the format of Exhibit 1-8, page 20.
2. Prepare the income statement of Grayson Architecture, Inc., for the month ended May 31, 2007. List expenses in decreasing order by amount. (p. 22)
3. Prepare the statement of retained earnings of Grayson Architecture, Inc., for the month ended May 31, 2007. (p. 22)
4. Prepare the balance sheet of Grayson Architecture, Inc., at May 31, 2007. (p. 22)

Business transactions and analysis

P1-37B Pellegrini Electronics Corporation was recently formed. The balance of each item in the company's accounting equation follows for May 4 and for each of the following days:

	Cash	Accounts Receivable	Supplies	Land	Accounts Payable	Common Stock	Retained Earnings
May 4	$2,000	$7,000	$ 800	$11,000	$3,800	$5,000	$12,000
7	6,000	3,000	800	11,000	3,800	5,000	12,000
12	4,000	3,000	800	11,000	1,800	5,000	12,000
17	4,000	3,000	1,100	11,000	2,100	5,000	12,000
19	5,000	3,000	1,100	11,000	2,100	6,000	12,000
20	3,900	3,000	1,100	11,000	1,000	6,000	12,000
22	9,900	3,000	1,100	5,000	1,000	6,000	12,000
25	9,900	3,700	400	5,000	1,000	6,000	12,000
26	9,300	3,700	1,000	5,000	1,000	6,000	12,000
30	4,300	3,700	1,000	5,000	1,000	6,000	7,000

Requirement

A single transaction took place on each day. Describe briefly the transaction that most likely occurred on each day, beginning with May 7. Indicate which accounts were increased or decreased and by what amount. No revenue or expense transactions occurred on these dates. (pp. 15–19)

Preparing the financial statements—simple situation

5

P1-38B Studio Gallery, Inc. provides pictures for high school yearbooks. The balance of retained earnings was $15,000 at December 31, 2008. At December 31, 2009, the business's accounting records show these balances:

Rent expense	$ 7,000	Common stock	$35,000
Cash	20,000	Accounts receivable	8,000
Dividends	16,000	Note payable	12,000
Accounts payable	6,000	Retained earnings	?
Advertising expense	4,000	Salary expense	22,000
Service revenue	74,000	Equipment	65,000

Prepare the following financial statements for Studio Gallery, Inc.

a. Income statement for the year ended December 31, 2009 (p. 22)

b. Statement of retained earnings for the year ended December 31, 2009. (p. 22)

c. Balance sheet at December 31, 2009 (p. 22)

Income statement, statement of retained earnings, balance sheet

P1-39B The amounts of (a) the assets and liabilities of Town & Country Realty, Inc. at December 31, 2007, and (b) the revenues and expenses of the company for the year ended on that date follow.

Note payable	$ 31,000	Accounts payable	$ 12,000
Property tax expense	2,000	Accounts receivable	3,000
Rent expense	14,000	Building	56,000
Salary expense	38,000	Cash	7,000
Service revenue	100,000	Equipment	13,000
Supplies	7,000	Interest expense	4,000
Utilities expense	3,000	Interest payable	1,000
Land	8,000	Dividends	32,000
Common stock	30,000		

The retained earnings balance was $13,000 one year ago, at December 31, 2006.

Requirements

1. Prepare the income statement of Town & Country Realty, Inc., for the year ended December 31, 2007. (p. 22)
2. Prepare the statement of retained earnings for the year ended December 31, 2007. (p. 22)
3. Prepare the balance sheet at December 31, 2007. (p. 22)

4. Answer these questions about the company.
   a. Was the result of operations for the year a profit or a loss? How much? (p. 22)
   b. Did stockholders drain off all the earnings for the year, or did they increase the company's stockholders' equity during the period? How would their actions affect the company's ability to borrow? (p. 22)

Balance sheet, entity concept

P1-40B Martha Agee operates Blinko Copy Center, Inc. She organized the business as a corporation on March 1, 2006. Blinko's first transaction was receipt of $25,000 cash from Agee and issuance of common stock to her. Consider the following facts at March 31, 2006:

a. Agee has $3,000 in her personal bank account and Blinko has $17,000 in its business bank account.
b. Office supplies on hand at the store total $1,000.
c. The business spent $15,000 for a Blinko franchise, which entitles it to use the corporate name. This franchise is an asset.
d. Blinko owes $34,000 on a note payable for some land acquired by the business for a total price of $60,000.
e. Agee owes $60,000 on a personal mortgage on her personal residence, which she acquired in 2004 for a total price of $100,000.
f. Agee owes $950 on her personal MasterCard.
g. Blinko acquired business furniture for $22,000 on March 26. Of this amount, the business owes $15,000 on account at March 31.

Requirements

1. Prepare the balance sheet of Blinko Copy Center, Inc., at March 31, 2006. (p. 22)
2. Identify the personal items that would not be reported on the balance sheet of the business. (pp. 11, 12, 22)

Correcting a balance sheet

5

P1-41B The bookkeeper of Dave Lundy Tax Service, Inc., P.C. prepared the balance sheet of the company while the accountant was ill. The balance sheet contains numerous errors. In particular, the bookkeeper knew that the balance sheet should balance, so he plugged in the stockholders' equity amount to achieve this balance. The stockholders' equity is totally incorrect. All other amounts are accurate, but some are out of place.

DAVE LUNDY TAX SERVICE, INC., PC
Balance Sheet
Month Ended Ocober 31, 2007

Assets		Liabilities	
Cash	$ 5,400	Notes receivable	$ 3,000
Insurance expense	300	Interest expense	600
Land	21,500	Office supplies	800
Salary expense	3,300	Accounts receivable	2,600
Office furniture	6,000	Note payable	21,000
Accounts payable	2,300		
Utilities expense	2,100	**Stockholders' Equity**	
Common stock	10,000	Retained earnings	22,900
Total assets	$50,900	Total liabilities	$50,900

Requirement

Prepare the correct balance sheet and date it correctly. Compute total assets, total liabilities, and total stockholders' equity. (p. 22)

Continuing Problem

For 24/7 practice, visit www.MyAccountingLab.com

Problem 1-42 is the first problem in a sequence that begins an accounting cycle. The cycle is continued in Chapter 2 and completed in Chapter 5.

Recording transactions and preparing a trial balance

P1-42 Redmon Consulting, Inc., began operations and completed these transactions during the first half of December:

Dec. 2	Received $10,000 cash and issued common stock.
2	Paid monthly office rent, $500.
3	Paid cash for a Dell computer, $2,000. This equipment is expected to remain in service for five years.
4	Purchased office furniture on account, $3,600. The furniture should last for five years.
5	Purchased supplies on account, $300.
9	Performed consulting service for a client on account, $1,700.
12	Paid utility expenses, $200.
18	Performed service for a client and received cash of $800.

Requirements

1. Analyze the effects of Redmon Consulting's transactions on the accounting equation. Use the format of Exhibit 1-8, page 20, and include these headings: Cash, Accounts Receivable, Supplies, Equipment, Furniture, Accounts Payable, Common Stock, and Retained Earnings.
2. Prepare the income statement of Redmon Consulting, Inc., for the month ended December 31, 2007. List expenses in decreasing order by amount. (p. 22)
3. Prepare the statement of retained earnings for the month ended December 31, 2007. (p. 22)
4. Prepare the balance sheet at December 31, 2007. (p. 22)

In Chapter 2, we will account for these same transactions a different way—as the accounting is actually performed in practice.

Apply Your Knowledge

Decision Cases

Accounting equation, evaluating performance

Case 1. This case follows up on the chapter-opening story about Sherman Lawn Service and DeFilippo Catering. It is now the end of the first year of operations, and both owners—Haig Sherman and Julie DeFilippo—want to know how well they came out at the end of the year. Neither business kept complete accounting records (even though Haig Sherman majored in accounting). Sherman and DeFilippo throw together the following data at year end:

Sherman Lawn Service:	
Total assets	$12,000
Owner equity	8,000
Total revenues	35,000
Total expenses	22,000
DeFilippo Catering:	
Total liabilities	$ 7,000
Owner equity	6,000
Total expenses	44,000
Net income	9,000

Working in the lawn-service business, Sherman has forgotten all the accounting he learned in college. DeFilippo majored in dietetics, so she never learned any accounting. To gain information for evaluating their businesses, they ask you several questions. For each answer, you must show your work to convince Sherman and DeFilippo that you know what you are talking about.

1. Which business has more assets? (pp. 13, 22)
2. Which business owes more to creditors? (pp. 13, 22)
3. In which business have the owners invested more? (pp. 13, 22)
4. Which business brought in more revenue? (pp. 13, 22)
5. Which business is more profitable? (p. 22)
6. Which of the foregoing questions do you think is most important for evaluating these two businesses? Why? (Challenge)
7. Which business looks better from a financial standpoint? (Challenge)

Measuring net income

5 6

Case 2. Dave and Reba Guerrera saved all their married life to open a bed and breakfast (B&B) named Tres Amigos. They invested $100,000 of their own money and the corporation issued common stock to them. The business then got a $100,000 bank loan for the $200,000 needed to get started. The corporation bought a run-down old Spanish colonial home in Tucson for $80,000. It cost another $50,000 to renovate. They found most of the furniture at antique shops and flea markets—total cost was $20,000. Kitchen equipment cost $10,000, and a Dell computer set cost $2,000.

continued . . .

Prior to the grand opening, the banker requests a report on their activities thus far. Tres Amigos' bank statement shows a cash balance of $38,000. They feel pretty good with that much net income in only six months. To better understand how well they are doing, they prepare the following income statement for presentation to the bank:

TRES AMIGOS BED AND BREAKFAST, INC. Income Statement Six Months Ended June 30, 2007	
Revenues:	
Investments by owner	$100,000
Bank loan	100,000
Total revenues	200,000
Expenses:	
Cost of the house	$ 80,000
Repairs to the house	50,000
Furniture expense	20,000
Kitchen equipment expense	10,000
Computer expense	2,000
Total expenses	162,000
Net income	38,000

1. Suppose you are the Guerreras' banker, and they have given you this income statement. Would you congratulate them on their net income? If so, explain why. If not, how would you advise them to measure the net income of the business? Does the amount of cash in the bank measure net income? Explain. (Challenge)

2. Prepare Tres Amigos' balance sheet from their data. There are no retained earnings yet. (p. 22)

Ethical Issues

Ethical Issue 1. The board of directors of Xiaping Trading Company is meeting to discuss the past year's results before releasing financial statements to the public. The discussion includes this exchange:

Wai Lee, company president: "This has not been a good year! Revenue is down and expenses are way up. If we're not careful, we'll report a loss for the third year in a row. I can temporarily transfer some land that I own into the company's name, and that will beef up our balance sheet. Brent, can you shave $500,000 from expenses? Then we can probably get the bank loan that we need."

Brent Ray, company chief accountant: "Wai Lee, you are asking too much. Generally accepted accounting principles are designed to keep this sort of thing from happening."

Requirements

1. What is the fundamental ethical issue in this situation? (Challenge)

2. Discuss how Wai Lee's proposals violate generally accepted accounting principles. Identify each specific concept or principle involved. (pp. 11, 12)

Ethical Issue 2. The tobacco companies have paid billions because of smoking-related illnesses. In particular, **Philip Morris,** a leading cigarette manufacturer, paid over $3 billion in one year.

Requirements

1. Suppose you are the chief financial officer (CFO) responsible for the financial statements of Philip Morris. What ethical issue would you face as you consider what to report in your company's annual report about the cash payments? What is the ethical course of action for you to take in this situation? (Challenge)
2. What are some of the negative consequences to Philip Morris for not telling the truth? What are some of the negative consequences to Philip Morris for telling the truth? (Challenge)

Financial Statement Case

Identifying items from a company's financial statements

This and similar cases in later chapters focus on the financial statement of a real company—**Amazon.com, Inc.,** the Internet shopping leader. As you work each case, you will gain confidence in your ability to use the financial statements of real companies.

Refer to Amazon.com's financial statements in Appendix A at the end of the book.

Requirements

1. How much in cash (including cash equivalents) did Amazon have on December 31, 2005?
2. What were the company's total assets at December 31, 2005? At December 31, 2004?
3. Write the company's accounting equation at December 31, 2005, by filling in the dollar amounts:

   ASSETS = LIABILITIES + STOCKHOLDERS' EQUITY

4. Identify net sales (revenue) for the year ended December 31, 2005. How much did total revenue increase or decrease from 2004 to 2005?
5. How much net income or net loss did Amazon earn for 2005 and for 2004? Based on net income, was 2005 better or worse than 2004?

Team Projects

Project I. You are opening Quail Creek Pet Kennel, Inc. Your purpose is to earn a profit, and you organize as a corporation.

1. Make a detailed list of 10 factors you must consider to establish the business.
2. Identify 10 or more transactions that your business will undertake to open and operate the kennel.

continued . . .

3. Prepare the Quail Creek Pet Kennel, Inc., income statement, statement of retained earnings, and balance sheet at the end of the first month of operations before you have had time to pay all the business's bills. Use made-up figures and include a complete heading for each financial statement. Date the balance sheet as of January 31, 20XX.

4. Discuss how you will evaluate the success of your business and how you will decide whether to continue its operation.

Project 2. You are promoting a rock concert in your area. Your purpose is to earn a profit, and you organize Concert Enterprises as a corporation.

Requirements

1. Make a detailed list of 10 factors you must consider to establish the business.

2. Describe 10 of the items your business must arrange in order to promote and stage the rock concert.

3. Prepare your business's income statement, statement of retained earnings, and balance sheet on June 30, 20XX, immediately after the rock concert and before you have had time to pay all the business's bills and to collect all receivables. Use made-up amounts, and include a complete heading for each financial statement. For the income statement and the statement of retained earnings, assume the period is the three months ended June 30, 20XX.

4. Assume that you will continue to promote rock concerts if the venture is successful. If it is unsuccessful, you will terminate the business within three months after the concert. Discuss how you will evaluate the success of your venture and how you will decide whether to continue in business.

For Internet Exercises, Excel in Practice, and additional online activities, go to the Web site www.prenhall.com/horngren

Quick Check Answers

1. *d* 2. *a* 3. *d* 4. *c* 5. *c* 6. *b* 7. *d* 8. *a* 9. *b* 10. *c*

Chapter 1: Demo Doc

Transaction Analysis Using Accounting Equation/Financial Statement Preparation

Demo Doc: To make sure you understand this material, work through the following demonstration "demo doc" with detailed comments to help you see the concept within the framework of a worked-through problem.

Learning Objectives 4, 5

On March 1, 2008, David Richardson incorporated a painting business near an historical housing district. David was the sole shareholder of the company, which he named DR Painting, Inc. During March 2008, DR Painting engaged in the following transactions:

a. DR Painting received cash of $40,000 from David Richardson and issued common stock to David.

b. The business paid $20,000 cash to acquire a truck.

c. The business purchased supplies costing $1,800 on account.

d. The business painted a house for a client and received $3,000 cash.

e. The business painted a house for a client for $4,000. The client agreed to pay next week.

f. The business paid $800 cash toward the supplies purchased in transaction c.

g. The business paid employee salaries of $1,000 in cash.

h. The business paid cash dividends of $1,500.

i. The business collected $2,600 from the client in transaction e.

j. David paid $100 cash for personal groceries.

Requirements

1. Analyze the preceding transactions in terms of their effects on the accounting equation of DR Painting, Inc. Use Exhibit 1-8 (p. 20) as a guide, but show balances only after the last transaction.

2. Prepare the income statement, statement of retained earnings, and balance sheet of the business after recording the transactions. Use Exhibit 1-9 (p. 20) in the text as a guide.

Chapter 1: Demo Doc Solutions

Requirement 1

Analyze the preceding transactions in terms of their effects on the accounting equation of DR Painting, Inc. Use Exhibit 1-8 (p. 20) as a guide, but show balances only after the last transaction.

Part 1	Part 2	Part 3	Part 4	Demo Doc Complete

a. DR Painting received $40,000 cash from David Richardson and issued common stock to David.

The business is receiving cash from a stockholder, so this is a recordable transaction for DR Painting.

The business's Cash (an asset) is increased by $40,000 and Common Stock (stockholders' equity) is also increased by $40,000.

The effect of this transaction on the accounting equation is:

	ASSETS	+	LIABILITIES	=	STOCKHOLDERS' EQUITY	TYPE OF STOCKHOLDERS' EQUITY TRANSACTION
	Cash	+		=	Common Stock	
a.	+40,000				+40,000	*Issued stock*
	40,000			=	*40,000*	

To record this in the table, we add $40,000 under Assets: Cash, and add $40,000 under Stockholders' Equity: Common Stock. To the right of the transaction, we write "Issued stock" to help us keep track of changes in the equity of the business. Before we move on, we should double-check to see that the left side of the equation equals the right side. It is important to remember that the equation must always balance after each transaction is recorded.

b. The business paid $20,000 cash to acquire a truck.

The Truck (an asset) is increased by $20,000, while Cash (an asset) decreases by $20,000.

The effect of this transaction on the accounting equation is:

	ASSETS				LIABILITIES +	STOCKHOLDERS' EQUITY	TYPE OF STOCKHOLDERS' EQUITY TRANSACTION
	Cash	+	Truck	=		Common Stock	
a.	40,000					40,000	*Issued stock*
b.	−20,000	+	20,000				
Bal.	20,000		20,000	=		40,000	
			40,000	=	*40,000*		

Note that transactions do not have to affect both sides of the equation. However, the accounting equation *always* holds, so *both sides must always balance.* It helps to check that this is true after every transaction.

c. The business purchased supplies costing $1,800 on account.

The supplies are an asset that is increased by $1,800. However, the supplies were not paid for in cash, but instead *on account*. This relates to accounts *pay*able (because it will have to be *paid* later). Because we now have *more* money that has to be paid later, it is an increase to Accounts Payable (a liability) of $1,800.

The effect of this transaction on the accounting equation is:

	ASSETS			=	LIABILITIES	+	STOCKHOLDERS' EQUITY
	Cash	+ Supplies +	Truck		Accounts Payable	+	Common Stock
Bal.	20,000		20,000	=			40,000
c.		+1,800			+1,800		
Bal.	20,000	1,800	20,000	=	1,800		40,000 Bal.
			41,800	=	*41,800*		

Remember that the supplies will be recorded as an asset until the time that they are used by the business (the adjustment will be addressed in a later chapter). The obligation to pay the $1,800 will remain in Accounts Payable until it is paid.

d. The business painted a house for a client and received cash of $3,000.

When the business paints houses, it means that it is doing work, or performing services, for clients, which is the way that the business makes money. By performing services, the business is earning service revenues (as opposed to *sales* revenues).

This means that there is an increase in Service Revenues (which increases Retained Earnings) of $3,000. Because the clients paid in cash, there is also an increase in Cash (an asset) of $3,000.

Remember: Revenues *increase* net income, which increases Retained Earnings.

The effect of this transaction on the accounting equation is:

	ASSETS			=	LIABILITIES	+	STOCKHOLDERS' EQUITY		TYPE OF STOCKHOLDERS' EQUITY TRANSACTION
	Cash	+ Supplies	+ Truck	=	Accounts Payable	+	Common Stock	+ Retained Earnings	
Bal.	20,000	1,800	20,000	=	1,800		40,000		
d.	+3,000							+3,000	*Service revenue*
Bal.	23,000	1,800	20,000	=	1,800		40,000	3,000	
			44,800	=	*44,800*				

Note that we write "Service revenue" to the right of the Retained Earnings column to record the type of transaction.

e. The business painted a house for a client for $4,000. The client agreed to pay next month.

This transaction is similar to transaction **d**, except that the business is not receiving the cash immediately. Does this mean that we should wait to record the revenue when the cash is received? No, DR Painting should recognize the revenue when the service is performed, regardless of whether it has received the cash.

Again, the business is performing services for clients, which means that it is earning service revenues. This results in an increase to Service Revenue (Retained Earnings) of $4,000.

However, this time the client did not pay in cash but instead agreed to pay later. This is the same as charging the services *on account*. This is money that the business will *receive* in the future (when the customers eventually pay), so it is called accounts *receiv*able. Accounts Receivable (an asset) is increasing by $4,000. Accounts Receivable represents amounts owed to the business and decreases when a customer pays.

The effect of this transaction on the accounting equation is:

	ASSETS				= LIABILITIES +	STOCKHOLDERS' EQUITY		TYPE OF STOCKHOLDERS' EQUITY TRANSACTION
	Cash	Accounts Receivable	Supplies	Truck	Accounts Payable	Common Stock	Retained Earnings	
Bal.	23,000		1,800	20,000	1,800	40,000	3,000	
e.		+4,000					+4,000	*Service revenue*
Bal.	23,000	4,000	1,800	20,000 =	1,800	40,000	7,000	
				48,800 =	*48,800*			

f. The business paid $800 cash toward the supplies purchased in transaction c.

Think of Accounts Payable (a liability) as a list of companies to whom the business will *pay* money at some point in the future. In this particular problem, the business owes money to the company from which it purchased supplies on account in transaction c. When the business *pays* the money in full, they can cross this company off of the list. Right now, the business is paying only *part* of the money owed.

This is a decrease to Accounts Payable (a liability) of $700 and a decrease to Cash (an asset) of $700. Because the business is only paying part of the money they owe to the supply store, the balance of Accounts Payable is $1,800 – $800 = $1,000.

You should note that this transaction does not affect Supplies because we are not buying more supplies. We are simply paying off a liability, not acquiring more assets or incurring a new expense.

The effect of this transaction on the accounting equation is:

	ASSETS				= LIABILITIES +	STOCKHOLDERS' EQUITY		TYPE OF STOCKHOLDERS' EQUITY TRANSACTION
	Cash	Accounts Receivable	Supplies	Truck	Accounts Payable	Common Stock	Retained Earnings	
Bal.	23,000	4,000	1,800	20,000	1,800	40,000	7,000	
f.	–800				–800			
Bal.	22,200	4,000	1,800	20,000 =	1,000	40,000	7,000	
				48,000 =	*48,000*			

g. The business paid employee salaries of $1,000 cash.

The work the employees have given to the business has *already been used*. By the end of March, DR Painting has had the employees working and painting for customers for the entire month. This means that the *benefit* of the work has already been received. This means that it is a salary *expense.* So, Salary Expense would increase by $1,000, which is a decrease to stockholders' equity.

Remember: Expenses *decrease* net income, which decreases Retained Earnings. The salaries were paid in cash, so Cash (an asset) is also decreased by $1,000. The effect of this transaction on the accounting equation is:

	ASSETS				= LIABILITIES	+ STOCKHOLDERS' EQUITY		TYPE OF STOCKHOLDERS' EQUITY TRANSACTION
	Cash	Accounts Receivable	Office Supplies	Truck	Accounts Payable	Common Stock	Retained Earnings	
Bal.	22,200	4,000	1,800	20,000	1,000	40,000	7,000	
g.	−1,000						−1,000	*Salary expense*
Bal.	21,200	4,000	1,800	20,000 =	1,000	40,000	6,000	
				47,000 =	*47,000*			

h. The business paid cash dividends of $1,500.

When the business pays cash, it is a recordable transaction. In this case, there is a decrease of $1,500 to Cash (an asset). David is an owner/shareholder of the corporation and is being given some of his value/ownership in cash. In other words, some of the *earnings* that were *retained* by the corporation are now being distributed to the shareholders. This results in a decrease of $1,500 to stockholders' equity, because Retained Earnings is decreasing.

You should note that *dividends are not an expense* because the cash is not used for operations. The cash dividends paid are for the owner's personal use rather than to earn revenue for the business.

The effect of this transaction on the accounting equation is:

	ASSETS				= LIABILITIES	+ STOCKHOLDERS' EQUITY		TYPE OF STOCKHOLDERS' EQUITY TRANSACTION
	Cash	Accounts Receivable	Office Supplies	Truck	Accounts Payable	Common Stock	Retained Earnings	
Bal.	21,200	4,000	1,800	20,000	1,000	40,000	6,000	
h.	−1,500						−1,500	*Dividends*
Bal.	19,700	4,000	1,800	20,000 =	1,000	40,000	4,500	
				45,500 =	*45,500*			

i. The business collected $2,600 from the client in transaction e.

Think of Accounts Receivable (an asset) as a list of clients from whom the business will *receive* money at some point in the future. Later, when the business collects (*receives*) the cash in full from any particular customer, they can cross that customer off the list.

In transaction **e**, DR Painting performed services for a client on account. Now, DR is receiving part of that money. This is a collection that decreases Accounts Receivable (an asset) by $2,600.

Because the cash is received, this is an increase to Cash (an asset) of $2,600.

The effect of this transaction on the accounting equation is:

	ASSETS				= LIABILITIES +	STOCKHOLDERS' EQUITY		TYPE OF STOCKHOLDERS' EQUITY TRANSACTION
	Cash	Accounts Receivable	Office Supplies	Truck	Accounts Payable	Common Stock	Retained Earnings	
Bal.	19,700	4,000	1,800	20,000	1,000	40,000	4,500	
i.	2,600	-2,600						*Dividends*
Bal.	22,300	1,400	1,800	20,000 =	1,000	40,000	4,500	
				45,500 =	*45,500*			

j. David paid $100 cash for personal groceries.

David is using $100 of *his own cash* for groceries. This is a *personal* expense for David's *personal* use that does not relate to the business and therefore is not a recordable transaction for the business. This transaction has no effect on the business's accounting equation. Had David used the *business's* cash to purchase groceries, *then* the business would record the transaction.

	ASSETS				= LIABILITIES +	EQUITY	
	Cash +	Accounts Receivable +	Supplies +	Truck =	Accounts Payable +	Common Stock +	Retained Earnings
a.	+$40,000					+$40,000	
b.	–$20,000			+$20,000			
c.			+$1,800		+$1,800		
d.	+$3,000						+$3,000
e.		+$4,000					+$4,000
f.	–$800				–$800		
g.	–$1,000						–$1,000
h.	–$1,500						–$1,500
i.	+$2,600	–$2,600					
j.	Not a transaction of business						
Bal.	$22,300	$1,400	$1,800	$20,000	$1,000	$40,000	$4,500
				$45,500	*$45,500*		

Requirement 2

Prepare the income statement, statement of retained earnings, and balance sheet of the business after recording the transactions. Use Exhibit 1-9 (p. 22) in the text as a guide.

Part 1	**Part 2**	Part 3	Part 4	Demo Doc Complete

Income Statement

The income statement is the first statement that can be prepared because the other financial statements rely upon the net income number calculated on the income statement.

The income statement reports the profitability of the business. To prepare an income statement, begin with the proper heading. A proper heading includes the name of the company (DR Painting, Inc.), the name of the statement (Income Statement), and the time period covered (Month Ended March 31, 2008). Notice that we are reporting income for a period of time, rather than a single date.

The income statement lists all revenues and expenses. It uses the following formula to calculate net income:

Revenues – Expenses = Net Income

First, you should list revenues. Second, list the expenses. Having trouble finding the revenues and expenses? Look in the equity column of the accounting equation. After you have listed and totaled the revenues and expenses, you subtract the total expenses from total revenues to determine net income or net loss. If you have a positive number, then you will record net income. A negative number indicates that expenses exceeded revenues, and you will record this as a net loss.

In the case of DR Painting, transactions **d** and **e** increased Service Revenue (by $3,000 and $4,000, respectively). This means that total Service Revenue for the month was $3,000 + $4,000 = $7,000.

The only expenses that were incurred were in transaction **g**, which resulted in a Salary Expense of $1,000. On the income statement, these would be recorded as follows:

DR PAINTING, INC. **Income Statement** Month Ended March 31, 2008		
Revenue:		
Service revenue		$ 7,000
Expenses:		
Salary expense	$ 1,000	
Total expenses		1,000
Net income		$ 6,000

Note the result is a net income of $6,000 ($7,000 – $1,000 = $6,000). You will use this amount on the statement of retained earnings.

Statement of Retained Earnings

Part 1	Part 2	**Part 3**	Part 4	Demo Doc Complete

The statement of retained earnings shows the changes in retained earnings for a period of time. To prepare a statement of retained earnings, begin with the proper heading. A proper heading includes the name of the company (DR Painting, Inc.), the name of the statement (Statement of Retained Earnings), and the time period covered (Month Ended March 31, 2008). As with the income statement, we are reporting Retained Earnings for a period of time, rather than a single date.

Net income is used on the statement of retained earnings to calculate the new balance in Retained Earnings. This calculation uses the following formula:

Beginning Retained Earnings
\+ Net Income (or – Net Loss)
– Dividends
Ending Retained Earnings

Start the body of the statement of retained earnings with the Retained Earnings at the beginning of the period (March 1). Then list net income. You should notice that the amount of net income comes directly from the income statement. Following net income you will list the dividends paid, which reduce Retained Earnings. Finally, total all amounts and compute the Retained Earnings at the end of the period.

In this case, because this is a new company, the beginning Retained Earnings is zero. Net income as reported on the income statement ($6,000) is added. In transaction **h**, the business paid cash dividends of $1,500. These dividends are deducted. The statement of retained earnings follows:

DR PAINTING, INC.
Statement of Retained Earnings
Month Ended March 31, 2008

Beginning retained earnings	$ 0
Add: Net income for the month	6,000
Less: Dividends paid	(1,500)
Retained earnings, March 31, 2008	$4,500

Note the result is a balance of $4,500 ($6,000 – $1,500 = $4,500) for Retained Earnings. You will use this amount on the balance sheet.

Balance Sheet

Part 1	Part 2	Part 3	**Part 4**	Demo Doc Complete

The balance sheet reports the financial position of the business. To prepare a balance sheet, begin with the proper heading. A proper heading includes the name of the company (DR Painting, Inc.), the name of the statement (Balance Sheet), and the time period covered (March 31, 2008). Unlike the income statement and statement of retained earnings, we are reporting the financial position of the company for a specific date rather than a period of time.

The balance sheet is a listing of all assets, liabilities, and equity, with the accounting equation verified at the bottom.

To prepare the body of the statement, begin by listing assets. Then you will record liabilities and stockholders' equity. Notice that the balance sheet is organized in the same order as the accounting equation. You should note that the amount of Retained Earnings comes directly from the ending Retained Earnings on your statement of retained earnings. You should then total both sides to make sure that they are equal. If they are not equal, then you will need to look for an error.

In this case, assets include the cash balance of $22,300, accounts receivable of $1,400, $1,800 worth of supplies, and the truck's value of $20,000, for a total of $45,500 in assets. Liabilities total $1,000, the balance of Accounts Payable account. The figures for assets and liabilities come directly from the accounting equation work sheet. From the statement of retained earnings, we have ending Retained Earnings of $4,500. There is also a balance of $40,000 in Common Stock. This gives us a total for liabilities and equity of $1,000 + $4,500 + $40,000 = $45,500, confirming that assets = liabilities + equity.

DR PAINTING, INC.
Balance Sheet
March 31, 2008

Assets		**Liabilities**	
Cash	$22,300	Accounts payable	$ 1,000
Accounts receivable	1,400		
Supplies	1,800	**Stockholders' Equity**	
Truck	20,000	Common stock	40,000
		Retained earnings	4,500
		Total stockholders' equity	44,500
		Total liabilities and	
Total assets	$45,500	stockholders' equity	$45,500

Part 1	Part 2	Part 3	Part 4	**Demo Doc Complete**

2 Recording Business Transactions

Learning Objectives

1. Use accounting terms
2. Apply the rules of debit and credit
3. Record transactions in the journal
4. Post from the journal to the ledger
5. Prepare and use a trial balance

Sherman Lawn Service and DeFilippo Catering are now up and running. Both businesses are buying supplies, earning revenues, collecting cash, and paying expenses. The proprietors, Haig Sherman and Julie DeFilippo, naturally want to know how they're doing.

In Chapter 1 Sherman and DeFilippo learned about the income statement and the balance sheet—two financial statements that help them measure progress. Sherman and DeFilippo also learned to record transactions in terms of the accounting equation. That procedure works well for a handful of transactions. But even Sherman Lawn Service or DeFilippo Catering would need a huge Excel spreadsheet to record all their transactions with the accounting equation. Fortunately, there's a better way.

In this chapter we show how accounting is actually done in business. This may be the most important chapter of the whole book. After you master this material, you'll have a foundation for learning accounting. But if you miss this, well, let's just say the picture won't be very pretty. Therefore, make sure you learn this material before you go on.

The following diagram summarizes the accounting process covered in this chapter.

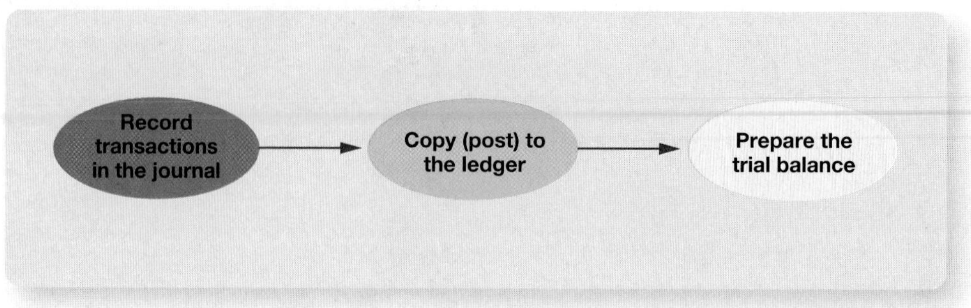

The Account, the Ledger, and the Journal

The basic summary device of accounting is the account. An **account** is the detailed record of all the changes that have occurred in a particular asset, liability, or owner's equity during a period. As we saw in Chapter 1, business transactions cause the changes.

1 Use accounting terms

Accountants record transactions first in a **journal**, which is the chronological record of transactions. Accountants then copy (post) the data to the book (or printout) of accounts called the **ledger**. A list of all the ledger accounts and their balances is called a **trial balance.**

Take a moment to memorize these important terms. You will be using them over and over again.

- **Account**—the detailed record of the changes in a particular asset, liability, or owner's equity
- **Ledger**—the book (or printout) holding all the accounts
- **Journal**—the chronological record of transactions
- **Trial balance**—the list of all the accounts with their balances

Accounts are grouped in three broad categories, according to the accounting equation:

Assets = Liabilities + Stockholders' Equity

Assets

Assets are economic resources that will benefit the business in the future. Most firms use the following asset accounts.

Cash

The Cash account is a record of the cash effects of transactions. Cash includes money, such as a bank balance, paper currency, coins, and checks. Cash is the most pressing need of start-up businesses such as Sherman Lawn Service and DeFilippo Catering.

Accounts Receivable

Most businesses sell goods or services in exchange for a promise of future cash receipts. Such sales are made on credit ("on account"), and Accounts Receivable is the account that holds these amounts. Most sales in the United States and in other developed countries are made on account.

Notes Receivable

A business may sell goods or services and receive a *promissory note.* A note receivable is a written pledge that the customer will pay a fixed amount of money by a certain date.

Prepaid Expenses

A business often pays certain expenses, such as rent and insurance, in advance. A *prepaid expense* is an asset because the prepayment provides a future benefit. Prepaid Rent, Prepaid Insurance, and Office Supplies are separate prepaid expense accounts. Your prepaid rent on your apartment or dorm room is an asset to you.

Land

The Land account shows the cost of land a business holds for use in operations. Land held for sale is different. Its cost is an investment.

Building

The cost of buildings—an office or a warehouse—appears in the Buildings account. Frito-Lay and The Coca-Cola Company own buildings around the world, where they make chips and drinks.

Equipment, Furniture, and Fixtures

A business has a separate asset account for each type of equipment—Computer Equipment, Office Equipment, and Store Equipment, for example. The Furniture account shows the cost of this asset.

Liabilities

Recall that a *liability* is a debt. A business generally has fewer liability accounts than asset accounts because the liabilities are summarized in a handful of accounts.

Accounts Payable

Accounts Payable are the opposite of Accounts Receivable. The promise to pay a debt arising from a credit purchase is an Account Payable. Such a purchase is said to be made on account. All companies from DeFilippo Catering to Coca-Cola to eBay, have Accounts Payable.

Notes Payable

Notes Payable are the opposite of Notes Receivable. Notes Payable represent debts the business owes because it signed promissory notes to borrow money or to purchase something.

Accrued Liabilities

An *accrued liability* is a liability for an expense that has not been paid. Taxes Payable, Interest Payable, and Salary Payable are accrued liability accounts.

Stockholders' Equity

The owners' claim to the assets of the business is called *stockholders' equity.* A corporation has separate accounts for the various elements of stockholders' equity.

Common Stock

The Common Stock account represents the paid-in capital of the corporation. All corporations have common stock, and the common stockholders are the owners of the business.

Retained Earnings

A business must earn a profit to remain in operation. The Retained Earnings account shows the cumulative net income earned by the corporation over its lifetime, minus cumulative net losses and dividends. The title Retained Earnings is thus well chosen—earnings kept by the business. We will be using this account more in the chapters to follow and include it here merely for completeness.

Dividends

The stockholders often demand cash from a corporation. After profitable operations, the board of directors may (or may not) declare a dividend to be paid in cash at a later date. Dividends are not required. They are optional and depend upon the action of the board of directors. The corporation can keep a separate account titled Dividends, which indicates a decrease in Retained Earnings.

Revenues

The increase in owner's equity created by delivering goods or services to customers is called *revenue.* The ledger contains as many revenue accounts as needed. Cookie Lapp Travel Design needs a Service Revenue account for amounts earned by providing travel services. If Cookie Lapp Travel lends money to an outsider, it needs an Interest Revenue account for the interest earned on the loan. If the business rents out a building to a tenant, it needs a Rent Revenue account.

Expenses

Expenses use up assets or create liabilities in the course of operating a business. Expenses have the opposite effect of revenues; expenses *decrease* owner's equity. A business needs a separate account for each type of expense, such as Salary Expense, Rent Expense, Advertising Expense, and Utilities Expense. Businesses strive to minimize their expenses in order to maximize net income—whether it's General Electric, Cookie Lapp Travel, or Sherman Lawn Service.

Exhibit 2-1 shows how asset, liability, and stockholders' equity accounts can be grouped in the ledger.

Chart of Accounts

The ledger contains the accounts grouped under these headings:

- Assets, Liabilities, and Stockholders' Equity
- Revenues and Expenses

Organizations use a **chart of accounts** to list all their accounts along with the account numbers.

Account numbers usually have two or more digits. Assets are often numbered beginning with 1, liabilities with 2, owner's equity with 3, revenues with 4, and expenses

EXHIBIT 2-1 **THE Ledger—Asset, Liability, and Stockholders' Equity Accounts**

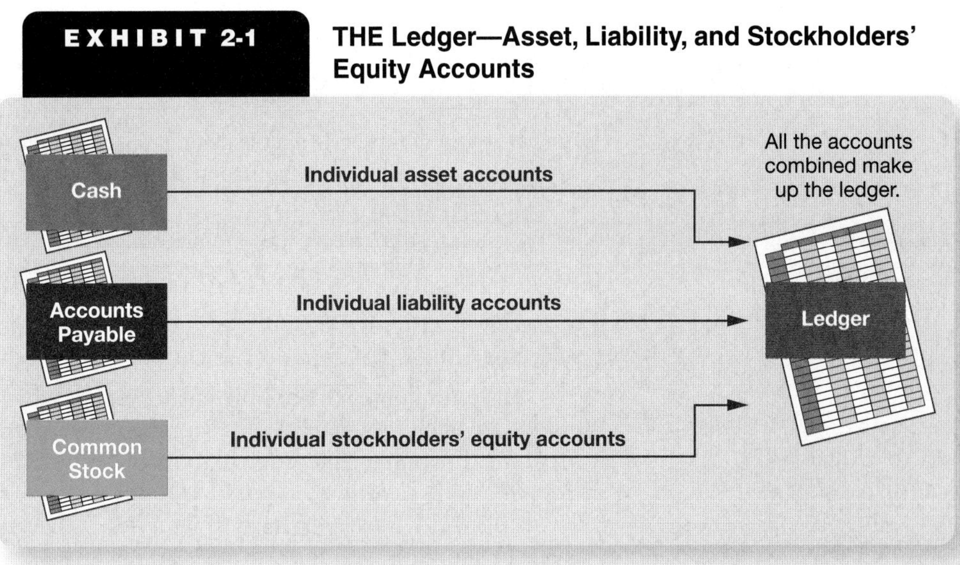

with 5. The second and third digits in an account number indicate where the account fits within the category. For example, Cash may be account number 101, the first asset account. Accounts Receivable may be account number 111, the second asset. Accounts Payable may be number 201, the first liability. All accounts are numbered by this system.

The chart of accounts for Cookie Lapp Travel Design appears in Exhibit 2-2. Notice the gap in account numbers between 121 and 141. Lapp may need to add another asset account. For example, she may start selling some type of inventory, account number 131.

EXHIBIT 2-2 **Chart of Accounts—Cookie Lapp Travel Design, Inc.**

Balance Sheet Accounts

Assets	Liabilities	Stockholders' Equity
101 Cash	201 Accounts Payable	301 Common Stock
111 Accounts Receivable	211 Salary Payable	311 Retained Earnings
121 Notes Receivable	221 Interest Payable	312 Dividends
141 Supplies	231 Notes Payable	
151 Furniture		
171 Building		
191 Land		

Income Statement Accounts
(Part of Stockholders' Equity)

Revenues	Expenses
401 Service Revenue	501 Rent Expense, Computer
411 Interest Revenue	502 Rent Expense, Office
	505 Salary Expense
	510 Depreciation Expense
	520 Utilities Expense
	530 Advertising Expense
	540 Supplies Expense

Double-Entry Accounting

As we saw in Chapter 1, accounting is based on transaction data, not on mere whim or opinion. Each business transaction has dual effects:

- The receiving side
- The giving side

For example, in the $30,000 cash receipt by Cookie Lapp Travel Design, the business:

- Received cash of $30,000
- Issued $30,000 of common stock

Accounting uses the double-entry system, which means that we record the dual effects of each transaction. As a result, every transaction affects at least two accounts. It would be incomplete to record only the giving side, or only the receiving side, of a transaction.

Consider a cash purchase of supplies. What are the dual effects? A cash purchase of supplies:

1. Increases supplies (you received supplies)
2. Decreases cash (you gave cash)

A credit purchase of equipment (a purchase on account):

1. Increases equipment (you received equipment)
2. Increases accounts payable (you gave your promise to pay in the future)

The T-Account

The most widely used form of account is called the *T-account* because it takes the form of the capital letter *T*. The vertical line divides the account into its left and right sides, with the title at the top. For example, the Cash account appears as follows.

Cash	
(Left side) Debit	(Right side) Credit

The left side of the account is called the **Debit** side, and the right side is called the **Credit** side. The words *debit* and *credit* are new. To become comfortable using them, remember that:

Debit = Left	Credit = Right

The terms *debit* and *credit* are deeply entrenched in business.[1] They are abbreviated as follows:

DR = Debit	CR = Credit

Increases and Decreases in the Accounts

2 Apply the rules of debit and credit

The account category (asset, liability, equity) governs how we record increases and decreases. For any given account, increases are recorded on one side, and decreases are recorded on the opposite side. The following T-accounts provide a summary.

[1]The words *debit* and *credit* abbreviate the Latin terms *debitum* and *creditum*. Luca Pacioli, the Italian monk who wrote about accounting in the 15th century, popularized these terms.

Assets	
Increase = Debit	Decrease = Credit

Liabilities and Stockholders' Equity	
Decrease = Debit	Increase = Credit

These are the *rules of debit and credit.* In your study of accounting, forget the general usage of credit and debit because accounting uses these terms in a specialized way. **Remember that *debit means left* and *credit means right.* Whether an account is increased or decreased by a debit or a credit depends on the type of account.**

In a computerized accounting system, the computer interprets debits and credits as increases or decreases. For example, a computer reads a debit to Cash as an increase. The computer reads a debit to Accounts Payable as a decrease.

Exhibit 2-3 shows the relationship between the accounting equation and the rules of debit and credit.

EXHIBIT 2-3 **The Accounting Equation and the Rules of Debit and Credit**

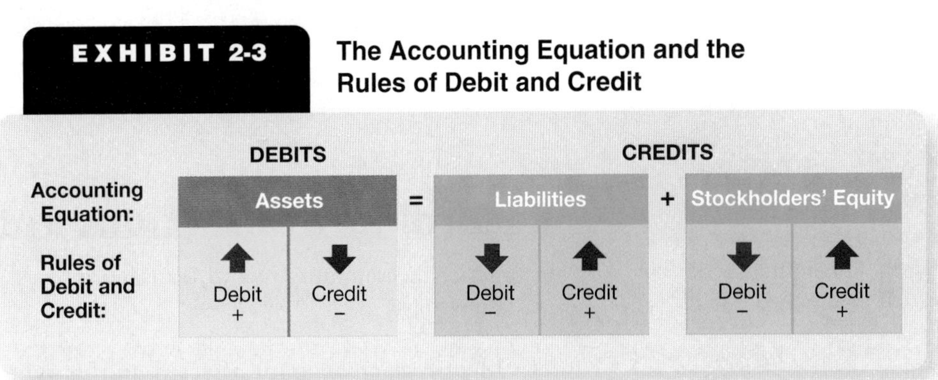

To illustrate the ideas diagrammed in Exhibit 2-3, reconsider the first transaction from Chapter 1. Cookie Lapp Travel Design received $30,000 cash and issued common stock. Which accounts of the business are affected?

The answer: The business's assets and equity would increase by $30,000, as the T-accounts show.

ASSETS = LIABILITIES + STOCKHOLDERS' EQUITY

Cash	
Debit for increase, 30,000	

Common Stock	
	Credit for increase, 30,000

The amount remaining in an account is called its *balance.* The first transaction gives Cash a $30,000 debit balance and Common Stock a $30,000 credit balance. Exhibit 2-4 illustrates the accounting equation after Cookie Lapp Travel Design's first two transactions.

The second transaction is a $20,000 purchase of land. After transaction 2, Cash has a $10,000 debit balance, Land has a debit balance of $20,000, and Common Stock has a $30,000 credit balance.

We create accounts as needed. The process of creating a new account is called *opening the account.* For transaction 1, we opened the Cash account and the Common Stock. For transaction 2, we opened the Land account.

EXHIBIT 2-4 **The Accounting Equation after the First Two Transactions of Cookie Lapp Travel Design, Inc.**

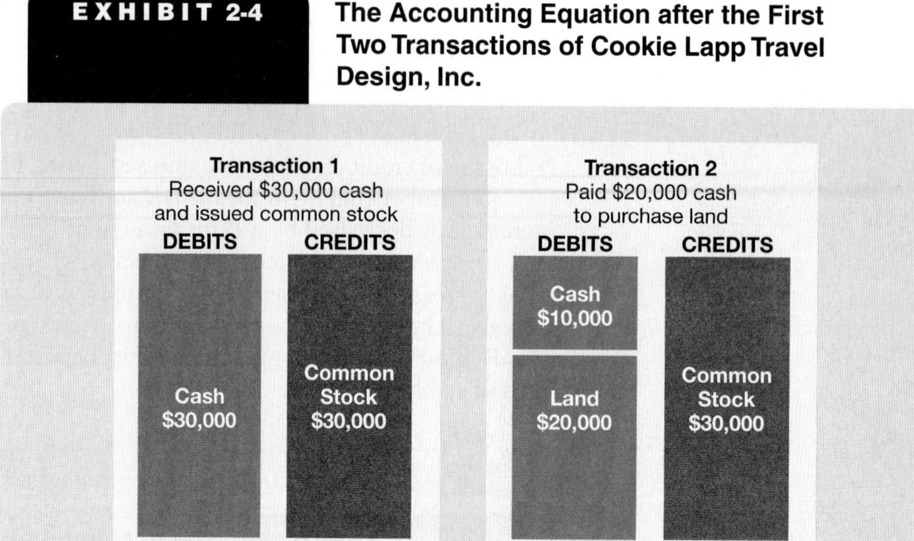

Recording Transactions in the Journal

3 Record transactions in the journal

In practice, accountants record transactions in a *journal.* The journalizing process has three steps:

1. Identify each account affected and its type (asset, liability, or stockholders' equity).
2. Determine whether each account is increased or decreased. Use the rules of debit and credit.
3. Record the transaction in the journal, including a brief explanation. The debit side of the entry is entered first. Total debits should always equal total credits. This step is also called "making the journal entry" or "journalizing the transaction."

These steps are the same whether computerized or manual.

Let's journalize the first transaction of Cookie Lapp Travel Design—the receipt of $30,000 cash and issuance of common stock.

STEP 1 The accounts affected by the receipt of cash and issuance of stock are *Cash* and *Common Stock.* Cash is an asset. Common Stock is equity.

STEP 2 Both accounts increase by $30,000. Therefore, we debit Cash, the asset, and we credit Common Stock, the equity account.

STEP 3 The journal entry is:

Journal **Page 1**

Date	Accounts and Explanation	Debit	Credit
Apr. 1[a]	Cash[b]	30,000[b]	
	Common Stock[c]		30,000[c]
	Issued stock.[d]		

Footnotes a, b, c, d, are explained as follows. The journal entry includes four parts:

a. Date of the transaction

b. Title of the account debited, along with the dollar amount

c. Title of the account credited, along with the dollar amount

d. Brief explanation of the transaction

Dollar signs are omitted because it's understood that the amounts are in dollars.

The journal entry presents the full story for each transaction. Exhibit 2-5 shows how Journal Page 1 looks after Cookie Lapp has recorded the first transaction.

EXHIBIT 2-5 **The Journal**

Journal **Page 1**

Date	Accounts and Explanation	Debit	Credit
Apr. 1	Cash	30,000	
	Common Stock		30,000
	Issued stock.		

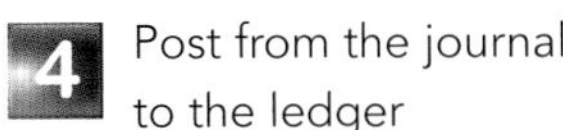

Posting (Copying Information) from the Journal to the Ledger

Journalizing a transaction records the data only in the journal—but not in the ledger. The data must also show up in the ledger and, therefore, must be copied to the ledger. The process of copying from the journal to the ledger is called **posting.** We *post* from the journal to the ledger.

Debits in the journal are posted as debits in the ledger and credits as credits—no exceptions. The first transaction of Cookie Lapp Travel Design is posted to the ledger in Exhibit 2-6.

Expanding the Rules of Debit and Credit: Revenues and Expenses

As we have noted, *revenues* are increases in equity by providing goods or services for customers. *Expenses* are decreases in equity from using up assets or increasing liabilities in the course of operations. Therefore, we must expand the accounting equation. There are several elements of stockholders' equity.

EXHIBIT 2-6 Making a Journal Entry and Posting to the Ledger

Journal Entry:

		Accounts and Explanation	Debit	Credit
		Cash	30,000	

Exhibit 2-7 shows revenues and expenses under stockholders' equity because they directly affect equity.

EXHIBIT 2-7 The Accounting Equation Includes Revenues and Expenses

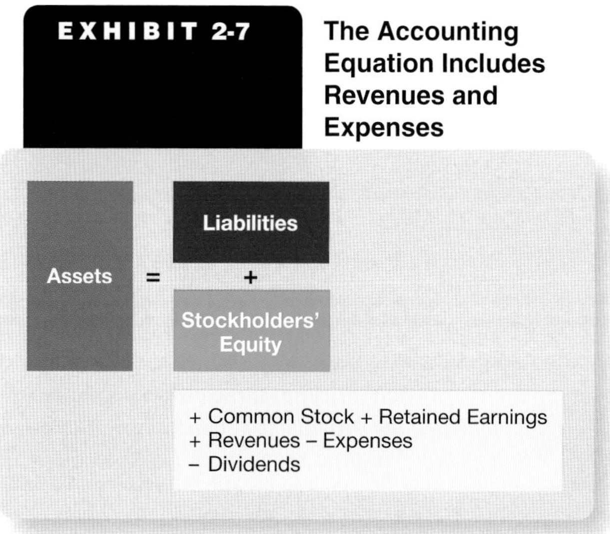

We can now express the rules of debit and credit in final form as shown in Exhibit 2-8. The accounting equation now includes revenues and expenses.

EXHIBIT 2-8 Final Rules of Debit and Credit

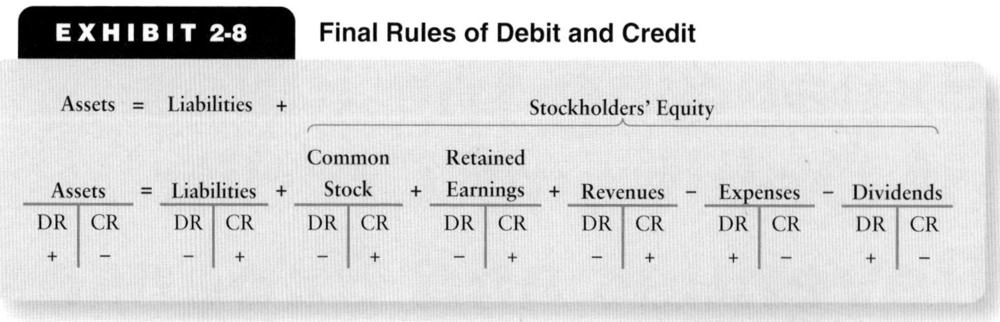

You can see that Expenses and Dividends are equity accounts that go against the grain. Expenses and Dividends are increased by debits rather than credits. As such, Expenses and Dividends are *negative* elements of equity.

The Normal Balance of an Account

An account's **normal balance** appears on the side—debit or credit—where we record an *increase*. For example, assets normally have a debit balance, so assets are *debit-balance accounts*. Liabilities and equity accounts normally have the opposite balance, so they are *credit-balance accounts*. Exhibit 2-9 illustrates the normal balances of assets, liabilities, and equity accounts. Again, Expenses and Dividends are equity accounts that have debit balances—unlike the other equity accounts.

EXHIBIT 2-9 **Normal Balances of the Accounts**

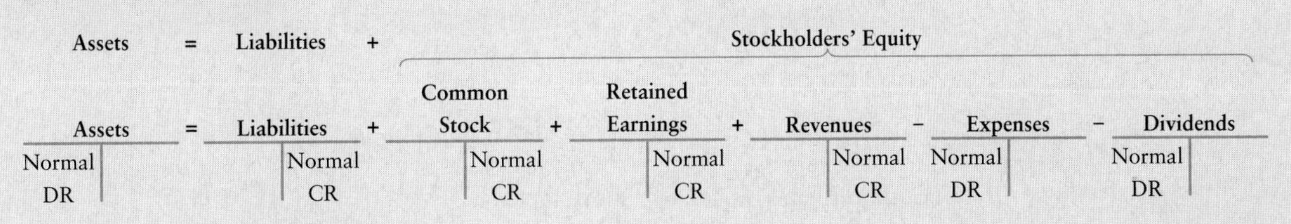

Revenues increase equity, so a revenue's normal balance is a credit. Expenses decrease equity, so an expense normally has a debit balance.

As we have seen, stockholders' equity includes:

Common Stock—a credit-balance account

Retained Earnings—a credit-balance account

Dividends—a debit-balance account

The sum of these three accounts should be a credit; for example,

Common Stock		Retained Earnings		Dividends	
	30,000		20,000	5,000	

Stockholders' Equity = $45,000, a credit

A debit account may occasionally have a credit balance. That indicates a negative amount of the item. For example, Cash will have a credit balance if the business overdraws its bank account. Also, the liability Accounts Payable—a credit balance account—will have a debit balance if the entity overpays its account. In other cases, an odd balance indicates an error. For example, a credit balance in Office Supplies, Furniture, or Buildings is an error because negative amounts of these assets make no sense.

Now let's put your new learning to practice. Let's account for the early transactions of Cookie Lapp Travel Design, Inc.

The Flow of Accounting Data

Exhibit 2-10 summarizes the flow of data through the accounting system. In the pages that follow, we record Cookie Lapp Travel Design's early transactions. Keep

EXHIBIT 2-10 Flow of Accounting Data from the Journal to the Ledger

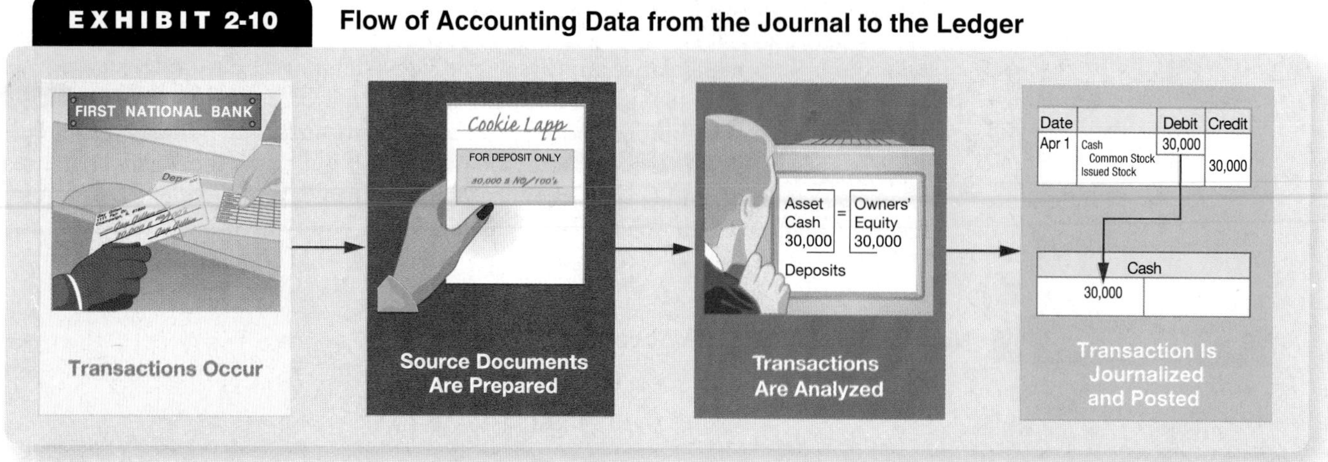

in mind that we are accounting for the travel agency. We are *not* accounting for Cookie Lapp's *personal* transactions.

Source Documents

Accounting data come from source documents, as shown in the second segment of Exhibit 2-10. There Cookie Lapp Travel Design received $30,000 and issued common stock to Lapp. The *bank deposit ticket* is the document that shows the amount of cash received by the business, and the stock certificate issued by the company shows the amount of stock issued. Based on these documents, Lapp can see how to record this transaction in the journal.

When Lapp buys supplies on account, the vendor sends Lapp an invoice requesting payment. The *purchase invoice* is the source document that tells Lapp to pay the vendor. The invoice shows what Lapp purchased and how much it cost—telling Lapp how to record the transaction.

Lapp may pay the account payable with a *bank check,* another source document. The check and the purchase invoice give Lapp the information she needs to record the cash payment accurately.

When Lapp provides travel service for a client, Lapp faxes a sales invoice to the client. Lapp's *sales invoice* is the source document that tells Lapp how much revenue to record.

There are many different types of source documents in business. In the transactions that follow, we illustrate some of the more common types of documents that Cookie Lapp Travel Design uses in its business.

Journalizing Transactions and Posting to the Ledger

Transaction 1

Cookie Lapp Travel Design received $30,000 cash from Lapp the stockholder and issued common stock to Lapp. The business deposited the money in its bank account, as proved by this deposit ticket.

DEPOSIT TICKET

Cookie Lapp Travel Design, Inc.
9000 CLARE BLVD.
Austin, TX 78702

DATE April 1, 2008

TEXAS FIRST STATE BANK
Box 1739 Terminal Annex
Austin, TX 78713

1: 1 2 200066 1: 1400‴0 3 8 5 7

CASH	CURRENCY		
	COIN		
LIST CHECKS SINGLY		30,000	00
TOTAL FROM OTHER SIDE			
TOTAL		30,000	00
LESS CASH RECEIVED			
NET DEPOSIT		30,000	00

The business increased cash, which is an asset, so we debit Cash. The business also increased stockholders' equity, so we credit Common Stock.

Journal Entry

	Account	Debit	Credit
	Cash	30,000	
	Common Stock		30,000
	Issued stock.		

Ledger Accounts

Cash		Common Stock	
(1) 30,000			(1) 30,000

Transaction 2

Lapp paid $20,000 cash for land. The purchase decreased cash; therefore, credit Cash. The asset, land, increased, so we debit the Land account.

Journal Entry

	Account	Debit	Credit
	Land	20,000	
	Cash		20,000
	Paid cash for land.		

Ledger Accounts

Cash		Land	
(1) 30,000	(2) 20,000	(2) 20,000	

Transaction 3

Lapp purchased $500 of office supplies on account, as shown on this purchase invoice.

INVOICE (purchase)

WHOLESALE OFFICE SUPPLY, INC.
500 HENDERSON ROAD
AUSTIN, TX 78722

Date: April 3, 2008
Terms: 30 days
Sold to: **COOKIE LAPP TRAVEL DESIGN**
9000 CLARE BLVD.
AUSTIN, TX 78702

Quantity	Item	Price	Total
38	Laser paper	$10	$380.00
8	Desk calendars	15	120.00
	Total amount due:		**$500.00**

The asset office supplies increased, so we debit Office Supplies. The liability accounts payable increased, so we credit Accounts Payable.

Journal Entry

	Accounts and Explanation	Debit	Credit
	Office Supplies	500	
	Accounts Payable		500
	Purchased supplies on account.		

Ledger Accounts

Office Supplies			
(3)	500		

Accounts Payable			
		(3)	500

Transaction 4

Lapp collected cash of $5,500 for service revenue that she earned by providing travel services for clients. The source document is Lapp's sales invoice.

INVOICE (sale)

COOKIE LAPP TRAVEL DESIGN, INC.
9000 CLARE BLVD.
Austin, TX 78702

Date: April 8, 2008
Sold to: **Allied Energy, Inc.**
325 Brooks Street

Invoice No: **15**
Service: Trip to Greece

PAID

Total amount due: $5,500

All accounts are due and payable within 30 days.

The asset cash increased, so debit Cash. Revenue increased, so credit Service Revenue.

Journal Entry

		Debit	Credit
	Cash	5,500	
	Service Revenue		5,500
	Performed service and received cash.		

Ledger Accounts

Cash

	Debit		Credit
(1)	30,000	(2)	20,000
(4)	5,500		

Service Revenue

	Debit		Credit
		(4)	5,500

In Chapter 1 we listed service revenue and expenses under Retained Earnings. Here we record the revenues and the expenses directly in their own accounts. There is no contradiction because revenues and expenses affect retained earnings as we will see in Chapter 4.

Transaction 5

Lapp performs service for clients and lets then pay later. She earned $3,000 of service revenue or account. This transaction increased Accounts Receivable, so we debit this asset. Service Revenue is increased with a credit.

Journal Entry

		Debit	Credit
	Accounts Receivable	3,000	
	Service Revenue		3,000
	Performed service on account.		

Ledger Accounts

Accounts Receivable

	Debit		Credit
(5)	3,000		

Service Revenue

	Debit		Credit
		(4)	5,500
		(5)	3,000

Transaction 6

Lapp paid the following cash expenses: Rent expense on a computer, $600; Office rent, $1,000; Salary expense, $1,200; Utilities expense, $400. Debit each expense account to record its increase. Credit Cash for its decrease.

Journal Entry

	Account	Debit	Credit
	Rent Expense, Computer	600	
	Rent Expense, Office	1,000	
	Salary Expense	1,200	
	Utilities Expense	400	
	Cash		3,200
	Paid cash expenses.		

Note: In practice, the business would record these expenses in four separate journal entries. Here we show them together to illustrate a *compound journal entry.*

Ledger Accounts

Cash

	Debit		Credit
(1)	30,000	(2)	20,000
(4)	5,500	(6)	3,200

Rent Expense, Computer

	Debit	Credit
(6)	600	

Rent Expense, Office

	Debit	Credit
(6)	1,000	

Salary Expense

	Debit	Credit
(6)	1,200	

Utilities Expense

	Debit	Credit
(6)	400	

Transaction 7

Lapp paid $300 on the account payable created in transaction 3. The paid check is Lapp's source document for this transaction.

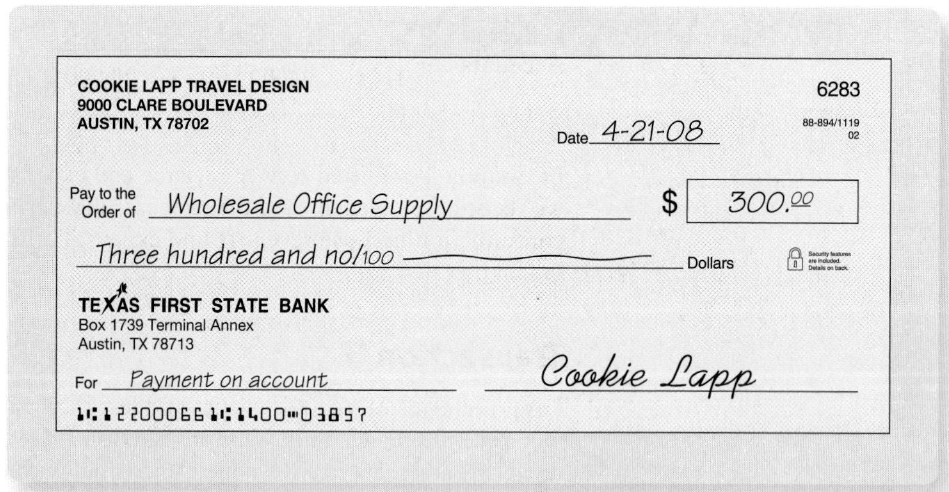
COOKIE LAPP TRAVEL DESIGN
9000 CLARE BOULEVARD
AUSTIN, TX 78702

6283

88-894/1119
02

Date 4-21-08

Pay to the Order of Wholesale Office Supply $ 300.00

Three hundred and no/100 Dollars

TEXAS FIRST STATE BANK
Box 1739 Terminal Annex
Austin, TX 78713

For Payment on account

Cookie Lapp

⑆1122000661⑆1400⑈03857

The payment decreased cash; therefore, credit Cash. The payment decreased accounts payable, so we debit that liability.

Journal Entry

	Account	Debit	Credit
	Accounts Payable	300	
	Cash		300
	Paid cash on account.		

Ledger Accounts

Cash			
(1)	30,000	(2)	20,000
(4)	5,500	(6)	3,200
		(7)	300

Accounts Payable			
(7)	300	(3)	500

Transaction 8

Cookie Lapp remodeled her home with personal funds. This is not a transaction of the travel agency, so there's no entry on the business's books.

Transaction 9

Lapp collected $2,000 cash from the client in transaction 5. Cash is increased, so debit Cash. Accounts receivable is decreased; credit Accounts Receivable.

Journal Entry

	Cash	2,000	
	Accounts Receivable		2,000
	Received cash on account.		

Note: This transaction has no effect on revenue; the related revenue was recorded in transaction 5.

Ledger Accounts

Cash			
(1)	30,000	(2)	20,000
(4)	5,500	(6)	3,200
(9)	2,000	(7)	300

Accounts Receivable			
(5)	3,000	(9)	2,000

Transaction 10

Lapp sells a parcel of land owned by the travel agency. The sale price, $9,000, equals her cost. Cash increased, so debit Cash. Land decreased; credit Land.

Journal Entry

	Cash	9,000	
	Land		9,000
	Sold land at cost.		

Ledger Accounts

Cash			
(1)	30,000	(2)	20,000
(4)	5,500	(6)	3,200
(9)	2,000	(7)	300
(10)	9,000		

Land			
(2)	20,000	(10)	9,000

Transaction 11

Lapp received a telephone bill for $100 and will pay this expense next month. There is no cash payment now. Utilities expense increased, so debit this expense. The liability accounts payable increased, so credit Accounts Payable.

Journal Entry

	Utilities Expense	100	
	Accounts Payable		100
	Received utility bill.		

Ledger Accounts

Accounts Payable			
(7)	300	(3)	500
		(11)	100

Utilities Expense			
(6)	400		
(11)	100		

Transaction 12

The business paid cash dividends of $2,000 to Cookie Lapp, the stockholder. Dividends decrease the entity's cash; therefore, credit Cash. Dividends also decrease stockholders' equity. Decreases in equity that result from dividends are debited to the Dividends account. Therefore, debit this account.

Journal Entry

	Dividends	2,000	
	Cash		2,000
	*Paid dividends.**		

*Companies first declare a dividends and then pay it. Here we simplify by referring to the payment only. Chapter 14 covers the details of accounting for dividends

Ledger Accounts

Cash			
(1)	30,000	(2)	20,000
(4)	5,500	(6)	3,200
(9)	2,000	(7)	300
(10)	9,000	(12)	2,000

Dividends			
(12)	2,000		

Each journal entry posted to the ledger is keyed by date or by transaction number. In this way, any transaction can be traced back and forth between the journal and the ledger. This helps locate any information you may need.

The Ledger Accounts After Posting

We next show the accounts of Cookie Lapp Travel Design after posting. The accounts are grouped under their headings in Exhibit 2-11.

Each account has a balance, denoted *Bal.* An account balance is the difference between the account's total debits and its total credits. For example, the $21,000 balance in the Cash account is the difference between:

- Total debits, $46,500 ($30,000 + $5,500 + $2,000 + $9,000)
- Total credits, $25,500 ($20,000 + $3,200 + $300 + $2,000)

We set a balance apart from the transaction amounts by a horizontal line. The final figure, below the horizontal line, is denoted as the balance (Bal.).

The Trial Balance

5 Prepare and use a trial balance

A **trial balance** summarizes the ledger by listing all the accounts with their balances—assets first, followed by liabilities and then stockholders' equity. In a manual accounting

EXHIBIT 2-11 Ledger Accounts After Posting

ASSETS

Cash

(1) 30,000	(2) 20,000
(4) 5,500	(6) 3,200
(9) 2,000	(7) 300
(10) 9,000	(12) 2,000
Bal. 21,000	

Accounts Receivable

(5) 3,000	(9) 2,000
Bal. 1,000	

Office Supplies

(3) 500	
Bal. 500	

Land

(2) 20,000	(10) 9,000
Bal. 11,000	

LIABILITIES

Accounts Payable

(7) 300	(3) 500
	(11) 100
	Bal. 300

STOCKHOLDERS' EQUITY*

Common Stock

	(1) 30,000
	Bal. 30,000

Dividends

(12) 2,000	
Bal. 2,000	

REVENUE

Service Revenue

	(4) 5,500
	(5) 3,000
	Bal. 8,500

EXPENSES

Rent Expense, Computer

(6) 600	
Bal. 600	

Rent Expense, Office

(6) 1,000	
Bal. 1,000	

Salary Expense

(6) 1,200	
Bal. 1,200	

Utilities Expense

(6) 400	
(11) 100	
Bal. 500	

*We add the Retained Earnings account in Chapter 3, when it arises at the end of the period.

system, the trial balance provides an accuracy check by showing whether total debits equal total credits. In all types of systems, the trial balance is a useful summary of the accounts and their balances. Exhibit 2-12 is the trial balance of Cookie Lapp Travel Design at April 30, 2008, end of the first month of operations.

A warning: Do not confuse the trial balance with the balance sheet. A trial balance is an internal document used only by company insiders. The public never sees a trial balance. Outsiders get only the company's financial statements.

EXHIBIT 2-12 Trial Balance

COOKIE LAPP TRAVEL DESIGN, INC.
Trial Balance
April 30, 2008

	Balance	
Account Title	Debit	Credit
Cash	$21,000	
Accounts receivable	1,000	
Office supplies	500	
Land	11,000	
Accounts payable		$ 300
Common stock		30,000
Dividends	2,000	
Service revenue		8,500
Rent expense, computer	600	
Rent expense, office	1,000	
Salary expense	1,200	
Utilities expense	500	
Total	$38,800	$38,800

Correcting Trial Balance Errors

Throughout the accounting process, total debits should always equal total credits. If not, there is an error. Computerized accounting systems eliminate many errors because most software won't let you make a journal entry that doesn't balance. But computers cannot *eliminate* all errors because humans can input the wrong data.

Errors can be detected by computing the difference between total debits and total credits on the trial balance. Then perform one or more of the following actions:

1. Search the trial balance for a missing account. For example suppose the accountant omitted Dividends from the trial balance in Exhibit 2-12. Total debits would then be $36,800 ($38,800 – $2,000). Trace each account from the ledger to the trial balance, and you will locate the missing account.
2. Divide the difference between total debits and total credits by 2. A debit treated as a credit, or vice versa, doubles the amount of error. Suppose the accountant posted a $500 credit as a debit. Total debits contain the $500, and total credits omit the $500. The out-of-balance amount is $1,000. Dividing the difference by 2 identifies the $500 amount of the transaction. Then search the trial balance for a $500 transaction and trace to the account affected.
3. Divide the out-of-balance amount by 9. If the result is evenly divisible by 9, the error may be a *slide* (example: writing $1,000 as $100) or a *transposition* (example: treating $1,200 as $2,100). Suppose Cookie Lapp printed the $2,000 Dividends as $20,000 on the trial balance—a slide-type error. Total debits would differ from total credits by $18,000 ($20,000 – $2,000 = $18,000). Dividing $18,000 by 9 yields $2,000, the correct amount of withdrawals. Trace $2,000 through the ledger until you reach the Dividends account. You have then found the error.

Details of Journals and Ledgers

In practice, the journal and the ledger provide details to create a "trail" through the records. Suppose a supplier bills us twice for an item that we purchased. To show we've already paid the bill, we must prove our payment. That requires us to use the journal and the ledger.

Details in the Journal

Exhibit 2-13 illustrates a transaction and then shows the journal with these details:

- The *transaction date,* April 1, 2008.
- The *accounts* debited and credited, along with their dollar amounts.
- The *posting reference,* abbreviated Post. Ref. Use of this column will become clear when we discuss details in the ledger, which come next.

EXHIBIT 2-13 Details of Journalizing and Posting

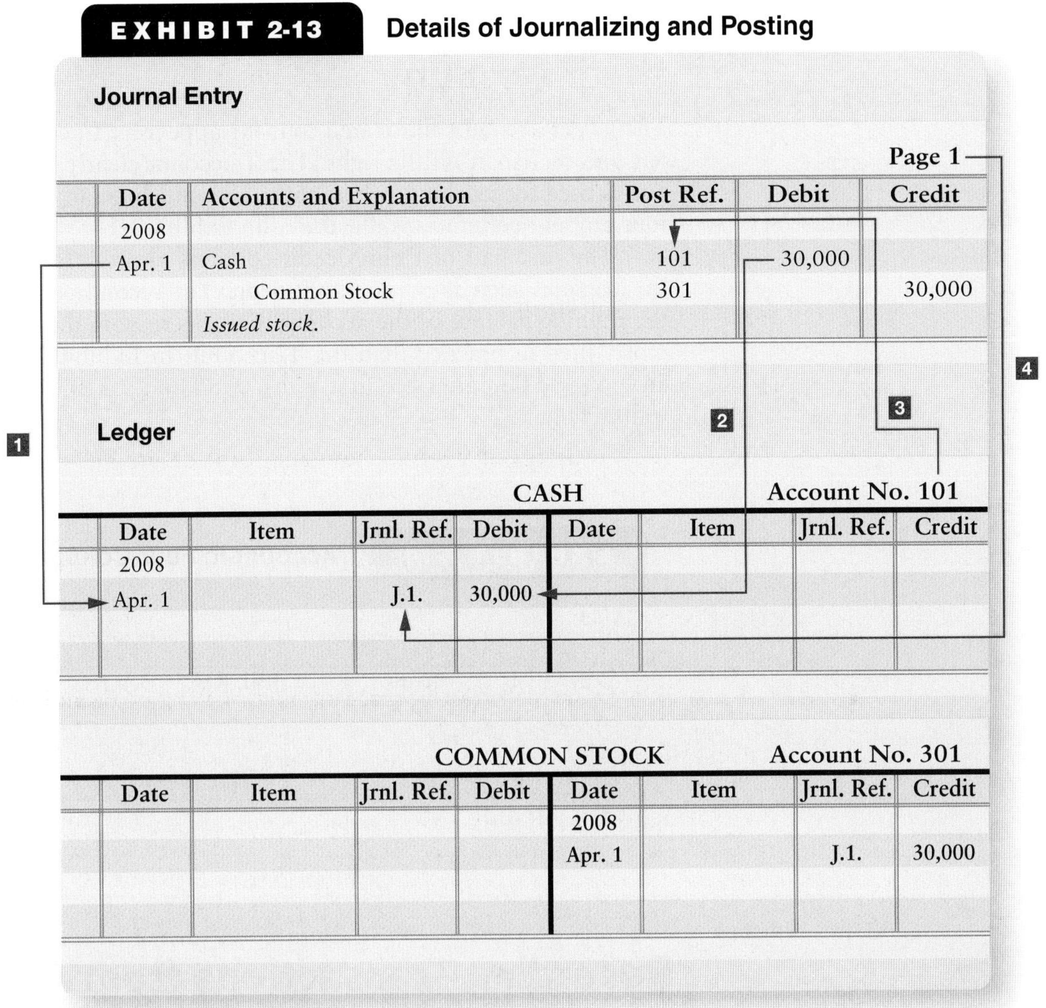

Journal Entry

Page 1

Date	Accounts and Explanation	Post Ref.	Debit	Credit
2008				
Apr. 1	Cash	101	30,000	
	Common Stock	301		30,000
	Issued stock.			

Ledger

CASH — Account No. 101

Date	Item	Jrnl. Ref.	Debit	Date	Item	Jrnl. Ref.	Credit
2008							
Apr. 1		J.1.	30,000				

COMMON STOCK — Account No. 301

Date	Item	Jrnl. Ref.	Debit	Date	Item	Jrnl. Ref.	Credit
				2008			
				Apr. 1		J.1.	30,000

Details in the Ledger

Posting means copying information from the journal to the ledger. But how do we handle the details? Exhibit 2-13 illustrates the steps, denoted by arrows:

Arrow **1**—Post the transaction **date** from the journal to the ledger.

Arrow **2**—Post the debit ($30,000) from the journal as a debit to the Cash account in the ledger. Likewise, post the credit (also $30,000) from the journal to the Common Stock account in the ledger. Now the ledger accounts have correct amounts.

Arrow **3**—Post the account numbers (**101** and **301**) from the ledger back to the journal. This step shows that the debit and the credit have both been posted to the ledger. **Post. Ref.** is the abbreviation for Posting Reference.

Arrow **4**—Post the page number from the journal to the ledger. **Jrnl. Ref.** means Journal Reference, and **J.1** refers to Journal Page **1**. This step shows where the data came from: Journal Page 1.

The Four-Column Account: An Alternative to the T-Account

The ledger accounts illustrated thus far appear as T-accounts, with the debit on the left and the credit on the right. The T-account clearly separates debits from credits and is used for teaching, where there isn't much detail. Another account format has four amount columns, as illustrated in Exhibit 2-14.

The first pair of Debit/Credit columns are for transaction amounts posted to the account, such as the $30,000 debit. The second pair of amount columns show the running balance of the account. For this reason, the four-column format is used more often in practice than the T-account. In Exhibit 2-14, Cash has a debit balance of $30,000 after the first transaction and a $10,000 balance after the second transaction.

EXHIBIT 2-14 **Account in Four-Column Format**

CASH — Account No. 101

Date	Item	Jrnl. Ref.	Debit	Credit	Balance Debit	Balance Credit
2008						
Apr. 1		J.1	30,000		30,000	
Apr. 3		J.1		20,000	10,000	

Recording Transactions from Actual Business Documents

In practice, businesses record transactions from the data of their actual documents such as bank deposit receipts and purchase invoices. When Cookie Lapp Travel Design collects cash for revenue earned, Lapp deposits the cash in the bank and gets a deposit receipt as shown in Exhibit 2-15.

EXHIBIT 2-15 **Actual Bank Deposit Receipt**

Thank You
FOR YOUR BUSINESS

TEXAS FIRST STATE BANK
Box 1739 Terminal Annex
Austin, TX 78702

CHECKING DEPOSIT RECEIPT UNLESS MARKED BELOW
☐ SAVINGS ☐ LOANS ☐ ____________

015 TFB 6-10-08 $225.00 4190-637-2

DEPOSITS MAY NOT BE AVAILABLE FOR IMMEDIATE WITHDRAWAL. BANK SYMBOL, TRANSACTION NUMBER AND AMOUNT OF DEPOSIT ARE SHOWN ABOVE.

Lapp's journal entry to record this cash receipt and revenue earned is

June 10	Cash	225.00	
	Service Revenue		225.00
	Performed service and received cash.		

To promote its business, Cookie Lapp Travel Design held a party and ordered flowers for table arrangements. Exhibit 2-16 shows the actual purchase invoice.

EXHIBIT 2-16 **Actual Purchase Invoice**

Rosetree Flower & Gift Shop **INVOICE**

P.O. BOX 76708
AUSTIN, TX 76708

Date	Invoice #
6/13/2008	193690

Bill to:	Ship to:	Delivered on:
Cookie Lapp Travel Design, Inc. 9000 Clare Blvd. Austin, TX 78702	Cookie Lapp Travel 9000 Clare Blvd. Austin, TX 78702	6/11/08

Quantity	Item Code	Description	Price Each	Amount
14	ARRANGEMENT	ARRANGEMENT - TABLES	9.00	126.00
	ARRANGEMENT	ARRANGEMENT - BLUE HYDRANGEA	100.00	100.00
		Sales Tax	8.25%	18.65
		THANK YOU FOR YOUR BUSINESS	**TOTAL**	244.65

In this purchase transaction, Cookie Lapp Travel Design purchased flowers costing $244.65 on account. Lapp recorded this promotion expense with the following journal entry:

June 13	Promotion Expense	244.65	
	Accounts Payable		244.65
	Purchased flowers on account.		

Lapp would record payment on June 30 as follows:

June 30	Accounts Payable	244.65	
	Cash		244.65
	Paid on account.		

Decision Guidelines

Analyzing and Recording Transactions

Suppose Julie DeFilippo in the chapter-opening story opens a small office and hires a helper to keep her books. QuickBooks software is used for the accounting.

DeFilippo offers you a job as accountant for this small business. The pay is good. Can you answer the manager's questions, which are outlined in the Decision Guidelines? If so, you may get the job.

Decision	Guidelines
• Has a transaction occurred?	If the event affects the entity's financial position and can be recorded reliably —*Yes* If either condition is absent—*No*
• Where to record the transaction?	In the *journal,* the chronological record of transactions
• What to record for each transaction?	Increases and/or decreases in all the accounts affected by the transaction
• How to record an increase/decrease in a (an)	Rules of debit and credit:

	Increase	**Decrease**
Asset	Debit	Credit
Liability	Credit	Debit
Stockholders' Equity	Credit	Debit
Revenue	Credit	Debit
Expense	Debit	Credit

Decision	Guidelines
• Where to store all the information for each account?	In the *ledger,* the record holding all the accounts
• Where to list all the accounts and their balances?	In the *trial balance*
• Where to report the results of operations?	In the income statement **(Revenues − Expenses = Net income or Net loss)**
• Where to report financial position?	In the balance sheet **(Assets = Liabilities + Stockholders' equity)**

Summary Problem

The trial balance of Reitmeier Service Center, Inc., on March 1, 2007, lists the entity's assets, liabilities, and owner's equity on that date.

		Balance	
	Account Title	Debit	Credit
	Cash	$ 26,000	
	Accounts receivable	4,500	
	Accounts payable		$ 2,000
	Common stock		28,500
	Total	$30,500	$30,500

During March, the business engaged in the following transactions:

a. Borrowed $45,000 from the bank and signed a note payable in the name of the business.

b. Paid cash of $40,000 to acquire land.

c. Performed service for a customer and received cash of $5,000.

d. Purchased supplies on credit, $300.

e. Performed customer service and earned revenue on account, $2,600.

f. Paid $1,200 on account.

g. Paid the following cash expenses: salaries, $3,000; rent, $1,500; and interest, $400.

h. Received $3,100 on account.

i. Received a $200 utility bill that will be paid next week.

j. Paid cash dividends of $1,800.

Requirements

1. Open the following accounts, with the balances indicated, in the ledger of Reitmeier Service Center. Use the T-account format.
   - **Assets**—Cash, $26,000; Accounts Receivable, $4,500; Supplies, no balance; Land, no balance
   - **Liabilities**—Accounts Payable, $2,000; Note Payable, no balance
   - **Stockholders' Equity**—Common Stock, $28,500; Dividends, no balance
   - **Revenues**—Service Revenue, no balance
   - **Expenses**—(none have balances) Salary Expense, Rent Expense, Utilities Expense, Interest Expense
2. Journalize each transaction. Key journal entries by transaction letter.
3. Post to the ledger.
4. Prepare the trial balance of Reitmeier Service Center, Inc., at March 31, 2007.

Solution

Requirement 1

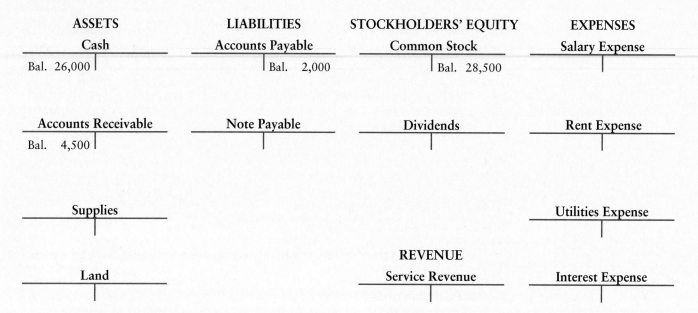

ASSETS

Cash	
Bal. 26,000	

Accounts Receivable	
Bal. 4,500	

Supplies	

Land	

LIABILITIES

Accounts Payable	
	Bal. 2,000

Note Payable	

STOCKHOLDERS' EQUITY

Common Stock	
	Bal. 28,500

Dividends	

REVENUE

Service Revenue	

EXPENSES

Salary Expense	

Rent Expense	

Utilities Expense	

Interest Expense	

Requirement 2

	Requirement 2		
a. Journal Entry	Cash	45,000	
	Note Payable		45,000
	Borrowed cash on note payable.		
b. Journal Entry	Land	40,000	
	Cash		40,000
	Purchased land.		
c. Journal Entry	Cash	5,000	
	Service Revenue		5,000
	Preformed service and received cash.		
d. Journal Entry	Supplies	300	
	Accounts Payable		300
	Purchased supplies on account.		
e. Journal Entry	Accounts Receivable	2,600	
	Service Revenue		2,600
	Performed service on account.		
f. Journal Entry	Accounts Payable	1,200	
	Cash		1,200
	Paid on account.		
g. Journal Entry	Salary Expense	3,000	
	Rent Expense	1,500	
	Interest Expense	400	
	Cash		4,900
	Paid expenses.		
h. Journal Entry	Cash	3,100	
	Accounts Receivable		3,100
	Received cash on account.		
i. Journal Entry	Utilities Expense	200	
	Accounts Payable		200
	Received utility bill.		
j. Journal Entry	Dividends	1,800	
	Cash		1,800
	Paid dividends.		

Requirement 3

ASSETS

Cash

Bal.	26,000	(b)	40,000
(a)	45,000	(f)	1,200
(c)	5,000	(g)	4,900
(h)	3,100	(j)	1,800
Bal.	31,200		

Accounts Receivable

Bal.	4,500	(h)	3,100
(e)	2,600		
Bal.	4,000		

Supplies

(d)	300		
Bal.	300		

Land

(b)	40,000		
Bal.	40,000		

LIABILITIES

Accounts Payable

(f)	1,200	Bal.	2,000
		(d)	300
		(i)	200
		Bal.	1,300

Note Payable

		(a)	45,000
		Bal.	45,000

STOCKHOLDERS' EQUITY

Common Stock

		Bal.	28,500

Dividends

(j)	1,800		
Bal.	1,800		

REVENUE

Service Revenue

		(c)	5,000
		(e)	2,600
		Bal.	7,600

EXPENSES

Salary Expense

(g)	3,000		
Bal.	3,000		

Rent Expense

(g)	1,500		
Bal.	1,500		

Interest Expense

(g)	400		
Bal.	400		

Utilities Expense

(i)	200		
Bal.	200		

Requirement 4

REITMEIER SERVICE CENTER, INC.
Trial Balance
March 31, 2007

	Balance	
Account Title	Debit	Credit
Cash	$31,200	
Accounts receivable	4,000	
Supplies	300	
Land	40,000	
Accounts payable		$ 1,300
Note payable		45,000
Common stock		28,500
Dividends	1,800	
Service revenue		7,600
Salary expense	3,000	
Rent expense	1,500	
Interest expense	400	
Utilities expense	200	
Total	$82,400	$82,400

Review *Recording Business Transactions*

Accounting Vocabulary

Account
The detailed record of the changes in a particular asset, liability, or owner's equity during a period. The basic summary device of accounting.

Chart of Accounts
List of all the accounts with their account numbers.

Credit
The right side of an account.

Debit
The left side of an account.

Journal
The chronological accounting record of an entity's transactions.

Ledger
The record holding all the accounts.

Normal Balance
The balance that appears on the side of an account—debit or credit—where we record increases.

Note Receivable
A written promise for future collection of cash.

Posting
Copying amounts from the journal to the ledger.

Trial Balance
A list of all the accounts with their balances.

Quick Check

1. Which sequence correctly summarizes the accounting process?
   a. Journalize transactions, post to the accounts, prepare a trial balance
   b. Post to the accounts, journalize transactions, prepare a trial balance
   c. Prepare a trial balance, journalize transactions, post to the accounts
   d. Journalize transactions, prepare a trial balance, post to the accounts

2. The left side of an account is used to record:
   a. Debit or credit, depending on the type of account
   b. Credits
   c. Debits
   d. Increases

3. Suppose Frazier Corporation has cash of $50,000, receivables of $60,000, and furniture totaling $200,000. The business owes $80,000 on account and has a $100,000 note payable. How much is Frazier's stockholders' equity?
   a. $20,000
   b. $130,000
   c. $180,000
   d. $310,000

4. Your business purchased supplies of $1,000 on account. The journal entry to record this transaction is:

a. Inventory	1,000	
Accounts Payable		1,000
b. Accounts Payable	1,000	
Supplies		1,000
c. Supplies	1,000	
Accounts Payable		1,000
d. Supplies	1,000	
Accounts Receivable		1,000

5. Which journal entry records your payment for the supplies purchased in transaction 4?

a. Accounts Payable	1,000	
Accounts Receivable		1,000
b. Supplies	1,000	
Cash		1,000
c. Cash	1,000	
Accounts Payable		1,000
d. Accounts Payable	1,000	
Cash		1,000

6. Posting a $1,000 purchase of supplies on account appears as follows:

a.

Supplies		Accounts Payable	
1,000			1,000

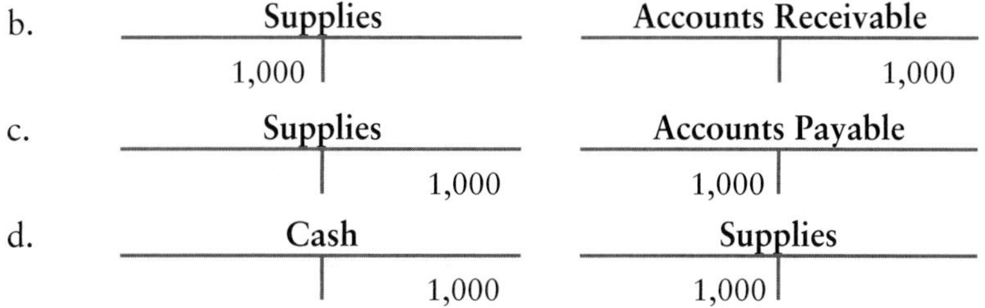

7. You paid $500 for supplies and purchased additional supplies on account for $700. Later you paid $300 of the accounts payable. What is the balance in your Supplies account?
   a. $500
   b. $900
   c. $1,500
   d. $1,200

8. **Kinko's Copies** recorded a cash collection on account by debiting Cash and crediting Accounts Payable. What will the trial balance show for this error?
   a. Too much for liabilities
   b. Too much for expenses
   c. The trial balance will not balance
   d. Too much for cash

9. Brett Wilkinson, Attorney, P.C., began the year with total assets of $120,000, liabilities of $70,000, and owner equity of $50,000. During the year he earned revenue of $110,000 and paid expenses of $30,000. The business paid cash dividends of $60,000. How much is the business's equity at year-end?
   a. $90,000
   b. $120,000
   c. $70,000
   d. $160,000

10. How would Brett Wilkinson record his expenses for the year in question 9?

a. Expenses	30,000	
Accounts Payable		30,000
b. Expenses	30,000	
Cash		30,000
c. Cash	30,000	
Expenses		30,000
d. Accounts Payable	30,000	
Cash		30,000

Answers are given after Apply Your Knowledge (p. 115).

Assess Your Progress

Short Exercises

Explaining the rules of debit and credit
2

S2-1 Aretha Franklin is tutoring Blaine McCormick, who is taking introductory accounting. Aretha explains to Blaine that *debits* are used to record increases in accounts and *credits* record decreases. Blaine is confused and seeks your advice.

- When are debits increases? When are debits decreases?
- When are credits increases? When are credits decreases?

Exhibit 2-8, page 70, gives the rules of debit and credit.

Using accounting terms
1

S2-2 Tighten your grip by filling in the blanks to review some key accounting definitions.

Rita Bowden is describing the accounting process for a friend who is a philosophy major. Rita states, "The basic summary device in accounting is the _____. The left side is called the _____ side, and the right side is called the _____ side. We record transactions first in a _____. Then we post (copy the data) to the _____. It is helpful to list all the accounts with their balances on a _____." (pp. 62–65)

Using accounting terms
1

S2-3 Accounting has its own vocabulary and basic relationships. Match the accounting terms at left with the corresponding definitions at right. (challenge)

_____ 1. Equity	A. Record of transactions
_____ 2. Debit	B. An asset
_____ 3. Expense	C. Left side of an account
_____ 4. Net income	D. Side of an account where increases are recorded
_____ 5. Ledger	E. Copying data from the journal to the ledger
_____ 6. Posting	F. Using up assets in the course of operating a business
_____ 7. Normal balance	G. Always a liability
_____ 8. Payable	H. Revenues − Expenses = _____
_____ 9. Journal	I. Book of accounts
_____ 10. Receivable	J. Assets – Liabilities = _____

Normal account balances
2

S2-4 Accounting records include three basic categories of accounts: assets, liabilities, and stockholders' equity. In turn, stockholders' equity holds the following categories: common stock, dividends, revenues, and expenses. Identify which categories of the accounts have a normal debit balance and which categories have a normal credit balance. (p. 69)

Recording transactions
3

S2-5 Mark Brown opened a medical practice in Alexandria, Virginia. Record the following transactions in the journal of Mark Brown, M.D., P.C. Include an explanation with each entry. (pp. 72–78)

continued . . .

9	Paid $100 on accounts payable.
17	Performed service for customers on account, $2,100.
23	Received $1,200 cash from a customer on account.
31	Paid the following expenses: salary, $1,200; rent, $500.

Requirement

Record the preceding transactions in the journal of Woodward Technology Solutions. Key transactions by date and include an explanation for each entry, as illustrated in the chapter. Use the following accounts: Cash; Accounts Receivable; Supplies; Building; Accounts Payable; Common Stock; Service Revenue; Salary Expense; Rent Expense. (pp. 72–78)

Posting to the ledger and preparing a trial balance

E2-19 Refer to Exercise 2-18 for the transactions of Woodward Technology Solutions, Inc.

Requirements

1. After journalizing the transactions of Exercise 2-18, post to the ledger, using T-account format. Key transactions by date. Date the ending balance of each account Aug. 31. (pp. 72–78).
2. Prepare the trial balance of Woodward Technology Solutions, Inc., at August 31, 2007. (p. 79)

Describing transactions and posting

E2-20 The journal of Alert Defensive Driving, Inc., includes the following entries for May 2006.

Journal Entry:

Page 5

Date	Accounts and Explanation	Post Ref.	Debit	Credit
May 2	Cash		20,000	
	Common Stock			20,000
9	Supplies		200	
	Accounts Payable			200
11	Accounts Receivable		2,600	
	Service Revenue			2,600
14	Rent Expense		3,200	
	Cash			3,200
22	Accounts Payable		300	
	Cash			300
25	Advertising Expense		400	
	Cash			400
27	Cash		1,400	
	Accounts Receivable			1,400
31	Fuel Expense		100	
	Accounts Payable			100

Requirements

1. Describe each transaction. (pp. 72–78)
2. Set up T-accounts using the following account numbers: Cash, 110; Accounts Receivable, 120; Supplies, 130; Accounts Payable, 210; Common Stock, 310; Service Revenue, 410; Rent Expense, 510; Advertising Expense, 520; Fuel Expense, 530. (p. 81)
3. Post to the accounts. Write dates and journal references in the accounts, as illustrated in Exhibit 2-13, page 81. Compute the balance of each account after posting. (p. 81)
4. Prepare the trial balance of Alert Defensive Driving, Inc., at May 31, 2006. (p. 79)

Journalizing transactions

3

E2-21 The first five transactions of Reed's Home Care Corporation, have been posted to the accounts as follows:

Cash			
(1)	12,000	(3)	40,000
(4)	37,000	(5)	6,000

Supplies			
(2)	400		

Equipment			
(5)	6,000		

Building			
(3)	40,000		

Accounts Payable			
		(2)	400

Note Payable			
		(4)	37,000

Common Stock			
		(1)	12,000

Requirement

Prepare the journal entries that served as the sources for the five transactions. Include an explanation for each entry as illustrated in the chapter. (pp. 72–78)

Preparing a trial balance

5

E2-22 Prepare the trial balance of Reed's Home Care Corporation at October 31, 2007, using the accounts from Exercise 2-21. (p. 79)

Preparing a trial balance

5

E2-23 The accounts of Mayflower Moving Company follow with their normal balances at December 31, 2006. The accounts are listed in no particular order.

Common stock	$ 48,700	Trucks	$125,000
Insurance expense	700	Fuel expense	2,000
Accounts payable	4,300	Dividends	6,000
Service revenue	86,000	Utilities expense	400
Building	44,000	Accounts receivable	9,400
Supplies expense	300	Note payable	60,000
Cash	5,000	Supplies	200
Salary expense	6,000		

Requirement

Prepare Mayflower's trial balance at December 31, 2006, listing accounts in proper sequence, as illustrated in the chapter. For example, Supplies comes before Trucks and Building. List the largest expense first, the second-largest expense next, and so on. (p. 79)

Recording transactions and using four-column accounts

E2-24 Open the following four-column accounts of Lee Bivona, CPA, P.C.: Cash; Accounts Receivable; Office Supplies; Office Furniture; Accounts Payable; Common Stock; Dividends; Service Revenue; Salary Expense; Rent Expense.

Journalize the following transactions and then post to the four-column accounts. Use the letters to identify the transactions. Keep a running balance in each account.

a. Bivona opened an accounting firm by investing $15,000 cash and office furniture valued at $5,400. The business issued $20,400 of common stock to Bivona.

b. Paid monthly rent of $1,500.

c. Purchased office supplies on account, $700.

d. Paid employee's salary, $1,800.

e. Paid $400 of the account payable created in transaction (c).

f. Performed accounting service on account, $5,600.

g. Paid cash dividends of $7,000.

Preparing a trial balance

E2-25 After recording and posting the transactions in Exercise 2-24, prepare the trial balance of Lee Bivona, CPA, P.C., at December 31, 2007.

Correcting errors in a trial balance

E2-26 The trial balance of Joy McDowell Tutoring Service, Inc., at March 31, 2009, does not balance:

Account Title	Balance Debit	Credit
Cash	$ 3,000	
Accounts receivable	2,000	
Supplies	600	
Computer equipment	26,000	
Accounts payable		$11,500
Common stock		11,600
Service revenue		9,700
Salary expense	1,700	
Rent expense	800	
Utilities expense	300	
Total	$34,400	$32,800

Investigation of the accounting records reveals that the bookkeeper:

a. Recorded a $400 cash revenue transaction by debiting Accounts Receivable. The credit entry was correct.

b. Posted a $1,000 credit to Accounts Payable as $100.

c. Did not record utilities expense or the related account payable in the amount of $200.

d. Understated Common Stock by $700.

Requirement

Prepare the correct trial balance at March 31, complete with a heading; journal entries are not required. (pp. 79–80)

Analyzing accounting errors

2 3 4 5

E2-27 Blenda Lozano has trouble keeping her debits and credits equal. During a recent month, Blenda made the following accounting errors:

a. In preparing the trial balance, Blenda omitted a $5,000 note payable. (p. 80)

b. Blenda posted a $700 utility expense as $70. The credit to Cash was correct.

c. In recording a $400 payment on account, Blenda debited Supplies instead of Accounts Payable. (p. 80)

d. In journalizing a receipt of cash for service revenue, Blenda debited Cash for $80 instead of the correct amount of $800. The credit was correct. (p. 80)

e. Blenda recorded a $120 purchase of supplies on account by debiting Supplies and crediting Accounts Payable for $210. (p. 80)

Requirements

1. For each of these errors, state whether total debits equal total credits on the trial balance.
2. Identify each account that has an incorrect balance, and indicate the amount and direction of the error (such as "Accounts Receivable $500 too high").

Computing financial statement amounts without a journal

5

E2-28 The owner of Jackson Lighting Company needs to compute the following summary information from the accounting records:

a. Net income for the month of July

b. Total cash paid during July

c. Cash collections from customers during July

d. Payments on account during July

The quickest way to compute these amounts is to analyze the following accounts:

Account	Balance		Additional Information for the Month of July
	June 30	July 31	
a. Retained Earnings	$ 9,000	$22,000	Dividends, $4,000
b. Cash	7,000	2,000	Cash receipts, $50,000
c. Accounts Receivable	24,000	26,000	Revenues on account, $75,000
d. Accounts Payable	11,000	20,000	Purchases on account, $40,000

The net income for July can be computed as follows:

Retained Earnings			
		June 30 Bal.	9,000
July Dividends	4,000	July Net Income	X = $17,000
		July 31 Bal.	22,000

Use a similar approach to compute the other three items. (Challenge)

Using actual business documents

3

E2-29 Suppose your name is Grant Schaeffer, and Advanced Automotive repaired your car. You settled the bill as noted on the following invoice. To you this is a purchase invoice. To Advanced Automotive, it's a sales invoice.

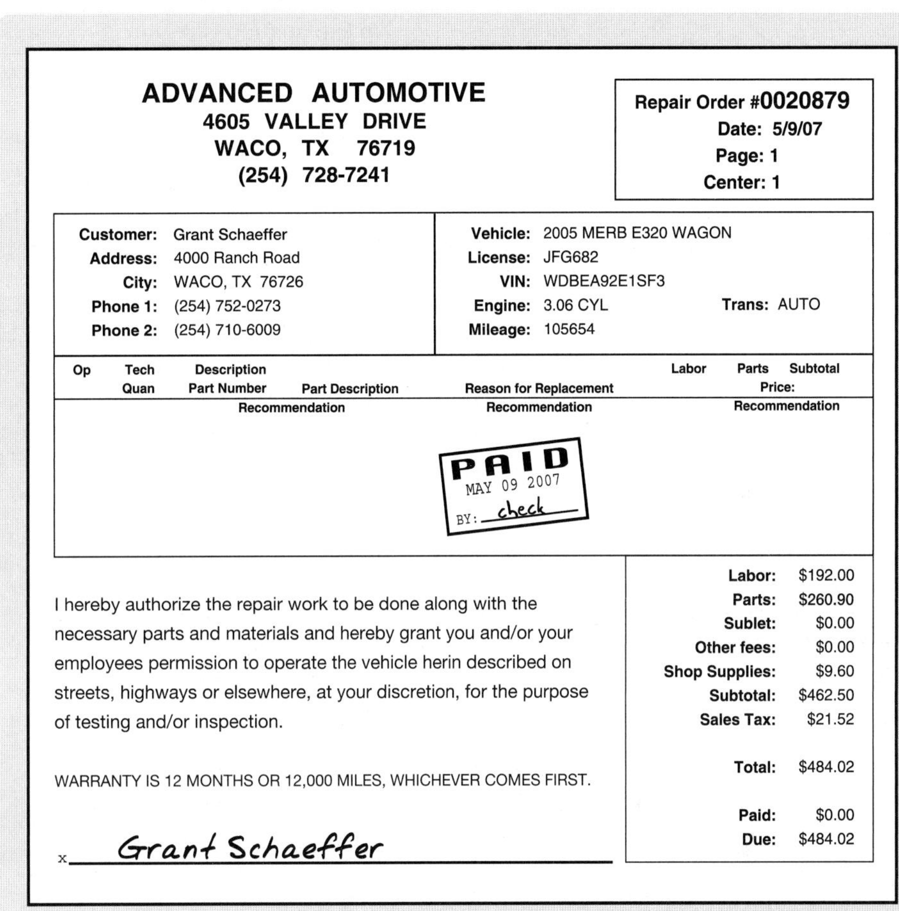

ADVANCED AUTOMOTIVE
4605 VALLEY DRIVE
WACO, TX 76719
(254) 728-7241

Repair Order #0020879
Date: 5/9/07
Page: 1
Center: 1

Customer:	Grant Schaeffer	**Vehicle:**	2005 MERB E320 WAGON
Address:	4000 Ranch Road	**License:**	JFG682
City:	WACO, TX 76726	**VIN:**	WDBEA92E1SF3
Phone 1:	(254) 752-0273	**Engine:**	3.06 CYL **Trans:** AUTO
Phone 2:	(254) 710-6009	**Mileage:**	105654

Op	Tech Quan	Description Part Number	Part Description Recommendation	Reason for Replacement Recommendation	Labor	Parts Price:	Subtotal Recommendation

PAID
MAY 09 2007
BY: check

I hereby authorize the repair work to be done along with the necessary parts and materials and hereby grant you and/or your employees permission to operate the vehicle herin described on streets, highways or elsewhere, at your discretion, for the purpose of testing and/or inspection.

WARRANTY IS 12 MONTHS OR 12,000 MILES, WHICHEVER COMES FIRST.

x Grant Schaeffer

Labor:	$192.00
Parts:	$260.90
Sublet:	$0.00
Other fees:	$0.00
Shop Supplies:	$9.60
Subtotal:	$462.50
Sales Tax:	$21.52
Total:	$484.02
Paid:	$0.00
Due:	$484.02

Journalize:

a. Your repair expense transaction. (pp. 82–83)

b. Advanced Automotive's service revenue transaction. (pp. 82–83)

Problems (Group A)

Using accounting terms and analyzing a trial balance

1

P2-30A →*Link Back to Chapter 1 (Balance Sheet, Income Statement).* Amber Shea, the principal stockholder of the Shea Law Firm, is considering adding another lawyer. Courtney Martinez is considering joining Shea and asks to see Shea's financial information. Shea gives Martinez the firm's trial balance, which follows. Help Martinez decide whether to join the firm by answering these questions for her.

1. How much are the firm's total assets? total liabilities? net income or net loss? (pp. 62–64)

continued . . .

2. Suppose Shea earned all the service revenue on account. Make a single journal entry to record the revenue, set up the two T-accounts affected, and post to those accounts. You may omit the explanation of the journal entry. (p. 72)
3. Make a single journal entry to record Shea's payment of utilities expense. No explanation is required.
4. In your own words, describe the accounting process that results in Shea's $12,000 balance for Cash. Use the following terms in your explanation: account, balance, journal ledger, post, and trial balance. (pp. 68–79).

SHEA LAW FIRM, P.C.
Trial Balance
December 31, 2008

Account Title	Balance Debit	Balance Credit
Cash	$ 12,000	
Accounts receivable	27,000	
Prepaid expenses	4,000	
Furniture	31,000	
Accounts payable		$ 35,000
Common stock		30,000
Dividends	53,000	
Service revenue		121,000
Rent expense	26,000	
Utilities expense	3,000	
Wage expense	23,000	
Supplies expense	7,000	
Total	$186,000	$186,000

Analyzing and journalizing transactions

P2-31A Showtime Amusements Company owns movie theaters. Showtime engaged in the following business transactions:

July	1	Darrell Palusky invested $350,000 personal cash in the business by depositing that amount in a bank account titled Showtime Amusements. The business issued common stock to Palusky.
	2	Paid $300,000 cash to purchase a theater building.
	5	Borrowed $220,000 from the bank. Palusky signed a note payable to the bank in the name of Showtime Amusements.
	10	Purchased theater supplies on account, $1,700.
	15	Paid $800 on account.
	15	Paid property tax expense on theater building, $1,200.
	16	Paid employee salaries, $2,800, and rent on equipment, $1,800. Make a single compound entry.

continued . . .

28	Paid cash dividends of $6,000.
31	Received $20,000 cash from service revenue and deposited that amount in the bank.

Showtime Amusements uses the following accounts: Cash; Supplies; Building; Accounts Payable; Notes Payable; Common Stock; Dividends; Service Revenue; Salary Expense; Rent Expense; Property Tax Expense.

Requirement

Journalize each transaction of Showtime Amusements Company as shown for July 1. Explanations are not required. (pp. 72–78)

July 1	Cash	350,000	
	Common Stock		350,000

Journalizing transactions, posting to T-accounts, and preparing a trial balance

P2-32A Doris Higgins started her practice as a design consultant on September 1 of the current year. During the first month of operations, the business completed the following transactions:

Sep. 1	Received $25,000 cash and issued common stock.
4	Purchased supplies, $200, and furniture, $1,800, on account.
6	Performed services for a law firm and received $4,000 cash.
7	Paid $20,000 cash to acquire land for a future office site.
10	Performed service for a hotel and received its promise to pay the $800 within one week.
14	Paid for the furniture purchased September 4 on account.
15	Paid secretary's salary, $600.
17	Received cash on account, $500.
20	Prepared a design for a school on account, $800.
28	Received $1,500 cash for consulting with **Procter & Gamble.**
30	Paid secretary's salary, $600.
30	Paid rent expense, $500.
30	Paid cash dividends of $2,000.

Requirement

Open the following T-accounts: Cash; Accounts Receivable; Supplies; Furniture; Land; Accounts Payable; Common Stock; Dividends; Service Revenue; Salary Expense; Rent Expense.

1. Record each transaction in the journal, using the account titles given. Key each transaction by date. Explanations are not required. (pp. 72–78)

continued . . .

2. Post the transactions to the T-accounts, using transaction dates as posting references in the ledger accounts. Label the balance of each account *Bal.*, as shown in the chapter. (pp. 72–78)
3. Prepare the trial balance of Doris Higgins, Designer, P.C., at September 30 of the current year. (p. 79)

Journalizing transactions, posting to accounts in four-column format, and preparing a trial balance

2, 3, 4, 5

P2-33A The trial balance of John Hilton, CPA, P.C., is dated January 31, 2007:

JOHN HILTON, CPA, P.C.
Trial Balance
January 31, 2007

		Balance	
Account Number	Account Title	Debit	Credit
11	Cash	$ 2,000	
12	Accounts receivable	9,500	
13	Supplies	800	
14	Land	18,600	
21	Accounts payable		$ 3,000
31	Common stock		27,900
32	Dividends		
41	Service revenue		
51	Salary expense		
52	Rent expense		
	Total	$30,900	$30,900

During February, Hilton or his business completed the following transactions:

Feb. 4	Hilton collected $3,500 cash from a client on account.
8	Performed tax services for a client on account, $7,000.
13	Paid business debt on account, $1,000.
18	Purchased office supplies on account, $100.
20	Paid cash dividends of $1,200.
21	Hilton paid for a deck for his private residence, using personal funds, $9,000.
22	Received cash of $5,500 for consulting work just completed.
28	Paid office rent, $800.
28	Paid employee salary, $1,800.

Requirements

1. Record the February transactions on page 3 of the business's journal. Include an explanation for each entry. (pp. 72–78)

continued . . .

2. Post the transactions to four-column accounts in the ledger, using dates, account numbers, journal references, and posting references. Open the ledger accounts listed in the trial balance, together with their balances at January 31. Enter *Bal.* (for January 31 balance) in the Item column, and place a check mark (✔) in the journal reference column for the January 31 balance in each account. (pp. 80–81)
3. Prepare the trial balance of John Hilton, CPA, P.C. at February 28, 2007.

Recording transactions; using four-column accounts; preparing a trial balance
2 3 5

P2-34A Maury Wills started an environmental consulting company and during the first month of operations (June 2008) the business completed the following transactions:

a. Wills began the business with an investment of $25,000 cash and a building valued at $30,000. The business issued $55,000 of common stock to Wills.
b. Purchased office supplies on account, $2,100.
c. Paid $18,000 for office furniture.
d. Paid employee's salary, $2,200.
e. Performed consulting service on account, $5,100.
f. Paid $800 of the account payable created in transaction (b).
g. Received a $600 bill for advertising expense that will be paid in the near future.
h. Performed consulting service for customers and received cash, $1,600.
i. Received cash on account, $1,200.
j. Paid the following cash expenses and made a single compound entry:
   (1) Rent on equipment, $700.
   (2) Utilities, $400.
k. Paid cash dividends of $1,000.

Requirements

1. Open the following four-column accounts: Cash; Accounts Receivable; Office Supplies; Office Furniture; Building; Accounts Payable; Common Stock; Dividends; Service Revenue; Salary Expense; Rent Expense; Advertising Expense; Utilities Expense.
2. Record each transaction in the journal. Use the letters to identify the transactions. (pp. 72–78)
3. Post to the accounts and keep a running balance for each account. (p. 80)
4. Prepare the trial balance of Wills Environmental Consulting Company at June 30, 2008. (p. 79)

Preparing the financial statements
5

P2-35A *Note:* Problem 2-35A should be used only in conjunction with Problem 2-34A.→ *Link Back to Chapter 1 (Income Statement, Statement of Retained Earnings, Balance Sheet).* Refer to Problem 2-34A. After

continued . . .

completing the trial balance in Problem 2-34A, prepare the following financial statements for Wills Consulting Company:

1. Income statement for the month ended June 30, 2008. (p. 22)
2. Statement of retained earnings for the month ended June 30, 2008. The beginning balance of retained earnings was $0. (p. 22)
3. Balance sheet at June 30, 2008. (p. 22)

Draw arrows to link the statements. If needed, use Exhibit 1-9, page 22, as a guide for preparing the financial statements.

Correcting errors in a trial balance

2 5

P2-36A The trial balance of URNO.1 Child Care, Inc., does not balance. The following errors are detected:

a. Cash is understated by $1,000.

b. A $2,000 debit to Accounts Receivable was posted as a credit.

c. A $1,000 purchase of supplies on account was neither journalized nor posted.

d. Equipment's cost is $75,000, not $85,000.

e. Salary expense is overstated by $100.

URNO.1 CHILD CARE
Trial Balance
June 30, 2008

Account Title	Balance Debit	Balance Credit
Cash	$ 3,000	
Accounts receivable	10,000	
Supplies	900	
Equipment	85,000	
Accounts payable		$ 55,000
Common stock		38,500
Dividends	2,100	
Service revenue		6,500
Salary expense	3,100	
Rent expense	1,000	
Total	$105,100	$100,000

Requirement

Prepare the correct trial balance at June 30. Journal entries are not required. (pp. 79, 81)

Problems (Group B)

Using accounting terms and analyzing a trial balance

P2-37B → *Link Back to Chapter 1 (Balance Sheet, Income Statement).* Judy Kroll, the principal stockholder of A+ Fire & Safety, is selling her interest in the business. Kroll offers the following trial balance to prospective buyers. Your best friend is considering buying out Kroll. He seeks your advice in interpreting this information.

continued . . .

A+ FIRE & SAFETY COMPANY
Trial Balance
December 31, 2007

Account Title	Balance Debit	Balance Credit
Cash	$ 7,000	
Accounts receivable	6,000	
Prepaid expenses	4,000	
Equipment	130,000	
Accounts payable		$ 31,000
Note payable		45,000
Common stock		33,000
Dividends	21,000	
Service revenue		112,000
Wage expense	38,000	
Rent expense	8,000	
Supplies expense	7,000	
Total	$221,000	$221,000

Requirements

Help your friend decide whether to buy A+ Fire & Safety by answering the following questions.

1. How much are the firm's total assets? total liabilities? net income or net loss? (pp. 62–64)
2. Suppose A+ earned all the service revenue on account. Make a single journal entry to record the revenue, set up the two T-accounts affected, and post to those accounts. You may omit the explanation of the journal entry. (p. 72)
3. Make a single journal entry to record A+'s payment of wage expense. Omit the explanation.
4. In your own words, describe the accounting process that results in A+'s $7,000 balance for Cash. Use the following terms in your explanation: account, balance, journal, ledger, post, and trial balance. (pp. 68–79)

Analyzing and journalizing transactions

P2-38B Dan Bell practices medicine under the business title Dan Bell, M.D., P.C. During April, the medical practice completed the following transactions:

April 1	Bell deposited $70,000 cash in the business bank account. The business issued common stock to Bell.
5	Paid monthly rent on medical equipment, $700.
9	Paid $22,000 cash to purchase land for an office site.
10	Purchased supplies on account, $1,200.
19	Borrowed $20,000 from the bank for business use. Bell signed a note payable to the bank in the name of the business.
22	Paid $1,000 on account.

continued . . .

30	Revenues earned during the month included $6,000 cash and $5,000 on account.
30	Paid employees' salaries ($2,400), office rent ($1,500), and utilities ($400). Make a single compound entry.
30	Paid cash dividends of $10,000.

Bell's business uses the following accounts: Cash; Accounts Receivable; Supplies; Land; Accounts Payable; Notes Payable; Common Stock; Dividends; Service Revenue; Salary Expense; Rent Expense; Utilities Expense.

Requirement

Journalize each transaction, as shown for April 1. Explanations are not required. (pp. 72–78)

April 1	Cash	70,000	
	Common Stock		70,000

Journalizing transactions, posting to T-accounts, and preparing a trial balance

P2-39B Laura Knipper opened a law office on January 2 of the current year. During the first month of operations, the business completed the following transactions:

January 2	Knipper deposited $36,000 cash in the business bank account Laura Knipper, Attorney, P.C., and the business issued common stock to Knipper.
3	Purchased supplies, $500, and furniture, $2,600, on account.
4	Performed legal service for a client and received cash, $1,500.
7	Paid cash to acquire land for a future office site, $22,000.
11	Prepared legal documents for a client on account, $900.
15	Paid secretary's salary, $570.
16	Paid for the furniture purchased January 3 on account.
18	Received $1,800 cash for helping a client sell real estate.
19	Defended a client in court and billed the client for $800.
29	Received cash on account, $400.
31	Paid secretary's salary, $570.
31	Paid rent expense, $700.
31	Paid cash dividends of $2,200.

Requirements

Open the following T-accounts: Cash; Accounts Receivable; Supplies; Furniture; Land; Accounts Payable; Common Stock; Dividends; Service Revenue; Salary Expense; Rent Expense.

1. Record each transaction in the journal, using the account titles given. Key each transaction by date. Explanations are not required. (pp. 72–78)

continued . . .

2. Post the transactions to T-accounts, using transaction dates as posting references in the ledger. Label the balance of each account *Bal.*, as shown in the chapter. (pp. 72–78)

3. Prepare the trial balance of Laura Knipper, Attorney, P.C., at January 31 of the current year. (p. 79)

Journalizing transactions, posting to accounts in four-column format, and preparing a trial balance

P2-40B The trial balance of Stephanie Stouse, Registered Dietician, P.C., at October 31, 2007, follows.

STEPHANIE STOUSE, REGISTERED DIETICIAN, P.C.
Trial Balance
October 31, 2007

		Balance	
Account Number	Account Title	Debit	Credit
11	Cash	$ 3,000	
12	Accounts receivable	8,000	
13	Supplies	600	
14	Equipment	15,000	
21	Accounts payable		$ 4,600
31	Common stock		22,000
32	Dividends		
41	Service revenue		
51	Salary expense		
52	Rent expense		
	Total	$26,600	$26,600

During November, Stouse or her business completed the following transactions:

Nov. 4	Collected $6,000 cash from a client on account.
7	Performed a nutritional analysis for a hospital on account, $5,700.
12	Stouse used personal funds to pay for the renovation of her private residence, $55,000.
16	Purchased office supplies on account, $800.
19	Paid cash dividends of $2,100 for personal use.
20	Paid business debt on account, $2,600.
24	Received $1,900 cash for consulting with **Kraft Foods.**
30	Paid office rent, $700.
30	Paid employee salary, $2,000.

Requirements

1. Record the November transactions on page 6 of the business's journal. Include an explanation for each entry. (pp. 72–78)

continued . . .

2. Post the transactions to four-column accounts in the ledger, using dates, account numbers, journal references, and posting references. Open the ledger accounts listed in the trial balance together with their balances at October 31. Enter *Bal.* (for October 31 balance) in the Item column, and place a check mark (✓) in the journal reference column for the October 31 balance of each account. (pp. 80–81)
3. Prepare the trial balance of Stephanie Stouse, Registered Dietician, P.C., at November 30, 2007.

Recording transactions; using four-column accounts; preparing a trial balance

P2-41B Vince Serrano started Serrano Carpet Installers, Inc., and during the first month of operations (January 2007) the business completed the following selected transactions:

a. Serrano began the business with an investment of $40,000 cash and a van (automobile) valued at $20,000. The business gave Serrano common stock worth $60,000.
b. Paid $32,000 for equipment.
c. Purchased supplies on account, $400.
d. Paid employee's salary, $1,300.
e. Received $800 for a carpet installation job.
f. Received a $500 bill for advertising expense that will be paid in the near future.
g. Paid the account payable created in transaction (c).
h. Installed carpet for a hotel on account, $6,300.
i. Received cash on account, $1,100.
j. Paid the following cash expenses and made a single compound entry:
   (1) Rent, $1,000.
   (2) Insurance, $600.
k. Paid cash dividends of $2,600.

Requirements

1. Open the following four-column accounts: Cash; Accounts Receivable; Supplies; Equipment; Automobile; Accounts Payable; Common Stock; Dividends; Service Revenue; Salary Expense; Rent Expense; Advertising Expense; Insurance Expense.
2. Record the transactions in the journal. Use the letters to identify the transactions. (pp. 72–78).
3. Post to the accounts and keep a running balance for each account. (p. 79)
4. Prepare the trial balance of Serrano Carpet Installers, Inc., at January 31, 2007. (p. 79)

Preparing the financial statements

5

P2-42B *Note:* Problem 2-42B should be used only in conjunction with Problem 2-41B.→ *Link Back to Chapter 1 (Income Statement, Statement of Retained Earnings, Balance Sheet)*. Refer to Problem 2-41B. After

continued . . .

completing the trial balance in Problem 2-41B, prepare the following financial statements for Serrano Carpet Installers, Inc.:

1. Income statement for the month ended January 31, 2007. (p. 22)
2. Statement of retained earnings for the month ended January 31, 2007. The beginning balance of retained earnings was $0. (p. 22)
3. Balance sheet at January 31, 2007. (p. 22)

Draw arrows to link the statements. If needed, use Exhibit 1-9, page 22, as a guide for preparing the financial statements.

Correcting errors in a trial balance
2 5

P2-43B The trial balance for Missing Link Exploration Company does not balance.

MISSING LINK EXPLORATION COMPANY
Trial Balance
March 31, 2007

Account Title	Balance Debit	Balance Credit
Cash	$ 6,200	
Accounts receivable	2,000	
Supplies	500	
Exploration equipment	22,300	
Computers	46,000	
Accounts payable		$ 2,700
Note payable		18,300
Common stock		50,800
Dividends	5,000	
Service revenue		4,900
Salary expense	1,300	
Rent expense	500	
Advertising expense	300	
Utilities expense	200	
Total	$84,300	$76,700

The following errors were detected:

a. The cash balance is overstated by $1,000.
b. Rent expense of $350 was erroneously posted as a credit rather than a debit.
c. A $6,900 credit to Service Revenue was not posted.
d. A $600 debit to Accounts Receivable was posted as $60.
e. The balance of Utilities Expense is understated by $60.
f. A $100 purchase of supplies on account was neither journalized nor posted.
g. Exploration equipment should be listed in the amount of $21,300.

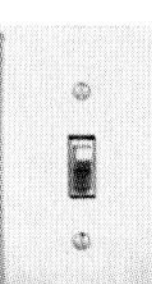

Requirement

Prepare the correct trial balance at March 31. Journal entries are not required. (pp. 79, 81)

for 24/7 practice, visit www.MyAccountingLab.com

Continuing Problem

Recording transactions and preparing a trial balance

2 3 4 5

Problem 2-44 continues with the consulting business of Carl Redmon, begun in Problem 1-42, page 46. Here you will account for Redmon Consulting's transactions as it's actually done in practice.

P2-44 Redmon Consulting, Inc., completed these transactions during the first half of December:

Dec. 2	Received $10,000 cash and issued common stock.
2	Paid monthly office rent, $500.
3	Paid cash for a Dell computer, $2,000. This equipment is expected to remain in service for five years.
4	Purchased office furniture on account, $3,600. The furniture should last for five years.
5	Purchased supplies on account, $300.
9	Performed consulting service for a client on account, $1,700.
12	Paid utility expenses, $200.
18	Performed service for a client and received cash of $800.

Requirements

1. Open T-accounts in the ledger: Cash; Accounts Receivable; Supplies; Equipment; Furniture; Accounts Payable; Common Stock; Dividends; Service Revenue; Rent Expense; Utilities Expense; and Salary Expense.
2. Journalize the transactions. Explanations are not required.
3. Post to the T-accounts. Key all items by date, and denote an account balance as *Bal.* Formal posting references are not required.
4. Prepare a trial balance at December 18. In the Continuing Problem of Chapter 3, we will add transactions for the remainder of December and prepare a trial balance at December 31.

Apply Your Knowledge

Decision Cases

Recording transactions directly in T-accounts, preparing a trial balance, and measuring net income or loss

Case 1. You have been requested by a friend named Dean McChesney to advise him on the effects that certain transactions will have on his business. Time is short, so you cannot journalize the transactions. Instead, you must analyze the transactions without a journal. McChesney will continue the business only if he can expect to earn monthly net income of $6,000. The business completed the following transactions during June:

a. McChesney deposited $10,000 cash in a business bank account to start the company. The company issued common stock to McChesney.

b. Paid $300 cash for supplies.

c. Incurred advertising expense on account, $700.

d. Paid the following cash expenses: secretary's salary, $1,400; office rent, $1,100.

e. Earned service revenue on account, $8,800.

f. Collected cash from customers on account, $1,200.

Requirements

1. Open the following T-accounts: Cash; Accounts Receivable; Supplies; Accounts Payable; Common Stock; Service Revenue; Salary Expense; Rent Expense; Advertising Expense. (pp. 72–78)
2. Post the transactions directly to the accounts without using a journal. Key each transaction by letter. Follow the format illustrated here for the first transaction.

Cash			
(a)	10,000		

Common Stock			
		(a)	10,000

3. Prepare a trial balance at June 30, 2009. List the largest expense first, the next largest second, and so on. The business name is A-Plus Travel Planners, Inc. (p. 79)
4. Compute the amount of net income or net loss for this first month of operations. Would you recommend that McChesney continue in business? (p. 22)

Using the accounting equation

Case 2. Answer the following questions. Consider each question separately. (Challenge)

1. Explain the advantages of double-entry bookkeeping over single-entry bookkeeping to a friend who is opening a used book store.
2. When you deposit money in your bank account, the bank credits your account. Is the bank misusing the word *credit* in this context? Why does the bank use the term *credit* to refer to your deposit, and not *debit?*

Ethical Issue

Better Days Ahead, a charitable organization, has a standing agreement with First National Bank. The agreement allows Better Days Ahead to overdraw its cash balance at the bank when donations are running low. In the past, Better Days Ahead managed funds wisely and rarely used this privilege. Jacob Henson has recently become the president of Better Days. To expand operations, Henson acquired office equipment and spent large amounts on fundraising. During Henson's presidency, Better Days Ahead has maintained a negative bank balance of approximately $10,000.

Requirement

What is the ethical issue in this situation? State why you approve or disapprove of Henson's management of Better Days Ahead's funds.

Financial Statement Case

Journalizing transactions for a company

This problem helps you develop skill in recording transactions by using a company's actual account titles. Refer to the **Amazon.com** financial statements in Appendix A. Assume that Amazon.com completed the following selected transactions during December 2005:

Dec. 1	Earned sales revenue and collected cash, $60,000.
9	Borrowed $200,000 by signing a note payable.
12	Purchased equipment on account, $10,000.
22	Paid half the account payable from December 12.
28	Paid electricity bill for $3,000 (this is an administrative expense)
31	Paid $100,000 of the note payable, plus interest expense of $1,000.

Requirement

Journalize these transactions, using the following account titles taken from the Amazon.com financial statements: Cash; Equipment; Accounts Payable; Note Payable; Sales Revenue; Administrative Expense; and Interest Expense. Explanations are not required.

Team Project

Contact a local business and arrange with the owner to learn what accounts the business uses.

Requirements

1. Obtain a copy of the business's chart of accounts.
2. Prepare the company's financial statements for the most recent month, quarter, or year. You may use either made-up account balances or balances supplied by the owner.

continued . . .

If the business has a large number of accounts within a category, combine related accounts and report a single amount on the financial statements. For example, the company may have several cash accounts. Combine all cash amounts and report a single Cash amount on the balance sheet.

You will probably encounter numerous accounts that you have not yet learned. Deal with these as best you can. The chart of accounts given in the inside covers of this book will be helpful.

Keep in mind that the financial statements report the balances of the accounts listed in the company's chart of accounts. Therefore, the financial statements must be consistent with the chart of accounts.

For Internet Exercises, Excel in Practice, and additional online activities, go to the Web site www.prenhall.com/horngren.

Quick Check Answers

1. *a* 2. *c* 3. *b* 4. *c* 5. *d* 6. *a* 7. *d* 8. *a* 9. *c* 10. *b*

Chapter 2: Demo Doc

Debit/Credit Transaction Analysis

Demo Doc: To make sure you understand this material, work through the following demonstration "demo doc" with detailed comments to help you see the concept within the framework of a worked-through problem.

Learning Objectives 1, 2, 3, 4

On September 1, 2008, Michael Moe incorporated Moe's Mowing, Inc., a company that provides mowing and landscaping services. During the month of September, the business incurred the following transactions:

a. To begin operations, Michael deposited $10,000 cash in the business's bank account. The business received the cash and issued common stock to Michael.

b. The business purchased equipment for $3,500 on account.

c. The business purchased office supplies for $800 cash.

d. The business provided $2,600 of services to a customer on account.

e. The business paid $500 cash toward the equipment previously purchased on account in transaction b.

f. The business received $2,000 in cash for services provided to a new customer.

g. The business paid $200 cash to repair equipment.

h. The business paid $900 cash in salary expense.

i. The business received $2,100 cash from customers on account.

j. The business paid cash dividends of $1,500.

Requirements

1. Create blank T-accounts for the following accounts: Cash, Accounts Receivable, Supplies, Equipment, Accounts Payable, Common Stock, Dividends, Service Revenue, Salary Expense, Repair Expense.

2. Journalize the transactions and show how they are recorded in T-accounts. Use the table in Exhibit 2-15 to help with the journal entries.

EXHIBIT 2-15 The Rules of Debit and Credit

	Increase	Decrease
Assets	debit	credit
Liabilities	credit	debit
Stockholders' Equity	credit	debit
Revenues	credit	debit
Expenses	debit	credit
Dividends	debit	credit

3. Total all of the T-accounts to determine their balances at the end of the month.

Demo Doc Solutions

Requirement 1

Create blank T-accounts for the following accounts: Cash, Accounts Receivable, Supplies, Equipment, Accounts Payable, Common Stock, Dividends, Service Revenue, Salary Expense, Repair Expense.

Part 1	Part 2	Part 3	Demo Doc Complete

Opening a T-account means drawing a blank account that looks like a capital "T" and putting the account title across the top. T-accounts give you a diagram of the additions and subtractions made to the accounts. For easy reference, they are usually organized into assets, liabilities, stockholders' equity, revenue, and expenses (in that order).

ASSETS = LIABILITIES + STOCKHOLDERS' EQUITY

Cash

Supplies

Accounts Payable

Common Stock

Dividends

Service Revenue

Accounts Receivable

Equipment

Salary Expense

Repair Expense

Requirement 2

Journalize the transactions and show how they are recorded in T-accounts.

Part 1	Part 2	Part 3	Demo Doc Complete

a. To begin operations, Michael deposited $10,000 cash in the business's bank account. The business received the cash and issued common stock to Michael.

First, we must determine which accounts are affected.

The business received $10,000 cash from its principal stockholder (Michael Moe). In exchange, the business issued common stock to Michael. So, the accounts involved are Cash and Common Stock.

The next step is to determine what type of accounts these are. Cash is an asset Common Stock is part of equity.

Next, we must determine if these accounts increased or decreased. From *the business's* point of view, Cash (an asset) has increased. Common Stock (equity) has also increased.

Now we must determine if these accounts should be debited or credited. According to the rules of debit and credit (see Exhibit 2-15 on p. 116), an increase in assets is a debit, while an increase in equity is a credit.

So, Cash (an asset) increases, which is a debit. Common Stock (equity) also increases, which is a credit.

The journal entry would be as follows:

a.		Cash (Asset, ↑; debit)	10,000	
		Common Stock (Equity, ↑; credit)		10,000
		Issued common stock.		

Note that the total dollar amounts of debits will equal the total dollar amounts of credits.

Remember to use the transaction letters as references. This will help as we post this entry to the T-accounts.

Each T-account has two sides for recording debits and credits. To record the transaction to the T-account, simply transfer the amount of the debit(s) to the correct account(s) as a debit (left-side) entry, and transfer the amount of the credit(s) to the correct account(s) as a credit (right-side) entry.

For this transaction, there is a debit of $10,000 to cash. This means that $10,000 is entered on the left side of the Cash T-account. There is also a credit of $10,000 to Common Stock. This means that $10,000 is entered on the right side of the Common Stock account.

Cash	
a. 10,000	

Common Stock	
	a. 10,000

b. The business purchased equipment for $3,500 on account.

The business received equipment in exchange for a promise to pay for the cost ($3,500) at a future date. So the accounts involved in the transaction are Equipment and Accounts Payable.

Equipment is an asset and Accounts Payable is a liability.

The asset Equipment has increased. The liability Accounts Payable has also increased.

Looking at Exhibit 2-15 (p. 116), an increase in assets (in this case, the increase in Equipment) is a debit, while an increase in liabilities (in this case, Accounts Payable) is a credit.

The journal entry would be as follows:

b.		Equipment (Asset, ↑; debit)	3,500	
		Accounts Payable (Liability, ↑; credit)		3,500
		Purchase of equipment on account.		

$3,500 is entered on the debit (left) side of the Equipment T-account. $3,500 is entered on the credit (right) side of the Accounts Payable account.

Equipment			
b.	3,500		

Accounts Payable			
		b.	3,500

c. The business purchased office supplies for $800 cash.

The business purchased supplies in exchange for cash ($800). So the accounts involved in the transaction are Supplies and Cash.

Supplies and Cash are both assets.

Supplies (an asset) has increased. Cash (an asset) has decreased.

Looking at Exhibit 2-15 (p. 116), an increase in assets is a debit, while a decrease in assets is a credit.

So the increase to Supplies (an asset) is a debit, while the decrease to Cash (an asset) is a credit.

The journal entry would be as follows:

c.		Supplies (Asset, ↑; debit)	800	
		Cash (Asset, ↓; credit)		800
		Purchase of supplies for cash.		

$800 is entered on the debit (left) side of the Supplies T-account. $800 is entered on the credit (right) side of the Cash account.

Cash			
a.	10,000	c.	800

Supplies			
c.	800		

Notice the $10,000 already on the debit side of the Cash account. This is from transaction **a.**

d. The business provided $2,600 of services to a customer on account.

The business received promises from customers to send cash ($2,600) next month in exchange for services rendered. So the accounts involved in the transaction are Accounts Receivable and Service Revenue.

Accounts Receivable is an asset and Service Revenue is revenue.

Accounts Receivable (an asset) has increased. Service Revenue (revenue) has also increased.

Looking at Exhibit 2-15 (p. 116), an increase in assets is a debit, while an increase in revenue is a credit.

So the increase to Accounts Receivable (an asset) is a debit, while the increase to Service Revenue (revenue) is a credit.

The journal entry is as follows:

d.		Accounts Receivable (Asset, ↑; debit)	2,600	
		Service Revenue (Revenue, ↑; credit)		2,600
		Provided services on account.		

$2,600 is entered on the debit (left) side of the Accounts Receivable T-account. $2,600 is entered on the credit (right) side of the Service Revenue account.

Accounts Receivable			
d.	2,600		

Service Revenue			
		d.	2,600

e. The business paid $500 cash toward the equipment previously purchased on account in transaction b.

The business paid *some* of the money that was owed on the purchase of equipment in transaction **b.** The accounts involved in the transaction are Accounts Payable and Cash.

Accounts Payable is a liability that has decreased. Cash is an asset that has also decreased.

Remember, the Accounts Payable account is a list of creditors to whom the business will have to make payments in the future (a liability). When the business makes these payments to the creditors, the amount of this account decreases, because the business now owes less (in this case, it reduces from $3,500—in transaction **b**—to $3,000).

Looking at Exhibit 2-15 (p. 116), a decrease in liabilities is a debit, while a decrease in assets is a credit.

So Accounts Payable (a liability) decreases, which is a debit. Cash (an asset) decreases, which is a credit.

e.		Accounts Payable (Liability, ↓; debit)	500	
		Cash (Asset, ↓; credit)		500
		Partial payment on Accounts Payable.		

$500 is entered on the debit (left) side of the Accounts Payable T-account. $500 is entered on the credit (right) side of the Cash account.

Cash			
a.	10,000		
		c.	800
		e.	500

Accounts Payable			
		b.	3,500
e.	500		

Again notice the amounts already in the T-accounts from previous transactions. We can tell which transaction caused each amount to appear by looking at the reference letter next to each number.

f. The business received $2,000 in cash for services provided to a new customer.

The business received cash ($2,000) in exchange for mowing and landscaping services rendered to clients. The accounts involved in the transaction are Cash and Service Revenue.

Cash is an asset that has increased and Service Revenue is revenue, which has also increased.

Looking at Exhibit 2-15 (p. 116), an increase in assets is a debit, while an increase in revenue is a credit.

So the increase to Cash (an asset) is a debit. The increase to Service Revenue (revenue) is a credit.

f.		Cash (Asset, ↑; debit)	2,000	
		Service Revenue (Equity, ↑; credit)		2,000
		Provided services for cash.		

$2,000 is entered on the debit (left) side of the Accounts Receivable T-account. $2,000 is entered on the credit (right) side of the Service Revenue account.

Cash

	Debit		Credit
a.	10,000		
		c.	800
		e.	500
f.	2,000		

Service Revenue

	Debit		Credit
		d.	2,600
		f.	2,000

Notice how we keep adding onto the T-accounts. The values from previous transactions are already in place.

g. The business paid $200 cash to repair equipment.

The business paid $200 cash to repair equipment. Because the benefit of the repairs has already been used, the repairs are recorded as Repair Expense. Because the repairs were paid in cash, the Cash account is also involved.

Repair Expense is an expense that has increased and Cash is an asset that has decreased.

Looking at Exhibit 2-15 (p. 116), an increase in expenses is a debit, while a decrease in an asset is a credit.

So Repair Expense (an expense) increases, which is debit. Cash (an asset) decreases, which is a credit.

g.		Repair Expense (Expense, ↑ ; debit)	200	
		Cash (Asset, ↓; credit)		200
		Payment for repairs.		

$200 is entered on the debit (left) side of the Repair Expense T-account. $200 is entered on the credit (right) side of the Cash account.

Cash

	Debit		Credit
a.	10,000		
		c.	800
		e.	500
f.	2,000		
		g.	200

Repair Expense

	Debit		Credit
g.	200		

h. The business paid $900 cash for salary expense.

The business paid employees $900 in cash. Because the benefit of the employees' work has already been used, their salaries are recorded as Salary Expense. Because the salaries were paid in cash, the Cash account is also involved.

Salary Expense is an expense that has increased and Cash is an asset that has decreased.

Looking at Exhibit 2-15 (p. 116), an increase in expenses is a debit, while a decrease in an asset is a credit.

In this case, Salary Expense (an expense) increases, which is a debit. Cash (an asset) decreases, which is a credit.

h.		Salary Expense (Expense, ↑; debit)	900	
		Cash (Asset, ↓; credit)		900
		Payment of salary using cash.		

$900 is entered on the debit (left) side of the Salary Expense T-account. $900 is entered on the credit (right) side of the Cash account.

Cash

	Debit		Credit
a.	10,000		
		c.	800
		e.	500
f.	2,000		
		g.	200
		h.	900

Salary Expense

	Debit		Credit
i.	900		

i. The business received $2,100 cash from customers on account.

The business received payments ($2,100) from customers for services previously provided in transaction **d.** The accounts involved in this transaction are Cash and Accounts Receivable.

Cash and Accounts Receivable are both assets.

The asset Cash has increased, and the asset Accounts Receivable has decreased.

Remember, Accounts Receivable is a list of customers from whom the business will receive money. When the business receives these payments from their customers, the amount of this account decreases, because the business now has less to receive in the future (in this case, it reduces from $2,600—in transaction **d**—to $500).

Looking at Exhibit 2-15 (p. 116), an increase in assets is a debit, while a decrease in assets is a credit.

So Cash (an asset) increases, which is a debit. Accounts Receivable (an asset) decreases, which is a credit.

i.		Cash (Asset, ↑; debit)	2,100	
		Accounts Receivable (Asset, ↓; credit)		2,100
		Receipt of payment from customer.		

$2,100 is entered on the debit (left) side of the Cash T-account. $2,100 is entered on the credit (right) side of the Accounts Receivable account.

Cash

	Debit		Credit
a.	10,000		
		c.	800
		e.	500
f.	2,000		
		g.	200
		h.	900
i.	2,100		

Accounts Receivable

	Debit		Credit
d.	2,600		
		i.	2,100

j. The business paid cash dividends of $1,500.

The business paid Michael dividends from the *earnings* it had *retained* on his behalf. This caused Michael's ownership interest (equity) to decrease. The accounts involved in this transaction are Dividends and Cash.

Dividends have increased and Cash is an asset that has decreased.

Looking at Exhibit 2-15 (p. 116), an increase in dividends is a debit, while a decrease in an asset is a credit.

Remember that Dividends are a negative element of stockholders' equity. Therefore, when Dividends increase, stockholders' equity decreases. So in this case, Dividends decrease equity with a debit. Cash (an asset) decreases with a credit.

j.		Dividends (Equity, ↓ ; debit)	1,500	
		Cash (Asset, ↓; credit)		1,500
		Paid dividends.		

$1,500 is entered on the debit (left) side of the Dividends T-account. $1,500 is entered on the credit (right) side of the Cash account.

Cash

	Debit		Credit
a.	10,000		
		c.	800
		e.	500
f.	2,000		
		g.	200
		h.	900
i.	2,100		
		j.	1,500

Dividends

	Debit		Credit
d.	1,500		

Now we will summarize all of the journal entries during the month:

Ref.	Accounts and Explanation	Debit	Credit
a.	Cash	10,000	
	Common Stock		10,000
	Issued common stock.		
b.	Equipment	3,500	
	Accounts Payable		3,500
	Purchase of equipment on account.		
c.	Supplies	800	
	Cash		800
	Purchase of supplies for cash.		
d.	Accounts Receivable	2,600	
	Service Revenue		2,600
	Provided services on credit.		
e.	Accounts Payable	500	
	Cash		500
	Partial payment on account.		
f.	Cash	2,000	
	Service Revenue		2,000
	Provided services for cash.		
g.	Repair Expense	200	
	Cash		200
	Payment for repairs.		
h.	Salary Expense	900	
	Cash		900
	Payment of salary.		
i.	Cash	2,100	
	Accounts Receivable		2,100
	Receipt of cash on account.		
j.	Dividends	1,500	
	Cash		1,500
	Paid dividends.		

Requirement 3

Total all of the T-accounts to determine their balances at the end of the month.

Part 1	Part 2	**Part 3**	Demo Doc Complete

To compute the balance in a T-account (total the T-account), add up the numbers on the debit/left side of the account and (separately) the credit/right side of the account. The difference between the total debits and total credits is the account's balance, which is placed on the side of the larger number (that is, the side with a balance). This gives the balance in the T-account (the net total of both sides combined).

For example, for the Cash account, the numbers on the left side total $10,000 + $2,000 + $2,100 = $14,100. The credit/right side = $800 + $500 + $200 + $900 + $1,500 = $3,900. The difference is $14,100 − $3,900 = $10,200. We put the $10,200 on the debit side because that was the side of the bigger number of $14,100. This is called a debit balance.

An easy way to think of totaling T-accounts is:

Beginning balance in T-account
+ Increases to T-account
– Decreases to T-account
T-account balance (total)

T-accounts after posting all transactions and totaling each account:

ASSETS = LIABILITIES + STOCKHOLDERS' EQUITY

Cash

Debit		Credit	
a.	10,000		
		c.	800
		e.	500
f.	2,000		
		g.	200
		h.	900
i.	2,100		
		j.	1,500
Bal.	10,200		

Supplies

Debit		Credit	
c.	800		
Bal.	800		

Accounts Payable

Debit		Credit	
		b.	3,500
e.	500		
		Bal.	3,000

Common Stock

Debit		Credit	
		a.	10,000
		Bal.	10,000

Dividends

Debit		Credit	
f.	1,500		
Bal.	1,500		

Service Revenue

Debit		Credit	
		d.	2,600
		f.	2,000
		Bal.	4,600

Accounts Receivable

Debit		Credit	
d.	2,600		
		i.	2,100
Bal.	500		

Equipment

Debit		Credit	
b.	3,500		
Bal.	3,500		

Salary Expense

Debit		Credit	
h.	900		
Bal.	900		

Repair Expense

Debit		Credit	
g.	200		
Bal.	200		

Part 1 | Part 2 | Part 3 | **Demo Doc Complete**

3 The Adjusting Process

Learning Objectives

1. Distinguish accrual accounting from cash-basis accounting
2. Apply the revenue and matching principles
3. Make adjusting entries
4. Prepare an adjusted trial balance
5. Prepare the financial statements from the adjusted trial balance

Chapter 1 introduced you to the accounting equation and the financial statements. Chapter 2 brought T-accounts, debits, credits, and the trial balance. You're now ready for the next step in the accounting cycle.

Sherman Lawn Service, Inc. and DeFilippo Catering, Inc. have well-oiled accounting systems. At the end of each period Haig Sherman and Julie DeFilippo need to measure their:

- net income
- financial position

Chapter 3 continues the accounting cycle by showing how to update the accounts at the end of the period. The process is called *adjusting the books,* and it requires special journal entries called *adjusting entries.*

Study this material carefully. It applies to small businesses like DeFilippo Catering and Cookie Lapp Travel Design and to giant companies such as eBay and PepsiCo. It also applies to the business you may operate some day.

Accounting Concepts and Principles

Accountants have concepts and principles to guide their work. Chief among these are:

- Accrual accounting versus cash-basis accounting
- The accounting period
- The revenue principle
- The matching principle

In this chapter, we apply these principles to Cookie Lapp Travel Design for the month of April. Coca-Cola, Toyota, and all other companies follow the same principles.

Accrual Accounting Versus Cash-Basis Accounting

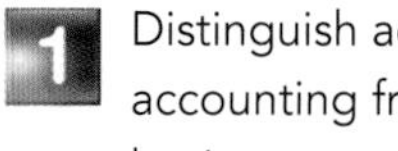
Distinguish accrual accounting from cash-basis accounting

There are two ways to do accounting:

- **Accrual accounting** records the effect of each transaction as it occurs. Most businesses use the accrual basis as covered in this book.
- **Cash-basis accounting** records only cash receipts and cash payments. It ignores receivables, payables, and depreciation. Only very small businesses use the cash basis of accounting.

Suppose Cookie Lapp Travel purchased $2,000 of office supplies on account. On the accrual basis, Lapp records this transaction as follows:

	Account	Debit	Credit
	Office Supplies	2,000	
	Accounts Payable		2,000
	Purchased supplies on account.		

In contrast, cash-basis accounting ignores this transaction because the business paid no cash. The cash basis records only cash receipts and cash payments. **In the cash basis,**

- Cash receipts are treated as revenues.
- Cash payments are treated as expenses.

Under the cash basis, Cookie Lapp Travel would record each cash payment as an expense. This is faulty accounting because Lapp acquired supplies, which are assets.

Now let's see how differently the accrual basis and the cash basis account for a revenue. Suppose Cookie Lapp Travel performed service and earned revenue but collected no cash. Under the accrual basis, Lapp records $10,000 of revenue on account as follows:

	Accounts Receivable	10,000	
	Service Revenue		10,000
	Earned revenue on account.		

Under the cash basis, the business would record no revenue because there is no cash receipt. Instead, Lapp would wait until she receives the cash. Then she would record the cash receipt as revenue. As a result, cash-basis accounting never reports accounts receivable from customers. In this case, cash-basis accounting shows the revenue in the wrong accounting period. Revenue should be recorded when it is earned, and that is how the accrual basis operates.

Exhibit 3-1 illustrates the difference between the accrual basis and the cash basis for a florist. Keep in mind that the accrual basis is the correct way to do accounting.

EXHIBIT 3-1 **Accrual Accounting Versus Cash-Basis Accounting**

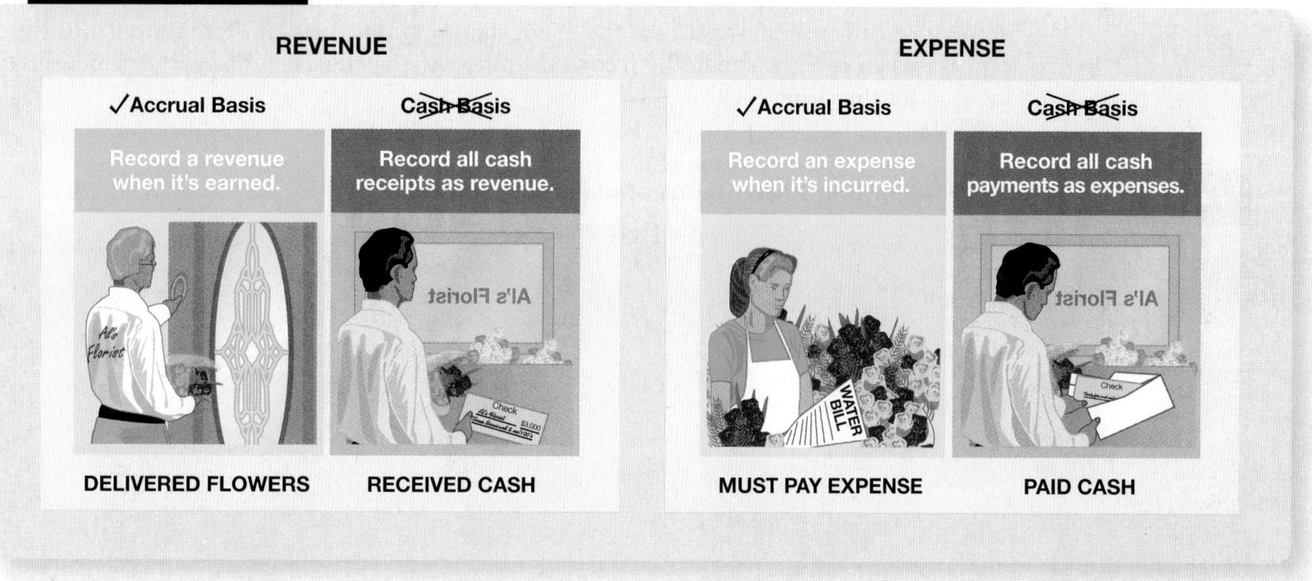

The Accounting Period

Cookie Lapp Travel Design will know for certain how well it has operated only after Lapp sells the assets, pays the liabilities, and gives any leftover cash to the owners. This process of going out of business is called *liquidation*. It is not practical to measure income this way because businesses need periodic reports on their affairs. Accountants slice time into small segments and prepare financial statements for specific periods.

The basic accounting period is one year, and all businesses prepare annual financial statements. For most companies, the annual accounting period runs the calendar year from January 1 through December 31. Other companies use a *fiscal year*, which ends on a date other than December 31. The year-end date is usually the low point in business activity for the year. Retailers are a notable example. For instance, Wal-Mart, JCPenney, and most other retailers use a fiscal year that ends on January 31 because their low point comes about a month after Christmas.

Companies also prepare financial statements for *interim* periods, such as monthly, quarterly, and semiannually. Most of our discussions are based on an annual accounting period, but everything can be applied to interim periods as well.

The Revenue Principle

2 Apply the revenue and matching principles

The **revenue principle** tells accountants:

- *When* to record revenue—that is, when to make a journal entry for a revenue
- The *amount* of revenue to record.

"Recording" something in accounting means to make an entry in the journal. That's where the process starts.

When to Record Revenue

The revenue principle says to record revenue when it has been earned—but not before. This occurs when the business has delivered a good or service to the customer. The company has done everything required by the sale agreement.

Exhibit 3-2 shows two situations that provide guidance on when to record revenue for Cookie Lapp Travel Design. The first situation illustrates when *not* to record revenue—because the client merely states his plan. Situation 2 illustrates when revenue should be recorded—after the travel agency has performed a service for the client.

EXHIBIT 3-2 **Recording Revenue: The Revenue Principle**

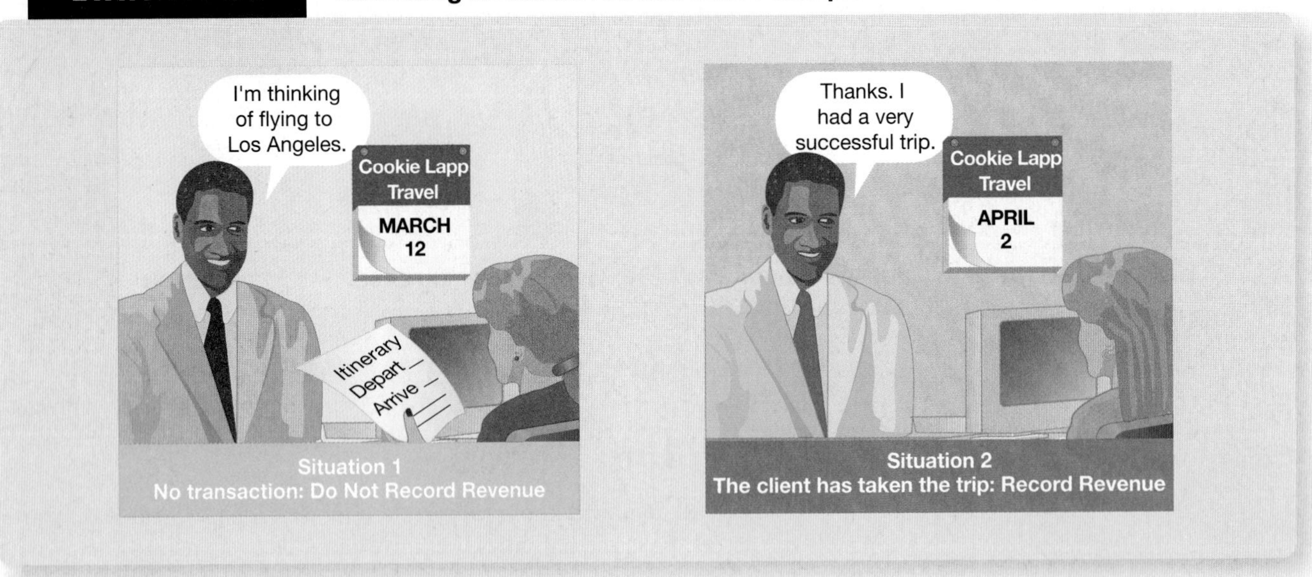

The Amount of Revenue to Record

Record revenue for the cash value of the item transferred to the customer. Suppose that to obtain a new client, Cookie Lapp performs travel service for the cut-rate price of \$100. Ordinarily, Lapp would have charged \$200 for this service. How much revenue should Lapp record? The answer is \$100 because that was the value of the transaction. Lapp will not receive \$200, so that is not the amount of revenue. She will receive only \$100 cash, so she records that amount of revenue.

The Matching Principle

The **matching principle** guides accounting for expenses. Recall that expenses—such as salaries, rent, utilities, and advertising—are assets used up and liabilities created in order to earn revenue. The matching principle directs accountants to:

1. Measure all the expenses incurred during the period.
2. Match the expenses against the revenues of the period.

To match expenses against revenues means to subtract expenses from revenues. The goal is to compute net income or net loss. Exhibit 3-3 illustrates the matching principle.

EXHIBIT 3-3 **Recording Expenses: The Matching Principle**

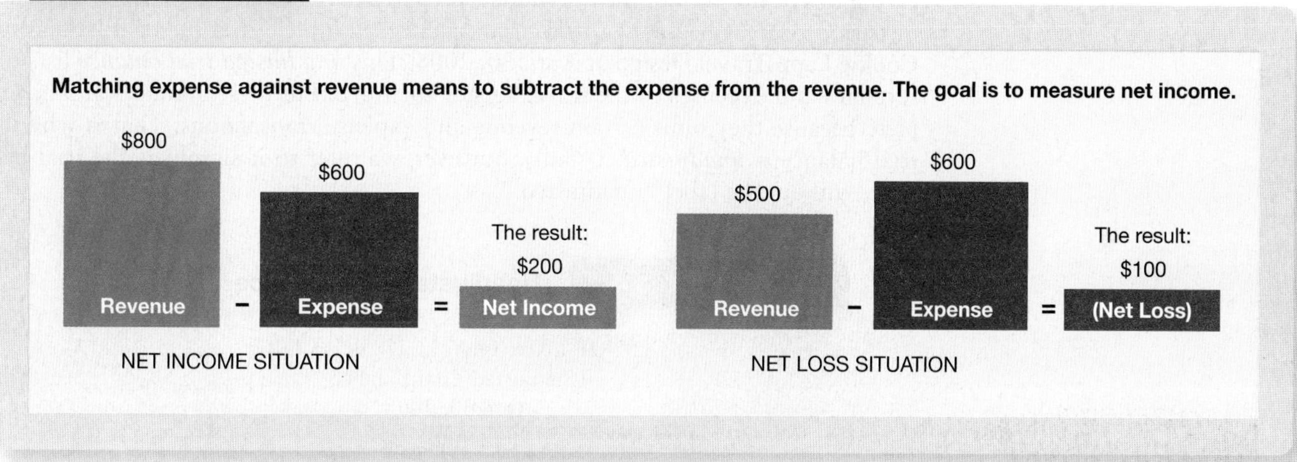

There is a natural link between some expenses and revenues. For example, Cookie Lapp Travel pays a commission to employees who sell the travel agency's services. *Cost of goods sold* is another example. If Toyota sells no automobiles, Toyota has no cost of goods sold.

Other expenses are not so easy to link to sales. For example, Cookie Lapp Travel Design's monthly rent expense occurs regardless of the revenues earned that month. The matching principle says to identify those expenses with a particular period, such as a month or a year. Lapp will record rent expense each month based on the lease agreement. Lapp also pays monthly salaries to her employee.

How does Cookie Lapp Travel Design bring its accounts up-to-date for the financial statements? To address this question, accountants use the time-period concept.

The Time-Period Concept

Owners need periodic readings on their business. The **time-period concept** ensures that information is reported often. To measure income, companies update their accounts at the end of each period. Cookie Lapp Travel provides an example of an expense accrual. At April 30, Lapp recorded salary expense of $900 that she owed her employee at the end of the month. Lapp's accrual entry was

Date	Accounts	Debit	Credit
Apr. 30	Salary Expense	900	
	Salary Payable		900
	Accrued salary expense.		

This entry assigns the salary expense to April because that was the month when the employee worked for the company. Without this entry, April's expenses would be understated, and net income would be overstated. The accrual entry also records the liability owed at April 30. Without this entry, total liabilities would be understated. The remainder of the chapter shows how to adjust the accounts and bring the books up-to-date.

Adjusting the Accounts

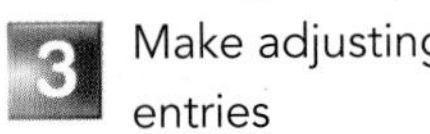

At the end of the period, the accountant prepares the financial statements. The end-of-period process begins with the trial balance. Exhibit 3-4 is the trial balance of Cookie Lapp Travel Design at April 30, 2008. This *unadjusted trial balance* lists the revenues and expenses of the travel agency for April. But these amounts are incomplete because they omit certain revenue and expense transactions. That is why the trial balance is *unadjusted*. Usually, however, we refer to it simply as the trial balance, without the label "unadjusted."

EXHIBIT 3-4 Unadjusted Trial Balance

COOKIE LAPP TRAVEL DESIGN, INC.
Unadjusted Trial Balance
April 30, 2008

Account	Debit	Credit
Cash	$24,800	
Accounts receivable	2,200	
Supplies	700	
Prepaid rent	3,000	
Furniture	18,000	
Accounts payable		$13,000
Unearned service revenue		600
Common stock		30,000
Retained earnings		2,600
Dividends	3,200	
Service revenue		7,000
Salary expense	900	
Utilities expense	400	
Total	$53,200	$53,200

Accrual accounting requires adjusting entries at the end of the period. We must have correct balances for the financial statements. To see why, consider the Supplies account in Exhibit 3-4.

Cookie Lapp Travel uses supplies during the month. This reduces the supplies on hand and creates an expense. It is a waste of time to record supplies expense every time it's used. But by the end of the month, the $700 of Supplies on the unadjusted trial balance (Exhibit 3-4) is out of date. So how does Lapp account for supplies expense? She must adjust the accounts at April 30.

Adjusting entries assign revenues to the period when they are earned and expenses to the period when they are incurred. Adjusting entries also update the asset and liability accounts. Adjustments are needed to properly measure two things:

1. Net income on the income statement and
2. Assets and liabilities on the balance sheet.

This end-of-period process is called *making the adjustments* or *adjusting the books.*

Prepaids and Accruals

The two basic categories of adjustments are *prepaids* and *accruals*. In a *prepaid* adjustment, the cash payment occurs before an expense is recorded. *Accrual* adjustments are the opposite. An accrual records an expense before the cash payment.

Adjusting entries fall into five categories:

1. Prepaid expenses
2. Depreciation
3. Accrued expenses
4. Accrued revenues
5. Unearned revenues

The core of this chapter shows how to account for these five types of adjusting entries.

Prepaid Expenses

Prepaid expenses are advance payments of expenses. Prepaid rent and prepaid insurance are examples. For example, McDonald's, the restaurant chain, makes prepayments for rent, insurance, and supplies. Keep in mind that prepaid expenses are assets, not expenses.

Prepaid Rent

Landlords require tenants to pay rent in advance. This prepayment creates an asset for the renter. Suppose Cookie Lapp Travel Design prepays three months' office rent on April 1, 2008. If the lease specifies a monthly rental of $1,000, the entry to record the payment is:

Date	Accounts and Explanation	Debit	Credit
Apr. 1	Prepaid Rent ($1,000 × 3)	3,000	
	Cash		3,000
	Paid rent in advance.		

After posting, Prepaid Rent has a $3,000 debit balance.

ASSETS

Prepaid Rent		
Apr. 1	3,000	

The trial balance at April 30, 2008, lists Prepaid Rent with a debit balance of $3,000 (Exhibit 3-4). Throughout April, Prepaid Rent maintains this balance. But $3,000 is *not* the amount of Prepaid Rent for the balance sheet at April 30. Why?

At April 30, Prepaid Rent should be decreased for the amount that has been used up. The used-up portion is one-third of the prepayment. Recall that an asset that has expired is an *expense*. The adjusting entry transfers $1,000 ($3,000 × 1/3) of the Prepaid Rent to Rent Expense. The adjusting entry is:

Apr. 30	Rent Expense ($3,000 × 1/3)	1,000	
	Prepaid Rent		1,000
	To record rent expense.		

After posting, Prepaid Rent and Rent Expense show correct ending balances:

ASSETS

Prepaid Rent

Apr. 1	3,000	Apr. 30	1,000
Bal.	2,000		

EXPENSES

Rent Expense

Apr. 30	1,000		
Bal.	1,000		

Correct asset amount: $2,000 → Total accounted for: $3,000 ← Correct expense amount: $1,000

The same analysis applies to the prepayment of three months of insurance. The only difference is in the account titles, which would be Prepaid Insurance instead of Prepaid Rent and Insurance Expense instead of Rent Expense. In a computerized system, the adjusting entry is programmed to recur automatically each accounting period.

The chapter Appendix 3A shows an alternative treatment of prepaid expenses. The end result on the financial statements is the same as illustrated here.

Supplies

Supplies are accounted for as prepaid expenses. On April 2, Cookie Lapp paid $700 for office supplies:

Apr. 2	Supplies	700	
	Cash		700
	Paid cash for supplies.		

The April 30 trial balance, therefore, lists Supplies with a $700 debit balance, as shown in Exhibit 3-4. But Lapp's April 30 balance sheet should *not* report supplies of $700. Why?

During April, the travel agency used supplies to conduct business. The cost of the supplies used becomes *supplies expense.* To measure supplies expense, Lapp counts the supplies on hand at the end of April. This is the amount of the asset still available to the business. Assume that supplies costing $600 remain at April 30. Supplies available minus supplies on hand measures supplies expense for the month ($100).

Asset available	–	Asset on hand at the end of the period	=	Expense (asset used during the period)
$700	–	$600	=	$100

The April 30 adjusting entry updates Supplies and records Supplies Expense for April as follows:

Apr. 30	Supplies Expense ($700 – $600)	100	
	Supplies		100
	To record supplies expense.		

After posting, Supplies and Supplies Expense hold correct ending balances:

ASSETS

Supplies

Apr. 2	700	Apr. 30	100
Bal.	600		

EXPENSES

Supplies Expense

Apr. 30	100	
Bal.	100	

Correct asset amount: $600 → Total accounted for: $700 ← Correct expense amount: $100

The Supplies account then enters May with a $600 balance, and the adjustment process is repeated each month.

Depreciation

Accrual accounting is clearly illustrated by depreciation. **Plant assets** are long-lived tangible assets used in the operation of a business. Examples include land, buildings, equipment, and furniture. As one accountant said, "All assets but land are on a march to the junkyard" because they decline in usefulness. This decline in usefulness of a plant asset is an expense, and accountants systematically spread its cost over its useful life. The allocation of a plant asset's cost to expense is called **depreciation.** Land is the exception. We record no depreciation for land.

Similarity to Prepaid Expenses

The concept of accounting for plant assets is the same as for a prepaid expense. The major difference is the length of time it takes for the asset to wear out. Prepaid expenses expire within a year, while plant assets remain useful for several years. On April 3 Cookie Lapp Travel purchased furniture for $18,000 and made this journal entry:

Apr. 3	Furniture	18,000	
	Cash		18,000
	Purchased furniture.		

After posting, the Furniture account has an $18,000 balance:

ASSETS

Furniture

Apr. 3	18,000	

Cookie Lapp believes the furniture will remain useful for 5 years and then be worthless. One way to compute depreciation is to divide the cost of the asset

($18,000) by its expected useful life (5 years). This procedure—called the straight-line method—computes depreciation of $3,600 per year ($18,000/5 years). Depreciation for each month is $300 ($3,600/12 months = $300 per month). Depreciation expense for April is recorded by this entry:

Apr. 30	Depreciation Expense—Furniture	300	
	Accumulated Depreciation—Furniture		300
	To record depreciation on furniture.		

The Accumulated Depreciation Account

Accumulated Depreciation is credited—not Furniture—because it's helpful to keep the original cost in the Furniture account. Managers can then refer to the Furniture account to see how much the asset cost. This information may help decide how much to pay for new furniture. The Accumulated Depreciation account holds the sum of all the depreciation recorded for the asset and the total increases over time.

Accumulated Depreciation is a contra asset, which means an asset account with a normal credit balance. A **contra account** has two main characteristics:

- A contra account follows a companion account.
- A contra account's normal balance (debit or credit) is opposite that of the companion.

Accumulated Depreciation is the contra account that follows Furniture. Furniture has a debit balance, so Accumulated Depreciation, a contra asset, has a credit balance. *All contra assets have credit balances.*

A business carries an accumulated depreciation account for each depreciable asset. If Cookie Lapp Travel has both a building and furniture, it will carry two accounts: Accumulated Depreciation—Building and Accumulated Depreciation—Furniture.

After posting the depreciation, Lapp's accounts appear as follows:

ASSETS

NORMAL ASSET

Furniture

Apr. 3	18,000	
Bal.	18,000	

CONTRA ASSET

Accumulated Depreciation—Furniture

	Apr. 30	300
	Bal.	300

EXPENSES

Depreciation Expense—Furniture

Apr. 30	300	
Bal.	300	

Book Value

The balance sheet reports both Furniture and Accumulated Depreciation. Because it's a contra account, Accumulated Depreciation is subtracted from Furniture. The resulting net amount (cost minus accumulated depreciation) of a plant asset is called its **book value**, as follows for Furniture:

Book value of plant assets:	
Furniture	$18,000
Less: Accumulated depreciation	(300)
Book value of the furniture	$17,700

Suppose the travel agency also owns a building that cost $48,000, with annual depreciation of $2,400. The amount of depreciation for one month would be $200 ($2,400/12), and the following entry records depreciation for April:

Apr. 30	Depreciation Expense—Building	200	
	Accumulated Depreciation—Building		200
	To record depreciation on building.		

The April 30 balance sheet would report plant assets as shown in Exhibit 3-5.

EXHIBIT 3-5 **Plant Assets on the Balance Sheet of Cookie Lapp Travel (April 30)**

Plant Assets		
Furniture	$18,000	
Less: Accumulated depreciation	(300)	$17,700
Building	$48,000	
Less: Accumulated depreciation	(200)	47,800
Plant assets, net		$65,500

Exhibit 3-6 shows how Fossil, the fashion watch company, reported Property, Plant, and Equipment as adapted from its annual report. The only new items are the last two. Leasehold improvements show Fossil's cost of changes made to the assets that Fossil leases. An example would be the cost to paint the Fossil logo on delivery trucks. The last item reports the cost of Fossil's plant assets that are under construction.

EXHIBIT 3-6 **Fossil Reports Property, Plant, and Equipment (Adapted)**

	(in millions)
Land	$ 8
Buildings	16
Furniture and fixtures	33
Computer equipment	19
Leasehold improvements	20
Construction in progress	27
	123
Less: Accumulated depreciation	(33)
Property, plant, and equipment, net	$ 90

Fossil's total cost of plant assets was $123 million, and Fossil has depreciated $33 million. The book value of the plant assets is, therefore, $90 million.

Now let's return to Cookie Lapp Travel Design.

Accrued Expenses

Businesses often have expenses before paying them. Consider an employee's salary. Lapp's salary expense grows as the employee works, so the expense is said to *accrue.* Another accrued expense is interest expense on a note payable. Interest accrues as the clock ticks. The term **accrued expense** refers to an expense the business has incurred but not yet paid. An accrued expense always creates a liability.

Companies don't make weekly journal entries to accrue expenses. That would waste time and money. Instead they wait until the end of the period. They make an adjusting entry to bring each expense (and the related liability) up-to-date for the financial statements.

Remember that prepaids and accruals are opposites.

- A *prepaid expense* is paid first and expensed later.
- An *accrued expense* is expensed first and paid later.

Now let's see how to account for accrued expenses.

Accruing Salary Expense

Suppose Cookie Lapp pays her employee a monthly salary of $1,800, half on the 15th and half on the last day of the month. Here is a calendar for April with the two paydays circled:

April						
S	M	T	W	T	F	S
					1	2
3	4	5	6	7	8	9
10	11	12	13	14	(15)	16
17	18	19	20	21	22	23
24	25	26	27	28	29	(30)

To illustrate a salary accrual, assume that if either payday falls on a weekend, Lapp pays the following Monday. During April, Lapp paid the first half-month salary on Friday, April 15, and made this entry:

Apr. 15	Salary Expense	900	
	Cash		900
	To pay salary.		

After posting, Salary Expense shows this balance:

EXPENSES

Salary Expense			
Apr. 15	900		

The trial balance at April 30 (Exhibit 3-4) includes Salary Expense, with a debit balance of $900. This is Lapp's salary expense for the first half of April. The second payment of $900 will occur in May, so Lapp must accrue salary expense for the second half of April. At April 30, Lapp makes this adjusting entry:

Apr. 30	Salary Expense	900	
	Salary Payable		900
	To accrue salary expense.		

After posting, Salary Expense and Salary Payable are up-to-date:

EXPENSES — Salary Expense

Apr. 15	900	
Apr. 30	900	
Bal.	1,800	

LIABILITIES — Salary Payable

	Apr. 30	900
	Bal.	900

Salary Expense holds a full month's salary, and Salary Payable shows the liability owed at April 30.

Accruing Interest Expense

Borrowing money creates a liability for a Note Payable. The entry to borrow $20,000 after signing a one-year note payable on December 1, 2008, is:

2008			
Dec. 1	Cash	20,000	
	Note Payable		20,000
	Borrowed money.		

Your interest on this note is payable one year later, on December 1, 2009. At December 31, 2008, the company must make an adjusting entry to record the interest expense that has accrued for the month of December. Assume one month's interest expense on this note is $100. Your December 31 adjusting entry to accrue interest expense is:

2008			
Dec. 31	Interest Expense	100	
	Interest Payable		100
	To accrue interest expense.		

After posting, Interest Expense and Interest Payable have these balances:

EXPENSES — Interest Expense

Dec. 31	100	
Bal.	100	

LIABILITIES — Interest Payable

	Dec. 31	100
	Bal.	100

Accrued Revenues

As we have just seen, expenses can occur before the cash payment, and that creates an accrued expense. Likewise, businesses also earn revenue before they receive the cash. This calls for an **accrued revenue**, which is a revenue that has been earned but not yet collected in cash.

Assume that Cookie Lapp Travel is hired on April 15 to perform travel services for San Jacinto College. Under this agreement, Lapp will earn $800 monthly. During April, Lapp will earn half a month's fee, $400, for work April 16 through April 30. On April 30, Lapp makes the following adjusting entry to accrue the revenue earned during April 16 through 30:

Apr. 30	Accounts Receivable ($800 × 1/2)	400	
	Service Revenue		400
	To accrue service revenue.		

The unadjusted trial balance in Exhibit 3-4 shows that Accounts Receivable has an unadjusted balance of $2,200. Service Revenue's unadjusted balance is $7,000. The adjustment updates both accounts.

ASSETS

Accounts Receivable

	Debit	Credit
	2,200	
Apr. 30	400	
Bal.	2,600	

REVENUES

Service Revenue

Debit		Credit
		7,000
	Apr. 30	400
	Bal.	7,400

Without the adjustment, Lapp's financial statements would understate both Accounts Receivable and Service Revenue. All accrued revenues are accounted for similarly: Debit a receivable and credit a revenue.

Now we turn to the final category of adjusting entries.

Unearned Revenues

Some businesses collect cash from customers in advance. Receiving cash before earning it creates a liability called **unearned revenue**; the company owes a product or a service to the customer. Only after completing the job will the business *earn* the revenue.

Suppose a law firm engages Cookie Lapp Travel to provide travel services, agreeing to pay her $600 monthly, beginning immediately. Lapp collects the first amount on April 20. Lapp records the cash receipt and a liability as follows:

Apr. 20	Cash	600	
	Unearned Service Revenue		600
	Collected revenue in advance.		

Now the liability account Unearned Service Revenue shows that Lapp owes $600.

LIABILITIES

Unearned Service Revenue

Debit		Credit
	Apr. 20	600

Unearned Service Revenue is a liability because it represents Lapp's obligation to perform service for a client.

The April 30 trial balance (Exhibit 3-4) lists Unearned Service Revenue with a $600 credit balance. During the last 10 days of the month—April 21 through April 30—Lapp will *earn* one-third (10 days divided by April's 30 days) of the $600, or $200. Therefore, Lapp makes the following adjustment to record earning $200 of revenue:

Apr. 30	Unearned Service Revenue ($600 × 1/3)	200	
	Service Revenue		200
	To record service revenue that was collected in advance.		

This adjusting entry shifts $200 from liability to revenue. Service Revenue increases by $200, and Unearned Service Revenue decreases by $200. Now both accounts are up-to-date at April 30:

LIABILITIES

Unearned Service Revenue

Apr. 30	200	Apr. 20	600
		Bal.	400

REVENUES

Service Revenue

			7,000
		Apr. 30	400
		Apr. 30	200
		Bal.	7,600

Correct liability amount: $400 → Total accounted for: $600 ← Correct revenue amount: $200

Remember this key point:

An unearned revenue is a liability, not a revenue.

An unearned revenue to one company is a prepaid expense to the company that paid in advance. Consider the law firm in the preceding example. The law firm had prepaid travel expense—an asset. Cookie Lapp Travel had unearned service revenue—a liability.

Exhibit 3-7 summarizes the timing of prepaid and accrual adjustments. Study the exhibit from left to right, and then move down. The chapter Appendix 3A shows an alternative treatment for unearned revenues.

Summary of the Adjusting Process

The adjusting process has two purposes:

1. Measure net income or net loss on the *income statement*. Every adjustment affects a *revenue* or an *expense*.
2. Update the *balance sheet*. Every adjustment affects an *asset* or a *liability*.

Exhibit 3-8 summarizes the effects of the various adjusting entries.

Exhibit 3-9 summarizes the adjusting entries of Cookie Lapp Travel Design at April 30. The adjustments are keyed by letter.

- Panel A gives the data for each adjustment.
- Panel B shows the adjusting entries.
- Panel C gives the accounts after posting.

EXHIBIT 3-7 Prepaid and Accrual Adjustments

PREPAIDS—Cash transaction comes *first*.

Prepaid Expenses	*Pay expense in advance and record an asset.*			*Record the expense later.*		
	Prepaid Rent	XXX		Rent Expense	XXX	
	Cash		XXX	Prepaid Rent		XXX
Unearned Revenues	*Receive cash in advance and record a liability.*			*Record the revenue later.*		
	Cash	XXX		Unearned Service Revenue	XXX	
	Unearned Service Revenue		XXX	Service Revenue		XXX

ACCRUALS—Cash transaction comes *later*.

Accrued Expenses	*Accrue an expense first.*			*Pay the liability later.*		
	Salary Expense	XXX		Salary Payable	XXX	
	Salary Payable		XXX	Cash		XXX
Accrued Revenues	*Accrue a revenue first.*			*Collect cash later.*		
	Interest Receivable	XXX		Cash	XXX	
	Interest Revenue		XXX	Interest Receivable		XXX

Source: The authors thank Darrel Davis and Alfonso Oddo for suggesting this exhibit.

EXHIBIT 3-8 Summary of Adjusting Entries

Category of Adjusting Entry	Debit	Credit
Prepaid expense	Expense	Asset
Depreciation	Expense	Contra asset
Accrued expense	Expense	Liability
Accrued revenue	Asset	Revenue
Unearned revenue	Liability	Revenue

Source: Adapted from material provided by Beverly Terry.

EXHIBIT 3-9 Journalizing and Posting the Adjusting Entries of Cookie Lapp Travel Design, Inc.

PANEL A—Information for Adjustments at April 30, 2008

a. Prepaid rent expired, $1,000.
b. Supplies expense, $100.
c. Depreciation on furniture, $300.
d. Accrued salary expense, $900.
e. Accrued service revenue, $400.
f. Service revenue that was collected in advance and now has been earned, $200.

PANEL B—Adjusting Entries

a.		Rent Expense	1,000	
		Prepaid Rent		1,000
		To record rent expense.		
b.		Supplies Expense	100	
		Supplies		100
		To record supplies used.		
c.		Depreciation Expense—Furniture	300	
		Accumulated Depreciation—Furniture		300
		To record depreciation on furniture.		
d.		Salary Expense	900	
		Salary Payable		900
		To accrue salary expense.		
e.		Accounts Receivable	400	
		Service Revenue		400
		To accrue service revenue.		
f.		Unearned Service Revenue	200	
		Service Revenue		200
		To record revenue that was collected in advance.		

EXHIBIT 3-9 continued

PANEL C—Ledger Accounts

Assets

Cash

	Debit		Credit
Bal.	24,800		

Accounts Receivable

	Debit		Credit
	2,200		
(e)	400		
Bal.	2,600		

Supplies

	Debit		Credit
	700	(b)	100
Bal.	600		

Prepaid Rent

	Debit		Credit
	3,000	(a)	1,000
Bal.	2,000		

Furniture

	Debit		Credit
Bal.	18,000		

Accumulated Depreciation—Furniture

	Debit		Credit
		(c)	300
		Bal.	300

Liabilities

Accounts Payable

	Debit		Credit
		Bal.	13,000

Salary Payable

	Debit		Credit
		(d)	900
		Bal.	900

Unearned Service Revenue

	Debit		Credit
(f)	200		600
		Bal.	400

Stockholders' Equity

Common Stock

	Debit		Credit
		Bal.	30,000

Retained Earnings

	Debit		Credit
		Bal.	2,600

Dividends

	Debit		Credit
(a)	3,200		

Revenue

Service Revenue

	Debit		Credit
			7,000
		(e)	400
		(f)	200
		Bal.	7,600

Expenses

Rent Expense

	Debit		Credit
(a)	1,000		
Bal.	1,000		

Salary Expense

	Debit		Credit
	900		
(d)	900		
Bal.	1,800		

Supplies Expense

	Debit		Credit
(b)	100		
Bal.	100		

Depreciation Expense—Furniture

	Debit		Credit
(c)	300		
Bal.	300		

Utilities Expense

	Debit		Credit
Bal.	400		

The Adjusted Trial Balance

This chapter began with the *unadjusted* trial balance (Exhibit 3-4). After the adjustments, the accounts appear as shown in Exhibit 3-9, Panel C. A useful step in preparing the financial statements is to list the accounts, along with their adjusted balances, on an **adjusted trial balance**. Exhibit 3-10 shows how to prepare the adjusted trial balance.

4 Prepare an adjusted trial balance

Exhibit 3-10 is a *work sheet*. We will continue this work sheet into Chapter 4. For now, simply note how clear this format is. The Account Titles and the Trial Balance are copied directly from the trial balance. The two Adjustments columns show the adjustment Debits and Credits. Each debit is identified by a letter keyed to Exhibit 3-9.

EXHIBIT 3-10 **Preparation of Adjusted Trial Balance**

COOKIE LAPP TRAVEL DESIGN, INC.
Preparation of Adjusted Trial Balance
April 30, 2008

	Trial Balance		Adjustments		Adjusted Trial Balance		
Account Title	Debit	Credit	Debit	Credit	Debit	Credit	
Cash	24,800				24,800		Balance Sheet (Exhibit 3-13)
Accounts receivable	2,200		(e) 400		2,600		Balance Sheet (Exhibit 3-13)
Supplies	700			(b) 100	600		Balance Sheet (Exhibit 3-13)
Prepaid rent	3,000			(a) 1,000	2,000		Balance Sheet (Exhibit 3-13)
Furniture	18,000				18,000		Balance Sheet (Exhibit 3-13)
Accumulated depreciation				(c) 300		300	Balance Sheet (Exhibit 3-13)
Accounts payable		13,000				13,000	Balance Sheet (Exhibit 3-13)
Salary payable				(d) 900		900	Balance Sheet (Exhibit 3-13)
Unearned service revenue		600	(f) 200			400	Balance Sheet (Exhibit 3-13)
Common stock		30,000				30,000	Statement of Retained Earnings (Exhibit 3-12)
Retained earnings		2,600				2,600	Statement of Retained Earnings (Exhibit 3-12)
Dividends	3,200				3,200		Statement of Retained Earnings (Exhibit 3-12)
Service revenue		7,000		(e) 400			Income Statement (Exhibit 3-11)
				(f) 200		7,600	Income Statement (Exhibit 3-11)
Rent expense			(a) 1,000		1,000		Income Statement (Exhibit 3-11)
Salary expense	900		(d) 900		1,800		Income Statement (Exhibit 3-11)
Supplies expense			(b) 100		100		Income Statement (Exhibit 3-11)
Depreciation expense			(c) 300		300		Income Statement (Exhibit 3-11)
Utilities expense	400				400		Income Statement (Exhibit 3-11)
Total	53,200	53,200	2,900	2,900	54,800	54,800	

The Adjusted Trial Balance columns give the adjusted account balances. Each amount in these columns is computed by combining the trial balance amounts plus or minus the adjustments. For example, Accounts Receivable starts with a debit balance of $2,200. Adding the $400 debit from adjustment (e) gives Accounts Receivable an adjusted balance of $2,600. Supplies begins with a debit balance of $700. After the $100 credit adjustment, Supplies has a $600 balance. More than one entry may affect a single account, such as for Service Revenue.

The Financial Statements

The April financial statements of Cookie Lapp Travel Design can be prepared from the adjusted trial balance in Exhibit 3-10. In the right margin, we see how the accounts are distributed to the financial statements. As always,

- the income statement (Exhibit 3-11) reports revenues and expenses.
- the statement of retained earnings (Exhibit 3-12) shows why retained earnings changed during the period.
- the balance sheet (Exhibit 3-13) reports assets, liabilities, and stockholders' equity.

Preparing the Statements

The financial statements should be prepared in this order:

5 Prepare the financial statements from the adjusted trial balance

1. Income statement—to determine net income
2. Statement of retained earnings—to compute ending retained earnings
3. Balance sheet—which needs the amount of ending retained earnings to achieve its balancing feature

All financial statements include these elements:

Heading

- Name of the entity—such as Cookie Lapp Travel Design, Inc.
- Title of the statement—income statement, balance sheet, and so on
- Date, or period, covered by the statement—April 30, 2008, or Month Ended April 30, 2008

Body of the statement

The income statement should list expenses in descending order by amount, as shown in Exhibit 3-11. But Miscellaneous Expense, a catchall category, usually comes last.

Relationships Among the Financial Statements

The arrows in Exhibits 3-11, 3-12, and 3-13 show how the financial statements relate to each other.

1. Net income from the income statement increases retained earnings. A net loss decreases retained earnings.
2. Ending retained earnings from the statement of retained earnings goes to the balance sheet and makes total liabilities plus stockholders' equity equal total assets.

To solidify your understanding of these relationships, trace net income from the income statement to the statement of retained earnings. Then trace ending stockholders' equity to the balance sheet.

EXHIBIT 3-11 The Income Statement Reports the Results of Operations

COOKIE LAPP TRAVEL DESIGN, INC. Income Statement Month Ended April 30, 2008		
Revenue:		
Service revenue		$7,600
Expenses:		
Salary expense	$1,800	
Rent expense	1,000	
Utilities expense	400	
Depreciation expense	300	
Supplies expense	100	
Total expenses		3,600
Net income		$4,000

EXHIBIT 3-12 Statement of Retained Earnings

COOKIE LAPP TRAVEL DESIGN, INC. Statement of Retained Earnings Month Ended April 30, 2008	
Retained earnings, April 1, 2008	$2,600
Add: Net income	4,000
	6,600
Less: Dividends	(3,200)
Retained earnings, April 30, 2008	$3,400

EXHIBIT 3-13 The Balance Sheet Reports Financial Position

COOKIE LAPP TRAVEL DESIGN, INC.
Balance Sheet
April 30, 2008

Assets			Liabilities	
Cash		$24,800	Accounts payable	$13,000
Accounts receivable		2,600	Salary payable	900
Supplies		600	Unearned service revenue	400
Prepaid rent		2,000	Total liabilities	14,300
Furniture	$18,000		**Stockholders' Equity**	
Less: Accumulated			Common stock	30,000
depreciation	(300)	17,700	Retained earnings	3,400
			Total stockholders' equity	33,400
			Total liabilities and	
Total assets		$47,700	stockholders' equity	$47,700

Ethical Issues in Accrual Accounting

Like all areas of business, accounting poses ethical challenges. Accountants must be honest in their work. Only with complete and accurate information can people make wise decisions. An example will illustrate.

Cookie Lapp Travel has done well as a business and wishes to open another office. Assume the company needs to borrow $30,000.

Suppose the travel agency understated expenses in order to inflate net income on the income statement. A banker could be tricked into lending the company money. Then if Lapp couldn't pay the loan, the bank would lose—all because the banker relied on incorrect accounting information.

Accrual accounting provides opportunities for unethical accounting. It would be easy for a dishonest businessperson to overlook depreciation expense at the end of the year. Failing to record depreciation would overstate net income and paint a rosy picture of the company's financial position. It is important for accountants to prepare accurate and complete financial statements because people rely on the data for their decisions.

Decision Guidelines

THE ACCOUNTING PROCESS

Take the role of Haig Sherman, who owns Sherman Lawn Service. Assume it's now the end of the first year, and Sherman wants to know where the business stands financially. The Decision Guidelines give a map of the accounting process to help Sherman manage the business.

Decision	Guidelines
Which basis of accounting better measures business income?	*Accrual basis,* because it provides more complete reports of operating performance and financial position
How to measure revenues?	Revenue principle—Record revenues only after they're earned
How to measure expenses?	Matching principle—Subtract expenses from revenues in order to measure net income
Where to start with the measurement of income at the end of the period?	Unadjusted trial balance, usually referred to simply as the *trial balance*
How to update the accounts for the financial statements?	*Adjusting entries* at the end of the period
What are the categories of adjusting entries?	Prepaid expenses Depreciation of plant assets Accrued expenses Accrued revenues Unearned revenues
How do the adjusting entries differ from other journal entries?	1. Adjusting entries are made only at the end of the period. 2. Adjusting entries never affect cash. 3. All adjusting entries debit or credit • At least one *income statement* account (a revenue or an expense), and • At least one *balance sheet* account (an asset or a liability)
Where are the accounts with their adjusted balances summarized?	*Adjusted trial balance,* which aids preparation of the financial statements

Summary Problem

The trial balance of Clay Employment Services, Inc., pertains to December 31, 2009, which is the end of Clay's annual accounting period. Data needed for the adjusting entries include:

a. Supplies on hand at year-end, $200.
b. Depreciation on furniture, $2,000.
c. Depreciation on building, $1,000.
d. Salaries owed but not yet paid, $500.
e. Accrued service revenue, $1,300.
f. $3,000 of the unearned service revenue has been earned.

Requirements

1. Open the ledger accounts with their unadjusted balances as for Accounts Receivable:

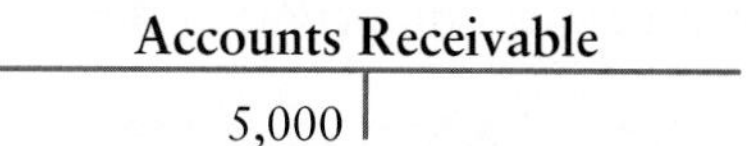

2. Journalize Clay's adjusting entries at December 31, 2009. Key entries by letter, as in Exhibit 3-9.
3. Post the adjusting entries.
4. Write the trial balance on a work sheet, enter the adjusting entries, and prepare an adjusted trial balance, as shown in Exhibit 3-10.
5. Prepare the income statement, the statement of owner's equity, and the balance sheet. Draw arrows linking the three financial statements.

CLAY EMPLOYMENT SERVICES, INC.
Trial Balance
December 31, 2009

	Balance	
Account Title	Debit	Credit
Cash	$ 6,000	
Accounts receivable	5,000	
Supplies	1,000	
Furniture	10,000	
Accumulated depreciation—furniture		$ 4,000
Building	50,000	
Accumulated depreciation—building		30,000
Accounts payable		2,000
Salary payable		
Unearned service revenue		8,000
Common stock		10,000
Retained earnings		2,000
Dividends	25,000	
Service revenue		60,000
Salary expense	16,000	
Supplies expense		
Depreciation expense—furniture and fixtures		
Depreciation expense—building		
Miscellaneous expense	3,000	
Total	$116,000	$116,000

Solution

Requirements 1 and 3

ASSETS

Cash

Bal. 6,000	

Accounts Receivable

5,000	
(e) 1,300	
Bal. 6,300	

Supplies

1,000	(a) 800
Bal. 200	

Furniture

Bal. 10,000	

Accumulated Depreciation—Furniture

	4,000
	(b) 2,000
	Bal. 6,000

Building

Bal. 50,000	

Accumulated Depreciation—Building

	30,000
	(c) 1,000
	Bal. 31,000

LIABILITIES

Accounts Payable

	Bal. 2,000

Salary Payable

	(d) 500
	Bal. 500

Unearned Service Revenue

(f) 3,000	8,000
	Bal. 5,000

STOCKHOLDERS' EQUITY

Common Stock

	Bal. 10,000

Retained Earnings

	Bal. 2,000

Dividends

Bal. 25,000	

REVENUE

Service Revenue

	60,000
	(e) 1,300
	(f) 3,000
	Bal. 64,300

EXPENSES

Salary Expense

16,000	
(d) 500	
Bal. 16,500	

Supplies Expense

(a) 800	
Bal. 800	

Depreciation Expense—Furniture

(b) 2,000	
Bal. 2,000	

Depreciation Expense—Building

(c) 1,000	
Bal. 1,000	

Miscellaneous Expense

Bal. 3,000	

Requirement 2

	2009			
a.	Dec. 31	Supplies Expense ($1,000 – $200)	800	
		Supplies		800
		To record supplies used.		
b.	31	Depreciation Expense—Furniture	2,000	
		Accumulated Depreciation—Furniture		2,000
		To record depreciation expense on furniture.		
c.	31	Depreciation Expense—Building	1,000	
		Accumulated Depreciation—Building		1,000
		To record depreciation expense on building.		
d.	31	Salary Expense	500	
		Salary Payable		500
		To accrue salary expense.		
e.	31	Accounts Receivable	1,300	
		Service Revenue		1,300
		To accrue service revenue.		
f.	31	Unearned Service Revenue	3,000	
		Service Revenue		3,000
		To record service revenue that was collected in advance.		

Requirement 4

CLAY EMPLOYMENT SERVICES, INC.
Preparation of Adjusted Trial Balance
December 31, 2009

	Trial Balance		Adjustments		Adjusted Trial Balance	
Account Title	Debit	Credit	Debit	Credit	Debit	Credit
Cash	6,000				6,000	
Accounts receivable	5,000		(e) 1,300		6,300	
Supplies	1,000			(a) 800	200	
Furniture	10,000				10,000	
Accumulated depreciation—furniture		4,000		(b) 2,000		6,000
Building	50,000				50,000	
Accumulated depreciation—building		30,000		(c) 1,000		31,000
Accounts payable		2,000				2,000
Salary payable				(d) 500		500
Unearned service revenue		8,000	(f) 3,000			5,000
Common stock		10,000				10,000
Retained earnings		2,000				2,000
Dividends	25,000				25,000	
Service revenue		60,000		(e) 1,300		
				(f) 3,000		64,300
Salary expense	16,000		(d) 500		16,500	
Supplies expense			(a) 800		800	
Depreciation expense—furniture			(b) 2,000		2,000	
Depreciation expense—building			(c) 1,000		1,000	
Miscellaneous expense	3,000				3,000	
Total	116,000	116,000	8,600	8,600	120,800	120,800

Requirement 5

CLAY EMPLOYMENT SERVICES, INC. Income Statement Year Ended December 31, 2009		
Revenue:		
Service revenue		$64,300
Expenses:		
Salary expense	$16,500	
Depreciation expense—furniture	2,000	
Depreciation expense—building	1,000	
Supplies expense	800	
Miscellaneous expense	3,000	
Total expenses		23,300
Net income		$41,000

CLAY EMPLOYMENT SERVICES, INC. Statement of Retained Earnings Year Ended December 31, 2009	
Retained earnings, January 1, 2009	$ 2,000
Add: Net income	41,000
	43,000
Less: Dividends	(25,000)
Retained earnings, December 31, 2009	$18,000

CLAY EMPLOYMENT SERVICES, INC.
Balance Sheet
December 31, 2009

Assets			Liabilities	
Cash		$ 6,000	Accounts payable	$ 2,000
Accounts receivable		6,300	Salary payable	500
Supplies		200	Unearned service revenue	5,000
Furniture	$10,000		Total liabilities	7,500
Less: Accumulated				
depreciation	(6,000)	4,000	**Stockholders' Equity**	
Building	$50,000		Common stock	10,000
Less: Accumulated			Retained earnings	18,000
depreciation	(31,000)	19,000	Total stockholders' equity	28,000
			Total liabilities and	
Total assets		$35,500	stockholders' equity	$35,500

Review *The Adjusting Process*

Accounting Vocabulary

Accrual Accounting
Accounting that records the impact of a business event as it occurs regardless of whether the transaction affected cash.

Accrued Expense
An expense that the business has incurred but not yet paid.

Accrued Revenue
A revenue that has been earned but not yet collected in cash.

Accumulated Depreciation
The cumulative sum of all depreciation expense recorded for an asset.

Adjusted Trial Balance
A list of all the accounts with their adjusted balances.

Adjusting Entry
Entry made at the end of the period to assign revenues to the period in which they are earned and expenses to the period in which they are incurred. Adjusting entries help measure the period's income and bring the related asset and liability accounts to correct balances for the financial statements.

Book Value (of a plant asset)
The asset's cost minus accumulated depreciation.

Cash-Basis Accounting
Accounting that records transactions only when cash is received or paid.

Contra Account
An account that always has a companion account and whose normal balance is opposite that of the companion account.

Deferred Revenue
A liability created when a business collects cash from customers in advance of doing work. Also called **unearned revenue**.

Depreciation
The allocation of a plant asset's cost to expense over its useful life.

Matching Principle
Guide to accounting for expenses. Identify all expenses incurred during the period, measure the expenses, and match them against the revenues earned during that same time period.

Plant Asset
Long-lived tangible assets—such as land, buildings, and equipment—used in the operation of a business.

Prepaid Expense
Advance payments of expenses. Examples include prepaid rent, prepaid insurance, and supplies.

Revenue Principle
The basis for recording revenues; tells accountants when to record revenue and the amount of revenue to record.

Time-Period Concept
Ensures that information is reported at regular intervals.

Unearned Revenue
A liability created when a business collects cash from customers in advance of doing work. Also called **deferred revenue**.

Quick Check

1. What are the distinctive features of accrual accounting and cash-basis accounting?
   a. Cash-basis accounting records all transactions.
   b. Accrual accounting records only receivables, payables, and depreciation.
   c. Accrual accounting is superior because it provides more information.
   d. All the above are true.

2. The revenue principle says
   a. Divide time into annual periods to measure revenue properly.
   b. Record revenue after you receive cash.
   c. Measure revenues and expenses in order to compute net income.
   d. Record revenue only after you have earned it.

3. Adjusting the accounts is the process of
   a. Zeroing out account balances to prepare for the next period
   b. Subtracting expenses from revenues to measure net income
   c. Recording transactions as they occur during the period
   d. Updating the accounts at the end of the period

4. Which types of adjusting entries are natural opposites?
   a. Prepaids and accruals
   b. Expenses and revenues
   c. Prepaids and depreciation
   d. Net income and net loss

5. Assume that the weekly payroll of Cookie Lapp Travel Design is $300. December 31, end of the year, falls on Monday, and Lapp will pay her employee on Friday for the full week. What adjusting entry will Lapp make on Monday, December 31?

a. Salary Expense	240	
Cash		240
b. Salary Expense	60	
Salary Payable		60
c. Salary Payable	300	
Salary Expense		300

   d. No adjustment is needed because the company will pay the payroll on Friday.

6. Body Studio gains a client who prepays $600 for a package of six physical training sessions. Body Studio collects the $600 in advance and will provide the training later. After two training sessions, what should Body Studio report on its income statement?
   a. Cash of $400
   b. Service revenue of $200
   c. Service revenue of $600
   d. Unearned service revenue of $200

7. Unearned revenue is always a (an)
   a. Asset
   b. Revenue
   c. Liability
   d. Stockholders' equity because you collected the cash in advance

8. Assume you prepay Body Studio for a package of six physical training sessions. Which type of account should you have in your records?
   a. Prepaid expense
   b. Accrued expense
   c. Accrued revenue
   d. Unearned revenue

9. The adjusted trial balance shows
   a. Amounts that may be out of balance
   b. Revenues and expenses only
   c. Amounts ready for the financial statements
   d. Assets, liabilities, and stockholders' equity only

10. Accounting data flow from the
    a. Balance sheet to the income statement
    b. Income statement to the statement of retained earnings
    c. Statement of retained earnings to the balance sheet
    d. Both b and c are correct

    Answers are given after Apply Your Knowledge (p. 180).

Assess Your Progress

Short Exercises

Comparing accrual accounting and cash-basis accounting

S3-1 Suppose you work summers house-sitting for people while they're away on vacation. Most of your customers pay you immediately after you finish a job. A few ask you to send them a bill. It is now June 30 and you have collected $600 from cash-paying customers. Your remaining customers owe you $500. How much service revenue would you have under the (a) cash basis and (b) accrual basis? Which method of accounting provides more information about your house-sitting business? Explain your answer. (pp. 128–129)

Accrual accounting versus cash-basis accounting for expenses

S3-2 The **Naman Howell Law Firm** uses a client database. Suppose Naman Howell paid $5,000 for a **Dell** computer. Describe how Naman Howell would account for the $5,000 expenditure under (a) the cash basis and (b) the accrual basis. State in your own words why the accrual basis is more realistic for this situation. (pp. 128–129)

Applying the revenue principle

S3-3 *Phoenix Magazine* sells annual subscriptions for the 12 monthly magazines mailed out each year. The company collects cash in advance and then mails out the magazines to subscribers each month.

Apply the revenue principle to determine (a) when Phoenix Magazine should record revenue for this situation and (b) the amount of revenue Phoenix should record for the magazines mailed out January through March. (pp. 130–131)

Applying the matching principle

S3-4 Suppose on January 1 you prepaid apartment rent of $3,600 for the full year. At September 30, what are your two account balances for this situation? Identify the two accounts and give their balances at September 30. (pp. 133–134)

Adjusting prepaid expenses

S3-5 On April 1 you prepaid six months of rent, $3,000. Give your adjusting entry to record rent expense at April 30. Include the date of the entry and an explanation. Then post to the two accounts involved, and show their balances at April 30. (pp. 133–134)

Recording depreciation

S3-6 On May 1 your company paid cash of $36,000 for computers that are expected to remain useful for three years. At the end of three years, the value of the computers is expected to be zero.

Make journal entries to record (a) purchase of the computers on May 1 and (b) depreciation on May 31. Include dates and explanations, and use the following accounts: Computer Equipment; Accumulated Depreciation—Computer Equipment; and Depreciation Expense—Computer Equipment. (pp. 135–136)

Adjusting entry; posting

S3-7 Refer to the data in Short Exercise 3-6.

1. Post to the accounts listed in Short Exercise 3-6, and show their balances at May 31. (p. 136)
2. What is the computer equipment's book value at May 31? (pp. 137–138)

Accruing interest expense

3

S3-8 Cookie Lapp Travel borrowed $50,000 on October 1 by signing a one-year note payable to Community One Bank. Lapp's interest expense for the remainder of the year (October through December) is $700.

1. Make Cookie Lapp's adjusting entry to accrue interest expense at December 31. Date the entry and include its explanation. (p. 139)
2. Post to the two accounts affected by the adjustment. (p. 139)

Accounting for unearned revenues

S3-9 **People Magazine** collects cash from subscribers in advance and then mails the magazines to subscribers over a one-year period. Give the adjusting entry that People Magazine makes to record the earning of $5,000 of Subscription Revenue that was collected in advance. Include an explanation for the entry, as illustrated in the chapter. (p. 141)

Preparing an adjusted trial balance

S3-10 Scissors Hair Stylists has begun the preparation of its adjusted trial balance as follows:

SCISSORS HAIR STYLISTS, INC.
Preparation of Adjusted Trial Balance
December 31, 2006

	Trial Balance		Adjustments		Adjusted Trial Balance	
Account Title	**Debit**	**Credit**	**Debit**	**Credit**	**Debit**	**Credit**
Cash	400					
Supplies	700					
Equipment	17,000					
Accumulated depreciation		1,000				
Accounts payable		200				
Interest payable						
Note payable		3,000				
Common stock		6,000				
Service revenue		12,000				
Rent expense	4,000					
Supplies expense						
Depreciation expense						
Interest expense	100					
Total	22,200	22,200				

Year-end data:

a. Supplies on hand, $200

b. Depreciation, $1,000

c. Accrued interest expense, $100

Complete Scissors' adjusted trial balance. Key each adjustment by letter. To save time, you may write your answers in the spaces provided on the adjusted trial balance given here.

Note: Short Exercises 3-11 and 3-12 should be used only after completing Short Exercise 3-10.

Computing net income

S3-11 Refer to the data in Short Exercise 3-10. Compute Scissors' net income for the year ended December 31, 2006. (pp. 146–147)

Computing total assets

5

S3-12 Refer to the data in Short Exercise 3-10. Compute Scissors' total assets at December 31, 2006. Remember that Accumulated Depreciation is a contra asset. (pp. 146–147)

Exercises

Cash basis versus accrual basis

E3-13 Best Yet Catering completed the following selected transactions during April:

Apr.	1	Prepaid rent for three months, $900.
	5	Paid electricity expenses, $300.
	9	Received cash for meals served to customers, $2,000.
	14	Paid cash for kitchen equipment, $3,000.
	23	Served a banquet on account, $3,000.
	30	Made the adjusting entry for rent (from April 1).
	30	Accrued salary expense, $900.

Show whether each transaction would be handled as a revenue or an expense using the accrual basis. Give the amount of revenue or expense for April. Journal entries are not required. Use the following format for your answer, and show your computations: (pp. 127–129)

Amount of Revenue (Expense) for April		
Date	**Revenue (Expense)**	**Accrual-Basis Amount of Revenue (Expense)**

Accrual accounting concepts and principles

1

E3-14 Identify the accounting concept or principle (there may be more than one) that gives the most direction on how to account for each of the following situations: (pp. 130–132)

a. The owner of a business desires *monthly* financial statements to measure the progress of the entity on an ongoing basis.

b. Expenses of the period total $5,500. This amount should be subtracted from revenue to compute the period's net income.

c. Expenses of $1,200 must be accrued in order to measure net income properly.

d. A customer states her intention to switch health clubs. Should the new health club record revenue based on this intention? Give the reason for your answer.

Cash versus accrual; applying the revenue principle

E3-15 Suppose you start up your own photography business to shoot videos at college parties. The freshman class pays you $100 in advance just to guarantee your services for its party. The sophomore class promises you a minimum of $250 for filming its formal, and you end up collecting cash of $400 for this party. Answer the following questions about the correct way to account for your revenue under the accrual basis.

continued . . .

a. When did you earn your revenue for both parties? What caused you to earn the revenue? Did you earn the revenue at the moment you received cash? (pp. 129–130)

b. In addition to cash, what type of account was created when you received $100 from the freshman class? Name the new account. (pp. 139–140)

Allocating prepaid expense to the asset and the expense

E3-16 Compute the amounts indicated by question marks for each of the following Prepaid Rent situations. For situations A and B, make the needed journal entry. Consider each situation separately. (pp. 133–134)

	Situation			
	A	B	C	D
Beginning Prepaid Rent	$ 800	$ 600	$ 400	$500
Payments for Prepaid Rent during the year	1,100	?	1,400	?
Total amount to account for	1,900	1,500	?	?
Ending Prepaid Rent	700	700	?	400
Rent Expense	$?	$ 800	$1,500	$900

Journalizing adjusting entries
3

E3-17 Journalize the adjusting entries for the following adjustments at January 31, end of the accounting period. (pp. 134–135, 143–144)

a. Depreciation, $700.

b. Prepaid rent expired, $300.

c. Interest expense accrued, $800.

d. Employee salaries owed for Monday through Thursday of a five-day workweek; weekly payroll, $10,000.

e. Unearned service revenue earned, $500.

Analyzing the effects of adjustments on net income
3

E3-18 Suppose the adjustments required in Exercise 3-17 were not made. Compute the overall overstatement or understatement of net income as a result of the omission of these adjustments. (Challenge)

Journalizing adjusting entries
3

E3-19 Journalize the adjusting entry needed at December 31 for each of the following independent situations. (pp. 133–134, 141)

a. On October 1, we collected $4,000 rent in advance, debiting Cash and crediting Unearned Rent Revenue. The tenant was paying one year's rent in advance. At December 31, we must account for the amount of rent we've earned.

b. Salary expense is $1,500 per day—Monday through Friday—and the business pays employees each Friday. This year December 31 falls on a Tuesday.

c. The unadjusted balance of the Supplies account is $3,100. Supplies on hand total $1,200.

d. Equipment was purchased last year at a cost of $10,000. The equipment's useful life is four years. Record the year's depreciation.

e. On September 1, when we prepaid $1,200 for a two-year insurance policy, we debited Prepaid Insurance and credited Cash.

Recording adjustments in T-accounts

E3-20 The accounting records of Meg Grayson, Architect, include the following unadjusted balances at March 31: Accounts Receivable, $1,000; Supplies, $600; Salary Payable, $0; Unearned Service Revenue, $400; Service Revenue, $4,700; Salary Expense, $1,200; Supplies Expense, $0. Grayson's accountant develops the following data for the March 31 adjusting entries:

a. Service revenue accrued, $600.

b. Unearned service revenue that has been earned, $200.

c. Supplies on hand, $500.

d. Salary owed to employee, $400.

Open a T-account for each account and record the adjustments directly in the accounts, keying each adjustment by letter. Show each account's adjusted balance. Journal entries are not required. (pp. 143–144)

Preparing an adjusted trial balance

E3-21 Merry Maids Company, the cleaning service, started the preparation of its adjusted trial balance as follows:

MERRY MAIDS COMPANY
Preparation of Adjusted Trial Balance
June 30, 2007

	Trial Balance		Adjustments		Adjusted Trial Balance	
Account Title	Debit	Credit	Debit	Credit	Debit	Credit
Cash	800					
Supplies	2,000					
Prepaid insurance	900					
Equipment	20,000					
Accumulated depreciation		3,000				
Accounts payable		2,100				
Salary payable						
Unearned service revenue		600				
Common stock		3,000				
Retained earnings		5,000				
Dividends	4,000					
Service revenue		22,000				
Salary expense	8,000					
Supplies expense						
Depreciation expense						
Insurance expense						
Total	35,700	35,700				

During the six months ended June 30, 2007, Merry Maids:

a. Used supplies of $1,500.

b. Used up prepaid insurance of $600.

c. Used up $500 of the equipment through depreciation.

d. Accrued salary expense of $300 that Merry Maids hasn't paid yet.

e. Earned $400 of the unearned service revenue.

continued . . .

Complete the adjusted trial balance. Key each adjustment by letter. To save time, you may write your answers directly in the spaces given here. (p. 145)

Using an adjusted trial balance
4

E3-22 Refer to the data is Exercise 3-21. Journalize the five adjustments, all dated June 30, 2007. Explanations are not required. (pp. 143–144)

Note: Exercise 3-23 should be used only in conjunction with Exercise 3-21.

Using an adjusted trial balance
4

E3-23 Refer to the data in Exercise 3-21.

a. Compute Merry Maids' net income for the period ended June 30, 2007. (pp. 146–147)

b. Compute Merry Maids' total assets at June 30, 2007. (pp. 146–147)

Adjusting the accounts
3 4

E3-24 The adjusted trial balance of Job Link Employment Service, Inc., is incomplete. Enter the adjustment amounts directly in the Adjustments columns below. (p. 145)

JOB LINK EMPLOYMENT SERVICE, INC.
Preparation of Adjusted Trial Balance
January 31, 2008

	Trial Balance		Adjustments		Adjusted Trial Balance	
Account Title	**Debit**	**Credit**	**Debit**	**Credit**	**Debit**	**Credit**
Cash	900				900	
Accounts receivable	4,500				5,600	
Supplies	1,000				700	
Equipment	32,300				32,300	
Accumulated depreciation		14,000				14,600
Salary payable						900
Common stock		10,000				10,000
Retained earnings		14,300				14,300
Dividends	5,100				5,100	
Service revenue		9,600				10,700
Salary expense	2,700				3,600	
Rent expense	1,400				1,400	
Depreciation expense					600	
Supplies expense					300	
Total	47,900	47,900			50,500	50,500

Journalizing adjustments
3 4

E3-25 Make the journal entry for each adjustment needed to complete the adjusted trial balance in Exercise 3-24. Date the entries and include explanations. (pp. 143–145)

Preparing the financial statements

E3-26 Refer to the adjusted trial balance in Exercise 3-24. Prepare the Job Link Employment Service income statement and statement of retained earnings for the month ended January 31, 2008, and its balance sheet on that date. Draw arrows linking the three statements. (pp. 146–147)

Preparing the income statement
5

E3-27 The accountant for John Eagle, CPA, P.C., has posted adjusting entries (a) through (e) to the accounts at December 31, 2007. Selected balance sheet accounts and all the revenues and expenses of the entity follow in T-account form.

Accounts Receivable

	Debit		Credit
	23,000		
(e)	1,000		

Supplies

	Debit		Credit
	1,000	(a)	400

Accumulated Depreciation—Equipment

	Debit		Credit
			5,000
		(b)	2,000

Accumulated Depreciation—Building

	Debit		Credit
			30,000
		(c)	5,000

Salary Payable

	Debit		Credit
		(d)	600

Service Revenue

	Debit		Credit
			105,000
		(e)	1,000

Salary Expense

	Debit		Credit
	28,000		
(d)	600		

Supplies Expense

	Debit		Credit
(a)	400		

Depreciation Expense—Equipment

	Debit		Credit
(b)	2,000		

Depreciation Expense—Building

	Debit		Credit
(c)	5,000		

Requirements

1. Prepare the income statement of John Eagle, CPA, P.C., for the year ended December 31, 2007. List expenses in order from the largest to the smallest. (pp. 146–147)
2. Were 2007 operations successful? Give the reason for your answer. (Challenge)

Preparing the statement of owner's equity

E3-28 Lake Air Interiors, Inc., began the year with retained earnings of $20,000. On July 12, Lake Air issued common stock and received $12,000 cash. The income statement for the year ended December 31, 2008, reported net income of $68,000. During 2008, Lake Air Interiors paid cash dividends of $4,000 each month.

Requirements

Prepare Lake Air Interiors, Inc.'s, statement of retained earnings for the year ended December 31, 2008. (pp. 146–147)

Computing financial statement amounts
5

E3-29 The adjusted trial balances of Pacific International at December 31, 2007, and December 31, 2006, include these amounts:

	2007	2006
Supplies	$ 2,000	$ 1,000
Salary payable	2,500	4,000
Unearned service revenue	13,000	16,000

continued . . .

Analysis of the accounts at December 31, 2007, reveals these transactions for 2007:

Cash payment for supplies	$ 6,000
Cash payments for salaries	47,000
Cash receipts in advance for service revenue	80,000

Compute the amount of supplies expense, salary expense, and service revenue to report on the Pacific International income statement for 2007. (pp. 133–141, 143–144)

Problems (Group A)

Applying accounting principles

P3-30A As the controller of Highland Academy, a private high school, you have hired a new bookkeeper, whom you must train. He objects to making an adjusting entry for accrued salaries at the end of the period. He reasons, "We will pay the salaries within a week or two. Why not wait until payment to record the expense? In the end, the result will be the same." Write a business memo to explain to the bookkeeper why the adjusting entry for accrued salary expense is needed. The format of a business memo follows. (pp. 127–129)

Date: ______________

To: New Bookkeeper

From: (Student Name)

Subject: Why the adjusting entry for salary expense is needed

Cash basis versus accrual basis

P3-31A Tee's Golf School completed the following transactions during January:

Jan. 1	Prepaid insurance for January through March, $300.
4	Performed service (gave golf lessons) on account, $2,200.
5	Purchased equipment on account, $1,900.
8	Paid property tax expense, $450.
11	Purchased office equipment for cash, $800.
19	Performed service and received cash, $700.
24	Collected $400 on account.
26	Paid account payable from January 5.

continued . . .

29	Paid salary expense, $900.
31	Recorded adjusting entry for January insurance expense (see Jan. 1).
31	Debited unearned revenue and credited revenue to adjust the accounts, $600.

Requirements

1. Show how each transaction would be handled using the accrual basis of accounting. Give the amount of revenue or expense for January. Journal entries are not required. Use the following format for your answer, and show your computations: (pp. 127–129)

Amount of Revenue (Expense) for January		
Date	Revenue (Expense)	Accrual-Basis Amount of Revenue (Expense)

2. Compute January net income or net loss under the accrual basis of accounting. (Challenge)
3. State why the accrual basis of accounting is preferable to the cash basis. (pp. 127–129)

Journalizing adjusting entries

3

P3-32A Journalize the adjusting entry needed on December 31, the end of the current year, for each of the following independent cases affecting Lindsey Landscaping. (pp. 133–134, 141)

a. Each Friday, Lindsey pays employees for the current week's work. The amount of the payroll is $5,000 for a five-day workweek. This year December 31 falls on a Monday. (p. 138)

b. Details of Prepaid Insurance are shown in the account:

Lindsey prepays a full year's insurance each year on January 1. Record insurance expense for the year ended December 31. (pp. 133–134)

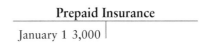

Prepaid Insurance	
January 1 3,000	

c. The beginning balance of Supplies was $3,800. During the year, Lindsey purchased supplies costing $5,000, and at December 31, the supplies on hand total $2,400. (p. 134)

d. Lindsey designed a landscape plan, and the client paid Lindsey $4,000 at the start of the project. Lindsey recorded this amount as Unearned Service Revenue. The job will take several months to complete, and Lindsey estimates that the company has earned three-fourths of the total revenue during the current year. (p. 141)

e. Depreciation for the current year includes: Equipment, $5,500; and Trucks, $3,000. Make a compound entry, as illustrated in Chapter 2. (pp. 74–75, 133–136)

Journalizing and posting adjustments to T-accounts; preparing the adjusted trial balance

P3-33A The trial balance of Dynaclean Air Purification Systems, Inc., at November 30, 2007, and the data needed for the month-end adjustments follow.

DYNACLEAN AIR PURIFICATION SYSTEMS, INC. Trial Balance November 30, 2007		
	Balance	
Account Title	**Debit**	**Credit**
Cash	$ 7,100	
Accounts receivable	19,800	
Prepaid rent	2,400	
Supplies	1,200	
Equipment	19,700	
Accumulated depreciation		$ 3,600
Accounts payable		3,300
Salary payable		
Unearned service revenue		2,800
Common stock		10,000
Retained earnings		30,000
Dividends	9,800	
Service revenue		15,600
Salary expense	3,800	
Rent expense		
Depreciation expense		
Advertising expense	1,500	
Supplies expense		
Total	$65,300	$65,300

Adjustment data at November 30:

a. Unearned service revenue still unearned, $1,100.

b. Prepaid rent still in force, $400.

c. Supplies used during the month, $1,000.

d. Depreciation for the month, $400.

e. Accrued advertising expense, $600. (Credit Accounts Payable.)

f. Accrued salary expense, $500.

Requirements

1. As directed by your instructor, open T-accounts (or four-column accounts) for the accounts listed in the trial balance, inserting their November 30 unadjusted balances. (pp. 82, 143–144)

2. Journalize the adjusting entries and post to the T-accounts. Key the journal entries and the posted amounts by letter. Show the ending balance of each account. (pp. 143–144)

continued . . .

If you are instructed to use four-column accounts, then post to the accounts and write "Balance" in the Item column for the November 30 unadjusted balance, as shown here for the Cash account:

ACCOUNT CASH

Date	Item	Jrnl. Ref.	Debit	Credit	Balance Debit	Balance Credit
Nov. 30	Balance				7,100	

Use the actual date (Nov. 30) for each posted amount. (pp. 82, 143–144)

3. Prepare the adjusted trial balance. (p. 145)
4. How will Dynaclean use the adjusted trial balance? (pp. 145–147)

Analyzing and journalizing adjustments
3

P3-34A Galaxy Theater Production Company unadjusted and adjusted trial balances at December 31, 2007, follow.

GALAXY THEATER PRODUCTION COMPANY
Adjusted Trial Balance
December 31, 2007

	Trial Balance		Adjusted Trial Balance	
Account Title	Debit	Credit	Debit	Credit
Cash	3,200		3,200	
Accounts receivable	5,200		11,200	
Supplies	1,200		300	
Prepaid insurance	2,600		2,300	
Equipment	21,600		21,600	
Accumulated depreciation		8,200		9,800
Accounts payable		4,400		4,400
Salary payable				1,000
Common stock		10,000		10,000
Retained earnings		4,400		4,400
Dividends	29,600		29,600	
Service revenue		68,000		74,000
Depreciation expense			1,600	
Supplies expense			900	
Utilities expense	5,000		5,000	
Salary expense	26,600		27,600	
Insurance expense			300	
Total	95,000	95,000	103,600	103,600

Requirements

Journalize the adjusting entries that account for the differences between the two trial balances. (pp. 143–144).

Preparing the financial statements from an adjusted trial balance
5

P3-35A The adjusted trial balance of Party Planners, Inc., at December 31, 2008, follows.

PARTY PLANNERS, INC.
Adjusted Trial Balance
December 31, 2008

	Balance	
Account Title	**Debit**	**Credit**
Cash	$ 12,300	
Accounts receivable	10,400	
Supplies	900	
Equipment	25,600	
Accumulated depreciation		$ 12,200
Accounts payable		3,600
Unearned service revenue		4,500
Salary payable		900
Note payable		15,000
Common stock		2,000
Retained earnings		8,000
Dividends	38,000	
Service revenue		63,700
Depreciation expense	5,300	
Salary expense	9,000	
Utilities expense	3,700	
Insurance expense	3,100	
Supplies expense	1,600	
Total	$109,900	$109,900

Requirements

1. Prepare Party Planners' 2008 income statement and statement of retained earnings and year-end balance sheet. List expenses in decreasing order on the income statement and show total liabilities on the balance sheet. Draw arrows linking the three financial statements. (pp. 146–147)
2. a. Which financial statement reports Party Planners' results of operations? Were 2008 operations successful? Cite specifics from the financial statements to support your evaluation. (pp. 146–147)

   b. Which statement reports the company's financial position? Does Party Planners' financial position look strong or weak? Give the reason for your evaluation. (pp. 146–147)

Preparing an adjusted trial balance and the financial statements

P3-36A Consider the unadjusted trial balance of Hummer Limo Service Company at October 31, 2007, and the related month-end adjustment data.

continued . . .

HUMMER LIMO SERVICE COMPANY
Trial Balance
October 31, 2007

Account Title	Balance Debit	Balance Credit
Cash	$ 6,300	
Accounts receivable	1,000	
Prepaid rent	3,000	
Supplies	600	
Automobile	72,000	
Accumulated depreciation		$ 3,000
Accounts payable		2,800
Salary payable		
Common stock		20,000
Retained earnings		53,000
Dividends	3,600	
Service revenue		9,400
Salary expense	1,400	
Rent expense		
Fuel expense	300	
Depreciation expense		
Supplies expense		
Total	$88,200	$88,200

Adjustment data:

a. Accrued service revenue at October 31, $2,000.

b. One-fifth of the prepaid rent expired during the month.

c. Supplies on hand October 31, $200.

d. Depreciation on automobile for the month. The auto's expected useful life is six years.

e. Accrued salary expense at October 31 for one day only. The five-day weekly payroll is $1,000.

Requirements

1. Write the trial balance on a work sheet, using Exhibit 3-10 as an example, and prepare the adjusted trial balance of Hummer Limo Service Company at October 31, 2007. Key each adjusting entry by letter. (p. 145)
2. Prepare the income statement and the statement of retained earnings for the month ended October 31, 2007, and the balance sheet at that date. Draw arrows linking the three financial statements. (pp. 146–147)

Problems (Group B)

Applying accounting principles

P3-37B Assume you own Bowen Electric Company, and you employ 10 people. Write a business memo to your assistant manager to explain the difference between the cash basis of accounting and the accrual basis. Mention

continued . . .

the roles of the revenue principle and the matching principle in accrual accounting. The format of a business memo follows. (pp. 127–129)

Date: ________________

To: Assistant Manager

From: (Student Name)

Subject: Difference between the cash basis and the accrual basis of accounting

Cash basis versus accrual basis

P3-38B Multiplex Medical Clinic completed these transactions during October:

Oct. 2	Prepaid insurance for October through December, $900.
4	Paid water bill, $200.
5	Performed services on account, $8,000.
9	Purchased medical equipment for cash, $1,400.
12	Received cash for services performed, $7,400.
14	Purchased office equipment on account, $300.
28	Collected $500 on account from October 5.
29	Paid salary expense, $1,100.
30	Paid account payable from October 14.
31	Recorded adjusting entry for October insurance expense (see October 2).
31	Debited unearned revenue and credited revenue in an adjusting entry, $700.

Requirements

1. Show how each transaction would be handled using the accrual basis of accounting. Give the amount of revenue or expense for October. Journal entries are not required. Use the following format for your answer, and show your computations: (pp. 127–129)

AMOUNT OF REVENUE (EXPENSE) FOR OCTOBER

Date	Revenue (Expense)	Accrual-Basis Amount of Revenue (Expense)

2. Compute October net income or net loss under the accrual basis of accounting. (Challenge)
3. Why is the accrual basis of accounting preferable to the cash basis? (pp. 127–129)

Journalizing adjusting entries

3

P3-39B Journalize the adjusting entry needed on December 31, end of the current year, for each of the following independent cases affecting Mid-America Water Park. (pp. 133–141)

a. Details of Prepaid Insurance are shown in the account:

Prepaid Insurance	
June 30 5,000	

continued . . .

Mid-America prepays a full year's liability insurance each year on June 30. Record insurance expense for the year ended December 31. (p. 138)

b. Mid-America pays employees each Friday. The amount of the weekly payroll is $2,000 for a five-day workweek. December 31 falls on a Wednesday. (p. 138)

c. Mid-America has borrowed money, signing a note payable. At December 31 Mid-America accrues interest expense of $300 that it will pay next year. (p. 140)

d. The beginning balance of Supplies was $1,000. During the year, Mid-America purchased supplies for $6,100, and at December 31 the supplies on hand total $2,100. (p. 134)

e. Mid-America is hosting a church group from Chicago. The tour operator paid Mid-America $12,000 as the service fee and Mid-America recorded this amount as Unearned Service Revenue. By December 31 Mid-America earned 60% of the total fee. (p. 141)

f. Depreciation for the current year includes Canoe Equipment, $3,800; and Trucks, $1,300. Make a compound entry, as illustrated in Chapter 2. (pp. 74–75, 135–136)

Journalizing and posting adjustments to T-accounts; preparing the adjusted trial balance

P3-40B The trial balance of Lexington Corporation at December 31, 2008, and the data needed for the month-end adjustments follow.

LEXINGTON CORPORATION
Trial Balance
December 31, 2008

Account Title	Balance Debit	Balance Credit
Cash	$ 12,200	
Accounts receivable	14,100	
Prepaid insurance	3,100	
Supplies	800	
Building	412,000	
Accumulated depreciation		$311,000
Accounts payable		1,900
Salary payable		
Unearned service revenue		2,300
Common stock		100,000
Retained earnings		15,000
Dividends	2,900	
Service revenue		17,800
Salary expense	2,100	
Insurance expense		
Depreciation expense		
Advertising expense	800	
Supplies expense		
Total	$448,000	$448,000

Adjustment data at December 31:

a. Prepaid insurance still in force, $600.

b. Supplies used during the month, $600.

continued . . .

c. Depreciation for the month, $900.
d. Accrued salary expense, $100.
e. Unearned service revenue still unearned, $1,100.

Requirements

1. As directed by your instructor, open T-accounts (or four-column accounts) for the accounts listed in the trial balance, inserting their December 31 unadjusted balances. (pp. 82, 143–144)
2. Journalize the adjusting entries and post to the T-accounts. Key the journal entries and the posted amounts by letter. Show the ending balance of each account. (pp. 143–144)

   If you are instructed to use four-column accounts, then post to the accounts and write "Balance" in the Item column for the December 31 unadjusted balance, as shown here for the Cash account:

   ACCOUNT CASH

					Balance	
Date	Item	Jrnl. Ref.	Debit	Credit	Debit	Credit
Dec. 31	Balance				12,200	

   Use the actual date (Dec. 31) for each posted amount. (pp. 82, 143–144)
3. Prepare the adjusted trial balance. (p. 145)
4. How will Lexington Corporation use the adjusted trial balance? (pp. 145–147)

Analyzing and journalizing adjustments
3

P3-41B Assume that a Blinko Copy Center, Inc., had the following unadjusted and adjusted trial balances at April 30, 2007.

BLINKO COPY CENTER, INC.
Adjusted Trial Balance
April 30, 2007

	Trial Balance		Adjusted Trial Balance	
Account Title	Debit	Credit	Debit	Credit
Cash	6,200		6,200	
Accounts receivable	6,000		6,900	
Supplies	1,000		300	
Prepaid rent	2,400		1,600	
Equipment	66,400		66,400	
Accumulated depreciation		16,000		17,200
Accounts payable		6,900		6,900
Salary payable				300
Common stock		55,000		10,000
Retained earnings				45,000
Dividends	3,600		3,600	
Service revenue		9,500		10,400
Salary expense	1,600		1,900	
Rent expense			800	
Depreciation expense			1,200	
Supplies expense			700	
Utilities expense	200		200	
Total	87,400	87,400	89,800	89,800

continued . . .

Requirements

Journalize the adjusting entries that account for the differences between the two trial balances. (pp. 133–140, 143–145)

Preparing the financial statements from an adjusted trial balance 5

P3-42B The adjusted trial balance of Snyder Piano Service, Inc., at December 31, 2007, follows.

SNYDER PIANO SERVICE, INC.
Adjusted Trial Balance
December 31, 2007

Account Title	Adjusted Trial Balance Debit	Credit
Cash	$ 8,300	
Accounts receivable	4,900	
Supplies	2,300	
Prepaid rent	1,600	
Equipment	7,700	
Accumulated depreciation		$ 4,900
Accounts payable		4,500
Unearned service revenue		600
Common stock		1,000
Retained earnings		2,000
Dividends	29,000	
Service revenue		66,000
Depreciation expense	2,300	
Rent expense	17,400	
Utilities expense	2,600	
Supplies expense	2,900	
Total	$79,000	$79,000

Requirements

1. Prepare the 2007 income statement, statement of retained earnings, and year-end balance sheet of Snyder Piano Service, Inc. List expenses in decreasing order on the income statement and show total liabilities on the balance sheet. Draw arrows linking the three financial statements. (pp. 146–147)
2. a. Which financial statement reports the company's results of operations? Were operations successful during 2007? Cite specifics from the financial statements to support your evaluation. (pp. 146–147)

   b. Which statement reports the company's financial position? Does its financial position look strong or weak? Give the reason for your evaluation. (pp. 146–147)

Preparing an adjusted trial balance and the financial statements

P3-43B The unadjusted trial balance of Solar Energy Company at July 31, 2007, and the related month-end adjustment data follow.

SOLAR ENERGY COMPANY
Trial Balance
July 31, 2007

Account Title	Balance Debit	Balance Credit
Cash	$ 8,900	
Accounts receivable	11,600	
Prepaid rent	4,000	
Supplies	800	
Equipment	28,800	
Accumulated depreciation		$ 3,500
Accounts payable		3,400
Salary payable		
Common stock		10,000
Retained earnings		29,100
Dividends	4,000	
Service revenue		15,000
Salary expense	2,400	
Rent expense		
Utilities expense	500	
Depreciation expense		
Supplies expense		
Total	$61,000	$61,000

Adjustment data:

a. Accrued service revenue at July 31, $2,000.

b. Prepaid rent expired during the month, $1,000.

c. Supplies on hand at July 31, $400.

d. Depreciation on equipment for the month, $300.

e. Accrued salary expense at July 31 for one day only. The five-day weekly payroll is $1,000.

For 24/7 practice, visit www.MyAccountingLab.com

Requirements

1. Using Exhibit 3-10 as an example, write the trial balance on a work sheet and prepare the adjusted trial balance of Solar Energy Company at July 31, 2007. Key each adjusting entry by letter. (p. 145)
2. Prepare the income statement and the statement of retained earnings for the month ended July 31, 2007, and the balance sheet at that date. Draw arrows linking the three statements. (pp. 146–147)

Continuing Problem

Problem 3-44 continues the Redmon Consulting, Inc., situation from Problem 2-44 of Chapter 2.

Adjusting the accounts, preparing an adjusted trial balance, and preparing the financial statements

P3-44 Refer to Problem 2-44 of Chapter 2. Start from the trial balance and the posted T-accounts that Redmon Consulting, Inc., prepared at December 18, as follows:

REDMON CONSULTING, INC.
Trial Balance
December 18, 2008

Account Title	Balance Debit	Balance Credit
Cash	$ 8,100	
Accounts receivable	1,700	
Supplies	300	
Equipment	2,000	
Accumulated depreciation		
Furniture	3,600	
Accumulated depreciation		
Accounts payable		$ 3,900
Salary payable		
Unearned service revenue		
Common stock		10,000
Retained earnings		
Dividends		
Service revenue		2,500
Rent expense	500	
Utilities expense	200	
Salary expense		
Depreciation expense—equipment		
Depreciation expense—furniture		
Supplies expense		
Total	$16,400	$16,400

Later in December, the business completed these transactions, as follows:

Dec. 21	Received $900 in advance for client service to be performed evenly over the next 30 days.
21	Hired a secretary to be paid $1,500 on the 20th day of each month. The secretary begins work immediately.
26	Paid $300 on account.
28	Collected $600 on account.
30	Paid cash dividends of $1,600.

continued . . .

Requirements

1. Open these additional T-accounts: Accumulated Depreciation—Equipment; Accumulated Depreciation—Furniture; Salary Payable; Unearned Service Revenue; Depreciation Expense—Equipment; Depreciation Expense—Furniture; Supplies Expense. (pp. 143–144)
2. Journalize the transactions of December 21 through 30. (pp. 72–78)
3. Post to the T-accounts, keying all items by date. (pp. 74–78)
4. Prepare a trial balance at December 31. Also set up columns for the adjustments and for the adjusted trial balance, as illustrated in Exhibit 3-10, page 145.
5. At December 31, Redmon gathers the following information for the adjusting entries:
   a. Accrued service revenue, $400.
   b. Earned $300 of the service revenue collected in advance on December 21.
   c. Supplies on hand, $100.
   d. Depreciation expense—equipment, $50; furniture, $60.
   e. Accrued $500 expense for secretary's salary.

   On your work sheet make these adjustments directly in the adjustments columns, and complete the adjusted trial balance at December 31. Throughout the book, to avoid rounding errors, we base adjusting entries on 30-day months and 360-day years. (p. 145)
6. Journalize and post the adjusting entries. In the accounts denote each adjusting amount as *Adj.* and an account balance as *Bal.* (pp. 143–144)
7. Prepare the income statement and the statement of retained earnings of Redmon Consulting, Inc., for the month ended December 31, and prepare the balance sheet at that date. Draw arrows linking the statements. (pp. 146–147)

Apply Your Knowledge

Decision Cases

Valuing a business on the basis of its net income

3 4

Case 1. Lee Nicholas has been the principal stockholder and has operated World.com Advertising, Inc., since its beginning 10 years ago. The company has prospered. Recently, Nicholas mentioned that he would sell the business for the right price.

Assume that you are interested in buying World.com Advertising, Inc. You obtain the most recent monthly trial balance, which follows. Revenues and expenses vary little from month to month, and January is a typical month. Your investigation reveals that the trial balance does *not* include monthly revenues of $3,800 and expenses of $1,100. Also, if you were to buy World.com Advertising, you would hire a manager so you could devote your time to other duties. Assume that this person would require a monthly salary of $5,000.

WORLD.COM ADVERTISING, INC.
Trial Balance
January 31, 2008

	Balance	
Account Title	Debit	Credit
Cash	$ 9,700	
Accounts receivable	14,100	
Prepaid expenses	2,600	
Building	221,300	
Accumulated depreciation		$ 68,600
Accounts payable		13,000
Salary payable		
Unearned service revenue		56,700
Common stock		50,000
Retained earnings		60,400
Dividends	9,000	
Service revenue		12,300
Rent expense		
Salary expense	3,400	
Utilities expense	900	
Depreciation expense		
Supplies expense		
Total	$261,000	$261,000

Requirements

1. Assume that the most you would pay for the business is 20 times the monthly net income *you could expect to earn* from it. Compute this possible price. (pp. 145–147)
2. Nicholas states that the least he will take for the business is an amount equal to the business's stockholders' equity balance on January 31. Compute this amount. (pp. 146–147)
3. Under these conditions, how much should you offer Nicholas? Give your reason. (Challenge)

Completing the accounting cycle to compute net income

3 5

Case 2. One year ago, Tyler Stasney founded Swift Classified Ads. Stasney remembers that you took an accounting course while in college and comes to you for advice. He wishes to know how much net income his business earned during the past year in order to decide whether to keep the company going. His accounting records consist of the T-accounts from his ledger, which were prepared by an accountant who moved to another city. The ledger at December 31 follows. The accounts have *not* been adjusted.

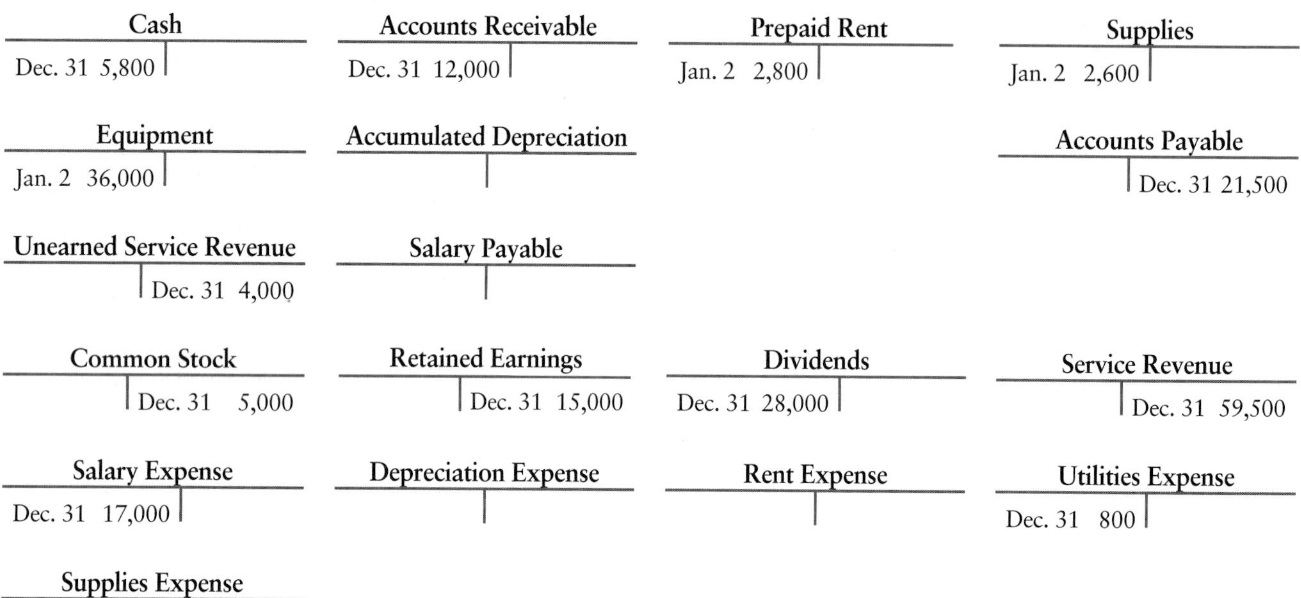

Cash
Dec. 31 5,800
Accounts Receivable
Dec. 31 12,000
Prepaid Rent
Jan. 2 2,800
Supplies
Jan. 2 2,600
Equipment
Jan. 2 36,000
Accumulated Depreciation
Accounts Payable
Dec. 31 21,500
Unearned Service Revenue
Dec. 31 4,000
Salary Payable
Common Stock
Dec. 31 5,000
Retained Earnings
Dec. 31 15,000
Dividends
Dec. 31 28,000
Service Revenue
Dec. 31 59,500
Salary Expense
Dec. 31 17,000
Depreciation Expense
Rent Expense
Utilities Expense
Dec. 31 800
Supplies Expense

Stasney indicates that at year-end, customers owe him $1,600 for accrued service revenue. These revenues have not been recorded. During the year, Stasney collected $4,000 service revenue in advance from customers, but he earned only $900 of that amount. Rent expense for the year was $2,400, and he used up $1,700 of the supplies. Stasney determines that depreciation on his equipment was $5,000 for the year. At December 31, he owes his employee $1,200 accrued salary.

Requirements

Help Stasney compute his net income for the year. Advise him whether to continue operating Swift Classified Ads. (pp. 143–147)

Ethical Issue

The net income of Steinbach & Sons, a department store, decreased sharply during 2007. Mort Steinbach, manager of the store, anticipates the need for a bank loan in 2008. Late in 2007, Steinbach instructs the store's accountant to record a $2,000 sale of furniture to the Steinbach family, even though the goods will not be shipped from the manufacturer until January 2008. Steinbach also tells the accountant *not* to make the following December 31, 2007, adjusting entries:

Salaries owed to employees	$900
Prepaid insurance that has expired	400

continued . . .

Requirements

1. Compute the overall effects of these transactions on the store's reported income for 2007. (pp. 143–147)
2. Why is Steinbach taking this action? Is his action ethical? Give your reason, identifying the parties helped and the parties harmed by Steinbach's action. (Challenge)
3. As a personal friend, what advice would you give the accountant? (Challenge)

Financial Statement Case

Journalizing and posting transactions and tracing account balances to the financial statements

Amazon.com—like all other businesses—makes adjusting entries prior to year-end in order to measure assets, liabilities, revenues, and expenses properly. Examine Amazon's balance sheet and Note 3. Pay particular attention to Accumulated Depreciation.

1. Open T-accounts for the following accounts with their balances at December 31, 2004 (amounts in millions, as in the Amazon.com financial statements):

Accumulated Depreciation	$ 177
Accounts Payable	1,142
Other Assets	42

2. Assume that during 2005 Amazon.com completed the following transactions (amounts in billions). Journalize each transaction (explanations are not required).
   a. Recorded depreciation expense, $46.
   b. Paid the December 31, 2004, balance of accounts payable.
   c. Purchased inventory on account, $1,366.
   d. Sold other assets and received cash of $5.
3. Post to the three T-accounts. Then the balance of each account should agree with the corresponding amount reported in Amazon's December 31, 2005, balance sheet. Check to make sure they do agree with Amazon's actual balances. You can find Accumulated Depreciation in Note 3.

Team Project

It's Just Lunch is a nationwide service company that arranges lunch dates for clients. It's Just Lunch collects cash up front for a package of dates. Suppose your group is opening an It's Just Lunch office in your area. You must make some important decisions—where to locate, how to advertise, and so on—and you must also make some accounting decisions. For example, what will be the end of your business's accounting year? How often will you need financial statements to evaluate operating performance and financial position? Will you use the cash basis or the accrual basis? When will you account for the revenue that the business earns? How will you account for the expenses?

continued . . .

Requirements

Write a report (or prepare an oral presentation, as directed by your professor) to address the following considerations:

1. Will you use the cash basis or the accrual basis of accounting? Give a complete explanation of your reasoning.
2. How often do you want financial statements? Why? Discuss how you will use each financial statement.
3. What kind of revenue will you earn? When will you record it as revenue? How will you decide when to record the revenue?
4. Prepare a made-up income statement for It's Just Lunch for the year ended December 31, 2008. List all the business's expenses, starting with the most important (largest dollar amount) and working through the least important (smallest dollar amount). Merely list the accounts. Dollar amounts are not required.

For Internet Exercises, Excel in Practice, and additional online activities, go to the Web site www.prenhall.com/horngren.

Quick Check Answers

1. *c* 2. *d* 3. *d* 4. *a* 5. *b* 6. *b* 7. *c* 8. *a* 9. *c* 10. *d*

Appendix 3A

Alternative Treatment of Prepaid Expenses and Unearned Revenues

Chapters 1 through 3 illustrate the most popular way to account for prepaid expenses and unearned revenues. This appendix illustrates an alternative approach.

Prepaid Expenses

Prepaid expenses are advance payments of expenses such as Prepaid Insurance, Prepaid Rent, and Prepaid Advertising. Supplies are also accounted for as prepaid expenses.

When a business prepays an expense—rent, for example—it can debit an *asset* account (Prepaid Rent), as illustrated on page 133.

Aug. 1	Prepaid Rent	XXX	
	Cash		XXX

Alternatively, it can debit an *expense* account to record this cash payment:

Aug. 1	Rent Expense	XXX	
	Cash		XXX

Either way, the business must adjust the accounts at the end of the period to report the correct amounts of the expense and the asset.

Prepaid Expense Recorded Initially as an Expense

Prepaying an expense creates an asset. However, the asset may be so short-lived that it will expire in the current accounting period—within one year or less. Thus, the accountant may decide to debit the prepayment to an expense account at the time of payment. A $6,000 cash payment for rent (one year, in advance) on August 1 may be debited to Rent Expense:

2006			
Aug. 1	Rent Expense	6,000	
	Cash		6,000

At December 31, only five months' prepayment has expired (for August through December), leaving seven months' rent still prepaid. In this case, the accountant must transfer 7/12 of the original prepayment of $6,000, or $3,500, to the asset account Prepaid Rent. At December 31, 2006, the business still has the benefit of the prepayment for January through July of 2007. The adjusting entry at December 31 is:

2006	Adjusting Entries		
Dec. 31	Prepaid Rent ($6,000 × 7/12)	3,500	
	Rent Expense		3,500

After posting, the two accounts appear as follows:

Prepaid Rent

2006			
Dec. 31 Adjusting	3,500		
Dec. 31 Balance	3,500		

Rent Expense

2006		2006	
Aug. 1 Payment	6,000	Dec. 31 Adjusting	3,500
Dec. 31 Balance	2,500		

The balance sheet at the end of 2006 reports Prepaid Rent of $3,500, and the income statement for 2006 reports Rent Expense of $2,500, regardless of whether the business initially debits the prepayment to an asset account or to an expense account.

Unearned (Deferred) Revenues

Unearned (deferred) revenues arise when a business collects cash before earning the revenue. Unearned revenues are liabilities because the business that receives cash owes the other party goods or services to be delivered later.

Unearned (Deferred) Revenue Recorded Initially as a Revenue

Receipt of cash in advance creates a liability, as discussed on page 000. Another way to account for the receipt of cash is to credit a *revenue account* when it receives the cash. If the business then earns all the revenue within the same period, no adjusting entry is needed at the end. However, if the business earns only part of the revenue that period, it must make an adjusting entry.

Suppose on October 1, 2006, a law firm records as service revenue the receipt of $9,000 cash for service revenue to be earned over nine months. The cash receipt entry is:

2006			
Oct. 1	Cash	9,000	
	Service Revenue		9,000

At December 31, the attorney has earned only 3/9 of the $9,000, or $3,000, for the months of October, November, and December. Accordingly, the law firm makes an adjusting entry to transfer the unearned portion (6/9 of $9,000, or $6,000) from the revenue account to a liability, as follows:

2006			
Dec. 31	Service Revenue ($9,000 × 6/9)	6,000	
	Unearned Service Revenue		6,000

The adjusting entry transfers the unearned portion to the liability account because the law firm still owes legal service to the client for January through June of 2007. After posting, the total amount ($9,000) is properly divided between the liability account ($6,000) and the revenue account ($3,000), as follows.

Unearned Service Revenue

	2006	
	Dec. 31 Adjusting	6,000
	Dec. 31 Balance	6,000

Service Revenue

2006		2006	
Dec. 31 Adjusting	6,000	Oct. 1 Receipt	9,000
		Dec. 31 Balance	3,000

The attorney's 2006 income statement reports service revenue of $3,000, and the balance sheet reports the unearned revenue of $6,000 as a liability. The result is the same whether the business initially credits a liability account or a revenue account.

Appendix 3A Assignments

Exercises

Recording supplies transactions two ways

E3A-1 At the beginning of the year, supplies of $1,100 were on hand. During the year, Damon Air Conditioning Service paid $5,400 for more supplies. At the end of the year, Damon has $800 of supplies on hand.

Requirements

1. Assume that Damon records supplies by initially debiting an *asset* account. Therefore, place the beginning balance in the Supplies T-account, and record the preceding entries directly in the accounts without using a journal.
2. Assume that Damon records supplies by initially debiting an *expense* account. Therefore, place the beginning balance in the Supplies Expense T-account, and record the preceding entries directly in the accounts without using a journal.
3. Compare the ending account balances under both approaches. Are they the same?

Recording unearned revenues two ways

E3A-2 At the beginning of the year, Avant Garde Advertising owed customers $2,700 for unearned service revenue collected in advance. During the year, Avant Garde received advance cash receipts of $7,000. At year-end, the liability for unearned revenue is $3,700.

Requirements

1. Assume that Avant Garde records unearned revenues by initially crediting a *liability* account. Open T-accounts for Unearned Service Revenue and Service Revenue, and place the beginning balance in Unearned Service Revenue. Journalize the cash collection and adjusting entries, and post their dollar amounts. As references in the T-accounts, denote a balance by *Bal.*, a cash receipt by *CR*, and an adjustment by *Adj.*
2. Assume that Avant Garde records unearned revenues by initially crediting a *revenue* account. Open T-accounts for Unearned Service

Revenue and Service Revenue, and place the beginning balance in Service Revenue. Journalize the cash collection and adjusting entries, and post their dollar amounts. As references in the T-accounts, denote a balance by *Bal.*, a cash receipt by *CR*, and an adjustment by *Adj.*

3. Compare the ending balances in the two accounts.

Problem

Recording prepaid rent and rent revenue collected in advance two ways

P3A-1 Smart Pages Pack'n Mail completed the following transactions during 2008:

Nov. 1	Paid $4,500 store rent covering the three-month period ending January 31, 2009.
Dec. 1	Collected $3,200 cash in advance from customers. The service revenue will be earned $800 monthly over the four-month period ending March 31, 2009.

Requirements

1. Journalize these entries by debiting an asset account for Prepaid Rent and by crediting a liability account for Unearned Service Revenue. Explanations are unnecessary.
2. Journalize the related adjustments at December 31, 2008.
3. Post the entries to the ledger accounts, and show their balances at December 31, 2008. Posting references are unnecessary.
4. Repeat requirements 1 through 3. This time, debit Rent Expense for the rent payment and credit Service Revenue for the collection of revenue in advance.
5. Compare the account balances in requirements 3 and 4. They should be equal.

Chapter 3: Demo Doc

Preparation of Adjusting Entries, Adjusted Trial Balance, and Financial Statements

Demo Doc: To make sure you understand this material, work through the following demonstration "demo doc" with detailed comments to help you see the concept within the framework of a worked-through problem.

Learning Objectives 3–5

Cloud Break Consulting, Inc., has the following information at June 30, 2008:

CLOUD BREAK CONSULTING, INC.
Unadjusted Trial Balance
June 30, 2008

	Balance	
Account Title	Debit	Credit
Cash	$131,000	
Accounts receivable	104,000	
Supplies	4,000	
Prepaid rent expense	27,000	
Land	45,000	
Building	300,000	
Accumulated depreciation—building		$155,000
Accounts payable		159,000
Unearned service revenue		40,000
Common stock		50,000
Retained earnings		52,000
Dividends	7,000	
Service revenue		450,000
Salary expense	255,000	
Rent expense	25,000	
Miscellaneous expense	8,000	
Total	$906,000	$906,000

Cloud Break must make adjusting entries for the following items:

a. Supplies on hand at year-end, $1,000.

b. Nine months of rent ($27,000) were paid in advance on April 1, 2008. No rent expense has been recorded since that date.

c. Depreciation expense has not been recorded on the building for the 2008 fiscal year. The building has a useful life of 25 years.

d. Employees work Monday through Friday. The weekly payroll is $5,000 and is paid every Friday. June 30, 2008, is a Thursday.

e. Service revenue of $15,000 must be accrued.

f. Cloud Break received $40,000 in advance for consulting services to be provided evenly from January 1, 2008 through August 31, 2008. None of the revenue from this client has been recorded.

Requirements

1. Open the ledger T-accounts with their unadjusted balances.

2. Journalize Cloud Break's adjusting entries at June 30, 2008, and post the entries to the T-accounts.

3. Total all of the T-accounts in the ledger.

4. Write the trial balance on a work sheet, enter the adjusting entries, and prepare an adjusted trial balance.

5. Prepare the income statement, the statement of retained earnings, and the balance sheet. Draw arrows linking the three financial statements.

Demo Doc Solution

Requirement 1

Open the ledger T-accounts with their unadjusted balances.

Part 1	Part 2	Part 3	Part 4	Part 5	Demo Doc Complete

Remember from Chapter 2 that opening a T-account means drawing a blank account that looks like a capital "T" and putting the account title across the top. To help find the accounts later, they are usually organized into assets, liabilities, stockholders' equity, revenue, and expenses (in that order). If the account has a starting balance, it ***must*** be put in on the correct side.

Remember that debits are always on the left side of the T-account and credits are always on the right side. This is true for *every* account.

The correct side to enter each account's starting balance is the side of *increase* in the account. This is because we expect all accounts to have a *positive* balance (that is, more increases than decreases).

For assets, an increase is a debit, so we would expect all assets to have a debit balance. For liabilities and stockholders' equity, an increase is a credit, so we would expect all of these accounts to have a credit balance. By the same reasoning, we expect revenues to have credit balances and expenses and dividends to have debit balances.

The unadjusted balances to be posted into the T-accounts are simply the amounts from the starting trial balance.

ASSETS

Cash	
Bal. 131,000	

Accounts Receivable	
104,000	

Supplies	
4,000	

Prepaid Rent	
Bal. 27,000	

Land	
Bal. 45,000	

Building	
Bal. 300,000	

Accumulated Depreciation—Building	
	Bal.155,000

LIABILITIES

Accounts Payable	
	Bal. 159,000

Unearned Service Revenue	
	Bal. 40,000

STOCKHOLDERS' EQUITY

Common Stock	
	Bal. 50,000

Retained Earnings	
	Bal. 52,000

Dividends	
Bal. 7,000	

REVENUE

Service Revenue	
	Bal. 450,000

EXPENSES

Salary Expense	
Bal. 255,000	

Rent Expense	
Bal. 25,000	

Miscellaneous Expense	
Bal. 8,000	

Requirement 2

Journalize Cloud Break's adjusting entries at June 30, 2008, and post the entries to the T-accounts.

Part 1	**Part 2**	Part 3	Part 4	Part 5	Demo Doc Complete

a. Supplies on hand at year-end, $1,000.

On June 30, 2008, the unadjusted balance in supplies was $4,000. However, a count shows that only $1,000 of supplies actually remains on hand. The supplies that are no longer there have been used. When assets/benefits are used, an expense is created.

Cloud Break's will need to make an adjusting journal entry to reflect the correct amount of supplies on the balance sheet.

Looking at the Supplies T-account:

Supplies			
Bal.	4,000		X
Bal.	1,000		

The supplies have decreased because they have been used up. The amount of the decrease is X. X = $4,000 − $1,000 = $3,000.

$3,000 of supplies expense must be recorded to show the value of supplies that have been used.

June 30	Supplies Expense ($4,000 – $1,000) (Expense,↑; debit)	3,000	
	Supplies (Asset,↓; credit)		3,000
	To record supplies expense.		

After posting, Supplies and Supplies Expense hold correct ending balances:

ASSETS

Supplies			
Bal	4,000	a.	3,000
Bal.	1,000		

EXPENSES

Supplies Expense			
a.	3,000		
Bal.	3,000		

b. Nine months of rent ($27,000) were paid in advance on April 1, 2008. No rent expense has been recorded since that date.

When something is prepaid, such as is common with rent or insurance, it is a *future* benefit (an asset) because the business is now entitled to receive goods or services for the terms of the prepayment. Once those goods or services are received (in this case, once Cloud Break has occupied the building being rented), this becomes a *past* benefit, and therefore an expense.

Cloud Break prepaid $27,000 for nine months of rent on April 1. This means that Cloud Break pays $27,000/9 = $3,000 a month for rent. At June 30, Prepaid Rent is adjusted for the amount of the asset that has been used up. Because Cloud Break has occupied the building being rented for three months, three months of the prepayment have been used. The amount of rent used is 3 × $3,000 = $9,000. Because that portion of the past benefit (asset) has expired, it becomes an expense (in this case, the adjustment transfers $9,000 from Prepaid Rent to Rent Expense).

This means that Rent Expense must be increased (a debit) and Prepaid Rent (an asset) must be decreased (a credit).

June 30	Rent Expense (Expense,↑; debit)	9,000	
	Prepaid Rent Expense (Asset,↓; credit)		9,000
	To record rent expense.		

ASSETS

Prepaid Rent Expense

Bal.	27,000		
		b.	9,000
Bal.	18,000		

EXPENSES

Rent Expense

Bal.	25,000	
b.	9,000	
Bal.	34,000	

c. Depreciation expense has not been recorded on the building for the 2008 fiscal year. The building has a useful life of 25 years.

Depreciation expense per year is calculated as:

$$\text{Depreciation expense per year} = \frac{\text{Original cost of asset}}{\text{Useful life of asset (in years)}}$$

The cost principle compels us to keep the original cost of a plant asset in that asset account. Because there is $300,000 in the building account, we know that this is the original cost of the building. We are told in the question that the building's useful life is 25 years.

Depreciation expense per year = $300,000/25 years = $12,000 per year

We will record depreciation of $12,000 in the adjusting journal entry.

The journal entry to record depreciation expense is *always* the same. It is only the *number* (dollar amount) in the entry that changes. There is always an increase to Depreciation Expense (a debit) and an increase to the contra-asset account of Accumulated Depreciation (a credit).

June 30	Depreciation Expense—Building (Expense,↑; debit)	12,000	
	Accumulated Depreciation—Building (Contra Asset,↑; credit)		12,000
	To record depreciation on building.		

ASSETS							EXPENSES	
ASSET			CONTRA ASSET					
Building			Accumulated Depreciation—Building				Depreciation Expense—Building	
Bal.	300,000		Bal.	155,000		c.	12,000	
			c.	12,000				
Bal.	300,000		Bal.	167,000		Bal.	12,000	

The book value of the building is its original cost (the amount in the Building T-account) minus the accumulated depreciation on the building.

Book value of plant assets:	
Building	$300,000
Less: Accumulated depreciation	(167,000)
Book value of the building	$133,000

d. Employees work Monday through Friday. The weekly payroll is $5,000 and is paid every Friday. June 30, 2008 is a Thursday.

Salary is an accrued expense. That is, it is a liability that incurs from an *expense* that hasn't been paid yet. Most employers pay their employees *after* the work has been done, so the work is a past benefit. So this expense (Salary Expense, in this case) grows until payday.

Cloud Break's employees are paid $5,000 for five days of work. That means they earn $5,000/5 = $1,000 per day. By the end of the day on Thursday, June 30, they have earned $1,000/day × 4 days = $4,000 of salary.

If the salaries have not been paid, then they are pay*able* (or in other words, they are *owed*) and must be recorded as some kind of payable account. You might be tempted to use accounts payable, but this account is usually reserved for *bills* received. But employees do not typically bill employers for their paychecks, they simply expect to be paid. The appropriate payable account for salaries is Salary Payable.

There is an increase to Salary Expense (a debit) and an increase to the liability Salary Payable (a credit) of $4,000.

June 30	Salary Expense (Expense, ↑; debit)	4,000	
	Salary Payable (Liability, ↑; credit)		4,000
	To accrue salary expense.		

EXPENSES				LIABILITIES	
Salary Expense				Salary Payable	
Bal.	255,000			d.	4,000
d.	4,000				
Bal.	259,000			Bal.	4,000

e. Service revenue of $15,000 must be accrued.

Accrued revenue is another way of saying "accounts receivable" (or receipt in the future). When *accrued* revenue is recorded, it means that accounts receivable is also recorded (that is, customers received goods or services from the business, but the business has not yet received the cash). The business is entitled to these receivables because the revenue has been earned.

Service Revenue must be increased by $15,000 (a credit) and the Accounts Receivable asset must be increased by $15,000 (a debit).

June 30	Accounts Receivable (Asset,↑; debit)	15,000	
	Service Revenue (Revenue,↑; credit)		15,000
	To accrue service revenue.		

ASSETS

Accounts Receivable

	Debit	Credit
	104,000	
e.	15,000	
Bal.	119,000	

REVENUES

Service Revenue

Debit		Credit
		450,000
	e.	15,000
	Bal.	465,000

f. Cloud Break received $40,000 in advance for consulting services to be provided evenly from January 1, 2008 through August 31, 2008. None of the revenue from this client has been recorded.

Cloud Break received cash in advance for work they had not yet performed for the client. By accepting the cash, Cloud Break also accepted the obligation to perform that work (or provide a refund if they did not). In accounting, an obligation is a liability. We call this liability "unearned revenue" because it *will* be revenue (after the work is performed) but it is not revenue *yet*.

The $40,000 paid in advance is still in the unearned revenue account. However, some of the revenue has been earned as of June 30. Six months of the earnings period have passed (January 1 through June 30), so six months worth of the revenue has been earned.

The entire revenue earnings period is eight months (January 1 through August 31), so the revenue earned per month is $40,000/8 = $5,000. The six months of revenue that have been earned are 6 × $5,000 = $30,000.

So Unearned Service Revenue, a liability, must be decreased by $30,000 (a debit). Because that portion of the revenue is now earned, it can be recorded as normal service revenue. Therefore, Service Revenue is increased by $30,000 (a credit).

June 30	Unearned Service Revenue (Liability, ↓; debit)	30,000	
	Service Revenue (Revenue,↑; credit)		30,000
	To record the earning of service revenue that was collected in advance.		

Essentially, the $30,000 has been shifted from "unearned revenue" to "earned" revenue.

LIABILITIES

Unearned Service Revenue

	Debit		Credit
		Bal.	40,000
f.	30,000		
		Bal.	10,000

REVENUES

Service Revenue

Debit		Credit
	Bal.	450,000
	e.	15,000
	f.	30,000
	Bal.	495,000

Now we will summarize all of the adjusting journal entries:

Ref.	Date	Accounts and Explanation	Debit	Credit
	2008			
a.	June 30	Supplies Expense ($4,000 – $3,000)	1,000	
		Supplies		1,000
		To record supplies used.		
b.	30	Rent Expense	9,000	
		Prepaid Rent		9,000
		To record rent expense.		
c.	30	Depreciation Expense—Building	12,000	
		Accumulated Depreciation—Building		12,000
		To record depreciation expense on building.		
d.	30	Salary Expense	4,000	
		Salary Payable		4,000
		To accrue salary expense.		
e.	30	Accounts Receivable	15,000	
		Service Revenue		15,000
		To accrue service revenue.		
f.	30	Unearned Service Revenue	30,000	
		Service Revenue		30,000
		To record the earning of service revenue that was collected in advance.		

Requirement 3

Total all of the T-accounts in the ledger.

Part 1	Part 2	**Part 3**	Part 4	Part 5	Demo Doc Complete

After posting all of these entries and totaling all of the T-accounts, we have:

ASSETS

Cash

Bal. 131,000	

Accounts Receivable

104,000	
e. 15,000	
Bal. 119,000	

Supplies

4,000	a. 3,000
Bal. 1,000	

Prepaid Rent

Bal. 27,000	
	b. 9,000
Bal. 18,000	

Land

Bal. 45,000	

Building

Bal. 300,000	

Accumulated Depreciation—Building

	155,000
	c. 12,000
	Bal. 167,000

LIABILITIES

Accounts Payable

	Bal. 159,000

Salary Payable

	d. 4,000
	Bal. 4,000

Unearned Service Revenue

f. 30,000	40,000
	Bal. 10,000

STOCKHOLDERS' EQUITY

Common Stock

	Bal. 50,000

Retained Earnings

	Bal. 52,000

Dividends

Bal. 7,000	

REVENUE

Service Revenue

	450,000
	e. 15,000
	f. 30,000
	Bal. 495,000

EXPENSES

Salary Expense

255,000	
d. 4,000	
Bal. 259,000	

Supplies Expense

a. 3,000	
Bal. 3,000	

Rent Expense

25,000	
b. 9,000	
Bal. 34,000	

Depreciation Expense—Building

c. 12,000	
Bal. 12,000	

Miscellaneous Expense

Bal. 8,000	

Requirement 4

Write the trial balance on a work sheet, enter the adjusting entries, and prepare an adjusted trial balance.

Part 1	Part 2	Part 3	**Part 4**	Part 5	Demo Doc Complete

First, we must copy the account titles and trial balance amounts directly from the trial balance (shown at the beginning of the question) into the Trial Balance section (columns). Place the amounts in the correct debit or credit column.

Next, we must record the adjusting journal entries in the correct debit or credit columns of the Adjustments section (columns) of the work sheet. Each entry should include a letter identifying the adjusting entry recorded.

Now calculate the new balances for each account by adding the debits and credits across. These should be the same balances that you calculated for the T-account in Requirement 3. Place these amounts into the Adjusted Trial Balance columns to give the adjusted account balances.

CLOUD BREAK CONSULTING, INC.
Preparation of Adjusted Trial Balance
June 30, 2008

	Trial Balance		Adjustments		Adjusted Trial Balance	
Account Title	Debit	Credit	Debit	Credit	Debit	Credit
Cash	131,000				131,000	
Accounts receivable	104,000		(e)15,000		119,000	
Supplies	4,000			(a) 3,000	1,000	
Prepaid rent expense	27,000			(b) 9,000	18,000	
Land	45,000				45,000	
Building	300,000				300,000	
Accumulated depreciation—building •		155,000		(c) 12,000		167,000
Accounts payable		159,000				159,000
Salary payable				(d) 4,000		4,000
Unearned service revenue		40,000	(f) 30,000			10,000
Common stock		50,000				50,000
Retained earnings		52,000				52,000
Dividends	7,000				7,000	
Service revenue		450,000		(e) 15,000		
				(f) 30,000		495,000
Salary expense	255,000		(d) 4,000		259,000	
Supplies expense			(a) 3,000		3,000	
Rent expense	25,000		(b) 9,000		34,000	
Depreciation expense—building			(c)12,000		12,000	
Miscellaneous expense	8,000				8,000	
Totals	906,000	906,000	73,000	73,000	937,000	937,000

You should be sure that the debit and credit columns equal before moving on to the next section.

Requirement 5

Prepare the income statement, the statement of retained earnings, and the balance sheet. Draw arrows linking the three financial statements.

Part 1	Part 2	Part 3	Part 4	**Part 5**	Demo Doc Complete

CLOUD BREAK CONSULTING, INC.
Income Statement
Year Ended June 30, 2008

Revenue:		
Service revenue		$495,000
Expenses:		
Salary expense	$259,000	
Rent expense	34,000	
Depreciation expense—building	12,000	
Supplies expense	3,000	
Miscellaneous expense	8,000	
Total expenses		316,000
Net income		$179,000

CLOUD BREAK CONSULTING, INC.
Statement of Retained Earnings
Year Ended June 30, 2008

Retained earnings, January 1, 2008	$ 52,000
Add: Net income	179,000
	231,000
Less: Dividends	(7,000)
Retained earnings, June 30, 2008	$224,000

CLOUD BREAK CONSULTING, INC.
Balance Sheet
June 30, 2008

Assets			**Liabilities**	
Cash		$131,000	Accounts payable	$159,000
Accounts receivable		119,000	Salary payable	4,000
Supplies		1,000	Unearned service revenue	10,000
Prepaid rent expense		18,000	Total liabilities	173,000
Land		45,000		
Building	$300,000		**Stockholders' Equity**	
Less: Accumulated			Common stock	50,000
depreciation	(167,000)	133,000	Retained earnings	224,000
			Total stockholders' equity	274,000
			Total liabilities and	
Total assets		$447,000	stockholders' equity	$447,000

Relationships Among the Financial Statements

The arrows in these statements show how the financial statements relate to each other. Follow the arrow that takes the ending balance of Retained Earnings to the balance sheet.

1. Net income from the income statements is reported as an increase to Retained Earnings on the statement of retained earnings. A net loss is recorded as a decrease to Retained Earnings.
2. Ending Retained Earnings from the statement of retained earnings is transferred to the balance sheet. The ending Retained Earnings is the final balancing amount for the balance sheet.

4 Completing the Accounting Cycle

Learning Objectives

1. Prepare an accounting work sheet
2. Use the work sheet
3. Close the revenue, expense, and dividend accounts
4. Classify assets and liabilities as current or long-term
5. Use the current ratio and the debt ratio to evaluate a company

What do football, baseball, basketball, and accounting have in common? They all start the first period with a score of zero.

Haig Sherman and Julie DeFilippo have operated Sherman Lawn Service and DeFilippo Catering, respectively, for a year. They took in revenue, incurred expenses, and earned net income during year 1. It's time to look ahead to the next period.

Should Sherman Lawn Service start year 2 with the net income that the business earned last year? No, Sherman must start from zero in order to measure its business performance in year 2. That requires Sherman to set his accounting scoreboard back to zero.

This process is called closing the books, and it's the last step in the accounting cycle. The **accounting cycle** is the process by which companies produce their financial statements.

Chapter 4 completes the accounting cycle by showing how to close the books. It begins with the adjusted trial balance, which you learned in Chapter 3. Here we extend to a more complete document called the accounting work sheet. Work sheets help by summarizing lots of data.

The Accounting Cycle

The accounting cycle starts with the beginning asset, liability, and owner's equity account balances left over from the preceding period. Exhibit 4-1 outlines the complete accounting cycle of Cookie Lapp Travel Design and every other business. Start with item 1 and move clockwise.

EXHIBIT 4-1 **The Accounting Cycle**

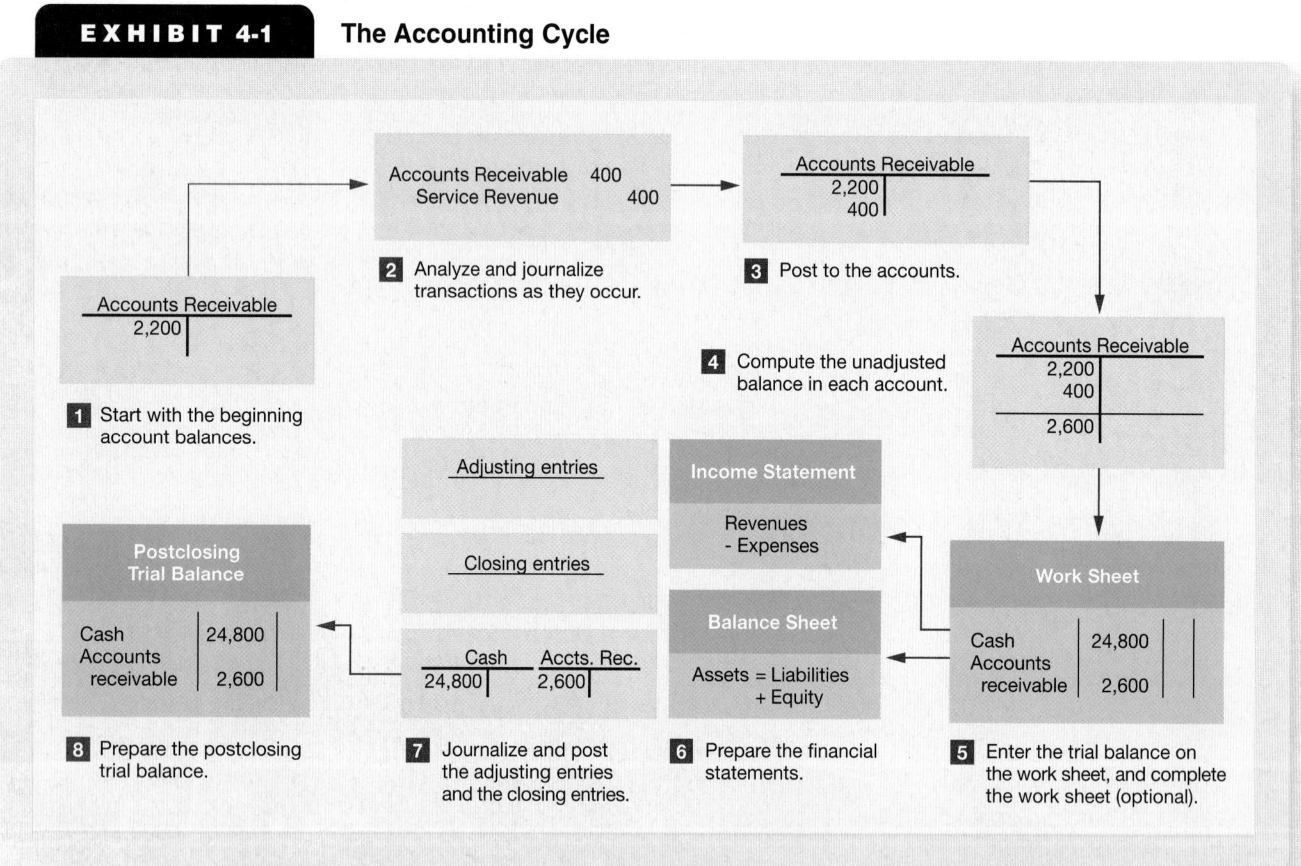

Accounting takes place at two different times:

- During the period—Journalizing transactions
  Posting to the accounts
- End of the period—Adjusting the accounts
  Closing the accounts
  Preparing the financial statements

The end-of-period work also readies the accounts for the next period. In Chapters 3 and 4, we cover the end-of-period accounting for a service business such as Sherman Lawn Service and Cookie Lapp Travel Design. Chapter 5 shows how a merchandising entity such as Wal-Mart or McDonald's adjusts and closes its books.

The Work Sheet

1 Prepare an accounting work sheet

Accountants often use a **work sheet**—a document with several columns—to summarize data for the financial statements. The work sheet is neither a journal, a ledger, nor a financial statement. It is merely a summary device that helps identify the accounts needing adjustment. An Excel spreadsheet works well for an accounting work sheet.

Exhibits 4-2 through 4-6 illustrate the development of a typical work sheet for Cookie Lapp Travel Design. The heading at the top displays the:

- Name of the business (Cookie Lapp Travel Design)
- Title of the document (Accounting Work Sheet)
- Period covered by the work sheet (Month ended April 30, 2008)

A step-by-step description of the work sheet follows, with all amounts given in Exhibits 4-2 through 4-6. Simply turn the acetate pages to follow from exhibit to exhibit.

Exhibit 4-2

1. **Enter the account titles and their unadjusted balances in the Trial Balance columns of the work sheet, and total the amounts.** The data come from the ledger accounts before any adjustments. Accounts are listed in proper order (Cash first, Accounts Receivable second, and so on). Total debits must equal total credits.

   An account with a zero balance (for example, Depreciation Expense) needs to be adjusted.

Exhibit 4-3

2. **Enter the adjusting entries in the Adjustments columns, and total the amounts.** Exhibit 4-3 includes the April adjusting entries that we made in Chapter 3.

   We can identify the accounts needing adjustment from the trial balance. Cash needs no adjustment because all cash transactions are recorded during the period. Consequently, Cash's balance is up-to-date.

   Accounts Receivable comes next. Has Cookie Lapp earned any revenue that she hasn't recorded? The answer is yes. At April 30, Lapp has earned $400 and will receive the cash later. For service revenue earned but not collected, Lapp debits Accounts Receivable and credits Service Revenue on the work sheet. A letter links the debit and the credit of each adjustment.

   By moving down the trial balance, Lapp identifies other accounts needing adjustment, such as Supplies. The business has used supplies during April, so Lapp debits Supplies Expense and credits Supplies. The other adjustments are analyzed and entered on the work sheet as we did in Chapter 3. After the adjustments are entered on the work sheet, the amount columns are totaled. Total debits must equal total credits.

Exhibit 4-4

3. **Compute each account's adjusted balance by combining the trial balance and adjustment figures. Enter each account's adjusted amount in the Adjusted Trial Balance columns.** Exhibit 4-4 shows the work sheet with the adjusted trial balance completed. For example, Cash is up-to-date, so it receives no adjustment. Accounts Receivable's adjusted balance of $2,600 is computed by adding the unadjusted amount of $2,200 to the $400 adjustment. For Supplies we subtract the $100 credit adjustment from the unadjusted balance of $700. An account may receive more than one adjustment, as for Service Revenue. On the adjusted trial balance, total debits must equal total credits.

Exhibit 4-5

4. **Extend (that is, copy) the asset, liability, and stockholders' equity amounts from the Adjusted Trial Balance to the Balance Sheet columns. Copy the revenue and expense amounts to the Income Statement columns. Total the statement columns.** Each account's balance should appear in only one column, as shown in Exhibit 4-5.

EXHIBIT 4-2 Trial Balance

COOKIE LAPP TRAVEL DESIGN, INC.
Accounting Work Sheet
Month Ended April 30, 2008

	Trial Balance		Adjustments		Adjusted Trial Balance		Income Statement		Balance Sheet	
Account Title	Dr.	Cr.	Dr.	Cr.	Dr.	Cr.	Dr.	Cr.	Dr.	Cr.
Cash	24,800									
Accounts receivable	2,200									
Supplies	700									
Prepaid rent	3,000									
Furniture	18,000									
Accumulated depreciation										
Accounts payable		13,000								
Salary payable										
Unearned service revenue		600								
Common stock		30,000								
Retained earnings		2,600*								
Dividends	3,200									
Service revenue		7,000								
Rent expense										
Salary expense	900									
Supplies expense										
Depreciation expense										
Utilities expense	400									
	53,200	53,200								
Net income										

*Assumed amount.

Write the account titles and their unadjusted balances in the Trial Balance columns of the work sheet. Total the amounts.

First, total the *income statement columns,* as follows:

Income Statement

■ Debits (Dr.) ⟶	Total expenses = $3,600	Difference = $4,000, a net income because total credits (revenues) exceed total debits (expenses)
■ Credits (Cr.) ⟶	Total revenues = $7,600	

Then total the *balance sheet* columns:

Balance Sheet

■ Debits (Dr.) ⟶	Total assets and dividends = $51,200	Difference = $4,000, a net income because total debits are greater
■ Credits (Cr.) ⟶	Total liabilities, stockholders' equity, and accumulated depreciation = $47,200	

Exhibit 4-6

5. **On the income statement, compute net income or net loss as total revenues minus total expenses. Enter net income as the balancing amount on the income statement. Also enter net income as the balancing amount on the balance sheet. Then total the financial statement columns.** Exhibit 4-6 presents the completed work sheet.

Revenue (total **credits** on the income statement)	$7,600
Less: Expenses (total **debits** on the income statement)	(3,600)
Net income	$4,000

Net Income

Net income of $4,000 is entered as a "plug figure" in the debit column of the income statement. This brings total debits up to total credits on the income statement. Net income is also entered as a "plug figure" in the credit column of the balance sheet. Net income brings the balance sheet into balance.

Net Loss

If expenses exceed revenues, the result is a net loss. In that event, print Net Loss on the work sheet. The net loss amount should be entered in the *credit* column of the income statement (to balance out) and in the *debit* column of the balance sheet (to balance out). After completion, total debits should equal total credits in the Income Statement columns and in the Balance Sheet columns.

Now practice what you've learned by working Summary Problem 1.

Summary Problem 1

The trial balance of Clay Employment Services, Inc., at December 31, 2009, follows.

CLAY EMPLOYMENT SERVICES, INC. Trial Balance December 31, 2009		
	Balance	
Account Title	Debit	Credit
Cash	$ 6,000	
Accounts receivable	5,000	
Supplies	1,000	
Furniture	10,000	
Accumulated depreciation—furniture		$ 4,000
Building	50,000	
Accumulated depreciation—building		30,000
Accounts payable		2,000
Salary payable		
Unearned service revenue		8,000
Common stock		10,000
Retained earnings		2,000
Dividends	25,000	
Service revenue		60,000
Salary expense	16,000	
Supplies expense		
Depreciation expense—furniture		
Depreciation expense—building		
Miscellaneous expense	3,000	
Total	$116,000	$116,000

Data needed for the adjusting entries include:

a. Supplies on hand at year-end, $200.

b. Depreciation on furniture, $2,000.

c. Depreciation on building, $1,000.

d. Salaries owed but not yet paid, $500.

e. Accrued service revenue, $1,300.

f. $3,000 of the unearned service revenue was earned during 2009.

Requirements

Prepare the accounting work sheet of Clay Employment Services, Inc., for the year ended December 31, 2009. Key each adjusting entry by the letter corresponding to the data given.

Solution

CLAY EMPLOYMENT SERVICES, INC.
Work Sheet
Year Ended December 31, 2009

	Trial Balance		Adjustments		Adjusted Trial Balance		Income Statement		Balance Sheet	
Account Title	Dr.	Cr.	Dr.	Cr.	Dr.	Cr.	Dr.	Cr.	Dr.	Cr.
Cash	6,000				6,000				6,000	
Accounts receivable	5,000		(e) 1,300		6,300				6,300	
Supplies	1,000			(a) 800	200				200	
Furniture	10,000				10,000				10,000	
Accumulated depreciation—furniture		4,000		(b) 2,000		6,000				6,000
Building	50,000				50,000				50,000	
Accumulated depreciation—building		30,000		(c) 1,000		31,000				31,000
Accounts payable		2,000				2,000				2,000
Salary payable				(d) 500		500				500
Unearned service revenue		8,000	(f) 3,000			5,000				5,000
Common stock		10,000				10,000				10,000
Retained earnings		2,000				2,000				2,000
Dividends	25,000				25,000				25,000	
Service revenue		60,000		(e) 1,300						
				(f) 3,000		64,300		64,300		
Salary expense	16,000		(d) 500		16,500		16,500			
Supplies expense			(a) 800		800		800			
Depreciation expense—furniture			(b) 2,000		2,000		2,000			
Depreciation expense—building			(c) 1,000		1,000		1,000			
Miscellaneous expense	3,000				3,000		3,000			
	116,000	116,000	8,600	8,600	120,800	120,800	23,300	64,300	97,500	56,500
Net income							41,000			41,000
							64,300	64,300	97,500	97,500

Completing the Accounting Cycle

2 Use the work sheet

The work sheet helps accountants prepare the financial statements, make the adjusting entries, and close the accounts. First, let's prepare the financial statements. We return to the running example of Cookie Lapp Travel Design, whose financial statements are given in Exhibit 4-7.

EXHIBIT 4-7 April Financial Statements of Cookie Lapp Travel Design, Inc.

COOKIE LAPP TRAVEL DESIGN, INC.
Income Statement
Month Ended April 30, 2008

Revenue:		
Service revenue		$7,600
Expenses:		
Salary expense	$1,800	
Rent expense	1,000	
Utilities expense	400	
Depreciation expense	300	
Supplies expense	100	
Total expensees		3,600
Net income		$4,000

COOKIE LAPP TRAVEL DESIGN, INC.
Statement of Retained Earnings
Month Ended April 30, 2008

Retained earnings, April 1, 2008	$2,600
Add: Net income	4,000
	6,600
Less: Dividends	(3,200)
Retained earnings, April 30, 2008	$3,400

COOKIE LAPP TRAVEL DESIGN, INC.
Balance Sheet
April 30, 2008

Assets			Liabilities	
Cash		$24,800	Accounts payable	$13,000
Accounts receivable		2,600	Salary payable	900
Supplies		600	Unearned service revenue	400
Prepaid rent		2,000	Total liabilities	14,300
Furniture	$18,000			
Less: Accumulated			**Stockholders' Equity**	
depreciation	(300)	17,700	Common stock	30,000
			Retained earnings	3,400
			Total stockholders' equity	33,400
			Total liabilities and	
Total assets		$47,700	stockholders' equity	$47,700

Preparing the Financial Statements

The work sheet shows the amount of net income or net loss for the period, but we still must prepare the financial statements. Exhibit 4-7 shows the April financial statements for Cookie Lapp Travel Design (based on data from the work sheet in Exhibit 4-6). We can prepare Lapp's financial statements immediately after completing the work sheet.

Recording the Adjusting Entries

Adjusting the accounts requires journalizing entries and posting to the accounts. The adjustments should be journalized after they are entered on the work sheet. Panel A of Exhibit 4-8 repeats Cookie Lapp's adjusting entries that we journalized in Chapter 3. Panel B shows the revenue and the expense accounts after all adjustments have been posted. Only the revenue and expense accounts are presented here to focus on the closing process. *Adj.* denotes an amount posted from an adjusting entry.

EXHIBIT 4-8 Journalizing and Posting the Adjusting Entries

PANEL A—Journalizing:

Adjusting Entries

Date	Accounts	Debit	Credit
Apr. 30	Accounts Receivable	400	
	Service Revenue		400
30	Supplies Expense	100	
	Supplies		100
30	Rent Expense	1,000	
	Prepaid Rent		1,000
30	Depreciation Expense	300	
	Accumulated Depreciation		300
30	Salary Expense	900	
	Salary Payable		900
30	Unearned Service Revenue	200	
	Service Revenue		200

PANEL B—Posting the Adjustments to the Revenue and Expense Accounts:

REVENUE

Service Revenue

Debit	Credit
	7,000
	Adj. 400
	Adj. 200
	Bal. 7,600

EXPENSES

Rent Expense

Debit	Credit
Adj. 1,000	
Bal. 1,000	

Salary Expense

Debit	Credit
900	
Adj. 900	
Bal. 1,800	

Supplies Expense

Debit	Credit
Adj. 100	
Bal. 100	

Depreciation Expense

Debit	Credit
Adj. 300	
Bal. 300	

Utilities Expense

Debit	Credit
400	
Bal. 400	

Accountants can use the work sheet to prepare monthly or quarterly statements without journalizing and posting the adjusting entries. Many companies journalize and post the adjusting entries (as in Exhibit 4-8) only at the end of the year.

Now we are ready to move to the last step—closing the accounts.

Closing the Accounts

3 Close the revenue, expense, and dividends accounts

Closing the accounts occurs at the end of the period. Closing gets the accounts ready for the next period and consists of journalizing and posting the closing entries. The closing process zeroes out all the revenues and all the expenses in order to measure each period's net income separately from all other periods.

Recall that the income statement reports net income for a specific period. For example, Cookie Lapp's net income for 2008 relates exclusively to 2008. At December 31, 2008, Lapp closes her revenue and expense accounts for the year. For this reason, revenues and expenses are called **temporary accounts**. For example, Lapp's balance of Service Revenue at April 30, 2008, is $7,600. This balance relates exclusively to April and must be zeroed out before Lapp records revenue for May.

The Dividends account is also temporary because it measures the dividends for only one period. The Dividends account is also closed at the end of the period.

To better understand the closing process, contrast the temporary accounts with the **permanent accounts**—the assets, liabilities, Common Stock, and Retained Earnings. These accounts are *not* closed at the end of the period because their balances are not used to measure income.

Consider Cash, Accounts Receivable, Accounts Payable, and Retained Earnings. These accounts carry over to the next period. For example, the Cash balance at December 31, 2008, becomes the beginning balance for 2009. Accounts Receivable at December 31, 2008, becomes the beginning balance for 2009. The same is true for all the other assets, all the liabilities, Common Stock and Retained Earnings.

Closing entries transfer the revenue, expense, and Dividends balances to the Retained Earnings account.

As an intermediate step the revenues and the expenses are transferred first to an account titled **Income Summary**. This temporary account collects the sum of all the expenses (a debit) and the sum of all the revenues (a credit). The Income Summary account is like a "holding tank" that shows the amount of net income or net loss of the current period. Its balance—net income or net loss—is then transferred (closed) to Retained Earnings. Exhibit 4-9 summarizes the closing process.

EXHIBIT 4-9 The Closing Process

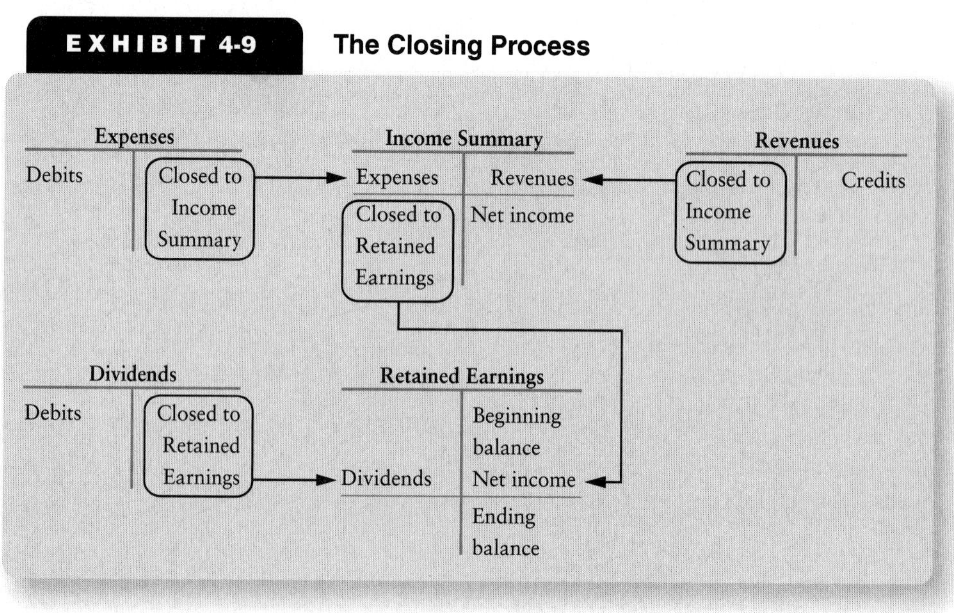

Start with Revenues at the far right and Expenses at the left. Then work toward the middle and down. Retained Earnings is the final account in the closing process.

Closing a Net Income

The steps in closing the books follow for a net income (the circled numbers are keyed to Exhibit 4-10).

1 Debit each *revenue* account for the amount of its credit balance. Credit Income Summary for the total of the revenues. This closing entry transfers total revenues to the *credit* side of Income Summary.

EXHIBIT 4-10 **Journalizing and Posting the Closing Entries**

PANEL A—Journalizing:

Closing Entries

	Date	Accounts	Debit	Credit
1	Apr. 30	Service Revenue	7,600	
		Income Summary		7,600
2	30	Income Summary	3,600	
		Rent Expense		1,000
		Salary Expense		1,800
		Supplies Expense		100
		Depreciation Expense		300
		Utilities Expense		400
3	30	Income Summary ($7,600 – $3,600)	4,000	
		Retained Earnings		4,000
4	30	Retained Earnings	3,200	
		Dividends		3,200

PANEL B—Posting:

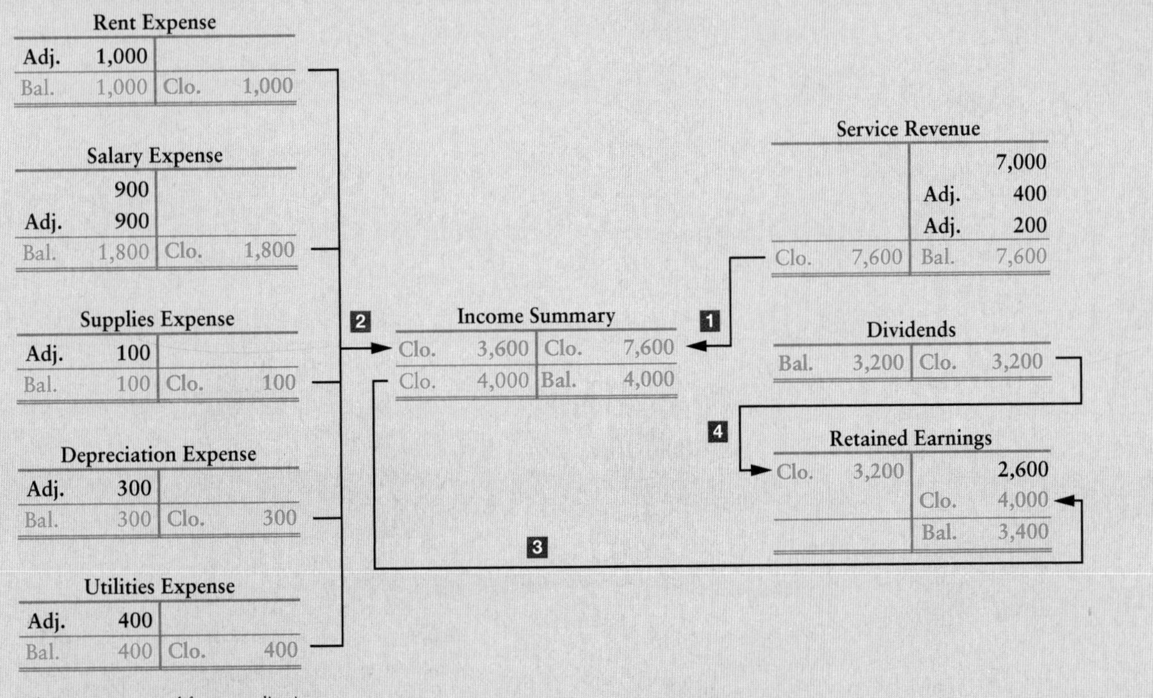

Adj. = Amount posted from an adjusting entry
Clo. = Amount posted from a closing entry
Bal. = Balance

2 Credit each *expense* account for the amount of its debit balance. Debit Income Summary for the total of the expenses. This closing entry transfers total expenses to the *debit* side of Income Summary.

3 The Income Summary account now holds the net income of the period, but only for a moment. To close net income, we debit Income Summary for the amount of its *credit balance,* and credit the Retained Earnings account. This closing entry transfers net income to Retained Earnings.

4 Credit the *Dividends* account for the amount of its debit balance. Debit the Retained Earnings account. This entry transfers the dividends to the *debit* side of Retained Earnings.

These steps are best illustrated with an example. Suppose Cookie Lapp Travel Design closes its books at the end of April. Exhibit 4-10 shows the complete closing process for Lapp's travel agency. Panel A gives the closing entries, and Panel B shows the accounts after posting.

After the closing entries, Retained Earnings ends with a balance of $3,400. Trace this balance to the statement of retained earnings and then to the balance sheet in Exhibit 4-7.

Closing a Net Loss

What would the closing entries be if Lapp's travel agency had suffered a net *loss* during April? Suppose expenses totaled $8,100 and revenues remained $7,600. In that case, the business suffered a net loss of $500 for April. The loss shows up as a debit balance in Income Summary, as follows:

Income Summary			
Expenses	8,100	Revenue	7,600
Net loss	500		

Closing entry **3** would then credit Income Summary for $500 and debit Retained Earnings, as follows:

3	Apr. 30	Retained Earnings	500	
		Income Summary		500

Then Income Summary is closed out and Retained Earnings has its ending balance, as follows:

Income Summary			
Expenses	8,100	Revenue	7,600
Net loss	500	Clo.	500

Retained Earnings			
Clo.	500		2,600
		Bal.	2,100

Finally, the Dividends balance would be closed to Retained Earnings, as before. Double underlines mean the account has a zero balance.

Postclosing Trial Balance

The accounting cycle can end with a **postclosing trial balance** (Exhibit 4-11). This optional step lists the accounts and their adjusted balances after closing.

Only assets, liabilities, Common Stock, and Retained Earnings accounts appear on the postclosing trial balance. No temporary accounts—revenues, expenses, or Dividends—are included because they've been closed. The ledger is up-to-date and ready for the next period.

EXHIBIT 4-11 Postclosing Trial Balance

COOKIE LAPP TRAVEL DESIGN, INC.
Postclosing Trial Balance
April 30, 2008

Cash	$24,800	
Accounts receivable	2,600	
Supplies	600	
Prepaid rent	2,000	
Furniture	18,000	
Accumulated depreciation		$ 300
Accounts payable		13,000
Salary payable		900
Unearned service revenue		400
Common stock		30,000
Retained earnings		3,400
Total	$48,000	$48,000

Reversing entries are special journal entries that key off the adjustments at the end of the period. Reversing entries ease the accounting of the next period. They are optional, and we cover them in Appendix 4A at the end of this chapter.

Classifying Assets and Liabilities

Classify assets and liabilities as current or long-term

Assets and liabilities are classified as either *current* or *long-term* to show their relative liquidity. **Liquidity** measures closeness to cash, and cash is the most liquid asset. Accounts receivable are relatively liquid because receivables are collected quickly. Supplies are less liquid, and furniture and buildings are even less liquid because of their long lives. A classified balance sheet lists assets in the order of their liquidity.

Assets

Current Assets

Current assets will be converted to cash, sold, or used up during the next 12 months or within the business's operating cycle if the cycle is longer than a year. The **operating cycle** is the time span when:

1. Cash is used to acquire goods and services.
2. These goods and services are sold to customers.
3. The business collects cash from customers.

For most businesses the operating cycle is a few months. Cash, Accounts Receivable, Supplies, and Prepaid Expenses are current assets. Merchandising entities such as

Home Depot, Sears, and Coca-Cola have another current asset: inventory. Inventory shows the cost of the goods the company holds for sale to customers.

Long-Term Assets

Long-term assets are all the assets other than current assets. One category of long-term assets is **plant assets** (also called **fixed assets** or property, plant, and equipment). Land, Buildings, Furniture, and Equipment are plant assets. Of these, Cookie Lapp Travel Design has only Furniture.

Other categories of long-term assets include Long-Term Investments and Other Assets (a catchall category). We discuss these categories in later chapters.

Liabilities

Owners need to know when they must pay each liability. Liabilities that are payable immediately create pressure, so the balance sheet lists liabilities in the order they must be paid. Balance sheets report two liability categories: *current liabilities* and *long-term liabilities.*

Current Liabilities

Current liabilities must be paid with cash or with goods and services within one year or within the entity's operating cycle if the cycle is longer than a year. Accounts Payable, Notes Payable due within one year, Salary Payable, Interest Payable, and Unearned Revenue are current liabilities.

Long-Term Liabilities

All liabilities that are not current are classified as **long-term liabilities.** Many notes payable are long-term. Some notes are payable in installments, with the first installment due within one year, the second due the second year, and so on. The first installment is a current liability, and the remaining amounts are long-term. A $100,000 note payable to be paid $10,000 per year over 10 years would include:

- A current liability of $10,000 for next year's payment, and
- A long-term liability of $90,000.

The Classified Balance Sheet

Thus far we have presented the *unclassified* balance sheet of Cookie Lapp Travel Design. We are now ready for the balance sheet that's actually used in practice—called a classified balance sheet. Exhibit 4-12 presents Cookie Lapp Travel Design's classified balance sheet.

Cookie Lapp Travel Design classifies each asset and each liability as current or long-term. The business could have labeled plant assets as *fixed assets.*

Balance Sheet Forms

The balance sheet of Cookie Lapp Travel Design in Exhibit 4-13 lists the assets at the top and the liabilities and stockholders' equity below. This arrangement is known as the *report form.* Lapp's balance sheet in Exhibit 4-12 lists the assets at the left and the liabilities and the equity at the right. That arrangement is known as the *account form.* Either form is acceptable; the report form is more popular.

EXHIBIT 4-12 Classified Balance Sheet in Account Form

COOKIE LAPP TRAVEL DESIGN, INC.
Balance Sheet
April 30, 2008

Assets			Liabilities	
Current assets:			Current liabilities:	
Cash		$24,800	Accounts payable	$13,000
Accounts receivable		2,600	Salary payable	900
Supplies		600	Unearned service revenue	400
Prepaid rent		2,000	Total current liabilities	14,300
Total current assets		30,000	Long-term liabilities (None)	0
Plant assets:			Total liabilities	14,300
Furniture	$18,000			
Less: Accumulated			**Stockholders' Equity**	
depreciation	(300)	17,700	Common stock	30,000
			Retained earnings	3,400
			Total stockholders' equity	33,400
			Total liabilities and	
Total assets		$47,700	stockholders' equity	$47,700

EXHIBIT 4-13 Classified Balance Sheet in Report Form

COOKIE LAPP TRAVEL DESIGN, INC.
Balance Sheet
April 30, 2008

Assets		
Current assets:		
Cash		$24,800
Accounts receivable		2,600
Supplies		600
Prepaid rent		2,000
Total current assets		30,000
Plant assets:		
Furniture	$18,000	
Less: Accumulated		
depreciation	(300)	17,700
Total assets		$47,700
Liabilities		
Current liabilities:		
Accounts payable		$13,000
Salary payable		900
Unearned service revenue		400
Total current liabilities		14,300
Long-term liabilities (None)		0
Stockholders' Equity		
Common stock		30,000
Retained earnings		3,400
Total stockholders' equity		33,400
Total liabilities and stockholders' equity		$47,700

Accounting Ratios

5 Use the current ratio and the debt ratio to evaluate a company

Accounting is designed to provide information for decision making by business owners, managers, and lenders. A bank considering lending money to Cookie Lapp must predict whether she can repay the loan. If Lapp already has a lot of debt, repayment is less certain than if she doesn't owe much money. To measure Cookie Lapp's financial position, decision makers use ratios that they compute from the company's financial statements. Two of the most widely used decision aids in business are the current ratio and the debt ratio.

Current Ratio

The **current ratio** measures a company's ability to pay its current liabilities. This ratio is computed as follows:

$$\text{Current ratio} = \frac{\text{Total current assets}}{\text{Total current liabilities}}$$

A company prefers to have a high current ratio because that means it has plenty of current assets to pay current liabilities. An increasing current ratio indicates improvement in ability to pay current debts. A decreasing current ratio signals deterioration in the ability to pay current liabilities.

A RULE OF THUMB A strong current ratio is 1.50, which indicates that the company has $1.50 in current assets for every $1.00 in current liabilities. A current ratio of 1.00 is considered low and somewhat risky.

Debt Ratio

A second decision aid is the **debt ratio**, which measures overall ability to pay debts. The debt ratio is computed as follows:

$$\text{Debt ratio} = \frac{\text{Total liabilities}}{\text{Total assets}}$$

The debt ratio indicates the proportion of a company's assets that are financed with debt. A *low* debt ratio is safer than a high debt ratio. Why? Because a company with low liabilities has low required payments. This company is unlikely to get into financial difficulty.

A RULE OF THUMB A debt ratio below 0.60, or 60%, is considered safe for most businesses. A debt ratio above 0.80, or 80%, borders on high risk.

Now study the Decision Guidelines feature, which summarizes what you have learned in this chapter.

Decision Guidelines

COMPLETING THE ACCOUNTING CYCLE

Suppose you own Sherman Lawn Service, DeFilippo Catering, or Cookie Lapp Travel Design. How can you measure the success of your business? The Decision Guidelines describe the accounting process you will use to provide the information for your decisions.

Decision	Guidelines
What document summarizes the effects of all the entity's transactions and adjustments throughout the period?	Accountant's *work sheet* with columns for • Trial balance • Adjustments • Adjusted trial balance • Income statement • Balance sheet
What is the last *major* step in the accounting cycle?	*Closing entries for the temporary accounts:* • Revenues } Income statement accounts • Expenses } • Dividends
Why close out the revenues, expenses, and dividends accounts?	Because these *temporary accounts* have balances that relate only to one accounting period and *do not* carry over to the next period.
Which accounts do *not* get closed out?	*Permanent (balance sheet) accounts:* • Assets • Liabilities • Common Stock and Retained Earnings The balances of these accounts *do* carry over to the next period.
How do businesses classify their assets and liabilities for reporting on the balance sheet?	*Current* (within one year or the entity's operating cycle if longer than a year), or *Long-term* (not current)
How do Haig Sherman, Julie DeFilippo, and Cookie Lapp evaluate their companies?	There are many ways, such as the company's net income (or net loss) on the income statement and the trend of net income from year to year. Another way to evaluate a company is based on the company's *financial ratios*. Two key ratios: $\text{Current ratio} = \frac{\text{Total current assets}}{\text{Total current liabilities}}$ The *current ratio* measures the ability to pay current liabilities with current assets. $\text{Debt ratio} = \frac{\text{Total liabilities}}{\text{Total assets}}$ The *debt ratio* measures the overall ability to pay liabilities. The debt ratio shows the proportion of the entity's assets that are financed with debt.

Summary Problem 2

Refer to the data in Problem 1 (Clay Employment Services, page 204–205).

Requirements

1. Journalize and post the adjusting entries. (Before posting to the accounts, enter into each account its balance as shown in the trial balance. For example, enter the $5,000 balance in the Accounts Receivable account before posting its adjusting entry.) Key adjusting entries by *letter*, as shown in the work sheet solution to Summary Problem 1. You can take the adjusting entries straight from the work sheet on page 204.
2. Journalize and post the closing entries. (Each account should carry its balance as shown in the adjusted trial balance.) To distinguish closing entries from adjusting entries, key the closing entries by *number*. Draw arrows to illustrate the flow of data, as shown in Exhibit 4-10. Indicate the balance of the Retained Earnings account after the closing entries are posted.
3. Prepare the income statement for the year ended December 31, 2009. List Miscellaneous Expense last among the expenses, a common practice.
4. Prepare the statement of retained earnings for the year ended December 31, 2009. Draw an arrow linking the income statement to the statement of retained earnings.
5. Prepare the classified balance sheet at December 31, 2009. Use the report form. All liabilities are current. Draw an arrow linking the statement of retained earnings to the balance sheet.

Solution

Requirement 1

Adjusting Entries

	Date	Accounts	Debit	Credit
a.	Dec. 31	Supplies Expense	800	
		Supplies		800
b.	31	Depreciation Expense—Furniture	2,000	
		Accumulated Depreciation—Furniture		2,000
c.	31	Depreciation Expense—Building	1,000	
		Accumulated Depreciation—Building		1,000
d.	31	Salary Expense	500	
		Salary Payable		500
e.	31	Accounts Receivable	1,300	
		Service Revenue		1,300
f.	31	Unearned Service Revenue	3,000	
		Service Revenue		3,000

Accounts Receivable

Debit	Credit
5,000	
(e) 1,300	
Bal. 6,300	

Supplies

Debit	Credit
1,000	(a) 800
Bal. 200	

Accumulated Depreciation—Furniture

Debit	Credit
	4,000
	(b) 2,000
	Bal. 6,000

Accumulated Depreciation—Building

Debit	Credit
	30,000
	(c) 1,000
	Bal. 31,000

Salary Payable

Debit	Credit
	(d) 500
	Bal. 500

Unearned Service Revenue

Debit	Credit
(f) 3,000	8,000
	Bal. 5,000

Service Revenue

Debit	Credit
	60,000
	(e) 1,300
	(f) 3,000
	Bal. 64,300

Salary Expense

Debit	Credit
16,000	
(d) 500	
Bal. 16,500	

Supplies Expense

Debit	Credit
(a) 800	
Bal. 800	

Depreciation Expense—Furniture

Debit	Credit
(b) 2,000	
Bal. 2,000	

Depreciation Expense—Building

Debit	Credit
(c) 1,000	
Bal. 1,000	

Requirement 2

		Closing Entries		
1.	Dec. 31	Service Revenue	64,300	
		Income Summary		64,300
2.	31	Income Summary	23,300	
		Salary Expense		16,500
		Supplies Expense		800
		Accumulated Depreciation—Furniture		2,000
		Accumulated Depreciation—Building		1,000
		Miscellaneous Expense		3,000
3.	31	Income Summary ($64,300 – $23,300)	41,000	
		Retained Earnings		41,000
4.	31	Retained Earnings	25,000	
		Dividends		25,000

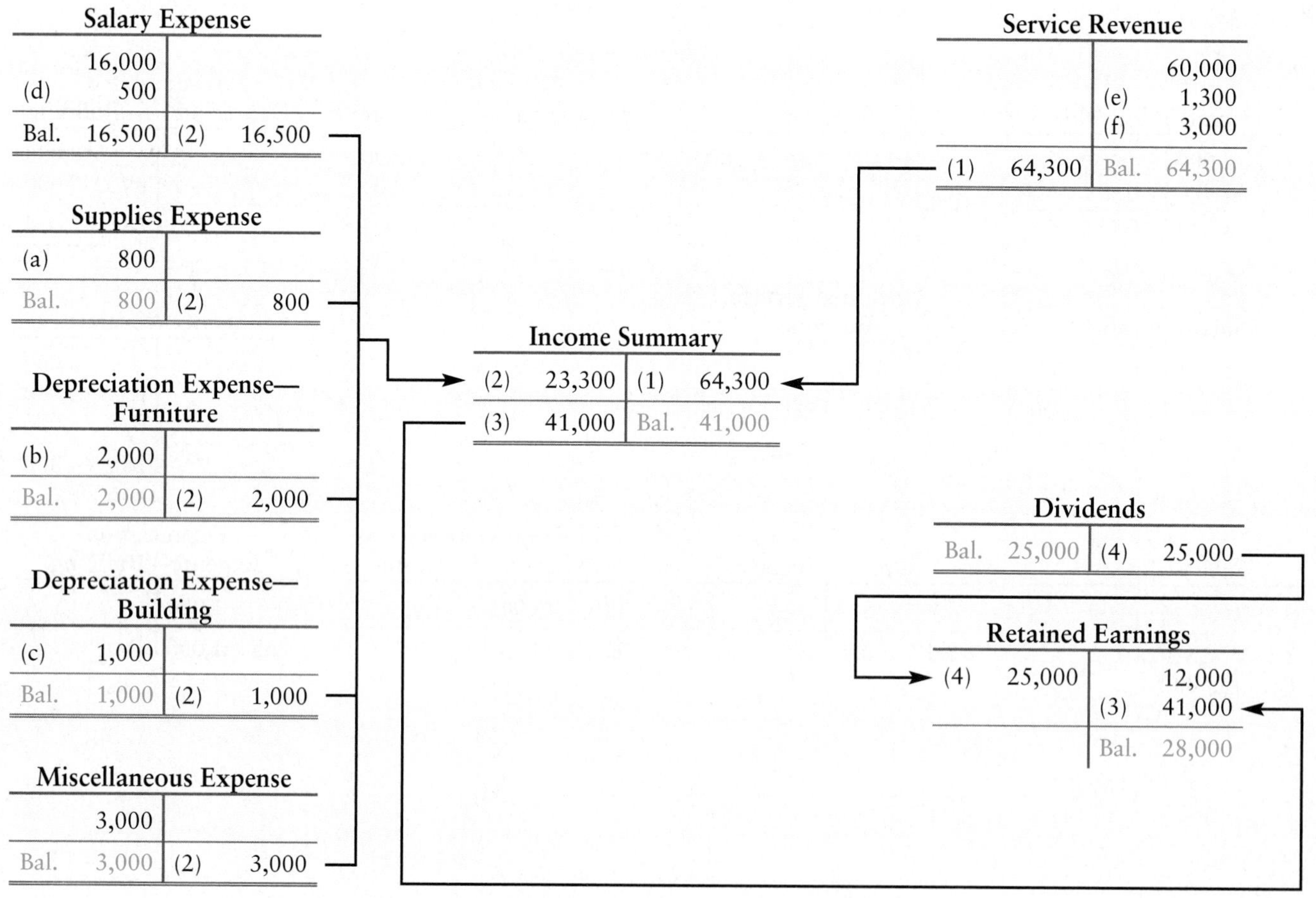

Requirement 3

CLAY EMPLOYMENT SERVICES, INC. Income Statement Year Ended December 31, 2009		
Revenue:		
Service revenue		$64,300
Expenses:		
Salary expense	$16,500	
Depreciation expense—furniture	2,000	
Depreciation expense—building	1,000	
Supplies expense	800	
Miscellaneous expense	3,000	
Total expenses		23,300
Net income		$41,000

Requirement 4

CLAY EMPLOYMENT SERVICES, INC. Statement of Retained Earnings Year Ended December 31, 2009	
Retained earnings, January 1, 2009	$ 2,000
Add: Net income	41,000
	43,000
Less: Dividends	(25,000)
Retained earnings, December 31, 2009	$18,000

Requirement 5

CLAY EMPLOYMENT SERVICES, INC. Balance Sheet December 31, 2009				
Assets			**Liabilities**	
Current assets:			Current liabilities:	
Cash		$ 6,000	Accounts payable	$ 2,000
Accounts receivable		6,300	Salary payable	500
Supplies		200	Unearned service	
Total current assets		12,500	revenue	5,000
Long-term assets:			Total current liabilities	7,500
Furniture	$10,000			
Less: Accumulated			**Stockholders' Equity**	
depreciation	(6,000)	4,000	Common stock	10,000
Building	$50,000		Retained earnings	18,000
Less: Accumulated			Total stockholders' equity	28,000
depreciation	(31,000)	19,000	Total liabilities and	
Total assets		$35,500	stockholders' equity	$35,500

Review *Completing the Accounting Cycle*

Accounting Vocabulary

Accounting Cycle
Process by which companies produce their financial statements for a specific period.

Closing the Accounts
Step in the accounting cycle at the end of the period. Closing the accounts consists of journalizing and posting the closing entries to set the balances of the revenue, expense, and dividend accounts to zero for the next period.

Closing Entries
Entries that transfer the revenue, expense, and dividend balances to the retained earnings account.

Current Asset
An asset that is expected to be converted to cash, sold, or consumed during the next 12 months, or within the business's normal operating cycle if the cycle is longer than a year.

Current Liability
A debt due to be paid with cash or with goods and services within one year or within the entity's operating cycle if the cycle is longer than a year.

Current Ratio
Current assets divided by current liabilities. Measures the company's ability to pay current liabilities from current assets.

Debt Ratio
Ratio of total liabilities to total assets. Tells the proportion of a company's assets that it has financed with debt.

Fixed Asset
Another name for property, plant, and equipment.

Income Summary
A temporary "holding tank" account into which revenues and expenses are transferred prior to their final transfer to the retained earnings account.

Liquidity
Measure of how quickly an item can be converted to cash.

Long-Term Asset
An asset other than a current asset.

Long-Term Liability
A liability other than a current liability.

Operating Cycle
Time span during which cash is paid for goods and services, which are then sold to customers from whom the business collects cash.

Permanent Accounts
Accounts that are *not* closed at the end of the period—the asset, liability, common stock, and retained earnings accounts.

Plant Asset
Another name for property, plant, and equipment.

Postclosing Trial Balance
List of the accounts and their balances at the end of the period after journalizing and posting the closing entries. This last step of the accounting cycle ensures that the ledger is in balance to start the next accounting period.

Reversing Entries
Special journal entries that ease the burden of accounting for transactions in the next period.

Temporary Accounts
The revenue and expense accounts that relate to a particular accounting period and are closed at the end of the period. For a corporation, the dividend account is also temporary.

Work Sheet
A columnar document designed to help move data from the trial balance to their financial statements.

Quick Check

1. Consider the steps in the accounting cycle in Exhibit 4-1, page 200. Which part of the accounting cycle provides information to help a business decide whether to expand its operations?
   a. Postclosing trial balance
   b. Adjusting entries
   c. Closing entries
   d. Financial statements

2. Which columns of the accounting work sheet show unadjusted amounts?
   a. Trial balance
   b. Adjustments
   c. Income Statement
   d. Balance Sheet

3. Which columns of the work sheet show net income?
   a. Trial Balance
   b. Adjustments
   c. Income Statement
   d. Both b and c

4. Which situation indicates a net loss on the income statement?
   a. Total debits equal total credits
   b. Total credits exceed total debits
   c. Total debits exceed total credits
   d. None of the above

5. Supplies has a $6,000 unadjusted balance on your trial balance. At year-end you count supplies of $2,000. What adjustment will appear on your work sheet?

a. Supplies	4,000	
Supplies Expense.........................		4,000
b. Supplies Expense	2,000	
Supplies......................................		2,000
c. Supplies Expense	4,000	
Supplies......................................		4,000

   d. No adjustment is needed because the Supplies account already has a correct balance.

6. Which of the following accounts is not closed?
   a. Accumulated Depreciation
   b. Service Revenue
   c. Depreciation Expense
   d. Dividends

7. What do closing entries accomplish?
   a. Transfer revenues, expenses, and Dividends to Retained Earnings
   b. Zero out the revenue, expense, and Dividends accounts

continued . . .

c. Bring the Retained Earnings account to its correct ending balance

d. All of the above

8. Which of the following is not a closing entry?

a. Income Summary..................................	XXX	
Rent Expense..................................		XXX
b. Retained Earnings	XXX	
Dividends		XXX
c. Service Revenue..................................	XXX	
Income Summary............................		XXX
d. Salary Payable	XXX	
Income Summary............................		XXX

9. Assets and liabilities are listed on the balance sheet in order of their

a. Purchase date

b. Liquidity

c. Balance

d. Adjustments

10. Sherman Lawn Service has cash of $300, receivables of $800, and supplies of $400. Sherman owes $500 on accounts payable and salary payable of $100. Sherman's current ratio is

a. 3.00

b. 0.31

c. 2.07

d. 2.50

Answers are given after Apply Your Knowledge (p. 246).

Assess Your Progress

Short Exercises

Explaining items on the work sheet
1

S4-1 ← *Link Back to Chapter 3 (Adjusting Entries).* Explain why the following accounts must be adjusted (pp. 132–133, 140):

a. Prepaid rent
b. Unearned service revenue
c. Supplies
d. Salary payable
e. Accumulated depreciation

Explaining items on the work sheet
1

S4-2 ← *Link Back to Chapters 2 and 3 (Definitions of Accounts).* Explain what the following terms mean (pp. 62–66, 136, 139–141)

a. Accounts receivable
b. Supplies
c. Prepaid rent
d. Furniture
e. Accumulated depreciation
f. Accounts payable
g. Unearned service revenue
h. Service revenue
i. Rent expense

Using the work sheet
1 2

S4-3 Answer the following questions:

1. What type of balance does the Retained Earnings account have—debit or credit? (pp. 69–71)
2. Which Income Statement account has the same type of balance as the Retained Earnings account? (pp. 69–71)
3. Which type of Income Statement account has the opposite type of balance as the Retained Earnings account? (pp. 69–70)
4. What do we call the difference between total debits and total credits on the Income Statement? Into what account is the difference figure closed at the end of the period? (pp. 206–207, 209)

Making closing entries
3

S4-4 It is December 31 and time for you to close the books.

Journalize the closing entries for Brett Kaufman Enterprises (p. 209):

a. Dividends, $6,000
b. Service revenue, $22,000
c. Make a single closing entry for all the expenses: Salary, $7,000; Rent, $4,000; Advertising, $3,000.
d. Income Summary

Analyzing the overall effect of the closing entries on the owner's capital account

S4-5 This exercise should be used in conjunction with Short Exercise 4-4.

1. Set up each T-account given in Short Exercise 4-4 and insert its adjusted balance as given (denote as *Bal.*) at December 31. Also set up a T-account for Retained Earnings, $25,000; and for Income Summary. Post the closing entries to the accounts, denoting posted amounts as *Clo.* (p. 209)
2. Compute the ending balance of Retained Earnings. (p. 209)

Making closing entries
3

S4-6 Riley Insurance Agency reported the following items at May 31:

Sales and marketing expense	$2,000	Cash	$1,000
Other assets	500	Service revenue	5,000
Depreciation expense	800	Accounts payable	300
Long-term liabilities	400	Accounts receivable	1,200

Make Riley's closing entries, as needed, for these accounts. (p. 209)

Posting closing entries

S4-7 This exercise should be used in conjunction with Short Exercise 4-6. Use the data in Short Exercise 4-6 to set up T-accounts for those accounts that Riley Insurance Agency closed out at May 31. Insert their account balances prior to closing, post the closing entries to these accounts, and show each account's ending balance after closing. Also show the Income Summary T-account. Denote a balance as *Bal.* and a closing entry amount as *Clo.* (p. 209)

Preparing a postclosing trial balance
3

S4-8 After closing its accounts at May 31, 2008, Hueske Electric Company had the following account balances:

Long-term liabilities	$ 500	Equipment	$4,000
Other assets	800	Cash	300
Accounts receivable	2,000	Service revenue	0
Total expenses	0	Retained earnings	1,400
Accounts payable	900	Supplies	100
Unearned service revenue	400	Accumulated depreciation	1,000
Common stock	3,000		

Prepare Hueske's postclosing trial balance at May 31, 2008. List accounts in proper order, as shown in Exhibit 4-11, p. 211.

Classifying assets and liabilities as current or long-term
4

S4-9 Ink Jet Printing reported the following (amounts in thousands).

Buildings	$4,000	Service revenue	$1,300
Accounts payable	400	Cash	200
Total expenses	1,050	Receivables	500
Accumulated depreciation	2,800	Interest expense	90
Accrued liabilities (such as		Equipment	800
Salary payable)	300	Prepaid expenses	100

1. Identify the assets (including contra assets) and liabilities. (p. 207)
2. Classify each asset and each liability as current or long-term. (pp. 212–213)

Classifying assets and liabilities as current or long-term

S4-10 ← *Link Back to Chapter 3 (Book Value).* Examine Ink Jet Printing's account balances in Short Exercise 4-9. Identify or compute the following amounts for Ink Jet:

a. Total current assets (pp. 212–213)
b. Total current liabilities (pp. 212–213)
c. Book value of plant assets (p. 135)
d. Total long-term liabilities (pp. 211–212)

Computing the current ratio and the debt ratio

S4-11 Heart of Texas Telecom had these account balances at December 31, 2007.

Note payable, long-term	$ 9,000	Accounts payable	$ 4,000
Prepaid rent	2,000	Accounts receivable	6,000
Salary payable	2,000	Cash	3,000
Service revenue	31,000	Depreciation expense	4,000
Supplies	1,000	Equipment	12,000

Compute Heart of Texas' current ratio and debt ratio. (p. 214)

Computing and using the current ratio and the debt ratio

5

S4-12 This exercise should be used in conjunction with Short Exercise 4-11.

1. How much in *current* assets does Heart of Texas Telecom have for every dollar of *current* liabilities that it owes? What ratio measures this relationship? (p. 214)
2. What percentage of Heart of Texas Telecom's total assets are financed with debt? What is the name of this ratio? (p. 214)
3. What percentage of Heart of Texas's total assets does the owner of the company actually own? (Challenge)

Exercises

Preparing a work sheet

1

E4-13 The trial balance of Wireless Solutions, Inc., follows.

WIRELESS SOLUTIONS, INC.
Trial Balance
November 30, 2007

	Balance	
Account Title	**Debit**	**Credit**
Cash	$ 3,500	
Accounts receivable	3,400	
Prepaid rent	1,200	
Supplies	3,300	
Equipment	34,100	
Accumulated depreciation		$ 1,800
Accounts payable		5,100
Salary payable		
Common stock		10,000
Retained earnings		26,000
Dividends	2,000	
Service revenue		7,100
Depreciation expense		
Salary expense	1,800	
Rent expense		
Utilities expense	700	
Supplies expense		
Total	$50,000	$50,000

Additional information at November 30, 2007:

a. Accrued service revenue, $300
b. Depreciation, $100
c. Accrued salary expense, $500
d. Prepaid rent expired, $800
e. Supplies used, $1,600

Requirements

Complete Wireless Solutions, Inc.'s, work sheet for the month ended November 30, 2007. How much was net income for November? (pp. 201–202)

Journalizing adjusting and closing entries

E4-14 Journalize Wireless Solutions, Inc.'s, adjusting and closing entries in Exercise 4-13. (pp. 208–209)

Posting adjusting and closing entries

E4-15 Set up T-accounts for those accounts affected by the adjusting and closing entries in Exercise 4-14. Post the adjusting and closing entries to the accounts; denote adjustment amounts by *Adj.*, closing amounts by *Clo.*, and balances by *Bal.* Double underline the accounts with zero balances after you close them, and show the ending balance in each account. (pp. 208–209)

Preparing a postclosing trial balance

E4-16 After completing Exercises 4-14 and 4-15, prepare the postclosing trial balance of Wireless Solutions, Inc., at November 30, 2007. (p. 210)

Adjusting the accounts

E4-17 ← *Link Back to Chapter 3 (Adjusting Entries).* Todd McKinney Magic Shows' records include the following account balances:

	December 31,	
	2006	2007
Prepaid rent	$400	$600
Unearned service revenue............	800	300

During 2007, McKinney recorded the following:

a. Prepaid annual rent of $6,000. (pp. 132–133)

b. Made the year-end adjustment to record rent expense of $5,800 for the year. (pp. 132–133)

c. Collected $4,000 cash in advance for service revenue to be earned later. (p. 140)

d. Made the year-end adjustment to record the earning of $4,500 service revenue that had been collected in advance. (p. 141)

Requirements

1. As directed by your instructor, set up T-accounts (p. 208) or four-column accounts (p. 82) for Prepaid Rent, Rent Expense, Unearned Service Revenue, and Service Revenue. Insert beginning and ending balances for Prepaid Rent and Unearned Service Revenue.
2. Journalize entries a through d above, and post to the accounts. Explanations are not required. Ensure that the ending balances for Prepaid Rent and Unearned Service Revenue agree with the December 31, 2007, balances given above. (pp. 133–134, 208)

Closing the books
3

E4-18 Refer to the Todd McKinney data in Exercise 4-17. After making the adjusting entries in Exercise 4-17, journalize McKinney's closing entries for revenue and expense at the end of 2007. Also set up T-accounts (p. 208) or four-column accounts (p. 82) for Rent Expense and Service Revenue and post the closing entries to these accounts. What are their balances after closing? (p. 209)

Identifying and journalizing entries
3

E4-19 From the following selected accounts of Pikasso Party Planning at June 30, 2008, prepare the entity's closing entries (p. 209):

Accounts receivable	$14,000	Retained earnings	$21,600
Depreciation expense	10,200	Service revenue	89,000
Rent expense	5,900	Unearned revenues	1,300
Dividends	40,000	Salary expense	12,500
Supplies	1,400	Supplies expense	3,900

Prepare a T-account for Retained Earnings. What is Pikasso's ending Retained Earnings balance at June 30, 2008? (p. 209)

Identifying and journalizing closing entries
3

E4-20 The accountant for Passport Photography has posted adjusting entries (a) through (e) to the following selected accounts at December 31, 2008.

Accounts Receivable	
41,000	
(a) 3,000	

Supplies	
4,000	(b) 2,000

Accumulated Depreciation—Furniture	
	5,000
	(c) 1,100

Accumulated Depreciation—Building	
	33,000
	(d) 6,000

Salary Payable	
	(e) 700

Retained Earnings	
	52,000

Dividends	
61,000	

Service Revenue	
	108,000
	(a) 3,000

Salary Expense	
26,200	
(e) 700	

Supplies Expense	
(b) 2,000	

Depreciation Expense—Furniture	
(c) 1,100	

Depreciation Expense—Building	
(d) 6,000	

Requirements

1. Journalize Passport Photography's closing entries at December 31, 2008. (p. 209)
2. Determine Passport's ending Retained Earnings balance at December 31, 2008. (p. 209)

Preparing a statement of retained earnings
3

E4-21 From the following accounts of Fleet Truck Wash, Inc., prepare the company's statement of retained earnings for the year ended December 31, 2007. (p. 207)

Retained Earnings			
Clo.	32,000	Jan. 1	164,000
		Clo.	140,000
		Bal.	272,000

Dividends			
Mar. 31	9,000		
Jun. 30	7,000		
Sep. 30	9,000		
Dec. 31	7,000		
Bal.	32,000	Clo.	32,000

Income Summary			
Clo.	88,000	Clo.	228,000
Clo.	140,000	Bal.	140,000

Making closing entries

2 3

E4-22 The adjusted trial balance and the income statement amounts from the April work sheet of Swift Sign Company follow:

Account Title	Adjusted Trial Balance		Income Statement	
Cash	$14,200			
Supplies	2,400			
Prepaid rent	1,100			
Equipment	52,000			
Accumulated depreciation		$ 6,000		
Accounts payable		4,600		
Salary payable		400		
Unearned service revenue		4,200		
Long-term note payable		5,000		
Common stock		15,000		
Retained earnings		24,800		
Dividends	1,000			
Service revenue		17,400		17,400
Salary expense	3,800		$ 3,800	
Rent expense	1,400		1,400	
Depreciation expense	300		300	
Supplies expense	400		400	
Utilities expense	800		800	
	$77,400	$77,400	6,700	17,400
Net income or net loss			?	?
			$17,400	$17,400

Requirements

1. Journalize Swift's closing entries at April 30. (p. 209)
2. How much net income or net loss did Swift earn for April? How can you tell? (pp. 202, 209)

Preparing a classified balance sheet

E4-23 Refer to Exercise 4-22.

Requirements

1. After solving Exercise 4-22, use the data in that exercise to prepare the classified balance sheet of Swift Sign Company at April 30 of the current year. Use the report form. You must compute the ending balance of Retained Earnings. (pp. 207, 213)
2. Compute Swift's current ratio and debt ratio at April 30. One year ago, the current ratio was 1.50 and the debt ratio was 0.30. Indicate whether Swift's ability to pay current and total debts has improved, deteriorated, or remained the same during the current year. (p. 214)

Computing financial statement amounts

2 4

E4-24 Data for the unadjusted trial balance of Planet Beach Tanning Salon at December 31, 2007 follow.

Cash	$ 3,000	Service revenue	$93,600
Equipment	66,200	Salary expense	42,700
Accumulated depreciation	21,800	Depreciation expense	
Accounts payable	6,100	Supplies expense	

Adjusting data for 2007 are:

a. Accrued service revenue, $3,100.

b. Supplies used in operations, $600.

c. Accrued salary expense, $1,400.

d. Depreciation expense, $4,000.

Lex Noonan, the principal stockholder, has received an offer to sell the company. He needs to know the net income for the year covered by these data.

Requirements

Without opening accounts, making journal entries, or using a work sheet, give Noonan the requested information. Prepare an income statement, and show all computations. (pp. 111, 207)

Problems (Group A)

Preparing a work sheet

1

P4-25A The trial balance of Victoria Motors, Inc., at June 30, 2008, follows.

VICTORIA MOTORS, INC.
Trial Balance
June 30, 2008

	Balance	
Account Title	Debit	Credit
Cash	$ 21,200	
Accounts receivable	37,800	
Supplies	17,600	
Prepaid insurance	2,300	
Equipment	32,600	
Accumulated depreciation		$ 26,200
Accounts payable		22,600
Wages payable		
Unearned service revenue		10,500
Common stock		5,000
Retained earnings		41,600
Dividends	4,200	
Service revenue		20,100
Depreciation expense		
Wage expense	3,200	
Insurance expense		
Rent expense	6,000	
Utilities expense	1,100	
Supplies expense		
Total	$126,000	$126,000

continued . . .

Additional data at June 30, 2008:

a. Depreciation on equipment, $600.
b. Accrued wage expense, $200.
c. Supplies on hand, $14,300.
d. Prepaid insurance expired during June, $500.
e. Unearned service revenue earned during June, $4,900.
f. Accrued service revenue, $1,100.

Requirements

Complete Victoria Motors, Inc.'s, work sheet for June. Key adjusting entries by letter. (p. 202)

Preparing a work sheet and the financial statements

1 2

P4-26A The unadjusted T-accounts of Paladdin Investment Advisers, Inc., at December 31, 2007, and the related year-end adjustment data follow.

Account	Debit	Credit
Cash	Bal. 15,000	
Accounts Receivable	Bal. 36,000	
Supplies	Bal. 9,000	
Equipment	Bal. 99,000	
Accumulated Depreciation		Bal. 13,000
Accounts Payable		Bal. 6,000
Salary Payable		
Unearned Service Revenue		Bal. 5,000
Note Payable, Long-Term		Bal. 60,000
Common Stock		Bal. 15,000
Retained Earnings		Bal. 21,000
Dividends	Bal. 62,000	
Service Revenue		Bal. 182,000
Salary Expense	Bal. 53,000	
Supplies Expense		
Depreciation Expense		
Interest Expense	Bal. 6,000	
Rent Expense	Bal. 15,000	
Insurance Expense	Bal. 7,000	

Adjustment data at December 31, 2007:

a. Unearned service revenue earned during the year, $1,000.
b. Supplies on hand, $1,000.
c. Depreciation for the year, $9,000.
d. Accrued salary expense, $1,000.
e. Accrued service revenue, $2,000.

Requirements

1. Enter the account data in the Trial Balance columns of a work sheet, and complete the work sheet. Key each adjusting entry by the letter corresponding to the data given. List all the accounts, including those with zero balances. Leave a blank line under Service Revenue. (p. 207)
2. Prepare the income statement, the statement of retained earnings, and the classified balance sheet in account format. (p. 207)
3. Did Paladdin have a good or a bad year during 2007? Give the reason for your answer. (Challenge)

Journalizing adjusting and closing entries

2 3

P4-27A The *unadjusted* trial balance of Glenn Real Estate Appraisal Company at June 30, 2009 follows.

GLENN REAL ESTATE APPRAISAL COMPANY
Trial Balance
June 30, 2009

Account Title	Balance Debit	Balance Credit
Cash	$ 12,300	
Accounts receivable	26,400	
Supplies	1,200	
Prepaid insurance	3,200	
Building	70,700	
Accumulated depreciation		$ 33,200
Land	30,000	
Accounts payable		39,100
Interest payable		1,400
Salary payable		
Common stock		8,000
Retained earnings		29,900
Dividends	45,300	
Service revenue		109,800
Salary expense	21,400	
Depreciation expense		
Insurance expense	3,100	
Utilities expense	4,300	
Supplies expense	3,500	
Total	$221,400	$221,400

Adjustment data at June 30, 2009:

a. Prepaid insurance expired, $3,000.
b. Accrued service revenue, $900.
c. Accrued salary expense, $700.
d. Depreciation for the year, $11,200.
e. Supplies used during the year, $200.

Requirements

1. Open T-accounts for Retained Earnings and all the accounts that follow on the trial balance. Insert their unadjusted balances. Also open a T-account for Income Summary, which has a zero balance. (p. 208)
2. Journalize the adjusting entries and post to the accounts that you opened. Show the balance of each revenue account and each expense account. (p. 208)
3. Journalize the closing entries and post to the accounts that you opened. Draw double underlines under each account balance that you close to zero. (p. 209)
4. Compute the ending balance of Retained Earnings. (p. 209)

Preparing an income statement

P4-28A Refer to the data for Glenn Real Estate Appraisal Company in Problem 4-27A. After journalizing and posting Glenn's adjusting and closing entries, prepare the company's income statement for the year ended June 30, 2009. List expenses in descending order—largest first, second-largest next, and so on. (p. 207)

Completing the accounting cycle

4-29A The trial balance of Road Runner Internet, Inc., at August 31, 2009, and the data for the month-end adjustments follow.

ROAD RUNNER INTERNET, INC.
Trial Balance
August 31, 2009

Account Title	Balance Debit	Balance Credit
Cash	$ 3,000	
Accounts receivable	6,500	
Prepaid rent	1,200	
Supplies	900	
Equipment	35,300	
Accumulated depreciation		$12,800
Accounts payable		4,200
Salary payable		
Unearned service revenue		8,900
Common stock		5,000
Retained earnings		5,400
Dividends	4,800	
Service revenue		27,300
Salary expense	2,100	
Rent expense	9,800	
Depreciation expense		
Supplies expense		
Total	$63,600	$63,600

Adjustment data:

a. Unearned service revenue still unearned at August 31, $6,500.

b. Prepaid rent still in force at August 31, $1,000.

c. Supplies used during the month, $500.

d. Depreciation for the month, $300.

e. Accrued salary expense at August 31, $400.

Requirements

1. Open the accounts listed in the trial balance and insert their August 31 unadjusted balances. Also open the Income Summary account. Use four-column accounts. Date the balances of the following accounts as of August 1: Prepaid Rent; Supplies; Equipment; Accumulated Depreciation; Unearned Service Revenue; and Retained Earnings. (p. 82)

   If your instructor so directs, use T-accounts. Date the balances of the following accounts as of August 1: Prepaid Rent; Supplies;

continued . . .

Equipment; Accumulated Depreciation; Unearned Service Revenue; and Retained Earnings. (p. 209)

2. Enter the trial balance on a work sheet and complete the work sheet of Road Runner Internet, Inc., for the month ended August 31, 2009. (p. 202)
3. Prepare the income statement, the statement of retained earnings, and the classified balance sheet in report form. (p. 207)
4. Using the work sheet data that you prepare, journalize and post the adjusting and closing entries. Use dates and show the ending balance of each account (pp. 82, 208–209)
5. Prepare a postclosing trial balance. (p. 210)

Preparing a classified balance sheet in report form

P4-30A Selected accounts of Blume Irrigation Systems at December 31, 2007, follow:

Common stock	$25,000	Accounts payable	$ 19,800
Note payable, long-term	37,800	Accounts receivable	26,600
Other assets	3,600	Accumulated depreciation—	
Prepaid insurance	7,700	equipment	7,800
Insurance expense	6,600	Accumulated depreciation—building	11,600
Salary expense	24,600	Retained earnings	72,100
Salary payable	3,900	Equipment	14,400
Supplies	2,500	Cash	6,500
Unearned service revenue	5,400	Service revenue	93,500
Interest payable	600	Building	122,700

Requirements

1. Prepare Blume's classified balance sheet in report form at December 31, 2007. Show totals for total assets, total liabilities, and total liabilities and stockholders' equity. (p. 213)
2. Compute Blume's current ratio and debt ratio at December 31, 2007. At December 31, 2006, the current ratio was 1.60 and the debt ratio was 0.35. Did the company's ability to pay both current and total debts improve or deteriorate during 2007? (p. 214)

Analyzing errors and journalizing adjusting entries

P4-31A ← *Link Back to Chapter 2 (Accounting Errors).* The accountant for William Smith, M.D., encountered the following situations while adjusting and closing the books at December 31. Consider each situation independently.

a. The accountant failed to make the following adjusting entries at December 31:
   1. Accrued salary expense, $600.
   2. Supplies expense, $1,100.
   3. Accrued interest expense on a note payable, $1,600.
   4. Depreciation of equipment, $400.
   5. Earned service revenue that had been collected in advance, $200.

   Compute the overall net income effect of these omissions. (p. 208, Challenge)

continued . . .

b. Record each adjusting entry identified in item a. (p. 208)

c. The $16,000 balance of Equipment was entered as $1,600 on the trial balance.

1. What is the name of this type of error? (p. 80)
2. Assume that this is the only error in the trial balance. Which will be greater, the total debits or the total credits, and by how much? (p. 80)
3. How can this type of error be identified? (p. 80)

d. A $500 credit to Accounts Receivable was posted as a debit.

1. At what stage of the accounting cycle will this error be detected? (p. 80)
2. Describe the technique for identifying the amount of the error. (p. 80)

Problems (Group B)

Preparing a work sheet

1

P4-32B The trial balance of Jane's Preschool, Inc., at May 31, 2008, follows.

JANE'S PRESCHOOL, INC.
Trial Balance
May 31, 2008

Account Title	Balance Debit	Balance Credit
Cash	$ 4,300	
Supplies	500	
Prepaid insurance	1,700	
Furniture	27,400	
Accumulated depreciation—furniture		$ 1,400
Building	53,900	
Accumulated depreciation—building		34,500
Accounts payable		13,300
Salary payable		
Unearned service revenue		8,800
Common stock		5,000
Retained earnings		15,000
Dividends	3,800	
Service revenue		16,800
Depreciation expense—furniture		
Depreciation expense—building		
Salary expense	2,100	
Insurance expense		
Utilities expense	1,100	
Supplies expense		
Total	$94,800	$94,800

Additional data at May 31, 2008.

a. Depreciation: furniture, $500; building, $400.

b. Accrued salary expense, $600.

continued . . .

c. Supplies on hand, $400.

d. Prepaid insurance expired, $300.

e. Unearned service revenue earned during May, $4,400.

Requirements

Complete Jane's work sheet for May. Key adjusting entries by letter. (p. 202)

Preparing a work sheet and the financial statements

1 2

P4-33B The unadjusted T-accounts of Investors Brokerage Company at December 31, 2007, and the related year-end adjustment data follow.

Account	Debit	Credit
Cash	Bal. 29,000	
Accounts Receivable	Bal. 44,000	
Supplies	Bal. 6,000	
Computers	Bal. 22,000	
Accumulated Depreciation		Bal. 12,000
Accounts Payable		Bal. 16,000
Salary Payable		
Unearned Service Revenue		Bal. 2,000
Note Payable, Long-Term		Bal. 40,000
Common Stock		Bal. 10,000
Retained Earnings		Bal. 31,000
Dividends	Bal. 54,000	
Service Revenue		Bal. 95,000
Salary Expense	Bal. 36,000	
Supplies Expense		
Depreciation Expense		
Interest Expense	Bal. 5,000	
Advertising Expense	Bal. 10,000	

Adjustment data at December 31, 2007.

a. Depreciation for the year, $5,000.

b. Supplies on hand, $2,000.

c. Accrued service revenue, $4,000.

d. Unearned service revenue earned during the year, $2,000.

e. Accrued salary expense, $1,000.

Requirements

1. Enter the account data in the trial balance columns of a work sheet, and complete the work sheet. Key each adjusting entry by the letter corresponding to the data given. List all the accounts, including those with zero balances. Leave a blank line under Service Revenue. (p. 202)
2. Prepare the income statement, the statement of retained earnings, and the classified balance sheet in account form. (p. 207)
3. Did Investors Brokerage Company have a good or a bad year during 2007? Give the reason for your answer. (Challenge)

Journalizing adjusting and closing entries

P4-34B The *unadjusted* trial balance of Jen Weaver Insurance Company at April 30, 2008, follows on the next page. Adjustment data at April 30, 2008, consist of

a. Accrued service revenue, $1,600.

b. Depreciation for the year: equipment, $1,000; building, $3,000.

continued . . .

c. Accrued salary expense, $800.
d. Unearned service revenue earned during the year, $1,100.
e. Supplies used during the year, $500.
f. Prepaid insurance expired, $700.

JEN WEAVER INSURANCE COMPANY Adjusted Trial Balance April 30, 2008		
	Balance	
Account Title	Debit	Credit
Cash	$ 4,500	
Accounts receivable	3,700	
Supplies	3,600	
Prepaid insurance	2,200	
Equipment	13,900	
Accumulated depreciation—equipment		$ 8,400
Building	74,300	
Accumulated depreciation—building		18,200
Accounts payable		19,500
Salary payable		800
Unearned service revenue		3,600
Common stock		10,000
Retained earnings		20,300
Dividends	27,500	
Service revenue		98,500
Salary expense	32,800	
Depreciation expense—equipment		
Depreciation expense—building		
Insurance expense	5,100	
Utilities expense	4,900	
Supplies expense	6,800	
Total	$179,300	$179,300

Requirements

1. Open T-accounts for Retained Earnings and all the accounts that follow on the trial balance. Insert their unadjusted balances. Also open a T-account for Income Summary, which has a zero balance. (p. 208)
2. Journalize the adjusting entries and post to the accounts that you opened. Show the balance of each revenue account and each expense account. (p. 208)
3. Journalize the closing entries and post to the accounts that you opened. Draw double underlines under each account balance that you close to zero. (p. 209)
4. Compute the ending balance of Retained Earnings. (p. 209)

Preparing an income statement
3

P4-35B Refer to the data for Jen Weaver Insurance Company in Problem 4-34B. After journalizing and posting Weaver's adjusting and closing entries, prepare the company's income statement for the year ended April 30, 2008. List expenses in descending order—that is, largest first, second-largest next, and so on. (p. 207)

Completing the accounting cycle

2 3 4

P4-36B The trial balance of Alpha Graphics Corp. at October 31, 2007, follows, along with the data for the month-end adjustments.

ALPHA GRAPHICS CORP.
Trial Balance
October 31, 2007

Account Title	Balance Debit	Balance Credit
Cash	$ 4,900	
Accounts receivable	15,310	
Prepaid rent	2,200	
Supplies	840	
Equipment	31,370	
Accumulated depreciation		$ 3,400
Accounts payable		7,290
Salary payable		
Unearned service revenue		5,300
Common stock		6,000
Retained earnings		22,290
Dividends	3,900	
Service revenue		17,100
Salary expense	2,860	
Rent expense		
Depreciation expense		
Supplies expense		
Total	$61,380	$61,380

Adjusting data at October 31:

a. Unearned service revenue still unearned, $800.

b. Prepaid rent still in force, $2,000.

c. Supplies used, $770.

d. Depreciation for the month, $250.

e. Accrued salary expense, $310.

Requirements

1. Open the accounts listed in the trial balance, inserting their October 31 unadjusted balances. Also open the Income Summary account. Use four-column accounts. Date the balances of the following accounts October 1: Prepaid Rent; Supplies; Equipment; Accumulated Depreciation; Unearned Service Revenue; and Retained Earnings. (p. 215)

   If your instructor so directs, use T-accounts. Date the balances of the following accounts as of October 1: Prepaid Rent; Supplies; Equipment; Accumulated Depreciation; Unearned Service Revenue; and Retained Earnings. (p. 208)

2. Enter the trial balance on a work sheet and complete the work sheet of Alpha Graphics Corp. for the month ended October 31, 2007. (p. 202)

3. Prepare the income statement, statement of retained earnings, and classified balance sheet in report form. (p. 207)

continued . . .

4. Using the work sheet data that you prepare, journalize and post the adjusting and closing entries. Use dates and show the ending balance of each account. (pp. 82, 208–209)
5. Prepare a postclosing trial balance. (p. 210)

Preparing a classified balance sheet in report form

P4-37B Selected accounts of Elevator Service Company, at December 31, 2008, follow.

Insurance expense	$ 600	Accounts payable	$34,700
Note payable, long-term	3,200	Accounts receivable	42,100
Other assets	2,300	Accumulated depreciation—building	47,300
Building	55,900	Common stock	15,000
Prepaid rent	4,700	Accumulated depreciation—	
Salary expense	17,800	equipment	7,700
Salary payable	3,500	Cash	12,000
Service revenue	71,100	Depreciation expense	1,900
Supplies	3,800	Retained earnings	31,900
Unearned service revenue	1,700	Equipment	24,200

Requirements

1. Prepare the company's classified balance sheet in report form at December 31, 2008. Show totals for total assets, total liabilities, and owner's equity. (p. 213)
2. Compute the company's current ratio and debt ratio at December 31, 2008. At December 31, 2007, the current ratio was 1.30 and the debt ratio was 0.55. Did the company's ability to pay debts improve, deteriorate, or remain the same during 2008? (p. 214)

Analyzing errors and journalizing adjusting entries 2

P4-38B ← *Link Back to Chapter 2 (Accounting Errors).* The accountant of Lancer Copy Center encountered the following situations while adjusting and closing the books at February 28. Consider each situation independently.

a. The accountant failed to make the following adjusting entries at February 28:
   1. Depreciation of equipment, $700.
   2. Earned service revenue that had been collected in advance, $2,000.
   3. Accrued service revenue, $1,400.
   4. Insurance expense, $300.
   5. Accrued interest expense on a note payable, $500.

   Compute the overall net income effect of these omissions. (p. 208, Challenge)
b. Record each of the adjusting entries identified in item a. (p. 149)
c. The $1,300 balance of Computer Software was entered as $13,000 on the trial balance.
   1. What is the name of this type of error? (p. 80)
   2. Assume that this is the only error in the trial balance. Which will be greater, the total debits or the total credits, and by how much? (p. 80)
   3. How can this type of error be identified? (p. 80)

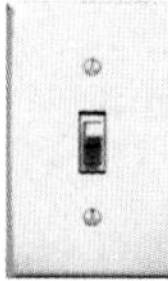

For 24-7 practice, visit www.MyAccountingLab.com

continued . . .

d. A $1,400 debit to Supplies was posted as $4,100.

1. At what stage of the accounting cycle will this error be detected? (p. 80)
2. What is the name of this type of error? Explain how to identify the error. (p. 80)

Continuing Problem

This problem continues the Redmon Consulting, Inc., situation begun in Problem 1-42 of Chapter 1 and continued from Problem 3-44 of Chapter 3.

Closing the books and preparing a classified balance sheet

3 4 5

P4-39 Refer to Problem 3-44 of Chapter 3. Start from the posted T-accounts and the *adjusted* trial balance that Redmon Consulting, Inc., prepared for the company at December 31:

REDMON CONSULTING, INC.
Adjusted Trial Balance
December 31, 2008

Account Title	Balance Debit	Balance Credit
Cash	$ 7,700	
Accounts receivable	1,500	
Supplies	100	
Equipment	2,000	
Accumulated depreciation—equipment		$ 50
Furniture	3,600	
Accumulated depreciation—furniture		60
Accounts payable		3,600
Salary payable		500
Unearned service revenue		600
Common stock		10,000
Retained earnings		
Dividends	1,600	
Service revenue		3,200
Rent expense	500	
Utilities expense	200	
Salary expense	500	
Depreciation expense—equipment	50	
Depreciation expense—furniture	60	
Supplies expense	200	
Total	$18,010	$18,010

Requirements

1. Journalize and post the closing entries at December 31. Denote each closing amount as *Clo.* and an account balance as *Bal.*
2. Prepare a classified balance sheet at December 31.
3. If your instructor assigns it, complete the accounting work sheet at December 31.

Apply Your Knowledge

Decision Case

Completing the accounting cycle to develop the information for a bank loan

One year ago, Ralph Collins founded Collins Consignment Sales Company, and the business has prospered. Collins comes to you for advice. He wishes to know how much net income the business earned during the past year. The accounting records consist of the T-accounts in the ledger, which were prepared by an accountant who has moved. The accounts at December 31 are shown below.

Collins indicates that, at year-end, customers owe him $1,000 accrued service revenue, which he expects to collect early next year. These revenues have not been recorded. During the year, he collected $4,100 service revenue in advance from customers, but the business has earned only $800 of that amount. Advertising expense for the year was $2,400, and he used up $2,100 of the supplies. Collins estimates that depreciation on equipment was $7,000 for the year. At December 31, he owes his employee $1,200 accrued salary. The company issued no stock during the year.

Collins expresses concern that dividends during the year might have exceeded the business's net income. To get a loan to expand the business, Collins must show the bank that the business's stockholders' equity has grown from its original $40,000 balance. Has it? You and Collins agree that you will meet again in one week.

Requirements

Prepare the financial statement that helps answer Collins's question. Can he expect to get the loan? Give your reason.

Account	Debit	Credit
Cash	Dec. 31 5,800	
Accounts Receivable	Dec. 31 12,300	
Prepaid Rent	Jan. 2 2,800	
Supplies	Jan. 2 2,600	
Equipment	Jan. 2 52,000	
Accumulated Depreciation		
Accounts Payable		Dec. 31 18,500
Salary Payable		
Unearned Service Revenue		Dec. 31 4,100
Common Stock		Jan. 2 40,000
Dividends	Dec. 31 50,000	
Service Revenue		Dec. 31 80,700
Salary Expense	Dec. 31 17,000	
Depreciation Expense		
Advertising Expense		
Utilities Expense	Dec. 31 800	
Supplies Expense		

Ethical Issue

← *Link Back to Chapter 3 (Revenue Principle).* Grant Film Productions wishes to expand and has borrowed $100,000. As a condition for making this loan, the bank requires that the store maintain a current ratio of at least 1.50.

Business has been good but not great. Expansion costs have brought the current ratio down to 1.40 at December 15. Rita Grant, owner of the business, is considering what might happen if she reports a current ratio of 1.40 to the bank. One course of action for Grant is to record in December $10,000 of revenue that the business will earn in January of next year. The contract for this job has been signed.

Requirements

1. Journalize the revenue transaction, and indicate how recording this revenue in December would affect the current ratio.
2. Discuss whether it is ethical to record the revenue transaction in December. Identify the accounting principle relevant to this situation, and give the reasons underlying your conclusion.

Financial Statement Case

Using a balance sheet

This case, based on the balance sheet of **Amazon.com** in Appendix A at the end of the book, will familiarize you with some of the assets and liabilities of that company. Use the Amazon.com balance sheet to answer the following questions.

Requirements

1. Which balance sheet format does Amazon.com use?
2. Name the company's largest current asset and largest current liability at December 31, 2005.
3. Compute Amazon's current ratios at December 31, 2005 and 2004. Did the current ratio improve, worsen, or hold steady during 2005?
4. Under what category does Amazon report furniture, fixtures, and equipment?
5. What was the cost of the company's fixed assets at December 31, 2005? What was the amount of accumulated depreciation? What was the book value of the fixed assets? See Note 3 for the data.

Team Project

Haig Sherman formed a lawn service business as a summer job. To start the business on May 1, he deposited $1,000 in a new bank account in the name of the business. The $1,000 consisted of a $600 loan from his father and $400 of his own money. The company, Sherman Lawn Service, Inc., issued $400 of common stock to Sherman. Sherman rented lawn equipment, purchased supplies, and hired other students to mow and trim customers' lawns.

At the end of each month, Sherman mailed bills to his customers. On August 31, he was ready to dissolve the business and return to college. Because he was so busy, he kept few records other than his checkbook and a list of receivables from customers.

At August 31, Sherman's checkbook shows a balance of $2,000, and customers still owe him $750. During the summer, he collected $5,500 from customers. His checkbook lists payments for supplies totaling $400, and he still has gasoline, weedeater cord, and other supplies that cost a total of $50. He paid his employees $1,800, and he still owes them $300 for the final week of the summer.

Sherman rented some equipment from Ludwig's Machine Shop. On May 1, he signed a six-month lease on mowers and paid $600 for the full lease period.

continued . . .

Ludwig's will refund the unused portion of the prepayment if the equipment is in good shape. In order to get the refund, Sherman has kept the mowers in excellent condition. In fact, he had to pay $300 to repair a mower.

To transport employees and equipment to jobs, Sherman used a trailer that he bought for $300. He figures that the summer's work used up one-third of the trailer's service potential. The business checkbook lists a payment of $500 for cash dividends during the summer. Sherman paid his father back during August.

Requirements

1. Prepare the income statement and the statement of retained earnings of Sherman Lawn Service, Inc., for the four months May through August.
2. Prepare the classified balance sheet of Sherman Lawn Service, Inc., at August 31.
3. Was Sherman's summer work successful? Give the reason for your answer.

For Internet Exercises, Excel in Practice, and additional online activities, go to the Web site www.prenhall.com/horngren.

Quick Check Answers

1. *d* 2. *a* 3. *c* 4. *c* 5. *c* 6. *a* 7. *d* 8. *d* 9. *b* 10. *d*

Reversing Entries: An Optional Step

Reversing entries are special journal entries that ease the burden of accounting for transactions in a later period. Reversing entries are the exact opposites of certain adjusting entries at the end of the prior period. Reversing entries are used most often in conjunction with accrual-type adjustments, such as accrued salary expense and accrued service revenue. *Generally accepted accounting principles do not require reversing entries. They are used only for convenience and to save time.*

Accounting for Accrued Expenses

To see how reversing entries work, return to Cookie Lapp's unadjusted trial balance at April 30 (Exhibit 4-2, page 202). Salary Expense has a debit balance of $900 for salaries paid during April. At April 30, the business still owes its employee an additional $900 for the last half of the month, so Lapp makes this adjusting entry:

Adjusting Entries			
Apr. 30	Salary Expense	900	
	Salary Payable		900

After posting, the accounts are updated at April 30.[1]

Salary Payable

	Apr. 30 Adj. 900
	Apr. 30 Bal. 900

Salary Expense

Paid during April, CP 900	
Apr. 30 Adj. 900	
Apr. 30 Bal. 1,800	

After the adjusting entry,

- The April income statement reports salary expense of $1,800.
- The April 30 balance sheet reports salary payable of $900.

The $1,800 debit balance of Salary Expense is closed at April 30, 2007, with this closing entry:

Closing Entries			
Apr. 30	Income Summary	1,800	
	Salary Expense		1,800

[1]Entry explanations used throughout this discussion are

Adj. = Adjusting entry
Bal. = Balance
Clo. = Closing entry
CP = Cash payment entry—a credit to Cash
CR = Cash receipt entry—a debit to Cash
Rev. = Reversing entry

After posting, Salary Expense has a zero balance as follows:

Salary Expense			
Paid during April, CP	900		
Apr. 30 Adj.	900		
Apr. 30 Bal.	1,800	Apr. 30 Clo.	1,800

Zero balance

Assume for this illustration that on May 5, the next payday, Lapp will pay the $900 of salary payable left over from April 30 plus $100 of salary expense for the first few days of May. Lapp's next payroll payment will be $1,000 ($900 + $100).

Accounting Without a Reversing Entry

On May 5, the next payday, Lapp pays the payroll of $1,000 and makes this journal entry:

Date	Account	Debit	Credit
May 5	Salary Payable	900	
	Salary Expense	100	
	Cash		1,000

This method of recording the cash payment is correct. However, it wastes time because Lapp must refer back to the April 30 adjustments. Otherwise, she does not know the amount of the debit to Salary Payable (in this example, $900). Searching April's adjusting entries wastes time and money. To save time, accountants can use reversing entries.

Making a Reversing Entry

A **reversing entry** switches the debit and the credit of a previous adjusting entry. *A reversing entry, then, is the exact opposite of a prior adjusting entry.* The reversing entry is dated the first day of the new period.

To illustrate reversing entries, recall that on April 30, Lapp made the following adjusting entry to accrue Salary Payable:

Adjusting Entries			
Apr. 30	Salary Expense	900	
	Salary Payable		900

The reversing entry simply reverses the debit and the credit of the adjustment:

Reversing Entries			
May 1	Salary Payable	900	
	Salary Expense		900

Observe that the reversing entry is dated the first day of the new period. It is the exact opposite of the April 30 adjusting entry. Ordinarily, the accountant who makes the adjusting entry also prepares the reversing entry at the same time. Lapp dates the reversing entry as of May 1 so that it affects only the new period. Note how the accounts appear after Lapp posts the reversing entry:

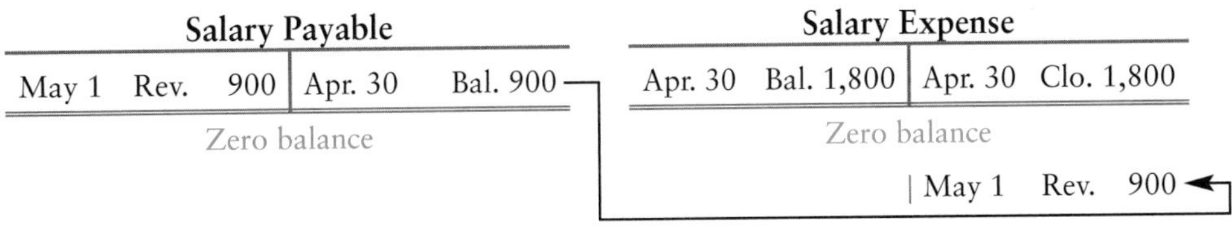

Salary Payable
May 1 Rev. 900
Apr. 30 Bal. 900
Zero balance
Salary Expense
Apr. 30 Bal. 1,800
Apr. 30 Clo. 1,800
Zero balance
May 1 Rev. 900

The arrow shows the transfer of the $900 credit balance from Salary Payable to Salary Expense. This credit balance in Salary Expense does not mean that the entity has negative salary expense, as you might think. Instead, the odd credit balance in the Salary Expense account is merely a temporary result of the reversing entry. The credit balance is eliminated on May 5, when Lapp pays the payroll and debits Salary Expense in the customary manner:

May 5	Salary Expense	1,000	
	Cash		1,000

This cash payment entry is posted as follows:

Salary Expense					
May 5	CP	1,000	May 1	Rev.	900
May 5	Bal.	100			

Now Salary Expense has its correct debit balance of $100, which is the amount of salary expense incurred in May. The $1,000 cash payment also pays the liability for Salary Payable so that Salary Payable has a zero balance, which is correct.

Appendix 4A Assignment

Problem

P4A-1 Refer to the data in Problem 4-29A, page 232.

Requirements

1. Open accounts for Salary Payable and Salary Expense. Insert their unadjusted balances at August 31, 2009.
2. Journalize adjusting entry (e) and the closing entry for Salary Expense at August 31. Post to the accounts.
3. On September 5, Road Runner Internet paid the next payroll amount of $500. This payment included the accrued amount at August 31, plus $100 for the first few days of September. Journalize this cash payment, and post to the accounts. Show the balance in each account.
4. Using a reversing entry, repeat requirements 1 through 3. Compare the balances of Salary Payable and Salary Expense after using a reversing entry with those balances computed without the reversing entry (as they appear in your answer to requirement 3).

Comprehensive Problem for Chapters 1–4

Journalizing, Posting, Work Sheet, Adjusting, Closing the Financial Statements

Dwyer Delivery Service, Inc., completed the following transactions during its first month of operations, January 2009.

a. Dwyer Delivery Service, Inc., a corporation, began operations by receiving $5,000 cash and a truck valued at $10,000. The business issued common stock to acquire these assets.

b. Paid $200 cash for supplies.

c. Prepaid insurance, $600.

d. Performed delivery services for a customer and received $700 cash.

e. Completed a large delivery job, billed the customer $2,000, and received a promise to collect the $2,000 within one week.

f. Paid employee salary, $800.

g. Received $900 cash for performing delivery services.

h. Collected $500 in advance for delivery service to be performed later.

i. Collected $2,000 cash from a customer on account.

j. Purchased fuel for the truck, paying $100 with a company credit card. Credit Accounts Payable.

k. Performed delivery services on account, $800.

l. Paid office rent, $500. This rent is not paid in advance.

m. Paid $100 on account.

n. Paid cash dividends of $1,900.

Requirements

1. Record each transaction in the journal, using the account titles given below. Key each transaction by its letter. Explanations are not required. (pp. 72–78, 132–135, 139–140)
2. Open the following T-accounts in this sequence:

Cash	Service Revenue
Accounts Receivable	Salary Expense
Supplies	Depreciation Expense
Prepaid Insurance	Insurance Expense
Delivery Truck	Fuel Expense
Accumulated Depreciation	Rent Expense
Accounts Payable	Supplies Expense
Salary Payable	
Unearned Service Revenue	
Common Stock	
Retained Earnings	
Dividends	
Income Summary	

Then post the transactions that you recorded in requirement 1. (pp. 72–78)

3. Prepare the trial balance of Dwyer Delivery Service, Inc., at the end of the month. Enter the trial balance on a 10-column accounting work sheet for the month ended January 31, 2009, listing all accounts in the sequence given above, including those accounts with zero balances. Then complete the work sheet using the following adjustment data at January 31. (p. 202)
   o. Accrued salary expense, $800
   p. Depreciation expense, $50
   q. Prepaid insurance expired, $150
   r. Supplies on hand, $100
   s. Unearned service revenue earned during January, $400
4. Prepare Dwyer Delivery Service, Inc.'s, income statement and statement of retained earnings for the month ended January 31, 2009 (page 206), and the classified balance sheet (page 213) on that date. On the income statement list expenses in decreasing order by amount—that is, the largest expense first, the smallest expense last. On the balance sheet, report assets at the left and liabilities and stockholders' equity at the right, as on page 206. Draw the arrows linking the three financial statements.
5. Journalize and post the adjusting entries. (p. 207)
6. Journalize and post the closing entries. Draw double underlines under the Withdrawals account, the Income Summary account, all the revenue accounts, and all the expense accounts to indicate their zero balances. (p. 209)
7. Prepare a post-closing trial balance at January 31, 2009. (pp. 210–211)

Chapter 4: Demo Doc

Accounting Work Sheets and Closing Entries

Demo Doc: To make sure you understand this material, work through the following demonstration "demo doc" with detailed comments to help you see the concept within the framework of a worked-through problem.

Learning Objectives 1–3

This question continues on from the Cloud Break Consulting, Inc., Demo Doc in Chapter 3 (pp. 185–186).

Use the data from the adjusted trial balance of Cloud Break Consulting, Inc., at June 30, 2008:

CLOUD BREAK CONSULTING, INC.
Adjusted Trial Balance
June 30, 2008

Account Title	Debit	Credit
Cash	$131,000	
Accounts receivable	119,000	
Supplies	1,000	
Prepaid rent expense	18,000	
Land	45,000	
Building	300,000	
Accumulated depreciation—building		$167,000
Accounts payable		159,000
Salary payable		4,000
Unearned service revenue		10,000
Common stock		50,000
Retained earnings		52,000
Dividends	7,000	
Service revenue		495,000
Salary expense	259,000	
Supplies expense	3,000	
Rent expense	34,000	
Depreciation expense—building	12,000	
Miscellaneous expense	8,000	
Totals	$937,000	$937,000

Requirements

1. Prepare Cloud Break's accounting work sheet showing the adjusted trial balance, the income statement accounts, and the balance sheet accounts.

2. Journalize and post Cloud Break's closing entries.

Chapter 4: Demo Doc Solution

Requirement 1

Prepare Cloud Break's accounting work sheet showing the adjusted trial balance, the income statement accounts, and the balance sheet accounts.

Part 1	Part 2	Part 3	Part 4	Part 5	Demo Doc Complete

The accounting work sheet is very similar to the adjusted trial balance; however, the work sheet has additional debit and credit columns for the income statement and balance sheet.

CLOUD BREAK CONSULTING, INC.
Work Sheet
June 30, 2008

	Adjusted Trial Balance		Income Statement		Balance Sheet	
Account Title	**Debit**	**Credit**	**Debit**	**Credit**	**Debit**	**Credit**
Cash	131,000					
Accounts receivable	119,000					
Supplies	1,000					
Prepaid rent	18,000					
Land	45,000					
Building	300,000					
Accumulated depreciation		167,000				
Accounts payable		159,000				
Salary payable		4,000				
Unearned service revenue		10,000				
Common stock		50,000				
Retained earnings		52,000				
Dividends	7,000					
Service revenue		495,000				
Salary expense	259,000					
Supplies expense	3,000					
Rent expense	34,000					
Depreciation expense	12,000					
Miscellaneous expense	8,000					
	937,000	937,000				

The accounts that belong on the income statement are put into the income statement columns and all other accounts are put into the balance sheet columns.

The income statement lists revenues and expenses. So Cloud Break's revenues (service revenues) and expenses (salary expense, supplies expense, rent expense,

continued . . .

depreciation expense, and miscellaneous expense) are copied over to the income statement columns:

CLOUD BREAK CONSULTING, INC.
Work Sheet
June 30, 2008

	Adjusted Trial Balance		Income Statement		Balance Sheet	
Account Title	**Debit**	**Credit**	**Debit**	**Credit**	**Debit**	**Credit**
Cash	131,000					
Accounts receivable	119,000					
Supplies	1,000					
Prepaid rent	18,000					
Land	45,000					
Building	300,000					
Accumulated depreciation		167,000				
Accounts payable		159,000				
Salary payable		4,000				
Unearned service revenue		10,000				
Common stock		50,000				
Retained earnings		52,000				
Dividends	7,000					
Service revenue		495,000		495,000		
Salary expense	259,000		259,000			
Supplies expense	3,000		3,000			
Rent expense	34,000		34,000			
Depreciation expense	12,000		12,000			
Miscellaneous expense	8,000		8,000			
	937,000	937,000	316,000	495,000		
Net income			179,000			
			495,000	495,000		

Net income is calculated by subtracting the expenses from the revenues, \$495,000 – \$316,000 = \$179,000. Notice that this is the same as net income from the income statement prepared in the Chapter 3 Demo Doc (p. 195).

The other accounts (assets, liabilities, and equity) are now copied over to the balance sheet columns.

CLOUD BREAK CONSULTING, INC.
Work Sheet
June 30, 2008

	Adjusted Trial Balance		Income Statement		Balance Sheet	
Account Title	**Debit**	**Credit**	**Debit**	**Credit**	**Debit**	**Credit**
Cash	131,000				131,000	
Accounts receivable	119,000				119,000	
Supplies	1,000				1,000	
Prepaid rent	18,000				18,000	
Land	45,000				45,000	
Building	300,000				300,000	
Accumulated depreciation		167,000				167,000
Accounts payable		159,000				159,000
Salary payable		4,000				4,000
Unearned service revenue		10,000				10,000
Common stock		50,000				50,000
Retained earnings		52,000				52,000
Dividends	7,000				7,000	
Service revenue		495,000		495,000		
Salary expense	259,000		259,000			
Supplies expense	3,000		3,000			
Rent expense	34,000		34,000			
Depreciation expense	12,000		12,000			
Miscellaneous expense	8,000		8,000			
	937,000	937,000	316,000	495,000	621,000	442,000
Net income			179,000			179,000
			495,000	495,000	621,000	621,000

Net income is added to the credit side of the balance sheet to make total credits equal total debits. This is because net income increases Retained Earnings (and therefore equity) as seen in requirement 2 of this Demo Doc (where the closing entries are journalized).

Requirement 2

Journalize and post Cloud Break's closing entries.

Part 1	**Part 2**	Part 3	Part 4	Part 5	Demo Doc Complete

We prepare closing entries to (1) clear out the revenue, expense, and dividends accounts to a zero balance in order to get them ready for the next period—that is, they must begin the next period empty so that we can evaluate each period's income separately from other periods. We also need to (2) update the Retained Earnings account by transferring all revenues, expenses, and dividends into it.

continued . . .

The Retained Earnings balance is calculated each year using the following formula:

Beginning retained earnings
+ Net income (or − Net loss)
− Dividends paid
Ending retained earnings

You can see this in the Retained Earnings T-account as well:

Retained Earnings	
	Beginning retained earnings
	Net income
Dividends	
	Ending retained earnings

This formula is the key to preparing the closing entries. We will use this formula, but we will do it *inside* the Retained Earnings T-account.

From the adjusted trial balance, we know that beginning Retained Earnings is $52,000. The first component of the formula is already in the T-account.

The next component is net income, which is *not* yet in the Retained Earnings account. There is no T-account with net income in it, but we can *create* one.

We will create a new T-account called *Income Summary*. We will place in the Income Summary account all the components of net income and come out with the net income number at the bottom. Remember:

Revenues − Expenses = Net income

This means that we need to get all of the revenues and expenses into the Income Summary account.

Let's look at the Service Revenue T-account:

Service Revenue	
	Bal. 495,000

In order to clear out all the income statement accounts so that they are empty to begin the next year, the first step is to debit each revenue account for the amount of its credit balance. Service Revenue has a *credit* balance of $495,000, so to bring that to zero, we need to *debit* Service Revenue for $495,000.

This means that we have part of our first closing entry:

1.		Service Revenue	495,000	
		???		495,000

What is the credit side of this entry? The reason we were looking at Service Revenue to begin with was to help calculate net income using the Income Summary account. So the other side of the entry must go to the Income Summary:

1.		Service Revenue	495,000	
		Income Summary		495,000

Part 1	Part 2	**Part 3**	Part 4	Part 5	Demo Doc Complete

The second step is to *credit* each expense account for the amount of its *debit* balance to bring each expense account to zero. In this case, we have five different expenses:

Salary Expense	
Bal. 259,000	

Supplies Expense	
Bal. 3,000	

Rent Expense	
Bal. 34,000	

Depreciation Expense	
Bal. 12,000	

Miscellaneous Expense	
Bal. 8,000	

The sum of all the expenses will go to the debit side of the Income Summary account:

2.		Income Summary	316,000	
		Salary Expense		259,000
		Supplies Expense		3,000
		Rent Expense		34,000
		Depreciation Expense		12,000
		Miscellaneous Expense		8,000

Part 1	Part 2	Part 3	**Part 4**	Part 5	Demo Doc Complete

Now let's look at the Income Summary account:

Income Summary	
	1. 495,000
2. 316,000	
	Bal. 179,000

Remember that the credit of $495,000 is from the first closing entry prepared at the beginning of this requirement.

The purpose of creating the Income Summary was to get the net income number into a single account. Notice that the Income Summary balance is the same net income number that appears on the income statement and in the accounting worksheet in Requirement 1.

Income Summary now has a *credit* balance of $179,000. The third step in the closing process is to transfer net income to the Retained Earnings account. To remove net income from the Income Summary, we must *debit* the Income Summary for $179,000:

3.		Income Summary	179,000	
		???		179,000

What is the credit side of this entry? It is Retained Earnings. The reason we created the (temporary) Income Summary account was to help calculate the profit or loss for the Retained Earnings account. So the credit side of the entry must go to Retained Earnings:

3.		Income Summary	179,000	
		Retained Earnings		179,000

This entry adds the net income to Retained Earnings. Notice that it also brings the Income Summary account to a zero balance.

Part 1	Part 2	Part 3	Part 4	**Part 5**	Demo Doc Complete

The last component of the Retained Earnings formula is dividends. There is already a Dividends account:

Dividends			
Bal.	7,000		

The final step in the closing process is to transfer Dividends to the debit side of the Retained Earnings account. The Dividends account has a *debit* balance of $7,000, so to bring that to zero, we need to *credit* Dividends by $7,000. The balancing debit will go to Retained Earnings:

4.		Retained Earnings	7,000	
		Dividends		7,000

This entry subtracts Dividends from the Retained Earnings account. Retained Earnings now holds the following data:

	Retained Earnings				
				52,000	**Beginning retained earnings**
			3.	179,000	**Net income**
Dividends	4.	7,000			
			Bal.	224,000	**Ending retained earnings**

The formula to update Retained Earnings has now been re-created inside the Retained Earnings T-account.

The following accounts are are included in the closing process:

Service Revenue

	Debit		Credit
			495,000
1.	495,000		
		Bal.	0

Salary Expense

	Debit		Credit
	259,000		
		2.	259,000
Bal.	0		

Supplies Expense

	Debit		Credit
	3,000		
		2.	3,000
Bal.	0		

Rent Expense

	Debit		Credit
	34,000		
		2.	34,000
Bal.	0		

Depreciation Expense

	Debit		Credit
	12,000		
		2.	12,000
Bal.	0		

Miscellaneous Expense

	Debit		Credit
	8,000		
		2.	8,000
Bal.	0		

Income Summary

	Debit		Credit
		1.	495,000
2.	316,000		
		Bal.	179,000
3.	179,000		
		Bal.	0

Dividends

	Debit		Credit
	7,000		
		4.	7,000
Bal.	0		

Retained Earnings

	Debit		Credit
			52,000
		3.	179,000
4.	7,000		
		Bal.	224,000

Notice that all the temporary accounts (the revenues, the expenses, Dividends, and Income Summary) now have a zero balance.

Part 1	Part 2	Part 3	Part 4	Part 5	**Demo Doc Complete**

5 Merchandising Operations

Learning Objectives

1. Account for the purchase of inventory
2. Account for the sale of inventory
3. Adjust and close the accounts of a merchandising business
4. Prepare a merchandiser's financial statements
5. Use gross profit percentage and inventory turnover to evaluate a business
6. Compute cost of goods sold in a periodic inventory system

Chapters 1–4 began with Sherman Lawn Service and DeFilippo Catering. You can identify with these businesses because you might operate a lawn service, a catering operation, or other small business. Sherman Lawn Service and DeFilippo Catering are similar. Both are proprietorships, and they follow the same accounting procedures.

Julie DeFilippo's catering business differs from the lawn service of Haig Sherman. Sherman provides a service for customers, whereas DeFilippo sells a product—food. Businesses that sell a product are called merchandisers because they sell merchandise, or goods, to customers.

In the early going we accounted for service companies, such as Sherman Lawn Service and Cookie Lapp Travel Design. That enabled us to focus on basic accounting:

- recording transactions
- adjusting and closing the books
- preparing the financial statements

These aspects of accounting are the same for service and merchandising entities.

Merchandisers have an additional asset—merchandise inventory—that service companies don't need. (We usually drop the term *merchandise* and refer simply to *inventory*). **Inventory** is defined as the merchandise that a company holds for sale to customers. For example, DeFilippo Catering must hold some food inventory in order to operate. Wal-Mart carries food inventory in addition to clothing, housewares, and school supplies. A Chevy dealer holds inventories of automobiles and auto parts.

Chapter 5 introduces merchandising. In this chapter we show how to account for the purchase and sale of inventory. We feature a small music store, and we use an actual business document to illustrate transactions.

Before launching into merchandising, let's compare service entities, with which you are familiar, to merchandising companies. Exhibit 5-1 shows how a service entity (on the left) differs from a merchandiser (on the right).

EXHIBIT 5-1 **Financial Statements of a Service Company and a Merchandiser**

SERVICE CO.* Balance Sheet June 30, 2008		MERCHANDISING CO.** Balance Sheet June 30, 2008	
Assets		**Assets**	
Current assets:		Current assets:	
Cash	$X	Cash	$X
Short-term investments	X	Short-term investments	X
Accounts receivable, net	X	Accounts receivable, net	X
Prepaid expenses	X	Inventory	X
		Prepaid expenses	X

*Such as Cookie Lapp Travel Design

**Such as Austin Sound, a music store in Austin, Texas

SERVICE CO. Income Statement Year Ended June 30, 2008		MERCHANDISING CO. Income Statement Year Ended June 30, 2008	
Service revenue	$XXX	Sales revenue	$X,XXX
Expenses:		Cost of goods sold	X
Salary expense	X	Gross profit	XXX
Depreciation expense	X	Operating expenses:	
Rent expense	X	Salary expense	X
Net income	$ X	Depreciation expense	X
		Rent expense	X
		Net income	$ X

What Are Merchandising Operations?

Merchandising consists of buying and selling products rather than services. Merchandisers have some new balance sheet and income statement items.

BALANCE SHEET:	**INCOME STATEMENT:**
• Inventory, an asset	• Sales revenue (often abbreviated as Sales)
	• Cost of goods sold, an expense

These items are highlighted in Exhibit 5-1 for Merchandising Co. Let's examine the operating cycle of a merchandising business.

The Operating Cycle of a Merchandising Business

The operating cycle of a merchandiser (see Exhibit 5-2):

1. Begins when the company purchases inventory
2. Then sells the inventory
3. And, last, collects cash from customers

EXHIBIT 5-2 **Operating Cycle of a Merchandiser**

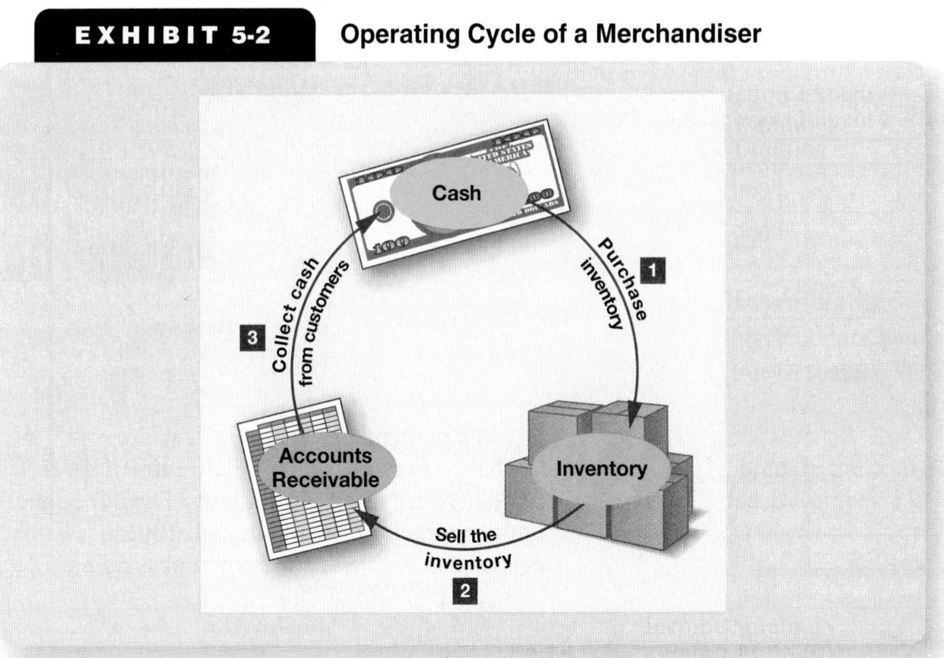

Now let's see how companies account for their inventory. We begin with journal entries. Then we post to the ledger accounts and, finally, prepare the financial statements.

Inventory Systems: Perpetual and Periodic

There are two main types of inventory accounting systems:

- Periodic system
- Perpetual system

The **periodic inventory system** is used for relatively inexpensive goods. A convenience store without optical-scanning cash registers doesn't keep a running record of every loaf of bread and every key chain that it sells. Instead, the business counts its inventory periodically to determine the quantities on hand. Restaurants and small retail stores also use the periodic system. Appendix 5B to this chapter (page 308) covers the periodic system, which is becoming less and less popular with the use of computers.

The **perpetual inventory system** keeps a running record of inventory and cost of goods sold. This system achieves control over the inventory. Even in a perpetual system, the business counts inventory at least once a year. The physical count establishes the correct amount of ending inventory for the financial statements and also serves as a check on the perpetual records.

The following chart compares the perpetual and periodic systems:

Perpetual Inventory System	Periodic Inventory System
• Keeps a running record of all inventory as it is bought and sold.	• Does *not* keep a running record of inventory on hand.

In both systems the inventory on hand is counted at least once each year.

Perpetual Inventory Systems

A modern perpetual inventory system records

- units purchased
- units sold
- the quantity of inventory on hand

Inventory systems are integrated with accounts receivable and sales. For example, Amazon.com's computers use bar codes to keep up-to-the-minute records and show the current inventory at any time.

In a perpetual system, the "cash register" at a Target store is a computer terminal that records sales and updates inventory records. Bar codes such as the one illustrated here are scanned by a laser. The bar coding represents inventory and cost data that keep track of each item. Most businesses use bar codes and computerized cash registers, so we cover the perpetual system.

Accounting for Inventory in the Perpetual System

The cycle of a merchandising entity begins with the purchase of inventory. In this section, we trace the steps that Austin Sound Center, a music store in Austin, Texas, takes to account for inventory. Austin Sound sells DVD players that it purchases from JDC.

1. JDC ships the inventory to Austin Sound and sends an invoice the same day. The **invoice** is the seller's request for payment from the buyer. An invoice is also called a *bill.* Exhibit 5-3 is the purchase invoice that Austin Sound received from JDC.
2. After the inventory is received, Austin Sound pays JDC.

EXHIBIT 5-3 **Purchase Invoice**

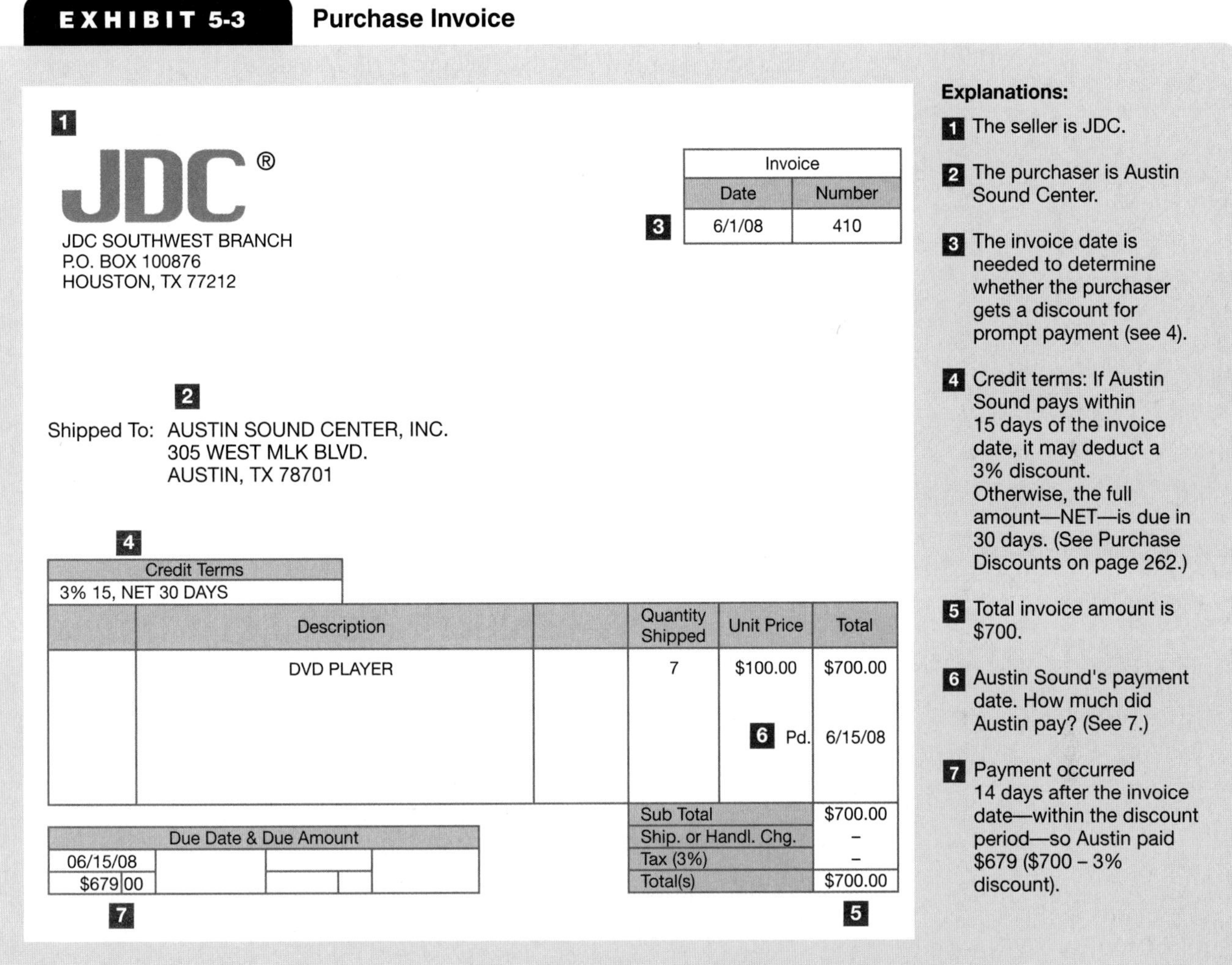

1

JDC®

JDC SOUTHWEST BRANCH
P.O. BOX 100876
HOUSTON, TX 77212

3

Invoice	
Date	Number
6/1/08	410

2

Shipped To: AUSTIN SOUND CENTER, INC.
305 WEST MLK BLVD.
AUSTIN, TX 78701

4

Credit Terms
3% 15, NET 30 DAYS

	Description		Quantity Shipped	Unit Price	Total
	DVD PLAYER		7	$100.00	$700.00
				6 Pd.	6/15/08
			Sub Total		$700.00
			Ship. or Handl. Chg.		–
			Tax (3%)		–
			Total(s)		$700.00

5

Due Date & Due Amount			
06/15/08			
$679 00			

7

Explanations:

1 The seller is JDC.

2 The purchaser is Austin Sound Center.

3 The invoice date is needed to determine whether the purchaser gets a discount for prompt payment (see 4).

4 Credit terms: If Austin Sound pays within 15 days of the invoice date, it may deduct a 3% discount. Otherwise, the full amount—NET—is due in 30 days. (See Purchase Discounts on page 262.)

5 Total invoice amount is $700.

6 Austin Sound's payment date. How much did Austin pay? (See 7.)

7 Payment occurred 14 days after the invoice date—within the discount period—so Austin paid $679 ($700 – 3% discount).

Purchase of Inventory

1 Account for the purchase of inventory

Here we use the actual invoice in Exhibit 5-3 to illustrate the purchasing process. Suppose Austin Sound receives the goods on June 3. Austin Sound records this purchase on account as follows:

June 3	Inventory	700	
	Accounts Payable		700
	Purchased inventory on account.		

The Inventory account is used only for goods purchased for resale. Supplies, equipment, and other assets are recorded in their own accounts. Inventory is an asset until it's sold.

Purchase Discounts

Many businesses offer customers a purchase discount for early payment. JDC's credit terms of "3% 15, NET 30 DAYS" mean that Austin Sound may deduct 3% if Austin pays within 15 days of the invoice date. Otherwise, the full amount—NET—is due in 30 days. These credit terms can also be expressed as "3/15, n/30."

Terms of "n/30" mean that no discount is offered and payment is due 30 days after the invoice date. Terms of *eom* mean that payment is due at the end of the current month.

Austin Sound paid within the discount period, so the cash payment entry is

June 15	Accounts Payable	700	
	Cash ($700 × 0.97)		679
	Inventory ($700 × 0.03)		21
	Paid within discount period.		

The discount is credited to Inventory because the discount decreases the cost, as shown in the Inventory account:

Inventory			
June 3	700	June 15	21
Bal.	679		

But if Austin Sound pays this invoice after the discount period, Austin Sound must pay the full $700. In that case, the payment entry is:

June 24	Accounts Payable	700	
	Cash		700
	Paid after discount period.		

Purchase Returns and Allowances

Businesses allow customers to *return* merchandise that is defective, damaged, or otherwise unsuitable. Or the seller may deduct an *allowance* from the amount the buyer owes. Purchase returns and allowances decrease the buyer's cost of the inventory.

Suppose a DVD player purchased by Austin Sound (Exhibit 5-3) was damaged in shipment. Austin returns the goods to JDC and records the purchase return as follows:

June 4	Accounts Payable	100	
	Inventory		100
	Returned inventory to seller.		

Transportation Costs

Someone must pay the transportation cost of shipping inventory from seller to buyer. The purchase agreement specifies FOB terms (*free on board*) to indicate who pays the freight. Exhibit 5-4 shows that:

- FOB shipping point means buyer pays the freight.
- FOB destination means seller pays the freight.

EXHIBIT 5-4 FOB Terms Determine Who Pays the Freight

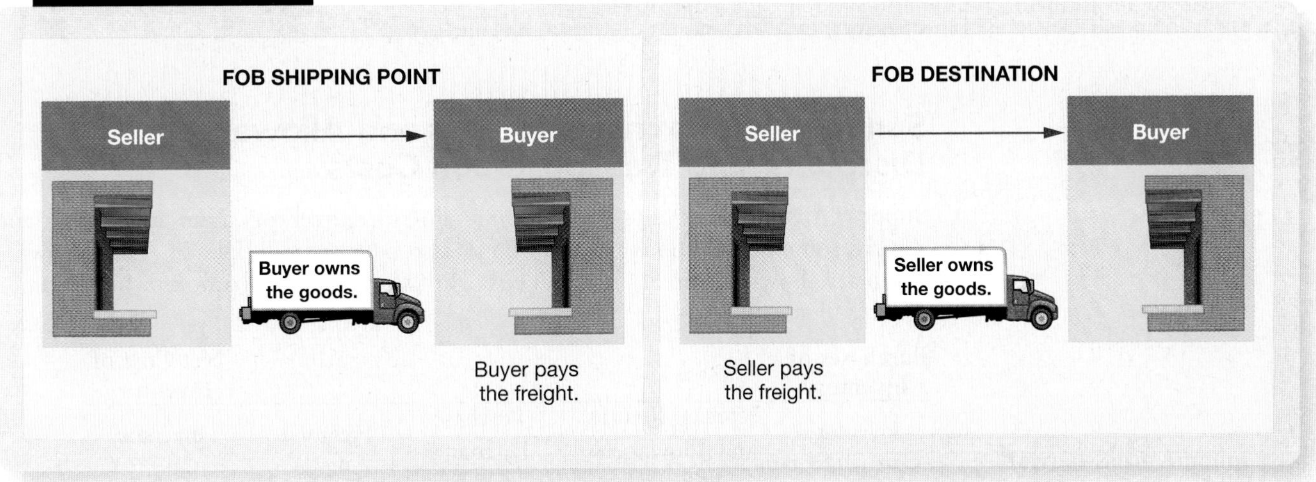

Freight costs are either freight in or freight out.

- *Freight in* is the transportation cost on *purchased goods.*
- *Freight out* is the transportation cost on *goods sold.*

FREIGHT IN FOB shipping point is most common. The buyer owns the goods while they are in transit, so the buyer pays the freight. Freight in becomes part of the cost of inventory and is, therefore, debited to the Inventory account. Suppose Austin Sound pays a $60 freight charge and makes this entry:

June 3	Inventory	60	
	Cash		60
	Paid a freight bill.		

The freight charge increases the net cost of the inventory to $660, as follows:

Inventory

June 3	Purchase	700	June 4	Return	100
June 3	Freight in	60			
Bal.	Net cost	660			

Discounts are computed only on the account payable to the seller ($600), not on the transportation costs, because there is no discount on freight.

Under FOB shipping point, the seller sometimes prepays the transportation cost as a convenience and lists this cost on the invoice. A $5,000 purchase of goods, coupled with a related freight charge of $400, would be recorded as follows:

June 20	Inventory ($5,000 + $400)	5,400	
	Accounts Payable		5,400
	Purchased inventory on account, including freight.		

If the buyer pays within the discount period, the discount will be computed on the $5,000 merchandise cost, not on the $5,400. For example, a 2% discount would be $100 ($5,000 × 0.02).

FREIGHT OUT The seller may pay freight charges to ship goods to customers. This is called *freight out.* Freight out is delivery expense to the seller. Delivery expense is an operating expense and is debited to the Delivery Expense account.

Summary of Purchase Returns and Allowances, Discounts, and Transportation Costs

Suppose Austin Sound buys $35,000 of audio/video inventory, takes a discount, and returns some of the goods. Austin Sound also pays some freight in. The following summary shows Austin Sound's net cost of this inventory. All amounts are assumed for this illustration.

Purchases of Inventory								Net Cost of Inventory
Inventory	−	Purchase Returns and Allowances	−	Purchase Discounts	+	Freight in	=	Inventory
$35,000	−	$700	−	$800	+	$2,100	=	$35,600

Inventory

Purchases of inventory	35,000	Purchase returns & allow.	700
Freight in	2,100	Purchase discount	800
Balance	35,600		

Sale of Inventory

Account for the sale of inventory

After a company buys inventory, the next step is to sell the goods. We shift now to the selling side and follow Austin Sound Center through a sequence of selling transactions.

The amount a business earns from selling merchandise inventory is called **sales revenue** (often abbreviated as **sales**). A sale also creates an expense, Cost of Goods Sold, as the seller gives up the asset Inventory. **Cost of goods sold** is the cost of inventory that has been sold to customers. Cost of goods sold (often abbreviated as **cost of sales**) is the merchandiser's major expense.

After making a sale on account, Austin Sound may experience any of the following:

- ***A sales return:*** The customer may return goods to Austin Sound.
- ***A sales allowance:*** Austin Sound may grant a sales allowance to reduce the cash to be collected from the customer.
- ***A sales discount:*** If the customer pays within the discount period—under terms such as 2/10, n/30—Austin Sound collects the discounted amount.
- ***Freight out:*** Austin Sound may have to pay delivery expense to transport the goods to the buyer.

Let's begin with a cash sale.

Cash Sale

Sales of retailers, such as Austin Sound, grocery stores, and Old Navy, are often for cash. Suppose Austin Sound made a $3,000 cash sale and issued the sales invoice in Exhibit 5-5.

EXHIBIT 5-5 Sales Invoice

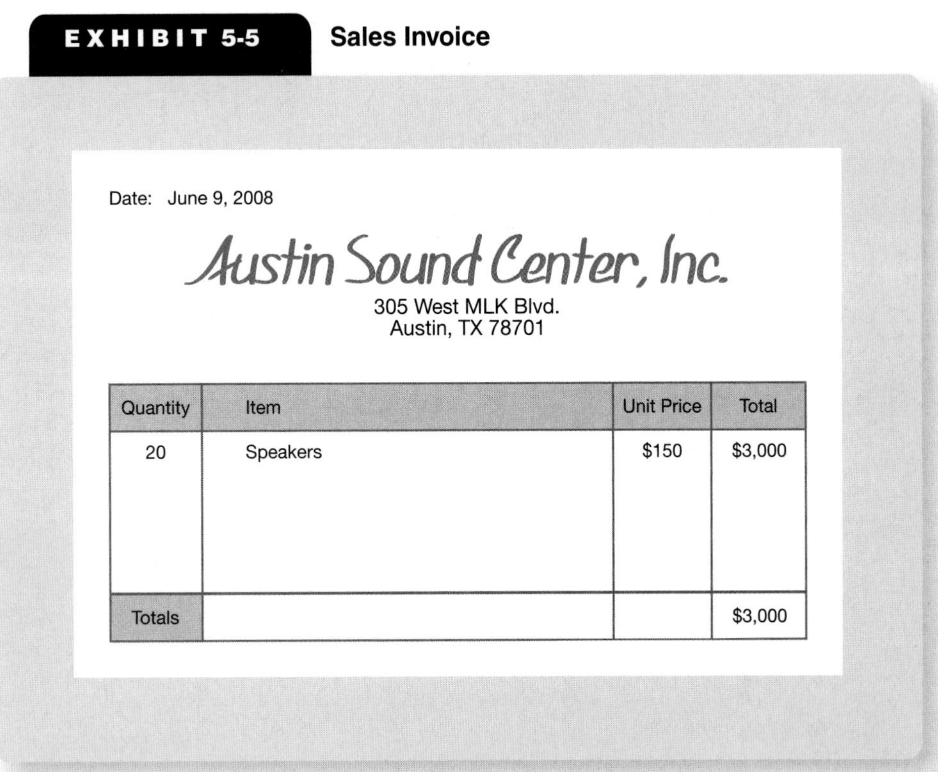

Date: June 9, 2008

Austin Sound Center, Inc.

305 West MLK Blvd.
Austin, TX 78701

Quantity	Item	Unit Price	Total
20	Speakers	$150	$3,000
Totals			$3,000

Cash sales of $3,000 are recorded by debiting Cash and crediting Sales Revenue as follows:

June 9	Cash	3,000	
	Sales Revenue		3,000
	Cash sale.		

Austin Sound sold goods and, therefore, must decrease the Inventory balance. Suppose these goods cost Austin $1,900. A second journal entry is needed to transfer the $1,900 cost of the goods from the Inventory account to Cost of Goods Sold, as follows:

June 9	Cost of Goods Sold	1,900	
	Inventory		1,900
	Recorded the cost of goods sold.		

The Cost of Goods Sold account keeps a current balance throughout the period. In this example, cost of goods sold is not $3,000, because that's the selling price of the goods. *Cost of goods sold is always based on the entity's cost, not the selling price.*

After posting, the Cost of Goods Sold account holds the cost of the inventory sold ($1,900 in this case):

Inventory		Cost of Goods Sold	
Purchases 50,000 (amount assumed)	Cost of sales 1,900 ⟷	June 9 1,900	

The computer automatically records the cost of goods sold entry. The cashier scans the bar code on the product and the computer performs this task.

Sale on Account

Most sales in the United States are made on account (on credit). A $5,000 sale on account is recorded as follows:

June 11	Accounts Receivable	5,000	
	Sales Revenue		5,000
	Sale on account.		

These goods cost the seller $2,900, so the related cost of goods sold entry is:

June 11	Cost of Goods Sold	2,900	
	Inventory		2,900
	Recorded the cost of goods sold.		

When the cash comes in, the seller records the cash receipt on account as follows:

June 19	Cash	5,000	
	Accounts Receivable		5,000
	Collection on account.		

Sales Discounts and Sales Returns and Allowances

We saw that purchase returns and allowances and purchase discounts decrease the cost of inventory purchases. In the same way, **sales returns and allowances** and **sales discounts** decrease the net amount of revenue earned on sales. Sales Returns and Allowances and Sales Discounts are contra accounts to Sales Revenue.

Sales Revenue − Sales Returns and Allowances − Sales Discounts = Net Sales Revenue[1]

Companies maintain separate accounts for Sales Discounts and Sales Returns and Allowances. Now let's examine a sequence of JDC sale transactions. Assume JDC is selling to Austin Sound Center.

On July 7, JDC sells stereo components for $7,200 on credit terms of 2/10, n/30. These goods cost JDC $4,700. JDC's entries to record this credit sale and the related cost of goods sold are:

July 7	Accounts Receivable	7,200	
	Sales Revenue		7,200
	Sale on account.		
7	Cost of Goods Sold	4,700	
	Inventory		4,700
	Recorded cost of goods sold.		

[1]Often abbreviated as Net sales.

SALES RETURNS Assume that the buyer returns $600 of the goods. JDC, the seller, records the sales return as follows:

July 12	Sales Returns and Allowances	600	
	Accounts Receivable		600
	Received returned goods.		

Accounts Receivable decreases because JDC will not collect cash for the returned goods.

JDC receives the returned merchandise and updates its inventory records. JDC must also decrease Cost of Goods Sold as follows (the returned goods cost JDC $400):

July 12	Inventory	400	
	Cost of Goods Sold		400
	Placed goods back in inventory.		

SALES ALLOWANCES Suppose JDC grants a $100 sales allowance for damaged goods. A sales allowance is recorded as follows:

July 15	Sales Returns and Allowances	100	
	Accounts Receivable		100
	Granted a sales allowance for damaged goods.		

There is no inventory entry for a sales allowance because the seller receives no returned goods from the customer.

After these entries are posted, Accounts Receivable has a $6,500 debit balance, as follows:

Accounts Receivable

July 7	Sale	7,200	July 12	Return	600
			15	Allowance	100
Bal.		6,500			

SALES DISCOUNTS On July 17, the last day of the discount period, JDC collects this receivable. JDC's cash receipt is $6,370 [$6,500 − ($6,500 × 0.02)], and the collection entry is:

July 17	Cash	6,370	
	Sales Discounts ($6,500 × 0.02)	130	
	Accounts Receivable		6,500
	Cash collection within the discount period.		

Now, JDC's Accounts Receivable balance is zero:

Accounts Receivable

July 7	Sale	7,200	July 12	Return	600
			15	Allowance	100
			17	Collection	6,500
Bal.		–0–			

Sales Revenue, Cost of Goods Sold, and Gross Profit

Net sales, cost of goods sold, and gross profit are key elements of profitability. Net sales revenue minus cost of goods sold is called **gross profit,** or **gross margin.**

Net sales – Cost of goods sold = Gross profit

Gross profit, along with net income, is a measure of business success. A sufficiently high gross profit is vital to a merchandiser.

The following example will clarify the nature of gross profit. Suppose JDC's cost to purchase a DVD is $15 and JDC sells the DVD for $20. JDC's gross profit per unit is $5, computed as follows:

Sales revenue earned by selling one DVD	**$20**
Less: Cost of goods sold for the DVD (what the DVD cost JDC)	**(15)**
Gross profit on the sale of one DVD	**$ 5**

The gross profit reported on JDC's income statement is the sum of the gross profits on the DVDs and all the other products the company sold during the year.

Let's put into practice what you've learned in the first half of this chapter.

Summary Problem 1

Suppose Liberty Sales Co. engaged in the following transactions during June of the current year:

June 3	Purchased inventory on credit terms of 1/10 net eom (end of month), $1,600.
9	Returned 40% of the inventory purchased on June 3. It was defective.
12	Sold goods for cash, $920 (cost, $550).
15	Purchased goods for $5,000. Credit terms were 3/15, net 30.
16	Paid a $260 freight bill on goods purchased.
18	Sold inventory for $2,000 on credit terms of 2/10, n/30 (cost, $1,180).
22	Received returned goods from the customer of the June 18 sale, $800 (cost, $480).
24	Borrowed money from the bank to take advantage of the discount offered on the June 15 purchase. Signed a note payable to the bank for the net amount, $4,850.
24	Paid supplier for goods purchased on June 15, less the discount.
28	Received cash in full settlement of the account from the customer who purchased inventory on June 18, less the return on June 22, and less the discount.
29	Paid the amount owed on account from the purchase of June 3, less the June 9 return.

Requirements

1. Journalize the preceding transactions for Liberty. Explanations are not required.
2. Set up T-accounts and post the journal entries to show the ending balances in the Inventory and the Cost of Goods Sold accounts.
3. Assume that the note payable signed on June 24 requires the payment of $90 interest expense. Was borrowing funds to take the cash discount a wise or unwise decision?

Solution

Requirement 1

Requirement 1			
June 3	Inventory	1,600	
	Accounts Payable		1,600
9	Accounts Payable ($1,600 × 0.40)	640	
	Inventory		640
12	Cash	920	
	Sales Revenue		920
12	Cost of Goods Sold	550	
	Inventory		550
15	Inventory	5,000	
	Accounts Payable		5,000
16	Inventory	260	
	Cash		260
18	Accounts Receivable	2,000	
	Sales Revenue		2,000
18	Cost of Goods Sold	1,180	
	Inventory		1,180
22	Sales Returns and Allowances	800	
	Accounts Receivable		800
22	Inventory	480	
	Cost of Goods Sold		480
24	Cash	4,850	
	Note Payable		4,850
24	Accounts Payable	5,000	
	Inventory ($5,000 × 0.03)		150
	Cash ($5,000 × 0.97)		4,850
28	Cash [($2,000 – $800) × 0.98]	1,176	
	Sales Discounts [($2,000 – $800) × 0.02]	24	
	Accounts Receivable ($2,000 – $800)		1,200
29	Accounts Payable ($1,600 – $640)	960	
	Cash		960

Requirement 2

Inventory

June 3	1,600	June 9	640
15	5,000	12	550
16	260	18	1,180
22	480	24	150
Bal.	4,820		

Cost of Goods Sold

June 12	550	June 22	480
18	1,180		
Bal.	1,250		

Requirement 3

Liberty's decision to borrow funds was wise because the discount received ($150) exceeded the interest paid ($90). Thus Liberty was $60 better off.

Adjusting and Closing the Accounts of a Merchandiser

3 Adjust and close the accounts of a merchandising business

A merchandiser adjusts and closes accounts the same way a service entity does. If a work sheet is used, the trial balance is entered, and the work sheet is completed to determine net income or net loss.

Adjusting Inventory Based on a Physical Count

The inventory account should stay current at all times. However, the actual amount of inventory on hand may differ from what the books show. Theft, damage, and errors occur. For this reason, businesses take a physical count of inventory at least once a year. The most common time to count inventory is at the end of the year. The business then adjusts the Inventory account based on the physical count.

At year end Austin Sound's Inventory account shows an unadjusted balance of $40,500.

Inventory		
	⋮	
Dec. 31	40,500	

With no shrinkage—due to theft or error—the business should have inventory costing $40,500. But on December 31, Austin Sound counts the inventory on hand, and the total cost comes to only $40,200.

INVENTORY BALANCE BEFORE ADJUSTMENT	−	ACTUAL INVENTORY ON HAND	=	ADJUSTING ENTRY TO INVENTORY
$40,500	−	$40,200	=	Credit of $300

Austin Sound records this adjusting entry for inventory shrinkage:

Dec. 31	Cost of Goods Sold	300	
	Inventory ($40,500 − $40,200)		300
	Adjustment for inventory shrinkage.		

This entry brings Inventory to its correct balance.

Inventory			
	⋮		
Dec. 31	40,500	Dec. 31 Adj.	300
Dec. 31 Bal.	40,200		

Austin Sound's other adjustments, plus a complete merchandising work sheet, are covered in Appendix 5A, pages 283–284, at the end of this chapter.

Closing the Accounts of a Merchandiser

Exhibit 5-6 presents Austin Sound, Inc.'s, closing entries, which are similar to those in Chapter 4, except for the new accounts (highlighted in color). All amounts are assumed for this illustration.

EXHIBIT 5-6 **Closing Entries for a Merchandiser**

Journal

		Closing Entries		
1.	Dec. 31	Sales Revenue	169,300	
		Income Summary		169,300
2.	31	Income Summary	116,200	
		Sales Discounts		1,400
		Sales Returns and Allowances		2,000
		Cost of Goods Sold		90,800
		Wage Expense		10,200
		Rent Expense		8,400
		Depreciation Expense		600
		Insurance Expense		1,000
		Supplies Expense		500
		Interest Expense		1,300
3.	31	Income Summary ($169,300 – $116,200)	53,100	
		Retained Earnings		53,100
4.	31	Retained Earnings	54,100	
		Dividends		54,100

Income Summary

Closing	116,200	Closing	169,300
Closing	53,100	Bal.	53,100

Retained Earnings

Closing	54,100	Bal.	15,900
		Closing	53,100
		Bal.	14,900

Dividends

Bal.	54,100	Closing	54,100

The first closing entry:

- debits all revenue accounts for their credit balances.
- credits Income Summary for total revenues ($169,300).

The second closing entry:

- debits Income Summary for total expenses plus the contra revenues ($116,200).
- credits the contra revenues (Sales Discounts and Sales Returns and Allowances) and all the expenses for their debit balances.

The last two closing entries:

- close net income from Income Summary to the Retained Earnings account.
- close Dividends into the Retained Earnings account.

Preparing a Merchandiser's Financial Statements

Exhibit 5-7 shows Austin Sound's financial statements for 2008.

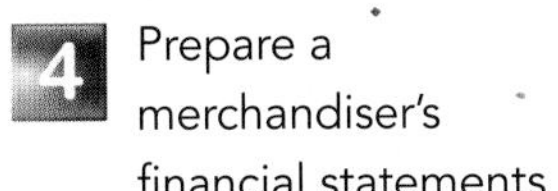

INCOME STATEMENT The income statement begins with sales, cost of goods sold, and gross profit. Then come the **operating expenses,** which are those expenses (other than cost of goods sold) that occur in the entity's major line of business.

Many companies report operating expenses in two categories:

- **Selling expenses** are expenses related to marketing the company's products—sales salaries; sales commissions; advertising; depreciation, rent, and utilities on store buildings; and delivery expense.
- **General expenses** include office expenses, such as the salaries of the executives and office employees; depreciation; rent; utilities; and property taxes on the home office building.

Gross profit minus operating expenses equals **operating income,** or **income from operations.** Operating income measures the results of the entity's major ongoing activities.

The last section of Austin Sound's income statement is **other revenue and expense.** This category reports revenues and expenses that fall outside its main operations. Examples include interest revenue, interest expense, and gains and losses on the sale of plant assets.

The bottom line of the income statement is net income:

Net income = Total revenues and gains − Total expenses and losses

We often hear the term *bottom line* to refer to a final result. The *bottom line* is net income on the income statement.

STATEMENT OF RETAINED EARNINGS A merchandiser's statement of retained earnings looks exactly like that of a service business.

BALANCE SHEET If the business is a merchandiser, the balance sheet shows inventory as a current asset. Service businesses have no inventory.

Income Statement Formats: Multi-Step and Single-Step

As we saw in Chapter 4, the balance sheet appears in two formats:

- The report format (assets on top, . . . , stockholders' equity at bottom)
- The account format (assets at left, liabilities and stockholders' equity at right)

continued on page 275 . . .

EXHIBIT 5-7 Financial Statements of Austin Sound Center

AUSTIN SOUND CENTER, INC.
Income Statement
Year Ended December 31, 2008

Sales revenue		$169,300
Less: Sales discounts	$(1,400)	
Sales returns and allowances	(2,000)	(3,400)
Net sales revenue		165,900
Cost of goods sold		90,800
Gross profit		75,100
Operating expenses:		
Wage expense	$10,200	
Rent expense	8,400	
Insurance expense	1,000	
Depreciation expense	600	
Supplies expense	500	20,700
Operating income		54,400
Other revenue and (expense):		
Interest expense		(1,300)
Net income		$ 53,100

AUSTIN SOUND CENTER, INC.
Statement of Retained Earnings
Year Ended December 31, 2008

Retained earnings, Dec. 31, 2007	$15,900
Add: Net income	53,100
	69,000
Less: Dividends	(54,100)
Retained earnings, Dec. 31, 2008	$14,900

AUSTIN SOUND CENTER, INC.
Balance Sheet
December 31, 2008

Assets			Liabilities	
Current Assets:			Current Liabilities:	
Cash		$ 2,800	Accounts payable	$39,500
Accounts receivable		4,600	Unearned sales revenue	700
Inventory		40,200	Wages payable	400
Prepaid insurance		200	Total current liabilities	40,600
Supplies		100	Long-term Liabilities:	
Total current assets		47,900	Note payable	12,600
Plant Assets:			Total liabilities	53,200
Furniture	$33,200			
Less: Accumulated			**Stockholders' Equity**	
depreciation	(3,000)	30,200	Common stock	10,000
			Retained earnings	14,900
			Total stockholders' equity	24,900
			Total liabilities and	
Total assets		$78,100	stockholders' equity	$78,100

There are also two formats for the income statement:

- The multi-step format
- The single-step format

The multi-step format is more popular.

Multi-Step Income Statement

A **multi-step income statement** lists several important subtotals. In addition to net income, it also reports gross profit and income from operations. The income statements presented thus far in this chapter have been multi-step. Austin Sound's multi-step income statement appears in Exhibit 5-7.

Single-Step Income Statement

The **single-step income statement** groups all revenues together and all expenses together without drawing other subtotals. Many companies use this format. The single-step format clearly distinguishes revenues from expenses and works well for service entities because they have no gross profit to report. Exhibit 5-8 shows a single-step income statement for Austin Sound.

EXHIBIT 5-8 **Single-Step Income Statement**

AUSTIN SOUND CENTER, INC.
Income Statement
Year Ended December 31, 2008

Revenues:		
Sales revenue		$169,300
Less: Sales discounts	$ 1,400	
Sales returns and allowances	2,000	(3,400)
Net sales revenue		165,900
Interest revenue		1,000*
Total revenues		166,900
Expenses:		
Cost of goods sold	$90,800	
Wage expense	11,200*	
Rent expense	8,400	
Interest expense	1,300	
Insurance expense	1,000	
Depreciation expense	600	
Supplies expenses	500	
Total expenses		113,800
Net income		$ 53,100

*Added or modified for this illustration.

Two Ratios for Decision Making

Inventory is the most important asset for a merchandiser. Business owners use several ratios to evaluate their operations, among them the gross profit percentage and the rate of inventory turnover.

5 Use gross profit percentage and inventory turnover to evaluate a business

The Gross Profit Percentage

Gross profit (gross margin) is net sales minus cost of goods sold. Merchandisers strive to increase the **gross profit percentage**, which is computed as follows:

For Austin Sound Center
(Exhibit 5-7)

$$\text{Gross profit percentage} = \frac{\text{Gross profit}}{\text{Net sales revenue}} = \frac{\$75{,}100}{\$165{,}900} = 0.453 = 45.3\%$$

The gross profit percentage (also called the *gross margin percentage*) is one of the most carefully watched measures of profitability. A small increase may signal an important rise in income, and vice versa for a decrease.

Exhibit 5-9 compares Austin Sound's gross margin to that of Target and Amazon.com.

EXHIBIT 5-9 Gross Profit on $1 of Sales for Three Merchandisers

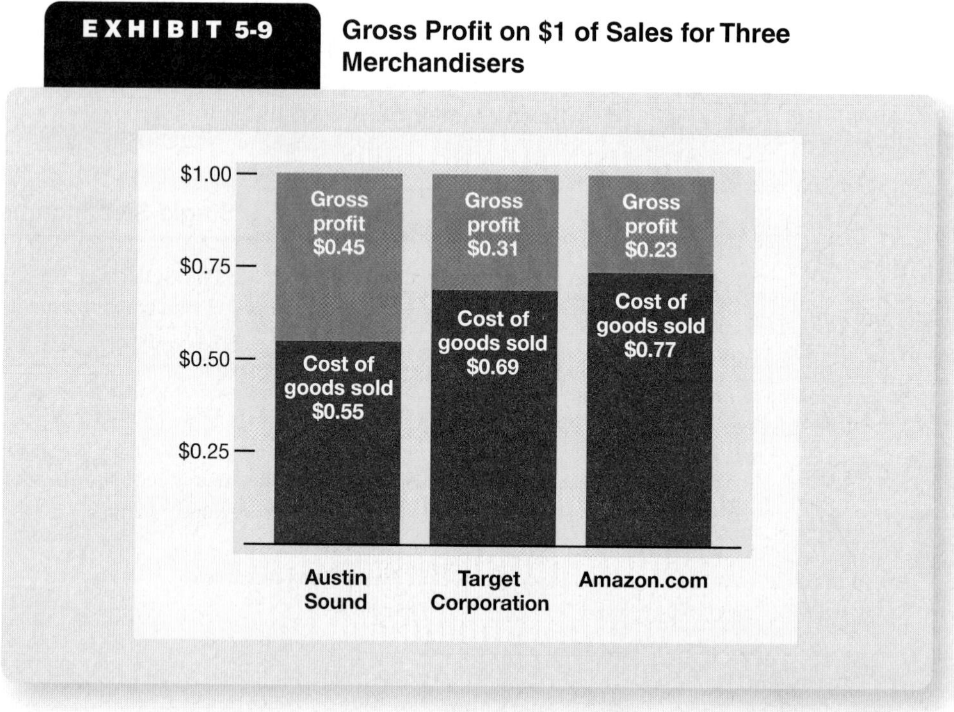

The Rate of Inventory Turnover

Owners and managers strive to sell inventory quickly because the inventory generates no profit until it is sold. The faster the sales, the higher the income. **Inventory turnover** measures how rapidly inventory is sold. It is computed as follows:

For Austin Sound Center
(Exhibit 5-7)

$$\text{Inventory turnover} = \frac{\text{Cost of goods sold}}{\text{Average inventory}} = \frac{\text{Cost of goods sold}}{(\text{Beginning inventory}^{*} + \text{Ending inventory}) / 2}$$

$$= \frac{\$90{,}800}{(\$38{,}600^{*} + \$40{,}200) / 2} = 2.3 \text{ times per year}$$

*Ending inventory from the preceding period. Amount assumed for this illustration.

A high turnover rate is desirable, and an increase in the turnover rate usually means higher profits. Exhibit 5-10 tells an interesting story. Amazon.com moves its merchandise much faster than Austin Sound.

EXHIBIT 5-10 Rate of Inventory Turnover for Two Merchandisers

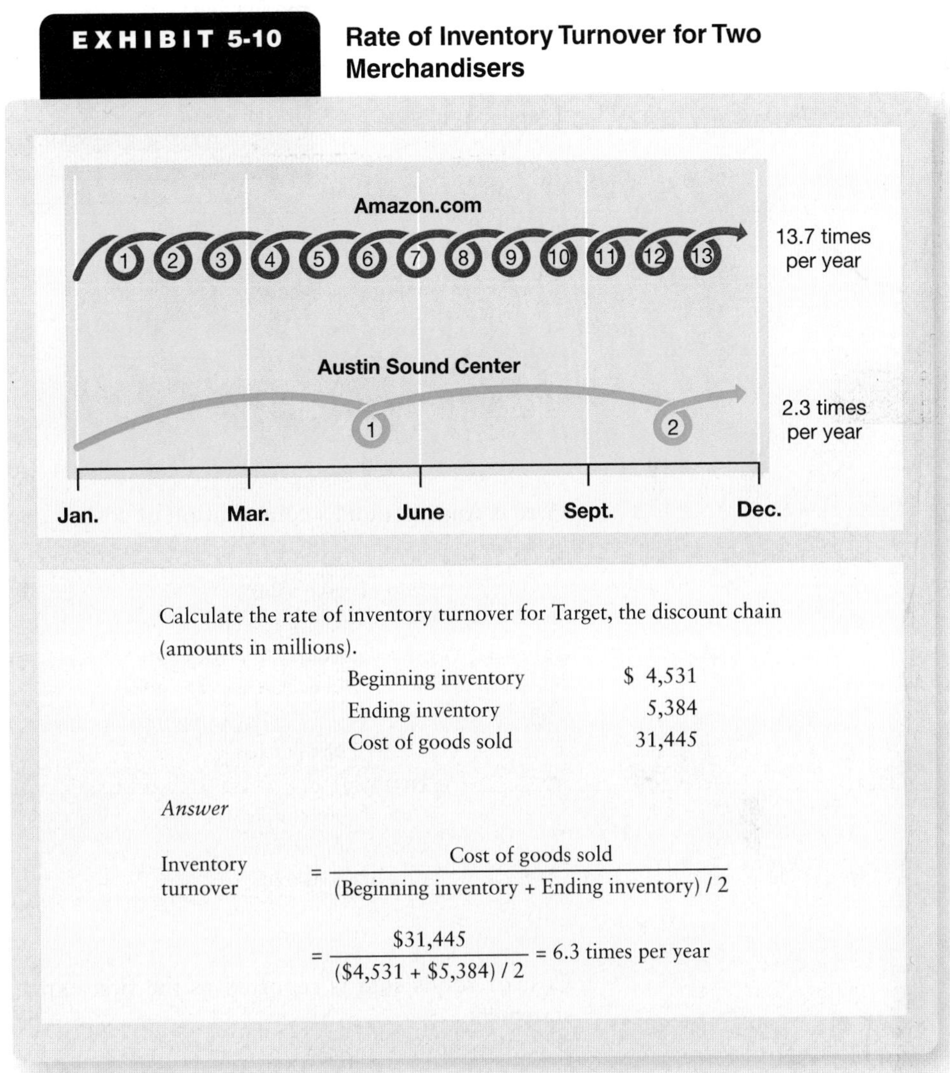

Calculate the rate of inventory turnover for Target, the discount chain (amounts in millions).

Beginning inventory	$ 4,531
Ending inventory	5,384
Cost of goods sold	31,445

Answer

$$\text{Inventory turnover} = \frac{\text{Cost of goods sold}}{(\text{Beginning inventory} + \text{Ending inventory}) / 2}$$

$$= \frac{\$31,445}{(\$4,531 + \$5,384) / 2} = 6.3 \text{ times per year}$$

Cost of Goods Sold in a Periodic Inventory System

6 Compute cost of goods sold in a periodic inventory system

The amount of cost of goods sold is the same regardless of the inventory system—perpetual or periodic. As we have seen under the perpetual system, cost of goods sold is simply the sum of the amounts posted to that account.

Cost of goods sold is computed differently under the periodic system. At the end of each period the company combines a number of accounts to compute cost of goods sold for the period. Exhibit 5-11 shows how to make the computation.

EXHIBIT 5-11 Measuring Cost of Goods Sold in the Periodic Inventory System

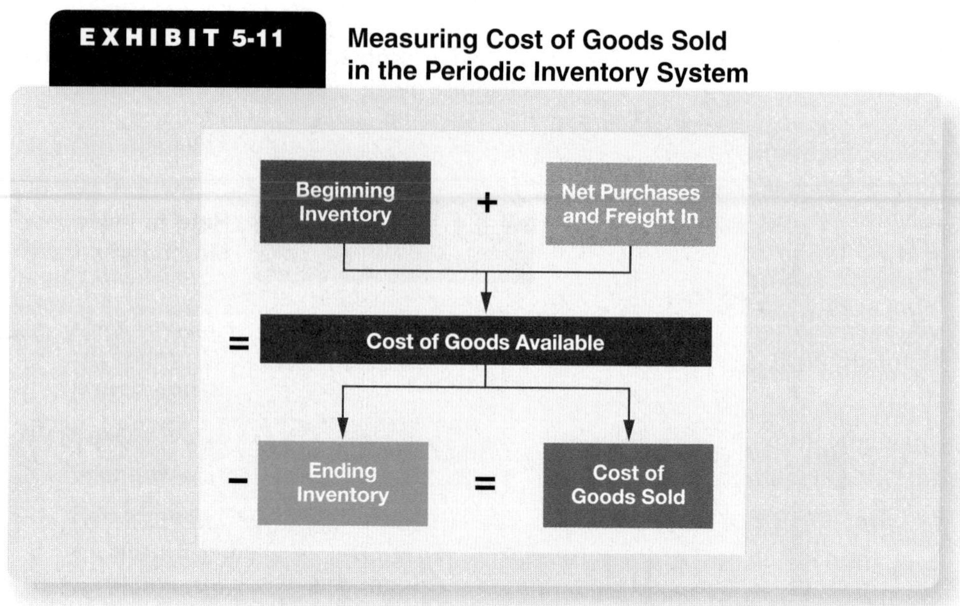

Here is Austin Sound's computation of cost of goods sold for 2008:

Cost of goods sold:		
Beginning inventory		$ 38,600
Purchases	$91,400	
Less: Purchase discounts	(3,000)	
Purchase returns and allowances	(1,200)	
Net purchases		87,200
Freight in		5,200
Cost of goods available		131,000
Less: Ending inventory		(40,200)
Cost of goods sold		$ 90,800

Cost of goods sold is reported as the first expense on the merchandiser's income statement.

Appendix 5B, pages 308–311, shows how to account for the purchase and the sale of inventory in the periodic inventory system.

Decision Guidelines

MERCHANDISING OPERATIONS AND THE ACCOUNTING CYCLE

Austin Sound and Cookie Lapp Travel Design are two very different companies. How do these two businesses differ? How are they similar? The Decision Guidelines answer these questions.

Decision	Guidelines

1. How do merchandisers differ from service entities?

- Merchandisers, such as Austin Sound, buy and sell *merchandise inventory.*
- Service entities, such as Cookie Lapp Travel Design, perform a *service.*

2. How do a merchandiser's financial statements differ from the statements of a service business?

Balance Sheet:

Merchandiser has *Inventory*, an asset.

Service business has *no* inventory.

Income Statement:

Merchandiser

Sales revenue	$XXX
– Cost of goods sold	(X)
= Gross profit	XX
– Operating expenses	(X)
= Net income	$ X

Service Business

Service revenue	$XX
– Operating expenses	(X)
= Net income	$ X

Statements of Owner's Equity:

No difference

3. Which type of inventory system to use?

- At all times the *perpetual system* shows the amount of *inventory* on hand (the asset) and the cost of goods sold (the expense).
- *Periodic system* shows the correct balances of inventory and cost of goods sold only after a count of the inventory, which occurs at least once each year.

4. How to format the merchandiser's income statement?

Multi-Step Format

Sales revenue	$XXX
– Cost of goods sold	(X)
= Gross profit	XX
– Operating expenses	(X)
= Operating income	X
+ Other revenues	X
– Other expenses	(X)
= Net income	$ X

Single-Step Format

Revenues:	Sales revenue	$ XXX
	Other revenues	X
	Total revenues	XXXX
Expenses:	Cost of goods sold	(X)
	Operating expenses	(X)
	Other expenses	(X)
	Total expenses	XXX
	Net income	$ X

5. How to evaluate merchandising operations?

Two key ratios

$$\text{Inventory} - \frac{\text{Purchase Returns}}{\text{and Allowances}} - \frac{\text{Purchas}}{\text{Discoun}}$$

$$\text{Inventory turnover}^{*} = \frac{\text{Cost of goods sold}}{\text{Average inventory}}$$

*In most cases—the higher, the better.

Summary Problem 2

The adjusted trial balance of Jan King Distributing Company follows.

JAN KING DISTRIBUTING COMPANY Adjusted Trial Balance December 31, 2007		
Cash	$ 5,600	
Accounts receivable	37,100	
Inventory	25,800	
Supplies	1,300	
Prepaid rent	1,000	
Furniture	26,500	
Accumulated depreciation		$ 23,800
Accounts payable		6,300
Salary payable		2,000
Interest payable		600
Unearned sales revenue		2,400
Note payable, long-term		35,000
Common stock		5,000
Retained earnings		17,200
Dividends	48,000	
Sales revenue		244,000
Interest revenue		2,000
Sales discounts	10,000	
Sales returns and allowances	8,000	
Cost of goods sold	81,000	
Salary expense	72,700	
Rent expense	7,700	
Depreciation expense	2,700	
Utilities expense	5,800	
Supplies expense	2,200	
Interest expense	2,900	
Total	$338,300	$338,300

Requirements

1. Journalize the closing entries at December 31. Post to the Income Summary account as an accuracy check on net income. The credit balance closed out of Income Summary should equal net income computed on the income statement. Also post to Retained Earnings, whose balance should agree with the amount reported on the balance sheet.
2. Prepare the company's single-step income statement, statement of retained earnings, and balance sheet in account form. Draw arrows linking the statements.
3. Compute the inventory turnover for 2007. Inventory at December 31, 2006, was $21,000. Turnover for 2006 was 3.0 times. Would you expect Jan King Distributing Company to be more profitable or less profitable in 2007 than in 2006? Give your reason.

Requirement 1

Closing Entries			
2007			
Dec. 31	Sales Revenue	244,000	
	Interest Revenue	2,000	
	Income Summary		246,000
31	Income Summary	193,000	
	Sales Discounts		10,000
	Sales Returns and Allowances		8,000
	Cost of Goods Sold		81,000
	Salary Expense		72,700
	Rent Expense		7,700
	Depreciation Expense		2,700
	Utilities Expense		5,800
	Supplies Expense		2,200
	Interest Expense		2,900
31	Income Summary ($246,000 – $193,000)	53,000	
	Retained Earnings		53,000
31	Retained Earnings	48,000	
	Dividends		48,000

Income Summary

Clo.	193,000	Clo.	246,000
Clo.	53,000	Bal.	53,000

Retained Earnings

			17,200
Dividends	48,000	Net inc.	53,000
		Bal.	22,200

Requirement 2

JAN KING DISTRIBUTING COMPANY Income Statement Year Ended December 31, 2007		
Revenues:		
Sales revenue		$244,000
Less: Sales discounts	$ (10,000)	
Sales returns and allowances	(8,000)	(18,000)
Net sales revenue		226,000
Interest revenue		2,000
Total revenue		228,000
Expenses:		
Cost of goods sold	$81,000	
Salary expense	72,700	
Rent expense	7,700	
Utilities expense	5,800	
Interest expense	2,900	
Depreciation expense	2,700	
Supplies expense	2,200	
Total expenses		175,000
Net income		$ 53,000

continued. . .

JAN KING DISTRIBUTING COMPANY Statement of Retained Earnings Year Ended December 31, 2007	
Retained earnings, Dec. 31, 2006	$17,200
Add: Net income	53,000
	70,200
Less: Dividends	(48,000)
Retained earnings, Dec. 31, 2007	$22,200

JAN KING DISTRIBUTING COMPANY Balance Sheet December 31, 2007				
Assets			**Liabilities**	
Current:			Current:	
Cash		$ 5,600	Accounts payable	$ 6,300
Accounts receivable		37,100	Salary payable	2,000
Inventory		25,800	Interest payable	600
Supplies		1,300	Unearned sales revenue	2,400
Prepaid rent		1,000	Total current liabilities	11,300
Total current assets		70,800	Long-term:	
Plant:			Note payable	35,000
Furniture	$26,500		Total liabilities	46,300
Less: Accumulated depreciation	(23,800)	2,700	**Stockholders' Equity**	
			Common stock	5,000
			Retained earnings	22,200
			Total stockholders' equity	27,200
Total assets		$73,500	Total liabilities and stockholders' equity	$73,500

Requirement 3

$$\text{Inventory turnover} = \frac{\text{Cost of goods sold}}{\text{Average inventory}} = \frac{\$81{,}000}{(\$21{,}000 + \$25{,}800) / 2} = 3.5 \text{ times}$$

The increase in the rate of inventory turnover from 3.0 to 3.5 suggests higher profits.

Appendix 5A

Work Sheet for a Merchandising Business

The work sheet of a merchandiser is similar to the work sheet for a service business. The main new account is the Inventory account, which must be adjusted based on a physical count, as discussed on page 271. Also, the merchandiser's work sheet carries the other new merchandising accounts (Sales Revenue, Cost of Goods Sold, and so on). Work sheet procedures are the same as for a service business. The sum of the Trial Balance amounts, plus or minus the adjustments, equal the Adjusted Trial Balance amounts. Then take the revenues and the expenses to the income statement and the assets, liabilities, and equity amounts to the balance sheet.

Exhibit 5A-1 is the work sheet of Austin Sound Center, Inc., for the year ended December 31, 2008.

EXHIBIT 5A-1 **Accounting Work Sheet for a Merchandising Business**

AUSTIN SOUND CENTER, INC.
Accounting Work Sheet
Year Ended December 31, 2008

	Trial Balance		Adjustments		Adjusted Trial Balance		Income Statement		Balance Sheet	
Account Title	**Debit**	**Credit**	**Debit**	**Credit**	**Debit**	**Credit**	**Debit**	**Credit**	**Debit**	**Credit**
Cash	2,800				2,800				2,800	
Accounts receivable	4,600				4,600				4,600	
Inventory	40,500			(a) 300	40,200				40,200	
Supplies	600			(e) 500	100				100	
Prepaid insurance	1,200			(c)1,000	200				200	
Furniture	33,200				33,200				33,200	
Accumulated depreciation		2,400		(d) 600		3,000				3,000
Accounts payable		39,500				39,500				39,500
Unearned sales revenue		2,000	(b)1,300			700				700
Wages payable				(f) 400		400				400
Note payable, long-term		12,600				12,600				12,600
Common stock		10,000				10,000				10,000
Retained earnings		15,900				15,900				15,900
Dividends	54,100				54,100				54,100	
Sales revenue		168,000		(b)1,300		169,300		169,300		
Sales discounts	1,400				1,400		1,400			
Sales returns and allowances	2,000				2,000		2,000			
Cost of goods sold	90,500		(a) 300		90,800		90,800			
Wage expense	9,800		(f) 400		10,200		10,200			
Rent expense	8,400				8,400		8,400			
Depreciation expense			(d) 600		600		600			
Insurance expense			(c)1,000		1,000		1,000			
Supplies expense			(e) 500		500		500			
Interest expense	1,300				1,300		1,300			
	250,400	250,400	4,100	4,100	251,400	251,400	116,200	169,300	135,200	82,100
Net income							53,100			53,100
							169,300	169,300	135,200	135,200

Adjustment data at December 31, 2008:

a. Actual inventory on hand, based on the physical count, $40,200. The unadjusted Inventory balance is $40,500, so we must adjust Inventory and Cost of Goods Sold by $300.

b. Unearned sales revenue that has been earned, $1,300.

c. Prepaid insurance expired, $1,000.

d. Depreciation, $600.

e. Supplies on hand, $100.

f. Accrued wages payable, $400.

A work sheet will aid the preparation of the closing entries (Exhibit 5-6, page 272) and the financial statements (Exhibit 5-7, page 274). However, the work sheet is optional.

Review *Merchandising Operations*

Accounting Vocabulary

Cost of Goods Sold
The cost of the inventory that the business has sold to customers. Also called **cost of sales**.

Cost of Sales
The cost of the inventory that the business has sold to customers. Also called **cost of goods sold**.

Gross Margin
Excess of net sales revenue over cost of goods sold. Also called **gross profit**.

Gross Margin Percentage
Gross profit divided by net sales revenue. A measure of profitability. Also called **gross profit percentage**.

Gross Profit
Excess of net sales revenue over cost of goods sold. Also called **gross margin**.

Gross Profit Percentage
Gross profit divided by net sales revenue. A measure of profitability. Also called **gross margin percentage**.

Income from Operations
Gross profit minus operating expenses plus any other operating revenues. Also called **operating income**.

Inventory
All the goods that the company owns and expects to sell in the normal course of operations.

Inventory Turnover
Ratio of cost of goods sold to average inventory. Measures the number of times a company sells its average level of inventory during a year.

Invoice
A seller's request for cash from the purchaser.

Multi-Step Income Statement
Format that contains subtotals to highlight significant relationships. In addition to net income, it reports gross profit and operating income.

Net Purchases
Purchases less purchase discounts and purchase returns and allowances.

Net Sales Revenue
Sales revenue less sales discounts and sales returns and allowances.

Operating Expenses
Expenses, other than cost of goods sold, that are incurred in the entity's major line of business. Examples include rent, depreciation, salaries, wages, utilities, and supplies expense.

Operating Income
Gross profit minus operating expenses plus any other operating revenues. Also called **income from operations**.

Other Expense
Expense that is outside the main operations of a business, such as a loss on the sale of plant assets.

Other Revenue
Revenue that is outside the main operations of a business, such as gain on the sale of plant assets.

Periodic Inventory System
A system in which the business does not keep a continuous record of inventory on hand. At the end of the period, it makes a physical count of on-hand inventory and uses this information to prepare the financial statements.

Perpetual Inventory System
The accounting inventory system in which the business keeps a running record of inventory and cost of goods sold.

Sales
The amount that a merchandiser earns from selling its inventory.

Sales Discount
Reduction in the amount receivable from a customer, offered by the seller as an incentive for the customer to pay promptly. A contra account to Sales Revenue.

Sales Returns and Allowances
Decreases in the seller's receivable from a customer's return of merchandise or from granting the customer an allowance from the amount owed to the seller. A contra account to Sales Revenue.

Sales Revenue
The amount that a merchandiser earns from selling its inventory. Also called **sales**.

Single-Step Income Statement
Format that groups all revenues together and then lists and deducts all expenses together without drawing any subtotals.

Quick Check

1. Which account does a merchandiser, but not a service company, use?
   a. Sales revenue
   b. Inventory
   c. Cost of goods sold
   d. All of the above

2. The two main inventory accounting systems are the:
   a. Purchase and sale
   b. Returns and allowances
   c. Cash and accrual
   d. Perpetual and periodic

3. The journal entry for the purchase of inventory on account is:

a. Inventory	XXX	
Accounts Payable		XXX
b. Accounts Payable	XXX	
Inventory		XXX
c. Inventory	XXX	
Accounts Receivable		XXX
d. Inventory	XXX	
Cash		XXX

4. JDC purchased inventory for $5,000 and also paid a $300 freight bill. JDC returned half the goods to the seller and later took a 2% purchase discount. What is JDC's cost of the inventory that it kept?
   a. $2,700
   b. $2,800
   c. $2,750
   d. $2,500

5. Suppose Austin Sound had sales of $300,000 and sales returns of $40,000. Cost of goods sold was $160,000. How much gross profit did Austin Sound report?
   a. $160,000
   b. $180,000
   c. $100,000
   d. $260,000

6. Suppose DeFilippo Catering's Inventory account showed a balance of $10,000 before the year-end adjustments. The physical count of goods on hand totaled $9,700. To adjust the accounts, DeFilippo would make this entry:

a. Inventory	300	
Accounts Receivable		300
b. Cost of Goods Sold	300	
Inventory		300
c. Inventory	300	
Cost of Goods Sold		300
d. Accounts Payable	300	
Inventory		300

7. Which account in question 6 would DeFilippo close at the end of the year?
   a. Cost of Goods Sold
   b. Accounts Receivable
   c. Accounts Payable
   d. Inventory

8. The final closing entry for a corporation is:

a. Dividends	XXX	
Retained Earnings		XXX
b. Retained Earnings....................	XXX	
Dividends.............................		XXX
c. Sales Revenue	XXX	
Income Summary		XXX
d. Income Summary.....................	XXX	
Expenses		XXX

9. Which subtotals appear on a multi-step income statement but not on a single-step income statement?
   a. Net sales and Cost of goods sold
   b. Operating expenses and Net income
   c. Cost of good sold and Net income
   d. Gross profit and Income from operations

10. Austin Sound made net sales of $85,000, and cost of goods sold totaled $51,000. Average inventory was $17,000. What was Austin Sound's gross profit percentage for this period?
    a. 34%
    b. 40%
    c. 60%
    d. 3.0 times

Answers are given after Apply Your Knowledge (p. 307).

Assess Your Progress

Short Exercises

Recording purchase and cash payment transactions

S5-1 You may have shopped at a Gap store. Suppose Gap purchased T-shirts on account for $10,000. Credit terms are 2/10, n/30. Gap paid within the discount period. Journalize the following transactions for Gap. (pp. 260–262)

a. Purchase of inventory.

b. Payment on account.

Accounting for the purchase of inventory—purchase discount

S5-2 Suppose Toys "Я" Us buys $100,000 worth of Lego toys on credit terms of 3/15, n/45. Some of the goods are damaged in shipment, so Toys "Я" Us returns $10,000 of the merchandise to Lego.

How much must Toys "Я" Us pay Lego

a. After the discount period? (p. 262)

b. Within the discount period? (p. 262)

Recording purchase, purchase return, and cash payment transactions

S5-3 Refer to the Toys "Я" Us situation in Short Exercise 5-2 and journalize the following transactions on the books of Toys "Я" Us. Explanations are not required. (pp. 260–262)

a. Purchase of the goods on May 6, 2005.

b. Return of the damaged goods on May 13.

c. Payment on May 15.

d. In the final analysis, how much did the inventory cost Toys "Я" Us?

Recording purchase transactions

S5-4 Suppose a Target store purchases $60,000 of women's sportswear on account from Tommy. Credit terms are 2/10, net 30. Target pays electronically, and Tommy receives the money on the tenth day.

Journalize Target's (a) purchase and (b) payment transactions. What was Target's net cost of this inventory? (pp. 260–262)

Note: Short Exercise 5-5 covers this same situation for the seller.

Recording sales, cost of goods sold, and cash collections

S5-5 Tommy sells $60,000 of women's sportswear to a Target store under credit terms of 2/10, net 30. Tommy's cost of the goods is $32,000, and Tommy collects cash from Target on the tenth day.

Journalize Tommy's (a) sale, (b) cost of goods sold, and (c) cash receipt. (pp. 265–268)

Note: Short Exercise 5-4 covers the same situation for the buyer.

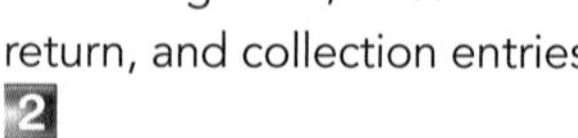

Recording sales, sales return, and collection entries

S5-6 Suppose Amazon.com sells 1,000 books on account for $10 each (cost of these books is $6,000). One hundred of these books (cost, $600) were damaged in shipment, so Amazon later received the damaged goods as sales returns. Then the customer paid the balance within the discount period. Credit terms were 2/15, net 30.

Journalize Amazon's (a) sale, (b) sale return, and (c) cash collection transactions. (pp. 265–268)

Computing net sales and gross profit

S5-7 Use the data in Short Exercise 5-6 to compute Amazon.com's (a) net sales revenue and (b) gross profit. (p. 268)

Adjusting inventory for shrinkage
3

S5-8 Patio Furniture's Inventory account at year-end appeared as follows:

Inventory	
Unadjusted balance 65,000	

The physical count of inventory came up with a total of $63,900. Journalize the adjusting entry. (pp. 271–273)

Closing the books
3

S5-9 Hayes RV Center, Inc., accounting records include the following accounts at December 31:

Cost of goods sold	$385,000	Accumulated depreciation	$ 38,000
Accounts payable	16,000	Cash	40,000
Rent expense	20,000	Sales revenue	700,000
Building	110,000	Depreciation expense	10,000
Retained earnings	40,000	Dividends	60,000
Inventory	260,000	Sales discounts	9,000
Common stock	100,000		

Journalize closing entries for Hayes': (p. 272)

a. Revenues

b. Expenses

c. Income Summary account

d. Dividends

Preparing a merchandiser's income statement
4

S5-10 Carolina Communications Corp. reported these figures in its financial statements (amounts in thousands):

Cash	$ 3,800
Total operating expenses	3,500
Accounts payable	4,000
Total stockholders' equity	4,200
Long-term notes payable	900
Inventory	400
Cost of goods sold	20,000
Equipment, net	3,700
Accrued liabilities	1,600
Net sales revenue	25,000
Accounts receivable	2,800

Prepare Carolina's multi-step income statement for the year ended January 31, 2007. (p. 274)

Preparing a merchandiser's balance sheet

S5-11 Use the data in Short Exercise 5-10 to prepare Carolina Communications Corp.'s classified balance sheet at January 31, 2007. Use the report form with all headings, and list accounts in proper order. (p. 274)

Computing the gross profit percentage and the rate of inventory turnover
5

S5-12 Refer to the Carolina Communications Corp. situation in Short Exercises 5-10 and 5-11. Compute the gross profit percentage and rate of inventory turnover for 2007. One year earlier, at January 31, 2006, Carolina's inventory balance was $300. (pp. 260–262, 276)

Computing cost of goods sold in a periodic inventory system
6

S5-13 T Wholesale Company began the year with inventory of $8,000. During the year, T purchased $90,000 of goods and returned $6,000 due to damage. T also paid freight charges of $1,000 on inventory purchases. At year-end T's adjusted inventory balance stood at $11,000. T uses the periodic inventory system.

Compute T's cost of goods sold for the year. (pp. 277–278)

Exercises

Journalizing transactions from a purchase invoice

E5-14 As the proprietor of Discount Tire Co., you received the following invoice from a supplier:

WHOLESALE DISTRIBUTORS, INC.
2600 Commonwealth Avenue
Boston, Massachusetts 02215

Invoice date: May 14, 2007

Sold to: Discount Tire Co.
4219 Crestwood Parkway
Lexington, Mass. 02173

Payment terms: 3/10 n/30

Description	Quantity Shipped	Price	Amount
P135–X4 Radials....................................	1	$37.24	$ 37.24
L912 Belted-bias....................................	8	41.32	330.56
R39 Truck tires....................................	10	60.02	600.20
Total..			$968.00

Due date:	Amount:
May 24, 2007	$938.96
May 25 through June 13, 2007	$968.00

Requirements

1. Discount received the invoice on May 15. Record the May 15 purchase on account. Carry amounts to the nearest cent throughout. (p. 260)
2. The P135–X4 Radial was ordered by mistake and was, therefore, returned to Wholesale Distributors. Journalize the return on May 19. (p. 262)
3. Record the May 22 payment of the net amount owed. (p. 262)

Journalizing purchase transactions

E5-15 On April 30, Boozer Jewelers purchased inventory of $6,000 on account from Van Dyke Diamonds, a jewelry importer. Terms were 3/15, net 45. The same day Boozer paid freight charges of $300. On receiving the goods, Boozer checked the order and found $1,000 of unsuitable merchandise. Boozer returned the unsuitable merchandise to Van Dyke on May 4. Then, on May 14, Boozer paid Van Dyke.

Requirements

Record the indicated transactions in the journal of Boozer Jewelers. Explanations are not required. (pp. 260–264)

Journalizing sales transactions

E5-16 Refer to the business situation in Exercise 5-15. Journalize the transactions of Van Dyke Diamonds. Van Dyke's cost of goods sold runs 60% of sales. Explanations are not required. (pp. 265–268)

Journalizing purchase and sales transactions

E5-17 Journalize, without explanations, the following transactions of Soul Art Gift Shop during the month of February: (pp. 260–268)

Feb. 3	Purchased $2,000 of inventory on account under terms of 2/10, n/eom (end of month) and FOB shipping point.
7	Returned $300 of defective merchandise purchased on February 3.
9	Paid freight bill of $50 on February 3 purchase.
10	Sold inventory on account for $3,100. Payment terms were 3/15 n/30. These goods cost Soul Art $1,700.
12	Paid amount owed on credit purchase of February 3, less the return and the discount.
16	Granted a sales allowance of $500 on the February 10 sale.
23	Received cash from February 10 customer in full settlement of her debt, less the allowance and the discount.

Adjusting and closing; computing gross profit

3

E5-18 Candy Creations' accounts at June 30 included these unadjusted balances:

Inventory	$ 5,600
Cost of goods sold	41,200
Sales revenue	86,900
Sales discounts	900
Sales returns and allowances	1,400

The physical count of inventory on hand added up to $5,400. This is the only adjustment needed.

a. Journalize the adjustment for inventory shrinkage. Include an explanation. (p. 272)

b. Journalize the closing entries for the appropriate accounts. (p. 272)

c. Compute the gross profit. (p. 274)

Computing inventory and cost of goods sold amounts

1 2

E5-19 Supply the missing income statement amounts in each of the following situations: (p. 274)

Sales	Sales Discounts	Net Sales	Cost of Goods Sold	Gross Profit
$91,500	$1,800	$89,700	$59,400	(a)
98,300	(b)	92,800	(c)	$33,000
62,400	2,100	(d)	44,100	(e)
(f)	3,000	(g)	72,500	39,600

Making closing entries

3

E5-20 Jackson Auto Glass, Inc.'s, accounting records carried the following selected accounts at January 31, 2008.

Inventory	$ 5,500	Selling expense	$ 6,800
Interest revenue	40	Sales revenue	38,400
Accounts payable	2,000	Interest expense	30
Cost of goods sold	27,000	Accounts receivable	600
Other expense	1,600	General and administrative expense	700
Dividends	300	Retained earnings	8,740

Requirements

1. Journalize all of Jackson's closing entries at January 31, 2008. (p. 274)
2. Set up T-accounts for Income Summary and Retained Earnings. Post to these accounts and take their ending balances. One year earlier, at January 31, 2007, the Retained Earnings balance was the $8,740 shown above. (p. 272)

Journalizing closing entries

3

E5-21 This exercise uses Appendix 5A, page 283. The trial balance and adjustments columns of the work sheet of Budget Business Systems Co. at March 31, 2007 follow.

	Trial Balance		Adjustments	
Account Title	Debit	Credit	Debit	Credit
Cash	2,100			
Accounts receivable	8,500		(a) 1,000	
Inventory	36,100			(b) 4,200
Supplies	13,000			(c) 7,600
Equipment	42,400			
Accumulated depreciation		11,200		(d) 2,200
Accounts payable		9,300		

continued...

Account Title	Trial Balance Debit	Trial Balance Credit	Adjustments Debit	Adjustments Credit
Salary payable				(e) 1,200
Note payable, long-term		7,500		
Common stock		6,000		
Retained earnings		27,900		
Dividends	45,000			
Sales revenue		233,000		(a) 1,000
Sales discounts	2,000			
Cost of goods sold	111,600		(b) 4,200	
Selling expense	21,000		(c) 5,200	
			(e) 1,200	
General expense	10,500		(c) 2,400	
			(d) 2,200	
Interest expense	2,700			
Total	294,900	294,900	16,200	16,200

Compute the adjusted balance for each account that must be closed. Then journalize Budget's closing entries at March 31, 2007. How much was Budget's net income or net loss? (pp. 272, 283)

Preparing a multi-step income statement

E5-22 Use the data in Exercise 5-21 to prepare the multi-step income statement of Budget Business Systems Co. for the year ended March 31, 2007. (p. 273–275)

Preparing a merchandiser's multi-step income statement to evaluate the business

E5-23 Selected amounts from the accounting records of Azalea Technology, Inc. follow.

Accounts payable	$16,200	Stockholders' equity, December 31, 2008	$126,070
Accumulated depreciation	18,700	Sales discounts	9,000
Cost of goods sold	99,400	Sales returns	4,600
General expenses	23,500	Sales revenue	241,000
Interest revenue	1,300	Selling expenses	37,800
Inventory, December 31, 2008	21,000	Unearned sales revenue	6,500
Inventory, December 31, 2007	26,400		

Requirements

1. Prepare Azalea Technology, Inc.'s, *multi-step* income statement for the year ended December 31, 2008. (p. 274)
2. Compute the rate of inventory turnover for 2008. Last year the turnover rate was 3.8 times. Does this trend suggest improvement or deterioration in inventory turnover? (p. 276)

Preparing a single-step income statement to evaluate the business

E5-24 Prepare Azalea Technology, Inc.'s, *single-step* income statement for 2008, using the data from Exercise 5-23. Compute the gross profit percentage, and compare it with last year's gross profit percentage of 50%. Does the trend in the gross profit percentage suggest better or worse profitability during the current year? (pp. 275, 276)

Computing gross profit percentage and inventory turnover

E5-25 Networking Systems earned sales revenue of $65 million in 2009. Cost of goods sold was $33 million, and net income reached $8 million, the company's highest ever. Total current assets included inventory of $3 million at December 31, 2009. Last year's ending inventory was $4 million. The managers of Networking Systems need to know the company's gross profit percentage and rate of inventory turnover for 2009. Compute these selected amounts. (p. 276)

Cost of goods sold in a periodic inventory system

6

E5-26 Baker Electric Co. uses the periodic inventory system. Baker reported these selected amounts at May 31, 2007:

Inventory, May 31, 2006	$19,000	Freight in	$ 4,000
Inventory, May 31, 2007	21,000	Sales revenue	170,000
Purchases (of inventory)	82,000	Sales discounts	3,000
Purchase discounts	2,000	Sales returns	15,000
Purchase returns	8,000	Stockholders' equity	52,000

Compute Baker's:

a. Net sales revenue (p. 274)
b. Cost of goods sold (p. 277)
c. Gross profit (p. 274)

Problems (Group A)

Explaining the perpetual inventory system

P5-27A Home Depot operates home-improvement stores across the country. Home Depot has a sophisticated perpetual inventory accounting system.

Requirements

You are the manager of a Home Depot store in Fort Lauderdale, Florida. Write a one-paragraph business memo to a new employee explaining how the company accounts for the purchase and sale of merchandise inventory. Use the following heading for your memo. (pp. 260–268)

Date: ____________

To: New Employee

From: Store Manager

Subject: Home Depot's perpetual inventory accounting system

Accounting for the purchase and sale of inventory

P5-28A The following transactions occurred between BMS Pharmaceuticals and VIP, the pharmacy chain, during October of the current year:

Oct. 6	VIP purchased $5,000 of merchandise from BMS on credit terms of 3/10, n/30, FOB shipping point. Separately, VIP paid a $500 bill for freight in. These goods cost BMS $2,100.
10	VIP returned $900 of the merchandise purchased on October 6. BMS accounted for the $900 sales return and placed the goods back in inventory (BMS's cost, $590).
15	VIP paid $3,000 of the invoice amount owed to BMS for the October 6 purchase, less the discount. This payment included none of the freight charge.
27	VIP paid the remaining amount owed to BMS for the October 6 purchase.

Requirements

Journalize these transactions, first on the books of VIP and second on the books of BMS Pharmaceuticals. (pp. 260–268)

Journalizing purchase and sale transactions

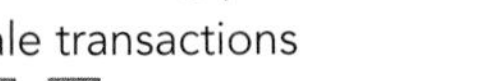

P5-29A Terry's Amusements completed in the following transactions during May:

May 1	Purchased supplies for cash, $300.
4	Purchased inventory on credit terms of 3/10 net eom, $6,000.
8	Returned half the inventory purchased on May 4. It was not the inventory ordered.
10	Sold goods for cash, $450 (cost, $250).
13	Sold inventory on credit terms of 2/15, n/45, $3,900 (cost, $1,800).
14	Paid the amount owed on account from May 4, less the return (May 8) and the discount.
17	Received defective inventory as a sales return from the May 13 sale, $900. Terry's cost of the inventory received was $600.
18	Purchased inventory of $5,000 on account. Payment terms were 2/10 net 30.
26	Paid the net amount owed for the May 18 purchase.
28	Received cash in full settlement of the account from the customer who purchased inventory on May 13, less the return and the discount.
29	Purchased inventory for cash, $2,000, plus freight charges of $160.

Requirements

Journalize the preceding transactions on the books of Terry's Amusements. (pp. 260–268)

Preparing a multi-step income statement

4

P5-30A The records of A-1 Publishers Company list the following selected accounts at November 30, 2007:

Selling expenses	$ 18,800	Inventory	$41,500
Furniture	37,000	Cash	36,000
Sales returns and allowances	3,200	Notes payable	21,600
Salary payable	800	Accumulated depreciation	23,600
Common stock	27,000	Cost of goods sold	52,000
Sales revenue	113,700	Sales discounts	2,100
Accounts payable	13,200	General expenses	9,300

Requirements

1. Prepare a multi-step income statement to show the computation of A-1 Publishers Company's net sales, gross profit, and net income for the month ended November 30, 2007. (p. 274)
2. M. Nolen, manager of the company, strives to earn gross profit of $50,000 and net income of $25,000 each month. Did he achieve these goals? Write a sentence to explain. (Challenge)

Preparing a multi-step income statement and a classified balance sheet

P5-31A ← *Link Back to Chapter 4 (Classified Balance Sheet).* The accounts of Northeast Electronics Company are listed along with their balances before closing at May 31, 2009.

Interest revenue	$ 400	Accounts payable	$ 16,900
Inventory	45,500	Accounts receivable	33,700
Note payable, long-term	45,000	Accumulated depreciation	38,000
Salary payable	2,800	Retained earnings, April 30, 2009	38,900
Sales discounts	2,400	Dividends	19,000
Sales returns and allowances	8,000	Cash	7,800
Sales revenue	296,600	Cost of goods sold	162,000
Selling expenses	37,900	Equipment	129,600
Supplies	5,900	General expenses	16,700
Unearned sales revenue	13,800	Common stock	15,000
Interest payable	1,100		

Requirements

1. Prepare Northeast Electronics Company's *multi-step* income statement for the month ended May 31, 2009: (p. 274)
2. Prepare Northeast Electronics Company's classified balance sheet in *report form* at May 31, 2009. Show your computation of the May 31 balance of Retained Earnings. (p. 274)

Preparing a single-step income statement and a classified balance sheet

P5-32A ← *Link Back to Chapter 4 (Classified Balance Sheet).*

Requirements

1. Use the data of Problem 5-31A to prepare a *single-step* income statement for the month ended May 31, 2009. (p. 275)
2. Prepare Northeast Electronics Company's classified balance sheet in *report format* at May 31, 2009. Show your computation of the May 31 balance of Retained Earnings. (p. 274)

Making closing entries; computing gross profit percentage, inventory turnover, and cost of goods sold

3 5 6

P5-33A The adjusted trial balance of Big Daddy Music Company at December 31, 2008, follows:

	Adjusted Trial Balance	
Account Title	Debit	Credit
Cash	4,000	
Accounts receivable	38,500	
Inventory	17,400	
Supplies	400	
Furniture	39,600	
Accumulated depreciation		8,700
Accounts payable		13,600
Salary payable		900
Unearned sales revenue		6,800
Note payable, long-term		15,000
Common stock		5,000
Retained earnings		31,400
Dividends	42,000	
Sales revenue		185,000
Sales returns	7,000	
Cost of goods sold	82,000	
Selling expense	19,000	
General expense	15,000	
Interest expense	1,500	
Total	266,400	266,400

Requirements

1. Journalize Big Daddy's closing entries. (p. 272)
2. Compute the gross profit percentage and the rate of inventory turnover for 2008. Inventory on hand one year ago, at December 31, 2007, was $12,600. For 2007, Big Daddy's gross profit percentage was 50%, and inventory turnover was 4.9 times. Do the trends in these ratios suggest improvement or deterioration in profitability? (p. 276)

continued. . .

3. Additional inventory data:

Purchases	$84,800	Purchase returns	$3,000
Purchase discounts	1,000	Freight in	6,000

Compute Big Daddy's cost of goods sold under the periodic inventory system. Does your computed amount agree with Big Daddy's adjusted balance of cost of goods sold? It should. (p. 277)

Preparing a merchandiser's work sheet

P5-34A This problem is based on Appendix 5A, page 283. Harley's of Chicago, Inc.'s, trial balance pertains to December 31, 2009.

HARLEY'S OF CHICAGO, INC. Trial Balance December 31, 2009		
Cash	$ 7,000	
Accounts receivable	4,000	
Inventory	73,000	
Prepaid rent	5,000	
Equipment	22,000	
Accumulated depreciation		$ 8,000
Accounts payable		6,000
Salary payable		
Note payable, long-term		18,000
Common stock		10,000
Retained earnings		40,000
Dividends	39,000	
Sales revenue		170,000
Cost of goods sold	67,000	
Salary expense	24,000	
Rent expense	7,000	
Utilities expense	3,000	
Depreciation expense		
Interest expense	1,000	
Total	$252,000	$252,000

Adjustment data at December 31, 2009:

a. Prepaid rent expired, $3,000.

b. Depreciation, $5,000.

c. Accrued salaries, $1,000.

d. Inventory on hand, $71,000.

Requirements

Complete Harley's accounting work sheet for the year ended December 31, 2009. Key adjusting entries by letter. (p. 283)

Journalizing the adjusting and closing entries of a merchandising business

P5-35A Refer to the data in Problem 5-34A.

1. Journalize Harley's adjusting and closing entries. (pp. 272–283)
2. Determine the December 31, 2009, balance of Retained Earnings. (pp. 272–274)

Problems (Group B)

Explaining the perpetual inventory system

1 2

P5-36B Scooter Mike sells pocket rockets, mini choppers, and all-terrain vehicles. The company has launched a new advertising campaign to introduce its products to the public.

Requirements

Scooter Mike expects to grow rapidly and to increase its level of inventory. As the chief accountant of this company, you wish to install a perpetual inventory system. Write a one-paragraph business memo to the company president to explain how that system would work for the purchase and sale of inventory. Use the following heading for your memo: (pp. 259–261)

Date: ____________________

To: Company President

From: Chief Accountant

Subject: How a perpetual inventory system works for purchases and sales

Accounting for the purchase and sale of inventory

P5-37B Assume the following transactions occurred between Heights Pharmacy and Procter & Gamble (P&G), the consumer products company, during August of the current year.

Aug. 8	Heights Pharmacy purchased $3,000 of merchandise from P&G on credit terms of 2/10, n/30, FOB shipping point. Separately, Heights paid a $100 bill for freight in. These goods cost P&G $900).
11	Heights returned $1,000 of the merchandise purchased on August 8. P&G accounted for the sales return and placed the goods back in inventory (P&G's cost, $400).
17	Heights paid $1,500 of the invoice amount owed to P&G for the August 8 purchase, less the discount. This payment included none of the freight charge.
26	Heights paid the remaining amount owed to P&G for the August 8 purchase.

continued. . .

Requirements

Journalize these transactions, first on the books of Heights Pharmacy and second on the books of Procter & Gamble. (pp. 260–268)

Journalizing purchase and sale transactions

P5-38B Alpha Graphics completed in the following transactions during September:

Sept.	2	Purchased inventory for cash, $740.
	5	Purchased store supplies on credit terms of net eom, $600.
	8	Purchased inventory of $3,000, plus freight charges of $200. Credit terms are 3/15, n/30.
	9	Sold goods for cash, $1,200. Alpha Graphics' cost of these goods was $700.
	11	Returned $1,000 of the inventory purchased on September 8. It was damaged.
	12	Purchased inventory on credit terms of 3/10, n/30, $3,800.
	14	Sold inventory on credit terms of 2/10, n/30, $9,600 (cost $5,000).
	16	Paid utilities expense, $275.
	20	Received returned inventory from the September 14 sale, $400. Alpha Graphics shipped the wrong goods by mistake. Alpha Graphics' cost of the inventory received was $250.
	21	Paid supplier for goods purchased on September 8 less the return (September 11) and the discount.
	23	Received $6,860 cash in partial settlement of his account from the customer who purchased inventory on September 14. Granted the customer a 2% discount and credited his account receivable for $7,000.
	30	Paid for the store supplies purchased on September 5.

Requirements

Journalize the preceding transactions on the books of Alpha Graphics. (pp. 260–268)

Preparing a multi-step income statement

4

P5-39B The records of Steubs Environmental Solutions Co. at June 30, 2008, list the following selected accounts:

Cash	$ 22,300	Inventory	$28,500
Note payable	4,300	Equipment	51,600
Sales revenue	206,000	Cost of goods sold	95,000
Salary payable	1,800	Accumulated depreciation	6,900
Common stock	5,600	Sales discounts	3,400
Sales returns and allowances	11,500	General expenses	16,300
Selling expenses	19,800	Accounts payable	23,800

continued. . .

Requirements

1. Prepare a multi-step income statement to show the computation of Steubs Environmental Solutions Co.'s net sales, gross profit, and net income for the year ended June 30, 2008. (p. 274)
2. Marty Steubs, manager of the business, strives to earn gross profit of $90,000 and net income of $50,000. Did he achieve these goals? Write a sentence or two to explain. (Challenge)

Preparing a multi-step income statement and a classified balance sheet
4

P5-40B ← *Link Back to Chapter 4 (Classified Balance Sheet).* The accounts of Mackey Home Center, Inc., are listed along with their balances before closing at July 31, 2008.

Accounts payable	$ 27,300	Inventory	$ 87,300
Accounts receivable	48,600	Note payable, long-term	60,000
Accumulated depreciation	116,400	Salary payable	6,100
Retained earnings, June 30	9,400	Sales discounts	1,100
Dividends	11,000	Sales returns and allowances	7,000
Cash	4,300	Sales revenue	268,200
Cost of goods sold	160,900	Selling expense	34,600
General expense	25,800	Building	126,000
Interest payable	3,000	Supplies	4,300
Interest revenue	1,200	Unearned sales revenue	9,300
Common stock	10,000		

Requirements

1. Prepare Mackey Home Center, Inc.'s, *multi-step* income statement for the month ended July 31, 2008. (p. 274)
2. Prepare Mackey's classified balance sheet in *report form* at July 31, 2008. Show your computation of the July 31 balance of Retained Earnings. (p. 274)

Preparing a single-step income statement and a classified balance sheet

P5-41B ← *Link Back to Chapter 4 (Classified Balance Sheet).*

Requirements

1. Use the data of Problem 5-40B to prepare Mackey Home Center, Inc.'s, *single-step* income statement for the month ended July 31, 2008. (p. 275)
2. Prepare Mackey's classified balance sheet in *report form* at July 31, 2008. Show your computation of the July 31 balance of Retained Earnings. (p. 275)

Making closing entries; computing gross profit percentage, inventory turnover, and cost of goods sold

P5-42B The adjusted trial balance of Arctic Cat RVs, Inc., at December 31, 2009, follows.

	Adjusted Trial Balance	
Account Title	**Debit**	**Credit**
Cash	7,000	
Accounts receivable	4,500	
Inventory	42,000	

continued. . .

Account Title	Adjusted Trial Balance Debit	Credit
Supplies	1,500	
Building	140,000	
Accumulated depreciation		29,000
Accounts payable		11,000
Salary payable		200
Unearned sales revenue		1,600
Note payable, long-term		30,000
Common stock		50,000
Retained Earnings		61,600
Dividends	45,000	
Sales revenue		201,400
Sales returns	14,000	
Cost of goods sold	101,000	
Selling expense	17,900	
General expense	9,900	
Interest expense	2,000	
Total	384,800	384,800

Requirements

1. Journalize Arctic Cat's closing entries. (p. 272)
2. Compute the gross profit percentage and the rate of inventory turnover for 2009. Inventory on hand at December 31, 2008, was $40,000. For 2008 Arctic Cat's gross profit percentage was 50% and the inventory turnover rate was 3.0 times. Do the trends in these ratios suggest improvement or deterioration in profitability? (p. 276)
3. Additional inventory data:

Purchases	$108,000	Purchase returns	$6,000
Purchase discounts	3,000	Freight in	4,000

Compute Arctic Cat's cost of goods sold under the periodic inventory system. Does your computed amount agree with Arctic Cat's adjusted balance of cost of goods sold? It should. (p. 277)

Preparing a merchandiser's work sheet

P5-43B This problem is based on Appendix 5A, page 283. The trial balance of Rustic Elegance, Inc., pertains to December 31, 2007.

RUSTIC ELEGANCE, INC. Trial Balance December 31, 2007		
Cash	$ 2,900	
Accounts receivable	10,100	
Inventory	71,000	
Prepaid insurance	3,200	
Furniture	23,900	
Accumulated depreciation		$ 7,000
Accounts payable		9,000
Salary payable		
Note payable, long-term		20,000
Common stock		10,000
Retained earnings		48,000
Dividends	36,300	
Sales revenue		190,000
Cost of goods sold	61,000	
Salary expense	46,500	
Rent expense	14,000	
Utilities expense	6,700	
Depreciation expense		
Insurance expense	5,300	
Interest expense	3,100	
Total	$284,000	$284,000

Adjustment data at December 31, 2007:

a. Prepaid insurance expired, $2,000.

b. Depreciation, $4,000.

c. Accrued salaries, $1,000.

d. Inventory on hand, $68,000.

Requirement

Complete the accounting work sheet of Rustic Elegance, Inc., for the year ended December 31, 2007. Key adjusting entries by letter. (p. 283)

Journalizing the adjusting and closing entries of a merchandising business

3

P5-44B Refer to the data in Problem 5-43B.

Requirements

1. Journalize the adjusting and closing entries of Rustic Elegance, Inc. (pp. 272, 283)
2. Determine the December 31, 2007, balance of Retained Earnings. (pp. 272, 283)

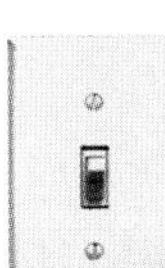

For 24/7 practice, visit www.MyAccountingLab.com

Continuing Problem

This problem completes the Redmon Consulting Company situation, begun in Problem 1-42 of Chapter 1 and continued through Chapters 2–4.

Accounting for both merchandising and service operations

P5-45 Redmon performs systems consulting. Redmon has also begun selling accounting software. During January, Redmon Consulting Company completed these transactions:

Jan. 2	Completed a consulting engagement and received cash of $7,200.
2	Prepaid three months' office rent, $1,500.
7	Purchased software inventory on account, $3,900, plus freight in, $100.
16	Paid employee salary, $1,400.
18	Sold software on account, $1,100 (cost $700).
19	Consulted with a client for a fee of $900 on account.
21	Paid on account, $2,000.
24	Paid utilities, $300.
28	Sold software for cash, $600 (cost $400).
31	Recorded these adjusting entries:
	Accrued salary expense, $1,400.
	Depreciation, $200.
	Expiration of prepaid rent, $500.
	Physical count of inventory, $2,800.

Requirements

1. Open the following selected T-accounts in the ledger: Cash; Accounts Receivable; Software Inventory; Prepaid Rent; Accumulated Depreciation; Accounts Payable; Salary Payable; Retained Earnings; Income Summary; Service Revenue; Sales Revenue; Cost of Goods Sold; Salary Expense; Rent Expense; Utilities Expense; and Depreciation Expense.
2. Journalize and post the January transactions. Key all items by date. Compute each account balance, and denote the balance as *Bal.*
3. Journalize and post the closing entries. Denote each closing amount as *Clo.* After posting all closing entries, prove the equality of debits and credits in the ledger.
4. Prepare the January income statement of Redmon Consulting Company. Use the single-step format.

Apply Your Knowledge

Decision Cases

Using the financial statements to decide on a business expansion

Case 1. ← *Link Back to Chapter 4 (Classified Balance Sheet. Current Ratio. Debt Ratio).* Jan Louis manages Poppa Rollo's Pizza, Inc., which has prospered during its second year of operation. Deciding whether to open another pizzeria, Louis has prepared the current income statement of the business. Louis read in an industry trade journal that a successful two-year-old pizzeria meets these criteria:

a. Gross profit percentage is at least 60%.

b. Net income is at least $90,000.

Louis believes the business meets both criteria. She intends to go ahead with the expansion plan and asks your advice on preparing the income statement in accordance with generally accepted accounting principles. When you point out that the statement includes errors, Louis assures you that all amounts are correct. But some items are listed in the wrong place.

Requirements

Prepare a multi-step income statement and make a recommendation about whether Louis should undertake the expansion. (p. 274)

POPPA ROLLO'S PIZZA, INC. Income Statement Year Ended December 31, 2008	
Sales revenue	$195,000
Gain on sale of land	24,600
Total revenue	219,600
Cost of goods sold	85,200
Gross profit	134,400
Operating expenses:	
Salary expense	35,600
Interest expense	6,000
Depreciation expense	4,800
Utilities expense	3,700
Total operating expense	50,100
Income from operations	84,300
Other revenue:	
Sales returns	10,700
Net income	$ 95,000

Expanding a business

Case 2. Bill Hildebrand and Melissa Nordhaus opened Party-Time T-Shirts to sell T-shirts for parties at their college. The company completed the first year of operations, and the owners are generally pleased with operating results, as shown by the following income statement:

continued...

PARTY-TIME T-SHIRTS **Income Statement** Year Ended December 31, 2007	
Net sales revenue	$350,000
Cost of goods sold	210,000
Gross margin	140,000
Operating expenses:	
Selling expense	40,000
General expense	25,000
Net income	$ 75,000

Hildebrand and Nordhaus are considering how to expand the business. They each propose a way to increase profits to $100,000 during 2008.

a. Hildebrand believes they should advertise more heavily. He believes additional advertising costing $20,000 will increase net sales by 30% and leave general expense unchanged.

b. Nordhaus proposes selling higher-margin merchandise, such as party dresses. An importer can supply a minimum of 1,000 dresses for $40 each; Party-Time can mark these dresses up 100% and sell them for $80. Nordhaus realizes they will have to advertise the new merchandise, and this advertising will cost $5,000. Party-Time can expect to sell only 80% of these dresses during the coming year.

Requirements

Help Hildebrand and Nordhaus determine which plan to pursue. Prepare a single-step income statement for 2008 to show the expected net income under each plan. (p. 273–275)

Ethical Issue

Dobbs Wholesale Antiques makes all sales under terms of FOB shipping point. The company usually receives orders for sales approximately one week before shipping inventory to customers. For orders received late in December, Kathy Dobbs, the owner, decides when to ship the goods. If profits are already at an acceptable level, Dobbs delays shipment until January. If profits for the current year are lagging behind expectations, Dobbs ships the goods during December.

Requirements

1. Under Dobbs FOB policy, when should the company record a sale?
2. Do you approve or disapprove of Dobbs' manner of deciding when to ship goods to customers and record the sales revenue? If you approve, give your reason. If you disapprove, identify a better way to decide when to ship goods. (There is no accounting rule against Dobbs' practice.)

Financial Statement Case

Closing entries for a well-known company

This case uses both the income statement (statement of operations) and the balance sheet of Amazon.com in Appendix A at the end of the book. It will help you understand the closing process of a business.

Requirements

1. Journalize Amazon.com's closing entries for the revenues and expenses of 2005. Show all amounts in millions as in the Amazon financial statements. You may be unfamiliar with certain revenues and expenses, but treat each item on the income statement as either a revenue or an expense. For example, Net Sales is the first revenue, and Interest Income is also a revenue. The last revenue is Cumulative Effect of Change in Accounting Principle. A loss is like an expense. In your closing entries ignore all subtotals such as Gross Profit, Total Operating Expenses, and Net Loss.
2. Create a T-account for Income Summary, post to that account, and then close Income Summary. How much was closed to Retained Earnings? How is the amount that was closed to Retained Earnings labeled on the income statement?

Team Project

With a small team of classmates, visit one or more merchandising businesses in your area. Interview a responsible official of the company to learn about its inventory policies and accounting system. Obtain answers to the following questions, write a report, and be prepared to make a presentation to the class if your instructor so directs:

Requirements

1. What merchandise inventory does the business sell?
2. From whom does the business buy its inventory? Is the relationship with the supplier new or longstanding?
3. What are the FOB terms on inventory purchases? Who pays the freight, the buyer or the seller? Is freight a significant amount? What percentage of total inventory cost is the freight?
4. What are the credit terms on inventory purchases—2/10, n/30, or other? Does the business pay early to get purchase discounts? If so, why? If not, why not?
5. How does the business actually pay its suppliers? Does it mail a check or pay electronically? What is the actual payment procedure?
6. Which type of inventory accounting system does the business use—perpetual or periodic? Is this system computerized?
7. How often does the business take a physical count of its inventory? When during the year is the count taken? Describe the count procedures followed by the company.
8. Does the manager use the gross profit percentage and the rate of inventory turnover to evaluate the business? If not, show the manager how to use these ratios in decision making.
9. Ask any other questions your group considers appropriate.

For Internet Exercises, Excel in Practice, and additional online activities, go to the Web site www.prenhall.com/horngren.

Quick Check Answers

1. *d* 2. *d* 3. *a* 4. *c* 5. *c* 6. *b* 7. *a* 8. *b* 9. *d* 10. *b*

Appendix 5B

Accounting for Merchandise in a Periodic Inventory System

Some businesses find it too expensive to invest in a perpetual inventory system. These businesses use a periodic system.

Recording the Purchase of Inventory

All inventory systems use the Inventory account. But in a periodic system, purchases, purchase discounts, purchase returns and allowances, and transportation costs are recorded in separate accounts. Let's account for Austin Sound Center's purchase of the JDC goods in Exhibit 5B-1.

EXHIBIT 5B-1 **Purchase Invoice**

1

JDC SOUTHWEST BRANCH
P.O. BOX 100876
HOUSTON, TX 77212

	Invoice	
	Date	Number
3	6/1/08	410

2

Shipped To: AUSTIN SOUND CENTER, INC.
305 WEST MLK BLVD.
AUSTIN, TX 78701

4

Credit Terms
3% 15, NET 30 DAYS

	Description		Quantity Shipped	Unit Price	Total
	DVD PLAYER		7	$100.00	$700.00
				6 Pd.	6/15/08

Due Date & Due Amount			
06/15/08			
$679 00			

7

Sub Total	$700.00
Ship. or Handl. Chg.	–
Tax (3%)	–
Total(s)	$700.00

5

Explanations:

1 The seller is JDC.

2 The purchaser is Austin Sound Center.

3 The invoice date is needed to determine whether the purchaser gets a discount for prompt payment (see 4).

4 Credit terms: If Austin Sound pays within 15 days of the invoice date, it may deduct a 3% discount. Otherwise, the full amount—NET—is due in 30 days. (See Purchase Discounts on page 309.)

5 Total invoice amount is $700.

6 Austin Sound's payment date. How much did Austin pay? (See 7.)

7 Payment occurred 14 days after the invoice date—within the discount period—so Austin paid $679 ($700 – 3% discount).

Recording Purchases and Purchase Discounts

The following entries record the purchase and payment on account within the discount period. Austin Sound received the goods on June 3 and paid within the discount period.

June 3	Purchases	700	
	Accounts Payable		700
	Purchased inventory on account.		
June 15	Accounts Payable	700	
	Cash ($700 × 0.97)		679
	Purchase Discounts ($700 × 0.03)		21
	Paid within discount period.		

Recording Purchase Returns and Allowances

Suppose that, prior to payment, Austin Sound returned to JDC goods costing $100 and also received from JDC a purchase allowance of $10. Austin Sound would record these transactions as follows:

June 4	Accounts Payable	100	
	Purchase Returns and Allowances		100
	Returned inventory to seller.		
4	Accounts Payable	10	
	Purchase Returns and Allowances		10
	Received a purchase allowance.		

During the period, the business records the cost of all inventory bought in the Purchases account. The balance of Purchases is a *gross* amount because it does not include subtractions for discounts, returns, or allowances. **Net purchases** is the remainder after subtracting the contra accounts from Purchases:

Purchases (*debit*)
– Purchase Discounts (*credit*)
– Purchase Returns and Allowances (*credit*)
= Net purchases (a *debit* subtotal, not a separate account)

Recording Transportation Costs

Under the periodic system, costs to transport purchased inventory from seller to buyer are debited to a separate Freight In account, as shown for a $60 freight bill:

June 3	Freight In	60	
	Cash		60
	Paid a freight bill.		

Recording the Sale of Inventory

Recording sales is streamlined in the periodic system. With no running record of inventory to maintain, we can record a $3,000 sale as follows:

June 9	Accounts Receivable	3,000	
	Sales Revenue		3,000
	Sale on account.		

There is no accompanying entry to Inventory and Cost of Goods Sold in the periodic system.

Accounting for sales discounts and sales returns and allowances is the same as in a perpetual inventory system (pages 259–277), except that there are no entries to Inventory or Cost of Goods Sold.

Cost of goods sold (also called *cost of sales*) is the largest single expense of most businesses that sell merchandise, such as Austin Sound and Gap, Inc. It is the cost of the inventory the business has sold to customers. In a periodic system, cost of goods sold must be computed as shown in Exhibit 5-11, page 278.

Exhibit 5B-2 summarizes this appendix by showing Austin Sound's net sales revenue, cost of goods sold, and gross profit on the income statement for the periodic system. (All amounts are assumed.)

EXHIBIT 5B-2 **Partial Income Statement—Periodic Inventory System**

AUSTIN SOUND CENTER, INC.
Income Statement
Year Ended December 31, 2008

Sales revenue			$169,300
Less: Sales discounts			(1,400)
Sales returns and allowances			(2,000)
Net sales revenue			$165,900
Cost of goods sold:			
Beginning inventory		$38,600	
Purchases	$91,400		
Less: Purchase discounts	(3,000)		
Purchase returns and allowances	(1,200)		
Net purchases		87,200	
Freight in		5,200	
Cost of goods available		131,000	
Less: Ending inventory		(40,200)	
Cost of goods sold			90,800
Gross profit			$ 75,100

Appendix 5B Assignments

Exercises

Journalizing purchase transactions

E5B-1 On April 30, Stanley & Weaver Jewelers purchased inventory of $8,000 on account from Intergem Jewels, a jewelry importer. Terms were 3/15, net 45. On receiving the goods, Stanley & Weaver checked the order and found $1,000 of unsuitable merchandise. Therefore, Stanley & Weaver returned $1,000 of merchandise to Intergem on May 4.

On May 14, Stanley & Weaver paid the net amount owed from April 30, less the return.

Requirements

Record the indicated transactions in the journal of Stanley & Weaver Jewelers. Use the periodic inventory system. Explanations are not required. (pp. 309–310)

Journalizing sale transactions

E5B-2 Refer to the business situation in Exercise 5B-1. Journalize the transactions of Intergem Jewels. Explanations are not required. (pp. 266–268, 309–310)

Problem

Journalizing purchase and sale transactions

P5B-1 Assume that the following transactions occurred between Providence Medical Supply and a Walgreen's drug store during November of the current year.

Nov. 6	Walgreen's purchased $6,200 of merchandise from Providence Medical Supply on credit terms 2/10, n/30, FOB shipping point. Separately, Walgreen's paid freight in of $300.
10	Walgreen's returned $900 of the merchandise to Providence.
15	Walgreen's paid $3,000 of the invoice amount owed to Providence for the November 6 purchase, less the discount.
27	Walgreen's paid the remaining amount owed to Providence for the November 6 purchase.

Requirements

Journalize these transactions, first on the books of the Walgreen's drug store and second on the books of Providence Medical Supply. Use the periodic inventory system.

Comprehensive Problem for Chapters 1–5

Completing a Merchandiser's Accounting Cycle

The end-of-month trial balance of St. James Technology, Inc., at January 31, 2009, follows. Additional data at January 31, 2009:

a. Supplies consumed during the month, $1,500. Half is selling expense, and the other half is general expense.

b. Depreciation for the month: building, $4,000; furniture, $4,800. One-fourth of depreciation is selling expense, and three-fourths is general expense.

c. Unearned sales revenue earned during January, $4,580.

d. Accrued salaries, a general expense, $1,150.

e. Inventory on hand, $63,720. St. James uses the perpetual inventory system.

Requirements

1. Using four-column accounts, open the accounts listed on the trial balance, inserting their unadjusted balances. Date the balances of the following accounts January 1: Supplies; Building; Accumulated Depreciation—Building; Furniture; Accumulated Depreciation—Furniture; Unearned Sales Revenue; Common Stock; and Retained Earnings. Date the balance of Dividends, January 31. Also open the Income Summary account. (p. 82)
2. Enter the trial balance on an accounting work sheet, and complete the work sheet for the month ended January 31, 2009. St. James Technology, Inc., groups all operating expenses under two accounts, Selling Expense and General Expense. Leave two blank lines under Selling Expense and three blank lines under General Expense. (p. 283)

ST. JAMES TECHNOLOGY, INC. Trial Balance January 31, 2009		
Cash	$ 16,430	
Accounts receivable	19,090	
Inventory	65,400	
Supplies	2,700	
Building	188,170	
Accumulated depreciation—building		$ 36,000
Furniture	45,600	
Accumulated depreciation—furniture		5,800
Accounts payable		28,300
Salary payable		
Unearned sales revenue		6,560
Note payable, long-term		87,000
Common stock		50,000
Retained earnings		94,980
Dividends	9,200	
Sales revenue		187,970
Sales discounts	7,300	
Sales returns and allowances	8,140	
Cost of goods sold	103,000	
Selling expense	21,520	
General expense	10,060	
Total	$496,610	$496,610

3. Prepare the company's *multi-step* income statement and statement of retained earnings for the month ended January 31, 2009. Also prepare the balance sheet at that date in *report* form. (p. 274)
4. Journalize the adjusting and closing entries at January 31. (pp. 208, 272)
5. Post the adjusting and closing entries, using dates. (pp. 208, 209)

6 Merchandise Inventory

Learning Objectives

1. Account for inventory by the FIFO, LIFO, and average-cost methods
2. Compare the effects of FIFO, LIFO, and average cost
3. Apply the lower-of-cost-or-market rule to inventory
4. Measure the effects of inventory errors
5. Estimate ending inventory by the gross profit method

Chapter 5 introduced the accounting for merchandise inventory. It showed how Austin Sound Center, a music store, recorded the purchase and sale of its inventory. Amazon.com, Wal-Mart, and Rocky Mountain Sportswear are other merchandising companies. The current chapter completes the accounting for merchandise inventory.

Rocky Mountain Sportswear (RMS) makes ski parkas for men, women, and children. RMS, like all other companies, may select from several different methods to account for its inventory. Inventory is the first area in which you must pick the accounting method you will use. In this chapter we use Rocky Mountain Sportswear to illustrate the different inventory accounting methods.

Get ready to learn a new vocabulary. By the time you complete this chapter, you'll be able to use new terms including *FIFO* and *LIFO.* You'll also be prepared to decide which accounting method is best for you if you ever start your own business.

First let's review how merchandise inventory affects a company. Exhibit 6-1 gives the merchandising section of Rocky Mountain Sportswear's balance sheet and income statement. Inventories, cost of goods sold, and gross profit are highlighted. These amounts (X, Y, and Z) are left blank to indicate that throughout the chapter we will be computing them using various accounting methods.

EXHIBIT 6-1 **Rocky Mountain Sportswear: Merchandising Sections of the Financial Statements**

ROCKY MOUNTAIN SPORTSWEAR COMPANY
Balance Sheet (partial)
December 31, 2008

Assets	
Current assets:	
Cash	$ 6,000
Short-term investments	3,000
Accounts receivable	12,000
Inventories	X
Prepaid expenses	4,000

ROCKY MOUNTAIN SPORTSWEAR COMPANY
Income Statement (partial)
Year Ended December 31, 2008

		(Millions)
Net sales		$80,000
Cost of goods sold		Y
Gross profit		Z

The remainder of the chapter explores how to compute these amounts in Exhibit 6-1:

- Ending inventory (X) on the balance sheet
- Cost of goods sold (Y) and gross profit (Z) on the income statement

We turn now to the different inventory costing methods.

Inventory Costing Methods

As we saw in Chapter 5,

$$\text{Ending inventory} = \frac{\text{Number of units}}{\textit{on hand}} \times \text{Unit cost}$$

$$\text{Cost of goods sold} = \frac{\text{Number of units}}{\textit{sold}} \times \text{Unit cost}$$

Companies determine the number of units from perpetual inventory records backed up by a physical count. The cost of each unit of inventory is:

Unit cost = Purchase price − Purchase discounts

Exhibit 6-2 gives the inventory data for a line of Rocky Mountain Sportswear (RMS) ski parkas.

EXHIBIT 6-2 Perpetual Inventory Record—Quantities Only

Item: Ski Parkas			
Date	**Quantity Purchased**	**Quantity Sold**	**Quantity on Hand**
Nov. 1			1
5	6		7
15		4	3
26	7		10
30		8	2
Totals	13	12	2

In this illustration, RMS began November with 1 ski parka on hand. RMS had 2 parkas at the end of the month. Assume that RMS's unit cost of each ski parka is $40. In this case,

Ending inventory	=	Number of units *on hand* (Exhibit 6-2)		Unit Cost		
		2	×	$40	=	$80

Cost of goods sold	=	Number of units *sold* (Exhibit 6-2)		Unit cost		
		12	×	$40	=	$480

What would ending inventory and cost of goods sold be if the cost of a ski parka increased from $40 to $50? Companies face price increases like this all the time. To determine inventory costs, the accounting profession has developed several costing methods.

Measuring inventory cost is easy when prices are constant. But unit cost often changes. A ski parka that cost RMS $40 in January may cost $45 in April. Suppose RMS sells 10,000 ski parkas in November. How many of the parkas cost $40? How many cost $45? To compute ending inventory and cost of goods sold, RMS must assign a specific unit cost to each item. The four costing methods GAAP allows are:

1. Specific unit cost
2. Average cost
3. First-in, first-out (FIFO) cost
4. Last-in, first-out (LIFO) cost

A company can use any of these methods to account for its inventory.

The **specific-unit-cost method** is also called the **specific-identification method.** This method uses the specific cost of each unit of inventory. Some businesses deal in unique inventory items, such as automobiles, jewels, and real estate. For instance, a

Chevrolet dealer may have two vehicles—a "stripped-down" model that costs $16,000 and a "loaded" model that costs $19,000. If the dealer sells the loaded model, cost of goods sold is $19,000. Suppose the stripped-down auto is the only unit left in inventory at the end of the period; ending inventory is $16,000.

Amazon.com uses the specific-unit-cost method to account for its inventory. But very few other companies use this method, so we shift to the more popular inventory costing methods. Exhibit 6-3 illustrates how each method works.

- Under FIFO, the cost of goods sold is based on the oldest purchases. In Exhibit 6-3, this is illustrated by the Cost of goods sold coming from the *bottom* of the container.
- Under LIFO, the cost of goods sold is based on the most recent purchases (new costs). This is illustrated by the Cost of goods sold coming from the *top* of the container.
- Under the average-cost method, the cost of goods sold is based on an average cost for the period. This is illustrated by the cost of goods sold coming from the *middle* of the container.

EXHIBIT 6-3 **Cost Flows for the Three Most Popular Inventory Methods**

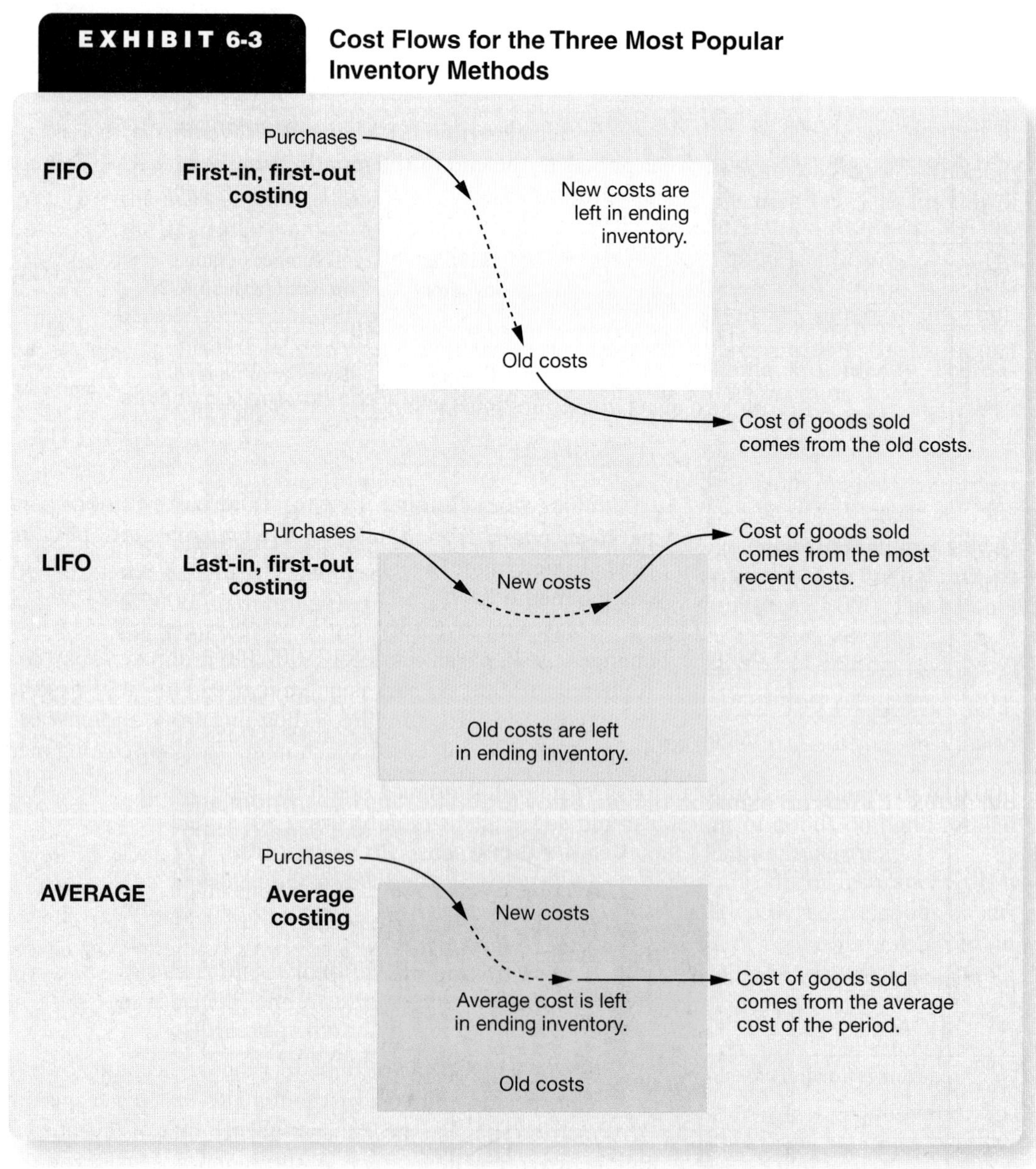

Now let's see how Rocky Mountain Sportswear would compute inventory amounts under FIFO, LIFO, and average costing. We use the following transaction data for all the illustrations:

ROCKY MOUNTAIN SPORTSWEAR SKI PARKA			
		Number of Units	Unit Cost
Nov. 1	Beginning inventory	1	$40
5	Purchase	6	45
15	Sale	4	
26	Purchase	7	50
30	Sale	8	

In the body of the chapter, we show inventory costing in a perpetual system. The chapter Appendix 6A (page 350) shows inventory costing in a periodic system.

Inventory Costing in a Perpetual System

The different inventory costing methods produce different amounts for:

- Ending inventory
- Cost of goods sold

Let's begin with the FIFO method.

First-In, First-Out (FIFO) Method

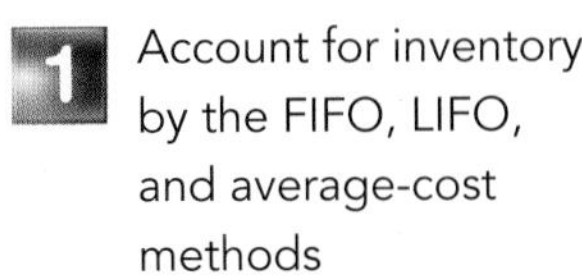

1
Account for inventory by the FIFO, LIFO, and average-cost methods

Rocky Mountain Sportswear (RMS) uses the **FIFO method** to account for its inventory. FIFO costing is consistent with the physical movement of inventory for most companies. That is, they sell their oldest inventory first. Under FIFO, the first costs incurred by RMS are the first costs assigned to cost of goods sold. FIFO leaves in ending inventory the last—the newest—costs. This is illustrated in the FIFO inventory record in Exhibit 6-4.

RMS began November with 1 ski parka that cost $40. After the November 5 purchase, the inventory on hand consists of 7 units.

7 units on hand	1 @ $40	=	$ 40
	6 @ $45	=	270
	Inventory on hand	=	$310

On November 15, RMS sold 4 units. Under FIFO, the first unit sold has the oldest cost ($40 per unit). The next 3 units sold cost $45 each. That leaves 3 units in inventory on hand at $45 each. The remainder of the inventory record follows the same pattern.

The FIFO monthly summary at November 30 is:

- Cost of goods sold: 12 units that cost a total of $560
- Ending inventory: 2 units that cost a total of $100

RMS measures cost of goods sold and inventory in this manner to prepare its financial statements.

EXHIBIT 6-4 Perpetual Inventory Record: FIFO

Ski Parkas

	Purchases			Cost of Goods Sold			Inventory on Hand		
Date	Quantity	Unit Cost	Total Cost	Quantity	Unit Cost	Total Cost	Quantity	Unit Cost	Total Cost
Nov. 1							1	$40	$40
5	6	$45	$270				1	40	40
							6	45	270
15				1	$40	$ 40			
				3	45	135	3	45	135
26	7	50	350				3	45	135
							7	50	350
30				3	45	135			
				5	50	250	2	50	100
30	13		$620	12		$560	2		$100

Journal Entries Under FIFO

The journal entries under FIFO follow the data in Exhibit 6-4. For example, on November 5, RMS purchased $270 of inventory and made the first journal entry. On November 15, RMS sold 4 ski parkas for the sale price of $80 each. RMS recorded the sale ($320) and the cost of goods sold ($175). The remaining journal entries (November 26 and 30) follow the inventory data in Exhibit 6-4.

The amounts unique to FIFO are highlighted for emphasis. All other amounts are the same for all three inventory methods.

FIFO Journal Entries: **(All purchases and sales on account. The sale price of a ski parka is $80 per unit.)**

Date	Account	Debit	Credit
Nov. 5	Inventory (6 × $45)	270	
	Accounts Payable		270
	Purchased inventory on account.		
15	Accounts Receivable (4 × $80)	320	
	Sales Revenue		320
	Sale on account.		
15	Cost of Goods Sold ($40 + $135)	175	
	Inventory		175
	Cost of goods sold.		
26	Inventory (7 × $50)	350	
	Accounts Payable		350
	Purchased inventory on account.		
30	Accounts Receivable (8 × $80)	640	
	Sales Revenue		640
	Sale on account.		
30	Cost of Goods Sold ($135 + $250)	385	
	Inventory		385
	Cost of goods sold.		

Last-In, First-Out (LIFO) Method

LIFO is the opposite of FIFO. Under **LIFO**, cost of goods sold comes from the newest—the most recent—purchases. Ending inventory comes from the oldest costs of the period. Exhibit 6-5 shows how LIFO works. Exhibit 6-5 gives a perpetual inventory record for the LIFO method.

EXHIBIT 6-5 **Perpetual Inventory Record: LIFO**

Ski Parkas

	Purchases			Cost of Goods Sold			Inventory on Hand		
Date	Quantity	Unit Cost	Total Cost	Quantity	Unit Cost	Total Cost	Quantity	Unit Cost	Total Cost
Nov. 1							1	$40	$40
5	6	$45	$270				1	40	40
							6	45	270
15				4	$45	$180	1	40	40
							2	45	90
26	7	50	350				1	40	40
							2	45	90
							7	50	350
30				7	50	350			
				1	45	45	1	40	40
							1	45	45
30	13		$620	12		$575	2		$85

Again, RMS had 1 ski parka at the beginning. After the purchase on November 5, RMS holds 7 units of inventory (1 @ $40 plus 6 @ $45). On November 15, RMS sells 4 units. Under LIFO, the cost of goods sold always comes from the newest purchase. That leaves 3 ski parkas in inventory on November 15.

3 units on hand	1 @ $40	=	$ 40
	2 @ $45	=	90
	Inventory on hand	=	$130

The purchase of 7 units on November 26 adds a new $50 layer to inventory. Now inventory holds 10 units.

10 units on hand	1 @ $40	=	$ 40
	2 @ $45	=	90
	7 @ $50	=	350
	Inventory on hand	=	$480

Then the sale of 8 units on November 30 peels back units in LIFO order. The LIFO monthly summary at November 30 is:

- Cost of goods sold: 12 units that cost a total of $575
- Ending inventory: 2 units that cost a total of $85

Under LIFO, RMS could measure cost of goods sold and inventory in this manner to prepare its financial statements.

Journal Entries Under LIFO

The journal entries under LIFO follow the data in Exhibit 6-5. On November 5, RMS purchased inventory of $270. The November 15 sale brought in sales revenue (4 units @ $80 = $320) and cost of goods sold ($180). The November 26 and 30 entries also come from the data in Exhibit 6-5. Amounts unique to LIFO are shown in color.

LIFO Journal Entries:	(All purchases and sales on account. The sale price of a ski parka is $80 per unit.)		
Nov. 5	Inventory (6 × $45)	270	
	Accounts Payable		270
	Purchased inventory on account.		
15	Accounts Receivable (4 × $80)	320	
	Sales Revenue		320
	Sale on account.		
15	Cost of Goods Sold	180	
	Inventory		180
	Cost of goods sold.		
26	Inventory (7 × $50)	350	
	Accounts Payable		350
	Purchased inventory on account.		
30	Accounts Receivable (8 × $80)	640	
	Sales Revenue		640
	Sale on account.		
30	Cost of Goods Sold ($350 + $45)	395	
	Inventory		395
	Cost of goods sold.		

Average-Cost Method

Suppose RMS uses the **average-cost method** to account for its inventory of ski parkas. With this method, the business computes a new average cost per unit after each purchase. Ending inventory and cost of goods sold are then based on the same average cost per unit. Exhibit 6-6 shows a perpetual inventory record for the

EXHIBIT 6-6 **Perpetual Inventory Record: Average Cost**

Ski Parkas

	Purchases			Cost of Goods Sold			Inventory on Hand		
Date	Quantity	Unit Cost	Total Cost	Quantity	Unit Cost	Total Cost	Quantity	Unit Cost	Total Cost
Nov. 1							1	$40.00	$ 40
5	6	$45	$270				7	44.29	310
15				4	$44.29	$177	3	44.29	133
26	7	50	350				10	48.30	483
30				8	48.30	386	2	48.30	97
30	13		$620	12		$563	2		$ 97

average-cost method. We round average unit cost to the nearest cent and total cost to the nearest dollar.

After each purchase, RMS computes a new average cost per unit. For example, on November 5, the new average unit cost is:

	Total cost of inventory on hand		Number of units on hand		Average cost per unit
Nov. 5	$40 + $270 = $310	÷	7 units	=	$44.29

The goods sold on November 15 are then costed out at $44.29 per unit. After each purchase, RMS computes a new average cost.

The average-cost summary at November 30 is:

- Cost of goods sold: 12 units that cost a total of $563
- Ending inventory: 2 units that cost a total of $97

Under the average-cost method, RMS could use these amounts to prepare its financial statements.

Journal Entries Under Average Costing

2 Compare the effects of FIFO, LIFO, and average cost

The journal entries under average costing follow the data in Exhibit 6-6. On November 5, RMS purchased $270 of inventory and made the first journal entry. On November 15, RMS sold 4 ski parkas for $80 each. RMS recorded the sale ($320) and the cost of goods sold ($177). The remaining journal entries (November 26 and 30) follow the data in Exhibit 6-6. Amounts unique to the average cost method are highlighted.

Average-Cost Journal Entries: (All purchases and sales on account. The sale price of a ski parka is $80 per unit.)			
Nov. 5	Inventory	270	
	Accounts Payable		270
	Purchased inventory on account.		
15	Accounts Receivable (4 × $80)	320	
	Sale Revenue		320
	Sale on account.		
15	Cost of Goods Sold	177	
	Inventory		177
	Cost of goods sold.		
26	Inventory	350	
	Accounts Payable		350
	Purchased inventory on account.		
30	Accounts Receivable (8 × $80)	640	
	Sales Revenue		640
	Sale on account.		
30	Cost of Goods Sold	386	
	Inventory		386
	Cost of goods sold.		

Comparing FIFO, LIFO, and Average Cost

Exhibit 6-7 shows that FIFO is the most popular inventory costing method. LIFO is next most popular and average cost ranks third.

EXHIBIT 6-7

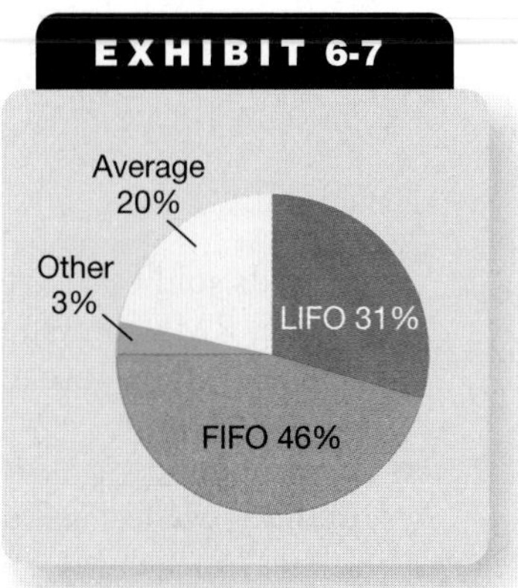

Use of the Various Inventory Methods

What leads Rocky Mountain Sportswear to select the FIFO method, General Electric to use LIFO, and Fossil (the watch company) to use average cost? The different methods have different benefits.

Exhibit 6-8 summarizes the results for the three inventory methods for RMS. It shows sales revenue, cost of goods sold, and gross profit for FIFO, LIFO, and average cost.

EXHIBIT 6-8 **Comparative Results for FIFO, LIFO, and Average Cost**

	FIFO	LIFO	Average
Sales revenue	$960	$960	$960
Cost of goods sold	560	575	563
Gross profit	$400	$385	$397

Exhibit 6-8 shows that FIFO produces the lowest cost of goods sold and the highest gross profit. Net income is also the highest under FIFO when inventory costs are rising. Many companies prefer high income in order to attract investors and borrow on good terms. FIFO offers this benefit.

LIFO results in the highest cost of goods sold and the lowest gross profit. That lets companies pay the lowest income taxes when inventory costs are rising. Low tax payments conserve cash and that's the main benefit of LIFO. The downside of LIFO is that the company reports low net income.

The average-cost method generates amounts that fall between the extremes of FIFO and LIFO. Companies that seek a "middle-ground" solution, therefore, use the average-cost method for inventory.

Summary Problem 1

Fossil specializes in designer watches and leather goods. Assume Fossil began June holding 10 wristwatches that cost $50 each. Fossil sells these watches for $100 each. During June, Fossil bought and sold inventory as follows:

June 3	Sold 8 units for $100 each
16	Purchased 10 units @ $55 each
23	Sold 8 units for $100 each

Requirements

1. Prepare a perpetual inventory record for Fossil under:
   - FIFO
   - LIFO
   - Average Cost

   Round unit cost to the nearest cent and all other amounts to the nearest dollar.
2. Journalize all of Fossil's inventory transactions for June under all three costing methods.
3. Show the computation of gross profit for each method.
4. Which method maximizes net income? Which method minimizes income taxes?

continued. . .

Solution

1. Perpetual inventory records:

FIFO

Wristwatches

Date	Purchases			Cost of Goods Sold			Inventory on Hand		
	Quantity	Unit Cost	Total Cost	Quantity	Unit Cost	Total Cost	Quantity	Unit Cost	Total Cost
June 1							10	$50	$500
3				8	$50	$400	2	50	100
16	10	$55	$550				2	50	100
							10	55	550
23				2	50	100			
				6	55	330	4	55	220
30				16		$830	4		$220

LIFO

Wristwatches

Date	Purchases			Cost of Goods Sold			Inventory on Hand		
	Quantity	Unit Cost	Total Cost	Quantity	Unit Cost	Total Cost	Quantity	Unit Cost	Total Cost
June 1							10	$50	$500
3				8	$50	$400	2	50	100
16	10	$55	$550				2	50	100
							10	55	550
23				8	55	440	2	50	100
							2	55	110
30				16		$840	4		$210

AVERAGE COST

Wristwatches

Date	Purchases			Cost of Goods Sold			Inventory on Hand		
	Quantity	Unit Cost	Total Cost	Quantity	Unit Cost	Total Cost	Quantity	Unit Cost	Total Cost
June 1							10	$50.00	$500
3				8	$50.00	$400	2	50.00	100
16	10	$55	$550				12	54.17	650
23				8	54.17	433	4	54.17	217
30				16		$833	4		217

2. Journal Entries:

		FIFO		LIFO		Average	
June 3	Accounts Receivable	800		800		800	
	Sales Revenue		800		800		800
3	Cost of Goods Sold	400		400		400	
	Inventory		400		400		400
16	Inventory	550		550		550	
	Accounts Payable		550		550		550
23	Accounts Receivable	800		800		800	
	Sales Revenue		800		800		800
30	Cost of Goods Sold	430		440		433	
	Inventory		430		440		433

3. Gross Profit:

	FIFO	LIFO	Average
Sales revenue ($800 + $800)	$1,600	$1,600	$1,600
Cost of goods sold ($400 + $430)	830		
($400 + $440)		840	
($400 + $433)			833
Gross profit	$ 770	$ 760	$ 767

4. FIFO maximizes net income.
LIFO minimizes income taxes.

Accounting Principles and Inventories

Several accounting principles affect inventories. Among them are consistency, disclosure, materiality, and accounting conservatism.

Consistency Principle

The **consistency principle** states that businesses should use the same accounting methods from period to period. Consistency helps investors compare a company's financial statements from one period to the next.

Suppose you are analyzing a company's net income over a two-year period. The company switched from LIFO to FIFO. Its net income increased dramatically but only as a result of the change in inventory method. If you did not know of the change, you might believe that the company's income really increased. Therefore, companies must report any changes in the accounting methods they use. Investors need this information to make wise decisions about the company.

Disclosure Principle

The **disclosure principle** holds that a company should report enough information for outsiders to make wise decisions about the company. In short, the company should report *relevant, reliable,* and *comparable* information about itself. This means disclosing the method being used to account for inventories. Suppose a banker is comparing two companies—one using LIFO and the other FIFO. The FIFO company reports higher net income, but only because it uses the FIFO method. Without knowledge of these accounting methods, the banker could lend money to the wrong business.

Materiality Concept

The **materiality concept** states that a company must perform strictly proper accounting *only* for significant items. Information is significant—or, in accounting terms, *material*—when it would cause someone to change a decision. The materiality concept frees accountants from having to report every last item in strict accordance with GAAP.

Accounting Conservatism

Conservatism in accounting means exercising caution in reporting items in the financial statements. Conservatism says,

- "Anticipate no gains, but provide for all probable losses."
- "If in doubt, record an asset at the lowest reasonable amount and a liability at the highest reasonable amount."
- "When there's a question, record an expense rather than an asset."

The goal of conservatism is to report realistic figures.

Other Inventory Issues

In addition to the FIFO, LIFO, and average cost methods, accountants face other inventory issues. This section covers:

- The lower-of-cost-or-market rule
- Effects of inventory errors
- Ethical issues
- Estimating ending inventory

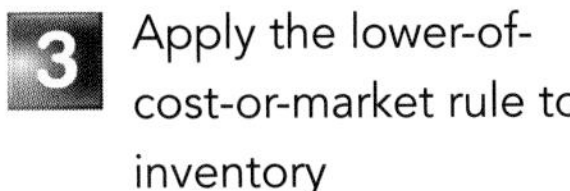

Apply the lower-of-cost-or-market rule to inventory

Lower-of-Cost-or-Market Rule

The **lower-of-cost-or-market rule** (abbreviated as **LCM**) shows accounting conservatism in action. LCM requires that inventory be reported in the financial statements at whichever is lower—

- the historical cost of the inventory or
- the market value of the inventory

For inventories, *market value* generally means *current replacement cost* (that is, the cost to replace the inventory on hand). If the replacement cost of inventory falls below its historical cost, the business must write down the inventory value. On the balance sheet the business reports ending inventory at its LCM value.

Suppose Rocky Mountain Sportswear paid $3,000 for inventory. By December 31, the inventory can now be replaced for $2,200, and the decline in value appears permanent. Market value is below cost, and the entry to write down the inventory to LCM follows:

	Cost of Goods Sold (cost, $3,000 – market, $2,200)	800	
	Inventory		800
	To write inventory down to market value.		

In this case, Rocky Mountain Sportswear's balance sheet would report this inventory as follows:

Balance Sheet	
Current assets:	
Inventory, at market	
(which is lower than FIFO cost)	$2,200

Companies often disclose LCM in notes to their financial statements, as shown here for Rocky Mountain Sportswear:

NOTE 2: STATEMENT OF SIGNIFICANT ACCOUNTING POLICIES

Inventories. Inventories are carried at the *lower of cost or market.* Cost is determined using the first-in, first-out method.

Effects of Inventory Errors

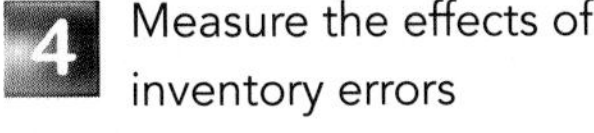

Measure the effects of inventory errors

Businesses count their inventory at the end of the period. For the financial statements to be accurate, it's important to get a correct count of ending inventory. This can be difficult for a company with far-flung operations.

An error in ending inventory creates a whole string of errors. To illustrate, suppose Rocky Mountain Sportswear accidentally counted too much ending inventory. Therefore, ending inventory is overstated on the balance sheet. The following diagram shows how an overstatement of ending inventory affects cost of goods sold, gross profit, and net income:

	Ending Inventory Overstated
Sales revenue	Correct
Cost of goods sold:	
Beginning inventory	Correct
Net purchases	Correct
Cost of goods available	Correct
Ending inventory	ERROR: Overstated
Cost of goods sold	Understated
Gross profit	Overstated
Operating expenses	Correct
Net income	Overstated

Understating the ending inventory—reporting the inventory too low—has the opposite effect, as shown here:

	Ending Inventory Understated
Sales revenue	Correct
Cost of goods sold:	
Beginning inventory	Correct
Net purchases	Correct
Cost of goods available	Correct
Ending inventory	ERROR: Understated
Cost of goods sold	Overstated
Gross profit	Understated
Operating expenses	Correct
Net income	Understated

Recall that one period's ending inventory becomes the next period's beginning inventory. Thus, an error in ending inventory carries over into the next period. Exhibit 6-9 illustrates the effect of an inventory error. Period 1's ending inventory is overstated by $5,000; period 1's ending inventory should be $10,000. The error carries over to period 2. Period 3 is correct. In fact, both Period 1 and Period 2 should look like Period 3.

Ending inventory is *subtracted* to compute cost of goods sold in one period and the same amount is *added* as beginning inventory the next period. Therefore, an inventory error cancels out after two periods. The overstatement of cost of goods sold in period 2 counterbalances the understatement for period 1. Thus, total gross profit for the two periods combined is correct. These effects are summarized in Exhibit 6-10.

Ethical Issues

No area of accounting has a deeper ethical dimension than inventory. Companies whose profits are lagging can be tempted to "cook the books." An increase in reported income will make the business look more successful than it really is.

There are two main schemes for cooking the books. The easiest way is to overstate ending inventory. In Exhibit 6-10, we saw how an inventory error affects net income.

continued after the exhibits on page 331. . .

EXHIBIT 6-9 Inventory Errors: An Example

	Period 1		Period 2		Period 3	
	Ending Inventory Overstated by $5,000		*Beginning* Inventory Overstated by $5,000		Correct	
Sales revenue		$100,000		$100,000		$100,000
Cost of goods sold:						
Beginning inventory	$10,000		$ 15,000		$ 10,000	
Net purchases	50,000		50,000		50,000	
Cost of goods available	60,000		65,000		60,000	
Ending inventory	(15,000)		(10,000)		(10,000)	
Cost of goods sold		45,000		55,000		50,000
Gross profit		$ 55,000		$ 45,000		$ 50,000
	$100,000 (Periods 1 and 2 combined)					

The correct gross profit is $50,000 for each period.

Source: The authors thank Carl High for this example.

EXHIBIT 6-10 Effects of Inventory Errors

	Period 1		Period 2	
	Cost of Goods Sold	Gross Profit and Net Income	Cost of Goods Sold	Gross Profit and Net Income
Period 1 Ending inventory *overstated*	Understated	Overstated	Overstated	Understated
Period 1 Ending inventory *understated*	Overstated	Understated	Understated	Overstated

The second way to cook the books involves sales. Datapoint Corporation and MiniScribe, both computer-related concerns, were charged with creating fictitious sales to boost reported profits.

Datapoint is alleged to have hired drivers to transport its inventory around the city so that the goods could *not* be counted. Datapoint's plan seemed to create the impression that the inventory must have been sold. The scheme broke down when the trucks returned the goods to Datapoint. The sales returns were much too high to be realistic, and the sales proved to be phony.

MiniScribe is alleged to have cooked its books by shipping boxes of bricks labeled as computer parts. The scheme boomeranged when MiniScribe had to record the sales returns. In virtually every area, accounting imposes a discipline that brings out the facts sooner or later.

Estimating Ending Inventory

5 Estimate ending inventory by the gross profit method

Often a business must *estimate* the value of its ending inventory. Suppose Rocky Mountain Sportswear suffers a fire loss and must estimate the value of the inventory destroyed. Or a company needs monthly financial statements.

The **gross profit method** provides a way to estimate inventory as follows:

Beginning inventory
+ Net purchases
= Cost of goods available
– Ending inventory
= Cost of goods sold

Rearranging *ending inventory* and *cost of goods sold* helps to estimate ending inventory:

Beginning inventory
+ Net purchases
= Cost of goods available
– Cost of goods sold (Sales – Gross profit = COGS)
= Ending inventory

Suppose a fire destroys your inventory. To collect insurance, you must estimate the cost of the inventory destroyed. Using your normal *gross profit percent* (that is, gross profit divided by net sales revenue), you can estimate cost of goods sold. Then subtract cost of goods sold from goods available to estimate ending inventory. Exhibit 6-11 illustrates the gross profit method (amounts assumed for this illustration):

EXHIBIT 6-11 **Gross Profit Method of Estimating Inventory (amounts assumed)**

Beginning inventory		$14,000
Net purchases		66,000
Cost of goods available		80,000
Estimated cost of goods sold:		
Sales revenue	$100,000	
Less: Estimated gross profit of 40%	(40,000)	
Estimated cost of goods sold		(60,000)
Estimated cost of *ending inventory*		$20,000

Decision Guidelines

GUIDELINES FOR INVENTORY MANAGEMENT

Assume you are starting a business to sell school supplies to your college friends. You'll need to stock computer disks, notebooks, and other inventory items. To manage the business, you'll also need some accounting records. Here are some of the decisions you'll face.

Decision	Guidelines	System or Method
Which inventory system to use?	• Expensive merchandise • Cannot control inventory by visual inspection	→ Perpetual system
	• Can control inventory by visual inspection	→ Periodic system
Which costing method to use?	• Unique inventory items	→ Specific unit cost
	• The most current cost of ending inventory • Maximizes reported income when costs are rising	→ FIFO
	• The most current measure of cost of goods sold and net income • Minimizes income tax when costs are rising	→ LIFO
	• Middle-of-the-road approach for income tax and net income	→ Average-cost method
How to estimate the cost of ending inventory?	• The cost-of-goods-sold model provides the framework	→ Gross profit method

Summary Problem 2

Suppose a division of IBM that handles computer parts has these inventory records for January 2008:

Date	Item	Quantity	Unit Cost	Sale Price
Jan. 1	Beginning inventory.............	100 units	$ 8	
10	Purchase..............................	60 units	9	
15	Sale......................................	70 units		$20
21	Purchase..............................	100 units	10	
30	Sale......................................	90 units		25

Operating expense for January was $1,900.

Requirement

Prepare the January income statement in multi-step format. Show amounts for FIFO, LIFO, and average cost. Label the bottom line "Operating income." (Round the average cost per unit to three decimal places and all other figures to whole-dollar amounts.) Show your computations, and use the cost-of-goods-sold model from pages 325 and 326 to compute cost of goods sold.

Solution

IBM
Income Statement for Computer Parts
Month Ended January 31, 2008

	FIFO		LIFO		Average Cost	
Sales revenue		$3,650		$3,650		$3,650
Cost of goods sold:						
Beginning inventory	$ 800		$ 800		$ 800	
Net purchases	1,540		1,540		1,540	
Cost of goods available	2,340		2,340		2,340	
Ending inventory	(1,000)		(800)		(900)	
Cost of goods sold		1,340		1,540		1,440
Gross profit		2,310		2,110		2,210
Operating expenses		1,900		1,900		1,900
Operating income		$ 410		$ 210		$ 310

Computations

Sales revenue:	(70 × $20) + (90 × $25)	= $3,650
Beginning inventory:	100 × $8	= $800
Purchases:	(60 × $9) + (100 × $10)	= $1,540
Ending inventory:		
FIFO	100* × $10	= $1,000
LIFO	100 × $8	= $800
Average cost:	100 × $9**	= $900

*Number of units in ending inventory = 100 + 60 − 70 + 100 − 90 =100
**Average cost per unit = $2,340/260 units† = $9
†Number of units available = 100 + 60 + 100 = 260.

Review Merchandise Inventory

Accounting Vocabulary

Average-Cost Method
Inventory costing method based on the average cost of inventory during the period. Average cost is determined by dividing the cost of goods available for sale by the number of units available.

Conservatism
Reporting the least favorable figures in the financial statements.

Consistency Principle
A business should use the same accounting methods and procedures from period to period.

Disclosure Principle
A business's financial statements must report enough information for outsiders to make knowledgeable decisions about the company.

First-In, First-Out (FIFO) Inventory Costing Method
Inventory costing method: The first costs into inventory are the first costs out to cost of goods sold. Ending inventory is based on the costs of the most recent purchases.

Gross Profit Method
A way to estimate inventory on the basis of the cost-of-goods-sold model: Beginning inventory + Net purchases = Cost of goods available for sale. Cost of goods available for sale – Cost of goods sold = Ending inventory.

Last-In, First-Out (LIFO) Inventory Costing Method
Inventory costing method: The last costs into inventory are the first costs out to cost of goods sold. Leaves the oldest costs—those of beginning inventory and the earliest purchases of the period—in ending inventory.

Lower-of-Cost-or-Market (LCM) Rule
Rule that an asset should be reported in the financial statements at whichever is lower—its historical cost or its market value.

Materiality Concept
A company must perform strictly proper accounting only for items that are significant to the business's financial situations.

Specific-Identification Method
Inventory costing method based on the specific cost of particular units of inventory. Also called the **specific-identification method**.

Specific-Unit-Cost Method
Inventory costing method based on the specific cost of particular units of inventory. Also called the **specific-identification method**.

Quick Check

1. T. J. Bronson made sales of $9,300 and ended April with inventories totaling $900. Cost of goods sold was $6,000. Total operating expenses were $2,700. How much net income did Bronson earn for the month?
   a. $600
   b. $900
   c. $3,300
   d. $6,600

2. Which inventory costing method assigns to ending inventory the newest—the most recent—costs incurred during the period?
   a. Specific unit cost
   b. Last-in, first-out (LIFO)
   c. First-in, first-out (FIFO)
   d. Average cost

3. Assume Amazon.com began June with 10 units of inventory that cost a total of $190. During June, Amazon purchased and sold goods as follows:

June 8	Purchase..........................	30 units @ $20
14	Sale	25 units @ $40
22	Purchase..........................	20 units @ $22
27	Sale	30 units @ $40

   Under the FIFO inventory method, how much is Amazon's cost of goods sold for the sale on June 14?
   a. $490
   b. $500
   c. $790
   d. $1,000

4. After the purchase on June 22, what is Amazon's cost of the inventory on hand? Amazon uses FIFO.
   a. $300
   b. $740
   c. $440
   d. $720

5. Under the FIFO method, Amazon's journal entry (entries) on June 14 is (are):

a. Accounts Receivable	490	
Inventory.....................................		490
b. Accounts Receivable	1,000	
Sales Revenue		1,000
c. Cost of Goods Sold	490	
Inventory.....................................		490

   d. Both b and c are correct.

6. Which inventory costing method results in the lowest net income during a period of rising inventory costs?
   a. Specific unit cost
   b. First-in, first-out (FIFO)
   c. Last-in, first-out (LIFO)
   d. Average cost

7. Suppose Amazon.com used the average-cost method and the perpetual inventory system. Use the Amazon data in question 3 to compute the average unit cost of the company's inventory on hand at June 8. Round unit cost to the nearest cent.
   a. $19.00
   b. $19.75
   c. $20.00
   d. Cannot be determined from the data given

8. Which of the following is most closely linked to accounting conservatism?
   a. Consistency principle
   b. Disclosure principle
   c. Lower-of-cost-or-market rule
   d. Materiality concept

9. At December 31, 2008, McAdam Company overstated ending inventory by $40,000. How does this error affect cost of goods sold and net income for 2008?
   a. Understates costs of goods sold
      Overstates net income
   b. Overstates cost of goods sold
      Understates net income
   c. Overstates both cost of goods sold and net income
   d. Leaves both cost of goods sold and net income correct because the errors cancel each other

10. Suppose Rockey Mountain Sportswear (RMS) suffered a fire loss and needs to estimate the cost of the goods destroyed. Beginning inventory was $100,000, net purchases totaled $600,000, and sales came to $1,000,000. RMS's normal gross profit percentage is 50%. Use the gross profit method to estimate the cost of the inventory lost in the fire.
    a. $350,000
    b. $300,000
    c. $250,000
    d. $200,000

Answers are given after Apply Your Knowledge (p. 349).

Assess Your Progress

Short Exercises

Perpetual inventory record—FIFO

S6-1 Shepherd Cycles uses the FIFO inventory method. Shepherd started June with 10 bicycles that cost $70 each. On June 16, Shepherd bought 20 bicycles at $80 each. On June 30, Shepherd sold 25 bicycles. Prepare Shepherd's perpetual inventory record. (pp. 319–321)

Perpetual inventory record—LIFO

S6-2 Use the Shepherd Cycles data in Short Exercise 6-1 to prepare a perpetual inventory record for the LIFO method. (p. 321)

Perpetual inventory record—average cost

S6-3 Use the Shepherd Cycles data in Short Exercise 6-1 to prepare a perpetual inventory record for the average-cost method. Round average cost per unit to the nearest cent and all other amounts to the nearest dollar. (pp. 322–323)

Recording inventory transactions—FIFO

S6-4 Use the Shepherd Cycles data in Short Exercise 6-1 to journalize

1. The June 16 purchase of inventory on account. (pp. 319–321)
2. The June 30 sale of inventory on account. Shepherd sold each bicycle for $140. (pp. 319–321)
3. Cost of goods sold under FIFO. (pp. 319–321)

Comparing cost of goods sold under FIFO and LIFO

S6-5 Answer these questions in your own words:

1. Why does FIFO produce the lowest cost of goods sold during a period of rising prices? (pp. 324–325)
2. Why does LIFO produce the highest cost of goods sold during a period of rising prices? (pp. 324–325)

Comparing ending inventory under FIFO and LIFO

S6-6 Explain in your own words which inventory method results in the highest, and the lowest, cost of ending inventory. Prices are rising. Exhibits 6-4, page 320, and 6-5, page 321, provide the needed information.

Applying the lower-of-cost-or-market rule

S6-7 Assume that a King Burger restaurant has the following perpetual inventory record for hamburger patties:

HAMBURGER PATTIES

Date	Purchases	Cost of Goods Sold	Inventory on Hand
May 9	$500		$500
22		$300	$200
31	$200		$400

At May 31, the accountant for the restaurant determines that the current replacement cost of the ending inventory is $450. Make any adjusting entry needed to apply the lower-of-cost-or-market rule. Then report inventory on the balance sheet. King Burger uses the average-cost method. (p. 329)

Applying the lower-of-cost-or-market rule

S6-8 Use the perpetual inventory record given in Short Exercise 6-7. Assume that the accountant determines that the current replacement cost of the ending inventory is $360. Make any adjusting entry needed to apply the lower-of-cost-or-market rule. Then report inventory on the balance sheet. King Burger uses the average-cost method. (p. 329)

Effect of an inventory error—one year only
4

S6-9 Van Dyke Copier inventory data for the year ended December 31, 2008, follow.

Sales revenue	$50,000
Cost of goods sold:	
Beginning inventory	$ 4,200
Net purchases	27,400
Cost of goods available	31,600
Less: Ending inventory	(4,600)
Cost of goods sold	27,000
Gross profit	$23,000

Assume that the ending inventory was accidentally overstated by $1,000. What are the correct amounts of cost of goods sold and gross profit? (p. 331)

Next year's effect of an inventory error
4

S6-10 Refer back to the Van Dyke Copier inventory data in Short Exercise 6-9. How would the inventory error affect Van Dyke's cost of goods sold and gross profit for the year ended December 31, 2009? (p. 331)

Estimating ending inventory by the gross profit method
5

S6-11 Carpetmaster began the year with inventory of $350,000. Inventory purchases for the year total $1,600,000, and cost of goods sold will be $1,750,000. How much is Carpetmaster's estimated cost of ending inventory? Use the gross profit method. (p. 332)

Estimating ending inventory by the gross profit method

S6-12 Leather Goods Company began the year with inventory of $50,000 and purchased $250,000 of goods during the year. Sales for the year are $500,000, and Leather Goods' gross profit percentage is 55% of sales. Compute the estimated cost of ending inventory by the gross profit method. (p. 332)

Exercises

Measuring ending inventory and cost of goods sold in a perpetual system—FIFO
1

E6-13 Hyatt Magic carries an inventory of putters and other golf clubs. Hyatt uses the FIFO method and a perpetual inventory system. Company records indicate the following for a particular line of Hyatt Magic putters:

Date	Item	Quantity	Unit Cost
Nov. 1	Balance	5	$70
6	Sale	3	
8	Purchase	10	79
17	Sale	4	
30	Sale	5	

Requirement

Prepare a perpetual inventory record for the putters. Then determine the amounts Hyatt Magic should report for ending inventory and cost of goods sold by the FIFO method. (pp. 319–321)

Recording perpetual inventory transactions
1

E6-14 After preparing the FIFO perpetual inventory record in Exercise 6-13, journalize Hyatt Magic's November 8 purchase of inventory on account and November 17 cash sale (sale price of each putter was $120). (pp. 319–321)

Measuring ending inventory and cost of goods sold in a perpetual system—LIFO

1

E6-15 Refer to the Hyatt Magic inventory data in Exercise 6-13. Assume that Hyatt Magic uses the LIFO cost method. Prepare Hyatt's perpetual inventory record for the putters on the LIFO basis. Then identify the cost of ending inventory and cost of goods sold for the month. (p. 321)

Applying the average-cost method in a perpetual inventory system

E6-16 Refer to the Hyatt Magic inventory data in Exercise 6-13. Assume that Hyatt Magic uses the average-cost method. Prepare Hyatt's perpetual inventory record for the putters on the average-cost basis. Round average cost per unit to the nearest cent and all other amounts to the nearest dollar. Then identify the cost of ending inventory and cost of goods sold for the month (pp. 322–323)

Recording perpetual inventory transactions

E6-17 Accounting records for Jim's Shopping Bags yield the following data for the year ended December 31, 2008.

Inventory, December 31, 2007	$ 8,000
Purchases of inventory (on account)	49,000
Sales of inventory—80% on account; 20% for cash (cost $41,000)	75,000
Inventory, December 31, 2008	?

Requirements

1. Journalize Jim's inventory transactions in the perpetual system. (pp. 319–321)
2. Report ending inventory on the balance sheet, and sales, cost of goods sold, and gross profit on the income statement. (p. 316)

Comparing FIFO and LIFO amounts for ending inventory

2

E6-18 Assume that a Toys "Я" Us store bought and sold a line of dolls for inventory during December as follows:

Beginning inventory	10 units @ $9
Sale	6 units
Purchase	15 units @ $12
Sale	14 units

Toys "Я" Us uses the perpetual inventory system. Compute the cost of ending inventory under (a) FIFO and (b) LIFO. You will need to prepare a perpetual inventory record for LIFO.

Which method results in higher cost of ending inventory? (pp. 319, 321)

Comparing FIFO and LIFO amounts for cost of goods sold

E6-19 Use the data in Exercise 6-18 to compute the cost of goods sold under (a) FIFO and (b) LIFO. You will need a complete perpetual inventory record for LIFO. Which method results in the higher cost of goods sold? (pp. 319, 321)

Comparing FIFO, LIFO, and average-cost amounts

2

E6-20 Assume that a Goodyear Tire store completed the following perpetual inventory transactions for a line of tires.

Beginning inventory	20 tires @ $60
Purchase	8 tires @ $75
Sale	15 tires @ $110

Compute cost of goods sold and gross profit under (a) FIFO, (b) LIFO, and (c) average cost (round average cost per unit to the nearest cent and all other amounts to the nearest dollar). (pp. 319–323)

Determining amounts for the income statement; periodic system

1

E6-21 This exercise is based on the Appendix 6A. Supply the missing amounts for each of the following companies (p. 350):

Company	Net Sales	Beginning Inventory	Net Purchases	Ending Inventory	Cost of Goods Sold	Gross Profit
Ash	$101,000	$21,000	$62,000	$19,000	(a)	$37,000
Elm	(b)	25,000	93,000	(c)	$94,000	43,000
Fir	94,000	(d)	54,000	22,000	62,000	(e)
Oak	84,000	10,000	(f)	8,000	(g)	47,000

Prepare the income statement for Ash Company, which uses the periodic inventory system. Include a complete heading and show the full computation of cost of goods sold. Ash's operating expenses for the year were $11,000. (p. 251)

Applying the lower-of-cost-or-market rule to inventories

3

E6-22 Eagle Resources, which uses the FIFO method, has these account balances at December 31, 2008, prior to releasing the financial statements for the year:

Inventory

Beg. bal. 12,000	
⁝	
End bal. 14,000	

Cost of Goods Sold

⁝	
Bal. 72,000	

Sales Revenue

	⁝
	Bal. 118,000

Eagle has determined that the replacement cost (current market value) of the December 31, 2008, ending inventory is $13,000.

Requirement

Prepare Eagle Resources' balance sheet at December 31, 2008, to show how Eagle would apply the lower-of-cost-or-market rule to inventories. Include a complete heading for the statement. (p. 329)

Applying the lower-of-cost-or-market rule to inventories 3

E6-23 Nutriset Foods reports inventory at the lower of average cost or market. Prior to releasing its March 2008 financial statements, Nutriset's *preliminary* income statement, before the year-end adjustments, appears as follows:

NUTRISET FOODS Income Statement (partial)	
Sales revenue	$118,000
Cost of goods sold	48,000
Gross profit	$ 70,000

Nutriset has determined that the replacement cost of ending inventory is $18,000. Cost is $21,000.

Requirement

Show how Nutriset should report sales, cost of goods sold, and gross profit. (pp. 324–325)

Measuring the effect of an inventory error 4

E6-24 Poiláne Bakery reported sales revenue of $28,000 and cost of goods sold of $12,000. Compute Poiláne's correct gross profit if the company made each of the following accounting errors. Show your work.

a. Ending inventory is overstated by $3,000. (pp. 329–330)

b. Ending inventory is understated by $3,000. (pp. 329–330)

Correcting an inventory error—two years 4

E6-25 Whole Foods Grocery reported the following comparative income statement for the years ended September 30, 2008 and 2007.

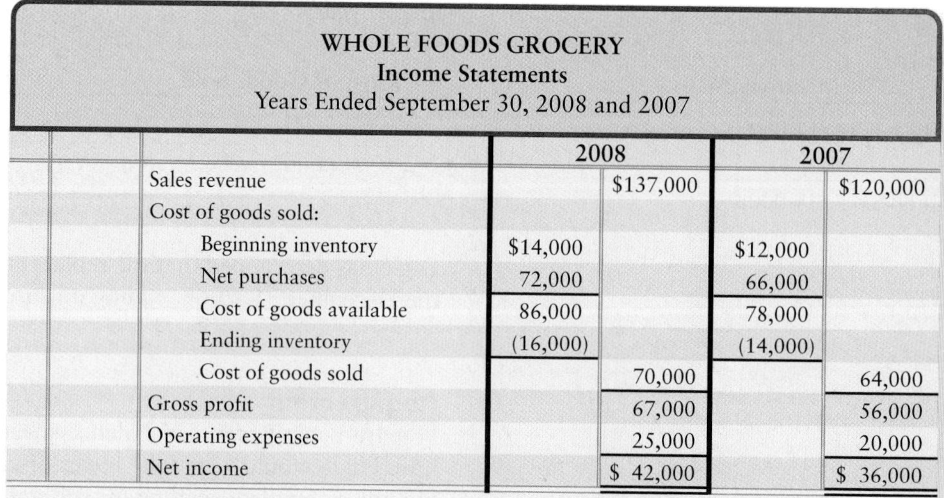

WHOLE FOODS GROCERY Income Statements Years Ended September 30, 2008 and 2007	2008		2007	
Sales revenue		$137,000		$120,000
Cost of goods sold:				
Beginning inventory	$14,000		$12,000	
Net purchases	72,000		66,000	
Cost of goods available	86,000		78,000	
Ending inventory	(16,000)		(14,000)	
Cost of goods sold		70,000		64,000
Gross profit		67,000		56,000
Operating expenses		25,000		20,000
Net income		$ 42,000		$ 36,000

continued. . .

During 2008, Whole Foods discovered that ending 2007 inventory, as previously reported, was overstated by $3,000. Prepare the corrected comparative income statement for the two-year period, complete with a heading for the statement. What was the effect of the error on net income for the two years combined? Explain your answer. (p. 330–331)

Estimating ending inventory by the gross profit method

5

E6-26 Toyota holds inventory all over the world. Assume that the records for an auto part show the following:

Beginning inventory................................	$ 150,000
Net purchases..	800,000
Net sales..	1,000,000
Gross profit rate.....................................	40%

Suppose this inventory, stored in the United States, was lost in a fire. Estimate the amount of the loss to Toyota. Use the gross profit method. (p. 332)

Estimating ending inventory by the gross profit method

5

E6-27 Chick Landscaping and Nursery began January with inventory of $47,000. During January, Chick made net purchases of $33,000 and had net sales of $60,000. For the past several years, Chick's gross profit has been 35% of sales. Use the gross profit method to estimate the cost of the ending inventory for the monthly financial statements. (p. 332)

Problems (Group A)

Using the perpetual inventory system—FIFO

1

P6-28A Ornamental Iron Works, which uses the FIFO method, began August with 50 units of iron inventory that cost $40 each. During August, the company completed these inventory transactions:

		Units	Unit Cost	Unit Sale Price
Aug. 3	Sale......................	40		$70
8	Purchase	80	$44	
21	Sale......................	70		75
30	Purchase	10	48	

Requirements

1. Prepare a perpetual inventory record for the inventory. (pp. 319–321)
2. Determine the company's cost of goods sold for August. (pp. 319–321)
3. Compute gross profit for August. (pp. 319–321)

Accounting for inventory using the perpetual system—LIFO

1

P6-29A Toy World began January with an inventory of 20 crates of toys that cost a total of $1,100. During the month, Toy World purchased and sold merchandise on account as follows:

Purchase 1	30 crates @ $65	Purchase 2	70 crates @ $70
Sale 1	40 crates @ sale price of $100	Sale 2	75 crates @ sale price of $110

Toy World uses the LIFO method.

continued. . .

Cash payments on account totaled $6,300. Operating expenses for the month were $3,600, with two-thirds paid in cash and the rest accrued as Accounts Payable.

Requirements

1. Prepare a perpetual inventory record, at LIFO cost, for this merchandise. (p. 321)
2. Make journal entries to record Toy World's transactions. (p. 321)

Accounting for inventory in a perpetual system—average-cost

1

P6-30A Refer to the Toy World situation in Problem 6-29A. Keep all the data unchanged, except that Toy World now uses the average-cost method.

Requirements

1. Prepare a perpetual inventory record at average cost. Round average unit cost to the nearest cent and all other amounts to the nearest dollar. (pp. 322–323)
2. Prepare a multi-step income statement for Toy World for the month ended January 31, 2007. (p. 316)

Applying the lower-of-cost-or-market rule to inventories

3

P6-31A Some of L&M Electronics' merchandise is gathering dust. It is now December 31, 2008, and the current replacement cost of the ending inventory is $25,000 below L&M's cost of the goods, which was $100,000. Before any adjustments at the end of the period, the company's Cost of Goods Sold account has a balance of $600,000.

What action should L&M Electronics take in this situation, if any? Give any journal entry required. At what amount should L&M report Inventory on the balance sheet? At what amount should the company report Cost of Goods Sold on the income statement? Discuss the accounting principle or concept that is most relevant to this situation. (p. 329)

Correcting inventory errors over a three-year period

4

P6-32A Lake Air Carpets' books show the following data (in thousands). In early 2009, auditors found that the ending inventory for 2006 was understated by $8 thousand and that the ending inventory for 2008 was overstated by $4 thousand. The ending inventory at December 31, 2007, was correct.

(Thousands)	2008		2007		2006	
Net sales revenue		$360		$285		$244
Cost of goods sold:						
Beginning inventory	$ 65		$ 55		$ 70	
Net purchases	195		135		130	
Cost of goods available	260		190		200	
Less: Ending inventory	(70)		(65)		(55)	
Cost of goods sold		190		125		145
Gross profit		170		160		99
Operating expenses		113		109		76
Net income		$ 57		$ 51		$ 23

continued. . .

Requirements

1. Show corrected income statements for the three years. (pp. 330–331)
2. State whether each year's net income—before your corrections—is understated or overstated. For each incorrect figure, indicate the amount of the understatement or overstatement. (pp. 330–331)

Estimating ending inventory by the gross profit method; preparing the income statement

5

P6-33A Party Time Costumes estimates its inventory by the gross profit method. The gross profit has averaged 50% of net sales. The company's inventory records reveal the following data (amounts in thousands):

Inventory, July 1	$ 360
Transactions during July:	
Purchases	3,700
Purchase discounts	20
Purchase returns	10
Sales	6,430
Sales returns	30

Requirements

1. Estimate the July 31 inventory, using the gross profit method. (p. 332)
2. Prepare the July income statement through gross profit for Party Time Costumes. (pp. 274, 334)

Problems (Group B)

Accounting for inventory in a perpetual system—FIFO

1

P6-34B Hobart Sign Company began with an inventory of 50 signs that cost a total of $1,500. Hobart purchased and sold merchandise on account as follows:

Purchase 1	60 signs @ $35
Sale 1	100 signs @ $60
Purchase 2	90 signs @ $40
Sale 2	70 signs @ $70

Hobart uses the FIFO cost method. Cash payments on account totaled $5,000. Operating expenses were $2,700; Hobart paid two-thirds in cash and accrued the rest as Accounts Payable.

Requirements

1. Prepare a perpetual inventory record, at FIFO cost, for this merchandise. (pp. 319–321)
2. Make journal entries to record the company's transactions. (pp. 319–321)

Accounting for inventory in a perpetual system—average cost

1

P6-35B Refer to the Hobart Sign Company situation in Problem 6-34B. Keep all the data unchanged, except that Hobart now uses the average-cost method.

continued. . .

Requirements

1. Prepare a perpetual inventory record at average cost. Round average unit cost to the nearest cent and all other amounts to the nearest dollar. (pp. 322–323)
2. Prepare a multi-step income statement for Hobart Sign Company for the month ended February 28, 2008. (p. 274)

Using the perpetual inventory system—LIFO

1

P6-36B La Tapatía Mexican Foods, which uses the LIFO method, began March with 50 units of food inventory that cost $15 each. During March, LaTapatía completed these inventory transactions:

		Units	Unit Cost	Unit Sale Price
March 2	Purchase.............	12	$20	
8	Sale	40		$36
17	Purchase.............	30	25	
22	Sale	31		40

Requirements

1. Prepare a perpetual inventory record for the inventory. (p. 321)
2. Determine LaTapatía's cost of goods sold for March. (p. 321)
3. Compute gross profit for March. (p. 316)

Applying the lower-of-cost-or-market rule to inventories

3

P6-37B Some of Lamar Scuba Center's merchandise is gathering dust. It is now December 31, 2009. The current replacement cost of Lamar's ending inventory is $15,000 below Lamar's cost of the goods, which was $90,000. Before any adjustments at the end of the period, the Cost of Goods Sold account has a balance of $400,000.

What action should Lamar take in this situation, if any? Give any journal entry required. At what amount should Lamar report Inventory on the balance sheet? At what amount should the company report Cost of Goods Sold on the income statement? Discuss the accounting principle or concept that is most relevant to this situation. (p. 329)

Correcting inventory errors over a three-year period

4

P6-38B The accounting records of Juniper Cove Music Store show these data (in thousands):

	2008		2007		2006	
Net sales revenue		$210		$165		$170
Cost of goods sold:						
Beginning inventory................	$ 20		$ 25		$ 40	
Net purchases........................	135		100		90	
Cost of goods available	155		125		130	
Less: Ending inventory	(30)		(20)		(25)	
Cost of goods sold..................		125		105		105
Gross profit..............................		85		60		65
Operating expenses....................		58		32		29
Net income		$ 27		$ 28		$ 36

continued. . .

In early 2009, auditors discovered that the ending inventory for 2006, as reported here, was understated by $6 thousand and that the ending inventory for 2008 was overstated by $7 thousand. The ending inventory at December 31, 2007, was correct.

Requirements

1. Show corrected income statements for the three years. (pp. 330–331)
2. State whether each year's net income as reported here is understated or overstated. For each incorrect net income figure, indicate the amount of the understatement or overstatement. (pp. 329–331)

Estimating ending inventory by the gross profit method; preparing the income statement

P6-39B Audio-Video estimates its inventory by the gross profit method when preparing monthly financial statements. For the past two years, gross profit has averaged 22% of net sales. The company's inventory records reveal the following data (amounts in thousands):

Inventory, March 1	$ 690
Transactions during March:	
Purchases	6,500
Purchase discounts	150
Purchase returns	10
Sales	8,610
Sales returns	110

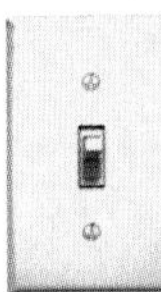

For 24/7 practice, visit www.MyAccountingLab.com

Requirements

1. Estimate the March 31 inventory using the gross profit method. (p. 332)
2. Prepare the March income statement through gross profit for Audio Video. (p. 316)

Apply Your Knowledge

Decision Cases

Making inventory decisions 2

Case 1. Assume you are opening a Bed Bath & Beyond store. To finance the business, you need a $500,000 loan, and your banker requires a set of forecasted financial statements. Assume you are preparing the statements and must make some decisions about how to do the accounting for the business. Answer the following questions (refer back to Chapter 5 if necessary):

1. Which type of inventory system will you use? Give your reason. (p. 259)
2. Show how to compute net purchases and net sales. How will you treat the cost of transportation-in? (pp. 264–267)
3. How often do you plan to do a physical count of inventory on hand? What will the physical count accomplish? (pp. 270–271)
4. Inventory costs are rising. Which inventory costing method will you use in order to:
   a. Maximize net income? (pp. 324–325)
   b. Pay the least amount of income tax? (pp. 324–325)

Increasing net income 2

Case 2. Suppose you manage Campbell Appliance. The store's summarized financial statements for 2008, the most recent year, follow:

CAMPBELL APPLIANCE
Income Statement
Year Ended December 31, 2008

	(Thousands)
Sales	$800
Cost of goods sold	660
Gross profit	140
Operating expenses	100
Net income	$ 40

CAMPBELL APPLIANCE
Balance Sheet
December 31, 2008

(Thousands)	Assets	Liabilities and Equity	
Cash	$ 30	Accounts payable	$ 35
Inventories	75	Note payable	280
Land and buildings, net	360	Total liabilities	315
		Stockholder equity	150
Total assets	$465	Total liabilities and equity	$465

Assume that you need to double net income. To accomplish your goal, it will be very difficult to raise the prices you charge because there is a Best Buy nearby. Also, you have little control over your cost of goods sold because the appliance manufacturers set the price you must pay.

Identify several strategies for doubling net income. (Challenge)

Ethical Issue

During 2008, Crop-Paper-Scissors, a craft store, changed to the LIFO method of accounting for inventory. Suppose that during 2009, Crop-Paper-Scissors switched back to the FIFO method and the following year switches back to LIFO again.

Requirements

1. What would you think of a company's ethics if it changed accounting methods every year?
2. What accounting principle would changing methods every year violate?
3. Who can be harmed when a company changes its accounting methods too often? How?

Financial Statement Case

Analyzing inventories
3 4 5

The notes are an important part of a company's financial statements, giving valuable details that would clutter the tabular data presented in the statements. This case will help you learn to use a company's inventory notes. Refer to the Amazon.com financial statements and related notes in Appendix A at the end of the book, and answer the following questions:

Requirements

1. How much was the Amazon.com merchandise inventory at December 31, 2005? At December 31, 2004?
2. Which cost method does Amazon use for inventories? How does Amazon value its inventories? See Note 1.
3. By rearranging the cost-of-goods-sold formula, you can compute purchases, which are not reported in the Amazon statements. How much were Amazon's inventory purchases during 2005?

Team Project

Link Back to Chapter 5 (Gross Profit Percentage and Inventory Turnover). Obtain the annual reports of as many companies as you have team members—one company per team member. Most companies post their financial statements on their Web sites.

Requirements

1. Identify the inventory method used by each company.
2. Compute each company's gross profit percentage and rate of inventory turnover for the most recent two years.
3. For the industries of the companies you are analyzing, obtain the industry averages for gross profit percentage and inventory turnover from Robert Morris Associates, *Annual Statement Studies;* Dun and Bradstreet, *Industry Norms and Key Business Ratios;* or Leo Troy, *Almanac of Business and Industrial Financial Ratios.*
4. How well does each of your companies compare to the average for its industry? What insight about your companies can you glean from these ratios?

For Internet Exercises, Excel in Practice, and additional online activities, go to the Web site www.prenhall.com/horngren.

Quick Check Answers

1. *a* 2. *c* 3. *a* 4. *b* 5. *d* 6. *c* 7. *b* 8. *c* 9. *a* 10. *d*

Appendix 6A

Accounting for Inventory in a Periodic System

We described the periodic inventory system briefly in Chapter 5. Accounting is simpler in a periodic system because the company keeps no daily running record of inventory on hand. The only way to determine the ending inventory and cost of goods sold in a periodic system is to count the goods—usually at the end of the year. The periodic system works well for a small business, in which the owner can control inventory by visual inspection.

This appendix illustrates how the periodic system works. The accounting in a periodic system is similar to a perpetual system, except:

1. The periodic system uses four additional accounts:
   - **Purchases**—this account holds the cost of inventory as it's purchased. Purchases carries a debit balance.
   - **Purchase Discounts**—this contra account carries a credit balance.
   - **Purchase Returns and Allowances**—this contra account carries a credit balance.
   - **Transportation-in**—this account holds the transportation cost paid on inventory purchases. It carries a debit balance.

   In the perpetual system, all these costs go into the Inventory account.

2. The end-of-period entries are more extensive in the periodic system because we must close out the beginning inventory balance and set up the cost of the ending inventory. This appendix illustrates the closing process for the periodic system.

3. Cost of goods sold in a periodic system is computed by the following formula (using assumed amounts for this illustration):

Beginning inventory (ending inventory from the preceding period)	$ 5,000
Net purchases (often abbreviated as Purchases)	20,000*
Cost of goods available	25,000
Less: Ending inventory (on hand at the end of the current period)	(7,000)
Cost of goods sold	$18,000

*Net purchases is determined as follows (all amounts assumed):

Purchases	$21,000
Less: Purchase discounts	(2,000)
Purchase returns and allowances	(5,000)
Add: Transportation-in	6,000
Net purchases	$20,000

Inventory Costing in the Periodic System

The various costing methods (FIFO, LIFO, and average) in a periodic inventory system follow the pattern illustrated earlier for the perpetual system. To show how the periodic system works, we use the same Rocky Mountain Sportswear data that we used for the perpetual system, as follows:

ROCKY MOUNTAIN SPORTSWEAR SKI PARKA

		Number of Units	Unit Cost
Nov. 1	Beginning inventory	1	$40
5	Purchase	6	45
26	Purchase	7	50
30	Ending inventory	2	?

We use these data to illustrate:

- FIFO
- LIFO
- Average cost

For all three methods cost of goods available is always the sum of beginning inventory plus net purchases:

Beginning inventory (1 unit @ $40)	$ 40
Net purchases (6 units @ $45) + (7 units @ $50)	620
Cost of goods available (14 units)	$660

The different methods—FIFO, LIFO, and average cost—compute different amounts for ending inventory and cost of goods sold.

First-In, First-Out (FIFO) Method

Under FIFO, the ending inventory comes from the newest—the most recent—purchases, which cost $50 per unit. FIFO is illustrated in the box that follows on the next page.

Last-In, First-Out (LIFO) Method

Under LIFO, the ending inventory comes from the oldest cost of the period—in this case the beginning inventory that cost $40 per unit, plus the first purchase at $45. The LIFO illustration follows on the next page.

Average-Cost Method

In the average-cost method, we compute a single average cost per unit for the entire period:

Cost of goods available	÷	Number of units available	=	Average cost per unit
$660	÷	14 units	=	$47.14

Then apply this average cost to compute ending inventory and cost of goods sold, as shown in the far right column:

	FIFO	LIFO	Average
Cost of goods available	$660	$660	$660
Less: Ending inventory			
FIFO (2 units @ $50)	(100)		
LIFO (1 unit @ $40 1 unit @ $45)		(85)	
Average (2 units @ $47.14)			(94)
Cost of goods sold	$560	$575	$566

Comparing the Perpetual and Periodic Inventory Systems

Exhibit 6A-1 provides a side-by-side comparison of the perpetual and the periodic inventory systems. It gives the:

- Journal entries
- Ledger accounts
- Reporting in the financial statements

EXHIBIT 6A-1 **Comparing the Perpetual and Periodic Inventory Systems (all amounts assumed for this illustration)**

JOURNAL ENTRIES

Perpetual System			Periodic System		
Inventory	$570,000		Purchases	$570,000	
Accounts Payable		570,000	Accounts Payable		$570,000
Purchased on account.			*Purchased inventory on account.*		
Accounts Payable	20,000		Accounts Payable	20,000	
Inventory		20,000	Purchase Returns and Allowances		20,000
Returned damaged goods to seller.			*Returned damaged goods to seller.*		
Accounts Receivable	900,000		Accounts Receivable	900,000	
Sales Revenue		900,000	Sales Revenue		900,000
Sale on account.			*Sale on account.*		
Cost of Goods Sold	530,000		No entry for cost of goods sold.		
Inventory		530,000			
Cost of goods sold.					

CLOSING ENTRIES

End of the Period			End of the Period		
			1. Cost of Goods Sold	$100,000	
			Inventory (beginning)		$100,000
			Transfer beginning inventory to cost of goods sold.		
			2. Inventory (ending)	120,000	
			Cost of Goods Sold		120,000
			Record ending inventory based on a physical count.		
			3. Cost of Goods Sold	550,000	
			Purchase Returns and Allowances	20,000	
			Purchases		570,000
			Transfer net purchases to cost of goods sold.		
1. Income Summary	530,000		4. Income Summary	530,000	
Cost of Goods Sold		530,000	Cost of Goods Sold		530,000
Close cost of goods sold.			*Close cost of goods sold.*		
			($100,000 – $120,000 + $550,000 = $530,000)		

EXHIBIT 6A-1 Continued

LEDGER ACCOUNTS

Perpetual System				Periodic System			
Inventory		Cost of Goods Sold		Inventory		Cost of Goods Sold	
100,000	20,000	530,000	530,000	100,000*	100,000	100,000	120,000
570,000	530,000			120,000		550,000	530,000
120,000							

*Beginning inventory was $100,000.

REPORTING IN THE FINANCIAL STATEMENTS

Perpetual System

Income Statement

Sales revenue	$900,000
Cost of goods sold	530,000
Gross profit	$370,000

Balance Sheet

Current assets:

Cash	$ XXX
Accounts receivable	XXX
Inventory	120,000

Periodic System

Income Statement

Sales revenue			$900,000
Cost of goods sold:			
Beginning inventory		$ 100,000	
Purchases	$570,000		
Less: Purchase returns and allowances	(20,000)	550,000	
Cost of goods available		650,000	
Less: Ending inventory		(120,000)	
Cost of goods sold			530,000
Gross profit			$370,000

Balance Sheet

Current assets:

Cash	$ XXX
Accounts receivable	XXX
Inventory	120,000

Appendix 6A Assignments

Exercises

Determining ending inventory and cost of goods sold by four methods—periodic system. 1

E6A-1 The periodic inventory records of Flexon Prosthetics indicate the following at October 31:

Oct. 1	Beginning inventory	9 units @ $60
8	Purchase	4 units @ 60
15	Purchase	10 units @ 70
26	Purchase	3 units @ 80

At October 31 Flexon counts 8 units of inventory on hand.

continued. . .

Requirements

Compute ending inventory and cost of goods sold, using each of the following methods.

1. Average cost (round average unit cost to the nearest cent) (pp. 350–351)
2. First-in, first-out (pp. 350–351)
3. Last-in, first-out (pp. 350–351)

Journalizing purchase, sale, and closing entries—periodic system

E6A-2 Flexon Prosthetics uses the periodic inventory system. Journalize Flexon Prosthetics'

a. Purchase of inventory on account, $1,180. (pp. 353–354)

b. Sale of inventory for $3,000. (pp. 353–354)

c. Closing entries: (pp. 353–354)

(1) Beginning inventory, $540.

(2) Ending inventory at FIFO cost, $590.

(3) Purchases, $1,180.

(4) Cost of goods sold at FIFO cost, $1,130.

Include an explanation for each entry.

Problem

Computing inventory by three methods—periodic system

P6A-1 A Best Yet Electronic Center began December with 100 units of inventory that cost $75 each. During December, the store made the following purchases:

Dec. 3	20 @ $80
12	50 @ 82
18	80 @ 85

Best Yet uses the periodic inventory system, and the physical count at December 31 indicates that 110 units of inventory are on hand.

Requirements

1. Determine the ending inventory and cost-of-goods-sold amounts for the December financial statements under the average cost, FIFO, and LIFO methods. (pp. 350–351)
2. Sales revenue for December totaled $25,000. Compute Best Yet's gross profit for December under each method. (pp. 353–354)
3. Which method will result in the lowest income taxes for Best Yet? Why? Which method will result in the highest net income for Best Yet? Why? (pp. 324–325, 353–354)

7 Internal Control and Cash

Learning Objectives

1. Define internal control
2. Describe good internal control procedures
3. Prepare a bank reconciliation and the related journal entries
4. Apply internal controls to cash receipts
5. Apply internal controls to cash payments
6. Make ethical business judgments

In the preceding chapter your business, In Motion, imprinted logos on T-shirts for groups around your campus. Operating out of your apartment, the business has been successful. Last year sales totaled $100,000, and your net income was $25,000. Not bad for a college student.

Suppose you are graduating and you want to expand the business. A college buddy wants into the action and has agreed to join In Motion. He can sell T-shirts around neighboring colleges and also help with the handling and delivery of inventory. In addition, he made an A in ACC 110, so you'll let him do the accounting.

With boxes of T-shirts crammed into every corner, your apartment is a bit cozy. You will need to rent warehouse space or possibly buy a building. Expansion will bring a new set of challenges:

- How will you safeguard In Motion's assets?
- How will you ensure that your friend follows policies that are best for the business? ■

This chapter presents a framework for dealing with these issues. It also shows how to account for cash, the most liquid of all assets.

Internal Control

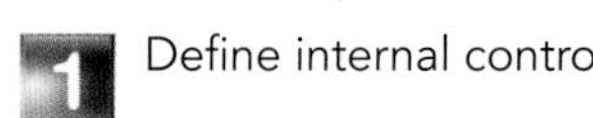

A key responsibility of a business owner is to control operations. Owners set goals, they hire managers to lead the way, and employees carry out the plan. **Internal control** is the organizational plan and all the related measures designed to:

1. **Safeguard assets.** A company must safeguard its assets; otherwise it's throwing away resources. If you fail to safeguard your cash, it will slip away.
2. **Encourage employees to follow company policy.** Everyone in an organization needs to work toward the same goal. With a friend operating part of In Motion, it's important for both of you to pursue the same goal. It's also important for you to develop policies so that you treat all customers similarly.
3. **Promote operational efficiency.** You cannot afford to waste resources. You work hard to make a sale, and you don't want to waste any of the benefits. If you can buy a T-shirt for $3, why pay $3.50? Eliminate waste, and increase your profits.
4. **Ensure accurate, reliable accounting records.** Good records are essential. Without reliable records, you cannot tell which part of the business is profitable and which part needs improvement. You could be losing money on every T-shirt you sell—unless you keep good records for the cost of your products.

How critical are internal controls? They're so important that the U.S. Congress passed a law that requires public companies—those that sell their stock to the public—to maintain a system of internal controls.

The Sarbanes-Oxley Act (SOX)

The Enron and WorldCom accounting scandals rocked the United States. Enron overstated profits and went out of business almost overnight. WorldCom (now MCI) reported expenses as assets and overstated both profits and assets. The company is just now emerging from bankruptcy. Sadly, the same accounting firm, Arthur Andersen, had audited both companies' financial statements. Arthur Andersen then closed its doors.

As the scandals unfolded, many people asked, "How can these things happen? Where were the auditors?" To address public concern, Congress passed the Sarbanes-Oxley Act, abbreviated as SOX. SOX revamped corporate governance in the United States and affected the accounting profession. Here are some of the SOX provisions:

1. Public companies must issue an internal control report, and the outside auditor must evaluate the client's internal controls.
2. A new body, the Public Company Accounting Oversight Board, oversees the work of auditors of public companies.

3. Accounting firms may not both audit a public client and also provide certain consulting services for the same client.

4. Stiff penalties await violators—25 years in prison for securities fraud; 20 years for an executive making false sworn statements.

Recently, the former chief executive of WorldCom was convicted of securities fraud and sentenced to 25 years in prison. The top executives of Enron were also sent to prison. You can see that internal controls and related matters can have serious consequences.

Exhibit 7-1 diagrams the shield that internal controls provide for an organization. Protected by the wall, people do business securely. How does a business achieve good internal control? The next section identifies the components of internal control.

EXHIBIT 7-1 **The Shield of Internal Control**

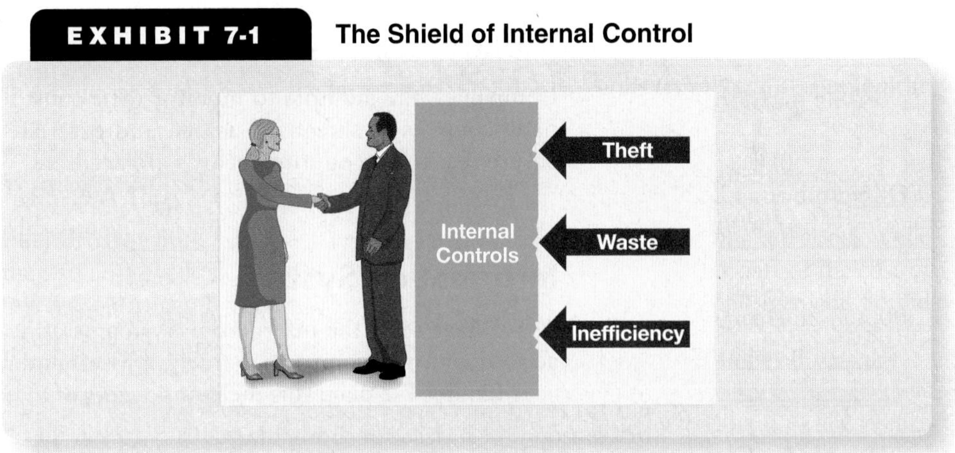

The Components of Internal Control

A business can achieve its internal control objectives by applying five components:

- Control environment
- Risk assessment
- Control procedures
- Monitoring of controls
- Information system

Control Environment

The control environment is the "tone at the top" of the business. It starts with the owner and the top managers. They must behave honorably to set a good example for company employees. The owner must demonstrate the importance of internal controls if he or she expects the employees to take the controls seriously. Former executives of Enron, WorldCom, and Tyco failed to establish a good control environment and are in prison as a result.

Risk Assessment

A company must identify its risks. For example, Kraft Foods faces the risk that its food products may harm people. American Airlines planes may go down, and all companies face the risk of bankruptcy. Companies facing difficulties are tempted to falsify the financial statements to make themselves look better than they really are.

Control Procedures

These are the procedures designed to ensure that the business's goals are achieved. Examples include assigning responsibilities, separating duties, and using security devices to protect inventory from theft. The next section discusses internal control procedures.

Monitoring of Controls

Companies hire auditors to monitor their controls. Internal auditors monitor company controls to safeguard assets, and external auditors monitor the controls to ensure that the accounting records are accurate.

Information System

As we have seen, the information system is critical. The owner of a business needs accurate information to keep track of assets and measure profits and losses.

Exhibit 7-2 diagrams the components of internal control.

EXHIBIT 7-2 The Components of Internal Control

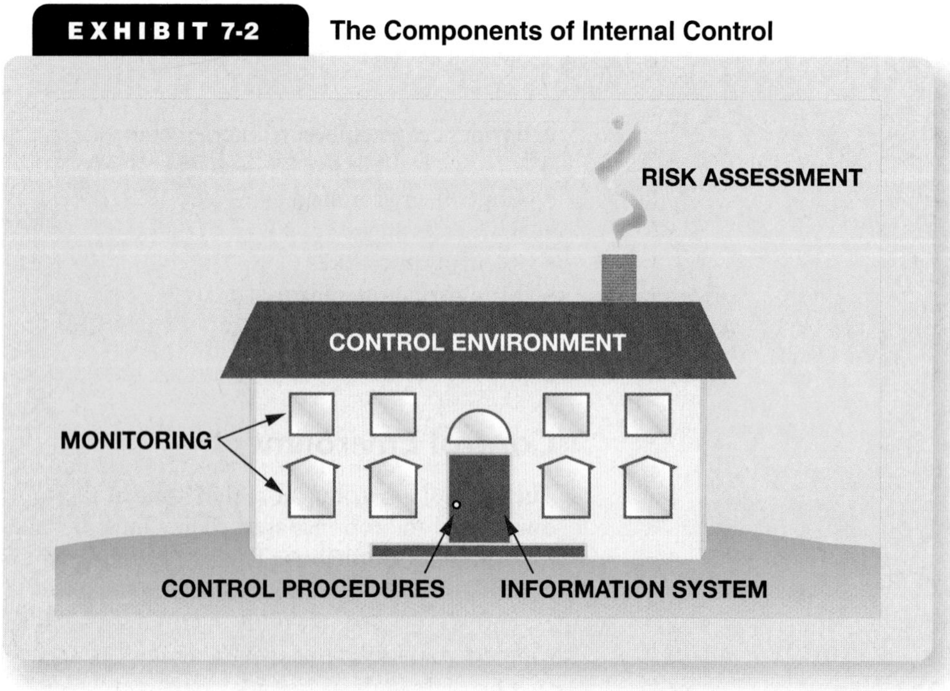

Internal Control Procedures

2 Describe good internal control procedures

Whether the business is In Motion (your T-shirt business), Microsoft, or an Exxon gas station, you need the following internal control procedures.

Competent, Reliable, and Ethical Personnel

Employees should be *competent, reliable,* and *ethical.* Paying good salaries will attract high-quality employees. You also must train them to do the job and supervise their work. This will build a competent staff.

Assignment of Responsibilities

In a business with good internal controls, no important duty is overlooked. Each employee has certain responsibilities. At In Motion, you'll be the boss because you own the business. Suppose you write the checks in order to control cash payments. You may let your friend do the accounting. In a large company the person in charge of writing checks is called the **treasurer**. The chief accounting officer is called the **controller**. With clearly assigned responsibilities, all important jobs get done.

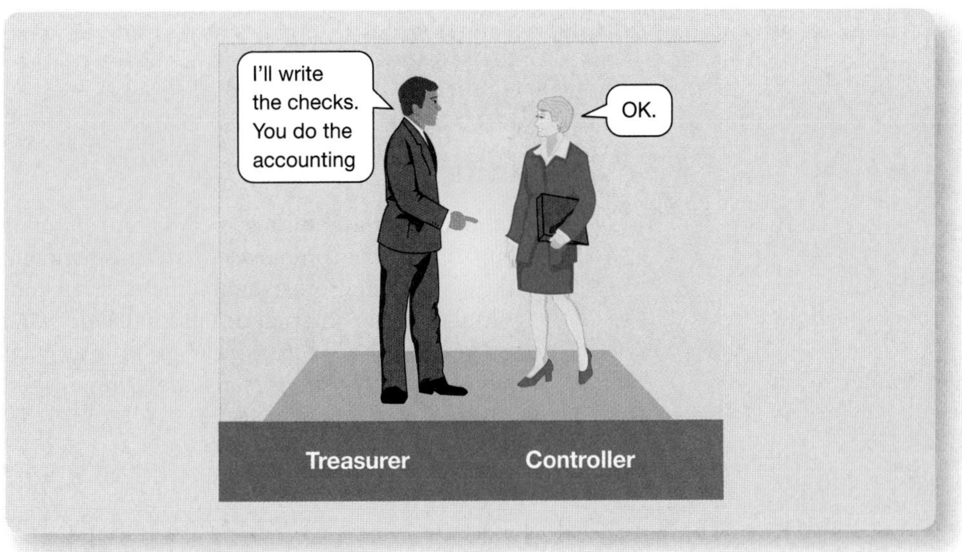

Separation of Duties

Smart management divides responsibility between two or more people. *Separation of duties* limits fraud and promotes the accuracy of the accounting records. Separation of duties can be divided into two parts:

1. **Separate operations from accounting.** Accounting should be completely separate from the operating departments, such as production and sales. What would happen if sales personnel recorded the company's revenue? Sales figures would be inflated, and top managers wouldn't know how much the company actually sold. This is why you should separate accounting and sales duties.

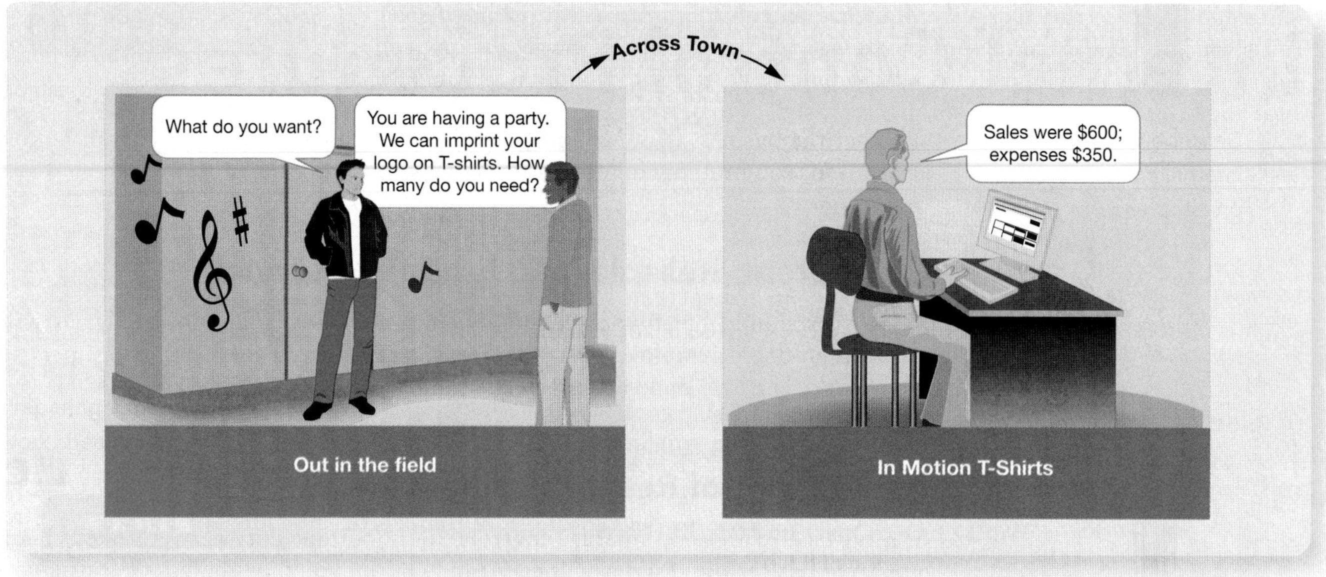

2. **Separate the custody of assets from accounting.** Accountants must not handle cash, and cashiers must not have access to the accounting records. If one employee has both duties, that person can steal cash and conceal the theft. The treasurer of a company handles cash, and the controller accounts for the cash. Neither person has both responsibilities. In an actual case, the cashier had access to his company's accounting records. With both duties, he was able to steal $600,000 and make bogus accounting entries to cover the theft.

Audits

To validate their accounting records, most companies have an audit. An **audit** is an examination of the company's financial statements and accounting system. To evaluate the system, auditors examine the internal controls.

Audits can be internal or external. *Internal auditors* are employees of the business. They ensure that employees are following company policies and operations are running efficiently. Auditors also determine whether the company is following legal requirements.

External auditors are completely independent of the business. They are hired to determine that the company's financial statements agree with generally accepted accounting principles. Auditors also suggest improvements that help the business run smoothly.

Documents

Documents provide the details of business transactions. Documents include invoices and fax orders. Documents should be prenumbered to prevent theft and inefficiency. A gap in the numbered sequence draws attention.

In a bowling alley a key document is the score sheet. The manager can compare the number of games scored with the amount of cash received. Multiply the number of games by the charge per game and compare the revenue with cash receipts. You can see whether the business is collecting all the revenue.

Bowling Scorecard **101**

Ron		SCORE
X \ — X X \ X \ — X		113
Sue		
X X X X X X X X X X		300
Games	Charge per Game	Total Revenue
2	$3	$6

Electronic Devices

Accounting systems are relying less on documents and more on digital storage devices. For example, retailers such as Target Stores and Macy's control inventory by attaching an electronic sensor to merchandise. The cashier removes the sensor. If a customer tries to leave the store with the sensor attached, an alarm sounds. According to Checkpoint Systems, these devices reduce theft by as much as 50%.

Other Controls

Businesses keep important documents in *fireproof vaults. Burglar alarms* protect buildings, and *security cameras* protect other property. *Loss-prevention specialists* train employees to spot suspicious activity.

Employees who handle cash are in a tempting position. Many businesses purchase *fidelity bonds* on cashiers. The bond is an insurance policy that reimburses the company for any losses due to employee theft. Before issuing a fidelity bond, the insurance company investigates the employee's record.

Mandatory vacations and *job rotation* improve internal control. Companies move employees from job to job. This improves morale by giving employees a broad view of the business. Also, knowing someone else will do your job next month keeps you honest.

Internal Controls for E-Commerce

E-commerce creates its own risks. Hackers may gain access to confidential information such as account numbers and passwords.

Pitfalls

E-commerce pitfalls include:

- Stolen credit-card numbers
- Computer viruses and Trojans
- Phishing expeditions

Stolen Credit-Card Numbers Suppose you buy CDs from EMusic.com. To make the purchase, your credit-card number must travel through cyberspace. Wireless networks (Wi-Fi) are creating new security hazards.

Amateur hacker Carlos Salgado, Jr., used his home computer to steal 100,000 credit-card numbers with a combined limit exceeding $1 billion. Salgado was caught when he tried to sell the numbers to an undercover FBI agent.

Computer Viruses and Trojans A **computer virus** is a malicious program that (a) enters program code without consent and (b) performs destructive actions. A **Trojan** hides inside a legitimate program and works like a virus. Viruses can destroy or alter data, make bogus calculations, and infect files. Most firms have found a virus in their system.

Suppose the U.S. Department of Defense takes bids for a missile system. Raytheon and Lockheed-Martin are competing for the contract. A hacker infects Raytheon's system and alters Raytheon's design. Then the government labels the Raytheon design as flawed and awards the contract to Lockheed.

Phishing Expeditions Thieves phish by creating bogus Web sites, such as AOL4Free.com. The neat-sounding Web site attracts lots of visitors, and the thieves obtain account numbers and passwords from unsuspecting people. They then use the data for illicit purposes.

Security Measures

To address the risks posed by e-commerce, companies have devised a number of security measures, including

- Encryption
- Firewalls

ENCRYPTION The server holding confidential information may not be secure. One technique for protecting customer data is encryption. **Encryption** rearranges messages by a mathematical process. The encrypted message can't be read by those who don't know the code. An accounting example uses check-sum digits for account numbers. Each account number has its last digit equal to the sum of the previous digits. For example, consider Customer Number 2237, where 2 + 2 + 3 = 7. Any account number that fails this test triggers an error message.

FIREWALLS **Firewalls** limit access into a local network. Members can access the network but nonmembers can't. Usually several firewalls are built into the system. Think of a fortress with multiple walls protecting the king's chamber in the center. At the point of entry, passwords, PINs (personal identification numbers), and signatures are used. More sophisticated firewalls are used deeper in the network. Start with Firewall 3, and work toward the center.

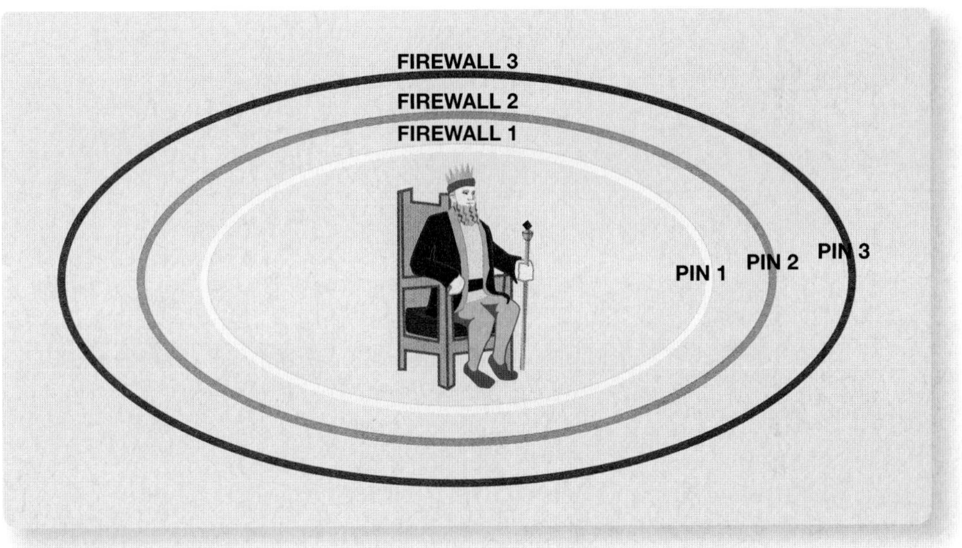

The Limitations of Internal Control—Costs and Benefits

Unfortunately, most internal controls can be overcome. Collusion—two or more people working together—can beat internal controls. Consider Galaxy Theater. Ralph and Lana can design a scheme in which Ralph sells tickets and pockets the cash from 10 customers. Lana, the ticket taker, admits 10 customers without tickets. Ralph and Lana split the cash. To prevent this situation, the manager must take additional steps, such as matching the number of people in the theater against the number of ticket stubs retained. But that takes time away from other duties.

The stricter the internal control system, the more it costs. A complex system of internal control can strangle the business with red tape. How tight should the controls be? Internal controls must be judged in light of their costs and benefits. An example of a good cost/benefit relationship: A security guard at a Wal-Mart store costs about $28,000 a year. On average, each guard prevents about $50,000 of theft. The net savings to Wal-Mart is $22,000.

The Bank Account as a Control Device

Cash is the most liquid asset because it's the medium of exchange. Cash is easy to conceal and relatively easy to steal. As a result, most businesses create specific controls for cash.

Keeping cash in a *bank account* helps control cash because banks have established practices for safeguarding customers' money. The documents used to control a bank account include the:

- Signature card
- Deposit ticket
- Check
- Bank statement
- Bank reconciliation

Signature Card

Banks require each person authorized to sign on an account to provide a *signature card*. This protects against forgery.

Deposit Ticket

Banks supply standard forms such as *deposit tickets*. The customer fills in the amount of each deposit. As proof of the transaction, the customer keeps a deposit receipt.

Check

To pay cash, the depositor writes a **check**, which tells the bank to pay the designated party a specified amount. There are three parties to a check:

- the *maker*, who signs the check
- the *payee*, to whom the check is paid
- the *bank* on which the check is drawn

Exhibit 7-3 shows a check drawn by In Motion T-Shirts, the maker. The check has two parts, the check itself and the *remittance advice* below. This optional attachment tells the payee the reason for the payment.

Bank Statement

Banks send monthly statements to customers. A **bank statement** reports what the bank did with the customer's cash. The statement shows the account's beginning and ending balances, cash receipts, and payments. Included with the statement are

EXHIBIT 7-3 **Check with Remittance Advice**

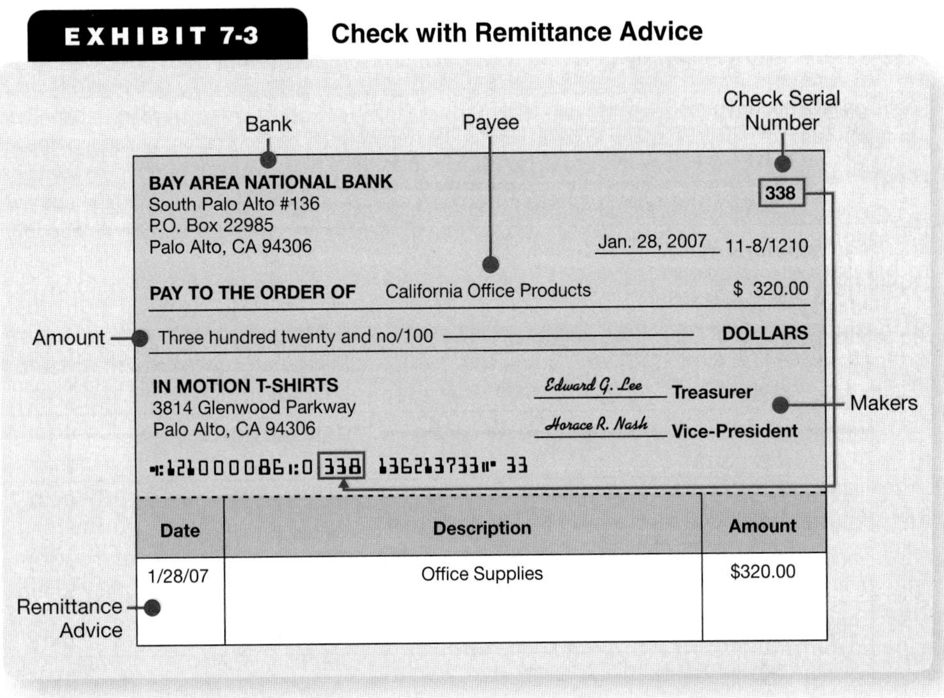

copies of the maker's *canceled checks* (or the actual paid checks). Exhibit 7-4 is the January bank statement of In Motion T-shirts.

Electronic funds transfer (EFT) moves cash by electronic communication. It is cheaper to pay without having to mail a check, so many people pay their mortgage, rent, and insurance by EFT.

The Bank Reconciliation

There are two records of a business's cash:

1. The Cash account in the company's general ledger. Exhibit 7-5 (page 369) shows that In Motion's ending cash balance is $3,340.
2. The bank statement, which shows the cash receipts and payments transacted through the bank. In Exhibit 7-4 (page 368), the bank shows an ending balance of $5,900 for In Motion T-shirts.

The books and the bank statement usually show different cash balances. Differences arise because of a time lag in recording transactions—two examples:

- When you write a check, you immediately deduct it in your checkbook. But the bank does not subtract the check from your account until it pays the check—a few days later. Likewise, you immediately add the cash receipt for all your deposits. But it may take a day or two for the bank to add deposits to your balance.
- Your EFT payments and cash receipts are recorded by the bank before you learn of them.

To ensure accurate cash records, you need to update your checkbook—either online or after you receive your bank statement. The result of this updating process creates a **bank reconciliation**, which you must prepare. The bank reconciliation explains all differences between your cash records and your bank balance. The person who prepares the bank reconciliation should have no other cash duties. Otherwise, he or she can steal cash and manipulate the reconciliation to conceal the theft.

EXHIBIT 7-4 Bank Statement

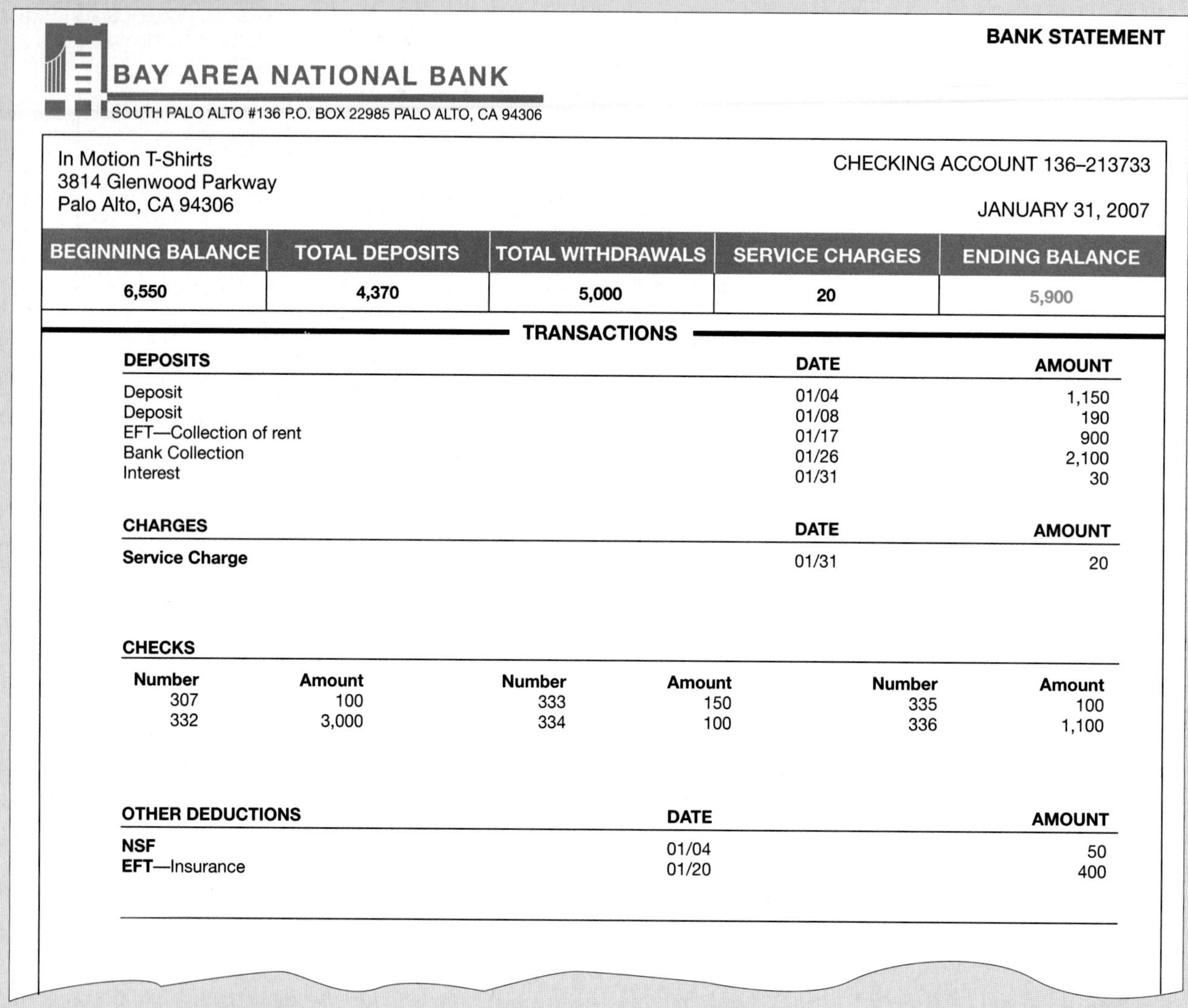

BANK STATEMENT

BAY AREA NATIONAL BANK

SOUTH PALO ALTO #136 P.O. BOX 22985 PALO ALTO, CA 94306

In Motion T-Shirts
3814 Glenwood Parkway
Palo Alto, CA 94306

CHECKING ACCOUNT 136–213733

JANUARY 31, 2007

BEGINNING BALANCE	TOTAL DEPOSITS	TOTAL WITHDRAWALS	SERVICE CHARGES	ENDING BALANCE
6,550	4,370	5,000	20	5,900

TRANSACTIONS

DEPOSITS	DATE	AMOUNT
Deposit	01/04	1,150
Deposit	01/08	190
EFT—Collection of rent	01/17	900
Bank Collection	01/26	2,100
Interest	01/31	30

CHARGES	DATE	AMOUNT
Service Charge	01/31	20

CHECKS

Number	Amount	Number	Amount	Number	Amount
307	100	333	150	335	100
332	3,000	334	100	336	1,100

OTHER DEDUCTIONS	DATE	AMOUNT
NSF	01/04	50
EFT—Insurance	01/20	400

Preparing the Bank Reconciliation

3 Prepare a bank reconciliation and the related journal entries

Here are the items that appear on a bank reconciliation. They all cause differences between the bank balance and the book balance. (We call your checkbook record the "Books.")

Bank Side of the Reconciliation

1. Items to show on the *Bank* side:
   a. **Deposits in transit** (outstanding deposits). You have recorded these deposits, but the bank has not. Add deposits in transit.
   b. **Outstanding checks.** You have recorded these checks, but the bank has not yet paid them. Subtract outstanding checks.
   c. **Bank errors.** Correct all bank errors on the Bank side of the reconciliation.

EXHIBIT 7-5 Cash Records of In Motion T-Shirts

General Ledger:

ACCOUNT Cash

Date	Item	Debit	Credit	Balance
2007				
Jan. 1	Balance			6,550
2	Cash receipt	1,150		7,700
7	Cash receipt	190		7,890
31	Cash payments		6,150	1,740
31	Cash receipt	1,600		3,340

Cash Payments:

Check No.	Amount	Check No.	Amount
332	$3,000	337	$ 280
333	510	338	320
334	100	339	250
335	100	340	490
336	1,100	Total	$6,150

Book Side of the Reconciliation

2. Items to show on the *Book* side:
   a. **Bank collections.** Bank collections are cash receipts that the bank has recorded for your account. But you haven't recorded the cash receipt yet. Many businesses have their customers pay directly to their bank. This is called a *lock-box system* and reduces theft. An example is a bank's collecting a note receivable for you. Add bank collections.
   b. **Electronic funds transfers.** The bank may receive or pay cash on your behalf. An EFT may be a cash receipt or a cash payment. Add EFT receipts and subtract EFT payments.
   c. **Service charge.** This cash payment is the bank's fee for processing your transactions. Subtract service charges.
   d. **Interest revenue on your checking account.** You earn interest if you keep enough cash in your account. The bank statement tells you of this cash receipt. Add interest revenue.
   e. **Nonsufficient funds (NSF) checks** are your earlier cash receipts that have turned out to be worthless. NSF checks (sometimes called *hot checks*) are treated as cash payments on your bank reconciliation. Subtract NSF checks.
   f. **The cost of printed checks.** This cash payment is handled like a service charge. Subtract this cost.
   g. **Book errors.** Correct all book errors on the Book side of the reconciliation.

Bank Reconciliation Illustrated

The bank statement in Exhibit 7-4 shows that the January 31 bank balance of In Motion T-shirts is $5,900 (upper right corner). However, the company's Cash account has a balance of $3,340, as shown in Exhibit 7-5. This situation calls for a bank reconciliation. Exhibit 7-6, panel A, lists the reconciling items for your easy reference, and panel B shows the completed reconciliation.

EXHIBIT 7-6 Bank Reconciliation

PANEL A—Reconciling Items

Bank side:

1. Deposit in transit, $1,600.
2. Bank error: The bank deducted $100 for a check written by another company. Add $100 to the bank balance.
3. Outstanding checks—total of $1,340.

Check No.	Amount
337	$280
338	320
339	250
340	490

Book side:

4. EFT receipt of your rent revenue, $900.
5. Bank collection of your note receivable, $2,100.
6. Interest revenue earned on your bank balance, $30.
7. Book error: You recorded check no. 333 for $510. The amount you actually paid Brown Company on account was $150. Add $360 to your book balance.
8. Bank service charge, $20.
9. NSF check from L. Ross, $50. Subtract $50 from your book balance.
10. EFT payment of insurance expense, $400.

PANEL B—Bank Reconciliation

IN MOTION T-SHIRTS
Bank Reconciliation
January 31, 2007

Bank			Books		
Balance, January 31		$5,900	**Balance, January 31**		$3,340
Add:			Add:		
1. Deposit in transit		1,600	4. EFT receipt of rent revenue		900
2. Correction of bank error		100	5. Bank collection of note		
		7,600	receivable		2,100
			6. Interest revenue earned on		
			bank balance		30
			7. Correction of book error—		
			overstated our check no. 333		360
Less:					6,730
3. Outstanding checks					
No. 337	$280		Less:		
No. 338	320		8. Service charge	$ 20	
No. 339	250		9. NSF check	50	
No. 340	490	(1,340)	10. EFT payment of insurance expense	400	(470)
Adjusted bank balance		$6,260	**Adjusted bank balance**		$6,260

These amounts should agree.

SUMMARY OF THE VARIOUS RECONCILING ITEMS:

BANK BALANCE—ALWAYS

- *Add* deposits in transit.
- *Subtract* outstanding checks.
- *Add* or *subtract* corrections of bank errors.

BOOK BALANCE—ALWAYS

- *Add* bank collections, interest revenue, and EFT receipts.
- *Subtract* service charges, NSF checks, and EFT payments.
- *Add* or *subtract* corrections of book errors.

Journalizing Transactions from the Reconciliation

The bank reconciliation is an accountant's tool separate from the journals and ledgers. It does *not* account for transactions in the journal. To get the transactions into the accounts, we must make journal entries and post to the ledger. All items on the Book side of the bank reconciliation require journal entries.

The bank reconciliation in Exhibit 7-6 requires In Motion to make journal entries to bring the Cash account up-to-date. Numbers in parentheses correspond to the reconciling items listed in Exhibit 7-6, Panel A.

4.	Jan. 31	Cash	900	
		Rent Revenue		900
		Receipt of monthly rent.		
5.	31	Cash	2,100	
		Notes Receivable		2,100
		Note receivable collected by bank.		
6.	31	Cash	30	
		Interest Revenue		30
		Interest earned on bank balance.		
7.	31	Cash	360	
		Accounts Payable—Brown Co.		360
		Correction of check no. 333.		
8.	31	Miscellaneous Expense[1]	20	
		Cash		20
		Bank service charge.		
9.	31	Accounts Receivable—L. Ross	50	
		Cash		50
		NSF check returned by bank.		
10.	31	Insurance Expense		
		Cash	400	
		Payment of monthly insurance.		400

[1]Miscellaneous Expense is debited for the bank service charge because the service charge pertains to no particular expense category.

The entry for the NSF check (entry 9) needs explanation. Upon learning that L. Ross's $50 check to us was not good, we must credit Cash to update the Cash account. Unfortunately, we still have a receivable from Ross, so we must debit Accounts Receivable—L. Ross to reinstate our receivable from Ross.

Online Banking

Online banking allows you to pay bills and view your account electronically. You don't have to wait until the end of the month to get a bank statement. With online banking you can reconcile transactions at any time and keep your account current whenever you wish. Exhibit 7-7 shows a page from the account history of Toni Anderson's bank account.

The account history—like a bank statement—lists deposits, checks, EFT payments, ATM withdrawals, and interest earned on your bank balance.

EXHIBIT 7-7 Online Banking—Account History (like a Bank Statement)

Account History for Toni Anderson Checking # 5401-632-9
as of Close of Business 07/27/2007

Account Details

Current Balance $4,136.08

Date ↓	Description	Withdrawals	Deposits	Balance
	Current Balance			**$4,136.08**
07/27/07	DEPOSIT		1,170.35	
07/26/07	28 DAYS-INTEREST		2.26	
07/25/07	Check #6131 View Image	443.83		
07/24/07	Check #6130 View Image	401.52		
07/23/07	EFT PYMT CINGULAR	61.15		
07/22/07	EFT PYMT CITICARD PAYMENT	3,172.85		
07/20/07	Check #6127 View Image	550.00		
07/19/07	Check #6122 View Image	50.00		
07/16/07	Check #6116 View Image	2,056.75		
07/15/07	Check #6123 View Image	830.00		
07/13/07	Check #6124 View Image	150.00		
07/11/07	ATM 4900 SANGER AVE	200.00		
07/09/07	Check #6119 View Image	30.00		
07/05/07	Check #6125 View Image	2,500.00		
07/04/07	ATM 4900 SANGER AVE	100.00		
07/01/07	DEPOSIT		9,026.37	

FDIC EQUAL HOUSING LENDER

E-Mail

But the account history doesn't show your beginning balance, so you can't work from your beginning balance to your ending balance.

Summary Problem 1

The cash account of Baylor Associates at February 28, 2007, follows.

Cash			
Feb. 1	Bal. 3,995	Feb. 3	400
6	800	12	3,100
15	1,800	19	1,100
23	1,100	25	500
28	2,400	27	900
Feb. 28	Bal. 4,095		

Baylor Associates received the bank statement on February 28, 2007 (negative amounts are in parentheses):

Bank Statement for February 2007

Beginning balance		
Deposits:		$3,995
Feb. 7	$ 800	
15	1,800	
24	1,100	3,700
Checks (total per day):		
Feb. 8	$ 400	
16	3,100	
23	1,100	(4,600)
Other items:		
Service charge		(10)
NSF check from M. E. Crown		(700)
Bank collection of note receivable for the company		1,000
EFT—monthly rent expense		(330)
Interest revenue earned on account balance		15
Ending balance		$3,070

Additional data:
Baylor deposits all cash receipts in the bank and makes all payments by check.

Requirements

1. Prepare the bank reconciliation of Baylor Associates at February 28, 2007.
2. Journalize the entries based on the bank reconciliation.

Solution

Requirement 1

BAYLOR ASSOCIATES Bank Reconciliation February 28, 2007		
Bank:		
Balance, February 28, 2007		$3,070
Add: Deposit of February 28 in transit		2,400
		5,470
Less: Outstanding checks issued on Feb. 25 ($500)		
and Feb. 27 ($900)		(1,400)
Adjusted bank balance, February 28, 2007		$4,070
Books:		
Balance, February 28, 2007		$4,095
Add: Bank collection of note receivable		1,000
Interest revenue earned on bank balance		15
		5,110
Less: Service charge	$ 10	
NSF check	700	
EFT—Rent expense	330	(1,040)
Adjusted book balance, February 28, 2007		$4,070

Requirement 2

Date	Accounts and Explanation	Debit	Credit
Feb. 28	Cash	1,000	
	Note Receivable		1,000
	Note receivable collected by bank.		
28	Cash	15	
	Interest Revenue		15
	Interest earned on bank balance.		
28	Miscellaneous Expense	10	
	Cash		10
	Bank service charge.		
28	Accounts Receivable—M. E. Crown	700	
	Cash		700
	NSF check returned by bank.		
28	Rent Expense	330	
	Cash		330
	Monthly rent expense.		

Internal Control over Cash Receipts

4 Apply internal controls to cash receipts

All cash receipts should be deposited for safekeeping in the bank—quickly. Companies receive cash over the counter and through the mail. Each source of cash has its own security measures.

Cash Receipts over the Counter

Exhibit 7-8 illustrates a cash receipt over the counter in a department store. The point-of-sale terminal (cash register) provides control over the cash receipts. Consider a Macy's store. For each transaction, Macy's issues a receipt to ensure that each sale is recorded. The cash drawer opens when the clerk enters a transaction, and the machine records it. At the end of the day, a manager proves the cash by comparing the cash in the drawer against the machine's record of sales. This step helps prevent theft by the clerk.

EXHIBIT 7-8 Cash Receipts over the Counter

At the end of the day—or several times a day if business is brisk—the cashier deposits the cash in the bank. The machine tape then goes to the accounting department for the journal entry to record sales revenue. These measures, coupled with oversight by a manager, discourage theft.

Cash Receipts by Mail

Many companies receive cash by mail. Exhibit 7-9 shows how companies control cash received by mail. All incoming mail is opened by a mailroom employee. The mailroom then sends all customer checks to the treasurer, who has the cashier deposit the money in the bank. The remittance advices go to the accounting department for journal entries to Cash and customer accounts. As a final step, the controller compares the following records for the day:

- Bank deposit amount from the treasurer
- Debit to Cash from the accounting department

The debit to Cash should equal the amount deposited in the bank. All cash receipts are safe in the bank, and the company books are up-to-date.

EXHIBIT 7-9 Cash Receipts by Mail

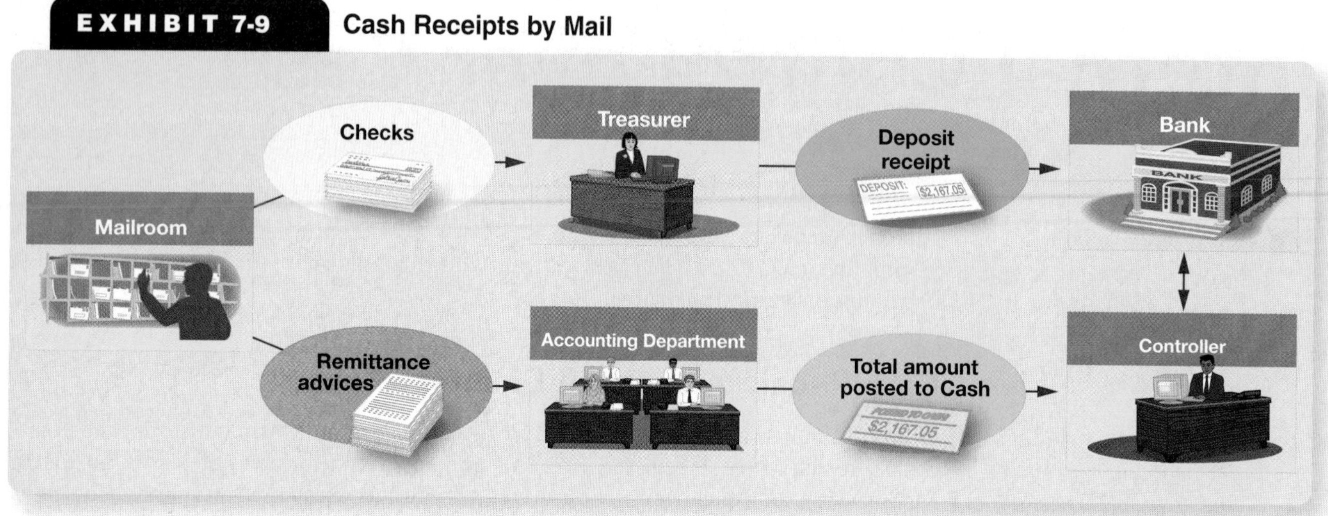

Many companies use a lock-box system. Customers send their checks directly to the company's bank account. Internal control is tight because company personnel never touch incoming cash. The lock-box system puts your cash to work immediately.

Internal Control over Cash Payments

5 Apply internal controls to cash payments

Companies make most payments by check. They also pay small amounts from a petty cash fund. Let's begin with cash payments by check.

Controls over Payment by Check

As we have seen, you need a good separation of duties between operations and writing checks for cash payments. Payment by check is an important internal control, as follows:

- The check provides a record of the payment.
- The check must be signed by an authorized official.
- Before signing the check, the official should study the evidence supporting the payment.

Controls over Purchase and Payment

To illustrate the internal control over cash payments by check, suppose In Motion T-Shirts buys its inventory from Hanes Textiles. The purchasing and payment process follows these steps, as shown in Exhibit 7-10. Start with the box for In Motion T-Shirts on the left side.

1 In Motion faxes a *purchase order* to Hanes Textiles. In Motion says, "Please send us 100 T-shirts."

2 Hanes Textiles ships the goods and faxes an *invoice* back to In Motion. Hanes sent the goods.

EXHIBIT 7-10 Cash Payments by Check

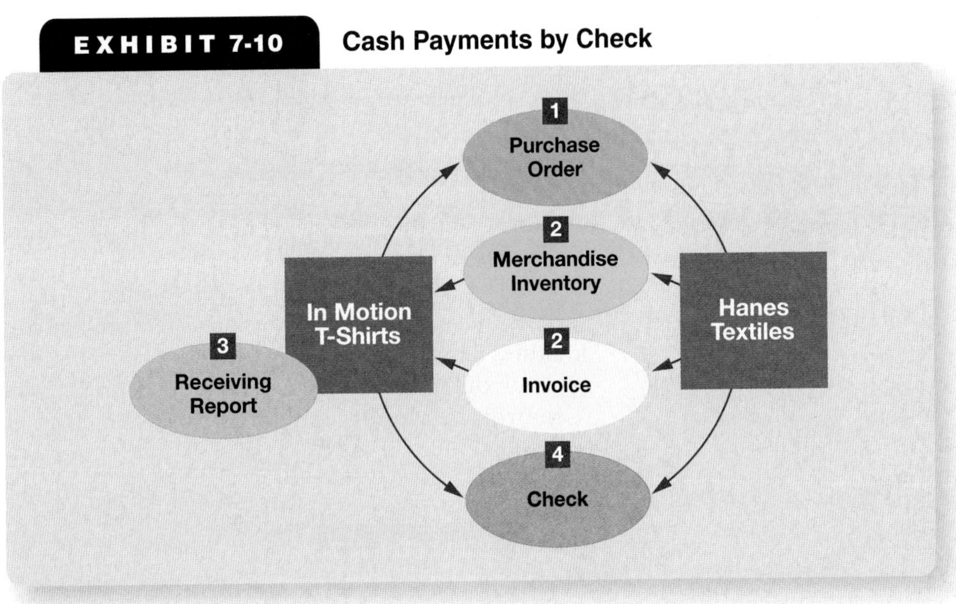

3 In Motion receives the *inventory* and prepares a *receiving report*. In Motion got its T-shirts.

4 After approving all documents, In Motion sends a *check* to Hanes. In Motion says, "Okay, we'll pay you."

For good internal control, the purchasing agent should neither receive the goods nor approve the payment. If these duties aren't separated, a purchasing agent can buy goods and have them shipped to his or her home. Or a purchasing agent can spend too much on purchases, approve the payment, and split the excess with the supplier.

Exhibit 7-11 shows In Motion's payment packet of documents. Before signing the check, the controller or the treasurer should examine the packet to prove that all the documents agree. Only then does the company know that:

1. It received the goods ordered.
2. It is paying only for the goods received.

EXHIBIT 7-11 Payment Packet

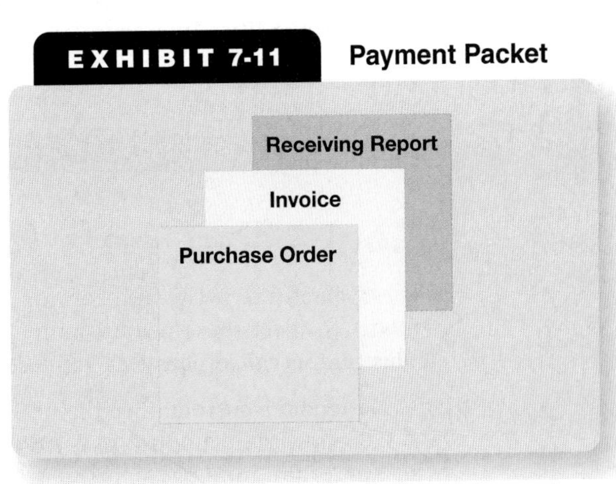

After payment, the check signer punches a hole through the payment packet. Dishonest people have been known to run a bill through twice for payment. This hole confirms that the bill has been paid.

The Voucher System

Many companies use the voucher system for internal control over cash payments. A **voucher** is a document authorizing a cash payment.

The voucher system uses (1) vouchers, (2) a voucher register (similar to a purchases journal), and (3) a check register (similar to a cash payments journal). All expenditures must be approved before payment. This approval takes the form of a voucher.

Exhibit 7-12 illustrates the voucher of In Motion T-Shirts. To enhance internal control, In Motion could add this voucher to the payment packet illustrated in Exhibit 7-11.

EXHIBIT 7-12 Voucher

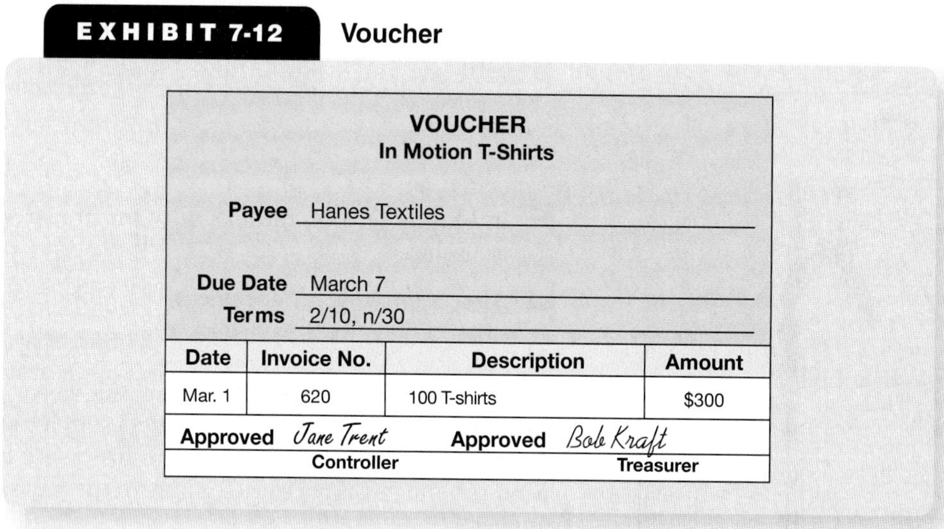
VOUCHER
In Motion T-Shirts

Payee Hanes Textiles

Due Date March 7
Terms 2/10, n/30

Date	Invoice No.	Description	Amount
Mar. 1	620	100 T-shirts	$300

Approved *Jane Trent* Controller — Approved *Bob Kraft* Treasurer

Streamlined Procedures

Technology is streamlining payment procedures. Evaluated Receipts Settlement (ERS) compresses the approval process into a single step: compare the receiving report to the purchase order. If those documents match, that proves In Motion got the T-shirts it ordered. Then In Motion pays Hanes Textiles, the supplier.

An even more streamlined process bypasses people and documents altogether. In Electronic Data Interchange (EDI), Wal-Mart's computers communicate directly with the computers of suppliers like Hanes Textiles and Hershey Foods. When Wal-Mart's inventory of Hershey candy reaches a low level, the computer sends a purchase order to Hershey. Hershey ships the candy and invoices Wal-Mart electronically. Then an electronic fund transfer (EFT) sends Wal-Mart's payment to Hershey.

Controlling Petty Cash Payments

It is wasteful to write a check for a taxi fare or the delivery of a package across town. To meet these needs, companies keep cash on hand to pay small amounts. This fund is called **petty cash** and needs controls such as the following:

- Designate a custodian of the petty cash fund.
- Keep a specific amount of cash on hand.
- Support all fund payments with a petty cash ticket.

Setting Up the Petty Cash Fund

The petty cash fund is opened when you write a check for the designated amount. Make the check payable to Petty Cash. On February 28, In Motion creates a petty cash fund of $200. The custodian cashes a $200 check and places the money in the fund. The journal entry is:

Feb. 28	Petty Cash	200	
	Cash in Bank		200
	To open the petty cash fund.		

For each petty cash payment, the custodian prepares a *petty cash ticket* like the one in Exhibit 7-13.

EXHIBIT 7-13 **Petty Cash Ticket**

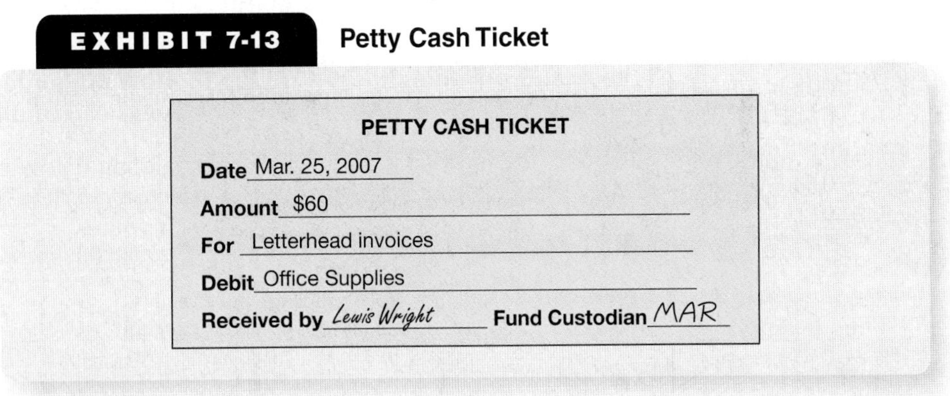
PETTY CASH TICKET

Date Mar. 25, 2007

Amount $60

For Letterhead invoices

Debit Office Supplies

Received by *Lewis Wright* Fund Custodian MAR

Signatures (or initials) identify the recipient of the cash and the fund custodian. The custodian keeps the petty cash tickets in the fund. The sum of the cash plus the total of the tickets should equal the fund balance ($200) at all times.

Maintaining the Petty Cash account at its designated balance is the nature of an **imprest system.** This clearly identifies the amount of cash for which the custodian is responsible, and that is the system's main internal control feature. Payments deplete the fund, so periodically it must be replenished.

Replenishing the Petty Cash Fund

On March 31 the petty cash fund holds

- $118 in petty cash
- $80 in petty cash tickets

You can see that $2 is missing:

Fund balance	$200
Cash on hand	$118
Petty cash tickets	80
Total accounted for	$198
Amount of cash missing	$ 2

To replenish the petty cash fund, you need to bring the cash on hand up to $200. The company writes a check, payable to Petty Cash, for $82 ($200 − $118). The fund custodian cashes this check and puts $82 back in the fund. Now the fund holds $200 cash as it should.

The petty cash tickets tell you what to debit, as shown in the entry to replenish the fund (items assumed for this illustration):

Mar. 31	Office Supplies	60	
	Delivery Expense	20	
	Cash Short and Over	2	
	Cash in Bank		82
	To replenish the petty cash fund.		

In this case, you lost $2. Losses are debited to a new account, Cash Short & Over.

At times the sum of cash in the petty cash fund ($118) plus the tickets ($90) may exceed the fund balance ($200). That situation creates a gain, which is credited to Cash Short & Over, as follows (using assumed amounts):

Mar. 31	Office Supplies	60	
	Delivery Expense	30	
	Cash		82
	Cash Short and Over		8
	To replenish the petty cash fund.		

Over time the Cash Short & Over account should net out to a zero balance. If not, you need to find a new petty cash custodian.

The Petty Cash account keeps its $200 balance at all times. Petty Cash is debited only when the fund is started (see the February 28 entry) or when its amount is changed. If the business raises the fund amount from $200 to $250, this would require a $50 debit to Petty Cash.

Reporting Cash on the Balance Sheet

Cash is the first asset listed on the balance sheet because it's the most liquid asset. Businesses often have many bank accounts and several petty cash funds. But they combine all cash amounts into a single total called "Cash and Cash Equivalents" for reporting on the balance sheet.

Cash equivalents include liquid assets such as time deposits, which are interest-bearing accounts that can be withdrawn with no penalty. Time deposits are sufficiently liquid to be reported along with cash. The balance sheet of In Motion T-Shirts reported the following current assets:

IN MOTION T-SHIRTS Balance Sheet December 31, 2008	
Assets	
Current assets:	
Cash and cash equivalents	$ 800
Short-term investments	1,000
Accounts receivable	2,000
Inventories	3,200
Prepaid insurance	400
Total current assets	$7,400

In Motion's cash balance means that In Motion has $800 available for immediate use. Cash that is restricted should not be reported as a current asset. For example, the bank may require you to keep a *compensating balance* on deposit in order to borrow from the bank. The compensating balance is not included in the cash amount on the balance sheet because it's not available for immediate use.

Ethics and Accounting

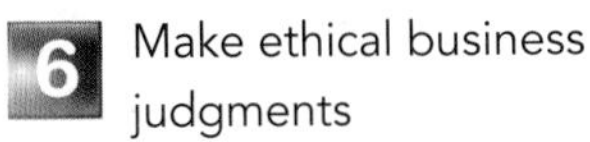
6 Make ethical business judgments

Roger Smith, the former chairman of General Motors, said, "Ethical practice is [. . .] good business." Smith knows that unethical behavior doesn't work. Sooner or later it comes back to haunt you. Moreover, ethical behavior wins out in the long run because it is the right thing to do.

Corporate and Professional Codes of Ethics

Most companies have a code of ethics to encourage employees to behave ethically. But codes of ethics are not enough by themselves. Owners and managers must set a high ethical tone, as we saw in the section on Control Environment. The owner must make it clear that the company will not tolerate unethical conduct.

As professionals, accountants are expected to maintain higher standards than society in general. Their ability to do business depends entirely on their reputation. Most independent accountants are members of the American Institute of Certified Public Accountants and must abide by the *AICPA Code of Professional Conduct.* Accountants who are members of the Institute of Management Accountants are bound by the *Standards of Ethical Conduct for Management Accountants.*

Ethical Issues in Accounting

In many situations, the ethical choice is easy. For example, stealing cash is both unethical and illegal. In other cases, the choices are more difficult. But in every instance, ethical judgments boil down to a personal decision: What should I do in a given situation? Let's consider three ethical issues in accounting.

Situation 1

Grant Busby is preparing the income tax return of a client who has earned more income than expected. On January 2, the client pays for advertising and asks Busby to backdate the expense to the preceding year. Backdating the deduction would lower the client's immediate tax payments. After all, there is a difference of only two days between January 2 and December 31. This client is important to Busby. What should he do?

Busby should refuse the request because the transaction took place in January of the new year.

What control device could prove that Busby behaved unethically if he backdated the transaction in the accounting records? An IRS audit could prove that the expense occurred in January rather than in December. Falsifying IRS documents is both unethical and illegal.

Situation 2

Diane Scott's software company owes $40,000 to Bank of America. The loan agreement requires Scott's company to maintain a current ratio (current assets divided by current liabilities) of 1.50 or higher. At present, the company's current ratio is 1.40. At this level, Scott is in violation of her loan agreement. She can increase the current ratio to 1.53 by paying off some current liabilities right before year-end. Is it ethical to do so?

Yes, because the action is a real business transaction.

Scott should be aware that paying off the liabilities is only a delaying tactic. It will hold off the bank for now, but the business must improve in order to keep from violating the agreement in the future.

Situation 3

David Duncan, the lead auditor of Enron Corporation, thinks Enron may be understating the liabilities on its balance sheet. Enron's transactions are very complex, and outsiders may never figure this out. Duncan asks his firm's Standards Committee how he should handle the situation. They reply, "Require Enron to report all its liabilities." Enron is Duncan's most important client, and Enron is pressuring him to certify the liabilities. Duncan can rationalize that Enron's reported amounts are okay. What should Duncan do? To make his decision, Duncan could follow the framework outlined in the following Decision Guidelines feature.

Decision Guidelines

Framework for Making Ethical Judgments

Weighing tough ethical judgments requires a decision framework. Answering these four questions will guide you through tough decisions. Let's apply them to David Duncan's situation.

Question	Decision Guidelines
1. What is the ethical issue?	1. *Identify the ethical issue.* The root word of ethical is *ethics*, which Webster's dictionary defines as "the discipline dealing with what is good and bad and with moral duty and obligation." Duncan's ethical dilemma is to decide what he should do with the information he has uncovered.
2. What are Duncan's options?	2. *Specify the alternatives.* For David Duncan, the alternatives include (a) go along with Enron's liabilities as reported or (b) force Enron to report higher amounts of liabilities.
3. What are the possible consequences?	3. *Assess the possible outcomes.* a. If Duncan certifies Enron's present level of liabilities—and if no one ever objects—Duncan will keep this valuable client. But if Enron's actual liabilities turn out to be higher than reported, Enron investors may lose money and take Duncan to court. That would damage his reputation as an auditor and hurt his firm. b. If Duncan follows his company policy, he must force Enron to increase its reported liabilities. That will anger the company, and Enron may fire Duncan as its auditor. In that case, Duncan will save his reputation, but it will cost him some business in the short run.
4. What shall I do?	4. *Make the decision.* In the end Duncan went along with Enron and certified the company's liabilities. He went directly against his firm's policies. Enron later admitted understating its liabilities, Duncan had to retract his audit opinion, and Duncan's firm, Arthur Andersen, collapsed quickly. Duncan should have followed company policy. Rarely is one person smarter than a team of experts. Duncan got out from under his firm's umbrella of protection, and it cost him and many others dearly.

Summary Problem 2

Abbey Company established a $300 petty cash fund. James C. Brown (JCB) is the fund custodian. At the end of the week, the petty cash fund contains the following:

a. Cash: $163

b. Petty cash tickets, as follows:

No.	Amount	Issued to	Signed by	Account Debited
44	$14	B. Jarvis	B. Jarvis and JCB	Office Supplies
45	39	S. Bell	S. Bell	Delivery Expense
47	43	R. Tate	R. Tate and JCB	—
48	33	L. Blair	L. Blair and JCB	Travel Expense

Requirements

1. Identify three internal control weaknesses revealed in the given data.
2. Prepare the general journal entries to record:
   a. Establishment of the petty cash fund.
   b. Replenishment of the fund. Assume that petty cash ticket no. 47 was issued for the purchase of office supplies.
3. What is the balance in the Petty Cash account immediately before replenishment? Immediately after replenishment?

Solution

Requirement 1

The three internal control weaknesses are

1. Petty cash ticket no. 46 is missing. There is no indication of what happened to this ticket. The company should investigate.
2. The petty cash custodian (JCB) did not sign petty cash ticket no. 45. This omission may have been an oversight on his part. However, it raises the question of whether he authorized the payment. Both the fund custodian and the recipient of cash should sign the ticket.
3. Petty cash ticket no. 47 does not indicate which account to debit. What did Tate do with the money, and what account should be debited? See 2b above.

Requirement 2

Petty cash journal entries:

a. Entry to establish the petty cash fund:

Account	Debit	Credit
Petty Cash	300	
Cash in Bank		300

b. Entry to replenish the fund:

Account	Debit	Credit
Office Supplies ($14 + $43)	57	
Delivery Expense	39	
Travel Expense	33	
Cash Short and Over	8	
Cash in Bank		137

Requirement 3

The balance in Petty Cash is *always* its specified balance, in this case $300.

Review Internal Control and Cash

Accounting Vocabulary

Audit
An examination of a company s financial statements and the accounting system.

Bank Collection
Collection of money by the bank on behalf of a depositor.

Bank Reconciliation
Document explaining the reasons for the difference between a depositor's cash records and the depositor's cash balance in its bank account.

Bank Statement
Document the bank uses to report what it did with the depositor's cash. Shows the bank account beginning and ending balance and lists the month's cash transactions conducted through the bank.

Check
Document that instructs a bank to pay the designated person or business a specified amount of money.

Computer Virus
A malicious program that (a) reproduces itself, (b) enters program code without consent, and (c) performs destructive actions.

Controller
The chief accounting officer of a company.

Deposit in Transit
A deposit recorded by the company but not yet by its bank.

Electronic Funds Transfer (EFT)
System that transfers cash by electronic communication rather than by paper documents.

Encryption
Rearranging plain-text messages by a mathematical process, the primary method of achieving confidentiality in e-commerce.

Firewalls
Devices that enable members of a local network to access the Internet but keep nonmembers out of the network.

Imprest System
A way to account for petty cash by maintaining a constant balance in the petty cash account, supported by the fund (cash plus payment tickets) totaling the same amount.

Internal Control
Organizational plan and all the related measures adopted by an entity to safeguard assets, encourage employees to follow company policy, promote operational efficiency, and ensure accurate and reliable accounting records.

Nonsufficient Funds (NSF) Check
A "hot" check; one for which the maker's bank account has insufficient money to pay the check.

Outstanding Check
A check issued by the company and recorded on its books but not yet paid by its bank.

Petty Cash
Fund containing a small amount of cash that is used to pay for minor expenditures.

Treasurer
In a large company, the person in charge of writing checks.

Trojan
A malicious program that hides inside a legitimate program and works like a virus.

Voucher
Instrument authorizing a cash payment.

Quick Check

1. Which of the following is not part of the definition of internal control?
   a. Safeguard assets
   b. Encourage employees to follow company policy
   c. Separation of duties
   d. Promote operational efficiency

2. Internal auditors focus on _____; external auditors are more concerned with _____. Fill in the blanks.
   a. cash receipts; cash payments
   b. e-commerce; fraud
   c. documents; records
   d. operations; financial statements

3. Darice Goodrich receives cash from customers. Her other assigned job is to post the collections to customer accounts receivable. Her company has weak
   a. Ethics
   b. Assignment of responsibilities
   c. Separation of duties
   d. Computer controls

4. Encryption
   a. Creates firewalls to protect data
   b. Cannot be broken by hackers
   c. Avoids the need for separation of duties
   d. Rearranges messages by a special process

5. The document that explains all differences between the company's cash records and the bank's figures is called a
   a. Bank statement
   b. Bank collection
   c. Bank reconciliation
   d. Electronic fund transfer

6. Which items appear on the Book side of a bank reconciliation?
   a. Outstanding checks
   b. Deposits in transit
   c. Both a and b
   d. None of the above

7. Which items appear on the Bank side of a bank reconciliation?
   a. Outstanding checks
   b. Deposits in transit
   c. Both a and b
   d. None of the above

8. Navarro Company's Cash account shows an ending balance of $770. The bank statement shows a $20 service charge and an NSF check for $100. A $250 deposit is in transit, and outstanding checks total $400. What is Navarro's adjusted cash balance?
   a. $530
   b. $650
   c. $680
   d. $1,050

9. After performing a bank reconciliation, we need to journalize
   a. All items on the Bank side of the reconciliation
   b. All items on the Book side of the reconciliation
   c. All items on the reconciliation
   d. No items from the reconciliation because the cash transactions need no adjustments.

10. Separation of duties is important for internal control of
   a. Cash receipts
   b. Cash payments
   c. Neither of the above
   d. Both a and b

   Answers are given after Apply Your Knowledge (p. 403).

Assess Your Progress

Short Exercises

Definition of internal control

S7-1 Internal controls are designed to safeguard assets, encourage employees to follow company policies, promote operational efficiency, and ensure accurate records. Which objective is most important? Which must the internal controls accomplish for the business to survive? Give your reason. (p. 358)

Applying the definition of internal control

1

S7-2 How does the Sarbanes-Oxley Act relate to internal controls? Be specific. (p. 358)

Characteristics of an effective system of internal control

2

S7-3 Explain in your own words why separation of duties is often described as the cornerstone of internal control for safeguarding assets. Describe what can happen if the same person has custody of an asset and also accounts for the asset. (p. 362)

Characteristics of an effective system of internal control

2

S7-4 How do external auditors differ from internal auditors? How does an external audit differ from an internal audit? How are the two types of audits similar? (pp. 362–363)

Aspects of a bank reconciliation

3

S7-5 Answer the following questions about the bank reconciliation: (pp. 367–372)

1. Is the bank reconciliation a journal, a ledger, an account, or a financial statement? If none of these, what is it? (pp. 367–372)
2. What is the difference between a bank statement and a bank reconciliation?

Preparing a bank reconciliation

S7-6 The Cash account of Ranger Security Systems reported a balance of $2,480 at May 31. There were outstanding checks totaling $900 and a May 31 deposit in transit of $200. The bank statement, which came from Park Cities Bank, listed a May 31 balance of $3,800. Included in the bank balance was a collection of $630 on account from Kelly Brooks, a Ranger customer who pays the bank directly. The bank statement also shows a $20 service charge and $10 of interest revenue that Ranger earned on its bank balance. *Prepare Ranger's bank reconciliation at May 31.* (p. 370)

Recording transactions from a bank reconciliation

S7-7 After preparing Ranger Security Systems' bank reconciliation in Short Exercise 7-6, journalize the company's transactions that arise from the bank reconciliation. Date each transaction May 31, and include an explanation with each entry. (p. 371)

Control over cash receipts

S7-8 Diedre Chevis sells furniture for DuBois Furniture Company. Chevis is having financial problems and takes $500 that she received from a customer. She rang up the sale through the cash register. What will alert Betsy DuBois, the owner, that something is wrong? (p. 375)

Control over cash receipts by mail

S7-9 Review the internal controls over cash receipts by mail. Exactly what is accomplished by the final step in the process, performed by the controller? (p. 375)

Internal control over payments by check
5

S7-10 A purchasing agent for Westgate Wireless receives the goods that he purchases and also approves payment for the goods. How could this purchasing agent cheat his company? How could Westgate avoid this internal control weakness? (p. 376)

Petty cash
5

S7-11 Record the following petty cash transactions of Lexite Laminated Surfaces in general journal form (explanations are not required): (p. 379)

April 1	Established a petty cash fund with a $200 balance.
30	The petty cash fund has $19 in cash and $187 in petty cash tickets that were issued to pay for Office Supplies ($117) and Entertainment Expense ($70). Replenished the fund with $181 of cash and recorded the expenses.

Making an ethical judgment
6

S7-12 Gwen O'Malley, an accountant for Ireland Limited, discovers that her supervisor, Blarney Stone, made several errors last year. Overall, the errors overstated the company's net income by 20%. It is not clear whether the errors were deliberate or accidental. What should O'Malley do? (p. 383)

Exercises

Identifying and correcting an internal control weakness

E7-13 Lane & Goble Bookstore has a liberal return policy. A customer can return any product for a full refund within 30 days of purchase. When a customer returns merchandise, Lane & Goble policy specifies:

- Store clerk issues a prenumbered return slip and refunds cash from the cash register. Keep a copy of the return slip for review by the manager.
- Store clerk places the returned goods back on the shelf as soon as possible. Lane & Goble uses a perpetual inventory system.

1. How can a dishonest store clerk steal from Lane & Goble? What part of company policy enables the store clerk to steal without getting caught? (pp. 361–363)
2. How can Lane & Goble improve its internal controls to prevent this theft? (pp. 361–363)

Identifying internal control strengths and weaknesses

E7-14 The following situations suggest a strength or a weakness in internal control. Identify each as *strength* or *weakness,* and give the reason for your answer.

a. Top managers delegate all internal control procedures to the accounting department. (p. 360)

b. The accounting department orders merchandise and approves invoices for payment. (pp. 361–362)

c. Cash received over the counter is controlled by the sales clerk, who rings up the sale and places the cash in the register. The sales clerk matches the total recorded by the register to each day's cash sales. (p. 375)

d. The officer who signs checks need not examine the payment packet because he is confident the amounts are correct. (p. 376)

Identifying internal controls

E7-15 Identify the missing internal control procedure in the following situations. Consider each situation separately. Select from these characteristics:

- Assignment of responsibilities
- Separation of duties
- Audits
- Electronic controls
- Other controls (specify)

a. While reviewing the records of Discount Pharmacy, you find that the same employee orders merchandise and approves invoices for payment. (pp. 361–362)

b. Business is slow at Fun City Amusement Park on Tuesday, Wednesday, and Thursday nights. To reduce expenses, the owner decides not to use a ticket taker on those nights. The ticket seller (cashier) is told to keep the tickets as a record of the number sold. (pp. 361–362)

c. The same trusted employee has served as cashier for 10 years. (p. 364)

d. When business is brisk, Stop-n-Go deposits cash in the bank several times during the day. The manager at one store wants to reduce the time employees spend delivering cash to the bank, so he starts a new policy. Cash will build up over weekends, and the total will be deposited on Monday. (pp. 374–375)

e. Grocery stores such as **Safeway** and **Meijer's** purchase most merchandise from a few suppliers. At another grocery store, the manager decides to reduce paperwork. He eliminates the requirement that the receiving department prepare a receiving report listing the goods actually received from the supplier. (p. 376–377)

Classifying bank reconciliation items

E7-16 The following items could appear on a bank reconciliation:

a. Outstanding checks
b. Deposits in transit
c. NSF check
d. Bank collection of our note receivable
e. Interest earned on bank balance
f. Service charge
g. Book error: We credited Cash for $200. The correct amount was $2,000
h. Bank error: The bank decreased our account for a check written by another customer

Requirements

Classify each item as (1) an addition to the book balance, (2) a subtraction from the book balance, (3) an addition to the bank balance, or (4) a subtraction from the bank balance. (p. 370)

Preparing a bank reconciliation

3

E7-17 D. J. Hunter's checkbook lists the following:

Date	Check No.	Item	Check	Deposit	Balance
9/1					$ 525
4	622	Art Café	$ 19		506
9		Dividends received		$ 116	622
13	623	General Tire Co.	43		579
14	624	ExxonMobil	58		521
18	625	Cash	50		471
26	626	Woodway Baptist Church	75		396
28	627	Bent Tree Apartments	275		121
30		Paycheck		1,209	1,330

Hunter's September bank statement shows the following:

Balance				$525
Add: Deposits				116
Debit checks:	No.	Amount		
	622	$19		
	623	43		
	624	68*		
	625	50		(180)
Other charges:				
Printed checks			$18	
Service charge			12	(30)
Balance				$431

*This is the correct amount for check number 624.

Requirements

Prepare Hunter's bank reconciliation at September 30. How much cash does Hunter actually have on September 30? (p. 370)

Preparing a bank reconciliation

3

E7-18 Fred Midas operates four bowling alleys. He just received the October 31 bank statement from City National Bank, and the statement shows an ending balance of $900. Listed on the statement are an EFT rent collection of $400, a service charge of $12, NSF checks totaling $74, and a $9 charge for printed checks. In reviewing his cash records, Midas identifies outstanding checks totaling $467 and a deposit in transit of $1,788. During October, he recorded a $290 check by debiting Salary Expense and crediting Cash for $29. Midas's Cash account shows an October 31 balance of $2,177. *Prepare the bank reconciliation at October 31.* (p. 370)

Making journal entries from a bank reconciliation

E7-19 Using the data from Exercise 7-18, make the journal entries Midas should record on October 31. Include an explanation for each entry. (p. 371)

Using a bank reconciliation as a control device
3

E7-20 Lynn Cavender owns Cavender's Boot City. She fears that a trusted employee has been stealing from the company. This employee receives cash from customers and also prepares the monthly bank reconciliation. To check up on the employee, Cavender prepares her own bank reconciliation, as follows. This reconciliation is both complete and accurate.

CAVENDER'S BOOT CITY
Bank Reconciliation
August 31, 2007

Bank		Books	
Balance, August 31	$ 1,500	Balance, August 31	$1,000
Add: Deposit in transit	400	Add: Bank collection	820
		Interest revenue	10
Less: Outstanding checks	(1,100)	Less: Service charge	(30)
Adjusted bank balance	$ 800	Adjusted book balance	$1,800

Which side of the reconciliation shows the true cash balance? What is Cavender's true cash balance? Does it appear that the employee has stolen from the company? If so, how much? Explain your answer. (p. 370)

Evaluating internal control over cash receipts

4

E7-21 When you check out at a Target store, the cash register displays the amount of the sale. It also shows the cash received and any change returned to you. Suppose the register also produces a customer receipt but keeps no internal record of the transactions. At the end of the day, the clerk counts the cash in the register and gives it to the cashier for deposit in the company bank account.

Write a memo to the store manager. Identify the internal control weakness over cash receipts, and explain how the weakness gives an employee the opportunity to steal cash. State how to prevent such a theft. (p. 375)

Accounting for petty cash
5

E7-22 Joy's Dance Studio created a $200 impress petty cash fund. During the month, the fund custodian authorized and signed petty cash tickets as follows:

Petty Cash Ticket No.	Item	Account Debited	Amount
1	Delivery of programs to customers	Delivery Expense	$22
2	Mail package	Postage Expense	42
3	Newsletter	Supplies Expense	34
4	Key to closet	Miscellaneous Expense	16
5	Computer diskettes	Supplies Expense	8

Requirements

Make the general journal entries to (a) create the petty cash fund and (b) record its replenishment. Cash in the fund totals $75, so $3 is missing. Include explanations. (pp. 379–381)

Control over petty cash
5

E7-23

1. Explain how an *imprest* petty cash system works. (p. 379)
2. Steppin' Out Night Club maintains an imprest petty cash fund of $100, which is under the control of Brenda Montague. At November 30, the fund holds $20 cash and petty cash tickets for office supplies, $60; and delivery expense, $25.
   Journalize (**a**) establishment of the petty cash fund on November 1 and (**b**) replenishment of the fund on November 30. (pp. 379–381)
3. Prepare a T-account for Petty Cash, and post to the account. What is Petty Cash's balance at all times? (pp. 380–381)

Evaluating the ethics of conduct by government legislators
6

E7-24 Members of the U.S. House of Representatives wrote a quarter million dollars of checks on the House bank without having the cash in their accounts. In effect, these representatives were borrowing money from each other on an interest-free, no-service-charge basis. The House closed its bank after these events were featured on FOX, CNN, ABC, and NBC.

Requirements

Suppose you are a new congressional representative from your state. Apply the ethical judgment framework outlined in the Decision Guidelines to decide whether you would intentionally write NSF checks through the House bank. (p. 383)

Problems (Group A)

Identifying the characteristics of an effective internal control system

P7-25A An employee of Kindler Orthopedics stole thousands of dollars from the company. Suppose Kindler has installed a new system of internal controls. As a consultant for Kindler Orthopedics, write a memo to the board of directors explaining how internal controls safeguard assets. (pp. 361–366)

Correcting internal control weaknesses

P7-26A Each of the following situations has an internal control weakness.

a. Rite-Way Applications sells accounting software. Recently, development of a new program stopped while the programmers redesigned Rite-Way's accounting system. Rite-Way's accountants could have performed this task. (p. 361)

b. Betty Grable has been your trusted employee for 30 years. She performs all cash-handling and accounting duties. Ms. Grable just purchased a new Lexus and a new home in an expensive suburb. As owner of the company you wonder how she can afford these luxuries because you pay her only $35,000 a year and she has no source of outside income.

c. Sanchez Hardwoods, a private company, falsified sales and inventory figures in order to get an important loan. The loan went through, but Sanchez later went bankrupt and couldn't repay the bank. (pp. 361–362)

d. The office supply company where Champs Sporting Goods purchases sales receipts recently notified Champs that its documents were not prenumbered. Alex Champ, the owner, replied that he never uses the receipt numbers. (p. 363)

e. Discount stores such as Target make most of their sales for cash, with the remainder in credit-card sales. To reduce expenses, one store manager ceases purchasing fidelity bonds on the cashiers. (p. 364)

continued . . .

Requirements
1. Identify the missing internal control characteristics in each situation.
2. Identify the possible problem caused by each control weakness.
3. Propose a solution to each internal control problem.

Preparing a bank reconciliation
3

P7-27A The March cash records of Tru-Value Insurance follow.

	Cash Receipts (CR)	Cash Payments (CP)	
Date	Cash Debit	Check No.	Cash Credit
Mar. 4	$2,716	1416	$ 8
9	544	1417	775
14	896	1418	88
17	367	1419	126
31	2,038	1420	970
		1421	200
		1422	2,267

Tru-Value's Cash account shows a balance of $6,172 on March 31. On March 31, Tru-Value received the following bank statement.

Bank Statement for March

Beginning balance			$4,045
Deposits and other Credits:			
Mar. 1	EFT	$ 625	
5		2,716	
10		544	
15		896	
18		367	
31	BC	1,000	6,148
Checks and other Debits:			
Mar. 8	NSF	$ 441	
11 (check no. 1416)		8	
19	EFT	340	
22 (check no. 1417)		775	
29 (check no. 1418)		88	
31 (check no. 1419)		216	
31	SC	25	(1,893)
Ending balance			$8,300

Explanations: BC—bank collection; EFT—electronic funds transfer; NSF—nonsufficient funds checks; SC—service charge.

Additional data for the bank reconciliation:

a. The EFT deposit was a receipt of rent revenue. The EFT debit was payment of insurance expense.

b. The NSF check was received from a customer.

continued . . .

c. The $1,000 bank collection was for a note receivable.

d. The correct amount of check 1419 is $216. Tru-Value mistakenly recorded the check for $126.

Requirements

Prepare the bank reconciliation of Tru-Value Insurance at March 31, 2008. (p. 370)

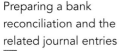

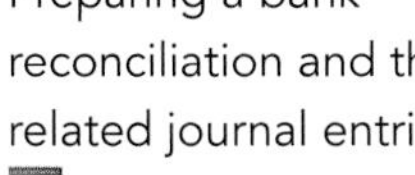
Preparing a bank reconciliation and the related journal entries

P7-28A The May 31 bank statement of Multi-Plex Healthcare has just arrived from First State Bank. To prepare the bank reconciliation, you gather the following data.

a. The May 31 bank balance is $12,209.

b. The bank statement includes two charges for NSF checks from customers. One is for $67, and the other for $195.

c. The following Multi-Plex checks are outstanding at May 31:

Check No.	Amount
616	$405
802	74
806	36
809	161
810	229
811	48

d. Multi-Plex collects from a few customers by EFT. The May bank statement lists a $200 EFT deposit for a collection on account.

e. The bank statement includes two special deposits that Multi-Plex hasn't recorded yet: $900, for dividend revenue, and $16, the interest revenue Multi-Plex earned on its bank balance during May.

f. The bank statement lists a $7 subtraction for the bank service charge.

g. On May 31, the Multi-Plex treasurer deposited $381, but this deposit does not appear on the bank statement.

h. The bank statement includes a $410 deduction for a check drawn by Multi-State Freight Company. Multi-Plex notified the bank of this bank error.

i. Multi-Plex's Cash account shows a balance of $11,200 on May 31.

Requirements

1. Prepare the bank reconciliation for Multi-Plex Healthcare at May 31. (p. 370)
2. Record the entries called for by the reconciliation. Include an explanation for each entry. (p. 371)

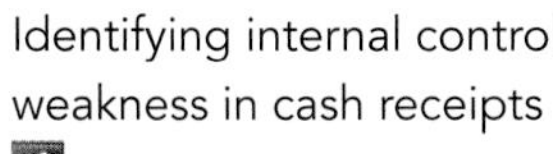
Identifying internal control weakness in cash receipts
4

P7-29A Pendley Productions makes all sales on credit. Cash receipts arrive by mail. Larry Padgitt in the mailroom opens envelopes and separates the checks from the accompanying remittance advices. Padgitt forwards the checks to another employee, who makes the daily bank deposit but has

continued . . .

no access to the accounting records. Padgitt sends the remittance advices, which show cash received, to the accounting department for entry in the accounts. Padgitt's only other duty is to grant sales allowances to customers. (A *sales allowance* decreases the amount receivable.) When Padgitt receives a customer check for less than the full amount of the invoice, he records the sales allowance and forwards the document to the accounting department.

Requirements

You are a new employee of Pendley Productions. Write a memo to Paulette Pendley, owner of the business, identifying the internal control weakness in this situation. State how to correct the weakness. (pp. 266–267, 361–362, 375)

Accounting for petty cash transactions
5

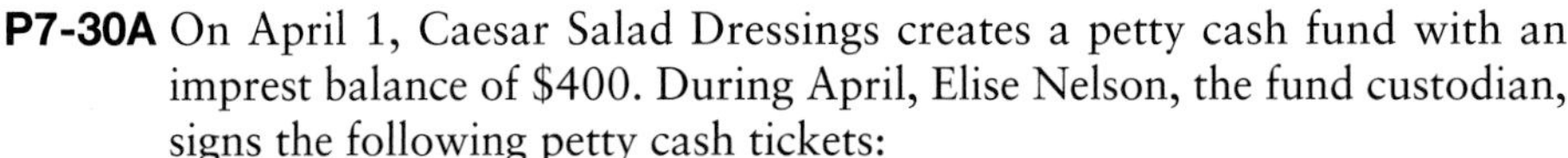

P7-30A On April 1, Caesar Salad Dressings creates a petty cash fund with an imprest balance of $400. During April, Elise Nelson, the fund custodian, signs the following petty cash tickets:

Petty Cash Ticket Number	Item	Amount
101	Office supplies	$86
102	Cab fare for executive	25
103	Delivery of package across town	37
104	Dinner money for city manager to entertain the mayor	80
105	Inventory	85

On April 30, prior to replenishment, the fund contains these tickets plus cash of $90. The accounts affected by petty cash payments are Office Supplies Expense, Travel Expense, Delivery Expense, Entertainment Expense, and Inventory.

Requirements

1. Explain the characteristics and the internal control features of an imprest fund. (p. 379)
2. On April 30, how much cash should the petty cash fund hold before it's replenished? (p. 379)
3. Make general journal entries to (**a**) create the fund and (**b**) replenish it. Include explanations. (pp. 379–381)
4. Make the May 1 entry to increase the fund balance to $500. Include an explanation, and briefly describe what the custodian does. (p. 379)

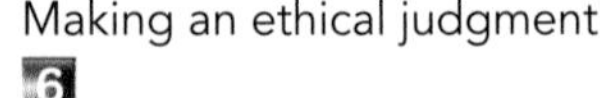

Making an ethical judgment
6

P7-31A Federal Credit Bank has a loan receivable from Subway Construction Company. Subway is late making payments to the bank, and Milton Reed, a Federal Credit Bank vice president, is helping Subway restructure its debt. Reed learns that Subway is depending on landing a contract from Starstruck Theater, another Federal Credit Bank client. Reed also serves as Starstruck's loan officer at the bank. In this capacity, he is aware that Starstruck is considering declaring bankruptcy. Reed has been

continued . . .

a great help to Subway, and Subway's owner is counting on him to carry the company through this difficult restructuring. To help the bank collect on this large loan, Reed has a strong motivation to help Subway survive.

Apply the ethical judgment framework from the chapter to help Reed plan his next action. (p. 383)

Problems (Group B)

Identifying the characteristics of an effective internal control system

P7-32B Sunburst Technology prospered during the recent economic expansion. Business was so good that the company used very few internal controls. A recent decline in the high-tech sector of the economy brought a cash shortage. Adam Klaus, the company owner, is looking for ways to save money.

As a consultant for Sunburst Technology, write a memo to convince Klaus of the company's need for a system of internal control. Be specific in explaining how an internal control system could save the company money. Include the definition of internal control, and briefly discuss the characteristics of an effective internal control system, beginning with competent, reliable, and ethical personnel. (pp. 358–366)

Correcting internal control weaknesses

P7-33B Each of the following situations has an internal control weakness.

a. Architects use paraprofessional employees to perform routine tasks. For example, a draftsman might prepare drawings to assist an architect. In the architecture firm of Lee & Dunham, Joseph Lee, the senior partner, turns over some of his high-level design work to less-qualified draftsmen. (p. 361)

b. Jim Alexander owns Central Forwarding, a storage company. His staff consists of 12 employees, and he manages the office. Often, Alexander's work requires him to travel. When he returns from business trips, the work in the office has not progressed much. In his absence, senior employees take over office management and neglect their regular duties. One employee could manage the office. (p. 361)

c. Aimee Atkins has worked for Michael Riggs, M.D., for many years. Atkins performs all accounting duties, including opening the mail, making the bank deposits, writing checks, and preparing the bank reconciliation. Riggs trusts Atkins completely. (pp. 361–362)

d. Computer programmers for Internet Solutions work under intense pressure. Facing tight deadlines, they sometimes bypass company policies and write programs without securing customer accounts receivable data. (pp. 364–366)

e. In evaluating internal control over cash payments, an auditor learns that the purchasing agent is responsible for purchasing diamonds for use in the company's manufacturing process. The purchasing agent also approves the invoices for payment and signs the checks. (p. 364)

Requirements

1. Identify the missing internal control characteristic in each situation.
2. Identify the possible problem caused by each control weakness.
3. Propose a solution to each internal control problem.

Preparing a bank reconciliation

3

P7-34B The cash records of Dunlap Dollar Stores for April follow.

Cash Receipts (CR)		Cash Payments (CP)	
Date	Cash Debit	Check No.	Cash Credit
Apr. 2	$4,170	3113	$ 890
8	500	3114	140
10	550	3115	1,930
16	2,180	3116	660
22	1,850	3117	1,470
29	1,060	3118	1,000
30	330	3119	630
		3120	1,670
		3121	100
		3122	2,410

Dunlap's Cash account shows a balance of $13,640 at April 30.

On April 30, Dunlap received the following bank statement:

Bank Statement for April

Beginning balance			$13,900
Deposits and other Credits:			
Apr. 1	EFT	$ 300	
4		4,170	
9		500	
12		550	
17		2,180	
22	BC	1,300	
23		1,850	10,850
Checks and other Debits:			
Apr. 7 (check no. 3113)		$ 890	
13 (check no. 3115)		1,390	
14	NSF	900	
15 (check no. 3114)		140	
18 (check no. 3116)		660	
21	EFT	200	
26 (check no. 3117)		1,470	
30 (check no. 3118)		1,000	
30	SC	20	(6,670)
Ending balance			$18,080

Explanations: BC—bank collection; EFT—electronic funds transfer; NSF—nonsufficient funds checks; SC—service charge.

Additional data for the bank reconciliation:

a. The EFT deposit was a receipt of rent. The EFT debit was an insurance payment.

b. The NSF check was received from a customer.

c. The $1,300 bank collection was for a note receivable.

d. The correct amount of check number 3115 is $1,390. (Dunlap mistakenly recorded the check for $1,930.)

continued . . .

Requirements

Prepare Dunlap's bank reconciliation at April 30, 2008. (p. 370)

Preparing a bank reconciliation and the related journal entries 3

P7-35B The August 31 bank statement of Ward's Supercenter has just arrived from United Bank. To prepare the Ward's bank reconciliation, you gather the following data:

a. Ward's Cash account shows a balance of $2,420 on August 31.

b. The bank statement includes two NSF checks from customers: $395 and $147.

c. Ward's pays rent expense ($750) and insurance expense ($290) each month by EFT.

d. The Ward checks below are outstanding at August 31.

Check No.	Amount
237	$ 49
288	141
291	578
293	11
294	609
295	8
296	101

e. The bank statement includes a deposit of $1,200, collected on our note receivable by the bank.

f. The bank statement shows that Ward earned $18 of interest on its bank balance during August.

g. The bank statement lists a $10 bank service charge.

h. On August 31, Ward deposited $316, but this deposit does not appear on the bank statement.

i. The bank statement includes a $300 deposit that Ward did not make. The bank erroneously credited Ward's account for another customer's deposit.

j. The August 31 bank balance is $3,527.

Requirements

1. Prepare the bank reconciliation for Ward's Supercenter at August 31. (p. 370)
2. Record the journal entries that bring the book balance of Cash into agreement with the adjusted book balance on the reconciliation. Include an explanation for each entry. (p. 371)

Identifying internal control weakness in cash receipts

P7-36B Advanced Audio Productions makes all sales on account. Cash receipts arrive by mail. James Gilette opens envelopes and separates the checks from the accompanying remittance advices. Gilette forwards the checks to another employee, who makes the daily bank deposit but has no access to the accounting records. Gilette sends the remittance advices, which show the cash received, to the accounting department for entry in the accounts. Gilette's only other duty is to grant sales allowances to customers. (A *sales*

continued . . .

allowance decreases the amount receivable.) When he receives a customer check for less than the full amount of the invoice, he records the sales allowance and forwards the document to the accounting department.

Requirements

You are the new controller of Advanced Audio Productions. Write a memo to the company president identifying the internal control weakness in this situation. State how to correct the weakness. (pp. 266–267, 361–362, 375)

Accounting for petty cash transactions

P7-37B Suppose that on June 1, Cool Gyrations, a disc jockey service, creates a petty cash fund with an imprest balance of $300. During June, Carol McColgin, fund custodian, signs the following petty cash tickets:

Petty Cash Ticket Number	Item	Amount
1	Postage for package received	$18
2	Decorations and refreshments for office party	13
3	Two boxes of stationery	20
4	Printer cartridges	27
5	Dinner money for sales manager entertaining a customer	50

On June 30, prior to replenishment, the fund contains these tickets plus cash of $170. The accounts affected by petty cash payments are Office Supplies Expense, Entertainment Expense, and Postage Expense.

Requirements

1. Explain the characteristics and the internal control features of an imprest fund. (p. 379)
2. On June 30, how much cash should this petty cash fund hold before it's replenished? (p. 379)
3. Make general journal entries to (**a**) create the fund and (**b**) replenish it. Include explanations. (pp. 379–381)
4. Make the entry on July 1 to increase the fund balance to $350. Include an explanation, and briefly describe what the custodian does. (p. 379)

Making an ethical judgment

6

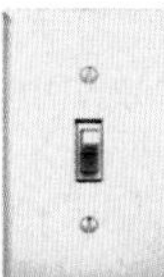

for 24-7 practice, visit www.MyAccountingLab.com

P7-38B Mike Schoenfeld is vice president of Lancer Bank in Shreveport, Louisiana. Active in community affairs, Schoenfeld serves on the board of directors of Baker Publishing Company. Baker is expanding and relocating its plant. At a recent meeting, board members decided to buy 15 acres of land on the edge of town. The owner of the property, Jack Fletcher, is a customer of Lancer Bank. Fletcher is completing a divorce, and Schoenfeld knows that Fletcher is eager to sell his property. In view of Fletcher's difficult situation, Schoenfeld believes Fletcher would accept almost any offer for the land. Realtors have appraised the property at $5 million.

Apply the ethical judgment framework from the Decision Guidelines (page 383) to help Schoenfeld decide what his role should be in Baker's attempt to buy the land from Fletcher.

Apply Your Knowledge

Decision Cases

Using internal controls
1 2

Case 1. Go to sarbox.org, the Web site for the Sarbanes-Oxley Act. Surf around for information on internal control, write a report of your findings, and present it to your class (if required by your instructor).

Correcting an internal control weakness

Case 2. This case is based on an actual situation. Centennial Construction Company, headquartered in Dallas, built a Rodeway Motel 35 miles north of Dallas. The construction foreman, whose name was Slim Chance, hired the 40 workers needed to complete the project. Slim had the construction workers fill out the necessary tax forms, and he sent their documents to the home office.

Work on the motel began on April 1 and ended September 1. Each week, Slim filled out a time card of hours worked by each employee during the week. Slim faxed the time sheets to the home office, which prepared the payroll checks on Friday morning. Slim drove to the home office on Friday, picked up the payroll checks, and returned to the construction site. At 5 P.M. on Friday, Slim distributed payroll checks to the workers.

a. Describe in detail the main internal control weakness in this situation. Specify what negative result(s) could occur because of the internal control weakness. (pp. 361–362, 376)

b. Describe what you would do to correct the internal control weakness. (pp. 361–362, 376)

Using the bank reconciliation to detect a theft
3

Case 3. San Diego Harbor Tours has poor internal control over cash. Ben Johnson, the owner, suspects the cashier of stealing. Here are some details of company cash at September 30.

a. The Cash account in the ledger shows a balance of $6,450.

b. The September 30 bank statement shows a balance of $4,300. The bank statement lists a $200 bank collection, a $10 service charge, and a $40 NSF check.

c. At September 30, the following checks are outstanding:

Amount
$100
300
600
200

d. There is a $3,000 deposit in transit at September 30.

e. The cashier handles all incoming cash and makes bank deposits. He also writes checks and reconciles the monthly bank statement.

Johnson asks you to determine whether the cashier has stolen cash from the business and, if so, how much. Perform your own bank reconciliation using the format illustrated in the chapter. There are no bank or book errors. Explain how Johnson can improve his internal controls. (pp. 367–370)

Ethical Issue

Internal control over cash payments; ethical considerations

Mel O'Conner owns rental properties in Michigan. Each property has a manager who collects rent, arranges for repairs, and runs advertisements in the local newspaper. The property managers transfer cash to O'Conner monthly and prepare their own bank reconciliations. The manager in Lansing has been stealing from the company. To cover the theft, he understates the amount of the outstanding checks on the monthly bank reconciliation. As a result, each monthly bank reconciliation appears to balance. However, the balance sheet reports more cash than O'Conner actually has in the bank. In negotiating the sale of the Lansing property, O'Conner is showing the balance sheet to prospective investors.

Requirements

1. Identify two parties other than O'Conner who can be harmed by this theft. In what ways can they be harmed?
2. Discuss the role accounting plays in this situation.

Financial Statement Case

Internal controls and cash

1

Study the audit opinion (labeled Report of Ernst & Young LLP) of Amazon.com and the Amazon financial statements given in Appendix A at the end of this book. Answer the following questions about the company.

Requirements

1. What is the name of Amazon.com's outside auditing firm (independent registered public accounting firm)? What office of this firm signed the audit report? How long after the Amazon year-end did the auditors issue their opinion?
2. Who bears primary responsibility for the financial statements? How can you tell?
3. Does it appear that the Amazon internal controls are adequate? How can you tell?
4. What standard of auditing did the outside auditors use in examining the Amazon financial statements? By what accounting standards were the statements evaluated?
5. By how much did Amazon's cash balance (including cash equivalents) change during 2005? What were the beginning and ending cash balances?

Team Project

You are promoting a rock concert in your area. Each member of your team will invest $10,000 of their hard-earned money in this venture. It is April 1, and the concert is scheduled for June 30. Your promotional activities begin immediately, and ticket sales start on May 1. You expect to sell all the business's assets, pay all the liabilities, and distribute all remaining cash to the group members by July 31.

Requirements

Write an internal control manual that will help safeguard the assets of the business. The starting point of the manual is to assign responsibilities among the group members. Authorize individuals, including group members and any outsiders that you need to hire, to perform specific jobs. Separate duties among the group and any employees.

For Internet Exercises, Excel in Practice, and additional online activities, go to the Web site www.prenhall.com/horngren.

Quick Check Answers

1. *c* 2. *d* 3. *c* 4. *d* 5. *c* 6. *d* 7. *c* 8. *b* 9. *b* 10. *d*

8 Receivables

Learning Objectives

1. Design internal controls for receivables
2. Use the allowance method to account for uncollectibles
3. Understand the direct write-off method for uncollectibles
4. Account for notes receivable
5. Report receivables on the balance sheet
6. Use the acid-test ratio and days' sales in receivables to evaluate a company

Your business, In Motion T-shirts, is doing well—so well in fact that your college has ordered 50 T-shirts with the college logo on it. The dean will give a T-shirt to all new faculty members. This is quite a vote of confidence, and the free publicity may bring in more business. But there's a hitch.

The college can't pay you immediately. It usually takes around 30 days to clear the paperwork and cut a check. Can you wait 30 days to get your money?

Most businesses face this situation. There are both advantages and disadvantages to extending credit to customers. In the case of your college, the pluses outweigh the minuses so, sure, you'll let them pay you later.

The main advantage of selling on credit (selling on account) is expanding your customer base; you can increase sales that way. The disadvantages are that you have to wait to receive cash and some customers may never pay you. You wind up eating some of the receivables.

A *receivable* arises when you sell goods or services to another party on credit. The receivable is the seller's claim for the amount of the transaction. A receivable also arises when you loan money to another party. Each credit transaction involves two parties:

- The **creditor**, who obtains a receivable (an asset)
- The **debtor**, who has a payable (a liability)

Your receivable is an asset, just as cash is. But the receivable is slightly different: It's very close to cash, but it's not cash yet. This chapter focuses on accounting for receivables.

Receivables: An Introduction

Types of Receivables

Receivables are monetary claims against others. The two major types of receivables are:

- accounts receivable
- notes receivable

Accounts receivable, also called *trade receivables,* are amounts to be collected from customers. Accounts Receivable serves as a *control account* because it summarizes the total of your receivables. Companies also keep a *subsidiary ledger* of the receivable from each customer. This is illustrated as follows:

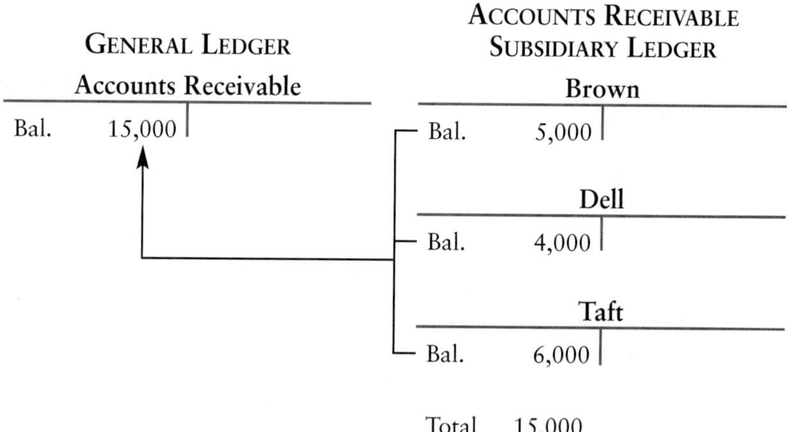

Notes receivable are more formal than accounts receivable, and notes include a charge for interest. The debtor of a note promises to pay the creditor a definite sum at a future date—the *maturity* date. A written document known as a *promissory note* serves as the evidence. Notes receivable due within one year or less are *current assets.* Notes due beyond one year are *long-term.*

Other receivables make up a miscellaneous category that may include loans to employees. Usually, other receivables are long-term, but they're current assets if due within one year or less. Receivables can be reported as shown in Exhibit 8-1. All the receivables are highlighted for emphasis.

EXHIBIT 8-1 **Receivables on the Balance Sheet**

EXAMPLE COMPANY Assets Date		
Assets		
Current assets:		
Cash		$X,XXX
Accounts receivable	$X,XXX	
Less: Allowance for uncollectible accounts	(XXX)	X,XXX
Notes receivable, short-term		X,XXX
Inventories		X,XXX
Prepaid expenses		X,XXX
Total		X,XXX
Investments and long-term receivables:		
Investments		X,XXX
Notes receivable, long-term		X,XXX
Other receivables		X,XXX
Total		X,XXX
Plant assets:		
Property, plant, and equipment		X,XXX
Total assets		$X,XXX

Establishing Internal Control over Collection of Receivables

Design internal controls for receivables

Businesses that sell on credit receive cash by mail, so internal control over collections is important. A critical element of internal control is the separation of cash-handling and cash-accounting duties. Consider the following case.

> Butler Supply Co. is family-owned and has loyal workers. Most company employees have been with the Butlers for years. The company makes 90% of its sales on account.
>
> The office staff consists of a bookkeeper and a supervisor. The bookkeeper maintains the accounts receivable subsidiary ledger and makes the daily bank deposit. The supervisor manages the office.

Can you spot the internal control weakness here? The bookkeeper has access to the accounts receivable and also handles cash. The bookkeeper could steal a customer check and write off the customer's account as uncollectible.[1] Unless someone reviews the bookkeeper's work, the theft may go undetected.

How can Butler Supply correct this control weakness? *The bookkeeper should not be allowed to handle cash.* The supervisor should make all bank deposits. A bank lock box would achieve the same result. In a lock-box system, customers send cash directly to the bank, and that keeps the bookkeeper's hands off the cash.

[1]The bookkeeper would need to forge the endorsement on the check and deposit it in a bank account that he controls.

Managing the Collection of Receivables: The Credit Department

Most companies have a credit department to evaluate customers. The extension of credit requires a balancing act. The company doesn't want to lose sales to good customers, but it also wants to avoid uncollectible receivables.

For good internal control over cash collections, the credit department should have no access to cash. For example, if a credit employee handles cash, he might pocket money received from a customer. He could then label the customer's account as uncollectible, and the company would write off the account receivable, as discussed in the next section. The company would stop billing that customer, and the employee would have covered his theft. For this reason, a sharp separation of duties is important.

The Decision Guidelines feature identifies the main issues in controlling and managing receivables. These guidelines serve as a framework for the remainder of the chapter.

Decision Guidelines

CONTROLLING, MANAGING, AND ACCOUNTING FOR RECEIVABLES

Butler Supply, In Motion T-Shirts, and all other companies that sell on credit face the same accounting challenges.

The main issues in *controlling* and *managing* receivables, plus a plan of action, follow.

Issue	Action
Extend credit only to customers who are most likely to pay.	Run a credit check on prospective customers.
Separate cash-handing, credit, and accounting duties to keep employees from stealing cash collected from customers.	Design the internal control system to separate duties.
Pursue collection from customers to maximize cash flow.	Keep a close eye on collections from customers.

The main issues in *accounting* for receivables, and the related plan of action, are as follows:

Issue	Action
Report receivables at their *net realizable value,* that is, the amount we expect to collect.	Estimate the allowance for uncollectible receivables. The *balance sheet* reports receivables at net realizable value (accounts receivable minus the allowance for uncollectibles).
Report the expense associated with failure to collect your receivables. This expense is called uncollectible-account expense.	The *income statement* reports the expense of failing to collect from customers (uncollectible-account expense).

Accounting for Uncollectibles (Bad Debts)

Selling on credit (on account) creates an account receivable. The revenue—service revenue or sales revenue—is recorded as follows (amounts assumed):

	Accounts Receivable	6,000	
	Service Revenue		6,000
	Performed service on account.		

	Accounts Receivable	10,000	
	Sales Revenue		10,000
	Sold goods on account.		

The business collects cash for most accounts receivable and makes this entry (amount assumed):

	Cash	10,000	
	Accounts Receivable		10,000
	Collected cash on account.		

Selling on credit brings both a benefit and a cost.

- **The benefit:** Increase revenues and profits by making sales to a wider range of customers.
- **The cost:** Some customers don't pay, and that creates an expense. The expense is called **uncollectible-account expense, doubtful-account expense,** or **bad-debt expense.**

To account for uncollectible receivables, you can use the allowance method or, in certain limited cases, the direct write-off method. We begin with the allowance method because it represents GAAP for most companies.

The Allowance Method

Most companies use the **allowance method** to measure bad debts. The key concept is to record uncollectible-account expense in the same period as the sales revenue. The business doesn't wait to see which customers will not pay. Instead, it records an expense on the basis of estimates developed from past experience.

Record Uncollectible-Account Expense for the estimated amount and set up **Allowance for Uncollectible Accounts** (or **Allowance for Doubtful Accounts**), a contra account to Accounts Receivable. The allowance is the amount the business expects *not* to collect. Subtracting the allowance from Accounts Receivable yields the net amount you expect to collect. Here are In Motion's final figures after all adjustments as reported on the balance sheet (amounts assumed):

Balance sheet (partial):	
Accounts receivable	$2,800
Less: Allowance for uncollectible accounts	(400)
Accounts receivable, net	$2,400

Interpretation: Customers owe In Motion $2,800, of which you expect to collect $2,400. You estimate that In Motion will not collect $400 of these receivables.

Another way for In Motion to report receivables follows.

Accounts receivable, net of allowance for uncollectible accounts of $400	$2,400

The income statement reports Uncollectible-Account Expense (Doubtful-Account Expense) among the operating expenses.

In the sections that follow, we show how to arrive at these amounts.

Estimating Uncollectibles

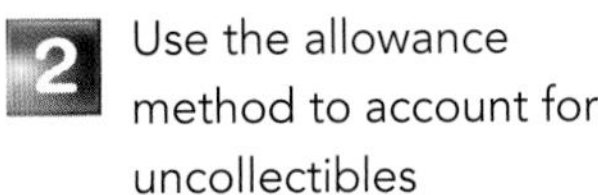

Use the allowance method to account for uncollectibles

How are uncollectible receivables estimated? Companies use their past experience. There are two basic ways to estimate uncollectibles:

- Percent-of-sales
- Aging-of-accounts-receivable

Both approaches work with the allowance method, and both normally require an adjusting entry at the end of the period.

Percent-of-Sales Method

The **percent-of-sales method** computes uncollectible-account expense as a percentage of net credit sales. This method is also called the **income-statement approach** because it focuses on the amount of expense. Assume it is December 31, 2007, and the accounts have these balances *before the year-end adjustments:*

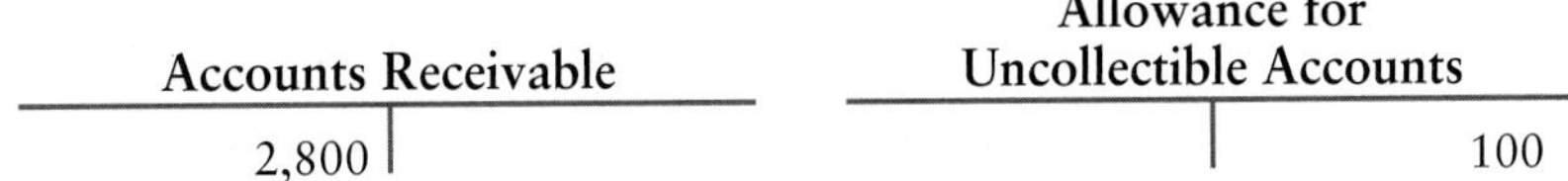

Accounts Receivable		Allowance for Uncollectible Accounts	
2,800			100

Interpretation: Accounts Receivable reports the amount that customers owe you. If you were to collect from all customers, you would receive $2,800. Allowance for Uncollectible Accounts should report the amount of the receivables that you expect *not* to collect.

Suppose it's clear to you that In Motion will *fail to collect* more than $100 of the receivables. The allowance is too low, so you need to bring it up to a more realistic credit balance. That requires an adjusting entry at the end of the period.

How the Percent-of-Sales Method Works

Based on prior experience, In Motion's uncollectible-account expense runs 2% of net credit sales, which totaled $15,000 for 2007. The adjusting entry records the following at year end:

2007			
Dec. 31	Uncollectible-Account Expense ($15,000 × 0.02)	300	
	Allowance for Uncollectible Accounts		300
	Recorded expense for the year.		

After posting, the accounts are ready for the balance sheet.

Accounts Receivable		Allowance for Uncollectible Accounts	
2,800			100
			Adj. 300
			End. Bal. 400

Net Accounts Receivable, $2,400

Now the allowance for uncollectible accounts is realistic. The balance sheet will report accounts receivable at the net amount of $2,400. The income statement will report uncollectible-account expense along with the other operating expenses.

Aging-of-Accounts-Receivable Method

The other approach for estimating uncollectible receivables is the **aging-of-accounts method.** This method is also called the **balance-sheet approach** because it focuses on accounts receivable. Assume it is December 31, 2007, and the accounts have these balances *before the year-end adjustments:*

Accounts Receivable		Allowance for Uncollectible Accounts	
2,800			100

Again, the allowance balance is too low. In the aging approach, you group individual accounts (Jones, Smith, etc.) according to how long they've been outstanding. The computer can sort customer accounts by age. Exhibit 8-2 shows how In Motion T-shirts groups its accounts receivable. This is called an aging schedule.

Interpretation: Customers owe you $2,800, but you expect not to collect $400 of this amount. These amounts appear in the lower right corner of the aging schedule that follows. Notice that the percentage uncollectible increases as a customer account gets older.

EXHIBIT 8-2 **Aging the Accounts Receivable of In Motion T-Shirts**

	Age of Account				
Customer Name	**1–30 Days**	**31–60 Days**	**61–90 Days**	**Over 90 Days**	**Total Balance**
Dean's Office	$ 500				$ 500
Phi Chi Fraternity	700				700
University Ministries	600				600
Drama Department			$340		340
Other accounts	60	$200		$400	660
Totals	$1,860	$200	$340	$400	$2,800
Estimated percentage uncollectible	× 1%	× 2%	× 5%	× 90%	
Allowance for Uncollectible Accounts balance	+ $ 19	+ $ 4	+ $ 17	+ $360	= $ 400

How the Aging Method Works

The aging method tells you what the credit balance of the allowance account needs to be—$400 in this case. The aging method works like this:

Allowance for Uncollectible Accounts:	
Credit balance needed	$400
Unadjusted balance already in the allowance	100
Adjusting entry for this amount	$300

To adjust the allowance, make this entry at year end:

2007			
Dec. 31	Uncollectible-Account Expense	300	
	Allowance for Uncollectible Accounts ($400 – $100)		300
	Adjusted the allowance account.		

After posting, the accounts are up-to-date and ready for the balance sheet.

Accounts Receivable

Debit	Credit
2,800	

Allowance for Uncollectible Accounts

Debit	Credit
	100
	Adj. 300
	End. Bal. 400

Net Accounts Receivable, $2,400

Report accounts receivable at *net realizable value* ($2,400) because that's the amount In Motion expects to collect in cash.

Using Percent-of-Sales and Aging Methods Together

In practice, companies use the percent-of-sales and the aging-of-accounts methods together.

- For *interim statements* (monthly or quarterly), companies use the percent-of-sales method because it is easier.
- At the end of the year, companies use the aging method to ensure that Accounts Receivable is reported at *net realizable value.*
- Using the two methods together provides good measures of both the expense and the asset. Exhibit 8-3 summarizes and compares the two methods.

EXHIBIT 8-3 **Comparing the Percent-of-Sales and Aging Methods**

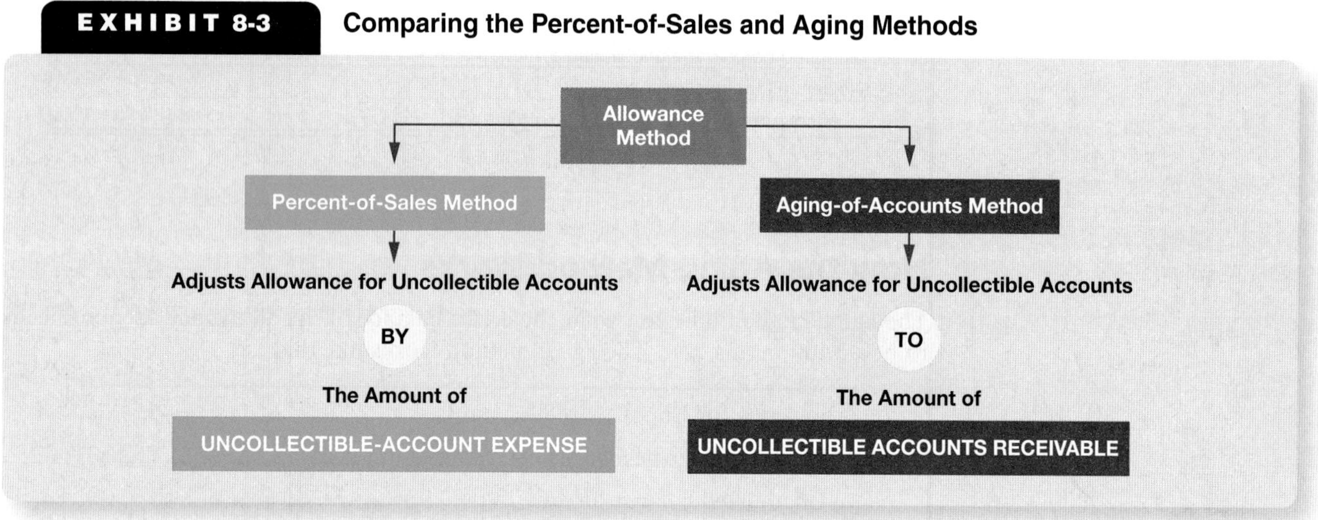

Writing Off Uncollectible Accounts

Early in 2008, In Motion T-shirts collects most of its accounts receivable and records the cash receipts as follows (amount assumed):

2008			
Jan.–Mar.	Cash	2,000	
	Accounts Receivable		2,000
	Collected on account.		

Suppose that, after repeated attempts, you finally decide that In Motion cannot collect a total of $200 from customers Andrews and Jones. You then write off the receivables from these customers, as follows:

2008			
Mar. 31	Allowance for Uncollectible Accounts	200	
	Accounts Receivable—Andrews		80
	Accounts Receivable—Jones		120
	Wrote off uncollectible accounts.		

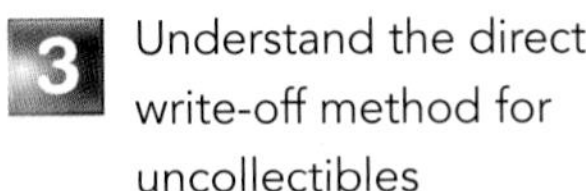

Understand the direct write-off method for uncollectibles

The Direct Write-Off Method

There is another way to account for uncollectible receivables that is unacceptable for most companies. It is called the **direct write-off method**. Under the direct write-off method, you wait until you decide that you'll never collect from the customer. Then you write off the customer's account receivable by debiting Uncollectible-Account Expense and crediting the customer's Account Receivable, as follows (using assumed data):

Date	Accounts and Explanation	Debit	Credit
2008			
Jan. 2	Uncollectible-Account Expense	110	
	Accounts Receivable—Smith		110
	Wrote off a bad account.		

The direct write-off method is defective for two reasons:

1. It does not set up an allowance for uncollectibles. As a result, the direct write-off method always reports the receivables at their full amount. Assets are overstated on the balance sheet.
2. It does not match uncollectible-account expense against revenue very well. In this example, In Motion made the sale to Smith in 2007 and should have recorded the uncollectible-account expense during 2007. That's the only way to measure net income properly. By recording the uncollectible-account expense in 2008, you would *overstate* net income in 2007 and *understate* net income in 2008. Both years' net income amounts are incorrect.

The direct write-off method is acceptable only when uncollectible receivables are very low. It works for retailers such as Wal-Mart, McDonald's, and Gap because those companies carry almost no receivables.

Recovery of Accounts Previously Written Off

When an account receivable is written off as uncollectible, the receivable does not die: The customer still owes the money. However, the company stops pursuing collection and writes off the account as uncollectible.

Some companies turn delinquent receivables over to an attorney and recover some of the cash. This is called *recovery of a bad account*. Let's see how to record the recovery of an account that we wrote off earlier. Recall that In Motion T-shirts wrote off the $80 receivable from customer Andrews (bottom of page 414). It is now January 4, 2009, and In Motion unexpectedly receives $80 from Andrews. To account for this recovery, you make two journal entries to (1) reverse the earlier write-off and (2) record the cash collection, as follows:

		Accounts and Explanation	Debit	Credit
1.		Accounts Receivable—Andrews	80	
		Allowance for Uncollectible Accounts		80
		Reinstated Andrews' account receivable.		
2.		Cash	80	
		Accounts Receivable—Andrews		80
		Collected on account.		

Credit-Card, Bankcard, and Debit-Card Sales

Credit-Card Sales

Credit-card sales are common in retailing. Customers present credit cards like American Express and Discover to pay for purchases. The credit-card company pays the seller and then bills the customer.

Credit cards offer the convenience of buying without having to pay cash immediately. An American Express customer receives a monthly statement from American Express, detailing each transaction. The customer can write one check to cover many purchases.

Retailers also benefit. They don't have to check each customer's credit rating. The credit-card company has already done so. Retailers don't have to keep accounts receivable records or pursue collection from customers.

The benefits do not come free. The seller receives less than 100% of the face value of the sale. The credit-card company takes a fee of 1% to 5% on the sale. Suppose you and your family have dinner at a Red Lobster restaurant. You pay the bill—$50—with a Discover card.

Customer pays $50

Seller collects $48

Credit-card company collects $2

Red Lobster's entry to record the $50 sale, subject to the credit-card company's 4% discount, is:

		Accounts Receivable—Discover	48	
		Credit-Card Discount Expense ($50 × 0.04)	2	
		Sales Revenue		50
		Recorded credit-card sales.		

On collection of the cash, Red Lobster records the following:

		Cash	48	
		Accounts Receivable—Discover		48
		Collected from Discover.		

Bankcard Sales

Most banks issue their own cards, known as *bankcards,* which operate much like credit cards. VISA and MasterCard are the two main bankcards. When an Exxon station makes a sale and takes a VISA card, the station receives cash at the point of sale. The cash received is less than the full amount of the sale because the bank deducts its fee. Suppose the Exxon station sells $150 of fuel to a family vacationing in its motor home. The station takes a VISA card, and the bank that issued the card charges a 2% fee. The Exxon station records the bankcard sale as follows:

	Account	Debit	Credit
	Cash	147	
	Bankcard Discount Expense ($150 × 0.02)	3	
	Sales Revenue		150
	Recorded a bankcard sale.		

Debit-Card Sales

Debit cards are fundamentally different from credit cards and bankcards. Using a debit card is like paying with cash, except that you don't have to carry cash or write a check.

At Target (or Kroger or Wal-Mart), the buyer "swipes" the card through a special terminal, and the buyer's bank balance is automatically decreased. Target's Cash account is increased immediately. Target doesn't have to deposit a check and wonder if it will bounce. With a debit card there is no third party, such as VISA or MasterCard, so there is no Bankcard Discount Expense.

Summary Problem 1

Monarch Map Company's balance sheet at December 31, 2007, reported the following:

Accounts receivable	$60,000
Allowance for uncollectible accounts	2,000

Requirements

1. How much of the receivable did Monarch expect to collect? Stated differently, what was the net realizable value of these receivables?

2. Journalize, without explanations, 2008 entries for Monarch:
   a. Total estimated Uncollectible-Account Expense was $2,400 for the first three quarters of the year, based on the percent-of-sales method.
   b. Write-offs of accounts receivable totaled $2,700.
   c. December 31, 2008, aging of receivables indicates that $2,200 of the receivables is uncollectible.

   Prepare a T-account for Allowance for Uncollectible Accounts, as follows:

Allowance for Uncollectible Accounts			
		Dec. 31, 2007 Bal.	2,000
2008 Write-offs	?	2008 Expense	?
		Bal. before Adj.	
		Dec. 31, 2008 Adj.	?
		Dec. 31, 2008 Bal.	2,200

   Post all three transactions to the allowance account.

3. Report Monarch's receivables and related allowance on the December 31, 2008, balance sheet. Accounts receivable total $63,000.
   What is the net realizable value of receivables at December 31, 2008? How much is uncollectible-account expense for 2008?

Solution

Requirement 1

Net realizable value of receivables ($60,000 − $2,000)	$58,000

Requirement 2

(a) Uncollectible-Account Expense	2,400	
Allowance for Uncollectible Accounts		2,400
(b) Allowance for Uncollectible Accounts	2,700	
Accounts Receivable		2,700
(c) Uncollectible-Account Expense ($2,200 − $1,700)	500	
Allowance for Uncollectible Accounts		500

Allowance for Uncollectible Accounts

		Dec. 31, 2007 Bal.	2,000
2008 Write-offs	2,700	2008 Expense	2,400
		Bal. before Adj.	1,700
		Dec. 31, 2008 Adj.	500
		Dec. 31, 2008 Bal.	2,200

Requirement 3

Accounts receivable	$63,000
Less: Allowance for uncollectible accounts	(2,200)
Accounts receivable, net	$60,800
Uncollectible-account expense for 2008 ($2,400 + $500)	$ 2,900

Notes Receivable: An Overview

Notes receivable are more formal than accounts receivable. The debtor signs a promissory note as evidence of the transaction. Before launching into the accounting, let's define the special terms used for notes receivable.

- **Promissory note:** A written promise to pay a specified amount of money at a particular future date.
- **Maker of the note (debtor):** The entity that signs the note and promises to pay the required amount; the maker of the note is the *debtor.*
- **Payee of the note (creditor):** The entity to whom the maker promises future payment; the payee of the note is the *creditor.*
- **Principal:** The amount loaned out by the payee and borrowed by the maker of the note.
- **Interest:** The revenue to the payee for loaning money; interest is expense to the debtor.
- **Interest period:** The period of time during which interest is computed. It extends from the original date of the note to the maturity date. Also called the **note term,** or simply the **time period.**
- **Interest rate:** The percentage rate of interest specified by the note. Interest rates are almost always stated for a period of one year. A 9% note means that the amount of interest for *one year* is 9% of the note's principal.
- **Maturity date:** The date when final payment of the note is due. Also called the **due date.**
- **Maturity value:** The sum of the principal plus interest due at maturity.

Exhibit 8-4 illustrates a promissory note. Study it carefully.

EXHIBIT 8-4 **A Promissory Note**

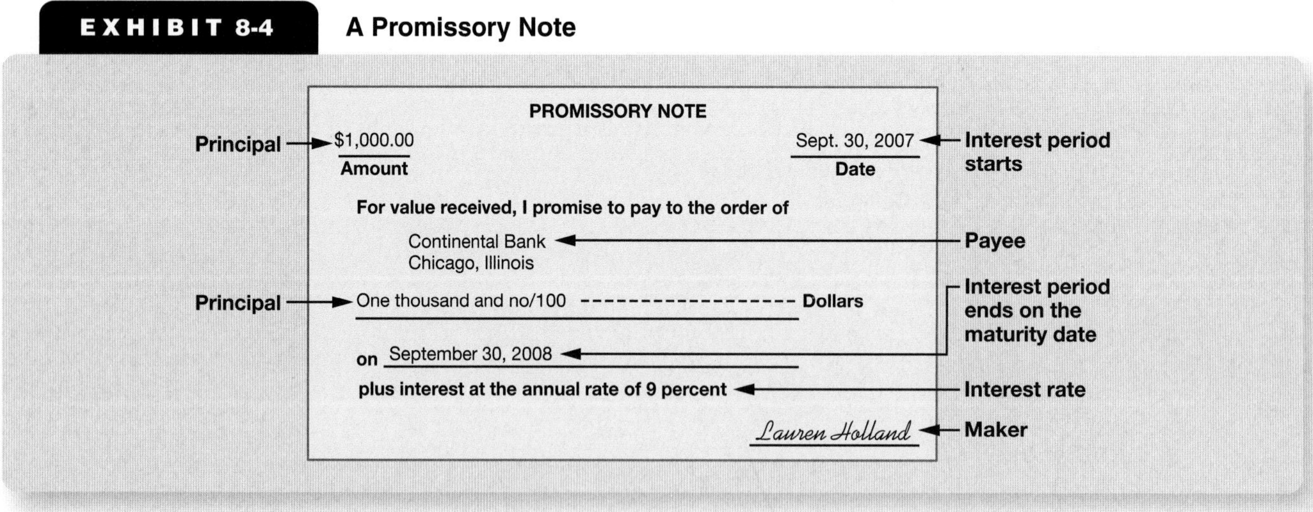
PROMISSORY NOTE

$1,000.00 Amount — Sept. 30, 2007 Date

For value received, I promise to pay to the order of

Continental Bank
Chicago, Illinois

One thousand and no/100 ------------------ Dollars

on September 30, 2008

plus interest at the annual rate of 9 percent

Lauren Holland

Identifying Maturity Date

Some notes specify the maturity date, as shown in Exhibit 8-4. Other notes state the period of the note in days or months. When the period is given in months, the note's maturity date falls on the same day of the month as the date the note was issued. A six-month note dated February 16 matures on August 16.

When the period is given in days, the maturity date is determined by counting the days from the date of issue. A 120-day note dated September 14, 2007, matures on January 12, 2008, as shown here:

Month	Number of Days	Cumulative Total
Sep. 2007	30 – 14 = 16	16
Oct. 2007	31	47
Nov. 2007	30	77
Dec. 2007	31	108
Jan. 2008	12	120

In counting the days remaining for a note, remember to:

- count the maturity date
- omit the date the note was issued

Computing Interest on a Note

The formula for computing the interest is:

AMOUNT OF INTEREST	=	PRINCIPAL	×	INTEREST RATE	×	TIME

Using the data in Exhibit 8-4, Continental Bank computes interest revenue for one year as:

AMOUNT OF INTEREST	=	PRINCIPAL	×	INTEREST RATE	×	TIME
$90		$1,000		0.09		1 yr

The maturity value of the note is $1,090 ($1,000 principal + $90 interest). The time element is 1 because the note's term is 1 year.

When the term of a note is stated in months, we compute the interest based on the 12-month year. Interest on a $2,000 note at 10% for three months is computed as:

AMOUNT OF INTEREST	=	PRINCIPAL	×	INTEREST RATE	×	TIME
$50		$2,000		0.10		3 / 12

When the interest period is stated in days, we sometimes compute interest based on a 360-day year rather than on a 365-day year.[2] The interest on a $5,000 note at 12% for 60 days can be computed as:

AMOUNT OF INTEREST	=	PRINCIPAL	×	INTEREST RATE	×	TIME
$100		$5,000		0.12		60 / 360

Keep in mind that interest rates are stated as an annual rate. Therefore, the time in the interest formula should also be expressed in terms of a year.

[2]A 360-day year eliminates some rounding, which is consistent with our use of whole-dollar amounts throughout this book.

Accounting for Notes Receivable

Recording Notes Receivable—Three Cases

4 Account for notes receivable

Consider the loan agreement shown in Exhibit 8-4. Lauren Holland signs the note, and Continental Bank gives Holland $1,000 cash. At maturity, Holland pays the bank $1,090 ($1,000 principal plus $90 interest). The bank's entries are:

Loan Out Money

2007			
Sep. 30	Note Receivable—L. Holland	1,000	
	Cash		1,000
	Loaned out money.		
2008			
Sep. 30	Cash	1,090	
	Note Receivable—L. Holland		1,000
	Interest Revenue ($1,000 × 0.09 × 1)		90
	Collected note receivable.		

Some companies sell merchandise in exchange for notes receivable. Assume that on October 20, 2009, General Electric sells household appliances for $15,000 to Dorman Builders. Dorman signs a 90-day promissory note at 10% annual interest. General Electric's entries to record the sale and collection from Dorman are:

Sell On A Note Receivable

2009			
Oct. 20	Note Receivable—Dorman Builders	15,000	
	Sales Revenue		15,000
	Made a sale.		
2010			
Jan. 18	Cash	15,375	
	Note Receivable—Dorman Builders		15,000
	Interest Revenue ($15,000 × 0.10 × 90/360)		375
	Collected note receivable.		

A company may accept a note receivable from a trade customer who fails to pay an account receivable. The customer signs a promissory note and gives it to the creditor. Suppose Sports Club cannot pay Hoffman Supply. Hoffman may accept a one-year, $4,000 note receivable, with 9% interest, from Sports Club. Hoffman's entry is:

Note Receivable On Account

2009			
Oct. 1	Note Receivable—Sports Club	4,000	
	Accounts Receivable—Sports Club		4,000
	Received a note on account.		

Accruing Interest Revenue

A note receivable may be outstanding at the end of an accounting period. The interest revenue earned on the note up to year-end is part of that year's earnings. Recall that interest revenue is earned over time, not just when cash is received.

Let's continue with the Hoffman Supply note receivable from Sports Club. Hoffman's accounting period ends December 31.

- How much of the total interest revenue does Hoffman earn in 2009 (for October, November, and December)?

$$\$4,000 \times .09 \times 3/12 = \$90$$

Hoffman makes this adjusting entry at December 31, 2009:

2009			
Dec. 31	Interest Receivable ($4,000 × 0.09 × 3/12)	90	
	Interest Revenue		90
	Accrued interest revenue.		

- How much interest revenue does Hoffman earn in 2010 (for January through September)?

$$\$4,000 \times .09 \times 9/12 = \$270$$

On the note's maturity date, Hoffman makes this entry:

2010			
Sep. 30	Cash [$4,000 + ($4,000 × 0.09)]	4,360	
	Note Receivable—Sports Club		4,000
	Interest Receivable ($4,000 × 0.09 × 3/12)		90
	Interest Revenue ($4,000 × 0.09 × 9/12)		270
	Collected note receivable plus interest.		

These entries assign the correct amount of interest to each year.

A company holding a note may need cash before the note matures. A procedure for selling the note, called discounting a note receivable, appears in the chapter Appendix 8A.

Dishonored Notes Receivable

If the maker of a note doesn't pay at maturity, the maker **dishonors** (**defaults on**) the note. Because the note has expired, it is no longer in force. But the debtor still owes the payee. The payee can transfer the note receivable amount to Accounts Receivable. Suppose Rubinstein Jewelers has a 6-month, 10% note receivable for $1,200 from Mark Adair, and Adair defaults. Rubinstein Jewelers will record the default as follows:

Feb. 3	Accounts Receivable—M. Adair	1,260	
	Note Receivable—M. Adair		1,200
	Interest Revenue ($1,200 × 0.10 × 6/12)		60
	Recorded a dishonored note receivable.		

Rubinstein will then bill Adair for the account receivable.

Reporting Receivables on the Balance Sheet

5 Report receivables on the balance sheet

On page 411 we showed two ways In Motion T-Shirts could report its accounts receivable, repeated here:

Balance Sheet (partial):	
Accounts receivable	$2,800
Less: Allowance for uncollectible accounts	(400)
Accounts receivable, net	$2,400
or	
Accounts receivable, net of allowance for doubtful accounts of $400	$2,400

Most companies use the second approach, but either is acceptable.

Computers and Accounts Receivable

Accounting for receivables by a company like M&M Mars requires thousands of postings for credit sales and cash collections. Manual accounting cannot keep up. However, Accounts Receivable can be computerized. At M&M Mars the order entry, shipping, and billing departments work together, as shown in Exhibit 8-5.

EXHIBIT 8-5 **Order Entry, Shipping, and Billing Working Together at M&M Mars**

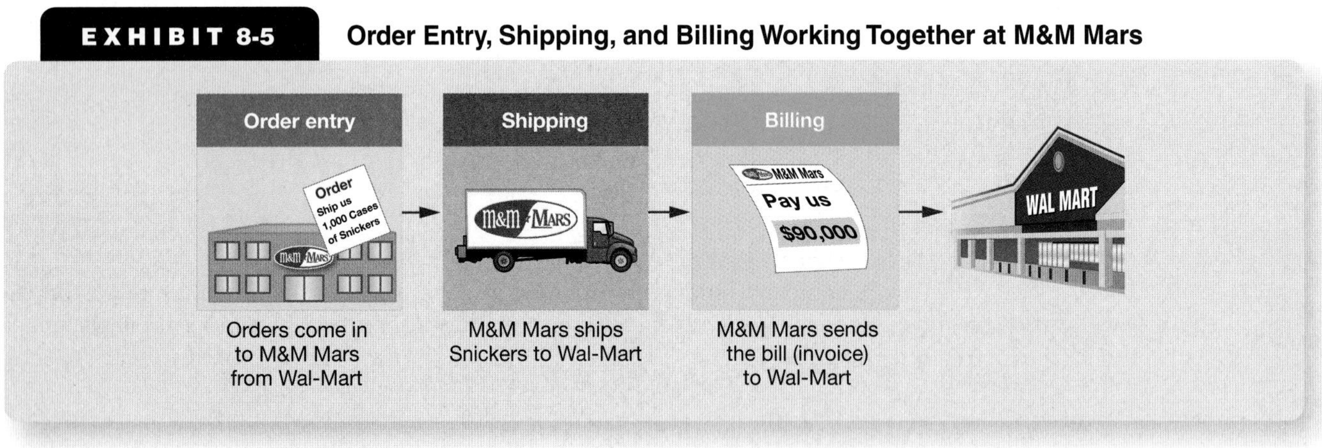

Using Accounting Information for Decision Making

The balance sheet lists assets in order of liquidity (closeness to cash):

- Cash comes first because it is the liquid asset.
- Short-term investments come next because they are almost as liquid as cash.

- Current receivables are less liquid than short-term investments because the company must collect the receivables.
- Merchandise inventory is less liquid than receivables because the goods must first be sold.

The balance sheet of In Motion T-Shirts provides an example in Exhibit 8-6. Focus on the current assets at December 31, 2007.

EXHIBIT 8-6 **In Motion T-Shirts Balance Sheet**

Assets	December 31, 2007	2006
Current assets:		
Cash	$ 800	$ 400
Short-term investments	1,500	300
Accounts receivable, net of allowance for doubtful accounts of $400 in 2007 and $300 in 2006	2,400	2,600
Inventory	800	600
Total current assets	5,500	3,900
Liabilities		
Current liabilities:		
Total current liabilities	$4,400	$2,900

Balance-sheet data become more useful by showing the relationships among assets, liabilities, and revenues. Let's examine two important ratios.

Acid-Test (or Quick) Ratio

6 Use the acid-test ratio and days' sales in receivables to evaluate a company

In Chapter 4, we discussed the current ratio, which measures ability to pay current liabilities with current assets. A more stringent measure of ability to pay current liabilities is the **acid-test** (or **quick**) **ratio.** The acid-test ratio reveals whether the entity can pay all its current liabilities if they come due immediately:

For In Motion T-Shirts (Exhibit 8-6)

$$\text{Acid-test ratio} = \frac{\text{Cash} + \begin{array}{c}\text{Short-term}\\\text{investments}\end{array} + \begin{array}{c}\text{Net current}\\\text{receivables}\end{array}}{\text{Total current liabilities}} = \frac{\$800 + \$1{,}500 + \$2{,}400}{\$4{,}400} = 1.07$$

The higher the acid-test ratio, the more able the business is to pay its current liabilities. In Motion's acid-test ratio of 1.07 means that In Motion has $1.07 of quick assets to pay each $1 of current liabilities. This is a strong position.

What is an acceptable acid-test ratio? That depends on the industry. Wal-Mart operates smoothly with an acid-test ratio of less than 0.20. Several things make this possible: Wal-Mart collects cash rapidly and has almost no receivables. The acid-test ratios for most department stores cluster about 0.80, while travel agencies average 1.10. In general, an acid-test ratio of 1.00 is considered safe.

Days' Sales in Receivables

After making a credit sale, the next step is to collect the receivable. **Days' sales in receivables**, also called the **collection period**, indicates how many days it takes to collect the average level of receivables. The shorter the collection period, the more quickly the organization can use its cash. The longer the collection period, the less cash is available for operations. Days' sales in receivables can be computed in two steps, as follows:[3]

For In Motion T-Shirts (Exhibit 8-6)

1. $$\text{One day's sales} = \frac{\text{Net sales (or Total revenues)}}{365 \text{ days}} = \frac{\$22{,}600^*}{365} = \$62 \text{ per day}$$

2. $$\text{Days' sales in average accounts receivable} = \frac{\text{Average net accounts receivable}}{\text{One day's sales}} = \frac{\left(\text{Beginning net receivables} + \text{Ending net receivables}\right) \div 2}{\text{One day's sales}}$$

$$= \frac{(\$2{,}400 + \$2{,}600)/2}{\$62} = 40 \text{ days}$$

*From In Motion's 2007 income statement, which is not reproduced here.

On average, it takes In Motion T-Shirts 40 days to collect its accounts receivable. The length of the collection period depends on the credit terms of the sale. For example, sales on net 30 terms should be collected within approximately 30 days. When there is a discount, such as 2/10, net 30, the collection period may be shorter. Credit terms of net 45 result in a longer collection period.

Investors and creditors do not evaluate a company on the basis of one or two ratios. Instead, they analyze all the information available. Then they stand back and ask, "What is our overall impression of this company?" We present all the financial ratios in Chapter 15. By the time you get to that point of your study, you'll have an overall view of the company.

[3]Days' sales in average receivables can also be computed in this one step:

$$\text{Days' sales in average receivables} = \frac{\text{Average net receivables}}{\text{Net sales}} \times 365$$

Decision Guidelines

ACCOUNTING FOR RECEIVABLES

The Decision Guidelines feature summarizes some key decisions for receivables.

Accounting for receivables is the same for In Motion T-Shirts as for a large company like M&M Mars. Suppose you decide that In Motion will sell on account, as most other companies do. How should you account for your receivables? These guidelines show the way.

Decision	Guidelines
ACCOUNTS RECEIVABLE How much of our receivables will we collect?	Less than the full amount of the receivables because we cannot collect from some customers.
How to report receivables at their net realizable value?	1. Use the *allowance method* to account for uncollectible receivables. Set up the allowance for Uncollectible Accounts. 2. Estimate uncollectibles by the a. *Percent-of-sales method* (income-statement approach) b. *Aging-of-accounts method* (balance-sheet approach) 3. Write off uncollectible receivables as they prove uncollectible. 4. $\text{Net accounts receivable} = \text{Accounts Receivable} - \text{Allowance for Uncollectible Accounts}$
Is there a simpler way to account for uncollectible receivables?	Yes, but it's unacceptable for most companies. The *direct write-off-method* uses no Allowance for Uncollectibles. It simply debits Uncollectible-Account Expense and credits a customer's Accounts Receivable to write it off when it has proved uncollectible. This method is acceptable only when uncollectibles are insignificant.
NOTES RECEIVABLE What two other accounts are related to notes receivable?	Notes receivable are related to: • Interest Revenue. • Interest Receivable (Interest revenue earned but not yet collected).
How to compute the interest on a note receivable?	**Amount of interest = Principal × Interest Rate × Time**
RECEIVABLES IN GENERAL How can you use receivables to evaluate a company's financial position?	• $\text{Acid-test ratio} = \dfrac{\text{Cash} + \text{Short-term investments} + \text{Net current receivables}}{\text{Total current liabilities}}$ • $\text{Day's sales in average receivables} = \dfrac{\text{Average net accounts receivable}}{\text{One day's sales}}$
How to report receivables on the balance sheet?	Accounts (or Notes) Receivable .... \$XXX Less: Allowance for uncollectible accounts ..... (X) Accounts (or notes) receivable, net .... \$ XX

Summary Problem 2

Suppose First Fidelity Bank engaged in the following transactions:

2007	
Apr. 1	Loaned out $8,000 to Bland Co. Received a six-month, 10% note.
Oct. 1	Collected the Bland note at maturity.
Dec. 1	Loaned $6,000 to Flores, Inc., on a 180-day, 12% note.
Dec. 31	Accrued interest revenue on the Flores note.
2008	
May 30	Collected the Flores note at maturity.

First Fidelity's accounting period ends on December 31.

Requirements

Explanations are not needed. Use a 360-day year to compute interest.

1. Record the 2007 transactions on April 1 through December 1 on First Fidelity's books.
2. Make the adjusting entry needed on December 31, 2007.
3. Record the May 30, 2008, collection of the Flores note.

Solution

Requirement 1

2007			
Apr. 1	Note Receivable—Bland Co.	8,000	
	Cash		8,000
Oct. 1	Cash ($8,000 + $400)	8,400	
	Note Receivable—Bland Co.		8,000
	Interest Revenue ($8,000 × 0.10 × 6/12)		400

Requirement 2

2007			
Dec. 1	Note Receivable—Flores, Inc.	6,000	
	Cash		6,000
31	Interest Receivable	60	
	Interest Revenue ($6,000 × 0.12 × 30/360)		60

Requirement 3

2008			
May 30	Cash [$6,000 + ($6,000 × .12 × 180/360)]	6,360	
	Note Receivable—Flores, Inc.		6,000
	Interest Receivable		60
	Interest Revenue ($6,000 × 0.12 × 150/360)		300

Review Receivables

Accounting Vocabulary

Acid-Test Ratio
Ratio of the sum of cash plus short-term investments plus net current receivables, to total current liabilities. Tells whether the entity could pay all its current liabilities if they came due immediately. Also called the **quick ratio**.

Aging-of-Accounts Methods
A way to estimate bad debts by analyzing individual accounts receivable according to the length of time they have been receivable from the customer. Also called the **balance-sheet approach**.

Allowance for Doubtful Accounts
A contra account, related to accounts receivable, that holds the estimated amount of collection losses. Also called **Allowance for Uncollectible Accounts**.

Allowance for Uncollectible Accounts
A contra account, related to accounts receivable, that holds the estimated amount of collection losses. Also called **Allowance for Doubtful Accounts**.

Allowance Method
A method of recording collection losses on the basis of estimates instead of waiting to see which customers the company will not collect from.

Bad-Debt Expense
Cost to the seller of extending credit. Arises from the failure to collect from credit customers. Also called **doubtful-account expense** or **uncollectible-account expense**.

Balance-Sheet Approach
A way to estimate bad debts by analyzing individual accounts receivable according to the length of time they have been receivable from the customer. Also called the **aging-of-accounts methods**.

Collection Period
Ratio of average net accounts receivable to one day s sales. Tells how many days' sales it takes to collect the average level of receivables. Also called the **days' sales in receivables**.

Creditor
The party to a credit transaction who sells goods or a service and obtains a receivable.

Days' Sales in Receivables
Ratio of average net accounts receivable to one day's sales. Tells how many days' sales it takes to collect the average level of receivables. Also called the **collection period**.

Debtor
The party to a credit transaction who makes a purchase and has a payable.

Default on a Note
Failure of a note's maker to pay a note receivable at maturity. Also called **dishonor of a note**.

Direct Write-Off Method
A method of accounting for uncollectible receivables, in which the company waits until the credit department decides that a customer's account receivable is uncollectible and then debits Uncollectible-Account Expense and credits the customer's Account Receivable.

Discounting a Note Receivable
Selling a note receivable before its maturity date.

Dishonor of a Note
Failure of a note's maker to pay a note receivable at maturity. Also called **default on a note**.

Doubtful-Account Expense
Cost to the seller of extending credit. Arises from the failure to collect from credit customers. Also called **uncollectible-account expense** or **bad-debt expense**.

Due Date
The date when final payment of the note is due. Also called the **maturity date**.

Income-Statement Approach
A method of estimating uncollectible receivables that calculates uncollectible-account expense. Also called the **percent-of-sales method**.

Interest
The revenue to the payee for loaning money; the expense to the debtor.

Interest Period
The period of time during which interest is computed. It extends from the original date of the note to the maturity date. Also called the **note term,** or simply **time period**.

Interest Rate
The percentage rate of interest specified by the note. Interest rates are almost always stated for a period of one year.

Maker of a Note
The person or business that signs the note and promises to pay the amount required by the note agreement: the debtor.

Maturity Date
The date when final payment of the note is due. Also called the **due date**.

Maturity Value
The sum of the principal plus interest due at maturity.

Note Term
The period of time during which interest is computed. It extends from the original date of the note to the maturity date. Also called the **interest period,** or simply **time period**.

Payee of a Note
The person or business to whom the maker of a note promises future payment: the creditor.

Percent-of-Sales Method
A method of estimating uncollectible receivables that calculates uncollectible-account expense. Also called the **income-statement approach**.

Principal
The amount loaned out by the payee and borrowed by the maker of the note.

Principal Amount
The amount loaned out by the payee and borrowed by the maker of the note.

Promissory Note
A written promise to pay a specified amount of money at a particular future date.

Quick Ratio
Ratio of the sum of cash plus short-term investments plus net current receivables, to total current liabilities. Tells whether the entity could pay all its current liabilities if they came due immediately. Also called the **acid-test ratio**.

Receivables
Monetary claims against a business or an individual.

Time Period
The period of time during which interest is computed. It extends from the original date of the note to the maturity date. Also called the **note term** or **interest period**.

Uncollectible-Account Expense
Cost to the seller of extending credit. Arises from the failure to collect from credit customers. Also called **doubtful-account expense** or **bad-debt expense**.

Quick Check

1. With good internal controls, the person who handles cash can also
   a. Account for cash receipts from customers
   b. Account for cash payments
   c. Issue credits to customers for sales returns
   d. None of the above

2. "Bad debts" are the same as
   a. Uncollectible accounts
   b. Doubtful accounts
   c. Neither of the above
   d. Both a and b

3. Which method of estimating uncollectible receivables focuses on Uncollectible-Account Expense for the income statement?
   a. Percent-of-sales approach
   b. Aging-of-accounts approach
   c. Net-realizable-value approach
   d. All of the above.

4. Your company uses the allowance method to account for uncollectible receivables. At the beginning of the year, Allowance for Uncollectibles had a credit balance of $1,100. During the year you recorded Uncollectible-Account Expense of $3,000 and wrote off bad receivables of $2,100. What is your year-end balance in Allowance for Uncollectibles?
   a. $1,000
   b. $2,000
   c. $3,100
   d. $3,200

5. Your ending balance of Accounts Receivable is $20,000. Use the data in the preceding question to compute the net realizable value of Accounts Receivable at year-end.
   a. $18,000
   b. $19,000
   c. $20,000
   d. $21,000

6. What is wrong with the direct write-off method of accounting for uncollectibles?
   a. The direct write-off method does not set up an allowance for uncollectibles.
   b. The direct write-off method overstates assets on the balance sheet.
   c. The direct write-off method does not match expenses against revenue very well.
   d. All of the above.

7. At December 31, you have a $10,000 note receivable from a customer. Interest of 8% has accrued for 6 months on the note. What will your financial statements report for this situation?
   a. Nothing, because you haven't received the cash yet.
   b. Balance sheet will report the note receivable of $10,000.
   c. Balance sheet will report the note receivable of $10,000 and interest receivable of $400.
   d. Income statement will report a note receivable of $10,000.

8. Return to the data in the preceding question. What will the income statement report for this situation?

   a. Nothing, because you haven't received the cash yet

   b. Interest revenue of $400

   c. Note receivable of $10,000

   d. Both b and c

9. At year-end, your company has cash of $10,000, receivables of $50,000, inventory of $40,000, and prepaid expenses totaling $5,000. Liabilities of $60,000 must be paid next year. What is your acid-test ratio?

   a. 0.83

   b. 1.00

   c. 1.67

   d. Cannot be determined from the data given

10. Return to the data in the preceding question. A year ago receivables stood at $70,000, and sales for the current year total $730,000. How many days did it take you to collect your average level of receivables?

    a. 45

    b. 35

    c. 30

    d. 20

Answers are given after Assess Your Progress (p. 451).

Assess Your Progress

Short Exercises

Internal control over the collection of receivables
1

S8-1 Jack Delaney is the accountant responsible for customer accounts in the accounts receivable subsidiary ledger. What duty will a good internal control system withhold from Delaney? Why? (p. 407)

Internal control over the credit department

S8-2 What job must be withheld from a company's credit department in order to safeguard its cash? If the credit department does perform this job, what can a credit department employee do to hurt the company? (pp. 408–409)

Applying the allowance method (percent-of-sales) to account for uncollectibles
2

S8-3 During its first year of operations, Signature Lamp Company earned revenue of $350,000 on account. Industry experience suggests that bad debts will amount to 2% of revenues. At December 31, 2008, accounts receivable total $40,000. The company uses the allowance method to account for uncollectibles.

1. Journalize Signature's uncollectible-account expense using the percent-of-sales method. (p. 412)
2. Show how to report accounts receivable on the balance sheet at December 31, 2008. Follow the first reporting format illustrated on page 411.

Applying the allowance method (percent-of-sales) to account for uncollectibles
2

S8-4 During 2009, Signature Lamp Company completed these transactions:

1. Sales revenue on account, $400,000 (ignore cost of goods sold). (p. 410)
2. Collections on account, $420,000. (p. 410)
3. Write-offs of uncollectibles, $6,000. (p. 414)
4. Uncollectible-account expense, 2% of sales revenue. (pp. 411–412)

Journalize Signature's 2009 transactions.

Applying the allowance method (aging-of-accounts) to account for uncollectibles
2

S8-5 Interstate Marble Importers had the following balances at December 31, 2007, before the year-end adjustments:

Accounts Receivable		Allowance for Uncollectible Accounts	
74,000			2,000

The aging of accounts receivable yields these data:

	Age of Accounts Receivable		
	0–60 Days	Over 60 Days	Total Receivables
Accounts receivable............	$70,000	$4,000	$74,000
Percent uncollectible	×2%	×20%	

continued . . .

1. Journalize Interstate's entry to adjust the allowance account to its correct balance at December 31, 2007. (pp. 413–414)
2. Prepare a T-account to compute the ending balance of Allowance for Uncollectible Accounts. (p. 413)

Applying the direct write-off method to account for uncollectibles
3

S8-6 Bob Rassler is an attorney in Los Angeles. Rassler uses the direct write-off method to account for uncollectible receivables.

At May 31, Rassler's accounts receivable totaled $14,000. During June, he earned revenue of $20,000 on account and collected $19,000 on account. He also wrote off uncollectible receivables of $2,000.

1. Use the direct write-off method to journalize Rassler's write-off of the uncollectible receivables. (pp. 415–416)
2. What is Rassler's balance of Accounts Receivable at June 30? Does he expect to collect all of this amount? Explain. (pp. 415–416)

Collecting a receivable previously written off
2

S8-7 University Cycle Shop had trouble collecting its account receivable from Lance Emmert. On January 19, University finally wrote off Emmert's $600 account receivable. University turned the account over to an attorney, who hounded Emmert for the rest of the year. On December 31, Emmert sent a $600 check to University Cycle Shop with a note that said, "Here's your money. Please call off your bloodhound!"

Journalize for University Cycle Shop:

Jan. 19	Write-off of Emmert's account against Allowance for Uncollectible Accounts. (pp. 415–416)
Dec. 31	Reinstatement of Emmert's account. (pp. 415–416)
31	Collection of cash from Emmert. (pp. 415–416)

Recording credit-card and bankcard sales
3

S8-8 Restaurants do a large volume of business by credit cards and bankcards. Suppose a Chili's restaurant had these transactions on a Saturday:

American Express credit-card sales..............	$10,000
VISA bankcard sales....................................	8,000

Suppose American Express charges merchants 2% and VISA charges $1\frac{1}{2}$%. Record these sale transactions for the restaurant. (p. 417)

Computing interest amounts on notes receivable
4

S8-9 For each of the following notes receivable, compute the amount of interest revenue earned during 2008. Use a 360-day year, and round to the nearest dollar. (pp. 421–422)

	Principal	Interest Rate	Interest Period During 2008
Note 1	$ 50,000	10%	3 months
Note 2	10,000	9%	60 days
Note 3	15,000	12%	75 days
Note 4	100,000	8%	6 months

Accounting for a note receivable
4

S8-10 Lantana Bank & Trust Company lent $100,000 to Ben Milam on a 90-day, 10% note. Record the following transactions for the bank (explanations are not required):

a. Lending the money on May 6. (pp. 421–422)

b. Collecting the principal and interest at maturity. Specify the date. For the computation of interest, use a 360-day year. (pp. 421–422)

Reporting receivables and other accounts in the financial statements
5

S8-11 Concentra Medical Center included the following items in its financial statements:

Allowance for doubtful accounts	$ 120	Service revenue	$14,400
Cash	1,150	Other assets	350
Accounts receivable	2,580	Cost of services sold and	
Accounts payable	1,020	other expenses	12,800
Notes payable	3,280		

1. How much net income did Concentra earn for the month? (p. 22)
2. Show two ways Concentra can report receivables on its classified balance sheet. (p. 424)

Using the acid-test ratio and days' sales in receivables to evaluate a company
6

S8-12 Avant Garde Clothiers reported the following items at February 28, 2008 (amounts in thousands, with last year's—2007—amounts also given as needed):

Accounts payable	$ 400	Accounts receivable, net:	
Cash	210	February 28, 2008	$ 220
Inventories:		February 28, 2007	150
February 28, 2008	190	Cost of goods sold	1,200
February 28, 2007	160	Short-term investments	160
Net sales revenue	2,190	Other current assets	90
Long-term assets	410	Other current liabilities	140
Long-term liabilities	170		

Compute Avant Garde's (a) acid-test ratio and (b) days' sales in average receivables for 2008. Evaluate each ratio value as strong or weak. Avant Garde sells on terms of net 30. (pp. 425–426)

Computing key ratios for a company
6

S8-13 Use the data in Short Exercise 8-12 to compute the following 2008 ratios for Avant Garde Clothiers. Round decimals to two places.

a. Current ratio (p. 214)

b. Debt ratio (p. 214)

c. Gross profit percentage (p. 276)

d. Rate of inventory turnover (p. 276)

Exercises

Identifying and correcting an internal control weakness

E8-14 Suppose Toyota is opening a regional office in St. Louis. Lesa Carter, the office manager, is designing the internal control system. Carter proposes the following procedures for credit checks on new customers, sales on account, cash collections, and write-offs of uncollectible receivables.

- The credit department runs a credit check on all customers who apply for credit. When an account proves uncollectible, the credit department authorizes the write-off of the account receivable.
- Cash receipts come into the credit department, which separates the cash received from the customer remittance slips. The credit department lists all cash receipts by customer name and amount of cash received.
- The cash goes to the treasurer for deposit in the bank. The remittance slips go to the accounting department for posting to customer accounts.
- The controller compares the daily deposit slip to the total amount posted to customer accounts. Both amounts must agree.

Identify the internal control weakness in this situation, and propose a way to correct it. (pp. 407–409)

Using the allowance method for bad debts (percent-of-sales)

E8-15 At September 30, Eagle Mountain Flagpoles had Accounts Receivable of $28,000 and Allowance for Uncollectible Accounts of $1,000. During October, Eagle Mountain recorded

- Sales of $180,000 ($160,000 on account; $20,000 for cash)
- Collections on account, $130,000
- Uncollectible-account expense, estimated as 2% of credit sales
- Write-offs of uncollectible receivables, $2,400

Requirements

1. Journalize sales, collections, uncollectible-account expense by the allowance method (percent-of-sales method), and write-offs of uncollectibles during October. (pp. 411–412, 415–416)
2. Prepare T-accounts to show the ending balances in Accounts Receivable and Allowance for Uncollectible Accounts. Compute *net* accounts receivable at October 31. How much does Eagle Mountain expect to collect? (pp. 418–420)

Using the direct write-off method for bad debts

3

E8-16 Refer to Exercise 8-15.

Requirements

1. Record uncollectible-account expense for October using the direct write-off method. (pp. 415–416)
2. What balance of accounts receivable does Eagle Mountain report on its Oct. 31 balance sheet under the direct write-off method? Does it expect to collect the full amount? (pp. 415–416)

Using the aging method to estimate bad debts

E8-17 At December 31, 2008, the Accounts Receivable balance of Easy Card is $300,000. The Allowance for Doubtful Accounts has a $8,900 credit balance. Easy Card prepares the following aging schedule for its accounts receivable:

continued . . .

Accounts Receivable	Age of Accounts			
	1–30 Days	31–60 Days	61–90 Days	Over 90 Days
$300,000..........................	$140,000	$80,000	$70,000	$10,000
Estimated percent uncollectible	0.5%	2.0%	6.0%	50%

Requirements

1. Journalize the year-end adjusting entry for doubtful accounts on the basis of the aging schedule. Show the T-account for the Allowance at December 31, 2008. (p. 413)
2. Show how Easy Card will report Accounts Receivable on its December 31, 2008 balance sheet. (pp. 413–414)

Sales, write-offs, and bad-debt recovery
2

E8-18 High Performance Cell Phones sold $20,000 of merchandise to Avery Trucking Company on account. Avery fell on hard times and paid only $6,000 of the account receivable. After repeated attempts to collect, High Performance finally wrote off its accounts receivable from Avery. Six months later High Performance received Avery's check for $14,000 with a note apologizing for the late payment.

Journalize for High Performance:

- Sale on account, $20,000. (Ignore cost of goods sold.) (p. 410)
- Collection of $6,000 on account. (p. 410)
- Write-off of the remaining portion of the Avery account receivable. High Performance uses the allowance method for uncollectibles. (p. 414)
- Reinstatement of Avery's account receivable. (p. 414)
- Collection in full from Avery, $14,000. (pp. 415–416)

Computing note receivable amounts

E8-19 On April 30, 2007, Synergy Bank loaned $80,000 to Kim Sperry on a one-year, 9% note.

Requirements

1. Compute the interest for the years ended December 31, 2007 and 2008 for the Sperry note. (p. 421)
2. Which party has a (p. 420)
   a. Note receivable? c. Interest revenue?
   b. Note payable? d. Interest expense?
3. How much in total would Sperry pay the bank if he pays off the note early—say, on November 30, 2007? (p. 421)

Recording notes receivable and accruing interest revenue

E8-20 Journalize the following transactions of Mediterranean Importers, which ends its accounting year on June 30: (pp. 421–423)

Apr. 1	Loaned $10,000 cash to Carroll Fadal on a one-year, 8% note.
June 6	Sold goods to Turf Masters, receiving a 90-day, 10% note for $9,000.
30	Made a single compound entry to accrue interest revenue on both notes. Use a 360-day year for interest computations.

Recording bankcard sales and a note receivable, and accruing interest revenue
4

E8-21 Record the following transactions in the journal of Top Dog Running Shoes: (pp. 421–423)

2008	
Feb. 12	Recorded MasterCard bankcard sales of $100,000, less a 2% discount.
Aug. 1	Loaned $20,000 to Jean Porter, an executive with the company, on a one-year, 12% note.
Dec. 31	Accrued interest revenue on the Porter note.
2009	
Aug. 1	Collected the maturity value of the Porter note.

Recording note receivable transactions

E8-22 High-Pressure Steam Cleaning performs service on account. When a customer account becomes four months old, High-Pressure converts the account to a note receivable. During 2008, the company completed these transactions:

June 29	Performed service on account for Montclair Club, $15,000. (p. 410)
Nov. 1	Received a $15,000, 60-day, 10% note from Montclair Club in satisfaction of its past-due account receivable. (pp. 422–423)
Dec. 31	Collected the Montclair Club note at maturity. (pp. 422–423)

Requirements

Record the transactions in High-Pressure's journal.

Evaluating ratio data
6

E8-23 Cherokee Carpets reported the following amounts in its 2009 financial statements. The 2008 figures are given for comparison.

	2009		2008	
Current assets:				
Cash		$ 3,000		$ 10,000
Short-term investments		23,000		11,000
Accounts receivable	$60,000		$74,000	
Less: Allowance for uncollectibles	(7,000)	53,000	(6,000)	68,000
Inventory		192,000		189,000
Prepaid insurance		2,000		2,000
Total current assets		$273,000		$280,000
Total current liabilities		$104,000		$107,000
Net sales		$730,000		$732,000

continued . . .

Requirements

1. Determine whether Cherokee's acid-test ratio improved or deteriorated from 2008 to 2009. How does Cherokee's acid-test ratio compare with the industry average of 0.80? (p. 425)
2. Compare the days' sales in receivables for 2009 with Cherokee's credit terms of net 30. (p. 426)

Collection period for receivables

6

E8-24 Swift Media Sign Company sells on account. Recently, Swift reported these figures:

	2008	2007
Net sales	$600,060	$570,000
Receivables at end of year	42,800	38,200

Requirements

1. Compute Swift's average collection period on receivables during 2008. (p. 425)
2. Suppose Swift's normal credit terms for a sale on account are "2/10 net 30." How well does Swift's collection period compare to the company's credit terms? Is this good or bad for Swift? Explain. (p. 425)

Problems (Group A)

Controlling cash receipts from customers

1

P8-25A Mail Plus performs mailing services on account, so virtually all cash receipts arrive in the mail. Gina Star, the owner, has just returned from a meeting with new ideas for the business. Among other things, Star plans to institute stronger internal controls over cash receipts from customers.

Requirement

Assume you are Gina Star. Write a memo to outline procedures that will ensure (1) all cash receipts are deposited in the bank and (2) all cash receipts are posted as credits to customer accounts receivable. Use the following format for your memo. (p. 407)

MEMO

Date:

To:

From:

Subject:

Accounting for uncollectibles by the allowance and direct write-off methods

P8-26A On February 28, Tradewinds Sailing Supplies had a \$75,000 debit balance in Accounts Receivable and a \$2,200 credit balance in Allowance for Uncollectible Accounts. During March, Tradewinds made

- Sales on account, \$410,000
- Collections on account, \$419,000
- Write-offs of uncollectible receivables, \$7,000

Requirements

1. Record sales and collections on account. Then record uncollectible-account expense and write-offs of customer accounts using the *allowance* method. Uncollectible-account expense was estimated at 2% of credit sales. Show all March activity in Accounts Receivable, Allowance for Uncollectible Accounts, and Uncollectible-Account Expense (post to these T-accounts). (pp. 410, 411–412, 414)
2. Suppose Tradewinds used a different method to account for uncollectible receivables. Record sales and collections on account. Then record uncollectible-account expense for March using the *direct write-off* method. Post to Accounts Receivable and Uncollectible-Account Expense and show their balances at March 31. (pp. 415–416)
3. What amount of uncollectible-account expense would Tradewinds report on its March income statement under each of the two methods? Which amount better matches expense with revenue? Give your reason. (pp. 411–412, 415–416)
4. What amount of *net* accounts receivable would Tradewinds report on its March 31 balance sheet under each of the two methods? Which amount is more realistic? Give your reason. (pp. 415–416, 419)

Using the percent-of-sales and aging methods for uncollectibles

P8-27A At September 30, the accounts of Aguilar Outsourcing Solutions include the following:

Accounts Receivable	\$65,000
Allowance for Uncollectible Accounts (credit balance)	1,100

During the last quarter of 2009, Aguilar completed the following selected transactions:

Dec. 22	Wrote off accounts receivable as uncollectible: Transnet, \$300; Webvan, \$100; and Alpha Group, \$600.
Dec. 31	Recorded uncollectible-account expense based on the aging of receivables, as follows:

	Age of Accounts			
Accounts Receivable	1–30 Days	31–60 Days	61–90 Days	Over 90 Days
\$55,000	\$30,000	\$10,000	\$10,000	\$5,000
Estimated percent uncollectible	0.5%	1.0%	4%	50%

continued . . .

Requirements

1. Record the transactions in the journal. (p. 413)
2. Open the Allowance for Uncollectible Accounts, and post entries affecting that account. Keep a running balance. (pp. 82, 418)
3. Show how Aguilar should report accounts receivable on its December 31, 2009, balance sheet. Use the first reporting format at the top of page 411.

Using the percent-of-sales method for uncollectibles
2 5

P8-28A Showbiz Sportswear completed the following selected transactions during 2008 and 2009:

2008	
Dec. 31	Estimated that uncollectible-account expense for the year was 1% of credit sales of $450,000 and recorded that amount as expense. Use the allowance method.
31	Made the closing entry for uncollectible-account expense.
2009	
Feb. 4	Sold inventory to Marian Holt, $1,500 on account. Ignore cost of goods sold.
July 1	Wrote off Marian Holt's account as uncollectible after repeated efforts to collect from her.
Nov. 19	Received $1,500 from Marian Holt, along with a letter apologizing for being so late. Reinstated Holt's account in full, and recorded the cash receipt.
Dec. 31	Made a compound entry to write off the following accounts as uncollectible: Kaycee Britt, $2,300; Tim Sands, $500; and Anna Chin, $1,200.
31	Estimated that uncollectible-account expense for the year was 1% on credit sales of $480,000 and recorded the expense.
31	Made the closing entry for uncollectible-account expense.

Requirements

1. Open general ledger accounts for Allowance for Uncollectible Accounts and Uncollectible-Account Expense. Keep running balances. All accounts begin with a zero balance. (pp. 82, 413)
2. Record the transactions in the general journal, and post to the two ledger accounts. (pp. 207, 410, 414)
3. The December 31, 2009, balance of Accounts Receivable is $164,500. Show how Accounts Receivable would be reported on the balance sheet at that date. Use the first reporting format on page 411.

Accounting for notes receivable, including accruing interest revenue

P8-29A Kelly Realty loaned money and received the following notes during 2008.

Note	Date	Principal Amount	Interest Rate	Term
(1)	Aug. 1	$12,000	9%	1 year
(2)	Oct. 31	11,000	12%	3 months
(3)	Dec. 19	15,000	10%	30 days

continued . . .

Requirements

For each note, compute interest using a 360-day year. Explanations are not required.

1. Determine the due date and maturity value of each note. (p. 420)
2. Journalize a single adjusting entry at December 31, 2008, to record accrued interest revenue on all three notes. (pp. 422–423)
3. For note (1), journalize the collection of principal and interest at maturity. (pp. 422–423)

Accounting for notes receivable, dishonored notes, and accrued interest revenue

P8-30A Record the following transactions in the general journal of Dvorak Interiors. Round all amounts to the nearest dollar. Explanations are not required. (pp. 209, 422–423, 423–424)

2007	
Dec. 21	Received a $4,400, 30-day, 9% note on account from Monica Lee.
31	Made an adjusting entry to accrue interest on the Lee note.
31	Made a closing entry for interest revenue.
2008	
Jan. 20	Collected the maturity value of the Lee note.
Sept. 14	Loaned $6,000 cash to Bullseye Investors, receiving a three-month, 13% note.
30	Received a $1,600, 60-day, 16% note for a sale to Chuck Powers. Ignore cost of goods sold.
Nov. 29	Chuck Powers dishonored his note at maturity; wrote off the note as uncollectible, debiting Allowance for Uncollectible Notes.
Dec. 14	Collected the maturity value of the Bullseye Investors note.

Journalizing uncollectibles, notes receivable, and accrued interest revenue

P8-31A Speedo Paint Company completed the following selected transactions:

2007	
Dec. 1	Sold inventory to Brent Estes, receiving a $16,000, three-month, 12% note. Ignore cost of goods sold.
31	Made an adjusting entry to accrue interest on the Estes note.
31	Made an adjusting entry to record uncollectible-account expense based on an aging of accounts receivable. The aging schedule shows that $12,800 of accounts receivable will not be collected. Prior to this adjustment, the credit balance in Allowance for Uncollectible Accounts is $11,100.
2008	
Mar. 1	Collected the maturity value of the Estes note.
July 21	Sold merchandise to Ann Mellon, receiving a 60-day, 9% note for $22,000. Ignore cost of goods sold.
Sep. 19	Mellon dishonored her note (failed to pay) at maturity; we converted the maturity value of the note to an account receivable.

continued . . .

Nov. 21	Loaned $40,000 cash to Air Control Co., receiving a 90-day, 9% note.
Dec. 2	Collected in full on account from Ann Mellon.
31	Accrued the interest on the Air Control note.

Requirement

Record the transactions in the journal of Speedo Paint Company. Explanations are not required. (pp. 413, 422–424)

Using ratio data to evaluate a company's financial position

P8-32A The comparative financial statements of 4th Gear Website Design for 2008, 2007, and 2006 include the data shown here:

	(In thousands)		
	2008	2007	2006
Balance sheet			
Current assets:			
Cash	$ 20	$ 20	$ 10
Short-term investments	70	100	60
Receivables, net	190	150	120
Inventories	420	380	340
Prepaid expenses	30	30	20
Total current assets	$ 730	$ 680	$ 550
Total current liabilities	$ 480	$ 410	$ 380
Income statement			
Sales revenue	$2,600	$2,500	$1,900

Requirements

1. Compute these ratios for 2008 and 2007:
   a. Current ratio (p. 214)
   b. Acid-test ratio (p. 425)
   c. Days' sales in receivables (p. 426)
2. Write a memo explaining to Les Arnold, the company owner, which ratios improved from 2007 to 2008 and which ratios deteriorated. Discuss whether this trend is favorable or unfavorable for the company. Use the memo format shown for Problem 8-25A, page 439.

Problems (Group B)

Controlling cash receipts from customers

P8-33B Stained Glass Crafters performs all work on account, with regular monthly billing to customers. M. C. Perry, the accountant, opens the mail. Company procedure requires him to separate customer checks from the remittance slips and then post collections to customer accounts. Perry deposits the checks in the bank. He computes each day's total amount posted to

continued . . .

customer accounts and matches this total to the bank deposit slip. This procedure is intended to ensure that all receipts are deposited in the bank.

Requirement

As a consultant hired by Stained Glass Crafters, write a memo to management evaluating the company's internal controls over cash receipts from customers. If the system is effective, identify its strong features. If the system has flaws, propose a way to strengthen the controls. Use the memo format that follows. (p. 407)

MEMO	
Date:	
To:	
From:	
Subject:	

Accounting for uncollectibles by the allowance and direct write-off methods

P8-34B On May 31, Rosetree Floral Supply had a $160,000 debit balance in Accounts Receivable and a $6,400 credit balance in Allowance for Uncollectible Accounts. During June, Rosetree made:

- Sales on account, $560,000
- Collections on account, $601,000.
- Write-offs of uncollectible receivables, $8,000

Requirements

1. Record sales and collections on account. Then record uncollectible-account expense (2% of credit sales) and write-offs of customer accounts for June using the *allowance* method. Show all June activity in Accounts Receivable, Allowance for Uncollectible Accounts, and Uncollectible-Account Expense (post to these T-accounts). (pp. 410–412, 414)
2. Suppose Rosetree used a different method to account for uncollectible receivables. Record sales and collections on account. Then record uncollectible-account expense for June using the *direct write-off* method. Post to Accounts Receivable and Uncollectible-Account Expense and show their balances at June 30. (pp. 415–416)
3. What amount of uncollectible-account expense would Rosetree report on its June income statement under each of the two methods? Which amount better matches expense with revenue? Give your reason. (pp. 411–412, 415–416)
4. What amount of *net* accounts receivable would Rosetree report on its June 30 balance sheet under each of the two methods? Which amount is more realistic? Give your reason. (pp. 415–416, 419)

Using the percent-of-sales and aging methods for uncollectibles

P8-35B At September 30, the accounts of East Terrace Medical Center (ETMC) include the following:

Accounts Receivable	$143,000
Allowance for Uncollectible Accounts (credit balance).........	3,200

During October through December, ETMC completed the following selected transactions:

Dec. 28	Wrote off as uncollectible the $1,500 account receivable from Brown Co. and the $1,100 account receivable from Jacob Weiss.
Dec. 31	Recorded uncollectible-account expense based on the aging of accounts receivable, which follows:

	Age of Accounts			
Accounts Receivable	1–30 Days	31–60 Days	61–90 Days	Over 90 Days
$163,000.........................	$100,000	$40,000	$14,000	$9,000
Estimated percent uncollectible	0.1%	1%	10%	30%

Requirements

1. Record the transactions in the journal. (pp. 413, 414)
2. Open the Allowance for Uncollectible Accounts, and post entries affecting that account. Keep a running balance. (pp. 82, 418)
3. Show how East Terrace Medical Center should report accounts receivable on its balance sheet at December 31, 2007. Use the first reporting format at the top of page 411.

Using the percent-of-sales method for uncollectibles

2 5

P8-36B Dialex Watches completed the following transactions during 2007 and 2008:

2007	
Dec. 31	Estimated that uncollectible-account expense for the year was 1% on credit sales of $400,000, and recorded that amount as expense. Use the allowance method.
31	Made the closing entry for uncollectible-account expense.
2008	
Jan. 17	Sold inventory to Mitch Vanez, $600, on account. Ignore cost of goods sold.
June 29	Wrote off the Mitch Vanez account as uncollectible after repeated efforts to collect from him.
Aug. 6	Received $600 from Mitch Vanez, along with a letter stating his apology for paying late. Reinstated Vanez's account in full and recorded the cash collection.
Dec. 31	Made a compound entry to write off the following accounts as uncollectible: Bernard Klaus, $1,700; Marie Monet, $1,300.

continued . . .

2008	
Dec. 31	Estimated that uncollectible-account expense for the year was 1% on credit sales of $480,000, and recorded that amount as expense.
31	Made the closing entry for uncollectible-account expense.

Requirements

1. Open general ledger accounts for Allowance for Uncollectible Accounts and Uncollectible-Account Expense. Keep running balances. All accounts begin with a zero balance. (pp. 82, 418)
2. Record the transactions in the general journal, and post to the two ledger accounts. (pp. 209, 410–414)
3. The December 31, 2008, balance of Accounts Receivable is $139,000. Show how Accounts Receivable would be reported on the balance sheet at that date. Use the first reporting format at the top of page 411.

Accounting for notes receivable, including accruing interest revenue
4

P8-37B Bank of Nashville received the following notes during 2008.

Note	Date	Principal Amount	Interest Rate	Term
(1)	Dec. 11	$13,000	9%	1 year
(2)	Nov. 30	12,000	12%	6 months
(3)	Dec. 7	9,000	10%	60 days

Requirements

For each note compute interest using a 360-day year. Explanations are not required.

1. Determine the due date and maturity value of each note. (p. 420)
2. Journalize a single adjusting entry at December 31, 2008, to record accrued interest revenue on all three notes. (pp. 422–423)
3. For note (1), journalize the collection of principal and interest at maturity. (pp. 422–423)

Accounting for notes receivable, dishonored notes, and accrued interest revenue

P8-38B Record the following transactions in the general journal of Renschler Communication. Explanations are not required. (pp. 209, 414, 422–423)

2007	
Dec. 19	Received a $5,000, 60-day, 12% note on account from Video Productions.
31	Made an adjusting entry to accrue interest on the Video Productions note.
31	Made a closing entry for interest revenue.

continued . . .

2008	
Feb. 17	Collected the maturity value of the Video Productions note.
June 1	Loaned $10,000 cash to Blues Brothers, receiving a 6-month, 11% note.
Oct. 31	Received a $1,500, 60-day, 12% note for a sale to Mark Phipps. Ignore cost of goods sold.
Dec. 1	Collected the maturity value of the Blues Brothers note.
30	Mark Phipps dishonored his note at maturity; wrote off the note receivable as uncollectible, debiting Allowance for Uncollectible Notes.

Journalizing uncollectibles, notes receivable, and accrued interest revenue

P8-39B Assume that La-Z Recliner Chairs completed the following selected transactions:

2007	
July 1	Sold goods to Wal-Mart, receiving a $40,000, 9-month, 9% note. Ignore cost of goods sold.
Dec. 31	Made an adjusting entry to accrue interest on the Wal-Mart note.
31	Made an adjusting entry to record uncollectible-account expense based on an aging of accounts receivable. The aging schedule shows that $14,400 of accounts receivable will not be collected. Prior to this adjustment, the credit balance in Allowance for Uncollectible Accounts is $11,300.
2008	
Apr. 1	Collected the maturity value of the Wal-Mart note.
June 23	Sold merchandise to Artesian Corp., receiving a 60-day, 10% note for $9,000. Ignore cost of goods sold.
Aug. 22	Artesian Corp. dishonored (failed to pay) its note at maturity; we converted the maturity value of the note to an account receivable.
Nov. 16	Loaned $20,000 cash to Crane, Inc., receiving a 90-day, 12% note.
Dec. 5	Collected in full on account from Artesian Corp.
31	Accrued the interest on the Crane, Inc., note.

Requirement

Record the transactions in the journal of La-Z Recliner Chairs. Explanations are not required. (pp. 413, 422–424)

Using ratio data to evaluate a company's financial position

P8-40B The comparative financial statements of Lomax Cosmetic Supply for 2009, 2008, and 2007 include the following selected data:

continued . . .

	(In thousands)		
	2009	2008	2007
Balance sheet			
Current assets:			
Cash	$ 90	$ 80	$ 60
Short-term investments	140	170	126
Receivables, net	280	260	244
Inventories	360	340	300
Prepaid expenses	50	20	40
Total current assets	$ 920	$ 870	$ 770
Total current liabilities	$ 580	$ 600	$ 660
Income statement			
Sales revenue	$5,840	$5,110	$4,200

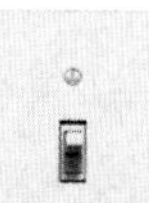

for 24/7 practice visit
www.MyAccountingLab.com

Requirements

1. Compute these ratios for 2009 and 2008:
   a. Current ratio (p. 214)
   b. Acid-test ratio (p. 425)
   c. Days' sales in receivables (p. 426)
2. Write a memo explaining to Sandra Lomax, the company owner, which ratios improved from 2008 to 2009 and which ratios deteriorated. Discuss whether this trend is favorable or unfavorable for the company. Use the memo format shown for Problem 8-33B, page 443.

Apply Your Knowledge

Decision Cases

Evaluating bankcard sales for profitability
2

Case 1. Weddings on Demand sells on account and manages its own receivables. Average experience for the past three years has been as follows:

	Total
Sales	$350,000
Cost of goods sold	210,000
Bad-debt expense	4,000
Other expenses	61,000

Mariel Picasso, the owner, is considering whether to accept bankcards (VISA, MasterCard) from customers because some are slow to pay. Typically, accepting bankcards increases total sales and cost of goods sold by 10%. But VISA and MasterCard charge approximately 2% of bankcard sales. If Picasso switches to bankcards, she'll no longer have bad-debt expense. She can also save $5,000 on other expenses. After the switchover to bankcards, Picasso expects cash sales of $200,000.

Requirement

Should Picasso start accepting bankcards? Show the computations of net income under her present arrangement and under the bankcard plan. (Challenge)

Comparing the allowance and direct write-off methods for uncollectibles

Case 2. Scribbles Stationery has always used the direct write-off method to account for uncollectibles. The company's revenues, bad-debt write-offs, and year-end receivables for the most recent year follow.

Year	Revenues	Write-Offs	Receivables at Year-End
2008	$150,000	$3,900	$14,000

Scribbles is applying for a bank loan, and the loan officer requires figures based on the allowance method of accounting for bad debts. In the past bad debts have run about 4% of revenues.

Requirements

Scribbles must give the banker the following information:

1. How much more or less would net income be for 2008 if Scribbles were to use the allowance method for bad debts? (pp. 411–412, 415–416)
2. How much of the receivables balance at the end of 2008 does Scribbles actually expect to collect? (pp. 411–412)

Compute these amounts, and then explain for Scribbles why net income is more or less using the allowance method versus the direct write-off method for uncollectibles.

Ethical Issue

E-Z Loan Co. makes loans to high-risk borrowers. E-Z borrows from its bank and then lends money to people with bad credit. The bank requires E-Z Loan to submit quarterly financial statements in order to keep its line of credit. E-Z's main asset is Notes Receivable. Therefore, Uncollectible-Note Expense and Allowance for Uncollectible Note are important accounts.

Slade McQueen, the owner of E-Z Loan Co., wants net income to increase in a smooth pattern, rather than increase in some periods and decrease in others. To report smoothly increasing net income, McQueen underestimates Uncollectible-Note Expense in some periods. In other periods, McQueen overestimates the expense. He reasons that over time the income overstatements roughly offset the income understatements.

Requirement

Is McQueen's practice of smoothing income ethical? Why or why not?

Financial Statement Case

Analyzing accounts receivable and uncollectibles
2 6

Use Amazon.com's balance sheet and the Note 1 data on "Allowance for Doubtful Accounts" in Appendix A at the end of this book.

1. Do accounts receivable appear to be an important asset for Amazon.com? What about Amazon's business affects the importance of accounts receivable?

2. Assume that all of "Accounts Receivable, Net and Other Current Assets" is accounts receivable. Further assume that gross receivables at December 31, 2005, were $317 million. Answer the following questions based on these data, plus what's reported on the balance sheet.
   a. How much did customers owe Amazon.com at December 31, 2005?
   b. How much did Amazon expect to collect from customers after December 31, 2005?
   c. Of the total receivable amount at December 31, 2005, how much did Amazon expect *not* to collect?

3. Compute Amazon.com's acid-test ratio at the end of 2005. Marketable securities are short-term investments. Assume that other current assets are zero. If all the current liabilities came due immediately, could Amazon pay them?

Team Project

Notes Receivable of the Bank. Bob Opper and Denise Shapp worked for several years as sales representatives for Xerox Corporation. During this time, they became close friends as they acquired expertise with the company's full range of copier equipment. Now they see an opportunity to put their experience to work and fulfill lifelong desires to establish their own business. Lakeside College, located in their city, is expanding, and there is no copy center within five miles of the campus. Business in the area is booming, and the population in this section of the city is growing.

continued . . .

Opper and Shapp want to open a copy center, similar to a FedEx Kinko's, near the campus. A small shopping center across the street from the college has a vacancy that would fit their needs. Opper and Shapp each have $20,000 to invest in the business, and they forecast the need for $30,000 to renovate the store. Xerox Corporation will lease two large copiers to them at a total monthly rental of $4,000. With enough cash to see them through the first six months of operation, they are confident they can make the business succeed. The two work very well together, and both have excellent credit ratings. Opper and Shapp must borrow $80,000 to start the business, advertise its opening, and keep it running for its first six months.

Assume the role of Opper and Shapp, the partners who will own Lakeside Copy Center.

1. As a group, visit a copy center to familiarize yourselves with its operations. If possible, interview the manager or another employee. Then write a loan request that Opper and Shapp will submit to a bank with the intent of borrowing $80,000 to be paid back over three years. The loan will be a personal loan to the partnership of Opper and Shapp, not to Lakeside Copy Center. The request should specify all the details of Opper's and Shapp's plan that will motivate the bank to grant the loan. Include a budgeted income statement for the first six months of the copy center's operation.

2. As a group, interview a loan officer in a bank. Have the loan officer evaluate your loan request. Write a report, or make a presentation to your class—as directed by your instructor—to reveal the loan officer's decision.

For Internet Exercises, Excel in Practice, and additional online activities, go to the Web site www.prenhall.com/horngren.

Quick Check Answers

1. *d* 2. *d* 3. *a* 4. *b* 5. *a* 6. *d* 7. *c* 8. *b* 9. *b* 10. *c*

Appendix 8A

Discounting a Note Receivable

A payee of a note receivable may need cash before the maturity date of the note When this occurs, the payee may sell the note, a practice called **discounting a note receivable**. The price to be received for the note is determined by present-value concepts. But the transaction between the seller and the buyer of the note can take any form agreeable to the two parties. Here we illustrate one procedure used for discounting short-term notes receivable. To receive cash immediately, the seller accepts a lower price than the note's maturity value.

To illustrate discounting a note receivable, suppose **General Electric** loaned \$15,000 to Dorman Builders on October 20, 2008. GE took a note receivable from Dorman. The maturity date of the 90-day 10% Dorman note is January 18, 2009. Suppose GE discounts the Dorman note at First City Bank on December 9, 2008, when the note is 50 days old. The bank applies a 12% annual interest rate to determine the discounted value of the note. The bank will use a discount rate that is higher than the note's interest rate in order to earn some interest on the transaction. The discounted value, called the *proceeds,* is the amount GE receives from the bank. The proceeds can be computed in five steps, as shown in Exhibit 8A-1.

EXHIBIT 8A-1 **Discounting (Selling) a Note Receivable: GE Discounts the Dorman Builders Note**

Step	Computation	
1. Compute the original amount of interest on the note receivable.	\$15,000 × 0.10 × 90/360	= \$375
2. Maturity value of the note = Principal + Interest	\$15,000 + \$375	= \$15,375
3. Determine the period (number of days, months, or years) the *bank* will hold the note (the discount period).	Dec. 9, 2008 to Jan. 18, 2009	= 40 days
4. Compute the bank's discount on the note. This is the bank's interest revenue from holding the note.	\$15,375 × 0.12 × 40/360	= \$205
5. Seller's proceeds from discounting the note receivable = Maturity value of the note – Bank's discount on the note.	\$15,375 – \$205	= \$15,170

The authors thank Doug Hamilton for suggesting this exhibit.

GE's entry to record discounting (selling) the note on December 9, 2008, is:

2008			
Dec. 9	Cash	15,170	
	Note Receivable—Dorman Builders		15,000
	Interest Revenue (\$15,170 – \$15,000)		170
	Discounted a note receivable.		

When the proceeds from discounting a note receivable are less than the principal amount of the note, the payee records a debit to Interest Expense for the amount of the difference. For example, GE could discount the note receivable for cash proceeds of $14,980. The entry to record this discounting transaction is:

2008			
Dec. 9	Cash	14,980	
	Interest Expense	20	
	Note Receivable—Dorman Builders		15,000
	Discounted a note receivable.		

Appendix 8A Assignments

Exercise

Notes receivable transactions

E8A-1 Big Tex Toys sells on account. When a customer account becomes three months old, Big Tex converts the account to a note receivable and immediately discounts the note to a bank. During 2009, Big Tex completed these transactions:

Aug. 29	Sold goods on account to V. Moyer, $5,000.
Dec. 1	Received a $5,000, 60-day, 10% note from Moyer in satisfaction of his past-due account receivable.
1	Sold the Moyer note by discounting it to a bank for $4,800.

Requirement

Record the transactions in Big Tex's journal.

Problem

Notes receivable transactions

P8A-1 A company received the following notes during 2008. The notes were discounted on the dates and at the rates indicated:

Note	Date	Principal Amount	Interest Rate	Term	Date Discounted	Discount Rate
(1)	Sept. 1	$8,000	9%	120 days	Nov. 2	12%
(2)	Aug. 19	9,000	8%	90 days	Aug. 30	10%
(3)	July 15	6,000	6%	6 months	Oct. 15	8%

Requirements

Identify each note by number, compute interest using a 360-day year, and round all interest amounts to the nearest dollar. Explanations are not required.

1. Determine the due date and maturity value of each note.
2. Determine the discount and proceeds from the sale (discounting) of each note.
3. Journalize the discounting of notes (1) and (2).

9 Plant Assets and Intangibles

Learning Objectives

1. Measure the cost of a plant asset
2. Account for depreciation
3. Select the best depreciation method for tax purposes
4. Account for the disposal of a plant asset
5. Account for natural resources
6. Account for intangible assets

Your business, In Motion T-Shirts, is at a crossroads. Thus far, you've hired outsiders to print logos on the T-shirts that you sell. By letting three printers compete against each other, you've been able to hold costs down. But two of the printers have gone out of business and the only one remaining has jacked up fees. What to do?

One option is to purchase screen-printing equipment and imprint the logos yourself. You'll have to pay $3,000 for the equipment, but the cost savings should recoup your outlay within a year. And you won't have to wait for others to get a job out. Go ahead. Take the plunge and buy the equipment.

Equipment is one type of plant asset. Others include land, buildings, and furniture. Often plant assets are referred to as Property, Plant, and Equipment.

Plant assets have some special characteristics. For example, you hold them for use in the business—not to sell as inventory. Also,

- Plant assets are relatively expensive, and their cost can be a challenge to determine.
- Plant assets last a long time—usually for several years. If plant assets wear out or become obsolete, you need to depreciate them.
- Plant assets may be sold or traded in. Accounting for the disposal of a plant asset is more complicated than selling inventory.

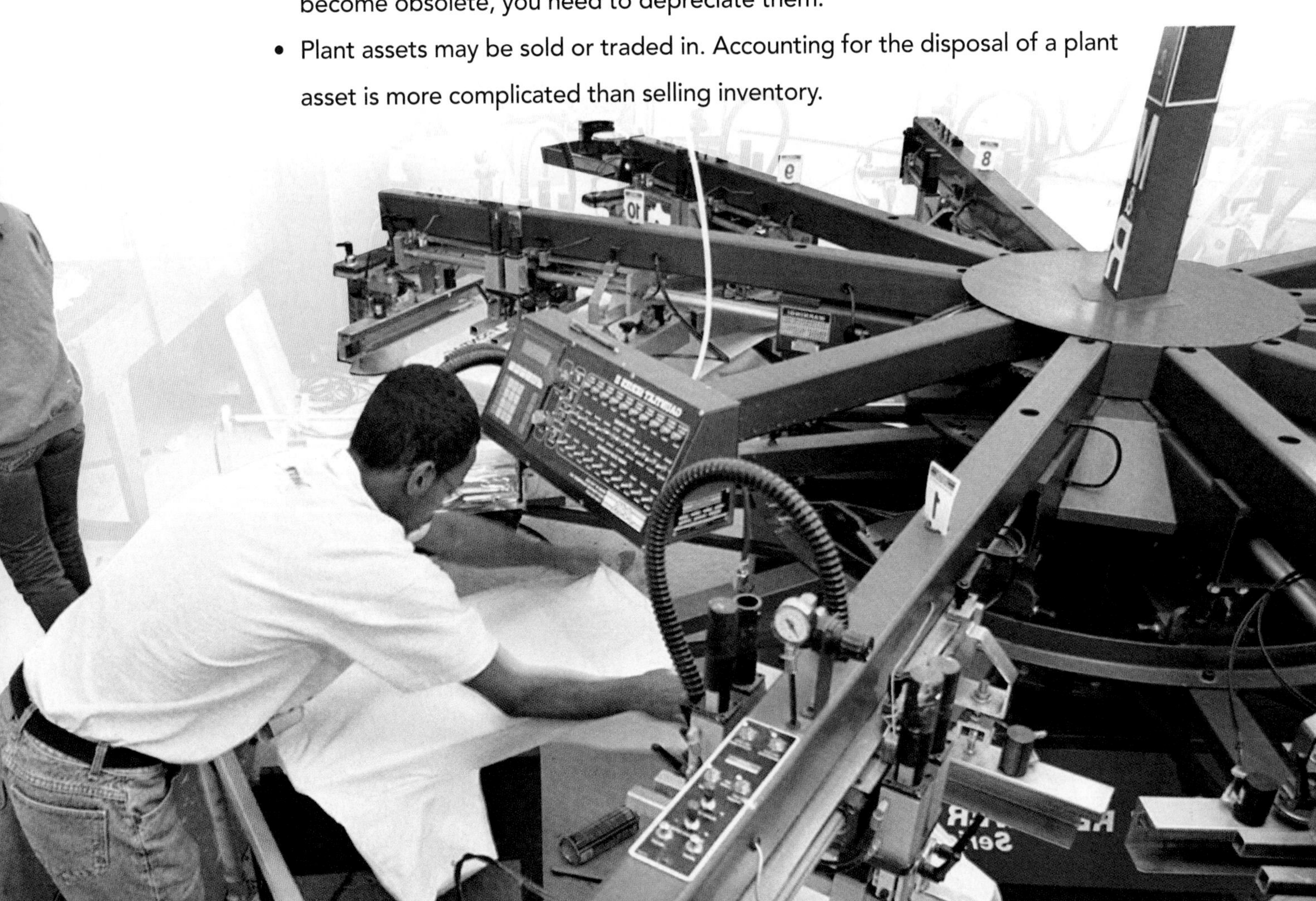

As you can see, plant assets pose some accounting challenges. This chapter addresses these issues and shows how to account for

1. Plant assets, which are useful because of their physical characteristics
2. **Intangible assets**, which have no physical form

Chapter 9 concludes our coverage of assets, except for investments. After completing this chapter, you should understand the various assets of a business and how to account for them. Let's begin with an example that is familiar to you.

Plant assets have their own terminology. Exhibit 9-1 shows which expense applies to each category of plant asset.

EXHIBIT 9-1 **Plant Assets and Their Related Expenses**

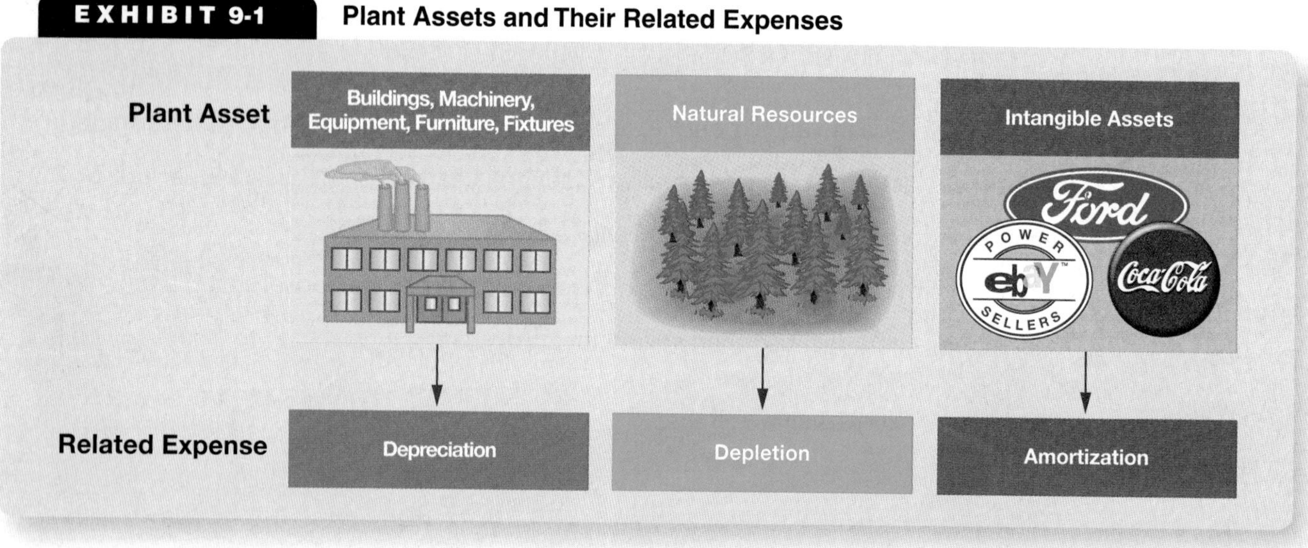

Measuring the Cost of a Plant Asset

1 Measure the cost of a plant asset

The *cost principle* says to carry an asset at its cost—the amount paid for the asset. The rule for measuring cost is:

$$\text{Cost of an asset} = \frac{\text{Sum of all the costs incurred to bring the asset}}{\text{to its intended purpose, net of all discounts}}$$

The *cost of a plant asset* is its purchase price plus taxes, purchase commissions, and all other amounts paid to ready the asset for its intended use. In Chapter 6, we applied this principle to inventory. These costs vary, so we discuss each asset individually.

Land and Land Improvements

The cost of land includes the following costs paid by the purchaser:

- purchase price
- brokerage commission
- survey and legal fees
- back property taxes
- cost of clearing the land and removing unwanted buildings

The cost of land is not depreciated.

The cost of land does **not** include the following costs:

- fencing
- paving
- sprinkler systems
- lighting

These separate plant assets—called *land improvements*—are subject to depreciation.

Suppose In Motion T-Shirts needs property and purchases land for $50,000. You also pay $4,000 in back property taxes, $2,000 in transfer taxes, $5,000 to remove an old building, and a $1,000 survey fee. What is your cost of this land? Exhibit 9-2 shows all the costs incurred to bring the land to its intended use, as follows:

EXHIBIT 9-2 Measuring the Cost of Land

Purchase price of land		$62,000
Add related costs:		
Back property taxes	$4,000	
Transfer taxes	2,000	
Removal of building	5,000	
Survey fee	1,000	
Total related costs		12,000
Total cost of land		$62,000

Suppose you sign a $50,000 note payable for the land and pay cash for the related costs. Your entry to record purchase of the land is:

	Land	62,000	
	Note Payable		50,000
	Cash		12,000

We would say that you *capitalized* the cost of the land at $62,000. This means that In Motion debited the Land account for $62,000.

Suppose you then pay $20,000 for fences, paving, lighting, and signs. The following entry records the cost of these land improvements.

	Land Improvements	20,000	
	Cash		20,000

Land and Land Improvements are two entirely separate assets. The cost of land improvements is depreciated over that asset's useful life.

Buildings

The cost of a building includes:

- architectural fees
- building permits
- contractor charges
- payments for material, labor, and overhead

The time to complete a building can be months, even years. If the company constructs its own assets, the cost of the building may include the cost of interest on borrowed money.

You may purchase an existing building. Its cost includes all the usual items, plus the cost to repair and renovate the building for its intended use.

Machinery and Equipment

The cost of machinery and equipment includes its:

- purchase price (less any discounts)
- transportation charges
- insurance while in transit
- sales and other taxes
- purchase commission
- installation costs
- cost of testing the asset before it is used

After the asset is up and running, we no longer capitalize these costs to the Equipment account. Thereafter, insurance, taxes, and maintenance costs are recorded as expenses.

There are many different kinds of equipment. In Motion T-Shirts has screen-printing equipment. American Airlines has airplanes, and Kinko's has copiers. Most businesses have computer equipment.

Furniture and Fixtures

Furniture and fixtures include desks, chairs, file cabinets, and display racks. The cost of furniture and fixtures includes the basic cost of each asset (less any discounts), plus all other costs to ready the asset for use.

A Lump-Sum (Basket) Purchase of Assets

A company may pay a single price for several assets as a group—a "basket purchase." For example, In Motion T-Shirts may pay one price for land and a building. For accounting, you must identify the cost of each asset, as shown in the following diagram. The total cost (100%) is divided among the assets according to their relative sales values. This is called the *relative-sales-value method*.

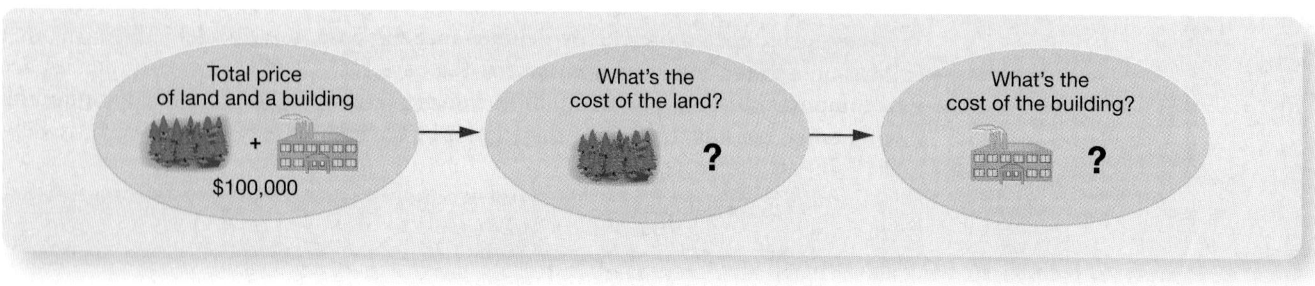

Suppose you purchase land and a building for your plant, and the combined purchase price is $100,000. An appraisal indicates that the land's market (sales) value is $30,000 and the building's market (sales) value is $90,000.

First, figure the ratio of each asset's market value to the total for both assets combined. The total appraised value is $120,000.

Land		Building		Total Market Value
$30,000	+	$90,000	=	$120,000

The land makes up 25% of the total market value, and the building 75%, as follows:

Asset	Market (Sales) Value	Percentage of Total Value	Total Purchase Price	Cost of Each Asset
Land	$ 30,000	$30,000/$120,000 = 25% ×	$100,000 =	$ 25,000
Building	90,000	$90,000/$120,000 = 75% ×	100,000 =	75,000
Total	$120,000	100%		$100,000

Suppose you pay cash. The entry to record the purchase of the land and building is:

	Land	25,000	
	Building	75,000	
	Cash		100,000

Capital Expenditures

Accountants divide expenditures on plant assets into two categories:

- Capital expenditures
- Expenses

Capital expenditures are debited to an asset account because they:

- Increase the asset's capacity or efficiency, or
- Extend the asset's useful life

Examples of capital expenditures include the purchase price plus all the other costs to bring an asset to its intended use, as discussed in the preceding sections. Also, an **extraordinary repair** is a capital expenditure because it adds to the asset's capacity or useful life.

Expenses, such as repair or maintenance expense, are *not* debited to an asset account because they merely maintain the asset in working order. Expenses are immediately subtracted from revenue. Examples include the costs of maintaining equipment, repairing a truck, and replacing its tires. These **ordinary repairs** are debited to Repair Expense.

Exhibit 9-3 shows some (a) capital expenditures and (b) expenses for a delivery truck.

Treating a capital expenditure as an expense, or vice versa, creates an accounting error. Suppose American Airlines makes a capital expenditure and expenses this

EXHIBIT 9-3 **Delivery-Truck Expenditures—Capital Expenditure or Expense?**

CAPITAL EXPENDITURE: Debit an Asset Account	EXPENSE: Debit Repair and Maintenance Expense
Extraordinary repairs:	*Ordinary repairs:*
Major engine overhaul	Repair of transmission or engine
Modification for new use	Oil change, lubrication, and so on
Addition to storage capacity	Replacement of tires or windshield
	Paint job

cost. This is an accounting error because the cost should have been debited to an asset. This error:

- overstates expenses
- understates net income

On the balance sheet, the Equipment account is understated.

Capitalizing an expense creates the opposite error. Expenses are understated, and net income is overstated. The balance sheet overstates assets.

Depreciation

As we've seen, **depreciation** is the allocation of a plant asset's cost to expense over its useful life. Depreciation matches the expense against the revenue to measure net income. Exhibit 9-4 illustrates depreciation for a Boeing 737 jet by American Airlines.

EXHIBIT 9-4

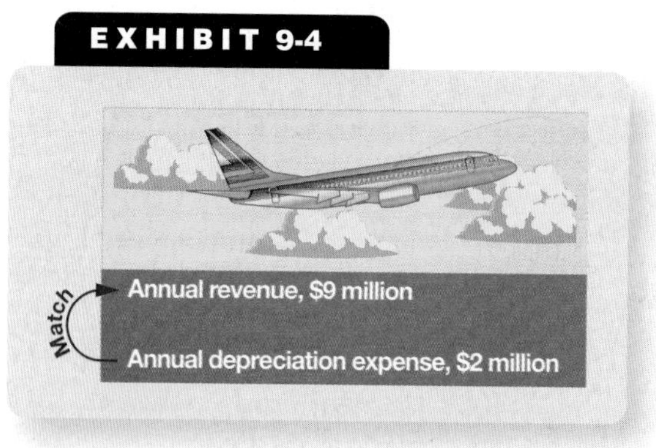

Depreciation and the Matching of Expense with Revenue

Suppose American buys a Boeing 737 jet. American believes it will get 10 years of service from the plane. Using the straight-line depreciation method, American expenses $\frac{1}{10}$ of the asset's cost in each of its 10 years of use.

Let's contrast what depreciation is with what it is *not.*

1. *Depreciation is not a process of valuation.* Businesses do not record depreciation based on the asset's market (sales) value.
2. *Depreciation does not mean that the business sets aside cash to replace an asset when it is used up.* Depreciation has nothing to do with cash.

Causes of Depreciation

All assets except land wear out. For some plant assets, *wear and tear* causes depreciation. For example, physical factors wear out the jets that American, Delta, and United fly. The screen printer you use at In Motion T-Shirts is also subject to physical wear and tear.

Assets such as computers and software may become *obsolete* before they wear out. An asset is obsolete when another asset can do the job more efficiently. Thus, an asset's useful life may be shorter than its physical life. Accountants usually depreciate computers over a short period—perhaps 2 to 4 years—even though they can be used longer. In all cases, the asset's cost is depreciated over its useful life.

Measuring Depreciation

Depreciation of a plant asset is based on three factors:

1. Cost
2. Estimated useful life
3. Estimated residual value

Cost is known. The other two factors are estimates.

Estimated useful life is the length of the service period expected from the asset. Useful life may be expressed in years, output, or miles. For example, a building's life is stated in years, an airplane in the number of miles it can fly, and a Xerox copier in the number of copies it can make.

Estimated residual value—also called **salvage value**—is the asset's expected cash value at the end of its useful life. A delivery truck's useful life may be 100,000 miles. At the end, the company will sell the truck. The expected cash receipt is the truck's estimated residual value. Estimated residual value is *not* depreciated because you expect to receive this amount at the end. If there's no residual value, then depreciate the full cost of the asset. Cost minus residual value is called **depreciable cost.**

Depreciation Methods

2 Account for depreciation

There are three major depreciation methods[1]:

- Straight-line
- Units-of-production
- Declining-balance

These methods work differently, but they all result in the same total depreciation. Exhibit 9-5 gives the data we will use for an American Airlines baggage-handling truck.

[1]We omit the sum-of-years'-digits method because only 7 of 600 companies in a recent poll used it.

EXHIBIT 9-5 Data for Recording Depreciation on a Truck

Data Item	Amount
Cost of truck	$41,000
Less: Estimated residual value	(1,000)
Depreciable cost	$40,000
Estimated useful life	
Years	5 years
Units of production	100,000 mi.

Straight-Line Method

The **straight-line (SL) method** allocates an equal amount of depreciation to each year. Depreciable cost is divided by useful life to determine annual depreciation. The equation for SL depreciation, applied to the American Airlines truck, is:

$$\text{Straight-line depreciation} = \frac{\text{Cost} - \text{Residual value}}{\text{Useful life, in years}} = \frac{\$41{,}000 - \$1{,}000}{5}$$
$$= \$8{,}000 \text{ per year}$$

The entry to record each year's depreciation is:

	Account	Debit	Credit
	Depreciation Expense	8,000	
	Accumulated Depreciation		8,000

This truck was purchased on January 1, 2008, and a *straight-line depreciation schedule* is given in Exhibit 9-6. The final column shows the asset's *book value,* which is cost less accumulated depreciation.

EXHIBIT 9-6 Straight-Line Depreciation for a Truck

		Depreciation for the Year						
Date	Asset Cost	Depreciation Rate		Depreciable Cost		Depreciation Expense	Accumulated Depreciation	Book Value
1-1-2008	$41,000							$41,000
12-31-2008		0.20*	×	$40,000	=	$8,000	$ 8,000	33,000
12-31-2009		0.20	×	40,000	=	8,000	16,000	25,000
12-31-2010		0.20	×	40,000	=	8,000	24,000	17,000
12-31-2011		0.20	×	40,000	=	8,000	32,000	9,000
12-31-2012		0.20	×	40,000	=	8,000	40,000	1,000

*1/5 year = 0.20 per year

As an asset is used, accumulated depreciation increases and book value decreases. See the Accumulated Depreciation and Book Value columns in Exhibit 9-6. An asset's final book value is *residual value* ($1,000 in Exhibit 9-6). At the end, the asset is said to be *fully depreciated.*

Units-of-Production (UOP) Method

The **units-of-production (UOP) method** allocates a fixed amount of depreciation to each *unit of output,* as illustrated in Exhibit 9-7:

$$\begin{array}{c}\text{Units-of-production}\\ \text{depreciation}\\ \text{per unit of output}\end{array} = \frac{\text{Cost} - \text{Residual value}}{\text{Useful life, in units of production}} = \frac{\$41{,}000 - \$1{,}000}{100{,}000 \text{ miles}}$$

$$= \$0.40 \text{ per mile}$$

EXHIBIT 9-7 Units-of-Production Depreciation for a Truck

Date	Asset Cost	Depreciation for the Year: Depreciation Per Unit		Number of Units		Depreciation Expense	Accumulated Depreciation	Book Value
1-1-2008	$41,000							$41,000
12-31-2008		$0.40	×	20,000	=	$ 8,000	$ 8,000	33,000
12-31-2009		0.40	×	30,000	=	12,000	20,000	21,000
12-31-2010		0.40	×	25,000	=	10,000	30,000	11,000
12-31-2011		0.40	×	15,000	=	6,000	36,000	5,000
12-31-2012		0.40	×	10,000	=	4,000	40,000	1,000

This truck is likely to be driven 20,000 miles the first year, 30,000 the second, 25,000 the third, 15,000 the fourth, and 10,000 during the fifth. The UOP depreciation each period varies with the number of units the asset produces. Exhibit 9-7 shows the *UOP depreciation schedule* for this asset.

Double-Declining Balance Method

Double-declining-balance depreciation is *accelerated.* An **accelerated depreciation method** writes off more depreciation near the start of an asset's life than straight-line does. The main accelerated method is **double-declining-balance (DDB)**. This method multiplies decreasing book value by a constant percentage that is 2 times the straight-line rate. DDB amounts can be computed in two steps:

1. Compute the straight-line depreciation rate per year. A 5-year asset has a straight-line rate of 1/5, or 20% per year. A 10-year asset has a straight-line rate of 1/10, or 10% per year, and so on.

   Multiply the straight-line rate by 2. The DDB rate for a 5-year asset is 40% per year (20% × 2 = 40%). For a 10-year asset, the DDB rate is 20% (10% × 2 = 20%).

2. Compute DDB depreciation for each year. Multiply the asset's book value (cost less accumulated depreciation) at the beginning of each year by the DDB rate.

Ignore residual value, except for the last year. The first-year depreciation for the truck in Exhibit 9-5 is:

$$\text{DDB depreciation for the first year} = \text{Asset book value at the beginning of the year} \times \text{DDB rate}$$

$$\$16,400 = \$41,000 \times 0.40$$

The same approach is used to compute DDB depreciation for each year, except for the final year.

Final-year depreciation is the amount needed to bring the asset to residual value. In the DDB schedule (Exhibit 9-8), final-year depreciation is $4,314—book value, $5,314, less the $1,000 residual value.

EXHIBIT 9-8 **Double-Declining-Balance Depreciation for a Truck**

		Depreciation for the Year							
Date	**Asset Cost**	**DDB Rate**		**Book Value**		**Depreciation Expense**	**Accumulated Depreciation**	**Book Value**
1-1-2008	$41,000							$41,000
12-31-2008		0.40	×	$41,000	=	$16,400	$16,400	24,600
12-31-2009		0.40	×	24,600	=	9,840	26,240	14,760
12-31-2010		0.40	×	14,760	=	5,904	32,144	8,856
12-31-2011		0.40	×	8,856	=	3,542	35,686	5,314
12-31-2012					=	4,314*	40,000	1,000

*Last-year depreciation is the "plug figure" needed to reduce book value to the residual amount ($5,314 – $1,000 = $4,314).

The DDB method differs from the other methods in two ways:

- Residual value is ignored at the start. In the first year, depreciation is computed on the asset's full cost.
- Final-year depreciation is the amount needed to bring the asset to residual value. Final-year depreciation is a "plug figure."

SWITCHOVER TO STRAIGHT-LINE Some companies change to the straight-line method during the next-to-last year of the asset's life. Let's use this plan to compute annual depreciation for 2011 and 2012. In Exhibit 9-8, at the end of 2010:

Book value = $8,856

Depreciable cost = $7,856 ($8,856 – $1,000)

Straight-line depreciation for 2004 and 2005

= $3,928 ($7,856 ÷ 2 years remaining)

Comparing Depreciation Methods

Let's compare the depreciation methods. Annual amounts vary, but total depreciation is $40,000 for all methods.

Amount of Depreciation per Year

Year	Straight-Line	Units-of-Production	Accelerated Method Double-Declining-Balance
1	$ 8,000	$ 8,000	$16,400
2	8,000	12,000	9,840
3	8,000	10,000	5,904
4	8,000	6,000	3,542
5	8,000	4,000	4,314
Total	$40,000	$40,000	$40,000

Which method is best? That depends on the asset. A business should match an asset's expense against the revenue that the asset produces.

Straight-Line

For an asset that generates revenue evenly over time, the straight-line method follows the matching principle. Each period shows an equal amount of depreciation.

Units-of-Production

The UOP method works best for an asset that depreciates due to wear and tear, rather than obsolescence. More use causes greater depreciation.

Double-Declining-Balance

The accelerated method (DDB) works best for assets that produce more revenue in their early years. Higher depreciation in the early years is matched against the greater revenue.

Comparisons

Exhibit 9-9 graphs annual depreciation for the three methods.

- Straight-line is flat because depreciation is the same each period.
- Units-of-production follows no pattern because depreciation varies with asset use.
- Accelerated depreciation is greater in the first year and less in the later years.

EXHIBIT 9-9 **Depreciation Patterns for the Various Methods**

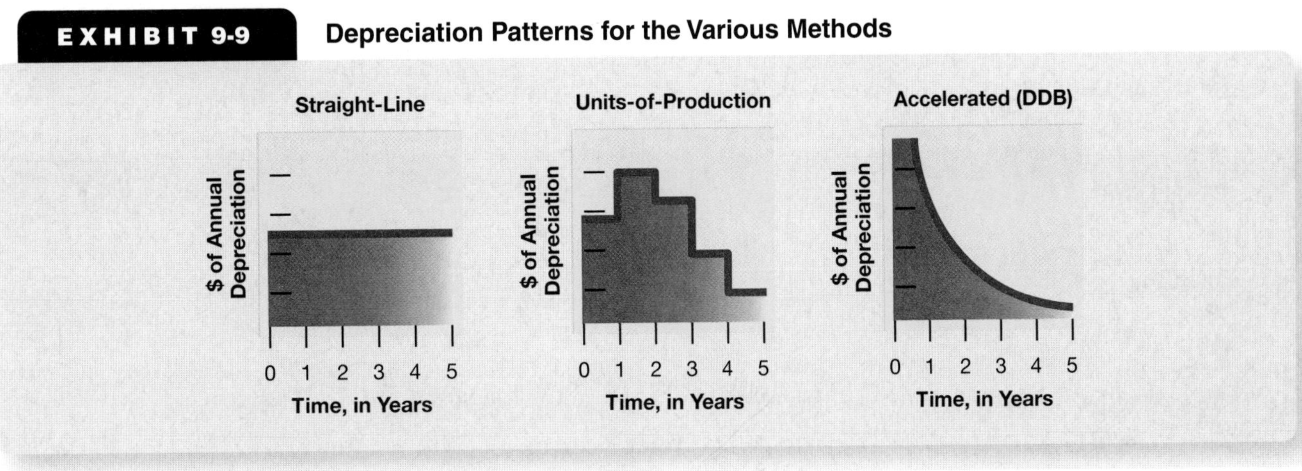

The straight-line depreciation method is most popular, used by the vast majority of companies. Exhibit 9-10 shows the percentages of companies that use each method.

EXHIBIT 9-10 Use of Depreciation Methods

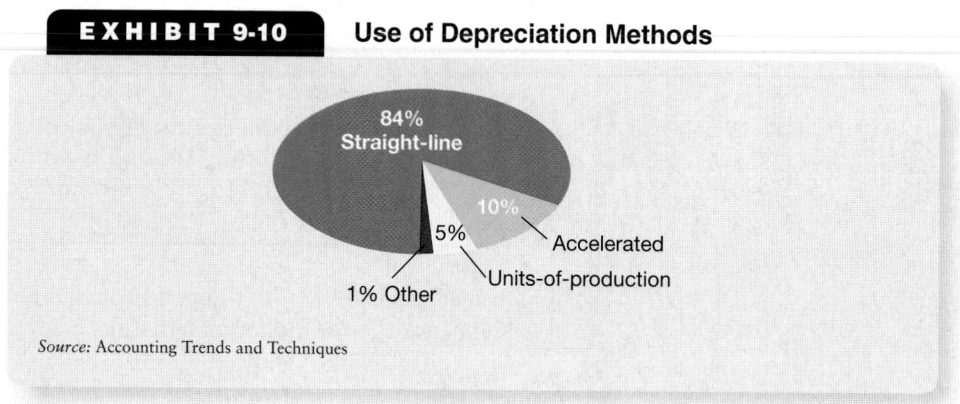

Source: Accounting Trends and Techniques

Summary Problem 1

Latté On Demand purchased a coffee drink machine on January 1, 2007, for \$44,000. Expected useful life is 10 years or 100,000 drinks, and residual value is \$4,000. Under three depreciation methods, annual depreciation and total accumulated depreciation at the end of 2007 and 2008 are as follows:

	Method A		Method B		Method C	
Year	Annual Depreciation Expense	Accumulated Depreciation	Annual Depreciation Expense	Accumulated Depreciation	Annual Depreciation Expense	Accumulated Depreciation
2007	\$1,200	\$1,200	\$8,800	\$ 8,800	\$4,000	\$4,000
2008	5,600	6,800	7,040	15,840	4,000	8,000

Requirements

1. Identify the depreciation method used in each instance, and show the equation and computation for each method. (Round to the nearest dollar.)
2. Assume use of the same method through 2009. Compute depreciation expense, accumulated depreciation, and asset book value for 2007 through 2009 under each method, assuming 12,000 units of production in 2009.

Solution

Requirement 1

Method A: Units-of-Production

$$\text{Depreciation per unit} = \frac{\$44{,}000 - \$4{,}000}{100{,}000 \text{ units}} = \$0.40$$

2007: \$0.40 × 3,000 units = \$1,200

2008: \$0.40 × 14,000 units = \$5,600

Method B: Double-Declining-Balance

$$\text{Rate} = \frac{1}{10 \text{ years}} \times 2 = 20\%$$

2007: 0.20 × \$44,000 = \$8,800

2008: 0.20 × (\$44,000 − \$8,800) = \$7,040

Method C: Straight-Line

Depreciable cost = \$44,000 − \$4,000 = \$40,000

Each year: \$40,000/10 years = \$4,000

Requirement 2

Method A: Units-of-Production

Year	Annual Depreciation Expense	Accumulated Depreciation	Book Value
Start			$44,000
2007	$1,200	$ 1,200	42,800
2008	5,600	6,800	37,200
2009	4,800	11,600	32,400

Method B: Double-Declining-Balance

Year	Annual Depreciation Expense	Accumulated Depreciation	Book Value
Start			$44,000
2007	$8,800	$ 8,800	35,200
2008	7,040	15,840	28,160
2009	5,632	21,472	22,528

Method C: Straight-Line

Year	Annual Depreciation Expense	Accumulated Depreciation	Book Value
Start			$44,000
2007	$4,000	$ 4,000	40,000
2008	4,000	8,000	36,000
2009	4,000	12,000	32,000

Computations for 2009:

Units-of-production	\$0.40 × 12,000 units = \$4,800
Double-declining-balance	0.20 × \$28,160 = \$5,632
Straight-line	\$40,000/10 years = \$4,000

Other Issues in Accounting for Plant Assets

Depreciation affects income taxes so you need to select the method that minimizes your taxes. Another issue is that you may have a gain or a loss when you sell a plant asset.

Depreciation and Income Taxes

3 Select the best depreciation method for tax purposes

As we just saw, most companies use straight-line depreciation for their financial statements. But to keep taxes low, they use accelerated depreciation.

Suppose you manage American Airline operations at Chicago O'Hare Airport. The IRS allows DDB depreciation, and you prefer DDB to straight-line. Why? Because DDB provides the fastest tax deductions and conserves cash. You can then invest the cash and earn more income. This is a common strategy.

To see how depreciation affects taxes and cash, recall our earlier depreciation for the American Airlines truck: First-year depreciation is:

- $8,000 under straight-line
- $16,400 under double-declining-balance

Which tax deduction do you prefer? DDB gives you a greater tax deduction and saves cash.

A special depreciation method called the *modified accelerated cost recovery system (MACRS)* is used for income tax purposes. Under MACRS, assets are divided into classes by asset life, as shown in Exhibit 9-11. MACRS depreciation is computed by the DDB method, the 150%-declining-balance method, or the straight-line method. Under 150% DB, the annual depreciation rate is computed by multiplying the straight-line rate by 1.50 (rather than by 2, as for DDB). For a 20-year asset, the straight-line rate is 0.05 (1/20 = 0.05), so the annual MACRS depreciation rate is 0.075 (0.05 × 1.50 = 0.075).

EXHIBIT 9-11 **Modified Accelerated Cost Recovery System (MACRS) Depreciation Method**

Class Identified by Asset Life (Years)	Representative Assets	Depreciation Method
3	Racehorses	DDB
5	Automobiles, light trucks	DDB
10	Equipment	DDB
20	Certain real estate	150% DB
27 1/2	Residential rental property	SL
39	Nonresidential rental property	SL

Depreciation for Partial Years

Companies purchase plant assets whenever they need them—such as February 8 or August 23. They don't wait until the beginning of a period. Therefore, companies develop policies to compute depreciation for partial years. Suppose In Motion T-Shirts purchases a building on July 1 for $100,000. The building's estimated life is 20 years, with estimated residual value of $40,000. How does In Motion compute depreciation for the year ended December 31?

Many companies compute partial-year depreciation by first calculating a full year's depreciation. They then multiply full-year depreciation by the fraction of the year that they used the asset. In this case you need to record 6 months' depreciation for July through December. Under the straight-line method, the year's depreciation for your building is $1,500, computed as follows:

$$\text{Full-year depreciation:} \quad \frac{\$100{,}000 - \$40{,}000}{20 \text{ years}} = \$3{,}000$$

$$\text{Partial-year depreciation:} \quad \$3{,}000 \times 6/12 = \$1{,}500$$

Another partial-year depreciation policy:

- Record a full month's depreciation on assets purchased on or before the 15th of the month, and
- Record no depreciation on assets bought after the 15th.

What if you buy an asset for $3,000 on August 22? In that case you record no depreciation for August. The year's depreciation is $1,000 for 4 months—September through December ($\$3{,}000 \times 4/12 = \$1{,}000$).

Partial-year depreciation is computed under DDB the same way: Apply the percentage of the year that the asset is used. Computers automatically calculate the depreciation expense for each period.

Changing the Useful Life of a Depreciable Asset

Estimating the useful life of a plant asset poses a challenge. As the asset is used, the business may change its estimated useful life. For example, American Airlines may find that its baggage-handling trucks are lasting 8 years instead of 5.

Accounting changes like this are common because no one has perfect foresight. When a company makes an accounting change, generally accepted accounting principles require the business to report the nature, reason, and effect of the accounting change.

For a change in accounting estimate, the asset's remaining depreciable book value is spread over the asset's remaining life. Suppose American Airlines used a truck for two years. Under the straight-line method, accumulated depreciation reached $16,000.

$$\begin{array}{c}\text{Straight-line}\\ \text{depreciation}\\ \text{for 2 years}\end{array} = \frac{\$41{,}000 - \$1{,}000}{5 \text{ years}} = \$8{,}000 \text{ per year} \times 2 \text{ years} = \$16{,}000$$

Remaining depreciable book value (cost *less* accumulated depreciation *less* residual value) is $24,000 ($41,000 − $16,000 − $1,000). Suppose American believes the truck will remain useful for 6 more years. At the start of year 3, the company would recompute depreciation as follows:

Remaining Depreciable Book Value	÷	(New) Estimated Useful Life Remaining	=	(New) Annual Depreciation
$24,000	÷	6 years	=	$4,000

In years 3 through 8, the yearly depreciation entry based on the new useful life is:

	Depreciation Expense—Truck	4,000	
	Accumulated Depreciation—Truck		4,000

Revised straight-line depreciation is computed as follows:

$$\text{Revised SL depreciation} = \frac{\text{Cost} - \text{Accumulated depreciation} - \text{New residual value}}{\text{Estimated remaining life in years}}$$

Using Fully-Depreciated Assets

A *fully-depreciated asset* is one that has reached the end of its *estimated* useful life. No more depreciation is recorded for the asset. If the asset is no longer useful, it is disposed of. But the asset may still be useful, and the company may continue using it. The asset account and its accumulated depreciation remain on the books, but no additional depreciation is recorded.

Disposing of a Plant Asset

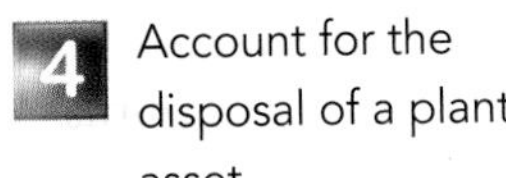

4 Account for the disposal of a plant asset

Eventually, an asset wears out or becomes obsolete. The owner may sell the asset or exchange it. If not, then it's junked. In all cases, you should bring depreciation up to date and then remove the asset from the books.

To record disposal,

- credit the asset account
- debit its accumulated depreciation

That gets the asset off the books.

Suppose you are disposing of equipment and final-year depreciation has just been recorded. Cost was $6,000, and there is no residual value. Accumulated depreciation, thus, totals $6,000. This asset cannot be sold or exchanged, so you have to junk it. The entry to record disposal is:

	Accumulated Depreciation—Equipment	6,000	
	Equipment		6,000
	To dispose of fully depreciated equipment.		

Now both accounts have a zero balance, as shown in the T-accounts.

Equipment		Accumulated Depreciation—Equipment	
6,000	6,000	6,000	6,000

If assets are junked before being fully depreciated, there's a loss equal to the asset's book value. Suppose store fixtures that cost $4,000 are junked at a loss. Accumulated depreciation is $3,000, and book value is therefore $1,000. Disposal generates a $1,000 loss, as follows:

	Accumulated Depreciation—Store Fixtures	3,000	
	Loss on Disposal of Store Fixtures	1,000	
	Store Fixtures		4,000
	To dispose of store fixtures.		

The loss is reported along with expenses on the income statement.

Selling a Plant Asset

Suppose you sell furniture on June 30, 2008, for $5,000 cash. The furniture cost $10,000 when purchased back in 2005. It has been depreciated straight-line over 10 years with no residual value.

First, update depreciation for 6 months—January through June. Your depreciation entry at June 30, 2008, is:

June 30	Depreciation Expense ($10,000/10 years × 6/12)	500	
	Accumulated Depreciation—Furniture		500
	To update depreciation.		

Now Furniture and Accumulated Depreciation are up-to-date.

Furniture

	Debit	Credit
Jan. 1, 2005	10,000	

Accumulated Depreciation—Furniture

Debit	Date	Credit
	Dec. 31, 2005	1,000
	Dec. 31, 2006	1,000
	Dec. 31, 2007	1,000
	June 30, 2008	500
	Balance	3,500

Book Value = $6,500

Book value of the furniture is $6,500. Suppose you sell it for $5,000 cash. The loss on the sale is $1,500, computed as follows:

Cash received from selling the asset		$5,000
Book value of asset sold:		
Cost	$10,000	
Less: Accumulated depreciation up to date of sale	(3,500)	6,500
Gain (loss) on sale of the asset		($1,500)

The entry to sell the furniture is:

June 30	Cash	5,000	
	Accumulated Depreciation—Furniture	3,500	
	Loss on Sale of Furniture	1,500	
	Furniture		10,000
	To sell furniture.		

When recording the sale of a plant asset, you must:

- Remove the balances from the asset account (Furniture, in this case) and its accumulated depreciation account.
- Record a gain or loss if the cash received differs from the asset's book value.

In the example we just completed, cash of $5,000 was less than book value of $6,500. The result was a loss of $1,500.

If the sale price had been \$7,500, there would have been a gain of \$1,000 (Cash, \$7,500 − asset book value, \$6,500). The entry to record this gain would be:

Date	Accounts	Debit	Credit
June 30	Cash	7,500	
	Accumulated Depreciation—Furniture	3,500	
	Furniture		10,000
	Gain on Sale of Furniture		1,000
	To sell furniture.		

Compute gain or loss on the sale of a plant asset as follows:

Gain (credit) = Sale proceeds > Book value
Loss (debit) = Sale proceeds < Book value

All gains and losses are reported on the income statement.

Exchanging Plant Assets

Businesses often trade in old plant assets for new ones. The most common exchange is a trade-in. For example, Domino's Pizza may trade in a five-year-old delivery car for a newer model. To record the exchange, Domino's must write off the old asset and its accumulated depreciation exactly as we just did for the disposal of furniture in the preceding section.

No Gain or Loss on Exchange

For most trade-ins, the business records the cost of the new asset at the book value of the old asset plus any cash payment. For example, assume Domino's old delivery car cost \$9,000 and has accumulated depreciation of \$8,000. Book value is therefore \$1,000. Domino's trades in the old auto and pays cash of \$10,000. Domino's records the trade-in with this journal entry:

Date	Accounts	Debit	Credit
	Delivery Auto (new)	11,000	
	Accumulated Depreciation (old)	8,000	
	Delivery Auto (old)		9,000
	Cash		10,000
	Traded in old delivery car for new auto.		

Domino's cost of the new car is \$11,000 (cash paid \$10,000, plus the book value of the old auto, \$1,000).

Loss on Exchange

A trade-in can result in a loss. That occurs when the market value of the new asset received is less than the total amount given—book value of old asset plus any cash paid. We never record an asset at more than its *market value*. To illustrate a loss, assume the market value of the new asset received in the preceding example is only $7,000. This situation creates a loss, computed as follows:

Market value of new auto received		$ 7,000
Value given:		
Book value of old auto traded in	$ 1,000	
Cash paid	10,000	11,000
(Loss) on exchange		$(4,000)

You would record this exchange with the following entry:

Delivery Auto (new)	7,000*	
Accumulated Depreciation (old)	8,000	
Loss on Exchange of Assets	4,000	
Delivery Auto (old)		9,000
Cash		10,000
Traded in old delivery car for new auto.		

*Maximum amount is the asset's market value.

Gains on asset exchanges occur less often.

Accounting for Natural Resources

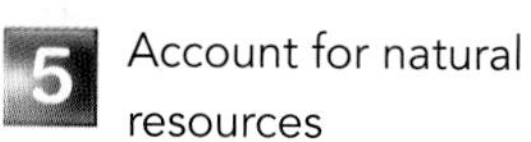
5 Account for natural resources

Natural resources are plant assets. Examples include iron ore, oil, natural gas, and timber. Natural resources are like inventories in the ground (oil) or on top of the ground (timber). Natural resources are expensed through *depletion*. **Depletion expense** is that portion of the cost of natural resources that is used up in a particular period. Depletion expense is computed by the units-of-production formula:

$$\text{Depletion expense} = \frac{\text{Cost} - \text{Residual value}}{\text{Estimated total units of natural resource}} \times \text{Number of units removed}$$

An oil well may cost $100,000 and hold 10,000 barrels of oil. Natural resources usually have no residual value. The depletion rate, thus, would be $10 per barrel ($100,000/10,000 barrels). If 3,000 barrels are extracted during the year, then depletion is $30,000 (3,000 barrels × $10 per barrel). The depletion entry is:

Depletion Expense (3,000 barrels × $10)	30,000	
Accumulated Depreciation—Oil		30,000

If 4,500 barrels are removed next year, depletion is $45,000 (4,500 barrels × $10 per barrel).

Accumulated Depletion is a contra account similar to Accumulated Depreciation. Natural resources can be reported on the balance sheet as shown for oil in the following example:

Property, Plant, and Equipment:		
Land		$ 40,000
Buildings	$ 80,000	
Equipment	20,000	
	100,000	
Less: Accumulated depreciation	(30,000)	70,000
Oil	$180,000	
Less: Accumulated depletion	(50,000)	130,000
Property, plant, and equipment, net		$240,000

Accounting for Intangible Assets

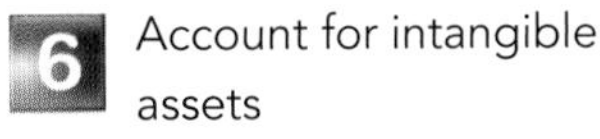

6 Account for intangible assets

As we saw earlier, *intangible assets* have no physical form. Instead, these assets convey special rights from patents, copyrights, trademarks, and so on.

In our technology-driven economy, intangibles are very important. Consider online pioneer eBay. The company has no physical products or equipment, but it helps people buy and sell everything from Batman toys to old picture frames. Each month eBay serves millions of customers. In a sense, eBay is a company of intangibles.

The intellectual capital of eBay or Intel is difficult to measure. But when one company buys another, we get a glimpse of the value of the acquired company. For example, America Online (AOL) acquired Time Warner. AOL said it would give $146 billion for Time Warner's net tangible assets of only $9 billion. Why so much for so little? Because Time Warner's intangible assets were worth billions. Intangibles can account for most of a company's market value, so companies must value their intangibles, just as they do inventory and equipment.

A *patent* is an intangible asset that protects a secret process or formula. The acquisition cost of a patent is debited to the Patents account. The intangible is expensed through **amortization**, the systematic reduction of the asset's carrying value on the books. Amortization applies to intangibles exactly as depreciation applies to equipment and depletion to oil and timber.

Amortization is computed over the asset's estimated useful life—usually by the straight-line method. Obsolescence often shortens an intangible's useful life. Amortization expense for an intangible asset can be credited directly to the asset with no accumulated amortization account. The residual value of most intangibles is zero.

Some intangibles have indefinite lives. For them, the company records no systematic amortization each period. Instead, it accounts for any decrease in the value of the intangible, as we shall see for goodwill.

Specific Intangibles

Patents, copyrights, trademarks, and franchises are intangible assets. Their accounting follows the pattern we illustrate for patents.

Patents

A **patent** is a federal government grant conveying an exclusive 20-year right to produce and sell an invention. The invention may be a product or a process—for example, the Dolby noise-reduction process. Like any other asset, a patent may be purchased. Suppose General Electric (GE) pays $200,000 to acquire a patent on January 1. GE believes this patent's useful life is 5 years. Amortization expense is $40,000 per year ($200,000/5 years). Acquisition and amortization entries for this patent are

Jan. 1	Patents	200,000	
	Cash		200,000
	To acquire a patent.		
Dec. 31	Amortization Expense—Patents ($200,000/5)	40,000	
	Patents		40,000
	To amortize the cost of a patent.		

At the end of the first year, GE will report this patent at $160,000 ($200,000 minus first-year amortization of $40,000), next year at $120,000, and so on.

Copyrights

A **copyright** is the exclusive right to reproduce and sell a book, musical composition, film, or other work of art or intellectual property. Copyrights also protect computer software programs, such as Microsoft Windows® and the Excel spreadsheet. Issued by the federal government, a copyright extends 70 years beyond the author's life.

A company may pay a large sum to purchase an existing copyright. For example, the publisher Simon & Schuster may pay $1 million for the copyright on a popular novel. Most copyrights have short useful lives.

Trademarks, Brand Names

Trademarks and **trade names** (also known as **brand names**) are assets that represent distinctive products or services, such as the CBS "eye" and NBC's peacock. Legally protected slogans include Chevrolet's "Like a Rock" and Avis Rent A Car's "We try harder." The cost of a trademark or trade name is amortized over its useful life.

Franchises, Licenses

Franchises and **licenses** are privileges granted by a private business or a government to sell goods or services under specified conditions. The Green Bay Packers football organization is a franchise granted by the National Football League. McDonald's restaurants and Holiday Inns are well-known business franchises. The acquisition cost of a franchise or license is amortized over its useful life.

Goodwill

Goodwill is truly a unique asset. *Goodwill* in accounting has a different meaning from the everyday phrase "goodwill among men." In accounting, **goodwill** is the excess of the cost to purchase another company over the market value of its net assets (assets minus liabilities).

Wal-Mart has expanded into Mexico. Suppose Wal-Mart acquired Monterrey Company. The sum of the market values of Monterrey's assets was $9 million and its liabilities totaled $1 million, so Monterrey's net assets totaled $8 million. Suppose Wal-Mart paid $10 million to purchase Monterrey Company. In this case, Wal-Mart paid $2 million for goodwill, computed as follows:

Purchase price to acquire Monterrey Company..........		$10 million
Market value of Monterrey Company's assets............	$9 million	
Less: Monterrey Company's liabilities........................	(1 million)	
Market value of Monterrey Company's net assets.......		8 million
Excess, called *goodwill*...		$ 2 million

Wal-Mart's entry to record the purchase of Monterrey, including the goodwill that Wal-Mart purchased, would be:

	Assets (Cash, Receivables, Inventories, Plant Assets, all at market value)	9,000,000	
	Goodwill	2,000,000	
	Liabilities		1,000,000
	Cash		10,000,000
	Purchased Monterrey Company.		

Goodwill has some special features:

1. Goodwill is recorded only by the company that purchases another company. An outstanding reputation may create goodwill, but that company never records goodwill for its own business. Instead, goodwill is recorded *only* by the acquiring entity when it buys another company.
2. According to generally accepted accounting principles (GAAP), goodwill is *not* amortized. Instead, the acquiring company measures the current value of its goodwill each year. If the goodwill has increased in value, there is nothing to record. But if goodwill's value has decreased, then the company records a loss and writes the goodwill down. For example, suppose Wal-Mart's goodwill—purchased above—is worth only $1,500,000 at the end of the first year. In that case, Wal-Mart would make this entry:

	Loss on Goodwill	500,000	
	Goodwill ($2,000,000 – $1,500,000)		500,000
	Recorded loss on goodwill.		

Wal-Mart would then report this goodwill at its current value of $1,500,000.

Accounting for Research and Development Costs

Accounting for research and development (R&D) costs is one of the toughest issues the accounting profession has faced. R&D is the lifeblood of companies such as Procter & Gamble, General Electric, Intel, and Boeing. But, in general, companies don't report R&D assets on their balance sheets because GAAP requires companies to expense R&D costs as they incur those costs.

Ethical Issues

The main ethical issue in accounting for plant assets is whether to capitalize or expense a cost. In this area, companies have split personalities. On the one hand, they want to save on taxes. This motivates them to expense all costs and decrease taxable income. But they also want to look as good as possible, with high net income and huge assets.

In most cases, a cost that is capitalized or expensed for tax purposes must be treated the same way in the financial statements. What, then, is the ethical path? Accountants should follow the general guidelines for capitalizing a cost:

Capitalize all costs that provide a future benefit.
Expense all other costs.

Many companies have gotten into trouble by capitalizing costs that were really expenses. They made their financial statements look better than the facts warranted. WorldCom committed this type of accounting fraud, and its former top executives are now in prison as a result. There are very few cases of companies getting into trouble by following the general guidelines, or even by erring on the side of accounting conservatism. It works.

Decision Guidelines

Accounting for Plant Assets and Related Expenses

The Decision Guidelines summarize key decisions a company makes in accounting for plant assets. Suppose you buy a T-Shirts Plus or a Curves International franchise and invest in related equipment. You have some decisions to make about how to account for the franchise and the equipment. The Decision Guidelines will help you maximize your cash flow and do the accounting properly.

Decision	Guidelines
Capitalize or expense a cost?	General rule: Capitalize all costs that provide *future benefit.* Expense all costs that provide *no future benefit.*
Capitalize or expense:	
• Cost associated with a new asset?	Capitalize all costs that bring the asset to its intended use.
• Cost associated with an existing asset?	Capitalize only those costs that add to the asset's usefulness or its useful life. Expense all other costs as repairs or maintenance.
Which depreciation method to use:	
• For financial reporting?	Use the method that best matches depreciation expense against the revenues produced by the asset.
• For income tax?	Use the method that produces the fastest tax deductions (MACRS). A company can use different depreciation methods for the financial statements and for income tax purposes. In the United States, this practice is considered both legal and ethical.

Summary Problem 2

The following figures appear in the Answers to Summary Problem 1, Requirement 2, on page 468.

	Method B: Double-Declining-Balance			Method C: Straight-Line		
Year	Annual Depreciation Expense	Accumulated Depreciation	Book Value	Annual Depreciation Expense	Accumulated Depreciation	Book Value
Start			$44,000			$44,000
2007	$8,800	$ 8,800	35,200	$4,000	$ 4,000	40,000
2008	7,040	15,840	28,160	4,000	8,000	36,000
2009	5,632	21,472	22,528	4,000	12,000	32,000

Latté on Demand purchased equipment on January 1, 2007. Management has depreciated the equipment by using the double-declining-balance method. On July 1, 2009, the company sold the equipment for $27,000 cash.

Requirements

1. Suppose the income tax authorities permit a choice between the two depreciation methods shown. Which method would you select for income tax purposes? Why?
2. Record Latté on Demand's depreciation for 2009 and the sale of the equipment on July 1, 2009.

Solution

Requirement 1

Select the double-declining balance method. For tax purposes, most companies select accelerated depreciation because it results in the fastest write-offs. Accelerated depreciation minimizes taxable income and income tax payments in the early years of the asset's life, thereby conserving cash.

Requirement 2

To record depreciation to date of sale and the sale of the Latté on Demand equipment:

Date	Accounts	Debit	Credit
2009			
Jan. 1	Depreciation Expense ($5,632 × 1/2 year)	2,816	
	Accumulated Depreciation		2,816
	To update depreciation.		
July 1	Cash	27,000	
	Accumulated Depreciation ($15,840 + $2,816)	18,656	
	Equipment		44,000
	Gain on Sale of Equipment		1,656
	To record sale of equipment.		

Review *Plant Assets and Intangibles*

Accounting Vocabulary

Accelerated Depreciation Method
A depreciation method that writes off more of the asset's cost near the start of its useful life than the straight-line method does.

Amortization
Systematic reduction of the asset's carrying value on the books. Expense that applies to intangibles in the same way depreciation applies to plant assets and depletion to natural resources.

Brand Names
Assets that represent distinctive identifications of a product or service.

Capital Expenditure
Expenditure that increases the capacity or efficiency of an asset or extends its useful life. Capital expenditures are debited to an asset account.

Copyright
Exclusive right to reproduce and sell a book, musical composition, film, other work of art, or computer program. Issued by the federal government, copyrights extend 70 years beyond the author's life.

Depletion Expense
Portion of a natural resource's cost used up in a particular period. Computed in the same way as units-of-production depreciation.

Depreciable Cost
The cost of a plant asset minus its estimated residual value.

Depreciation
The allocation of a plant asset's cost to expense over its useful life.

Double-Declining-Balance (DDB) Method
An accelerated depreciation method that computes annual depreciation by multiplying the asset's decreasing book value by a constant percent that is two times the straight-line rate.

Estimated Residual Value
Expected cash value of an asset at the end of its useful life. Also called **salvage value**.

Estimated Useful Life
Length of the service period expected from an asset. May be expressed in years, units of output, miles, or another measure.

Extraordinary Repair
Repair work that generates a capital expenditure.

Franchise
Privileges granted by a private business or a government to sell a product or service under specified conditions.

Goodwill
Excess of the cost of an acquired company over the sum of the market values of its net assets (assets minus liabilities).

Intangibles
Assets with no physical form. Valuable because of the special rights they carry. Examples are patents and copyrights.

Licenses
Privileges granted by a private business or a government to sell a product or service under specified conditions.

Ordinary Repair
Repair work that is debited to an expense account.

Patent
A federal government grant giving the holder the exclusive right to produce and sell an invention for 20 years.

Plant Assets
Long-lived tangible assets, such as land, buildings, and equipment, used to operate a business.

Salvage Value
Expected cash value of an asset at the end of its useful life. Also called **estimated residual value**.

Straight-Line (SL) Depreciation Method
Depreciation method in which an equal amount of depreciation expense is assigned to each year of asset use.

Trademarks
Assets that represent distinctive identifications of a product or service.

Trade Names
Assets that represent distinctive identifications of a product or service.

Units-of-Production (UOP) Depreciation Method
Depreciation method by which a fixed amount of depreciation is assigned to each unit of output produced by an asset.

Quick Check

1. Which cost is not recorded as part of the cost of a building?
   a. Annual building maintenance
   b. Construction materials and labor
   c. Earthmoving for the building's foundation
   d. Real estate commission paid to buy the building

2. FedEx bought two used Boeing airplanes. Each plane was worth \$35 million, but the owner sold the combination for \$60 million. How much is FedEx's cost of each plane?
   a. \$60 million
   b. \$70 million
   c. \$30 million
   d. \$35 million

3. How should you record a capital expenditure?
   a. Debit an asset
   b. Debit an expense
   c. Debit a liability
   d. Debit capital

4. Which method always produces the most depreciation in the first year?
   a. Straight-line
   b. Double-declining-balance
   c. Units-of-production
   d. All produce the same total depreciation

5. A FedEx jet costs \$50 million and is expected to fly 500 million miles during its 10-year life. Residual value is expected to be zero because the plane was used when acquired. If the plane travels 20 million miles the first year, how much depreciation should FedEx record under the units-of-production method?
   a. \$2 million
   b. \$5 million
   c. \$10 million
   d. Cannot be determined from the data given

6. Which depreciation method would you prefer to use for income tax purposes? Why?
   a. Straight-line because it is simplest
   b. Units-of-production because it best tracks the asset's use
   c. Double-declining-balance because it gives the fastest tax deductions for depreciation
   d. Double-declining-balance because it gives the most total depreciation over the asset's life

7. A copy machine cost $40,000 when new and has accumulated depreciation of $35,000. Suppose Kinko's junks this machine, receiving nothing. What is the result of the disposal transaction?
   a. No gain or loss
   b. Gain of $5,000
   c. Loss of $35,000
   d. Loss of $5,000

8. Suppose Kinko's in the preceding question sold the machine for $5,000. What is the result of this disposal transaction?
   a. Gain of $2,000
   b. Loss of $2,000
   c. Gain of $3,000
   d. No gain or loss

9. Which method is used to compute depletion?
   a. Depletion method
   b. Units-of-production method
   c. Straight-line method
   d. Double-declining-balance method

10. Which intangible asset is recorded only as part of the acquisition of another company?
   a. Patent
   b. Copyright
   c. Goodwill
   d. Franchise

Answers are given after Apply Your Knowledge (p. 497).

Assess Your Progress

Short Exercises

Measuring the cost of a plant asset

S9-1 This chapter lists the costs included for the acquisition of land. First is the purchase price, which is obviously included in the cost of the land. The reasons for including the other costs are not so obvious. For example, removing a building looks more like an expense. State why the costs listed are included as part of the cost of the land. After the land is ready for use, will these costs be capitalized or expensed? (p. 456)

Lump-sum purchase of assets

S9-2 In Motion T-Shirts pays $150,000 for a group purchase of land, building, and equipment. At the time of your acquisition, the land has a market value of $80,000, the building $60,000, and the equipment $20,000. Journalize the lump-sum purchase of the three assets for a total cost of $150,000. You sign a note payable for this amount. (p. 458)

Capitalizing versus expensing plant-asset costs

S9-3 Texas Aero repaired one of its Boeing 737 aircraft at a cost of $250,000. Texas Aero erroneously capitalized this cost as part of the cost of the plane. How will this accounting error affect Texas Aero's net income? Ignore depreciation. (p. 460)

Computing depreciation by three methods—first year only

S9-4 At the beginning of the year, Texas Aero purchased a used Boeing jet for $35,000,000. Texas Aero expects the plane to remain useful for five years (6 million miles) and to have a residual value of $5,000,000. The company expects the plane to be flown 1 million miles the first year.

1. Compute Texas Aero's *first-year* depreciation on the plane using the following methods:
   a. Straight-line (p. 462)
   b. Units-of-production (p. 463)
   c. Double-declining-balance (p. 464)
2. Show the airplane's book value at the end of the first year under the straight-line method. (p. 462)

Computing depreciation by three methods—second year

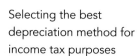

S9-5 At the beginning of 2007, Texas Aero purchased a used **Boeing** jet at a cost of $35,000,000. Texas Aero expects the plane to remain useful for five years (6 million miles) and to have a residual value of $5,000,000. Texas Aero expects the plane to be flown 1 million miles the first year and 1.5 million miles the second year. Compute *second-year* depreciation on the plane using the following methods:

a. Straight-line (p. 462)
b. Units-of-production (p. 463)
c. Double-declining-balance (p. 464)

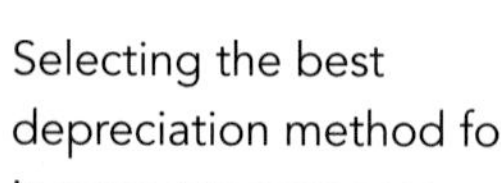

Selecting the best depreciation method for income tax purposes

S9-6 This exercise uses the Texas Aero data from Short Exercise 9-4. Texas Aero is deciding which depreciation method to use for income tax purposes.

1. Which depreciation method offers the tax advantage for the first year? Describe the nature of the tax advantage. (pp. 468–469)
2. How much extra depreciation will Texas Aero get to deduct for the first year as compared with the straight-line method? (pp. 462, 464)

Partial-year depreciation

S9-7 On March 31, 2008, FedEx Kinko's purchased a Xerox copy machine for $80,000. FedEx Kinko's expects the machine to last for five years and to have a residual value of $8,000. Compute depreciation on the machine for the year ended December 31, 2008, using the straight-line method. (pp. 469–470)

Computing and recording depreciation after a change in useful life

S9-8 Assume that the Chicago Cubs baseball organization paid $50,000 for a hot dog stand with a 10-year life and zero expected residual value. After using the hot dog stand for four years, the company determines that the asset will remain useful for only two more years. Record depreciation on the hot dog stand for year 5 by the straight-line method. (p. 471)

Recording a gain or loss on disposal of a plant asset

S9-9 Return to the American Airlines baggage-handling truck in Exhibit 9-7, page 463. Suppose American sold the truck on December 31, 2009, for $28,000 cash, after using the truck for two full years. Depreciation for 2009 has been recorded. Make the journal entry to record American's sale of the truck. (p. 473)

Exchanging plant assets

S9-10 Air & Sea Travel purchased a Dell Computer for $3,000, debiting Computer Equipment. During 2007 and 2008, Air & Sea recorded depreciation of $2,200 on the computer. In January 2009, Air & Sea traded in the computer for a new one, paying $2,500 cash. Journalize Air & Sea Travel's exchange of computers. (p. 473)

Accounting for the depletion of natural resources

S9-11 British Petroleum (BP) holds huge reserves of oil and gas assets. Assume that at the end of 2006, BP's cost of oil and gas reserves totaled $24 billion, representing 2.4 billion barrels of oil and gas.

1. Which depreciation method does BP use to compute depletion? (pp. 474–475)
2. Suppose BP removed 0.5 billion barrels of oil during 2007. Record depletion expense for 2007. (pp. 474–475)

Accounting for goodwill

S9-12 When one media company buys another, goodwill is often the most costly asset. Vector Advertising paid $210,000 to acquire *The Thrifty Nickel,* a weekly advertising paper. At the time of the acquisition, *The Thrifty Nickel*'s balance sheet reported total assets of $100,000 and liabilities of $60,000. The fair market value of *Thrifty Nickel* assets was $80,000.

1. How much goodwill did Vector Advertising purchase as part of the acquisition of *The Thrifty Nickel?* (pp. 476–477)
2. Journalize Vector's acquisition of *The Thrifty Nickel.* (pp. 476–477)

Accounting for patents and research and development cost
6

S9-13 This exercise summarizes the accounting for patents and for research and development.

During 2008, Digital Cable Company paid $50,000 to research and develop a new technology, and also purchased a patent for $10,000. Digital's service revenue for 2008 totaled $700,000, and selling expenses were $400,000. Digital expects the patent to have a useful life of five years. Prepare Digital Cable Company's income statement for the year ended December 31, 2008, complete with a heading. (pp. 22, 475–478)

Exercises

Determining the cost of plant assets

E9-14 Trautschold Furniture Co. purchased land, paying $80,000 cash plus a $300,000 note payable. In addition, Trautschold paid delinquent property tax of $2,000, title insurance costing $3,000, and $5,000 to level the land and remove an unwanted building. The company then constructed an office building at a cost of $500,000. It also paid $50,000 for a fence around the property, $10,000 for a sign near the entrance, and $6,000 for special lighting of the grounds. Determine the cost of the land, land improvements, and building. Which of these assets will Trautschold depreciate? (pp. 456–458)

Allocating cost to assets acquired in a lump-sum purchase

E9-15 Northwood Properties bought three lots in a subdivision for a lump-sum price. An independent appraiser valued the lots as follows:

Lot	Appraised Value
1	$50,000
2	60,000
3	70,000

Northwood paid $150,000 in cash. Record the purchase in the journal, identifying each lot's cost in a separate Land account. Round decimals to three places, and use your computed percentages throughout. (p. 458)

Distinguishing capital expenditures from expenses

E9-16 Classify each of the following expenditures as a capital expenditure or an expense related to machinery: (a) purchase price; (b) ordinary recurring repairs to keep the machinery in good working order; (c) lubrication before machinery is placed in service; (d) periodic lubrication after machinery is placed in service; (e) major overhaul to extend useful life by three years; (f) sales tax paid on the purchase price; (g) transportation and insurance while machinery is in transit from seller to buyer; (h) installation; (i) training of personnel for initial operation of the machinery; and (j) income tax paid on income earned from the sale of products manufactured by the machinery. (p. 450)

Capitalizing versus expensing costs; measuring the effect of an error

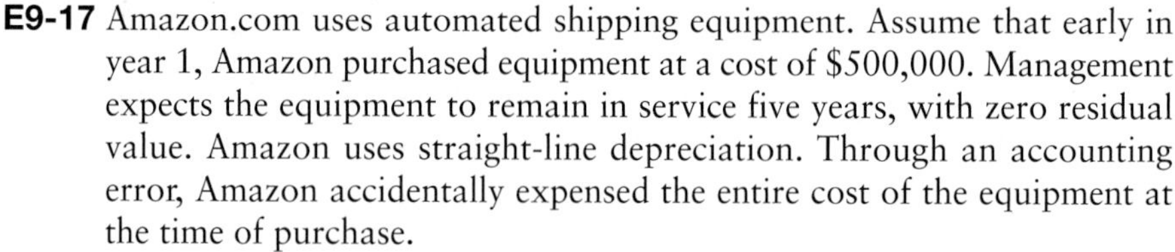

E9-17 Amazon.com uses automated shipping equipment. Assume that early in year 1, Amazon purchased equipment at a cost of $500,000. Management expects the equipment to remain in service five years, with zero residual value. Amazon uses straight-line depreciation. Through an accounting error, Amazon accidentally expensed the entire cost of the equipment at the time of purchase.

Requirements

Compute the overstatement or understatement in the following items immediately after purchasing the equipment:

1. Equipment (p. 460)
2. Net income (p. 460)

Explaining the concept of depreciation

E9-18 Ron Zander just slept through the class in which Professor Chen explained the concept of depreciation. Because the next test is scheduled for Friday, Zander telephones Sven Svensen to get his notes from the lecture. Svensen's notes are concise: "Depreciation—Sounds like Greek to me." Zander next tries Lisa Lake, who says she thinks depreciation is what happens when an asset wears out. Jason Gerbing is confident that depreciation is the process of creating a cash fund to replace an asset at the end of its useful life. Explain the concept of depreciation for Zander. Evaluate the explanations of Lake and Gerbing. Be specific. (pp. 460–461)

Computing depreciation amounts by three methods

E9-19 Pulley-Bone Fried Chicken bought equipment on January 2, 2007, for $15,000. The equipment was expected to remain in service 4 years and to perform 3,000 fry jobs. At the end of the equipment's useful life, Pulley-Bone estimates that its residual value will be $3,000. The equipment performed 300 jobs the first year, 900 the second year, 1,200 the third, and 600 the fourth year. Prepare a schedule of *depreciation expense* per year for the equipment under the three depreciation methods. After two years under double-declining-balance depreciation, the company switched to the straight-line method. Show your computations. (pp. 462–464)

Which method tracks the wear and tear on the equipment most closely? (p. 465)

Selecting the best depreciation method for income tax purposes

E9-20 Flips Gymnastics Center paid $140,000 for fitness equipment that is expected to have a 10-year life. The expected residual value is $40,000.

Select the appropriate MACRS depreciation method for income tax purposes. Then determine the extra amount of depreciation that Flips can deduct by using MACRS depreciation, versus straight-line, during the first two years of the equipment's life. (pp. 469–471)

Changing a plant asset's useful life

E9-21 A-1 Security Consultants purchased a building for $500,000 and depreciated it on a straight-line basis over a 40-year period. The estimated residual value was $100,000. After using the building for 15 years, A-1 realized that wear and tear on the building would wear it out before 40 years. Starting with the 16th year A-1 began depreciating the building over a revised total life of 25 years. Record depreciation on the building for years 15 and 16. (pp. 462, 471)

Analyzing the sale of a plant asset; DDB depreciation

E9-22 On January 2, 2006, Ditto Clothing Consignments purchased showroom fixtures for $10,000 cash, expecting the fixtures to remain in service 5 years. Ditto has depreciated the fixtures on a double-declining-balance basis, with zero residual value. On September 30, 2007, Ditto sold the fixtures for $6,200 cash. Record both depreciation for 2007 and sale of the fixtures on September 30, 2007. (p. 473)

Trade-in of office fixtures—two situations

E9-23 Community Bank recently traded in office fixtures. Here are the facts:

Old fixtures:

- Cost, $90,000
- Accumulated depreciation, $75,000

New fixtures:

- Cash paid, $100,000, plus the old fixtures

continued . . .

1. Record Community Bank's trade-in of old fixtures for new ones. (p. 473)
2. Now let's change one fact and see a different outcome. Community Bank feels compelled to do business with Lakeside Furniture, a bank customer, even though the bank can get the fixtures elsewhere at a better price. Community Bank is aware that the new fixtures' market value is only $110,000. Now record the trade-in. (p. 473)

Measuring a plant asset's cost, using UOP depreciation, and trading in an asset

E9-24 Covenant Trucking Company uses the units-of-production (UOP) depreciation method because UOP best measures wear and tear on the trucks. Consider these facts about one Mack truck in the company's fleet.

When acquired in 2006, the rig cost $350,000 and was expected to remain in service for 10 years or 1,000,000 miles. Estimated residual value was $100,000. The truck was driven 80,000 miles in 2006, 120,000 miles in 2007, and 160,000 miles in 2008. After 40,000 miles in 2009, the company traded in the Mack truck for a less-expensive Freightliner. Covenant also paid cash of $20,000. Determine Covenant's cost of the new truck. Journal entries are not required. (pp. 463, 473)

Recording natural resource assets and depletion

E9-25 Sierra Mountain Mining paid $428,500 for the right to extract mineral assets from a 200,000-ton deposit. In addition to the purchase price, Sierra also paid a $500 filing fee, a $1,000 license fee to the state of Nevada, and $70,000 for a geological survey of the property. Because Sierra purchased the rights to the minerals only, it expects the asset to have zero residual value. During the first year, Sierra removed 30,000 tons of the minerals. Make journal entries to record (a) purchase of the minerals (debit Mineral Asset), (b) payment of fees and other costs, and (c) depletion for the first year. (pp. 474–475)

Recording a patent, amortization, and a change in the asset's useful life

E9-26 1. Hewlett Packard (HP) manufactures printers. Assume that HP recently paid $600,000 for a patent on a new laser printer. Although it gives legal protection for 20 years, the patent is expected to provide a competitive advantage for only 8 years. Assuming the straight-line method of amortization, make journal entries to record (a) the purchase of the patent and (b) amortization for year 1. (pp. 475–476)

2. After using the patent for 4 years, HP learns at an industry trade show that another company is designing a more-efficient printer. On the basis of this new information, HP decides, starting with year 5, to amortize the remaining cost of the patent over 2 remaining years, giving the patent a total useful life of 6 years. Record amortization for year 5. (p. 471)

Measuring and recording goodwill

E9-27 PepsiCo, Inc., has acquired several other companies. Assume that PepsiCo purchased Kettle Chips Co. for $8 million cash. The book value of Kettle Chips' assets is $12 million (market value, $15 million), and it has liabilities of $10 million.

Requirements

1. Compute the cost of the goodwill purchased by PepsiCo.
2. Record the purchase of Kettle Chips by PepsiCo.

Problems (Group A)

Identifying the elements of a plant asset's cost

P9-28A Park and Fly, near an airport, incurred the following costs to acquire land, make land improvements, and construct and furnish a small building:

a. Purchase price of 3 acres of land	$ 60,000
b. Delinquent real estate taxes on the land to be paid by Park and Fly	3,700
c. Additional dirt and earthmoving	5,100
d. Title insurance on the land acquisition	1,000
e. Fence around the boundary of the property	44,200
f. Building permit for the building	200
g. Architect's fee for the design of the building	5,000
h. Signs near the approaches to the property	20,900
i. Materials used to construct the building	40,000
j. Labor to construct the building	30,000
k. Interest cost on construction loan for the building	3,800
l. Parking lots on the property	120,000
m. Lights for the parking lot	8,900
n. Salary of construction supervisor (10% to building; 90% to parking lot)	50,000
o. Furniture	6,000
p. Transportation of furniture from seller to the building	400
q. Landscaping (shrubs)	9,000

Park and Fly depreciates land improvements over 20 years, buildings over 30 years, and furniture over 8 years, all on a straight-line basis with zero residual value.

Requirements

1. Set up columns for Land, Land Improvements, Building, and Furniture. Show how to account for each cost by listing the cost under the correct account. Determine the total cost of each asset. (pp. 456–458)
2. All construction was complete and the assets were placed in service on March 31. Record partial-year depreciation for the year ended December 31. (pp. 462, 469–470)

Recording plant-asset transactions, exchange, and disposal

1 2 4

P9-29A Gretta Chun Associates surveys American eating habits. The company's accounts include Land, Buildings, Office Equipment, and Communication Equipment, with a separate accumulated depreciation account for each asset. During 2007, Chun completed the following transactions:

Jan.	1	Traded in old office equipment with book value of $11,000 (cost of $96,000 and accumulated depreciation of $85,000) for new equipment. Chun also paid $19,000 in cash. (p. 473)

continued . . .

Apr.	1	Acquired land and communication equipment in a group purchase. Total cost was $80,000 paid in cash. An independent appraisal valued the land at $90,000 and the communication equipment at $10,000. (p. 458)
Sep.	1	Sold a building that had cost $128,000 (accumulated depreciation of $100,000 through December 31 of the preceding year). Chun received $60,000 cash from the sale of the building. (p. 473) Depreciation is computed on a straight-line basis. The building has a 30-year useful life and a residual value of $20,000. (pp. 462–470)
Dec.	31	Recorded depreciations as follows: Communication equipment is depreciated by the straight-line method over a 5-year life with zero residual value. (pp. 462–470) Office equipment is depreciated straight-line over 6 years with $3,000 residual value. (pp. 462–470)

Requirement

Record the transactions in the journal of Gretta Chun Associates. Chun ends its accounting year on December 31.

Explaining the concept of depreciation

2

P9-30A The board of directors of Park Place Porsche is having a quarterly meeting. Accounting policies are on the agenda, and depreciation is being discussed. A new board member, an attorney, has some strong opinions about two aspects of depreciation policy. Jennifer Axelrod argues that depreciation must be coupled with a fund to replace company assets. Otherwise, there is no way to guarantee the replacement of worn-out assets, she argues. Axelrod also challenges the 3-year depreciable life of company computers. She states that the computers will last much longer and should be depreciated over at least 5 years.

Requirement

Write a memo to explain the concept of depreciation to Axelrod and to answer her arguments. Format your memo as follows: (pp. 460–461)

MEMO

To: ________________

From: ________________

Subject: ________________

Computing depreciation by three methods and the advantage of accelerated depreciation for tax purposes

P9-31A On January 2, 2006, Speedway Delivery Service purchased a truck at a cost of $63,000. Before placing the truck in service, Speedway spent $2,200 painting it, $800 replacing tires, and $4,000 overhauling the engine. The truck should remain in service for 6 years and have a residual value of $14,200. The truck's annual mileage is expected to be 18,000 miles in each of the first four years and 14,000 miles in each of the next two years—100,000 miles in total. In deciding which depreciation method to use, Jerry Speers, the general manager, requests a depreciation schedule for each of the depreciation methods (straight-line, units-of-production, and double-declining-balance).

Requirements

1. Prepare a depreciation schedule for each depreciation method, showing asset cost, depreciation expense, accumulated depreciation, and asset book value. (pp. 462–464)
2. Speedway prepares financial statements using the depreciation method that reports the highest net income in the early years of asset use. For income-tax purposes, the company uses the depreciation method that minimizes income taxes in the early years. Consider the first year that Speedway uses the truck. Identify the depreciation methods that meet the general manager's objectives, assuming the income tax authorities permit the use of any of the methods. (pp. 465, 468–469)

Accounting for natural resources and the related expenses

P9-32A Conseco Oil Company has an account titled Oil and Gas Properties. Conseco paid $6,000,000 for oil reserves holding an estimated 500,000 barrels of oil. Assume the company paid $550,000 for additional geological tests of the property and $450,000 to prepare for drilling. During the first year, Conseco removed 70,000 barrels of oil, which it sold on account for $30 per barrel. Operating expenses totaled $800,000, all paid in cash.

Requirements

1. Record all of Conseco's transactions, including depletion. (pp. 474–475)
2. Prepare the company's income statement for this oil and gas project for the first year. (p. 22)

Accounting for intangibles

P9-33A Central States Telecom provides communication services in Iowa, Nebraska, the Dakotas, and Montana. Central States purchased goodwill as part of the acquisition of Surety Wireless Company, which had these figures:

Book value of assets	$600,000
Market value of assets	900,000
Liabilities	540,000

continued . . .

Requirements

1. Make the journal entry to record Central States' purchase of Surety Wireless for $300,000 cash plus a $400,000 note payable. (pp. 476–477)
2. What special asset does Central States' acquisition of Surety Wireless identify? How should Central States Telecom account for this asset after acquiring Surety Wireless? Explain in detail. (pp. 476–477)

Reporting plant-asset transactions in the financial statements—a review

P9-34A On May 31, 2004, FedEx, the overnight shipper, had total assets of $19 billion and total liabilities of $11 billion. Included among the assets were property, plant, and equipment with a cost of $20 billion and accumulated depreciation of $11 billion. During the year ended May 31, 2004, FedEx earned total revenues of $25 billion and had total expenses of $24 billion.

Requirements

1. Show how FedEx would report property, plant, and equipment on its balance sheet at May 31, 2004. (pp. 474–475)
2. How much was FedEx's owners' equity at May 31, 2004? (pp. 13–14)
3. Did FedEx report net income or net loss on its 2004 income statement? Compute the amount. (p. 22)

Problems (Group B)

Identifying the elements of a plant asset's cost

1 2

P9-35B Vandergiff Jewelry incurred the following costs to acquire land, make land improvements, and construct and furnish a new building.

a. Purchase price of 4 acres of land	$ 85,000
b. Real estate commission	3,400
c. Landscaping (additional dirt and earthmoving)	8,100
d. Fence around the boundary of the property	9,900
e. Delinquent real estate taxes on the land to be paid by Vandergiff	5,900
f. Company signs at front of the property	9,700
g. Building permit for the building	500
h. Architect's fee for the design of the building	22,500
i. Labor to construct the building	169,000
j. Materials used to construct the building	215,000
k. Interest cost on construction loan for the building	9,000
l. Landscaping (shrubs)	6,400
m. Parking lot and concrete walks	29,700
n. Lights for the parking lot and walkways	10,300
o. Salary of construction supervisor (85% to building; 15% to parking lot and concrete walks)	40,000
p. Furniture for the building	117,800
q. Transportation and installation of furniture	2,200

continued . . .

Vandergriff depreciates land improvements over 20 years, buildings over 40 years, and furniture over 8 years, all on a straight-line basis with zero residual value.

Requirements

1. Set up columns for Land, Land Improvements, Building, and Furniture. Show how to account for each cost by listing the cost under the correct account. Determine the total cost of each asset. (pp. 456–458)
2. All construction was complete and the assets were placed in service on May 1. Record partial-year depreciation for the year ended December 31. (pp. 462, 469–470)

Recording plant-asset transactions, exchange, and disposal
1 2 4

P9-36B The accounts of Haley-Davis Printing Company include Land, Buildings, and Equipment. Haley-Davis has a separate accumulated depreciation account for each asset. During 2007, the company completed the following transactions:

Jan. 1	Traded in equipment with accumulated depreciation of \$90,000 (cost of \$130,000) for similar new equipment. Haley-Davis also paid \$80,000 cash. (p. 473)
July 1	Sold a building that cost \$550,000 and that had accumulated depreciation of \$250,000 through December 31 of the preceding year. Haley-Davis received \$100,000 cash and a \$200,000 note receivable. (p. 473) Depreciation is computed on a straight-line basis. The building has a 40-year useful life and a residual value of \$50,000. (pp. 355, 361)
Aug. 31	Purchased land and a building for a lump-sum payment of \$300,000. An independent appraisal valued the land at \$105,000 and the building at \$210,000. (p. 458)
Dec. 31	Recorded depreciation as follows: Equipment has an expected useful life of 1,000,000 units of output and estimated residual value of \$20,000. Depreciation is units-of-production. During the year, Haley-Davis produced 150,000 units of output. (pp. 463, 469–470) Depreciation on buildings is straight-line. The new building has a 40-year useful life and a residual value equal to \$50,000. (pp. 462, 469–470)

Requirement

Record the transactions in Haley-Davis's journal.

Explaining the concept of depreciation

P9-37B The board of directors of Computer Solutions is reviewing the 2007 annual report. A new board member—a professor—questions the company accountant about the depreciation. The professor wonders why depreciation has decreased from \$200,000 in 2005 to \$180,000 in 2006 to \$160,000 in 2007. He states that he could understand the decreasing amounts of depreciation if the company had been selling properties, but

continued . . .

that has not occurred. Further, growth in the city is increasing the values of property. He asks why the company is recording depreciation when property values are rising.

Requirement

Write a paragraph or two to explain the concept of depreciation and answer the professor's questions. Which depreciation method does Computer Solutions appear to be using? (pp. 460–464)

Computing depreciation by three methods and the advantage of accelerated depreciation for tax purposes

P9-38B On January 3, 2007, Joe Griffin Photography paid $224,000 for photo equipment. In addition to the purchase price, Griffin paid $700 transportation charges, $100 insurance for the equipment while in transit, $12,100 sales tax, and $3,100 for specialized training to be able to use the equipment. Griffin estimates that the equipment will remain in service 5 years and have a residual value of $20,000. The equipment should produce 50,000 photos the first year, with annual production decreasing by 5,000 photos during each of the next four years (that is, 45,000 photos in year 2; 40,000 in year 3; and so on—a total of 200,000 photos). In trying to decide which depreciation method to use, Griffin has requested a depreciation schedule for each of three depreciation methods (straight-line, units-of-production, and double-declining-balance).

Requirements

1. For each depreciation method, prepare a depreciation schedule showing asset cost, depreciation expense, accumulated depreciation, and asset book value. (pp. 462–464)
2. Griffin prepares financial statements using the depreciation method that reports the highest income in the early years. For income tax purposes, the company uses the method that minimizes income taxes in the early years. Consider the first year of using the equipment. Identify the depreciation methods that meet Griffin's objectives, assuming the income tax authorities permit the use of any of the methods. (pp. 465, 468–469)

Accounting for natural resources and the related expense

P9-39B RKI Properties' balance sheet includes a natural resource asset, Coal. RKI paid $600,000 cash for the right to work a mine with an estimated 100,000 tons of coal. The company paid $60,000 to remove unwanted buildings and $40,000 to prepare the surface for mining. RKI also signed a $50,000 note payable to an environmental company that will return the land to its original condition. During the first year, RKI removed 40,000 tons of coal, which it sold on account for $20 per ton. Operating expenses for the first year totaled $360,000, half paid in cash and half on account.

Requirements

1. Record all of RKI's transactions, including depletion, for the year. (pp. 474–475)
2. Prepare the company's income statement for the year. (p. 22)

Accounting for intangibles
6

P9-40B The balance sheet of MBC Television reports intangible assets. Assume that MBC purchased the intangibles as part of the acquisition of another company, which carried these figures:

Book value of assets........................	$ 800,000
Market value of assets	1,100,000
Liabilities..	400,000

Requirements

1. Make the journal entry to record MBC's purchase of the other company for $1,000,000, half in cash and half for a note payable. (pp. 476–477)
2. What special asset does MBC's acquisition of the other company identify? How should MBC account for this asset after acquiring the other company? Explain in detail. (pp. 476–477)

Reporting plant assets in the financial statements—a review

P9-41B At the end of 2004, PepsiCo had total assets of $28 billion and total liabilities of $14 billion. Included among the assets were property, plant, and equipment with a cost of $16 billion and accumulated depreciation of $8 billion. During 2004, PepsiCo earned total revenues of $29 billion and had total expenses of $25 billion.

for 24/7 practice visit www.MyAccountingLab.com

Requirements

1. Show how PepsiCo reported property, plant, and equipment on its balance sheet at December 31, 2004. What was the book value of property, plant, and equipment on that date? (pp. 474–475)
2. How much was PepsiCo's owners' equity at December 31, 2004? (pp. 13–14)
3. Did PepsiCo have net income or net loss for 2004? Compute the amount. (p. 22)

Apply Your Knowledge

Decision Case

Measuring profitability based on different inventory and depreciation methods 

Suppose you are considering investing in two businesses, Tiger Woods Enterprises and Phil Mickelson Systems. The two companies are virtually identical, and both began operations at the beginning of the current year. During the year, each company purchased inventory as follows:

Jan.	4	10,000 units at $4 =	$ 40,000
Apr.	6	5,000 units at 5 =	25,000
Aug.	9	7,000 units at 6 =	42,000
Nov.	27	10,000 units at 7 =	70,000
Totals		32,000	$177,000

During the first year, both companies sold 25,000 units of inventory.

In early January, both companies purchased equipment costing $143,000 (10-year estimated useful life and a $20,000 residual value). Woods uses the inventory and depreciation methods that maximize reported income (FIFO and straight-line). By contrast, Mickelson uses the inventory and depreciation methods that minimize income taxes (LIFO and double-declining-balance). Both companies' trial balances at December 31 included the following:

Sales revenue	$270,000
Operating expenses	80,700

Requirements

1. Prepare both companies' income statements. (p. 350)
2. Write an investment letter to address the following questions for your clients: Which company appears to be more profitable? Which company has more cash to invest in new projects? Which company would you prefer to invest in? Why? (pp. 324–325) Format your investment letter as follows:

INVESTMENT LETTER

To: Our clients

From: Student Name

Subject: Selecting Tiger Woods Enterprises or Phil Mickelson Systems for a long-term investment

Ethical Issue

Western Bank & Trust purchased land and a building for the lump sum of $3 million. To get the maximum tax deduction, Western allocated 90% of the purchase price to the building and only 10% to the land. A more realistic allocation would have been 70% to the building and 30% to the land.

continued . . .

Requirements

1. Explain the tax advantage of allocating too much to the building and too little to the land.
2. Was Western's allocation ethical? If so, state why. If not, why not? Identify who was harmed.

Financial Statement Case

Plant assets

Refer to the Amazon.com financial statements, including Notes 1 and 3, in Appendix A at the end of this book. Answer the following questions.

Requirements

1. Which depreciation method does Amazon.com use for reporting in the financial statements? What type of depreciation method does the company probably use for income tax purposes? Why is this method preferable for tax purposes?
2. Depreciation expense is embedded in the operating expense amounts listed on the income statement. Note 3 gives the amount of depreciation expense. What was the amount of depreciation for 2005? Record Amazon's depreciation expense for 2005.
3. The statement of cash flows reports the purchases of fixed assets. How much were Amazon's fixed asset purchases during 2005? Journalize the company's cash purchase of fixed assets.

Team Project

Requirements

Visit a local business.

1. List all its plant assets.
2. If possible, interview the manager. Gain as much information as you can about the business's plant assets. For example, try to determine the assets' costs, the depreciation method the company is using, and the estimated useful life of each asset category. If an interview is impossible, then develop your own estimates of the assets' costs, useful lives, and book values, assuming an appropriate depreciation method.
3. Determine whether the business has any intangible assets. If so, list them and learn as much as possible about their nature, cost, and estimated useful lives.
4. Write a detailed report of your findings and be prepared to present it to the class.

For Internet Exercises, Excel in Practice, and additional online activities, go to the Web site www.prenhall.com/horngren.

Quick Check Answers

1. *a* 2. *c* 3. *a* 4. *b* 5. *a* 6. *c* 7. *d* 8. *d* 9. *b* 10. *c*

10 Current Liabilities and Payroll

Learning Objectives

1. Account for current liabilities of known amount
2. Account for current liabilities that must be estimated
3. Compute payroll amounts
4. Record basic payroll transactions
5. Use a payroll system
6. Report current liabilities on the balance sheet

Cameras, computers, and cars carry warranties against defects. Most other new products do too. When you buy a new automobile, the manufacturer agrees to repair the car if something goes wrong. That may motivate you to select a Chevrolet over a Honda.

Product guarantees are called warranties, and warranties are an important liability for General Motors, Sony, and Dell. Warranties pose an accounting challenge because General Motors doesn't know which Chevys will have to be repaired. But it's almost certain that some cars will have problems, so GM goes ahead and records a warranty liability based on estimates. ■

In this chapter we will see how companies account for product warranties. You also will learn about accounts payable, payroll, and other current liabilities. Recall that *current liabilities* are obligations due within one year or within the company's operating cycle if it's longer than a year. Obligations due beyond that period are *long-term liabilities.*

Current Liabilities of Known Amount

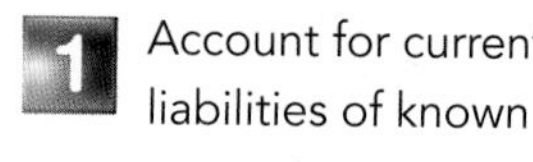

Account for current liabilities of known amount

The amounts of most liabilities are known. A few must be estimated. Let's begin with current liabilities of known amount.

Accounts Payable

Amounts owed for products or services purchased on account are *accounts payable.* We have seen many accounts payable illustrations in preceding chapters. General Motors Corporation (GM) reported accounts payable of $30 billion at December 31, 2005 (see Exhibit 10-1).

EXHIBIT 10-1 **How General Motors Reports Its Current Liabilities**

GENERAL MOTORS CORPORATION
Balance Sheet (partial; adapted)
December 31, 2005

Liabilities	*(In billions)*
Current Liabilities:	
Accounts payable	$ 30
Notes payable	286
Accrued expenses payable	84

One of GM's common transactions is the credit purchase of inventory. With accounts payable and inventory systems integrated, GM records the purchase of inventory on account as follows (amount assumed):

Oct. 19	Inventory	600	
	Accounts Payable		600
	Purchase on account.		

Then, to pay the liability, GM debits Accounts Payable and credits Cash.

Nov. 12	Accounts Payable	600	
	Cash		600
	Paid on account.		

Short-Term Notes Payable

Short-term notes payable are a common form of financing. Short-term notes payable are promissory notes that must be paid within one year. The following entries are typical for a short-term note used to purchase inventory:

2008			
Sep. 30	Inventory	8,000	
	Note Payable, Short-term		8,000
	Purchased inventory on a one-year, 10% note.		

At year-end it's necessary to accrue interest expense for 3 months as follows:

2008			
Dec. 31	Interest Expense ($8,000 × 0.10 × 3/12)	200	
	Interest Payable		200
	Accrued interest expense at year-end.		

The interest accrual at December 31, 2008, allocated $200 of the interest on this note to 2008. During 2009, the interest on this note is $600, as shown here.

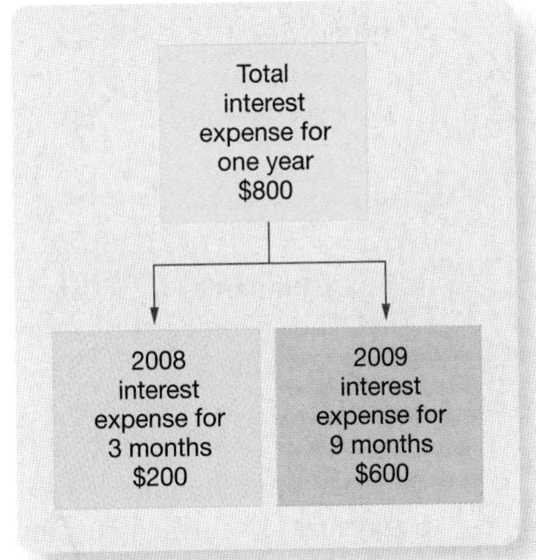

Payment of the note in 2009 is recorded as follows:

2009			
Sep. 30	Note Payable, Short-Term	8,000	
	Interest Payable	200	
	Interest Expense ($8,000 × 0.10 × 9/12)	600	
	Cash [$8,000 + ($8,000 × 0.10)]		8,800
	Paid note and interest at maturity.		

Sales Tax Payable

Most states levy sales tax on retail sales. Retailers collect the sales tax in addition to the price of the item sold. Sales Tax Payable is a current liability because the retailer must pay the state. Consider a McDonald's restaurant.

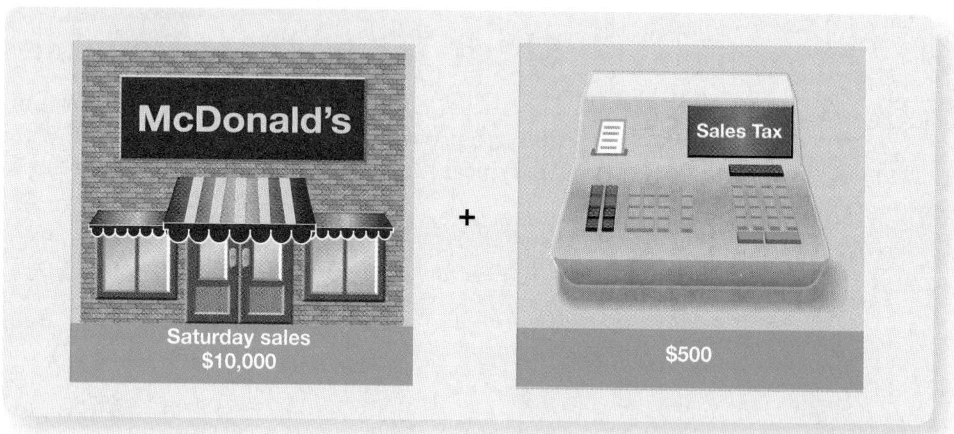

Suppose one Saturday's sales at a McDonald's restaurant totaled $10,000. McDonald's collected an additional 5% sales tax, which would equal $500 ($10,000 × 0.05). McDonald's would record that day's sales as follows:

Sales Tax Payable is a current liability.

	Cash ($10,000 × 1.05)	10,500	
	Sales Revenue		10,000
	Sales Tax Payable ($10,000 × 0.05)		500
	To record cash sales and the related sales tax.		

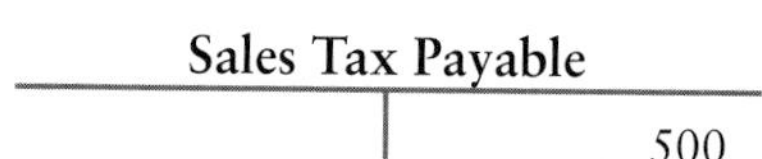

Companies forward the sales tax to the state at regular intervals. To pay the tax, they debit Sales Tax Payable and credit Cash.

Current Portion of Long-Term Notes Payable

Some long-term notes payable are paid in installments. The **current portion of notes payable** (also called **current maturity**) is the principal amount payable within one year—a current liability. The remaining portion is long-term. At the end of the year, the company may make an adjusting entry to shift the current installment of the long-term note payable to a current liability account, as follows (amount assumed):

Dec. 31	Long-Term Note Payable	10,000	
	Current Portion of Note Payable		10,000
	Transferred current portion of note to a current liability account.		

Accrued Expenses (Accrued Liabilities)

An **accrued expense** is an expense that has not yet been paid. That's why accrued expenses are also called **accrued liabilities.** Accrued expenses typically occur with the passage of time, such as interest on a note payable.

Like most other companies, General Motors has accrued liabilities for salaries payable and interest payable. We illustrated accounting for interest payable in the middle of page 501.

Payroll, also called **employee compensation,** also creates accrued expenses. For service organizations—such as CPA firms and travel agencies—payroll is *the* major expense. The second half of this chapter covers payroll liabilities.

Unearned Revenues

Unearned revenue is also called *deferred revenue.* The business has received cash in advance and, therefore, has an obligation to provide goods or services to the customer. Let's consider an example.

Sports Illustrated (SI) sells magazine subscriptions and collects cash in advance. By receiving cash before earning the revenue, SI has a liability for future issues of the magazine. The liability is called Unearned Sales Revenue.

Assume that SI charges $36 for a three-year subscription. SI's entry to record the receipt of cash in advance would be:

2006			
Jan. 1	Cash	36	
	Unearned Sales Revenue		36
	Received cash in advance.		

After receiving the cash on January 1, 2006, SI owes three years of magazines. SI's liability is:

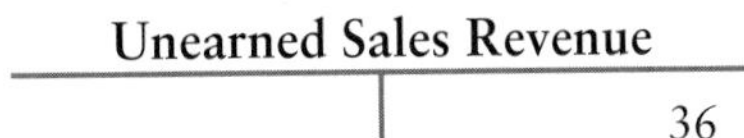

During 2006, SI delivers one-third of the magazines and earns $12 ($36 × 1/3) of the revenue. At December 31, 2006, SI makes the following adjusting entry to decrease the liability, and increase the revenue, as follows:

2006			
Dec. 31	Unearned Sales Revenue	12	
	Sales Revenue ($36 × 1/3)		12
	Earned revenue that was collected in advance.		

Now SI has earned $12 of the revenue and still owes subscribers $24 of magazines, as follows:

Sales Revenue			
		Dec. 31	12

Unearned Sales Revenue			
Dec. 31	12	Jan. 1	36
		Bal.	24

Current Liabilities That Must Be Estimated

2 Account for current liabilities that must be estimated

A business may know that a liability exists but not know the exact amount. It cannot simply ignore the liability. This liability must be reported on the balance sheet. A prime example is Estimated Warranty Payable, which is common for companies like General Motors and Sony.

Estimated Warranty Payable

Many companies guarantee their products against defects under *warranty* agreements. Ninety-day warranties and 1-year warranties are common.

The matching principle says to record the *warranty expense* in the same period that we record the revenue. The expense, therefore, occurs when you make a sale, not when you pay warranty claims. At the time of the sale, the company does not know the exact amount of warranty expense. But the business can estimate its warranty expense and the related liability.

Assume that Whirlpool Corporation, which manufactures appliances, made sales of $200,000 subject to product warranties. Whirlpool estimates that 3% of its products will require warranty payments. The company would record the sales and the warranty expense in the same period, as follows:

June 20	Accounts Receivable	200,000	
	Sales Revenue		200,000
	Sales on account.		
June 20	Warranty Expense ($200,000 × 0.03)	6,000	
	Estimated Warranty Payable		6,000
	To accrue warranty expense.		

Assume that Whirlpool's warranty payments total $5,800. Whirlpool repairs the defective appliances and makes this journal entry:

Dec. 11	Estimated Warranty Payable	5,800	
	Cash		5,800
	To pay warranty claims.		

Whirlpool's expense on the income statement is $6,000, the estimated amount, not the $5,800 actually paid. After paying for these warranties, Whirlpool's liability account has a credit balance of $200.

Estimated Warranty Payable		
5,800		6,000
	Bal.	200

Contingent Liabilities

A *contingent liability* is not an actual liability. Instead, it is a potential liability that depends on a *future* event. For example, suppose General Motors is sued because of its GMC trucks. GM thus faces a contingent liability, which may or may not become actual. If this lawsuit's outcome could hurt GM, it would be unethical for GM to withhold knowledge from investors and creditors.

Another contingent liability arises when you *cosign a note payable* for a friend. You have a contingent liability until the note comes due. If your friend pays off the note, the contingent liability vanishes. If not, you must pay the debt, and your liability becomes real.

The accounting profession divides contingent liabilities into three categories, as shown in Exhibit 10-2.

EXHIBIT 10-2 **Contingent Liabilities: Three Categories**

Likelihood of an Actual Loss	How to Report the Contingency
Remote	Ignore. *Example:* A frivolous lawsuit.
Reasonably possible	Describe the situation in a note to the financial statements. *Example:* The company is the defendant in a significant lawsuit and the outcome could go either way.
Probable, and the amount of the loss can be estimated	Record an expense and an actual liability, based on estimated amounts. *Example:* Warranty expense, as illustrated in the preceding section, beginning on page 514.

Stop and review what you have learned by studying the Decision Guidelines.

Decision Guidelines

ACCOUNTING FOR CURRENT LIABILITIES

Suppose you're in charge of accounting for your student service club. The club decides to borrow $1,000 for a Habitat for Humanity project. The bank requires your club's balance sheet. These Decision Guidelines will help you report current liabilities accurately.

Decision	Guidelines
What are the two main issues in accounting for current liabilities?	• *Recording* the liability in the journal • *Reporting* the liability on the balance sheet
What are the two basic categories of current liabilities?	• Current liabilities of *known amount:* Accounts payable Short-term notes payable Sales tax payable Current portion of notes payable Accrued expenses (accrued liabilities) Salary, wages, commission, and bonus payable Unearned revenues • Current liabilities that *must be estimated:* Estimated warranty payable

Summary Problem 1

Answer each question independently.

Requirements

1. A **Wendy's** restaurant made cash sales of $4,000 subject to a 5% sales tax. Record the sales and the related sales tax. Also record Wendy's payment of the tax to the state of South Carolina.
2. At December 31, 2006, Head Shapers Hair Salons reported a 6% long-term note payable as follows:

Current Liabilities	
Portion of long-term note payable due within one year..................	$ 10,000
Interest payable ($210,000 × 0.06 × 6/12)	6,300
Long-Term Liabilities	
Long-term note payable	$200,000

   Head Shapers pays interest on June 30 each year.

   Show how Head Shapers would report its liabilities on the year-end balance sheet one year later—December 31, 2007. The current maturity of the long-term note payable is $10,000 each year until the liability is paid off.

3. How does a contingent liability differ from an actual liability?

Solution

Requirement 1

	Accounts	Debit	Credit
	Cash ($4,000 × 1.05)	4,200	
	Sales Revenue		4,000
	Sales Tax Payable ($4,000 × 0.05)		200
	To record cash sales and sales tax.		
	Sales Tax Payable	200	
	Cash		200
	To pay sales tax.		

Requirement 2

Head Shapers' balance sheet at December 31, 2007:

Current Liabilities	
Portion of long-term note payable due within one year..................	$ 10,000
Interest payable ($200,000 × 0.06 × 6/12)	6,000
Long-Term Liabilities	
Long-term note payable	$190,000

Requirement 3

A contingent liability is a *potential* liability; the contingency may or may not become an actual liability.

Accounting for Payroll

3 Compute payroll amounts

Labor cost is so important that most businesses develop a special payroll system. There are numerous ways to express an employee's pay:

- *Salary* is pay stated at an annual, monthly, or weekly rate, such as $48,000 per year, $4,000 per month, or $1,000 per week.
- *Wages* are pay amounts stated at an hourly rate, such as $10 per hour.
- *Commission* is pay stated as a percentage of a sale amount, such as a 5% commission on a sale. A realtor, thus, earns $5,000 on a $100,000 sale of real estate.
- *Bonus* is pay over and above base salary (wage or commission). A bonus is usually paid for exceptional performance—in a single amount after year-end.
- *Benefits* are extra compensation—items that aren't paid directly to the employee. Benefits cover health, life, and disability insurance. The employer pays the insurance company, which then provides coverage for the employee. Another type of benefit sets aside money for the employee during his or her retirement.

Businesses pay employees at a base rate for a set period—called *straight time.* For additional hours—*overtime*—the employee may get a higher pay rate.

Lucy Childres is an accountant for Bobby Jones Golf Company. Her pay is as follows:

- Lucy earns a salary of $600 per week for straight time (40 hours), so her hourly pay rate is $15 ($600/40).
- The company pays *time-and-a-half* for overtime. That rate is 150% (1.5 times) the straight-time rate. Thus, Lucy earns $22.50 per hour of overtime ($15.00 × 1.5 = $22.50).
- For working 42 hours during a week, she earns gross pay of $645, computed as follows:

Straight-time pay for 40 hours	$600
Overtime pay for 2 overtime hours: 2 × $22.50	45
Gross pay	$645

Gross Pay and Net (Take-Home) Pay

Two pay amounts are important for accounting purposes:

- **Gross pay** is the total amount of salary, wages, commission, and bonus earned by the employee during a pay period. Gross pay is the amount before taxes or any other deductions. Gross pay is the employer's expense. In the preceding illustration, Lucy Childres's gross pay was $645.
- **Net pay**, also called **take-home pay**, is the amount the employee gets to keep. Take-home pay equals gross pay minus all deductions. The employer writes a paycheck to each employee for his or her take-home pay.

The federal government requires employers to deduct taxes from employee paychecks. Insurance companies and investment companies may also get some of the employee's pay. Amounts withheld from paychecks are called *withholding deductions.*

Payroll Withholding Deductions

Payroll withholding deductions are the difference between gross pay and take-home pay. They are withheld from paychecks and sent to the government, to insurance companies, and other entities. Payroll deductions fall into two categories:

- *Required deductions*, such as employee income tax and Social Security tax. Employees pay their income tax and Social Security tax through payroll deductions.
- *Optional deductions*, including insurance premiums, charitable contributions, and other amounts that are withheld at the employee's request.

After being withheld, payroll deductions become the liability of the employer, who then pays the outside party—taxes to the government and contributions to charitable organizations such as United Way.

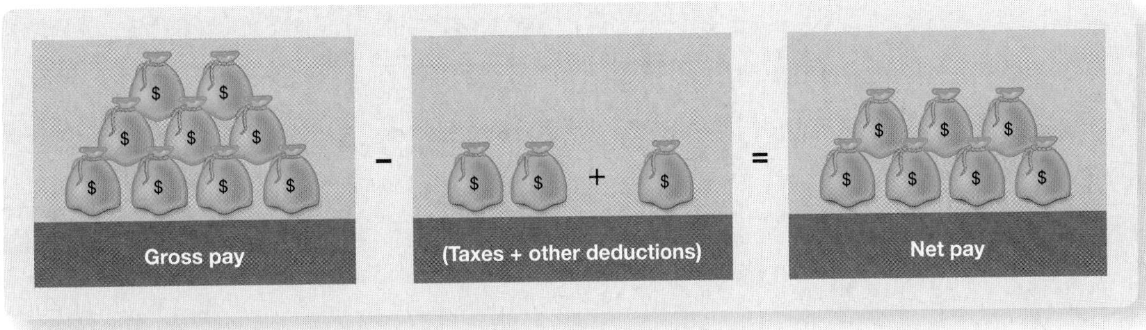

Required Withholding for Employee Income Tax

U.S. law requires companies to withhold income tax from employee paychecks. The income tax deducted from gross pay is called **withheld income tax**. The amount withheld depends on the employee's gross pay and on the number of *withholding allowances* he or she claims.

An employee files Form W-4 with his employer to indicate the number of allowances claimed for income-tax withholding. Each allowance lowers the amount of tax withheld.

- An unmarried taxpayer usually claims one allowance.
- A childless married couple, two allowances.
- A married couple with one child, three allowances, and so on.

Exhibit 10-3 shows a W-4 for R. C. Dean, who claims four allowances (line 5).

Required Withholding for Employee Social Security (FICA) Tax

The *Federal Insurance Contributions Act (FICA)*, also known as the Social Security Act, created the Social Security Tax. The Social Security program provides retirement, disability, and medical benefits. The law requires employers to withhold **Social Security (FICA) tax** from employees' paychecks. The FICA tax has two components:

1. Old age, survivors', and disability insurance (OASDI)
2. Health insurance (Medicare)

The amount of tax withheld varies from year to year. For 2008, the OASDI tax applies to the first $90,000 of employee earnings in a year. The taxable amount of

EXHIBIT 10-3 Form W-4

Cut here and give Form W-4 to your employer. Keep the top part for your records.

Form **W-4** Department of the Treasury Internal Revenue Service

Employee's Withholding Allowance Certificate

For Privacy Act and Paperwork Reduction Act Notice, see page 2.

OMB No. 1545-0010 **2006**

1 Type or print your first name and middle initial R.C.	Last name Dean	Your social security number 344 : 86 : 4529
Home address (number and street or rural route) 4376 Palm Drive	3 ☐ Single ☒ Married ☐ Married, but withhold at higher Single rate. **Note:** If married, but legally separated, or spouse is a nonresident alien, check the "Single" box.	
City or town, state, and ZIP code Fort Lauderdale, FL 33317	4 **If your last name differs from that shown on your social security card, check here. You must call 1-800-772-1213 for a new card.** ▶ ☐	

5 Total number of allowances you are claiming (from line **H** above **or** from the applicable worksheet on page 2) . . . 5 | 4

6 Additional amount, if any, you want withheld from each paycheck . . . . 6 | $

7 I claim exemption from withholding for 2003, and I certify that I meet **both** of the following conditions for exemption:
- Last year I had a right to a refund of **all** Federal income tax withheld because I had **no** tax liability **and**
- This year I expect a refund of **all** Federal income tax withheld because I expect to have **no** tax liability.

If you meet both conditions, write "Exempt" here . . . . ▶ 7

Under penalties of perjury, I certify that I am entitled to the number of withholding allowances claimed on this certificate, or I am entitled to claim exempt status.
Employee's signature
(Form is not valid unless you sign it.) ▶ R.C. Dean **Date ▶**

8 Employer's name and address (Employer: Complete lines 8 and 10 only if sending to the IRS.)	9 Office code (optional)	10 Employer identification number
Blumenthal's Crescent Square Shopping Center Fort Lauderdale, FL 33310	14	83 : 19475

Cat. No. 10220Q

earnings is adjusted annually. The OASDI tax rate is 6.2%. Therefore, the maximum OASDI tax that an employee paid in 2008 was $5,580 ($90,000 × 0.062).

The Medicare portion of the FICA tax applies to all employee earnings. This tax rate is 1.45%. An employee thus pays a combined FICA tax rate of 7.65% (6.2% + 1.45%) of the first $90,000 of annual earnings, plus 1.45% of earnings above $90,000.

To ease your computational burden, we assume that the FICA tax is 8% of the first $90,000 of employee earnings each year. (Use these numbers when you complete this chapter's assignments.) For each employee who earns $90,000 or more, we shall assume the employer withholds $7,200 ($90,000 × 0.08) and sends that amount to the federal government.

Assume that Rex Jennings, an employee, earned $85,000 prior to December. Jennings's salary for December is $10,000.

- How much of Jennings' pay is subject to FICA tax? Only $5,000—from $85,000 up to the $90,000 maximum.
- How much FICA tax will be withheld from Jennings's December paycheck? The computation follows.

Employee earnings subject to the tax in one year	$90,000
Employee earnings prior to the current month	−85,000
Current pay subject to FICA tax	$ 5,000
FICA tax rate	×0.08
FICA tax to be withheld from the current paycheck	$ 400

Optional Withholding Deductions

As a convenience to employees, companies withhold payroll deductions and then pay designated organizations according to employee instructions. Insurance premiums, retirement savings, union dues, and gifts to charities such as United Way are examples.

Many employers offer *cafeteria plans* that let workers select from a menu of insurance coverage. Suppose General Motors provides each employee with $500 of insurance coverage each month. One employee may use his $500 to purchase health insurance. Another may select disability coverage. A third worker may choose a combination of health insurance and disability coverage.

Summary of Gross Pay, Withholding Deductions, and Net (Take-Home) Pay

Suppose Rex Jennings has these amounts for his final pay period of the year (amounts assumed):

Gross pay		$10,000
Withholding deductions:		
Employee income tax (20%)	$2,000	
Employee FICA tax	400	
Employee co-pay for health insurance	180	
Employee contribution to United Way	20	
Total withholdings		2,600
Net (take-home) pay		$ 7,400

Employer Payroll Taxes

In addition to income tax and FICA tax, which are withheld from employee paychecks, *employers* must pay at least three payroll taxes. These taxes do *not* come out of employee paychecks.

1. Employer **Social Security (FICA) tax**
2. State **unemployment compensation tax**
3. Federal **unemployment compensation tax**

Employer FICA Tax

In addition to the employee's Social Security tax, the employer must pay an equal amount into the program. The Social Security system is funded by equal contributions from employer and employee. Using our 8% Social Security tax rate, the employer's maximum annual tax is $7,200 ($90,000 × 0.08) for each employee.

State and Federal Unemployment Compensation Taxes

State and federal unemployment taxes finance workers' compensation for people laid off from work. *In recent years, employers have paid a combined tax of 6.2% on the first $7,000 of each employee's annual earnings.* The proportion paid to the state is 5.4%, plus 0.8% to the federal government. For this payroll tax the employer uses two liability accounts:

- Federal Unemployment Tax Payable
- State Unemployment Tax Payable

Exhibit 10-4 shows a typical distribution of payroll costs for one employee. All amounts are assumed.

EXHIBIT 10-4 Typical Breakdown of Payroll Costs for One Employee

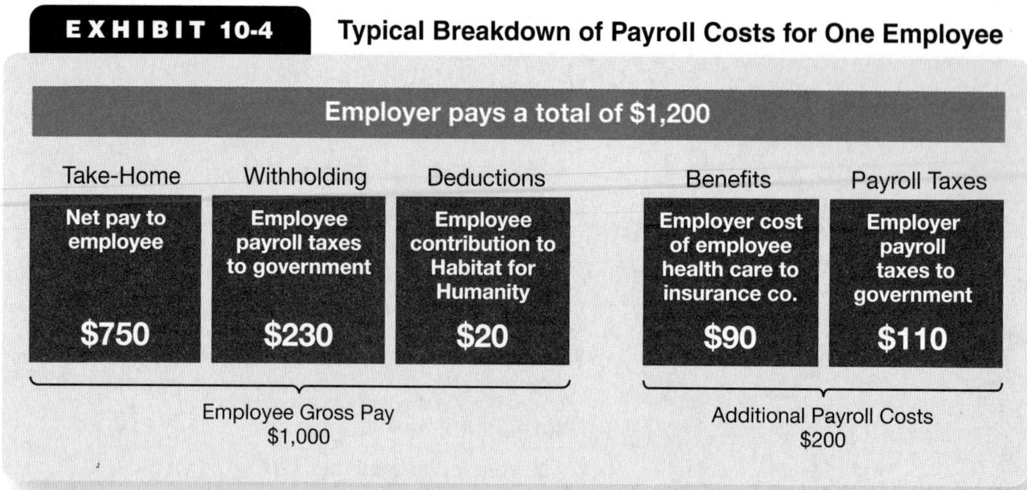

Payroll Accounting

4 Record basic payroll transactions

Exhibit 10-5 summarizes an employer's entries for a monthly payroll of $10,000. All amounts are assumed for illustration only.

- Entry A records *salary expense. Gross salary* is $10,000, and net (take-home) pay is $7,860. There is a payable to Habitat for Humanity because employees specify this charitable deduction.
- Entry B records *benefits* paid by the employer. This company pays for health and life insurance on its employees, a common practice. The employer also pays cash into retirement plans for the benefit of employees after they retire. 401(k) plans

EXHIBIT 10-5 Payroll Accounting by the Employer

	A. Salary Expense		
	Salary Expense (or Wage Expense or Commission Expense)	10,000	
	Employee Income Tax Payable		1,200
	FICA Tax Payable ($10,000 × 0.08)		800
	Payable to Habitat to Humanity		140
	Salary Payable to Employees (take-home pay)		7,860
	To record salary expense.		
	B. Benefits Expense		
	Health Insurance Expense	800	
	Life Insurance Expense	200	
	Retirement-Plan Expense	500	
	Employee Benefits Payable		1,500
	To record employee benefits payable by employer.		
	C. Payroll Tax Expense		
	Payroll Tax Expense	1,420	
	FICA Tax Payable ($10,000 × 0.08)		800
	State Unemployment Tax Payable ($10,000 × 0.054)		540
	Federal Unemployment Tax Payable ($10,000 × 0.008)		80
	To record employer's payroll taxes.		

are popular because they allow workers to specify where their retirement funds are invested.

- Entry C records the employer's *payroll tax expense,* which includes the employer's $800 FICA tax plus state and federal unemployment taxes.

The Payroll System

5 Use a payroll system

Good business requires paying employees accurately and on time. The components of the payroll system are:

- A payroll record
- Payroll checks
- Employee earnings record

Payroll Record

Each pay period the company organizes payroll data in a special journal called the *payroll record.* The payroll record works like a cash payments journal for recording payroll checks.

Exhibit 10-6 is a payroll record for Blumenthal's. The payroll record has sections for each employee's gross pay, withholding deductions, and net pay.

EXHIBIT 10-6 **Blumenthal's Payroll Record (Partial)**

Week Ended December 31, 2007

		Gross Pay			Withholding Deductions				Net Pay	
Employee Name	**Hours**	**Straight-Time**	**Overtime**	**Total**	**Federal Income Tax**	**FICA Tax**	**United Way**	**Total**	**Amount**	**Check No.**
Chen, W. L.*	40	500		500	71	40	3	114	386	1621
Dean, R. C.	46	400	90	490	59	39	2	100	390	1622
Ellis, M.	41	560	20	580	86	46		132	448	1623
Trimble, E. A.†	40	2,360		2,360	665		15	680	1,680	1641
Total		13,940	685	14,625	3,150	1,170	50	4,370	10,255	

*W. L. Chen earned gross pay of $500. His net pay was $386, paid with check number 1621.
†The business deducted no FICA tax from E. A. Trimble. She has already earned more than $90,000.
Note: For simplicity we combine OASDI and Medicare benefits under a single heading for FICA tax.

The payroll record gives the employer the information needed to record salary expense for the week, as follows:

Dec. 31	Salary Expense (gross pay)	14,625	
	Employee Income Tax Payable		3,150
	FICA Tax Payable		1,170
	Payable to United Way		50
	Salary Payable (net pay)		10,255

Payroll Checks

Most companies pay employees by check or by electronic fund transfer (EFT). A *paycheck* has an attachment that details the payroll amounts. These figures come from the payroll record in Exhibit 10-6. Exhibit 10-7 shows the payroll check to R. C. Dean for take home pay of $390.

EXHIBIT 10-7 **Payroll Check for Take-Home Pay**

Blumenthal's
Payroll Account
Fort Lauderdale, FL

1622

12/31 2007

Pay to the Order of R.C. Dean $ 390.00

Three hundred ninety & 00/100 .... **Dollars**

Republic Bank
Fort Lauderdale
Florida 33310

Anna Figaro **Treasurer**

•A111900031A 0787C50000454C

Pay			**Deductions**				**Net Pay**	**Check No.**
Straight time	Overtime	Gross	Income tax	FICA	United Way	Total		
400	90	490	59	39	2	100	390	1622

Earnings Record

The employer must file a payroll tax return with both federal and state governments. Exhibit 10-8 is the Form 941 that Blumenthal's filed with the Internal Revenue Service for the quarter ended December 31, 2007. These forms must be filed no later than one month after the end of a quarter.

The employer must also provide the employee with a wage and tax statement, Form W-2, at the end of the year. Exhibit 10-9 (on page 516) shows the earnings record of R. C. Dean for the last two weeks of 2007 and his totals for the year.

The employee earnings record is neither a journal nor a ledger, and it is not required by law. It merely helps the employer prepare payroll tax reports.

Exhibit 10-10, page 516, is the Wage and Tax Statement, Form W-2, for employee R. C. Dean. The employer prepares this statement and gives copies to the employee and to the Internal Revenue Service (IRS). Dean uses the W-2 to prepare his income tax return. The IRS uses the W-2 to ensure that Dean is paying income tax on all his income from that job.

Paying the Payroll

Up to this point, we have covered only the *recording* of payroll liabilities. We now turn to the *payment* of these liabilities. Most employers make three cash payments for payrolls:

- Net (take-home) pay to employees
- Employee benefits
- Payroll taxes and other payroll deductions

continued at bottom of page 515 . . .

EXHIBIT 10-8 Payroll Tax Return

Form **941 for 2007: Employer's Quarterly Federal Tax Return** 9901
(Rev. January 2005) Department of the Treasury — Internal Revenue Service OMB No. 1545-0029

Employer identification number [ ] [ ] – [ ] [ ] [ ] [ ] [ ] [ ] [ ]

Name (not your trade name)

Trade name (if any) Blumenthal's

Address Crescent Square Shopping Center
Number Street Suite or room number

Fort Lauderdale FL 33310-1234
City State ZIP code

Report for this Quarter ... (Check one.)
- [ ] 1: January, February, March
- [ ] 2: April, May, June
- [ ] 3: July, August, September
- [X] 4: October, November, December

Read the separate instructions before you fill out this form. Please type or print within the boxes.

Part 1: Answer these questions for this quarter.

Line	Description	Column 1		Column 2	Amount
1	Number of employees who received wages, tips, or other compensation for the pay period including: *Mar. 12* (Quarter 1), *June 12* (Quarter 2), *Sept. 12* (Quarter 3), *Dec. 12* (Quarter 4)				18
2	Wages, tips, and other compensation				113,654.
3	Total income tax withheld from wages, tips, and other compensation				18,168.
4	If no wages, tips, and other compensation are subject to social security or Medicare tax				[ ] Check and go to line 6.
5	Taxable social security and Medicare wages and tips:				
5a	Taxable social security wages	110,774.	× .124 =	13,736.	
5b	Taxable social security tips	.	× .124 =	.	
5c	Taxable Medicare wages & tips	113,654.	× .029 =	3,296.	
5d	Total social security and Medicare taxes (Column 2, lines 5a + 5b + 5c = line 5d)				17,032.
6	Total taxes before adjustments (lines 3 + 5d = line 6)				35,200.
7	Tax adjustments (If your answer is a negative number, write it in brackets.):				
7a	Current quarter's fractions of cents			.	
7b	Current quarter's sick pay			.	
7c	Current quarter's adjustments for tips and group-term life insurance			.	
7d	Current year's income tax withholding (Attach Form 941c)			.	
7e	Prior quarters' social security and Medicare taxes (Attach Form 941c)			.	
7f	Special additions to federal income tax (reserved use)			.	
7g	Special additions to social security and Medicare (reserved use)			.	
7h	Total adjustments (Combine all amounts: lines 7a through 7g.)				.
8	Total taxes after adjustments (Combine lines 6 and 7h.)				35,200.
9	Advance earned income credit (EIC) payments made to employees				– .
10	Total taxes after adjustment for advance EIC (lines 8 – 9 = line 10)				35,200.
11	Total deposits for this quarter, including overpayment applied from a prior quarter				35,200.
12	Balance due (lines 10 – 11 = line 12) Make checks payable to the *United States Treasury*				– .
13	Overpayment (If line 11 is more than line 10, write the difference here.)			– .	Check one [ ] Apply to next return. [ ] Send a refund.

Next →

For Privacy Act and Paperwork Reduction Act Notice, see the back of the Payment Voucher. Cat. No. 17001Z Form **941** (Rev. 1-2005)

Net (Take-Home) Pay to Employees

To pay employees, the company debits Salary Payable and credits Cash. Using Exhibit 10-6, the company journalizes net pay for the December 31 weekly payroll:

Date	Account	Debit	Credit
Dec. 31	Salary Payable	10,255	
	Cash		10,255

continued at bottom of page 516 . . .

EXHIBIT 10-9 Employee Earnings Record for 2007

EMPLOYEE NAME AND ADDRESS:					SOCIAL SECURITY NO.: 344-86-4529					
DEAN, R. C. 4376 PALM DRIVE FORT LAUDERDALE, FL 33317					MARITAL STATUS: MARRIED WITHHOLDING EXEMPTIONS: 4 PAY RATE: $400 PER WEEK JOB TITLE: SALESPERSON					
		Gross Pay			Withholding Deductions				Net Pay	
Week Ended	Hrs.	Straight-Time	Over-time	Total	Federal Income Tax	FICA Tax	United Way	Total	Amount	Check No.
Dec. 24	48	400	120	520	66	42	2	110	410	1598
Dec. 31	46	400	90	490	59	39	2	100	390	1622
Total		20,800	2,450	23,250	1,940	1,860	100	3,900	19,350	

EXHIBIT 10-10 Employee Wage and Tax Statement, Form W-2

a Control number 2222 Void ☐ For Official Use Only ▶ OMB No. 1545-0008		
b Employer identification number 83-19475	1 Wages, tips, other compensation 23,250.00	2 Federal income tax withheld 1,940
c Employer's name, address, and ZIP code Blumenthal's Crescent Square Shopping Center Fort Lauderdale, FL 33310-1234	3 Social security wages 23,250.00	4 Social security tax withheld 1,510
	5 Medicare wages and tips 23,250.00	6 Medicare tax withheld 350
	7 Social security tips	8 Allocated tips
d Employee's social security number 344-86-4529	9 Advance EIC payment	10 Dependent care benefits
e Employee's name (first, middle initial, last) R.C. Dean	11 Nonqualified plans	12 Benefits included in box 1
4376 Palm Drive Fort Lauderdale, FL 33317	13 See instrs. for box 13	14 Other
f Employee's address and ZIP code	15 Statutory employee ☐ Deceased ☐ Pension plan ☐	Legal rep. ☐ Deferred compensation ☐

16 State Employer's state ID no.	17 Sate wages, tips, etc	18 State income tax	19 Locality name	20 Local wages, tips, etc	21 Local income tax

Form **W-2** Wage and Tax Statement **2007**

Department of the Treasury—Internal Revenue Service

For Privacy Act and Paperwork Reduction Act Notice, see separate instructions.

Copy A For Social Security Administration—Send this entire page with Form W-3 to the Social Security Administration; photocopies are **not** acceptable.

Cat. No. 10134D

Benefits Paid to Insurance Companies and Investment Companies

The employer might pay for employees' insurance coverage and their retirement plans. If the total cash payment for these benefits is $1,500, the entry is:

Dec. 31	Employee Benefits Payable	1,500	
	Cash		1,500

Payroll Taxes and Other Deductions

The employer must send the government two sets of payroll taxes: those withheld from employees and those paid by the employer. From Exhibit 10-6, the business could record these tax payments as follows (the unemployment tax amounts are assumed):

Dec. 31	Employee Income Tax Payable	3,150	
	FICA Tax Payable ($1,170 × 2)	2,340	
	Payable to United Way	50	
	State Unemployment Tax Payable	100	
	Federal Unemployment Tax Payable	10	
	Cash		5,650

Internal Control over Payroll

There are two main controls for payroll:

- controls for efficiency
- controls to safeguard payroll disbursements

Controls for Efficiency

Reconciling the bank account can be time-consuming because there may be many outstanding paychecks. To limit the outstanding checks, a company may use two payroll bank accounts. It pays the payroll from one account one month and from the other account the next month. This way the company can reconcile each account every other month, and that decreases accounting expense.

Payroll transactions are ideal for computer processing. The payroll data are stored in a file, and the computer makes the calculations, prints paychecks, and updates all records electronically.

Controls to Safeguard Payroll Disbursements

The owner of a small business can monitor his or her payroll by personal contact with employees. Large companies cannot. A particular risk is that a paycheck may be written to a fictitious person and cashed by a dishonest employee. To guard against this, large businesses adopt strict internal controls for payrolls.

Hiring and firing employees should be separated from accounting and from passing out paychecks. Photo IDs ensure that only actual employees are paid. Employees clock in at the start and clock out at the end of the workday to prove their attendance and hours worked.

As we saw in Chapter 7, the foundation of internal control is separation of duties. This is why companies have separate departments for the following payroll functions:

- Human Resources hires and fires workers.
- Payroll maintains employee earnings records.
- Accounting records all transactions.
- Treasurer (or bursar) distributes paychecks to employees.

Reporting Current Liabilities

6 Report current liabilities on the balance sheet

At the end of each period, the company reports all of its current liabilities on the balance sheet. Bob May Homes had the current liabilities shown in Exhibit 10-11.

EXHIBIT 10-11 **Current Liabilities on the Balance Sheet**

Current Liabilities	
Accounts payable	$ 6,400
Current portion of note payable	5,000
Salary payable	3,800
Employee withheld income tax payable	400
Employee FICA tax payable	150*
Employer FICA tax payable	150*
Payable to United Way	100
Unearned revenue	4,500
Interest payable	5,700
Total current liabilities	$26,200
*These amounts can be combined and reported as "FICA Tax Payable"	$ 300

Ethical Issues in Reporting Liabilities

Accounting for liabilities poses an ethical challenge. Businesses like to show high levels of net income because that makes them look successful.

Owners and managers may be tempted to overlook some expenses and liabilities at the end of the accounting period. For example, a company can fail to accrue warranty expense. This will cause total expenses to be understated and net income to be overstated.

Contingent liabilities also pose an ethical challenge. Because contingencies are not real liabilities, they are easy to overlook. But a contingency can turn into a real liability and wreck the company. Successful people don't play games with their accounting. Falsifying financial statements can land a person in prison.

Now let's summarize the accounting for payroll by examining the Decision Guidelines.

Decision Guidelines

ACCOUNTING FOR PAYROLL

What decisions must General Motors make to account for payroll? Whether it's GM or your start-up business, the Decision Guidelines provide an outline for your actions.

Decision	Guidelines
What are the key elements of a payroll accounting system?	• Employee's Withholding Allowance Certificate, Form W-4 • Payroll record • Payroll checks • Employer's quarterly tax returns, Form 941 • Employee earnings record • Employee wage and tax statement, Form W-2
What are the key terms in the payroll area?	*Gross pay* (Total amount earned by the employee) – *Payroll withholding deductions:* **a.** Withheld income tax **b.** Withheld FICA (Social Security) tax—equal amount also paid by employer **c.** Optional withholding deductions (insurance, retirement, charitable contributions, union dues) = *Net (take-home) pay*
What is the employer's total payroll expense?	Total payroll expense = Gross pay + *Employee benefits* **a.** Insurance (health, life, and disability) **b.** Retirement benefits + *Employer payroll taxes* **a.** Employer FICA (Social Security) tax—equal amount also paid by employee **b.** Employer state and federal unemployment taxes
Where to report payroll costs?	• Payroll expenses on the income statement • Payroll liabilities on the balance sheet

Summary Problem 2

Rags-to-Riches, a clothing resale store, employs one salesperson, Dee Hunter. Hunter's straight-time salary is $400 per week, with time-and-a-half pay for hours above 40. Rags-to-Riches withholds income tax (10%) and FICA tax (8%) from Hunter's pay. Rags-to-Riches also pays payroll taxes for FICA (8%) and state and federal unemployment (5.4% and 0.8%, respectively). In addition, Rags-to-Riches contributes 6% of Hunter's gross pay into her retirement plan.

During the week ended December 26, Hunter worked 50 hours. Prior to this week, she had earned $22,000.

Requirements (Round all amounts to the nearest dollar.)

1. Compute Hunter's gross pay and net pay for the week.
2. Record the following payroll entries that Rags-to-Riches would make for:
   a. Hunter's gross pay, including overtime
   b. Expense for employee benefits
   c. Employer payroll taxes
   d. Payment of net pay to Hunter
   e. Payment for employee benefits
   f. Payment of all payroll taxes
3. How much was Rags-to-Riches' total payroll expense for the week?

Solution

Requirement 1

Gross pay:	Straight-time pay for 40 hours		$400
	Overtime pay:		
	Rate per hour ($400/40 × 1.5)	$15	
	Hours (50 − 40)	10	150
	Gross pay		$550
Net pay:	Gross pay		$550
	Less: Withheld income tax ($550 × 0.10)	$55	
	Withheld FICA tax ($550 × 0.08)	44	99
	Net pay		$451

Requirement 2

a.		Sales Salary Expense	550	
		Employee Income Tax Payable		55
		FICA Tax Payable		44
		Salary Payable		451
b.		Retirement-Plan Expense ($550 × 0.06)	33	
		Employee Benefits Payable		33
c.		Payroll Tax Expense	78	
		FICA Tax Payable ($550 × 0.08)		44
		State Unemployment Tax Payable ($550 × 0.054)		30
		Federal Unemployment Tax Payable ($550 × 0.008)		4
d.		Salary Payable	451	
		Cash		451
e.		Employee Benefits Payable	33	
		Cash		33
f.		Employee Income Tax Payable	55	
		FICA Tax Payable ($44 × 2)	88	
		State Unemployment Tax Payable	30	
		Federal Unemployment Tax Payable	4	
		Cash		177

Requirement 3

Rags-to-Riches incurred *total payroll expense* of $661 (gross pay of $550 + payroll taxes of $78 + benefits of $33). See entries (**a**) through (**c**).

Review *Current Liabilities and Payroll*

Accounting Vocabulary

Accrued Expense
An expense that the business has not yet paid. Also called **accrued liability**.

Accrued Liability
An expense that the business has not yet paid. Also called **accrued expense**.

Current Maturity
Amount of the principal that is payable within one year. Also called **current portion of notes payable**.

Current Portion of Notes Payable
Amount of the principal that is payable within one year. Also called **current maturity**.

Employee Compensation
A major expense. Also called **payroll**.

FICA Tax
Federal Insurance Contributions Act (FICA) tax, which is withheld from employees' pay. Also called **Social Security tax**.

Gross Pay
Total amount of salary, wages, commissions, or any other employee compensation before taxes and other deductions.

Net (Take-Home) Pay
Gross pay minus all deductions. The amount of compensation that the employee actually takes home.

Payroll
A major expense. Also called **employee compensation**.

Short-Term Note Payable
Promissory note payable due within one year, a common form of financing.

Social Security Tax
Federal Insurance Contributions Act (FICA) tax, which is withheld from employees' pay. Also called **FICA tax**.

Unemployment Compensation Tax
Payroll tax paid by employers to the government, which uses the money to pay unemployment benefits to people who are out of work.

Withheld Income Tax
Income tax deducted from employees' gross pay.

Quick Check

1. Known liabilities of uncertain amounts are
   a. Contingent liabilities
   b. Ignored (Record them when paid.)
   c. Reported on the balance sheet
   d. Reported only in the notes to the financial statements

2. On January 1, 2008, you borrowed $10,000 on a five-year, 8% note payable. At December 31, 2009, you should *record*
   a. Interest payable of $800
   b. Nothing (The note is already on the books.)
   c. Note receivable of $10,000
   d. Cash payment of $10,000

3. Your company sells $100,000 of goods and you collect sales tax of 3%. What current liability does the sale create?
   a. None; you collected cash up front.
   b. Unearned revenue of $3,000
   c. Sales tax payable of $3,000
   d. Sales revenue of $103,000

4. At December 31, your company owes employees for three days of the five-day workweek. The total payroll for the week is $8,000. What journal entry should you make at December 31?
   a. Nothing, because you will pay the employees on Friday

b. Salary Expense	4,800	
Salary Payable		4,800
c. Salary Expense	8,000	
Salary Payable		8,000
d. Salary Payable	4,800	
Salary Expense		4,800

5. What is unearned revenue?
   a. Receivable
   b. Current asset
   c. Revenue
   d. Current liability

6. General Electric (GE) owed Estimated Warranty Payable of $1,000 at the end of 2007. During 2008, GE made sales of $100,000 and expects product warranties to cost the company 3% of the sales. During 2008, GE paid $2,500 for warranties. What is GE's Estimated Warranty Payable at the end of 2008?
   a. $3,500
   b. $2,500
   c. $2,000
   d. $1,500

7. Payroll expenses include
   a. Salaries and wages
   b. Employee benefits
   c. Payroll taxes
   d. All of the above

8. What is the most that an employee paid the federal government for old age, survivors', and disability insurance (FICA tax) during 2008?
   a. $5,580.
   b. $90,000.
   c. Nothing. The employer paid it.
   d. There is no upper limit on FICA tax.

9. The document that an employer gives each employee at the end of the year to report annual earnings and taxes paid is the
   a. Form W-2
   b. Form W-4
   c. Payroll record
   d. Form 941

10. The *foundation* of internal control over payroll is
    a. Paying the correct amount of payroll tax
    b. Separating payroll duties
    c. Filing government tax forms on time
    d. Accurately computing gross pay, deductions, and net pay

Answers are given after Apply Your Knowledge (p. 541).

Assess Your Progress

Short Exercises

Accounting for a note payable
1

S10-1 On June 30, 2006, Cimmaron Co. purchased $8,000 of inventory on a 1-year, 9% note payable. Journalize the company's (a) accrual of interest expense on December 31, 2006, and (b) payment of the note plus interest on June 30, 2007. (pp. 501–502)

Reporting a short-term note payable and the related interest
1

S10-2 Refer to the data in Short Exercise 10-1. Show what Cimmaron reports for the note payable and related interest payable on its balance sheet at December 31, 2006, and on its income statement for the year ended on that date. (pp. 501–502)

Accounting for warranty expense and warranty payable
2

S10-3 Sierra Corporation guarantees its snowmobiles for three years. Company experience indicates that warranty costs will add up to 5% of sales.

Assume that the Sierra dealer in Colorado Springs made sales totaling $500,000 during January 2007, its first month of operations. The company received cash for 30% of the sales and notes receivable for the remainder. Warranty payments totaled $21,000 during 2007.

1. Record the sales, warranty expense, and warranty payments for Sierra. (p. 504)
2. Post to the Estimated Warranty Payable T-account. At the end of 2007, how much in estimated warranty payable does Sierra owe? (p. 504)

Applying GAAP; reporting warranties in the financial statements

S10-4 What amount of warranty expense will Sierra (in Short Exercise 10-3) report during 2007? Does the warranty expense for the year equal the year's cash payments for warranties? Which accounting principle addresses this situation? (p. 504)

Interpreting an actual company's contingent liabilities
2

S10-5 Harley-Davidson, Inc., the motorcycle manufacturer, included the following note (adapted) in its annual report:

Notes to Consolidated Financial Statements

Commitments and Contingencies (Adapted)

The Company self-insures its product liability losses in the United States up to $3 million.

Catastrophic coverage is maintained for individual claims in excess of $3 million up to $25 million.

1. Why are these *contingent* (versus real) liabilities? (pp. 505–506)
2. How can a contingent liability become a real liability for Harley-Davidson? What are the limits to the company's product liabilities in the United States? (pp. 505–506)

Short Exercise 10-6 begins a sequence of exercises that ends with Short Exercise 10-8.

Computing an employee's total pay
3

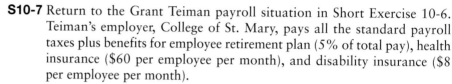

S10-6 Grant Teiman is paid $640 for a 40-hour workweek and time-and-a-half for hours above 40.

1. Compute Teiman's gross pay for working 50 hours during the first week of February. (pp. 508–509)
2. Teiman is single, and his income tax withholding is 10% of total pay. Teiman's only payroll deductions are payroll taxes. Compute Teiman's net (take-home) pay for the week. Use an 8% FICA tax rate, and carry amounts to the nearest cent. (pp. 509–511)

Computing the payroll expense of an employer
3

S10-7 Return to the Grant Teiman payroll situation in Short Exercise 10-6. Teiman's employer, College of St. Mary, pays all the standard payroll taxes plus benefits for employee retirement plan (5% of total pay), health insurance ($60 per employee per month), and disability insurance ($8 per employee per month).

Compute College of St. Mary's total expense of employing Grant Teiman for the 50 hours that he worked during the first week of February. Carry amounts to the nearest cent. (pp. 511–512)

Making payroll entries
4

S10-8 After solving Short Exercises 10-6 and 10-7, journalize for College of St. Mary the following expenses related to the employment of Grant Teiman.

a. Salary expense (pp. 511–512)
b. Benefits (pp. 511–512)
c. Employer payroll taxes (pp. 511–512)

Computing payroll amounts late in the year
3

S10-9 Suppose you work for KPMG, the accounting firm, all year and earn a monthly salary of $6,000. There is no overtime pay. Your withheld income taxes consume 15% of gross pay. In addition to payroll taxes, you elect to contribute 5% monthly to your retirement plan. KPMG also deducts $200 monthly for your co-pay of the health insurance premium.

Compute your net pay for November. Use an 8% FICA tax rate. (pp. 513–514)

Using a payroll system
5

S10-10 Refer to Blumenthal's payroll record in Exhibit 10-6, page 513.

1. How much was the company's total salary expense for the week?
2. How much cash did the employees take home for their work?
3. How much did *employees* pay this week for
   a. Federal income tax?
   b. FICA tax?

Internal controls over payroll disbursements
5

S10-11 What are some of the important elements of good internal control to safeguard payroll disbursements?

Reporting current liabilities
6

S10-12 Citadel Sporting Goods' payroll record for the week ended June 30, 2007, included these totals:

	Withholding Deductions				
Gross Pay	Federal Income Tax	FICA Tax	Habitat for Humanity	Total	Net Pay
$8,000	$790	$640	$110	$1,540	$6,460

In addition to the payroll liabilities shown here, Citadel has the following current liabilities at June 30, 2007:

Accounts payable	$29,000
Employer FICA tax payable	640

Prepare the current liabilities section of Citadel's balance sheet at June 30, 2007. List current liabilities in descending order, starting with the largest first, including the payroll liabilities. Show total current liabilities. (p. 518)

Exercises

Recording sales tax
1

E10-13 Make general journal entries to record the following transactions of Sagebrush Software. Explanations are not required.

March 31	Recorded cash sales of $200,000, plus sales tax of 8% collected for the state of Texas. (pp. 501–502)
April 6	Sent March sales tax to the state. (pp. 501–502)

Recording note payable transactions
1

E10-14 Journalize the following note payable transactions of Concilio Video Productions. Explanations are not required.

2007	
May 1	Purchased equipment costing $15,000 by issuing a one-year, 8% note payable. (pp. 501–502)
Dec. 31	Accrued interest on the note payable. (pp. 501–502)
2008	
May 1	Paid the note payable at maturity. (pp. 501–502)

Recording and reporting current liabilities
1

E10-15 TransWorld Publishing completed the following transactions during 2008:

Oct. 1	Sold a six-month subscription, collecting cash of $200, plus sales tax of 9%. (pp. 501–504)
Nov. 15	Remitted (paid) the sales tax to the state of Tennessee. (pp. 501–502)
Dec. 31	Made the necessary adjustment at year-end to record the amount of sales revenue earned during the year. (pp. 503–504)

continued . . .

Journalize these transactions (explanations are not required). Then report the liability on the company's balance sheet at December 31, 2008.

Accounting for warranty expense and warranty payable
2

E10-16 The accounting records of Durango Ceramics included the following at December 31, 2007:

Estimated Warranty Payable	
	Balance 3,000

In the past, Durango's warranty expense has been 6% of sales. During 2008, Durango made sales of $100,000 and paid $7,000 to satisfy warranty claims.

Requirements

1. Journalize Durango's warranty expense and warranty payments during 2008. Explanations are not required. (p. 504)
2. What balance of Estimated Warranty Payable will Durango report on its balance sheet at December 31, 2008? (p. 504)

Computing net pay
3

E10-17 Cappy Scanlan manages the women's sportswear department of Parisian Department Store in Seattle. She earns a base monthly salary of $750 plus a 10% commission on her personal sales. Through payroll deductions, Scanlan donates $25 per month to a charitable organization, and she authorizes Parisian to deduct $50 monthly for her co-pay of health insurance. Tax rates on Scanlan's earnings are 12% for income tax and 8% of the first $90,000 for FICA. During the first 11 months of the year, she earned $87,000.

Requirement

Compute Scanlan's gross pay and net (take-home) pay for December, assuming her sales for the month are $80,000. (p. 508)

Computing and recording gross pay and net pay

E10-18 Harold Sollenberger manages a Dairy Queen drive-in. His straight-time pay is $10 per hour, with time-and-a-half for hours in excess of 40 per week. Sollenberger's payroll deductions include withheld income tax of 9%, FICA tax of 8%, and a weekly deduction of $5 for a charitable contribution to United Fund. Sollenberger worked 50 hours during the week.

Requirements

1. Compute Sollenberger's gross pay and net pay for the week. Carry amounts to the nearest cent. (p. 508)
2. Journalize Dairy Queen's wage expense—including payroll deductions—for Sollenberger's work. An explanation is not required. (pp. 511–512)

Recording a payroll

E10-19 Pablo's Mexican Restaurants incurred salary expense of $65,000 for 2009. The payroll expense includes employer FICA tax of 8% in addition to state unemployment tax of 5.4% and federal unemployment tax

continued . . .

of 0.8%. Of the total salaries, $19,000 is subject to unemployment tax. Also, the company provides the following benefits for employees: health insurance (cost to the company, $2,060), life insurance (cost to the company, $350), and retirement benefits (cost to the company, 6% of salary expense).

Requirement

Record Pablo's expenses for employee benefits and for payroll taxes. Explanations are not required. (pp. 511–512)

Reporting payroll expense and liabilities

E10-20 Saturn Solartech has annual salary expense of $450,000. In addition, Saturn incurs payroll tax expense equal to 10% of the total payroll. At December 31, Saturn owes salaries of $8,000 and payroll taxes of $2,000.

Requirement

Show what Saturn will report for these facts on its income statement and year-end classified balance sheet. (p. 518)

Reporting current and long-term liabilities

E10-21 Optical Dispensary borrowed $300,000 on January 2, 2007, by issuing a 10% note payable that must be paid in three equal annual installments plus interest for the year. The first payment of principal and interest comes due January 2, 2008.

Requirement

Insert the appropriate amounts to show how Optical Dispensary should report its current and long-term liabilities. (pp. 502, 508)

	December 31		
	2007	2008	2009
Current liabilities:			
Current portion of note payable	$____	$____	$____
Interest payable................................	____	____	____
Long-term liabilities:			
Long-term note payable....................	____	____	____

Reporting current and long-term liabilities

E10-22 Oriental Rug Company completed these selected transactions during December 2006, its first month of operations.

a. Sales of $200,000 are subject to estimated warranty cost of 3%. (p. 504)

b. Pier 1 Imports ordered $15,000 of rugs. With its order, Pier 1 sent a check for $15,000 in advance. Oriental Rugs will ship the goods in January 2007. (pp. 503–504)

continued . . .

c. The December payroll of $90,000 is subject to employee withheld income tax of 9% and FICA tax of 8%. Oriental Rugs must also pay FICA tax of 8% plus state unemployment tax of 5.4% and federal unemployment tax of 0.8%. On December 31, Oriental Rugs pays employees their net pay, but accrues all tax amounts. (p. 511)

Requirement

Report each item at its correct amount on Oriental Rugs' balance sheet at December 31, 2006. Show total current liabilities. (p. 518)

Analyzing current liabilities; using the current ratio

E10-23 The comparative balance sheet of Paladin Security Services for two years reported these figures:

	2006	2005
Total current assets	$ 4,600	$ 4,100
Noncurrent assets	14,200	13,000
	$18,800	$17,100
Total current liabilities	$ 3,700	$ 4,800
Noncurrent liabilities	9,500	7,400
Owner's equity	5,600	4,900
	$18,800	$17,100

Compute Paladin's current ratio and debt ratio for both years. Did the ratios improve or deteriorate in 2006? Compute the debt ratio to 3 decimal places. (p. 214)

Recording current liabilities

E10-24 Eric O'Neill Associates reported short-term notes payable and salary payable as follows:

	December 31	
	2008	2007
Current liabilities (partial):		
Short-term notes payable	$16,500	$15,000
Salary payable	3,300	3,000

During 2008, O'Neill paid off both current liabilities that were left over from 2007. During 2008, O'Neill borrowed money on short-term notes payable and accrued salary expense during 2008.

Requirement

Journalize all four of these transactions for O'Neill during 2008. (pp. 501–502, 511–512, 515–517)

Problems (Group A)

Journalizing liability transactions

P10-25A The following transactions of Lexington Pharmacies occurred during 2006 and 2007:

2006	
Jan. 9	Purchased computer equipment at a cost of $8,000, signing a six-month, 8% note payable for that amount.
29	Recorded the week's sales of $60,000, three-fourths on credit, and one-fourth for cash. Sales amounts are subject to a 6% state sales tax.
Feb. 5	Sent the last week's sales tax to the state.
Feb. 28	Borrowed $200,000 on a 4-year, 9% note payable that calls for annual installment payments of $50,000 principal plus interest. Record the short-term and the long-term portions of the note payable in two separate accounts.
July 9	Paid the six-month, 8% note, plus interest, at maturity.
Aug. 31	Purchased inventory for $3,000, signing a six-month, 10% note payable.
Dec. 31	Accrued warranty expense, which is estimated at 3% of sales of $600,000.
31	Accrued interest on all outstanding notes payable. Make a separate interest accrual entry for each note payable.
2007	
Feb. 28	Paid the first installment and interest for one year on the 4-year note payable.
28	Paid off the 10% note plus interest at maturity.

Requirement

Record the transactions in Lexington's general journal. Explanations are not required. (pp. 501–502, 504)

Computing and recording a payroll

P10-26A The records of Georgia Tea & Coffee Company show the following figures:

Employee Earnings	
Straight-time earnings	$16,400
Overtime pay	(a)
Total employee earnings.............	(b)

continued . . .

Deductions and Net Pay	
Withheld income tax	$ 2,000
FICA tax	(c)
Charitable contributions	300
Medical insurance	600
Total deductions	5,400
Net pay	18,500
Accounts Debited	
Salary Expense	$ (d)

Requirements

1. Determine missing amounts (a) through (d). (pp. 509–511)
2. Journalize this payroll for the month. No explanation is required. (pp. 511–512)

Computing and recording payroll amounts

P10-27A Felix McKay is general manager of Moonwalk Tanning Salons. During 2008, McKay worked for the company all year at a $6,625 monthly salary. He also earned a year-end bonus equal to 10% of his salary.

McKay's federal income tax withheld during 2008 was $737 per month, plus $924 on his bonus check. State income tax withheld came to $43 per month, plus $67 on the bonus. The FICA tax withheld was 8% of the first $90,000 in annual earnings. McKay authorized the following payroll deductions: United Fund contribution of 1% of total earnings and life insurance of $19 per month.

Moonwalk incurred payroll tax expense on McKay for FICA tax of 8% of the first $90,000 in annual earnings. The company also paid state unemployment tax of 5.4% and federal unemployment tax of 0.8% on the first $7,000 in annual earnings. In addition, Moonwalk provides McKay with health insurance at a cost of $35 per month and retirement benefits. During 2008, Moonwalk paid $7,000 into McKay's retirement plan.

Requirements

1. Compute McKay's gross pay, payroll deductions, and net pay for the full year 2008. Round all amounts to the nearest dollar. (pp. 509–511)
2. Compute Moonwalk's total 2008 payroll expense for McKay. (pp. 511–512)
3. Make the journal entry to record Moonwalk's expense for McKay's total earnings for the year, his payroll deductions, and net pay. Debit Salary Expense and Bonus Expense as appropriate. Credit liability accounts for the payroll deductions and Cash for net pay. An explanation is not required. (pp. 511–512)

Journalizing, posting, and reporting liabilities

1 2 3 4 5 6

P10-28A The general ledger of Pack-N-Ship at June 30, the end of the company's fiscal year, includes the following account balances before adjusting entries.

Accounts Payable	$110,000
Current Portion of Note Payable	______
Interest Payable	______
Salary Payable	______
Employee Payroll Taxes Payable	______

continued . . .

Employer Payroll Taxes Payable................	$ ______
Unearned Rent Revenue............................	6,000
Long-Term Note Payable	200,000

The additional data needed to develop the adjusting entries at June 30 are as follows:

a. The long-term debt is payable in annual installments of $40,000 with the next installment due on July 31. On that date, Pack-N-Ship will also pay one year's interest at 9%. Interest was last paid on July 31 of the preceding year. Make the adjusting entry to shift the current installment of the long-term note payable to a current liability. Also accrue interest expense at year end. (pp. 502–504)

b. Gross salaries for the last payroll of the fiscal year totaled $5,100. Of this amount, employee payroll taxes payable were $1,100, and salary payable was $4,000. (pp. 501–512)

c. Employer payroll taxes payable were $900. (pp. 501–512)

d. On February 1, the company collected one year's rent of $6,000 in advance. (p. 503)

Requirements

1. Using four-column format, open the listed accounts, inserting the unadjusted June 30 balances. (p. 82)
2. Journalize and post the June 30 adjusting entries to the accounts that you opened. Key adjusting entries by letter.
3. Prepare the liabilities section of the balance sheet at June 30, 2008. Show total current liabilities and total liabilities. (p. 518)

Using a payroll record; recording a payroll
5

P10-29A The payroll records of Navasota Video Productions provide the following information for the weekly pay period ended December 29, 2007:

Employee	Hours Worked	Hourly Wage Rate	Federal Income Tax	United Way Contributions	Earnings Through Previous Week
Larry Fisher......	42	$40	$278	$35	$90,474
Felicia Jones......	47	8	87	4	23,154
Joe Opper.........	40	11	64	4	4,880
Sara Tate..........	46	35	288	8	88,600

Employees are paid wages at the rate of time-and-a-half for hours over 40 per week. Round all amounts to the nearest dollar, and show your computations. Explanations are not required for journal entries.

Requirements

1. Enter the appropriate information in a payroll record similar to Exhibit 10-6, page 513. In addition to the deductions listed, the employer also takes out FICA tax: 8% of the first $90,000 of each employee's annual earnings.

continued . . .

2. Record the payroll information in the general journal. (pp. 513–514)
3. The first payroll check is number 319, paid to Larry Fisher. Record the check numbers in the payroll record. Also, prepare the general journal entry to record payment of net wages payable to the employees. (pp. 513–517)
4. The employer's payroll taxes include FICA tax of 8% of the first $90,000 of each employee's wages. The employer also pays unemployment taxes of 6.2% (5.4% for the state and 0.8% for the federal government) on the first $7,000 of each employee's annual earnings. Record the employer's payroll taxes in the general journal. (pp. 501–502)

Reporting current liabilities

P10-30A Morrison's Gifts' accounting records provide the following liability data at year-end:

a. Sales of $400,000 were covered by Morrison's product warranty. At January 1, estimated warranty payable was $3,000. During the year, Morrison recorded warranty expense of $12,000 and paid warranty claims of $14,000. (p. 504)
b. December sales totaled $100,000, and Morrison collected an additional state sales tax of 7%. This amount will be sent to the state of Mississippi early in January. (pp. 501–502)
c. Morrison owes $100,000 on a note payable. At December 31, 6% interest on the full note and $20,000 of this principal are payable within one year. (pp. 501–502)
d. On November 30, Morrison received cash of $4,500 in advance for the rent on a building. This rent will be earned evenly over three months. (pp. 503–504)
e. On September 30, Morrison signed a six-month, 8% note payable to purchase equipment costing $30,000. The note requires payment of principal and interest at maturity. (pp. 501–502)

Requirement

For each item, indicate the account and the related amount to be reported as a *current* liability on Morrison's December 31 balance sheet.

Problems (Group B)

Journalizing liability transactions

P10-31B The following transactions of Pan-American Paper Company occurred during 2006 and 2007.

2006		
Feb.	3	Purchased equipment for $40,000, signing a six-month, 9% note payable.
	28	Recorded the week's sales of $60,000, one-third for cash, and two-thirds on credit. All sales amounts are subject to a 5% sales tax.
Mar.	7	Sent last week's sales tax to the state.

continued . . .

Apr. 30	Borrowed $100,000 on a long-term, 9% note payable that calls for annual payment of interest each April 30.
Aug. 3	Paid the six-month, 9% note at maturity.
Nov. 30	Purchased inventory at a cost of $7,000, signing a three-month, 6% note payable for that amount.
Dec. 31	Accrued warranty expense, which is estimated at 3% of sales of $200,000.
31	Accrued interest on all outstanding notes payable. Make a separate interest accrual entry for each note payable.
2007	
Feb. 28	Paid off the 6% inventory note, plus interest, at maturity.
Apr. 30	Paid the interest for one year on the long-term note payable.

Requirement

Record the transactions in Pan American's general journal. Explanations are not required. (pp. 501–502, 504)

Computing and recording a payroll

P10-32B The records of Lyndon Olson Political Consultants show the following figures:

Employee Earnings	
Straight-time earnings	$ (a)
Overtime pay	5,000
Total employee earnings	(b)
Deductions and Net Pay	
Withheld income tax	$ 9,000
FICA tax	6,000
Charitable contributions	(c)
Medical insurance	1,000
Total deductions	18,000
Net pay	64,000
Account Debited	
Salary Expense	$ (d)

Requirements

1. Determine missing amounts (a) through (d). (pp. 509–511)
2. Journalize Olson's payroll for the month. No explanation is required. (pp. 511–512)

Computing and recording payroll amounts

P10-33B Louann Winters is a vice president at Crossroads Bank. During 2008, Winters worked for the bank all year at a $6,500 monthly salary. She also earned a year-end bonus equal to 15% of her annual salary.

continued . . .

Winters' federal income tax withheld during 2008 was $820 per month, plus $2,480 on her bonus check. State income tax withheld came to $60 per month, plus $80 on the bonus. The FICA tax withheld was 8% of the first $90,000 of annual earnings. Winters authorized the following payroll deductions: United Fund contribution of 1% of total earnings and life insurance of $20 per month.

Crossroads Bank incurred payroll tax expense on Winters for FICA tax of 8% of the first $90,000 in total annual earnings. The bank also paid state unemployment tax of 5.4% and federal unemployment tax of 0.8% on the first $7,000 of annual earnings. The bank provided Winters with the following benefits: health insurance at a cost of $40 per month, and retirement benefits to be paid during her retirement. During 2008, the bank's cost of Winters's retirement plan was $4,000.

Requirements

1. Compute Winters' gross pay, payroll deductions, and net pay during 2008. Round all amounts to the nearest dollar. (pp. 509–511)
2. Compute the bank's total 2008 payroll expense for Winters. (pp. 511–512)
3. Make the journal entry to record the bank's expense for Winters' total earnings for the year, her payroll deductions, and net pay. Debit Salary Expense and Bonus Expense as appropriate. Credit liability accounts for the payroll deductions and Cash for net pay. An explanation is not required. (pp. 511–512)

Journalizing, posting, and reporting liabilities

P10-34B The Northwood Inn general ledger at September 30, 2008, the end of the company's fiscal year, includes the following account balances before adjusting entries.

Accounts Payable	$ 36,210
Current Portion of Note Payable	______
Interest Payable	______
Salary Payable	______
Employee Payroll Taxes Payable	______
Employer Payroll Taxes Payable	______
Unearned Rent Revenue	3,900
Long-Term Note Payable	100,000

The additional data needed to develop the adjusting entries at September 30 are as follows:

a. The long-term note payable is payable in annual installments of $50,000, with the next installment due on January 31, 2009. On that date, Northwood will also pay one year's interest at 6%. Interest was last paid on January 31. Make the adjusting entry to shift the current installment of the note payable to a current liability. Also accrue interest expense at year end. (pp. 501–502)

b. Gross salaries for the last payroll of the fiscal year were $4,300. Of this amount, employee payroll taxes payable were $950. (pp. 511–512)

continued . . .

c. Employer payroll taxes payable were $890. (pp. 511–512)

d. On August 1, the company collected six months' rent of $3,900 in advance. (p. 503)

Requirements

1. Using four-column format, open the listed accounts, inserting their unadjusted September 30 balances. (p. 82)
2. Journalize and post the September 30 adjusting entries to the accounts that you opened. Key adjusting entries by letter.
3. Prepare the liabilities section of Northwood Inn's balance sheet at September 30, 2008. Show total current liabilities and total liabilities. (p. 518)

Using a payroll record; recording a payroll

P10-35B The payroll records of Carolina Home Improvements provide the following information for the weekly pay period ended December 29, 2007:

Employee	Hours Worked	Weekly Salary	Federal Income Tax	Health Insurance	Earnings Through Previous Week
Cynthia Cooper.......	43	$ 400	$ 74	$16	$17,060
Tim LeMann	46	480	90	10	22,300
Ron Marx	48	1,400	319	46	88,000
Karen York..............	40	240	32	6	3,410

All employees are paid time-and-a-half for hours worked in excess of 40 per week.

Requirements

Round all amounts to the nearest dollar, and show your computations. Explanations are not required for journal entries.

1. Enter the appropriate information in a payroll record similar to Exhibit 10-6, page 513. In addition to the deductions listed, the employer also withholds FICA tax: 8% of the first $90,000 of each employee's annual earnings.
2. Record the payroll information in the general journal. (pp. 513–514)
3. The first payroll check is number 178, paid to Cooper. Record the check numbers in the payroll record. Also, prepare the general journal entry to record payment of net pay to the employees. (pp. 513–517)
4. The employer's payroll taxes include FICA of 8% of the first $90,000 of each employee's annual earnings. The employer also pays unemployment taxes of 6.2% (5.4% for the state and 0.8% for the federal government) on the first $7,000 of each employee's annual earnings. Record the employer's payroll taxes in the general journal. (pp. 511–512)

Reporting current liabilities

6

P10-36B Following are pertinent facts about events during the current year at Lafferty Trailers.

a. December sales totaled $300,000, and Lafferty collected sales tax of 5%. The sales tax will be sent to the state of Virginia early in January. (pp. 501–502)

continued . . .

b. Sales are covered by a Lafferty product warranty. At January 1, estimated warranty payable was $1,300. During the year, Lafferty recorded warranty expense of $7,900 and paid warranty claims of $8,100. (p. 504)

c. Lafferty owes $75,000 on a note payable. At December 31, 6% interest for the year plus $25,000 of this principal are payable within one year. (pp. 501–502)

d. On August 31, Lafferty signed a six-month, 6% note payable to purchase equipment costing $80,000. The note requires payment of principal and interest at maturity. (pp. 501–502)

e. On October 31, Lafferty received cash of $2,400 in advance for the rent on a building. This rent will be earned evenly over six months. (pp. 503–504)

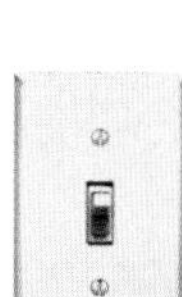

For 24/7 practice, visit www.MyAccountingLab.com

Requirement

For each item, indicate the account and the related amount to be reported as a *current* liability on Lafferty's December 31 balance sheet.

Apply Your Knowledge

Decision Cases

Identifying internal control weaknesses and their solution

Case 1. Golden Bear Construction Co. operates throughout California. The owner, Gaylan Beavers, employs 15 work crews. Construction supervisors report directly to Beavers, and the supervisors are trusted employees. The home office staff consists of an accountant and an office manager.

Because employee turnover is high in the construction industry, supervisors hire and fire their own crews. Supervisors notify the office of all personnel changes. Also, supervisors forward to the office the employee W-4 forms. Each Thursday, the supervisors submit weekly time sheets for their crews, and the accountant prepares the payroll. At noon on Friday, the supervisors come to the office to get paychecks for distribution to the workers at 5 p.m.

The company accountant prepares the payroll, including the paychecks. Beavers signs all paychecks. To verify that each construction worker is a bona fide employee, the accountant matches the employee's endorsement signature on the back of the canceled paycheck with the signature on that employee's W-4 form.

Requirements

1. Identify one way that a supervisor can defraud Golden Bear Construction under the present system.
2. Discuss a control feature that the company can use to *safeguard* against the fraud you identified in Requirement 1.

Contingent liabilities

2

Case 2. Microsoft Corporation is the defendant in numerous lawsuits claiming unfair trade practices. Microsoft has strong incentives not to disclose these contingent liabilities. However, GAAP requires that companies report their contingent liabilities.

Requirements

1. Why would a company prefer *not* to disclose its contingent liabilities?
2. Describe how a bank could be harmed if a company seeking a loan did not disclose its contingent liabilities.
3. What ethical tightrope must companies walk when they report contingent liabilities?

Ethical Issue

Bombadier Industries manufactures aircraft-related electronic devices. Bombadier borrows heavily to finance operations. Often Bombadier is profitable because it can earn operating income much higher than its interest expense. However, when the business cycle has turned down, the company's debt burden has pushed the company to the brink of bankruptcy. Operating income is sometimes less than interest expense.

Requirement

Is it unethical for managers to saddle a company with a high level of debt? Or is it just risky? Who can get hurt when a company takes on too much debt? Discuss.

Financial Statement Case

Current liabilities
1 6

Details about a company's liabilities appear in a number of places in the annual report. Use Amazon.com's financial statements, including Notes 1 and 4, to answer the following questions. Amazon's financial statements are in Appendix A at the end of this book.

Requirements

1. Give the breakdown of Amazon.com's current liabilities at December 31, 2005. Give the January 2006 entry to record the payment of accrued expenses and other current liabilities that Amazon owed at December 31, 2005.
2. At December 31, 2005, how much did Amazon owe customers for unearned revenue that Amazon had collected in advance? Which account on the balance sheet reports this liability?
3. How much was Amazon's long-term debt at December 31, 2005? Of this amount, how much was due within one year? How much was payable beyond one year in the future?

Team Projects

Project 1. In recent years, the airline industry has dominated headlines. Consumers are shopping Priceline.com and other Internet sites for the lowest rates. The airlines have also lured customers with frequent-flyer programs, which award free flights to passengers who accumulate specified miles of travel. Unredeemed frequent-flyer mileage represents a liability that airlines must report on their balance sheets, usually as Air Traffic Liability.

Southwest Airlines, a profitable, no-frills carrier based in Dallas, has been rated near the top of the industry. Southwest controls costs by flying to smaller, less-expensive airports; using only one model of aircraft; serving no meals; increasing staff efficiency; and having a shorter turnaround time on the ground between flights. The fact that most of the cities served by Southwest have predictable weather maximizes its on-time arrival record.

Requirements

With a partner or group, lead your class in a discussion of the following questions, or write a report as directed by your instructor.

1. Frequent-flyer programs have grown into significant obligations for airlines. Why should a liability be recorded for those programs? Discuss how you might calculate the amount of this liability. Can you think of other industries that offer incentives that create a similar liability?
2. One of Southwest Airlines' strategies for success is shortening stops at airport gates between flights. The company's chairman has stated, "What [you] produce is lower fares for the customers because you generate more revenue from the same fixed cost in that airplane." Look up *fixed cost* in the index of this book. What are some of the "fixed costs" of an airline? How can better utilization of assets improve a company's profits?

Project 2. Consider three different businesses:

a. A bank

b. A magazine publisher

c. A department store

Requirements

For each business, list all of its liabilities—both current and long-term. If necessary, study Chapter 13 on long-term liabilities. Then compare your lists to identify what liabilities the three business have in common. Also identify the liabilities that are unique to each type of business.

For Internet Exercises, Excel in Practice, and additional online activities go to the Web site www.prenhall.com/horngren.

Quick Check Answers

1. *c* 2. *a* 3. *c* 4. *b* 5. *d* 6. *d* 7. *d* 8. *a* 9. *a* 10. *b*

Comprehensive Problem for Chapters 7–10

Comparing Two Businesses

Suppose you created a software package, sold the business, and now are ready to invest in a resort property. Several locations look promising: Monterrey, California; Durango, Colorado; and Mackinac Island, Michigan. Each place has its appeal, but Durango wins out. Two small resorts are available in Durango. The property owners provide the following data:

	Gold Rush Resorts	Mountain Hideaway
Cash	$ 31,000	$ 63,000
Accounts receivable	20,000	18,000
Inventory	64,000	70,000
Land	270,000	669,000
Buildings	1,200,000	1,500,000
Accumulated depreciation—buildings	(20,000)	(100,000)
Furniture	750,000	900,000
Accumulated depreciation—furniture	(75,000)	(180,000)
Total assets	$2,240,000	$2,940,000
Total liabilities	$1,300,000	$1,000,000
Owner's equity	940,000	1,940,000
Total liabilities and owner's equity	$2,240,000	$2,940,000

Income statements for the last year report net income of $500,000 for Gold Rush Resorts and $400,000 for Mountain Hideaway.

Inventories

Gold Rush Resorts uses the FIFO inventory method, and Mountain Hideaway uses LIFO. If Gold Rush had used LIFO, its ending inventory would have been $7,000 lower. (pp. 324–325)

Plant Assets

Gold Rush Resorts uses the straight-line depreciation method and an estimated useful life of 40 years for buildings and 10 years for furniture. Estimated residual values are $400,000 for buildings and $0 for furniture. Gold Rush's buildings are 1 year old. (p. 462)

Mountain Hideaway uses the double-declining-balance method and depreciates buildings over 30 years. The furniture, also 1 year old, is being depreciated over 10 years. (p. 464)

Accounts Receivable

Gold Rush Resorts uses the direct write-off method for uncollectible receivables. Mountain Hideaway uses the allowance method. The Gold Rush owner estimates that $2,000 of the company's receivables are doubtful. Mountain Hideaway receivables are already reported at net realizable value. (pp. 410, 414)

Requirements

1. To compare the two resorts, convert Gold Rush Resorts' net income to the accounting methods and the estimated useful lives used by Mountain Hideaway.
2. Compare the two resorts' net incomes after you have revised Gold Rush's figures. Which resort looked better at the outset? Which looks better when they are placed on equal footing?

11 Corporations: Paid-In Capital and the Balance Sheet

Learning Objectives

1. Identify the characteristics of a corporation
2. Record the issuance of stock
3. Prepare the stockholders' equity section of a corporation balance sheet
4. Account for cash dividends
5. Use different stock values in decision making
6. Evaluate return on assets and return on stockholders' equity
7. Account for the income tax of a corporation

It's 6 A.M. and you've pulled an all-nighter studying for a history exam. Crammed full of facts, you need a break. Besides that you're hungry. Where can you get a cup of coffee and a quick bite? Many college students go to IHOP near the campus.

You probably never thought of the business aspect of IHOP. The company started as the International House of Pancakes in Toluca Lake, California. In 2001 IHOP opened its 1,000th restaurant. Like Amazon.com and Coca-Cola, IHOP is a corporation. From here on we'll focus on corporations, so this chapter marks a turning point.

We begin with the start-up of a corporation and also cover the corporate balance sheet. Fortunately, most of the accounting you've learned thus far also applies to corporations. First, however, let's take an overview of corporations with IHOP as the focus company.

Corporations: An Overview

Corporations dominate business activity in the United States. Proprietorships and partnerships are more numerous, but corporations do much more business and are larger. Most well-known companies, such as UPS and Intel, are corporations. Their full names include *Corporation* or *Incorporated* (abbreviated *Corp.* and *Inc.*) to show that they are corporations—for example, Intel Corporation and NIKE, Inc.

Characteristics of a Corporation

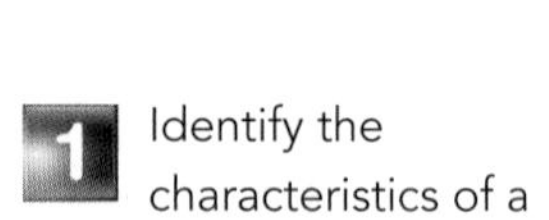

What makes the corporate form of organization so attractive? Several things. We now discuss corporations' advantages and disadvantages.

Separate Legal Entity

A corporation is a separate legal entity formed under the laws of a particular state. For example, the state of New York may grant a **charter**, a document that gives the owners permission to form a corporation. Neither a proprietorship nor a partnership requires a state charter, because in the eyes of the law they are the same as their owner(s). A corporation's owners are called **stockholders** or **shareholders**.

A corporation has many of the rights of a person. For example, a corporation may buy, own, and sell property. The assets and liabilities of IHOP belong to the corporation, not to its owners. The corporation may enter into contracts, sue, and be sued, just like an individual.

Continuous Life and Transferability of Ownership

The owners' equity of a corporation is divided into shares of **stock**. A corporation has a *continuous life* regardless of who owns the stock. By contrast, proprietorships and partnerships end when their ownership changes. Stockholders may sell or trade stock to another person, give it away, or bequeath it in a will. Transfer of the stock does not affect the continuity of the corporation.

No Mutual Agency

Mutual agency means that all the owners act as agents of the business. A contract signed by one owner is binding for the whole company. Mutual agency operates in partnerships but *not* in corporations. A stockholder of IHOP cannot commit IHOP to a contract (unless the person is also an officer of the company).

Limited Stockholder Liability

Stockholders have **limited liability** for corporation debts. That means they have no personal obligation for the corporation's liabilities. The most a stockholder can lose on an investment in a corporation is the amount invested. In contrast, proprietors and partners are personally liable for all the debts of their businesses, unless the partnership is a limited liability partnership (LLP).

The combination of limited liability and no mutual agency means that persons can invest in a corporation without fear of losing all their personal wealth if the business fails. This feature enables a corporation to raise more money than proprietorships and partnerships.

Separation of Ownership and Management

Stockholders own a corporation, but a *board of directors*—elected by the stockholders—appoints the officers to manage the business. Stockholders may invest $1,000 or $1 million without having to manage the company.

Corporate Taxation

Corporations are separate taxable entities. They pay several taxes not borne by proprietorships or partnerships, including an annual franchise tax levied by the state. The franchise tax keeps the corporate charter in force. Corporations also pay federal and state income taxes just as individuals do.

Corporate earnings are subject to **double taxation.**

- First, corporations pay income taxes on corporate income.
- Then the stockholders pay personal income tax on the cash dividends they receive from corporations.

Proprietorships and partnerships pay no business income tax. Instead, the tax falls solely on the owners.

Government Regulation

Because of stockholders' limited liability, outsiders can look no further than the corporation for payment of its debts. To protect persons who do business with corporations, government agencies monitor corporations. This *government regulation* can be expensive.

Exhibit 11-1 summarizes the advantages and disadvantages of corporations.

EXHIBIT 11-1 **Advantages and Disadvantages of a Corporation**

Advantages	Disadvantages
1. Corporations can raise more money than a proprietorship or partnership.	1. Ownership and management are separated.
2. Corporation has continuous life.	2. Double taxation.
3. The transfer of corporate ownership is easy.	3. Government regulation is expensive.
4. There's no mutual agency among the stockholders.	
5. Stockholders have limited liability.	

Organizing a Corporation

Organizing a corporation begins when the *incorporators* obtain a charter from the state. The charter **authorizes** the corporation to issue a certain number of shares of stock. The incorporators pay fees, sign the charter, and file documents; then the corporation becomes a legal entity. The stockholders agree to a set of **bylaws**, which act as their constitution.

Ultimate control of the corporation rests with the stockholders as they vote their shares of stock. Each share of stock carries one vote. The stockholders elect the **board of directors**, which:

- sets policy
- elects a **chairperson**, who is the most powerful person in the company
- appoints the **president**, who is in charge of day-to-day operations

Most corporations also have vice presidents. Exhibit 11-2 shows the authority structure in a corporation.

EXHIBIT 11-2 **Structure of a Corporation**

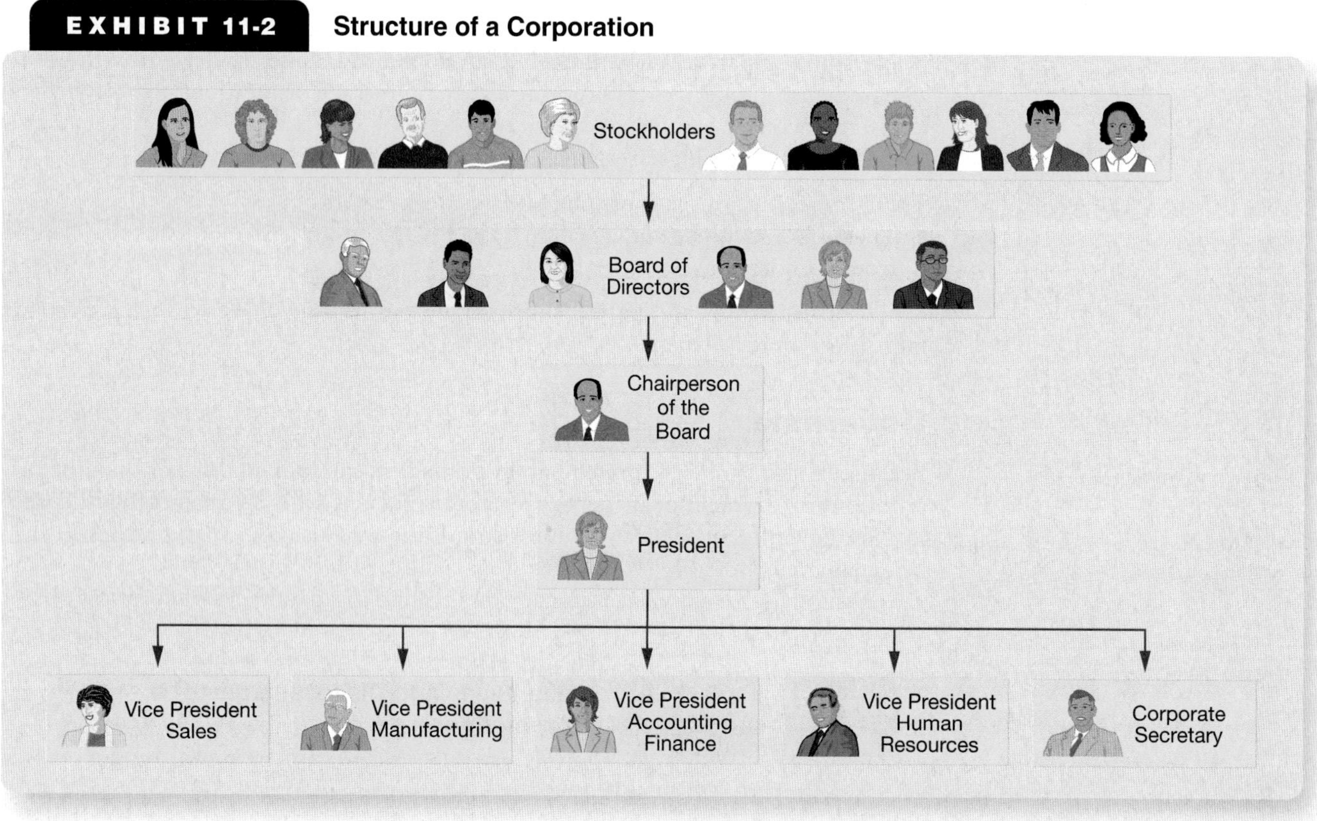

Capital Stock

A corporation issues *stock certificates* to the stockholders when they buy the stock. The stock represents the corporation's capital, so it is called *capital stock*. The basic unit of stock is a *share*. A corporation may issue a stock certificate for any number of shares. Exhibit 11-3 shows a stock certificate for 288 shares of Central Jersey Bancorp common stock. The certificate shows the:

- company name
- stockholder name
- number of shares owned by the stockholder

Stock that is held by the stockholders is said to be **outstanding**. The outstanding stock of a corporation represents 100% of its ownership.

EXHIBIT 11-3 Stock Certificate

Stockholders' Equity Basics

A corporation reports assets and liabilities exactly as for a proprietorship or a partnership. But the owners' equity of a corporation—called **stockholders' equity**—is reported differently. State laws require corporations to report their sources of capital because some of the capital must be maintained by the company. There are two basic sources:

- **Paid-in capital** (also called **contributed capital**) represents amounts received from the stockholders. Common stock is the main source of paid-in capital.
- **Retained earnings** is capital earned by profitable operations.

Exhibit 11-4 outlines a summarized version of the stockholders' equity of IHOP Corporation (amounts in millions):

EXHIBIT 11-4 Stockholders' Equity of IHOP Corporation (Adapted, with amounts in millions)

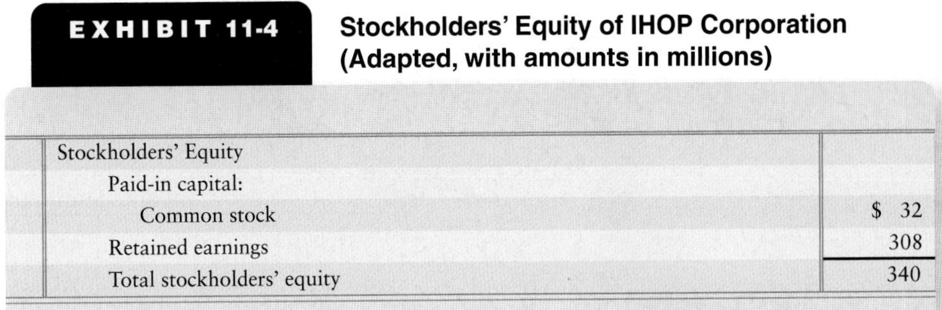

Stockholders' Equity	
Paid-in capital:	
Common stock	$ 32
Retained earnings	308
Total stockholders' equity	340

Paid-In Capital Comes from the Stockholders

Common stock is paid-in capital because it comes from the stockholders. Suppose IHOP is issuing common stock. IHOP's entry to record the receipt of $20,000 cash and the issuance of stock is:

Oct. 20	Cash	20,000	
	Common Stock		20,000
	Issued stock.		

Issuing stock increases both assets and stockholders' equity.

Retained Earnings Come from Profitable Operations

Profitable operations generate net income, which increases equity through a separate account called Retained Earnings.

Some people think of Retained Earnings as a fund of cash. It is not, because Retained Earnings is not an asset; it's an element of stockholders' equity. Retained Earnings has no particular relationship to cash or any other asset.

As we've just seen, a corporation needs at least two capital accounts:

- Common Stock
- Retained Earnings

Corporations close their revenues and expenses into Income Summary, and then they close net income to Retained Earnings. Let's assume IHOP's revenues were $500,000 and expenses totaled $400,000 for December. The closing entries would be:

Dec. 31	Sales Revenue	500,000	
	Income Summary		500,000
	To close sales revenue.		
31	Income Summary	400,000	
	Expenses (detailed)		400,000
	To close expenses.		

Now, Income Summary holds revenues, expenses, and net income.

Income Summary

Expenses	400,000	Revenues	500,000
		Balance (net income)	100,000

Finally, Income Summary's balance is closed to Retained Earnings.

Dec. 31	Income Summary	100,000	
	Retained Earnings		100,000
	To close net income to Retained Earnings.		

This closing entry completes the closing process. Income Summary is zeroed out, and Retained Earnings now holds net income, as follows:

Income Summary

Expenses	400,000	Revenues	500,000
Closing	100,000	Net income	100,000

Retained Earnings

		Closing (net income)	100,000

If IHOP has a net *loss*, Income Summary will have a debit balance, as follows:

Income Summary

Expenses	460,000	Revenues	400,000
Net loss	60,000		

To close this $60,000 loss, the final closing entry credits Income Summary and debits Retained Earnings as follows:

Dec. 31	Retained Earnings	60,000	
	Income Summary		60,000
	To close net loss *to Retained Earnings.*		

The accounts now have their final balances.

Income Summary

Expenses	460,000	Revenues	400,000
Net loss	60,000	Closing	60,000

Retained Earnings

Closing (net loss)	60,000		

A Retained Earnings Deficit

A loss may cause a debit balance in Retained Earnings. This condition—called a Retained Earnings **deficit**—is reported as a negative amount in stockholders' equity. HAL, Inc., which owns Hawaiian Airlines, Inc., reported this deficit:

Stockholders' Equity	**(In millions)**
Paid-in capital:	
Common stock	$ 50
Deficit	(193)
Total stockholders' equity	$(143)

A Corporation May Pay Dividends to the Stockholders

A profitable corporation may distribute cash to the stockholders. Such distributions are called **dividends**. Dividends are similar to a proprietor's withdrawals. Dividends decrease both assets and retained earnings. Most states prohibit using paid-in capital for dividends. Accountants, therefore, use the term *legal capital* to refer to the portion of stockholders' equity that cannot be used for dividends.

Stockholders' Rights

A stockholder has four basic rights, unless a right is withheld by contract:

1. **Vote.** Stockholders participate in management by voting on corporate matters. This is a stockholder's sole right to manage the corporation. Each share of stock carries one vote.
2. **Dividends.** Stockholders receive a proportionate part of any dividend. Each share of stock receives an equal dividend.
3. **Liquidation.** Stockholders receive their proportionate share of any assets remaining after the corporation pays its debts and liquidates (goes out of business).

A fourth right is usually withheld because it is rarely exercised.

4. **Preemption.** Stockholders can maintain their proportionate ownership in the corporation. Suppose you own 5% of a corporation's stock. If the corporation issues 100,000 new shares of stock, it must offer you the opportunity to buy 5% (5,000) of the new shares.

Classes of Stock

Corporations can issue different classes of stock. The stock of a corporation may be either:

- **common or preferred**
- **par or no-par**

Common Stock and Preferred Stock

Every corporation issues **common stock,** which represents the basic ownership of the corporation. The owners are the common stockholders. Some companies issue Class A common stock, which carries the right to vote. They may also issue Class B common stock, which may be nonvoting. There is a separate account for each class of stock.

Preferred stock gives its owners certain advantages over common. Most notably, preferred stockholders receive dividends before the common stockholders, and preferred receives assets before common if the corporation liquidates. Corporations pay a fixed dividend on preferred stock. Investors usually buy preferred stock to earn those fixed dividends. With these advantages, preferred stockholders take less investment risk than common stockholders.

Owners of preferred stock also have the four basic stockholder rights, unless a right is withheld. The right to vote is sometimes withheld from preferred stock. Companies may issue different series of preferred stock (Series A and Series B, for example). Each series is recorded in a separate account. Preferred stock is rarer than you might think. A recent survey of 600 corporations revealed that only 16% had some preferred stock outstanding (Exhibit 11-5).

EXHIBIT 11-5 Preferred Stock

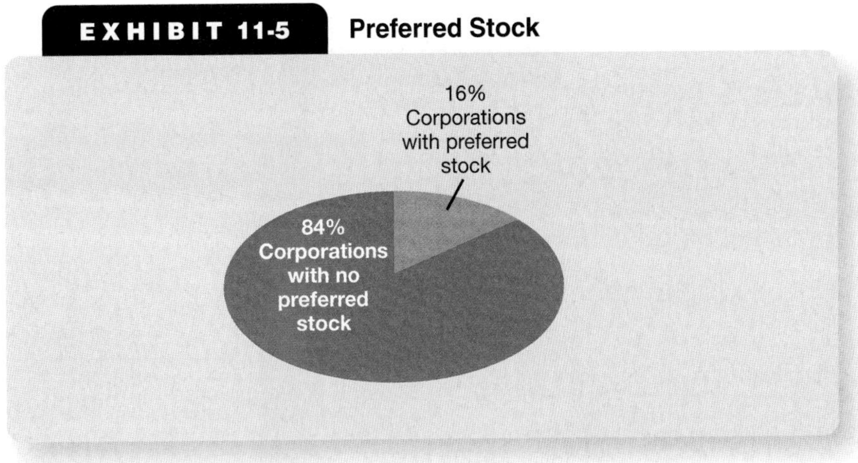

Par Value, Stated Value, and No-Par Stock

Stock may carry a par value or it may be no-par stock. **Par value** is an arbitrary amount assigned by a company to a share of its stock. Most companies set par value low to avoid legal difficulties from issuing their stock below par. Companies maintain a minimum amount of stockholders' equity for the protection of creditors, and this minimum represents the corporation's legal capital. **Legal capital** is usually the par value of the shares issued.

The par value of IHOP's common stock is $0.01 (1 cent) per share. Deere & Co., which makes John Deere tractors, and Whirlpool, the appliance company, have common stock with a par value of $1 per share. Par value of preferred stock can be higher—$25 or $100. Par value is used to compute dividends on preferred stock, as we shall see.

No-par stock does not have par value. Pfizer, the pharmaceutical company, has preferred stock with no par value. But some no-par stock has a **stated value**, which makes it similar to par-value stock. The stated value is an arbitrary amount similar to par value.

Issuing Stock

2 Record the issuance of stock

Corporations such as IHOP and Coca-Cola need huge quantities of money. They cannot finance all their operations through borrowing, so they raise capital by issuing stock. A company can sell its stock directly to stockholders or it can use the services of an *underwriter,* such as the brokerage firms Merrill Lynch and Morgan Stanley, Dean Witter. An underwriter usually agrees to buy all the stock it cannot sell to its clients.

The price that the corporation receives from issuing stock is called the *issue price.* Usually, the issue price exceeds par value because par value is quite low. In the following sections, we use IHOP to show how to account for the issuance of stock.

Issuing Common Stock

The Wall Street Journal is the most popular medium for advertising stock. The ads are called *tombstones.* Exhibit 11-6 reproduces IHOP's tombstone, which appeared in *The Wall Street Journal.*

EXHIBIT 11-6 Announcement of Public Offering of IHOP Stock (Adapted)

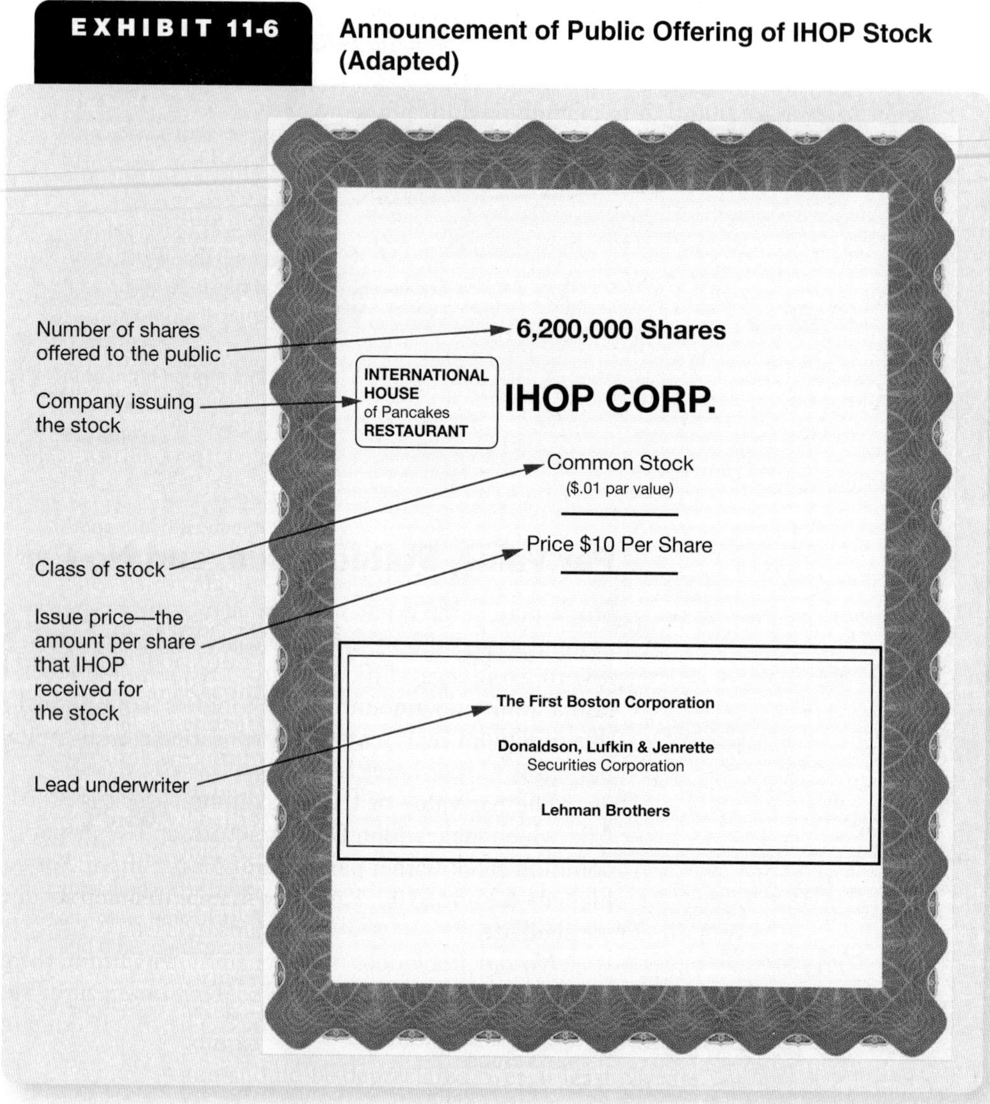

IHOP's tombstone shows that IHOP hoped to raise approximately $62 million of capital (6,200,000 shares × $10 per share). But in the final analysis, IHOP issued only 3.2 million of the shares and received cash of approximately $32 million.

Issuing Common Stock at Par

Suppose IHOP's common stock carried a par value of $10 per share. The stock issuance entry of 3.2 million shares would be:

Date	Accounts and Explanation	Debit	Credit
Jan. 31	Cash (3,200,000 × $10)	32,000,000	
	Common Stock		32,000,000
	Issued common stock at par.		

Issuing Common Stock at a Premium

Most corporations set par value low and issue common stock for a price above par. The amount above par is called a *premium*. IHOP's common stock has an actual par value of $0.01 (1 cent) per share. The $9.99 difference between the issue price ($10) and par value ($0.01) is a premium. Let's see how to account for the issuance of IHOP stock at a premium.

A premium on the sale of stock is not a gain, income, or profit for the corporation because the company is dealing with its own stockholders. This situation illustrates one of the fundamentals of accounting: *A company can have no profit or loss when buying or selling its own stock.*

With a par value of $0.01, IHOP's entry to record the issuance of its stock at $10 per share is:

Jul. 31	Cash (3,200,000 shares × $10 issue price)	32,000,000	
	Common Stock (3,200,000 shares × $0.01 par value)		32,000
	Paid-In Capital in Excess of Par—		
	Common (3,200,000 shares × $9.99 premium)		31,968,000
	Issued common stock at a premium.		

Paid-In Capital in Excess of Par is also called *Additional Paid-In Capital.*

IHOP Corp. would report stockholders' equity on its balance sheet as follows, assuming that its charter authorizes 40,000,000 shares of common stock and the balance of retained earnings is $308,000,000.

STOCKHOLDERS' EQUITY	
Paid-in capital:	
Common stock; $0.01 par; 40,000,000 shares authorized; 3,200,000 shares issued	$ 32,000
Paid-in capital in excess of par	31,968,000
Total paid-in capital	32,000,000
Retained earnings	308,000,000
Total stockholders' equity	$340,000,000

The balances of the Common Stock account and of Paid-In Capital in Excess of Par are computed as follows:

Common stock balance	=	Number of shares issued	×	Par value per share
$32,000	=	3,200,000	×	$0.01

Paid-In Capital in Excess of Par is the total amount received from issuing the common stock minus its par value, as follows:

Paid-In Capital in Excess of Par	=	Number of Shares issued	×	Premium per share
$31,968,000	=	3,200,000	×	$9.99

Altogether, total paid-in capital is the sum of:

Total paid-in capital	=	Common stock	+	Paid-In Capital in Excess of Par
$32,000,000	=	$32,000	+	$31,968,000

Issuing No-Par Stock

When a company issues no-par stock, it debits the asset received and credits the stock account. For no-par stock there can be no paid-in capital in excess of par.

Assume Rocky Mountain Corporation, which manufactures ski equipment, issues 4,000 shares of no-par common stock for $20 per share. The stock-issuance entry is:

Aug. 14	Cash (4,000 × $20)	80,000	
	Common Stock		80,000
	Issued no-par common stock.		

Regardless of the stock's price, Cash is debited and Common Stock is credited for the cash received.

Rocky Mountain's charter authorizes 10,000 shares of no-par stock, and the company has $150,000 in retained earnings. Rocky Mountain reports stockholders' equity on its balance sheet as follows:

STOCKHOLDERS' EQUITY	
Paid-in capital:	
Common stock, no par, 10,000 shares authorized, 4,000 shares issued	$ 80,000
Retained earnings	150,000
Total stockholders' equity	$230,000

Issuing No-Par Stock with a Stated Value

Accounting for no-par stock with a stated value is identical to accounting for par-value stock. No-par stock with a stated value uses an account titled Paid-In Capital in Excess of *Stated* Value.

Issuing Stock for Assets Other Than Cash

A corporation may issue stock for assets other than cash. It records the assets received at their current market value and credits the stock accounts accordingly. The assets' prior book value is irrelevant. Kahn Corporation issued 10,000 shares of its $1 par common stock for equipment worth $4,000 and a building worth $120,000. Kahn's entry is:

Nov. 30	Equipment	4,000	
	Building	120,000	
	Common Stock (10,000 × $1)		10,000
	Paid-In Capital in Excess of Par—		
	Common ($124,000 – $10,000)		114,000
	Issued common stock in exchange for equipment and a building.		

Issuing Preferred Stock

Accounting for preferred stock follows the pattern illustrated for common stock. Chiquita Brands, famous for bananas, has some preferred stock outstanding. Assume Chiquita issued 10,000 shares of preferred stock at par value of $10 per share. The issuance entry is:

July 31	Cash	100,000	
	Preferred Stock (10,000 shares × $10)		100,000
	Issued preferred stock.		

Most preferred stock is issued at par value. Therefore, Paid-In Capital in Excess of Par is rare for preferred stock. For this reason, we do not cover it in this book.

Ethical Considerations

Issuance of stock for *cash* poses no ethical challenge because the value of the asset received is clearly understood. Issuing stock for assets other than cash can pose a challenge. The company issuing the stock wants to look successful—record a large amount for the asset received and the stock issued. Why? Because large asset and equity amounts make the business look prosperous. The desire to look good can motivate a company to record a high amount for the assets.

A company is supposed to record an asset received at its current market value. But one person's evaluation of a building can differ from another's. One person may appraise the building at a market value of $4 million. Another may honestly believe the building is worth only $3 million. A company receiving the building in exchange for its stock must decide whether to record the building at $3 million, $4 million, or some other amount.

The ethical course of action is to record the asset at its current market value, as determined by independent appraisers. Corporations are rarely found guilty of *understating* their assets, but companies have been sued for *overstating* assets.

Review of Accounting for Paid-In Capital

3 Prepare the stockholders' equity section of a corporation balance sheet

Let's review the first half of this chapter by showing the stockholders' equity section of MedTech Corporation's balance sheet in Exhibit 11-7.

Observe the order of the equity accounts:

- Preferred stock
- Common stock at par value
- Paid-in capital in excess of par (belongs to the common stockholders)
- Retained earnings (after the paid-in capital accounts)

Many companies label Paid-In Capital in Excess of Par as **Additional Paid-In Capital** on the balance sheet. This amount is part of common equity, not preferred equity.

EXHIBIT 11-7 Part of MedTech.com Corporation's Balance Sheet

Stockholder's Equity	
Paid-in capital:	
Preferred stock, 5%, $100 par, 5,000 shares authorized 400 shares issued	$ 40,000
Common stock, $10 par, 20,000 shares authorized, 5,000 shares issued	50,000
Paid-in capital in excess of par—common	70,000
Total paid-in capital	160,000
Retained earnings	90,000
Total stockholders' equity	$250,000

The Decision Guidelines will solidify your understanding of stockholders' equity.

Decision Guidelines

THE STOCKHOLDERS' EQUITY OF A CORPORATION

Suppose you are interested in investing in stock. The following guidelines are relevant to your decision.

Decision	Guidelines
What are the two main segments of stockholders' equity?	• Paid-in capital • Retained earnings
Which is more permanent, paid-in capital or retained earnings?	Paid-in capital is more permanent because corporations can use retained earnings for dividends, which decreases the size of the company.
How are paid-in capital and retained earnings	
• Similar?	• Both represent stockholders' equity (ownership) of the corporation.
• Different?	• Paid-in capital and retained earnings come from different sources: a. *Paid-in capital* comes from the stockholders. b. *Retained earnings* comes from profitable operations.
What are the main categories of paid-in capital?	• Preferred stock • Common stock, plus paid-in capital in excess of par

Summary Problem 1

1. Is each of the following statements true or false?
   a. A stockholder may bind the corporation to a contract.
   b. The policy-making body in a corporation is called the board of directors.
   c. The owner of 100 shares of preferred stock has greater voting rights than the owner of 100 shares of common stock.
   d. Par-value stock is more valuable than no-par stock.
   e. Issuance of 1,000 shares of $5 par-value stock at $12 increases paid-in capital by $7,000.
   f. The issuance of no-par stock with a stated value is fundamentally different from issuing par-value stock.
   g. A corporation issues its preferred stock in exchange for land and a building with a combined market value of $200,000. This transaction increases the corporation's owners' equity by $200,000 regardless of the assets' prior book value.

2. Delphian Corporation has two classes of common stock. The company's balance sheet includes the following:

STOCKHOLDERS' EQUITY	
Paid-in capital:	
Class A common stock, voting, $1 par value, authorized and issued 1,200,000 shares	$ 1,200,000
Additional paid-in capital—Class A common	2,000,000
Class B common stock, nonvoting, no par value, authorized and issued 11,000,000 shares	55,000,000
	58,200,000
Retained earnings	800,000,000
Total stockholders' equity	$858,200,000

Requirements

a. Record the issuance of the Class A common stock.

b. Record the issuance of the Class B common stock.

c. What is the total paid-in capital of the company?

d. What was the average issue price of each share of Class B common stock?

Solution

1. Answers to true/false statements:
   a. False
   b. True
   c. False
   d. False
   e. False
   f. False
   g. True

2.

a.		Cash	3,200,000	
		Class A Common Stock		1,200,000
		Additional Paid-In Capital		2,000,000
		To record issuance of Class A common stock.		
b.		Cash	55,000,000	
		Class B Common Stock		55,000,000
		To record issuance of Class B common stock.		
c.		Total paid-in capital is $58,200,000 ($1,200,000 + $2,000,000 + $55,000,000).		
d.		Average issue price = $5 ($55,000,000/11,000,000 shares)		

Now let's see how to account for dividends.

Accounting for Cash Dividends

Corporations share their wealth with the stockholders through dividends. Corporations declare dividends from retained earnings and then pay with cash.

Dividend Dates

A corporation declares a dividend before paying it. Three dividend dates are relevant.

1. **Declaration date.** On the declaration date—say, May 1—the board of directors announces the intention to pay the dividend. The declaration of a cash dividend creates a liability for the corporation.
2. **Date of record.** Those stockholders holding the stock on the date of record—a week or two after declaration, say, May 15—will receive the dividend.
3. **Payment date.** Payment of the dividend usually follows the record date by a week or two—say, May 30.

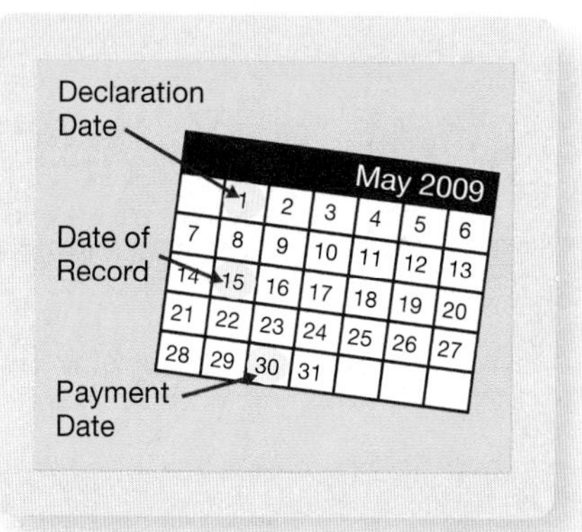

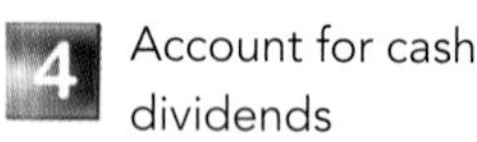
Account for cash dividends

Declaring and Paying Dividends

The cash dividend rate on *preferred stock* is often expressed as a percentage of the preferred-stock par value, such as 6%. But sometimes cash dividends on preferred stock are expressed as a dollar amount per share, such as $2 per share. Therefore, preferred dividends are computed two ways, depending on how the preferred-stock cash-dividend rate is expressed. Here are the two ways to compute preferred dividends, using new figures made up for this illustration:

1. **Par value of the preferred stock × Preferred dividend rate = Preferred dividend**

   Example: $100,000 × 6% (.06) = $6,000

2. **Number of shares of preferred stock outstanding × Preferred dividend rate = Preferred dividend**

   Example: 4,000 shares × $2 per share = $8,000

Cash dividends on *common stock* are computed the second way because cash dividends are not expressed as a percentage.

To account for the declaration of a cash dividend we debit Retained Earnings and credit Dividends Payable, as follows (amount assumed):[1]

May 1	Retained Earnings	20,000	
	Dividends Payable		20,000
	Declared a cash dividend.		

To pay the dividend, debit Dividends Payable and credit Cash.

May 30	Dividends Payable	20,000	
	Cash		20,000
	Paid the cash dividend.		

Dividends Payable is a current liability. When a company has issued both preferred and common, the preferred stockholders get their dividends first. The common stockholders receive dividends only if the total dividend is large enough to satisfy the preferred requirement. Let's see how dividends are divided between preferred and common.

Dividing Dividends Between Preferred and Common

Sierra Corp. has common stock plus 10,000 shares of preferred stock outstanding. The annual preferred dividend rate is $2 per share. Therefore, Sierra's annual dividend must exceed $20,000 for the common stockholders to get anything. Exhibit 11-8 shows the division of dividends between preferred and common for two situations.

EXHIBIT 11-8 **Dividing a Dividend Between Preferred Stock and Common Stock**

Case A: Total dividend of $8,000:	
Preferred dividend (the full $8,000 goes to preferred because the annual preferred dividend is $20,000)	$ 8,000
Common dividend (none because the total dividend did not cover the preferred dividend for the year)	0
Total dividend	$ 8,000
Case B: Total dividend of $50,000:	
Preferred dividend (10,000 shares × $2 per share)	$20,000
Common dividend ($50,000 – $20,000)	30,000
Total dividend	$50,000

If Sierra's dividend is large enough to cover the preferred dividend (Case B), the preferred stockholders get their regular dividend, and the common stockholders get

[1]Some accountants debit a Dividends account, which is closed to Retained Earnings. But most businesses debit Retained Earnings directly, as shown here.

the remainder. But if the year's dividend falls below the annual preferred amount (Case A), the preferred stockholders receive the entire dividend, and the common stockholders get nothing that year.

Dividends on Cumulative and Noncumulative Preferred

Preferred stock can be either:

- Cumulative or
- Noncumulative

Preferred is cumulative unless it's specifically designated as noncumulative. Most preferred stock is cumulative. Let's see how this plays out.

A corporation may fail to pay the preferred dividend. This is called *passing the dividend*, and the dividends are said to be *in arrears*. **Cumulative preferred** must receive all dividends in arrears before the common stockholders get a dividend.

The preferred stock of Sierra Corp. mentioned on page 564 is cumulative. How do we know this? Because preferred is not labeled as noncumulative.

Suppose Sierra passed the 2006 preferred dividend of $20,000. Before paying any common dividend in 2007, Sierra must first pay preferred dividends of $20,000 for 2006 and $20,000 for 2007, a total of $40,000. In 2007, Sierra declares a $50,000 dividend. How much of this dividend goes to preferred? How much goes to common? The allocation of this $50,000 dividend is:

	Total dividend		$50,000
	Preferred gets		
	2006: 10,000 shares × $2 per share	$20,000	
	2007: 10,000 shares × $2 per share	20,000	
	Total to preferred		40,000
	Common gets the remainder.		$10,000

Sierra's entry to record the declaration of this dividend is

2007			
Sep. 6	Retained Earnings	50,000	
	Dividends Payable, Preferred ($20,000 × 2)		40,000
	Dividends Payable Common ($50,000 – $40,000)		10,000
	Declared a cash dividend.		

If the preferred stock is ***noncumulative***, the corporation need not pay any dividends in arrears. Suppose Sierra's preferred stock was noncumulative and the company passed the 2006 dividend. The preferred stockholders would lose the 2006 dividend forever. Then, before paying any common dividends in 2007, Sierra would have to pay only the 2007 preferred dividend of $20,000.

Dividends in arrears are *not* a liability. A liability for dividends arises only after the board of directors declares the dividend. But a corporation reports cumulative preferred dividends in arrears in notes to the financial statements. This shows the common stockholders how much it will take for them to get any dividends.

Different Values of Stock

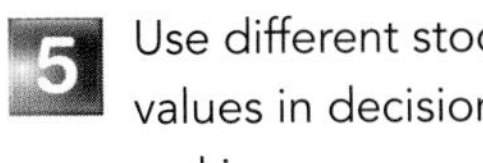

There are several different *stock values* in addition to par value. Market value and book value are used for decision making.

Market Value

Market value, or *market price,* is the price for which a person can buy or sell a share of stock. The corporation's net income and general economic conditions affect market value. The Internet and most newspapers report stock prices. Log on to any company's Web site to track its stock price. *In almost all cases, stockholders are more concerned about the market value of a stock than about any other value.*

When IHOP went public, its stock had a market price of $10 when it was issued. Shortly thereafter, IHOP's stock shot up to $36 per share. The purchase of 100 shares of IHOP stock at $36 would cost you $3,600 ($36 × 100), plus a commission. If you were selling 100 shares of IHOP stock, you would receive cash of $3,600 less a commission. The commission is the fee a stockbroker charges for buying or selling the stock. The price of a share of IHOP stock has fluctuated from $10 at issuance to a recent high of $50.50.

Book Value

Book value is the amount of owners' equity on the company's books for each share of its stock. If the company has only common stock outstanding, you can divide total stockholders' equity by the number of shares *outstanding*. A company with equity of $150,000 and 5,000 shares of common stock has a book value of $30 per share ($150,000/5,000 shares).

If the company has both preferred and common outstanding, preferred has first claim to the equity. Therefore, we subtract preferred equity from total equity to compute book value per share of common. To illustrate, Lille Corporation reports the following amounts:

STOCKHOLDERS' EQUITY	
Paid in capital:	
Preferred stock, 6%, $10 par, 5,000 shares issued	$ 50,000
Common stock, $1 par, 20,000 shares authorized, 10,000 shares issued	10,000
Paid-in capital in excess of par—common	170,000
Total paid-in capital	230,000
Retained earnings	420,000
Total stockholders' equity	$650,000

Last year's and this year's preferred dividends are in arrears.

Book value per share of common is computed as follows:

Preferred equity:	
Par value	$ 50,000
Cumulative dividends for two years: ($50,000 × .06 × 2)	6,000
Preferred equity	$ 56,000
Common equity:	
Total stockholders' equity	$650,000
Less preferred equity	−56,000
Common equity	$594,000
Book value per share of common ($594,000/10,000 shares)	$59.40

Book value may figure into the price to pay for a closely-held company, whose stock is not publicly traded. Also, a company may buy out a stockholder by paying the book value of the person's stock. This recently occurred for a friend of the coauthor of this book. The president retired, and his company bought him out at book value.

Some investors compare the book value of a stock with its market value. The idea is that a stock selling below book value is a good buy. But the book value/market value relationship is far from clear. Other investors believe that a stock selling below book value means the company must be having problems.

Exhibit 11-9 contrasts the book values and market values for the stocks of three well-known companies. In all three cases, market price far exceeds book value—a sign of success.

EXHIBIT 11-9 **Book Value and Market Value for Three Well-Known Companies**

	Book Value Per Share	Recent Stock Price
IHOP Corp.	$17.02	$40.98
Coca-Cola	6.61	43.81
Dell	2.61	35.20

Evaluating Operations

Investors are constantly comparing companies' profits. IHOP's net income isn't comparable with that of a new company because IHOP is established and the other company is just getting started. To compare companies, we need some standard profitability measures. Two important ratios are return on assets and return on common stockholders' equity.

Rate of Return on Total Assets

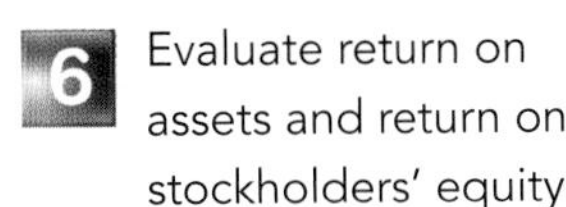

Evaluate return on assets and return on stockholders' equity

The **rate of return on total assets**, or simply **return on assets**, measures a company's success in using assets to earn income. Two groups invest money to finance a corporation:

- Stockholders
- Creditors

Net income and interest expense are the returns to these two groups. The stockholders earn the corporation's net income, and the creditors get its interest expense.

The sum of net income plus interest expense is the numerator of the return-on-assets ratio. The denominator is average total assets. Return on assets is computed as follows, using data from the 2004 annual report of IHOP Corp. (dollar amounts in millions):

$$\text{Rate of Return on Total Assets} = \frac{\text{Net Income} + \text{Interest Expense}}{\text{Average Total Assets}}$$

$$= \frac{\$33 + \$22}{(\$843 + \$822)/2} = \frac{\$55}{\$832.5} = 0.066$$

Net income and interest expense are taken from the income statement. Average total assets comes from the beginning and ending balance sheets.

What is a good rate of return on total assets? There is no single answer because rates of return vary widely by industry. In most industries, a 10% return on assets is considered good.

Rate of Return on Common Stockholders' Equity

Rate of return on common stockholders' equity, often shortened to **return on equity**, shows the relationship between net income available to the common stockholders and their average common equity. The numerator is net income minus preferred dividends. Preferred dividends are subtracted because the preferred stockholders have first claim to any dividends. The denominator is average *common stockholders' equity*—total equity minus preferred equity. IHOP's rate of return on common stockholders' equity for 2004 is computed as follows (amounts in millions):

$$\text{Rate of Return on Common Stockholders' Equity} = \frac{\text{Net Income} - \text{Preferred Dividends}}{\text{Average Common Stockholders' Equity}}$$

$$= \frac{\$33 - \$0}{(\$340 + \$382)/2} = \frac{\$33}{\$361} = 0.091$$

IHOP has no preferred stock, so preferred dividends are zero.

IHOP's rates of return carry both bad news and good news.

- The bad news is that these rates of return are low. Most companies strive for return on equity of 15% or higher. IHOP's 9.1% is disappointing.

- The good news is that return on equity exceeds return on assets. That means IHOP is earning more for its stockholders than it's paying for interest expense, and that's a healthy sign.

If return on assets ever exceeds return on equity, the company is in trouble. Why? Because the company's interest expense is greater than its return on equity. In that case, no investor would buy the company's stock. Return on assets should always be significantly lower than return on equity.

Accounting for Income Taxes by Corporations

7 Account for the income tax of a corporation

Corporations pay income tax just as individuals do, but not at the same rates. At this writing, the federal tax rate on most corporate income is 35%. Most states also levy a corporate income tax, so most corporations pay a combined federal and state income tax rate of approximately 40%.

To account for income tax, a corporation measures two income tax amounts:

- Income tax expense
- Income tax payable

In general, income tax expense and income tax payable can be computed as follows:[2]

Income tax *expense*	=	Income before tax from the income statement	×	Income tax rate

Income tax *payable*	=	Taxable income from the tax return filed with the IRS	×	Income tax rate

The income statement and the income tax return are entirely separate documents. You've been studying the income statement throughout this course. The tax return is new. It reports taxes to the IRS.

For most companies, income tax expense and income tax payable differ. The most important difference occurs when a corporation uses straight-line depreciation for the income statement and accelerated depreciation for the tax return.

Continuing with the IHOP illustration, suppose for 2008 that IHOP Corp. has

- Income before income tax of $55 million (This comes from the income statement.)
- Taxable income of $40 million (This comes from the tax return.)

IHOP will record income tax for 2008 as follows (dollar amounts in millions and assume an income tax rate of 40%):

Date	Accounts	Debit	Credit
2008			
Dec. 31	Income Tax Expense ($55 × 0.40)	22	
	Income Tax Payable ($40 × 0.40)		16
	Deferred Tax Liability		6
	Recorded income tax for the year.		

IHOP will pay the $16 million of Income Tax Payable within a few months. The Deferred Tax Liability account is long-term, so IHOP will pay this debt over a num-

[2]The authors thank Jean Marie Hudson for suggesting this presentation.

ber of years. For this situation IHOP's 2008 financial statements would report these figures (in millions):

Income Statement		Balance Sheet	
Income before income tax	$55	Current liabilities:	
Income tax expense	(22)	Income tax payable	$16
Net income	$33	Long-term liabilities:	
		Deferred tax liability	6*

* Assumes the beginning balance of Deferred tax liability was zero.

Decision Guidelines

DIVIDENDS, STOCK VALUES, EVALUATING OPERATIONS, AND CORPORATE INCOME TAX

Suppose you are considering buying some IHOP stock. You are naturally interested in how well the company is doing. Does IHOP pay dividends? What are IHOP's stock values? What are the rates of return on IHOP's assets and equity? The Decision Guidelines will help you evaluate the company.

Decision	Guidelines
Dividends	
Whether to declare a cash dividend?	• Must have enough retained earnings to declare the dividend. • Must have enough cash to pay the dividend.
What happens with a dividend?	• The IHOP board of directors declares the dividend. Then the dividend becomes a liability for IHOP. • The date of record fixes who will receive the dividend. • Payment of the dividend occurs later.
Who receives the dividend?	• Preferred stockholders get their dividends first. Preferred dividends have a specified rate. • Common stockholders receive the remainder.
Stock Values	
How much to pay for a stock?	Its market value.
How is book value used in decision making?	Can measure the value of a stock that is not traded on a stock exchange.
Evaluating Operations	
How to evaluate the operations of a corporation?	Two measures: • Rate of return on total assets (return on assets) • Rate of return on common equity (return on equity) For a healthy company, return on equity should exceed return on assets by a wide margin.
Accounting for Income Tax	
What are the three main tax accounts?	• Income tax expense • Income tax payable, a current liability • Deferred tax liability, usually long-term
How to measure	
• Income tax expense?	Income before income tax (from the income statement) × Income tax rate
• Income tax payable?	Taxable income (from the income tax return filed with the Internal Revenue Service) × Income tax rate
• Deferred tax liability?	Difference between income tax expense and income tax payable

Summary Problem 2

Use the following accounts and related balances to prepare the classified balance sheet of Fiesta, Inc., at September 30, 2007. Use the account format of the balance sheet.

Common stock, $1 par,		Long-term note payable	$ 70,000
50,000 shares authorized,		Inventory	85,000
20,000 shares issued	$20,000	Property, plant, and	
Salary payable	3,000	equipment, net	205,000
Cash	15,000	Accounts receivable, net	25,000
Accounts payable	20,000	Preferred stock, $2.50, no-par,	
Retained earnings	80,000	10,000 shares authorized,	
Paid-in capital in excess of		2,000 shares issued	50,000
par—common	75,000	Income tax payable	12,000

Solution

FIESTA, INC.
Balance Sheet
September 30, 2007

Assets		**Liabilities**		
Current:		Current:		
Cash	$ 15,000	Accounts payable		$ 20,000
Accounts receivable,		Salary payable		3,000
net	25,000	Income tax payable		12,000
Inventory	85,000	Total current liabilities		35,000
Total current		Long-term note payable		70,000
assets	125,000	Total liabilities		105,000
Property, plant, and				
equipment, net	205,000	**Stockholders' Equity**		
		Preferred stock, $2.50, no-par,		
		10,000 shares authorized,		
		2,000 shares issued	$ 50,000	
		Common stock, $1 par,		
		50,000 shares authorized,		
		20,000 shares issued	20,000	
		Paid-in capital in excess of		
		par—common	75,000	
		Total paid-in capital	145,000	
		Retained earnings	80,000	
		Total stockholders' equity		225,000
		Total liabilities and		
Total assets	$330,000	stockholders' equity		$330,000

Compute the book value per share of Fiesta's common stock. No preferred dividends are in arrears, and Fiesta has not declared the current-year dividend.

continued . . .

Preferred equity:	
Carrying value	$ 50,000
Cumulative dividend for the current year (2,000 shares × $2.50)	5,000
Preferred equity	$ 55,000
Common:	
Total stockholders' equity	$225,000
Less preferred equity	55,000)
Common equity	$170,000
Book value per share of common ($170,000/20,000 shares)	$ 8.50

Review Corporations: Paid-In Capital and the Balance Sheet

Accounting Vocabulary

Additional Paid-In Capital
The paid-in capital in excess of par, common plus other accounts combined for reporting on the balance sheet.

Authorization of Stock
Provision in a corporate charter that gives the state's permission for the corporation to issue—that is, to sell—a certain number of shares of stock.

Board of Directors
Group elected by the stockholders to set policy and to appoint the officers.

Book Value
Amount of owners' equity on the company's books for each share of its stock.

Bylaws
Constitution for governing a corporation.

Chairperson
Elected by a corporation's board of directors, the most powerful person in the corporation.

Charter
Document that gives the state's permission to form a corporation.

Common Stock
The class of stock that represents the basic ownership of the corporation.

Contributed Capital
Capital from investment by the stockholders. Also called **paid-in capital**.

Cumulative Preferred Stock
Preferred stock whose owners must receive all dividends in arrears before the corporation pays dividends to the common stockholders.

Deficit
Debit balance in the Retained Earnings account.

Dividends
Distributions by a corporation to its stockholders.

Double Taxation
Corporations pay their own income taxes on corporate income. Then the stockholders pay personal income tax on the cash dividends they receive from corporations.

Legal Capital
The portion of stockholders' equity that cannot be used for dividends.

Limited Liability
No personal obligation of a stockholder for corporation debts. A stockholder can lose no more on an investment in a corporation's stock than the cost of the investment.

Market Value
Price for which a person could buy or sell a share of stock.

Outstanding Stock
Stock in the hands of stockholders.

Paid-in Capital
Capital from investment by the stockholders. Also called **contributed capital**.

Par Value
Arbitrary amount assigned to a share of stock.

Preferred Stock
Stock that gives its owners certain advantages over common stockholders, such as the right to receive dividends before the common stockholders and the right to receive assets before the common stockholders if the corporation liquidates.

President
Chief operating officer in charge of managing the day-to-day operations of a corporation.

Rate of Return on Common Stockholders' Equity
Net income minus preferred dividends, divided by average common stockholders' equity. A measure of profitability. Also called **return on equity**.

Rate of Return on Total Assets
The sum of net income plus interest expense divided by average total assets. Measures the success a company has in using its assets to earn income for those financing the business. Also called **return on assets**.

Retained Earnings
Capital earned through profitable operation of the business.

Return on Assets
The sum of net income plus interest expense divided by average total assets. Measures the success a company has in using its assets to earn income for those financing the business. Also called **rate of return on total assets**.

Return on Equity
Net income minus preferred dividends, divided by average common stockholders' equity. A measure of profitability. Also called **rate of return on common stockholders' equity**.

Shareholder
A person who owns the stock of a corporation. Also called **stockholder**.

Stated Value
An arbitrary amount that accountants treat as though it were par value.

Stock
Shares into which the owners' equity of a corporation is divided.

Stockholder
A person who owns the stock of a corporation. Also called **shareholder**.

Stockholders' Equity
Owners' equity of a corporation.

Quick Check

1. Which characteristic of a corporation is most attractive?
   a. Double taxation
   b. Mutual agency
   c. Limited liability
   d. All of the above

2. Which corporate characteristic is a disadvantage?
   a. Double taxation
   b. Mutual agency
   c. Limited liability
   d. None of the above

3. The two basic sources of corporate capital are
   a. Paid-in capital and retained earnings
   b. Assets and equity
   c. Preferred and common
   d. Retained earnings and dividends

4. Which class of stockholders takes the greater investment risk?
   a. Common
   b. Preferred
   c. Neither; bondholders take the most risk
   d. Both preferred and common take equal risk

5. Suppose Pier 1 Imports issued 100,000 shares of \$0.05 par common stock at \$1 per share. Which journal entry correctly records the issuance of this stock?

a. Cash	100,000	
Common Stock		100,000
b. Common Stock	100,000	
Cash		5,000
Paid-In Capital in Excess of Par		95,000
c. Common Stock	100,000	
Cash		100,000
d. Cash	100,000	
Common Stock		5,000
Paid-In Capital in Excess of Par		95,000

6. Suppose IHOP issues common stock to purchase a building. IHOP should record the building at
   a. The par value of the stock given
   b. A value assigned by the board of directors
   c. Its market value
   d. Its book value

7. Chewning Corporation has 10,000 shares of 5%, $10 par preferred stock and 50,000 shares of common stock outstanding. Chewning declared no dividends in 2008. In 2009, Chewning declares a total dividend of $50,000. How much of the dividends go to the common stockholders?
   a. $50,000
   b. $40,000
   c. $10,000
   d. None; it all goes to preferred

8. Connor Health Foods has 10,000 shares of $1 par common stock outstanding, which was issued at $10 per share. Connor also has retained earnings of $80,000. How much is Connor's total stockholders' equity?
   a. $10,000
   b. $90,000
   c. $100,000
   d. $180,000

9. Dale Corporation has the following data:

Net income	$22,000	Average total assets	$300,000
Interest expense	8,000	Average common equity	100,000
Preferred dividends	10,000		

   Dale's return on assets is
   a. 15%
   b. 12%
   c. 10%
   d. 4%

10. A corporation's income tax payable is computed as:
   a. Income before tax × Income tax rate
   b. Taxable income × Income tax rate
   c. Net income × Income tax rate
   d. Return on equity × Income tax rate

Answers are given after Apply Your Knowledge (p. 595).

Assess Your Progress

Short Exercises

Authority structure in a corporation

S11-1 Answer these questions about corporations. (p. 548)

1. Who is the most powerful person in the corporation?
2. What group holds the ultimate power?
3. Who is in charge of day-to-day operations?
4. Who is in charge of accounting?

The balance sheets of a corporation and a proprietorship

S11-2 How does a proprietorship balance sheet differ from a corporation's balance sheet? How are the two balance sheets similar? (pp. 550–551)

Issuing stock

S11-3 Colorado Corporation has two classes of stock: Common, $1 par: Preferred, $20 par. Journalize Colorado's issuance of

a. 1,000 shares of common stock for $10 per share

b. 1,000 shares of preferred stock for a total of $20,000

Explanations are not required. (pp. 553–556)

Effect of a stock issuance

S11-4 IHOP issued common stock and received $32,000,000. The par value of the IHOP stock was only $32,000. Is the excess amount of $31,968,000 a profit to IHOP? Does the excess affect net income? If not, what was it? (pp. 553–554)

Issuing stock and interpreting stockholders' equity

S11-5 Smartpages.com issued stock during 2008 and reported the following on its balance sheet at December 31, 2008:

Common stock, $0.25 par value	
Authorized: 5,000 shares	
Issued: 3,000 shares	$ 750
Paid-in capital in excess of par	3,850
Retained earnings	24,500

Journalize the company's issuance of the stock for cash. (pp. 553–554)

Preparing the stockholders' equity section of a balance sheet

S11-6 Hillcrest Corporation reported the following accounts:

Cost of goods sold	$58,800	Accounts payable	$ 6,000
Paid-in capital in excess of par	17,000	Retained earnings	16,000
Common stock, $1 par,		Unearned revenue	5,200
40,000 shares issued	40,000	Total assets	?
Cash	24,000	Long-term note payable	7,600

continued . . .

Prepare the stockholders' equity section of the Hillcrest balance sheet. (pp. 553–554)

Using stockholders' equity data

S11-7 Use the Hillcrest Corporation data in Short Exercise 11-6 to compute Hillcrest's

a. Total liabilities (pp. 146–147)

b. Total assets (p. 13)

Accounting for cash dividends

S11-8 Java Company earned net income of $85,000 during the year ended December 31, 2008. On December 15, Java declared the annual cash dividend on its 4% preferred stock (par value, $100,000) and a $0.50 per share cash dividend on its common stock (50,000 shares). Java then paid the dividends on January 4, 2009.

Journalize for Java:

a. Declaring the cash dividends on December 15, 2008. (pp. 562–565)

b. Paying the cash dividends on January 4, 2009. (pp. 562–564)

Dividing cash dividends between preferred and common stock

S11-9 Sterling Trust has the following stockholders' equity:

Paid-in capital:	
Preferred stock, 5%, $10 par, 5,000 shares authorized, 4,000 shares issued	$ 40,000
Common stock, $0.10 par, 1,000,000 shares authorized and issued	100,000
Paid-in capital in excess of par—common	300,000
Total paid-in capital	440,000
Retained earnings	260,000
Total stockholders' equity	$700,000

Answer these questions about Sterling's dividends:

1. Is Sterling's preferred stock cumulative or noncumulative? How can you tell? (pp. 562–565)
2. Sterling declares cash dividends of $15,000 for 2006. How much of the dividends goes to preferred? How much goes to common? (pp. 564–565)
3. Sterling passed the preferred dividend in 2007 and 2008. In 2009 the company declares cash dividends of $15,000. How much of the dividend goes to preferred? How much goes to common? (p. 565)

Book value per share of common stock

S11-10 Refer to the stockholders' equity of Sterling Trust in Short Exercise 11-9. Sterling has not declared preferred dividends for 5 years (including the current year). Compute the book value per share of Sterling's common stock. (p. 566)

Computing return on assets and return on equity for a leading company

S11-11 Coca-Cola's 2004 financial statements reported the following items—with 2005 figures given for comparison (adapted, in millions):

	2004	2003
Balance sheet		
Total assets	$31,327	$27,342
Total liabilities	$15,392	$13,252
Total stockholders' equity (all common)	15,935	14,090
Total liabilities and equity	$31,327	$27,342
Income statement		
Net sales	$21,962	
Cost of goods sold	7,638	
Gross profit	14,324	
Selling, administrative, and general expenses	8,146	
Interest expense	196	
All other expenses	1,135	
Net income	$ 4,847	

Compute Coca-Cola's rate of return on total assets and rate of return on common stockholders' equity for 2004. Do these rates of return look high or low? (pp. 567–568)

Accounting for a corporation's income tax

S11-12 Foxey Flowers had income before income tax of $80,000 and taxable income of $70,000 for 2007, the company's first year of operations. The income tax rate is 40%.

1. Make the entry to record Foxey's income taxes for 2007. (pp. 568–569)
2. Show what Foxey Flowers will report on its 2007 income statement, starting with income before income tax. (pp. 568–569)

Exercises

Organizing a corporation

1

E11-13 Jack and Judy Myers are opening Parties on Demand. To buy stage props and other equipment they need outside capital, so they plan to organize the business as a corporation. They come to you for advice. Write a memorandum informing them of the steps in forming a corporation. Identify specific documents used in this process, and name the different parties involved in the ownership and management of a corporation. (pp. 547–548)

Issuing stock

E11-14 Mustang Properties completed the following stock issuance transactions:

June 19	Issued 1,000 shares of $1 par common stock for cash of $8 per share.
July 3	Sold 300 shares of $4.50, no-par preferred stock for $15,000 cash.
11	Received equipment with market value of $20,000. Issued 3,000 shares of the $1 par common stock.

continued . . .

Requirements

1. Journalize the transactions. Explanations are not required. (pp. 553–556)
2. How much paid-in capital did these transactions generate for Mustang Properties? (p. 554)

Recording issuance of no-par stock

E11-15 Manor House Restaurants issued 5,000 shares of no-par common stock for $6 per share. Record issuance of the stock if the stock (a) is true no-par stock and (b) has stated value of $2 per share. Which type of stock results in more total paid-in capital? (pp. 553–554)

Issuing stock to finance the purchase of assets

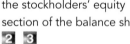

E11-16 This exercise shows the similarity and the difference between two ways for Mane Event Styling Salons, Inc., to acquire plant assets.

Case A—Issue stock and buy the assets in separate transactions:

Mane Event issued 10,000 shares of its $10 par common stock for cash of $700,000. In a separate transaction, Mane Event purchased a building for $500,000 and equipment for $200,000. Journalize the two transactions.

Case B—Issue stock to acquire the assets:

Mane Event issued 10,000 shares of its $10 par common stock to acquire a building valued at $500,000 and equipment worth $200,000. Journalize this single transaction.

Compare the balances in all accounts after making both sets of entries. Are the account balances similar or different? (pp. 553–556)

Issuing stock and preparing the stockholders' equity section of the balance sheet

E11-17 The charter for KXAS-TV authorizes the company to issue 100,000 shares of $3, no-par preferred stock and 500,000 shares of common stock with $1 par value. During its start-up phase, KXAS completed the following transactions:

Aug. 6	Issued 500 shares of common stock to the stockholders who organized the corporation, receiving cash of $13,000.
12	Issued 300 shares of preferred stock for cash of $20,000.
14	Issued 1,000 shares of common stock in exchange for land valued at $26,000.
31	Closed net income of $40,000 into Retained Earnings.

Requirements

1. Record the transactions in the general journal. (pp. 551–554)
2. Prepare the stockholders' equity section of the KXAS-TV balance sheet at August 31. (p. 556)

Stockholders' equity section of a balance sheet

E11-18 The charter of Maple Leaf Capital Corporation authorizes the issuance of 1,000 shares of preferred stock and 10,000 shares of common stock.

continued . . .

During a two-month period, Maple Leaf completed these stock-issuance transactions:

Nov. 23	Issued 2,000 shares of $1 par common stock for cash of $12.50 per share.
Dec. 12	Received inventory valued at $25,000 and equipment with market value of $16,000 for 3,000 shares of the $1 par common stock.
17	Issued 1,000 shares of 5%, $50 par preferred stock for $50 per share.

Requirement

Prepare the stockholders' equity section of the Maple Leaf Capital balance sheet for the transactions given in this exercise. Retained Earnings has a balance of $70,000. (pp. 556–557)

Paid-in capital for a corporation

E11-19 Ariba Corp. recently organized. The company issued common stock to an inventor in exchange for a patent with a market value of $50,000. In addition, Ariba received cash both for 2,000 shares of its $10 par preferred stock at par value and for 6,000 shares of its no-par common stock at $20 per share. Without making journal entries, determine the total *paid-in capital* created by these transactions. (pp. 556–557)

Stockholders' equity section of a balance sheet

E11-20 International Publishing Company has the following selected account balances at June 30, 2007. Prepare the stockholders' equity section of International's balance sheet. (pp. 556–557)

Inventory	$112,000	Common stock, no par	
Machinery and equipment	109,000	with $1 stated value,	
Preferred stock, 5%, 10 par,		100,000 shares authorized	
20,000 shares authorized,		and issued	$100,000
5,000 shares issued	50,000	Accumulated depreciation—	
Paid-in capital in excess of		machinery and equipment	62,000
stated value—common	90,000	Retained earnings	110,0000
Cost of goods sold	81,000		

Dividing dividends between preferred and common stock

E11-21 Waddell & Reed, Inc., has the following stockholders' equity:

Paid-in capital:	
Preferred stock, 8%, $10 par, 100,000 shares authorized, 20,000 shares issued	$ 200,000
Common stock, $0.50 par, 500,000 shares authorized, 300,000 shares issued	150,000
Paid-in capital in excess of par—common	600,000
Total paid-in capital	950,000
Retained earnings	150,000
Total stockholders' equity	$1,100,000

continued . . .

First, determine whether preferred stock is cumulative or noncumulative. Then compute the amount of dividends to preferred and to common for 2007 and 2008 if total dividends are $10,000 in 2007 and $50,000 in 2008. (pp. 562–565)

Computing dividends on preferred and common stock
4

E11-22 The following elements of stockholders' equity are adapted from the balance sheet of Volvo Marketing Corp.

Stockholders' Equity	
Preferred stock, 5% cumulative, $2 par, 50,000 shares issued	$100,000
Common stock, $0.10 par, 9,000,000 shares issued	900,000

Volvo paid no preferred dividends in 2008.

Requirement

Compute the dividends to preferred and common for 2009 if total dividends are $150,000. (p. 565)

Book value per share of common stock
5

E11-23 The balance sheet of Mark Todd Wireless, Inc., reported the following:

Preferred stock, $50 par value, 6%, 1,000 shares issued and outstanding	$ 50,000
Common stock, no par value, 10,000 shares authorized; 5,000 shares issued	222,000
Total stockholders' equity	$277,000

Assume that Todd has paid preferred dividends for the current year and all prior years (no dividends in arrears). Compute the book value per share of the common stock. (p. 567)

Book value per share of common stock; preferred dividends in arrears
5

E11-24 Refer to Exercise 11-23. Compute the book value per share of Todd's common stock if three years' preferred dividends (including dividends for the current year) are in arrears. (p. 567)

Evaluating profitability
6

E11-25 La Salle Exploration Company reported these figures for 2008 and 2007:

	2008	2007
Income statement:		
Interest expense	$ 12,400,000	$ 17,100,000
Net income	18,000,000	18,700,000

continued . . .

	2008	2007
Balance sheet:		
Total assets	$326,000,000	$317,000,000
Preferred stock, $2, no-par, 100,000 shares issued and outstanding	2,500,000	2,500,000
Common stockholders' equity	184,000,000	176,000,000
Total stockholders' equity	186,500,000	178,500,000

Compute rate of return on total assets and rate of return on common stockholders' equity for 2008. Do these rates of return suggest strength or weakness? Give your reason. (pp. 567–570)

Accounting for income tax by a corporation

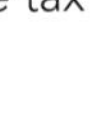

E11-26 The income statement of eBay, Inc., reported income before income tax of $400 million (rounded) during a recent year. Assume eBay's taxable income for the year was $344 million. The company's income tax rate was close to 37.5%.

1. Journalize eBay's entry to record income tax for the year. (pp. 568–569)
2. Show how eBay would report income tax expense on its income statement and income tax liabilities on its balance sheet. Complete the income statement, starting with income before tax. For the balance sheet, assume all beginning balances were zero. (pp. 568–569)

Problems (Group A)

Organizing a corporation

P11-27A Lance Lot and Arthur King are opening a FedEx Kinko's store. There are no competing copy shops in the area. Their fundamental decision is how to organize the business. Lot thinks the partnership form is best for their business. King favors the corporate form of organization. They seek your advice. (pp. 547–549)

Requirement

Write a memo to Lot and King to make them aware of the advantages and disadvantages of organizing the business as a corporation. Use the following format:

Date: ________________

To: Lance Lot and Arthur King

From: Student Name

Subject: Advantages and disadvantages of the corporate form of business organization

Journalizing corporation transactions and preparing the stockholders' equity section of the balance sheet 2 3

P11-28A A-Mobile Wireless needed additional capital to expand, so the business incorporated. The charter from the state of Georgia authorizes A-Mobile to issue 50,000 shares of 6%, \$100-par preferred stock and 100,000 shares of no-par common stock. A-Mobile completed the following transactions:

Dec. 2	Issued 20,000 shares of common stock for equipment with market value of \$100,000.
6	Issued 500 shares of preferred stock to acquire a patent with a market value of \$50,000.
9	Issued 12,000 shares of common stock for cash of \$60,000.

Requirements

1. Record the transactions in the general journal. (pp. 554–556)
2. Prepare the stockholders' equity section of the A-Mobile Wireless balance sheet at December 31. The ending balance of Retained Earnings is \$90,000. (pp. 556–557)

Issuing stock and preparing the stockholders' equity section of the balance sheet.

P11-29A Lockridge-Priest, Inc., was organized in 2008. At December 31, 2008, the Lockridge-Priest balance sheet reported the following stockholders' equity:

Paid-in capital:	
Preferred stock, 6%, \$50 par, 100,000 shares authorized, none issued	\$ —
Common stock, \$1 par, 500,000 shares authorized, 60,000 shares issued	60,000
Paid-in capital in excess of par—common	40,000
Total paid-in capital	100,000
Retained earnings	25,000
Total stockholders' equity	\$125,000

Requirements

1. During 2009, the company completed the following selected transactions. Journalize each transaction. Explanations are not required.
   a. Issued for cash 1,000 shares of preferred stock at par value. (pp. 555–556)
   b. Issued for cash 2,000 shares of common stock at a price of \$3 per share. (pp. 553–554)
   c. Net income for the year was \$75,000, and the company declared no dividends. Make the closing entry for net income. (pp. 551–552)
2. Prepare the stockholders' equity section of the Lockridge-Priest balance sheet at December 31, 2009. (pp. 556–557)

Stockholders' equity section of the balance sheet

P11-30A The following summaries for Centroplex Service, Inc., and Jacobs-Cathey Co. provide the information needed to prepare the stockholders' equity section of each company's balance sheet. The two companies are independent.

- *Centroplex Service, Inc.* Centroplex is authorized to issue 40,000 shares of $1 par common stock. All the stock was issued at $10 per share. The company incurred net losses of $50,000 in 2004 and $14,000 in 2005. It earned net income of $28,000 in 2006 and $176,000 in 2007. The company declared no dividends during the four-year period.
- *Jacobs-Cathey Co.* Jacobs-Cathey's charter authorizes the issuance of 50,000 shares of 5%, $15 par preferred stock and 500,000 shares of no-par common stock. Jacobs-Cathey issued 1,000 shares of the preferred stock at $15 per share. It issued 100,000 shares of the common stock for $200,000. The company's retained earnings balance at the beginning of 2007 was $120,000. Net income for 2007 was $90,000, and the company declared the specified preferred dividend for 2007. Preferred dividends for 2006 were in arrears.

Requirements

For each company, prepare the stockholders' equity section of its balance sheet at December 31, 2007. Show the computation of all amounts. Entries are not required. (pp. 556–557, 562–565)

Analyzing the stockholders' equity of a corporation

P11-31A Trane Comfort Specialists, Inc., reported the following stockholders' equity on its balance sheet at June 30, 2008.

Stockholders' Equity	
Paid-in capital:	
Preferred stock, 6%—Authorized 600,000 shares; issued 200,000 shares	$ 1,000,000
Common stock—$1 par value—Authorized 5,000,000 shares; issued 1,300,000	1,300,000
Additional paid-in capital, common	2,400,000
Total paid-in capital	4,700,000
Retained earnings	11,900,000
Total stockholders' equity	$16,600,000

Requirements

1. Identify the different issues of stock that Trane has outstanding. (pp. 558–561)
2. What is the par value per share of Trane's preferred stock?
3. Make two summary journal entries to record issuance of all the Trane stock for cash. Explanations are not required. (pp. 553–556)
4. No preferred dividends are in arrears. Journalize the declaration of a $500,000 dividend at June 30, 2008. Use separate Dividends Payable accounts for Preferred and Common. An explanation is not required. (pp. 562–564)

Preparing a corporation balance sheet; measuring profitability

P11-32A The following accounts and December 31, 2006, balances of New York Optical Corporation are arranged in no particular order.

Retained earnings	$145,000	Common stock, $5 par	
Inventory	101,000	100,000 shares authorized,	
Property, plant, and		22,000 shares issued	$110,000
equipment, net	278,000	Dividends payable	3,000
Prepaid expenses	13,000	Paid-in capital in excess	
Goodwill	63,000	of par—common	140,000
Accrued liabilities payable	17,000	Accounts payable	31,000
Long-term note payable	104,000	Preferred stock, 4%, $10, no-par	
Accounts receivable, net	102,000	25,000 shares authorized,	
Cash	43,000	5,000 shares issued	50,000

Requirements

1. Prepare the company's classified balance sheet in account format at December 31, 2006 (pp. 570–571)
2. Compute New York Optical's rate of return on total assets and rate of return on common stockholders' equity for the year ended December 31, 2006. For the rates of return, you will need these data: (pp. 567–570)

Total assets, Dec. 31, 2005	$502,000
Common equity, Dec. 31, 2005	305,000
Net income, 2006	47,000
Interest expense, 2006	3,000

3. Do these rates of return suggest strength or weakness? Give your reason. (pp. 568–570)

Computing dividends on preferred and common stock

4

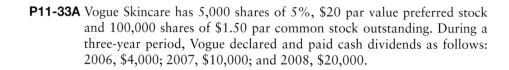

P11-33A Vogue Skincare has 5,000 shares of 5%, $20 par value preferred stock and 100,000 shares of $1.50 par common stock outstanding. During a three-year period, Vogue declared and paid cash dividends as follows: 2006, $4,000; 2007, $10,000; and 2008, $20,000.

Requirements

1. Compute the total dividends to preferred and to common for each of the three years if
   a. Preferred is noncumulative. (p. 469)
   b. Preferred is cumulative. (p. 469)
2. For case l.b., journalize the declaration of the 2008 dividends on December 22, 2008, and payment on January 14, 2009. Use separate Dividends Payable accounts for Preferred and Common. (p. 469)

Analyzing the stockholders' equity of a corporation

4 5

P11-34A The balance sheet of Beechcraft, Inc., reported the following:

Stockholders' Equity	
Paid-in capital:	
Preferred stock, \$5 par, 6%, 1,000 shares authorized and issued	\$ 5,000
Common stock, \$1 par, 40,000 shares authorized; 16,000 shares issued	16,000
Additional paid-in capital—common	214,000
	235,000
Retained earnings	70,000
Total stockholders' equity	\$305,000

Preferred dividends are in arrears for two years, including the current year. On the balance sheet date, the market value of the Beechcraft common stock was \$30 per share.

Requirements

1. Is the preferred stock cumulative or noncumulative? How can you tell? (p. 565)
2. What is the total paid-in capital of the company? (pp. 556–557)
3. What was the total market value of the common stock? (p. 566)
4. Compute the book value per share of the common stock. (p. 565)

Computing and recording a corporation's income tax

P11-35A The accounting records of Reflection Redwood Corporation provide income statement data for 2007.

Total revenue	\$930,000
Total expenses	700,000
Income before tax	\$230,000

Total expenses include depreciation of \$50,000 computed on the straight-line method. In calculating taxable income on the tax return, Reflection Redwood uses the modified accelerated cost recovery system (MACRS). MACRS depreciation was \$80,000 for 2007. The corporate income tax rate is 40%.

Requirements

1. Compute taxable income for the year. For this computation, substitute MACRS depreciation in place of straight-line depreciation. (pp. 568–569)
2. Journalize the corporation's income tax for 2007. (pp. 568–569)
3. Show how to report the two income tax liabilities on Redwood's classified balance sheet. (pp. 568–569)

Problems (Group B)

Organizing a corporation

1

P11-36B Sherry Taft and Laura Sims are opening Bank Compliance Consultants. The area is growing, and no competitors are located nearby. Their basic decision is how to organize the business. Taft thinks the partnership form is best. Sims favors the corporate form of organization. They seek your advice. (pp. 547–549)

Requirement

Write a memo to Taft and Sims to show them the advantages and disadvantages of organizing the business as a corporation. Use the following format for your memo:

Date: ______________

To: Sherry Taft and Laura Sims

From: Student Name

Subject: Advantages and disadvantages of the corporate form of business organization

Journalizing corporation transactions and preparing the stockholders' equity section of the balance sheet.

P11-37B Mailmax Direct is incorporated in the state of Arizona. The charter authorizes Mailmax to issue 1,000 shares of 6%, $100 par preferred stock and 250,000 shares of $10-par common stock. In its first month, Mailmax completed these transactions:

Jan. 3	Issued 9,000 shares of common stock for equipment with market value of $90,000.
12	Issued 500 shares of preferred stock to acquire a patent with a market value of $50,000.
28	Issued 1,500 shares of common stock for $11 cash per share.

Requirements

1. Record the transactions in the general journal. (pp. 553–554)
2. Prepare the stockholders' equity section of the Mailmax Direct, Inc., balance sheet at January 31. The ending balance of Retained Earnings is $43,500. (pp. 556–557)

Issuing stock and preparing the stockholders' equity section of the balance sheet

2 3

P11-38B Lieberman Corporation was organized in 2007. At December 31, 2007, Lieberman's balance sheet reported the following stockholders' equity:

Paid-in capital:	
Preferred stock, 5%, $10 par, 50,000 shares authorized, none issued	$ —
Common stock, $2 par, 100,000 shares authorized, 10,000 shares issued	20,000
Paid-in capital in excess of par—common	30,000
Total paid-in capital	50,000

continued . . .

Retained earnings (Deficit)	(5,000)
Total stockholders' equity	$45,000

Requirements

1. During 2008, Lieberman completed the following selected transactions. Journalize each transaction. Explanations are not required.
   a. Issued for cash 5,000 shares of preferred stock at par value. (pp. 555–556)
   b. Issued for cash 1,000 shares of common stock at a price of $7 per share. (pp. 553–554)
   c. Net income for the year was $100,000, and the company declared no dividends. Make the closing entry for net income. (pp. 551–552)
2. Prepare the stockholders' equity section of the Lieberman Corporation balance sheet at December 31, 2008. (pp. 556–557)

Stockholders' equity section of the balance sheet

P11-39B Stockholders' equity information for two independent companies, Monterrey Enterprises, Inc., and Guadalupe Corp., follow.

- *Monterrey Enterprises, Inc.* Monterrey is authorized to issue 60,000 shares of $5 par common stock. All the stock was issued at $12 per share. The company incurred a net loss of $40,000 in 2006. It earned net income of $30,000 in 2007 and $90,000 in 2008. The company declared no dividends during the three-year period.
- *Guadalupe Corp.* Guadalupe's charter authorizes the company to issue 10,000 shares of $2.50 preferred stock with par value of $50 and 120,000 shares of no-par common stock. *Guadalupe* issued 1,000 shares of the preferred stock at par. It issued 40,000 shares of the common stock for a total of $220,000. The company's Retained Earnings balance at the beginning of 2008 was $65,000, and net income for the year was $90,000. During 2008, the company declared the specified dividend on preferred and a $0.50 per share dividend on common. Preferred dividends for 2007 were in arrears.

Requirements

For each company, prepare the stockholders' equity section of its balance sheet at December 31, 2008. Show the computation of all amounts. Entries are not required. (pp. 556–557)

Analyzing the stockholders' equity of a corporation

P11-40B Crawford-Austin Properties included the following stockholders' equity on its year-end balance sheet at December 31, 2006.

Stockholders' Equity	
Paid-in capital:	
Preferred stock, 6%	$ 65,000
Common stock—par value $1 per share; 650,000 shares authorized, 230,000 shares issued	230,000
Paid-in capital in excess of par—common	70,000
Total paid-in capital	365,000

continued . . .

Retained earnings	2,000,000
Total stockholders' equity	$2,365,000

Requirements

1. Identify the different issues of stock that Crawford-Austin has outstanding. (pp. 551–552)
2. Is the preferred stock cumulative or noncumulative? How can you tell? (p. 565)
3. Give two summary journal entries to record issuance of all the Crawford-Austin stock. All the stock was issued for cash. Explanations are not required. (pp. 553–556)
4. Preferred dividends are in arrears for 2005 and 2006. Record the declaration of a $50,000 cash dividend on December 30, 2007. Use separate Dividends Payable accounts for Preferred and Common. An explanation is not required. (pp. 562–565)

Preparing a corporation balance sheet; measuring profitability

P11-41B The accounts and June 30, 2007, balances of Cromwell Company are arranged in no particular order:

Requirements

1. Prepare the company's classified balance sheet in account format at June 30, 2007. (pp. 570–571)

Accounts receivable, net	$46,000	Property, plant, and equipment, net	$231,000
Paid-in capital in excess of par—common	19,000	Common stock, $1 par, 500,000 shares authorized, 236,000 shares issued	236,000
Accrued liabilities payable	26,000	Dividends payable	9,000
Long-term note payable	12,000	Retained earnings	42,000
Inventory	81,000	Preferred stock, $0.10, no-par, 10,000 shares authorized and issued	25,000
Prepaid expenses	10,000		
Cash	10,000		
Accounts payable	31,000		
Trademark, net	22,000		

2. Compute Cromwell's rate of return on total assets and rate of return on common stockholders' equity for the year ended June 30, 2007. For the rates of return, you will need these data: (pp. 567–570)

Total assets, June 30, 2006	$404,000
Common equity, June 30, 2006	303,000
Net income, fiscal year 2007	31,000
Interest expense, fiscal year 2007	6,000

3. Do these rates of return suggest strength or weakness? Give your reason. (pp. 568–570)

Computing dividends on preferred and common stock

P11-42B FHA Loan Company has 10,000 shares of $3.50, no-par preferred stock and 50,000 shares of no-par common stock outstanding. FHA declared and paid the following dividends during a three-year period: 2006, $20,000; 2007, $100,000; and 2008, $150,000.

Requirements

1. Compute the total dividends to preferred stock and to common stock for each of the three years if
   a. Preferred is noncumulative. (p. 566)
   b. Preferred is cumulative. (p. 565)
2. For case 1.b., journalize the declaration of the 2008 dividends on December 28, 2008, and the payment on January 17, 2009. Use separate Dividends Payable accounts for Preferred and Common. (p. 565)

Analyzing the stockholders' equity of a corporation

P11-43B The balance sheet of Creative Communications, Inc., reported the following:

Stockholders' Equity	
Paid-in capital:	
Preferred stock; nonvoting; no par, $3; 8,000 shares issued	$320,000
Common stock; $1.50 par; 40,000 shares issued	60,000
Additional paid-in capital—common	240,000
	620,000
Retained earnings	130,000
Total stockholders' equity	$750,000

Preferred dividends are in arrears for three years including the current year. On the balance sheet date, the market value of the Creative Communications common stock is $14 per share.

Requirements

1. Is the preferred stock cumulative or noncumulative? How can you tell? (p. 565)
2. Which class of stockholders controls the company? Give your reason. (pp. 552–564)
3. What is the total paid-in capital of the company? (pp. 556–557)
4. What was the total market value of the common stock? (p. 566)
5. Compute the book value per share of the common stock. (p. 565)

Computing and recording a corporation's income tax

7

P11-44B The accounting records of Dwyer Minerals Corporation provide income statement data for 2008.

Total revenue	$680,000
Total expenses	460,000
Income before tax	$220,000

continued . . .

Total expenses include depreciation of $50,000 computed under the straight-line method. In calculating taxable income on the tax return, Dwyer uses MACRS. MACRS depreciation was $70,000 for 2008. The corporate income tax rate is 35%.

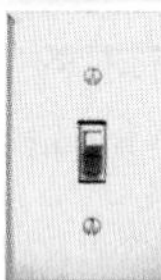

for 24/7 practice, visit www.MyAccountingLab.com

Requirements

1. Compute Dwyer's taxable income for the year. For this computation, substitute MACRS depreciation expense in place of straight-line depreciation. (pp. 568–569)
2. Journalize the corporation's income tax for 2008. (pp. 568–569)
3. Show how to report the two income tax liabilities on Dwyer's classified balance sheet. (pp. 568–569)

Apply Your Knowledge

Decision Cases

Evaluating alternative ways to raise capital
2 3

Case 1. Lena Esteé and Kathy Lauder have a patent on a new line of cosmetics. They need additional capital to market the products, and they plan to incorporate the business. They are considering the capital structure for the corporation. Their primary goal is to raise as much capital as possible without giving up control of the business. Esteé and Lauder plan to invest the patent in the company and receive 100,000 shares of the corporation's common stock. They've been offered $100,000 for the patent.

The corporation's plans for a charter include an authorization to issue 5,000 shares of preferred stock and 500,000 shares of $1 par common stock. Esteé and Lauder are uncertain about the most desirable features for the preferred stock. Prior to incorporating, they are discussing their plans with two investment groups. The corporation can obtain capital from outside investors under either of the following plans:

- *Plan 1.* Group 1 will invest $150,000 to acquire 1,500 shares of 6%, $100 par nonvoting, noncumulative preferred stock.
- *Plan 2.* Group 2 will invest $100,000 to acquire 1,000 shares of $5, no-par preferred stock and $70,000 to acquire 70,000 shares of common stock. Each preferred share receives 50 votes on matters that come before the stockholders.

Requirements

Assume that the corporation is chartered.

1. Journalize the issuance of common stock to Esteé and Lauder. Explanations are not required.
2. Journalize the issuance of stock to the outsiders under both plans. Explanations are not required.
3. Net income for the first year is $180,000 and total dividends are $30,000. Prepare the stockholders' equity section of the corporation's balance sheet under both plans.
4. Recommend one of the plans to Esteé and Lauder. Give your reasons.

Characteristics of corporations' capital stock

Case 2. Answering the following questions will enhance your understanding of the capital stock of corporations. Consider each question independently of the others.

1. Why are capital stock and retained earnings shown separately in the shareholders' equity section of the balance sheet?
2. Preferred shares have advantages with respect to dividends and corporate liquidation. Why would investors buy common stock when preferred stock is available?
3. Manuel Chavez, major shareholder of MC, Inc., proposes to sell some land he owns to the company for common shares in MC, Inc. What problem does MC, Inc., face in recording the transaction?
4. If you owned 100 shares of stock in Coca-Cola Company and someone offered to buy the stock for its book value, would you accept the offer? Why or why not?

Ethical Issue

Note: This case is based on an actual situation.

Stan Sewell paid $50,000 for a franchise that entitled him to market software programs in the countries of the European Union. Sewell intended to sell individual franchises for the major language groups of western Europe—German, French, English, Spanish, and Italian. Naturally, investors considering buying a franchise from Sewell asked to see the financial statements of his business.

Believing the value of the franchise to be greater than $50,000, Sewell sought to capitalize his own franchise at $500,000. The law firm of St. Charles & LaDue helped Sewell form a corporation chartered to issue 500,000 shares of common stock with par value of $1 per share. Attorneys suggested the following chain of transactions:

a. A third party borrows $500,000 and purchases the franchise from Sewell.

b. Sewell pays the corporation $500,000 to acquire all its stock.

c. The corporation buys the franchise from the third party, who repays the loan.

In the final analysis, the third party is debt-free and out of the picture. Sewell owns all the corporation's stock, and the corporation owns the franchise. The corporation's balance sheet lists a franchise acquired at a cost of $500,000. This balance sheet is Sewell's most valuable marketing tool.

Requirements

1. What is unethical about this situation?

2. Who can be harmed? How can they be harmed? What role does accounting play?

Financial Statement Case

Analyzing stockholders' equity

The Amazon.com financial statements appear in Appendix A at the end of this book. Answer the following questions about Amazon's stock. The Accumulated Deficit account is Retained Earnings with a negative balance.

Requirements

1. How much of Amazon's preferred stock was outstanding at December 31, 2005? How can you tell?

2. Examine Amazon.com's balance sheet. Which stockholders' equity account increased the most during 2005? What caused this increase? The statement of operations (income statement) helps to answer this question.

3. Use par value and the number of shares to show how to compute the balances in Amazon.com's Common Stock account at the end of both 2005 and 2004.

4. Would it be meaningful to compute Amazon.com's return on equity? Explain your answer.

Team Project

Competitive pressures are the norm in business. Lexus automobiles (made in Japan) have cut into the sales of Mercedes Benz (a German company), Jaguar (now a division of Ford), General Motors' Cadillac Division, and Ford's Lincoln Division. Dell, Gateway, and Compaq computers have siphoned business away from IBM. Foreign steelmakers have reduced the once-massive U.S. steel industry to a fraction of its former size.

Indeed, corporate downsizing has occurred on a massive scale. During the past few years, companies mentioned here have pared down their plant and equipment, laid off employees, or restructured operations.

Requirements

1. Identify all the stakeholders of a corporation and the stake each group has in the company. A *stakeholder* is a person or a group who has an interest (that is, a stake) in the success of the organization.

2. Identify several measures by which a corporation may be considered deficient and which may indicate the need for downsizing. How can downsizing help to solve this problem? Discuss how each measure can indicate the need for downsizing.

3. Debate the downsizing issue. One group of students takes the perspective of the company and its stockholders, and another group of students takes the perspective of other stakeholders of the company.

For Internet exercises, Excel in Practice, and additional online activities, go to the Web site www.prenhall.com/horngren.

Quick Check Answers

1. *c* 2. *a* 3. *a* 4. *a* 5. *d* 6. *c* 7. *b* 8. *d* 9. *c* 10. *b*

12 Corporations: Retained Earnings and the Income Statement

Learning Objectives

1 Account for stock dividends

2 Distinguish stock splits from stock dividends

3 Account for treasury stock

4 Report restrictions on retained earnings

5 Analyze a corporate income statement

Chapter 11 introduced corporations and covered the basics of stockholders' equity. Our feature company was IHOP, the restaurant chain. We saw that a corporation's balance sheet is the same as for a proprietorship or a partnership, except for owners' equity. Chapter 11 began with IHOP's issuance of common stock and also covered the declaration and payment of cash dividends.

This chapter takes corporate equity a few steps further, as follows:

Chapter 11 Covered	Chapter 12 Covers
Paid-in capital	Retained earnings
Issuing stock	Buying back a corporation's stock (treasury stock)
Cash dividends	Stock dividends and stock splits
Corporate balance sheet	Corporate income statement

Chapter 12 completes our discussion of corporate equity. It begins with *stock dividends* and *stock splits*—terms you've probably heard. Let's see what these terms mean.

Retained Earnings, Stock Dividends, and Stock Splits

We've seen that the owners' equity of a corporation is called *stockholders' equity* or *shareholders' equity*. Paid-in capital and retained earnings make up stockholders' equity. We studied paid-in capital in Chapter 11. Now let's focus on retained earnings.

Retained Earnings

Retained Earnings carries the balance of the business's accumulated lifetime net income less all net losses and less all dividends. A debit balance in Retained Earnings is called a *deficit*. Retained earnings deficits are rare because these companies go out of business. When you see a balance sheet, remember this about Retained Earnings:

1. **Credits to Retained Earnings arise only from net income.** Retained Earnings shows how much net income a corporation has earned and retained over its entire lifetime.
2. **The Retained Earnings account is not a reservoir of cash.** Retained Earnings represents no asset in particular. In fact, the corporation may have a large balance in Retained Earnings but insufficient cash to pay a dividend.

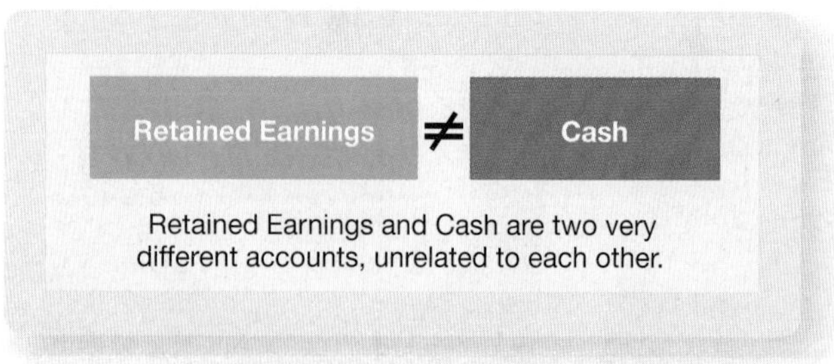

Retained Earnings
≠
Cash
Retained Earnings and Cash are two very different accounts, unrelated to each other.

3. Retained Earnings' ending balance is computed as follows (amounts assumed):

Beginning balance	$ 70,000
Add: Net income for the year	80,000
Less: Net loss (none this year)	
Dividends for the year	(50,000)
Ending balance	$100,000

Stock Dividends

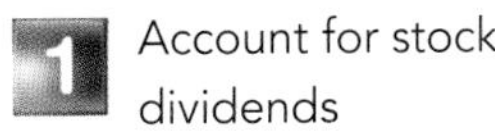

Account for stock dividends

A **stock dividend** is a distribution of a corporation's own stock to its stockholders. Unlike cash dividends, stock dividends do not give any assets to the stockholders. Stock dividends:

- Affect *only* stockholders' equity accounts (including Retained Earnings and Common Stock)
- Have *no* effect on total stockholders' equity
- Have *no* effect on assets or liabilities

As Exhibit 12-1 shows, a stock dividend decreases Retained Earnings and increases Common Stock. A stock dividend is a transfer from Retained Earnings to Common Stock. Total equity is unchanged.

EXHIBIT 12-1 **Effects of a Stock Dividend**

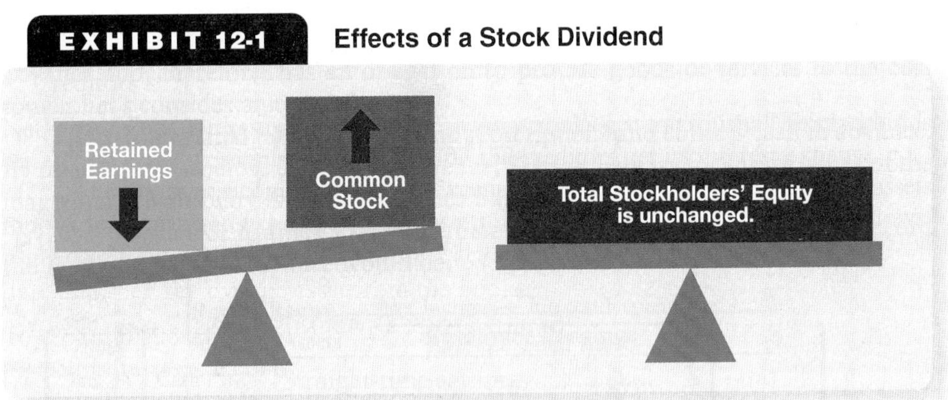

The corporation distributes stock dividends to stockholders in proportion to the number of shares they already own. Suppose you own 300 shares of IHOP common stock. If IHOP distributes a 10% stock dividend, you would receive 30 (300 × 0.10) additional shares. You would now own 330 shares of the stock. All other IHOP stockholders also receive additional shares equal to 10% of their holdings, so you are all in the same relative position after the dividend as before.

Why Issue Stock Dividends?

A company issues stock dividends for several reasons:

1. **To continue dividends but conserve cash.** A company may wish to continue dividends but need to keep its cash.
2. **To reduce the market price of its stock.** A stock dividend may cause the company's stock price to fall because of the increased supply of the stock. A share of IHOP stock has traded at $50 recently. Doubling the shares outstanding by issuing a stock dividend would drop IHOP's stock price to $25 per share. The objective is to make the stock less expensive and, thus, more attractive to investors.

Recording Stock Dividends

As with a cash dividend, there are three dates for a stock dividend:

- Declaration date
- Record date
- Distribution (payment) date

The board of directors announces the stock dividend on the declaration date. The date of record and the distribution date then follow.

The declaration of a stock dividend does *not* create a liability because the corporation is not obligated to pay assets. (Recall that a liability is a claim on *assets.*) With a stock dividend, the corporation has declared its intention to distribute its stock. Assume that IHOP has the following stockholders' equity prior to a stock dividend:

IHOP CORP. STOCKHOLDERS' EQUITY (ADAPTED, IN THOUSANDS)	
Paid-in capital:	
Common stock, $1 par, 1,000 shares authorized, 200 shares issued ..	$ 200
Paid-in capital in excess of par	31,800
Total paid-in capital	32,000
Retained earnings........	308,000
Total stockholders' equity	$340,000

The entry to record a stock dividend depends on its size. Generally accepted accounting principles distinguish between

- A *small* stock dividend (less than 20% to 25% of issued stock)
- A *large* stock dividend (25% or more of issued stock)

Stock dividends between 20% and 25% are rare.

SMALL STOCK DIVIDENDS—LESS THAN 20% TO 25% Small stock dividends are accounted for at their market value. Here's how the various accounts are affected:

- Retained Earnings is debited for the market value of the dividend shares.
- Common Stock is credited for the dividend stock's par value.
- Paid-In Capital in Excess of Par is credited for the remainder.

Assume IHOP distributes a stock dividend when the market value of IHOP common stock is $50 per share. Exhibit 12-2 illustrates the accounting for a 10% stock dividend.[1]

EXHIBIT 12-2 Accounting for a Stock Dividend

Small Stock Dividend—For Example, 10% (Amounts in thousands)		
Retained Earnings		
(200 × 0.10 × $50 market value)	1,000	
Common Stock		
(200 × 0.10 × $1 par)		20
Paid-In Capital in Excess of Par		980

A stock dividend does not affect assets, liabilities, or *total* stockholders' equity. A stock dividend merely rearranges the equity accounts, leaving total equity unchanged. Exhibit 12-3 shows IHOP's stockholders' equity after the stock dividend.

[1]A stock dividend can be recorded with two journal entries—for (1) the declaration and (2) the stock distribution. But most companies record stock dividends with a single entry on the date of distribution, as we illustrate here.

EXHIBIT 12-3 Stockholders' Equity after a Stock Dividend—IHOP Corporation

IHOP Corporation Stockholders' Equity (Adapted, in Thousands)	
Paid-in capital:	
Common stock, $1 par, 1,000 shares authorized,	
220 shares issued ($200 + $20)	$ 220
Paid-in capital in excess of par ($31,800 + $980)	32,780
Total paid-in capital	33,000
Retained earnings ($308,000 – $1,000)	307,000
Total stockholders' equity	$340,000

Observe that total stockholders' equity stays at $340,000.

LARGE STOCK DIVIDENDS—25% OR MORE Large stock dividends are rare, so we do not illustrate them. Instead of large stock dividends, companies split their stock, as we illustrate next.

Stock Splits

A **stock split** is fundamentally different from a stock dividend. A stock split increases the number of authorized, issued, and outstanding shares of stock. A stock split also decreases par value per share. For example, if IHOP splits its stock 2 for 1, the number of outstanding shares is doubled and par value per share is cut in half. A stock split also decreases the market price of the stock.

The market price of a share of IHOP common stock has been approximately $50. Assume that IHOP wishes to decrease the market price to approximately $25. IHOP can split its stock 2 for 1, and market price will drop to around $25. A 2-for-1 stock split means that IHOP will have twice as many shares of stock outstanding after the split as before, and each share's par value is cut in half. Assume that IHOP had issued 200,000 shares of $1 par common stock before the split. Exhibit 12-4 shows how a 2-for-1 split affects IHOP's equity.

EXHIBIT 12-4 A 2-for-1 Stock Split

IHOP Stockholders' Equity (Adapted, in Thousands)			
Before 2-for-1 Stock Split		**After 2-for-1 Stock Split**	
Paid-in capital:		Paid-in capital:	
Common stock, $1.00 par,		Common stock, $0.50 par,	
1,000 shares authorized,		2,000 shares authorized,	
200 shares issued	$ 200	400 shares issued	$ 200
Paid-in capital in excess		Paid-in capital in excess	
of par	31,800	of par	31,800
Total paid-in capital	32,000	Total paid-in capital	32,000
Retained earnings	308,000	Retained earnings	308,000
Total stockholders' equity	$340,000	Total stockholders' equity	$340,000

Study the exhibit and you'll see that a 2-for-1 stock split:

- Cuts par value per share in half
- Doubles the shares of stock authorized and issued
- Leaves all account balances and total equity unchanged

Because the stock split affects no account balances, no formal journal entry is needed. Instead, the split is recorded in a *memorandum entry* such as the following:

Aug. 19	Split the common stock 2 for 1. Called in the $1.00 par common stock and distributed two shares of $0.50 par common stock for each old share. Now 400 shares are outstanding.

Stock Dividends and Stock Splits Compared

2 Distinguish stock splits from stock dividends

Stock dividends and stock splits have some similarities and differences. Exhibit 12-5 summarizes their effects on stockholders' equity. For completeness, it also covers cash dividends.

EXHIBIT 12-5 **Effects of Dividends and Stock Splits**

Event	Common Stock	Paid-In Capital in Excess of Par	Retained Earnings	Total Stockholders' Equity
Cash dividend	No effect	No effect	Decrease	Decrease
Stock dividend	Increase	Increase	Decrease	No effect
Stock split	No effect	No effect	No effect	No effect

Treasury Stock

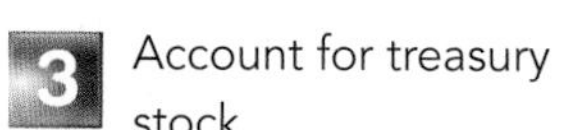
3 Account for treasury stock

A company's own stock that it has issued and later reacquired is called **treasury stock.**[2] In effect, the corporation holds the stock in its treasury. A corporation such as IHOP may purchase treasury stock for several reasons:

1. Management wants to increase net assets by buying low and selling high.
2. Management wants to support the company's stock price.
3. Management wants to avoid a takeover by an outside party.

Treasury stock transactions are common among corporations. A recent survey of 600 companies showed that 66% held treasury stock. Now let's see how to account for treasury stock.

Purchase of Treasury Stock

Jupiter Cable Company had the following stockholders' equity before purchasing treasury stock:

[2]We illustrate the *cost* method of accounting for treasury stock because it is used most widely. Intermediate accounting courses also cover an alternative method.

JUPITER CABLE COMPANY Stockholders' Equity [*Before* Purchase of Treasury Stock]	
Paid-in capital:	
Common stock, $1 par, 10,000 shares authorized and issued	$10,000
Paid-in capital in excess of par	12,000
Total paid-in capital	22,000
Retained earnings	23,000
Total stockholders' equity	$45,000

On March 31, Jupiter purchased 1,000 shares of treasury stock, paying $5 per share. Debit Treasury Stock and credit Cash as follows:

Date	Accounts and Explanation	Debit	Credit
Mar. 31	Treasury Stock (1,000 × $5)	5,000	
	Cash		5,000
	Purchased treasury stock.		

Treasury Stock	
5,000	

Treasury Stock Basics

Here are the basics of accounting for treasury stock:

- The Treasury Stock account has a debit balance, which is the opposite of the other equity accounts. Therefore, *Treasury Stock is contra equity.*
- Treasury stock is recorded at cost, without reference to par value.
- The Treasury Stock account is reported beneath Retained Earnings on the balance sheet, subtracted as follows:

JUPITER CABLE COMPANY Stockholders' Equity [*After* Purchase of Treasury Stock]	
Paid-in capital:	
Common stock, $1 par, 10,000 shares authorized and issued	$10,000
Paid-in capital in excess of par	12,000
Total paid-in capital	22,000
Retained earnings	23,000
Subtotal	45,000
Less: Treasury stock, 1,000 shares at cost	(5,000)
Total stockholders' equity	$40,000

Treasury stock decreases the company's stock that's outstanding, that is, held by the stockholders. We compute outstanding stock as follows:

$$\text{Outstanding stock} = \text{Issued stock} - \text{Treasury stock}$$

Outstanding shares are important because only outstanding shares have voting rights and receive cash dividends. Treasury stock doesn't carry a vote, and it gets no dividends.

Sale of Treasury Stock

Companies buy their treasury stock with a view toward reselling it. A company may sell treasury stock at its cost, above cost, or below cost.

Sale at Cost

If treasury stock is sold for cost—the same price the corporation paid for it—then debit Cash and credit Treasury Stock for the same amount.

Sale Above Cost

If treasury stock is sold for more than cost, the difference is credited to a new account, Paid-In Capital from Treasury Stock Transactions. This excess is additional paid-in capital because it came from the company's stockholders. It has no effect on net income. Suppose Jupiter Cable Company resold its treasury shares for $9 per share (cost was $5). The entry to sell treasury stock for a price above cost is:

Dec. 7	Cash (1,000 × $9)	9,000	
	Treasury Stock (1,000 × $5 cost)		5,000
	Paid-In Capital from Treasury Stock Transactions		4,000
	Sold treasury stock.		

Treasury Stock	
5,000	5,000
0	

Paid-In Capital from Treasury Stock Transactions is reported with the other paid-in capital accounts on the balance sheet, beneath Common Stock and Paid-In Capital in Excess of Par, as shown here:

JUPITER CABLE COMPANY Stockholders' Equity [*After* Purchase and Sale of Treasury Stock]	
Paid-in capital:	
Common stock, $1 par, 10,000 shares authorized and issued	$10,000
Paid-in capital in excess of par	12,000
Paid-in capital from treasury stock transactions	4,000
Total paid-in capital	26,000
Retained earnings	23,000
Total stockholders' equity	$49,000

Exhibit 12-6 tracks stockholders' equity to show how treasury stock transactions affect corporate equity.

EXHIBIT 12-6 Stockholders' Equity of Jupiter Cable Company

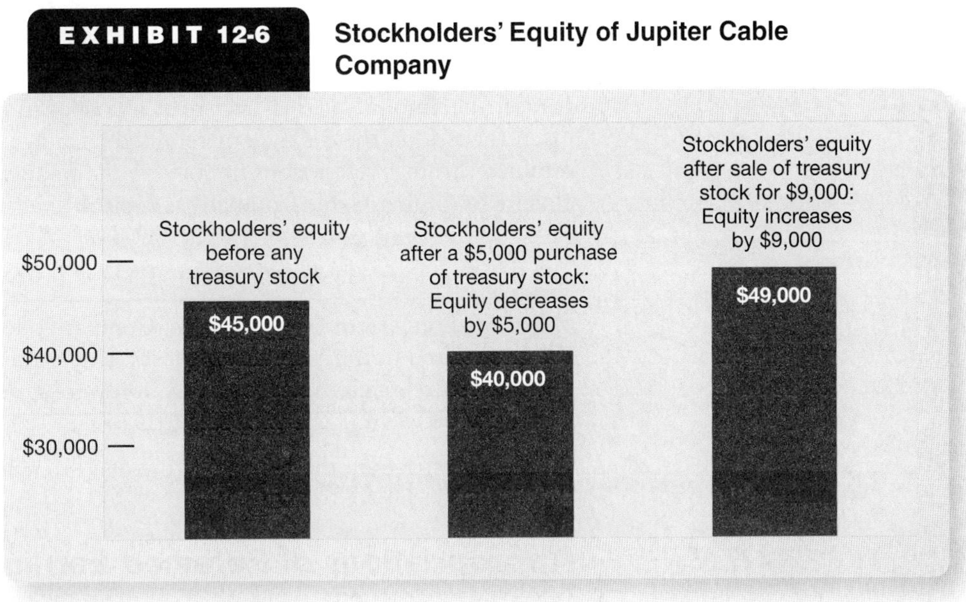

Sale Below Cost

The resale price of treasury stock can be less than cost. The shortfall is debited first to Paid-In Capital from Treasury Stock Transactions. If this account's balance is too small, then debit Retained Earnings for the remaining amount. We illustrate this situation in Summary Problem 1 on page 609.

Other Stockholders' Equity Issues

Companies may retire their stock, restrict retained earnings, and report stockholders' equity in a variety of ways. This section covers these reporting issues.

Retirement of Stock

Not all companies purchase their stock to hold it in the treasury. A corporation may retire its stock by canceling the stock certificates. Retired stock cannot be reissued.

Retirements of preferred stock are common as companies seek to avoid paying the preferred dividends. To purchase stock for retirement, debit the stock account—for example, Preferred Stock—and credit cash. That removes the retired stock from the company's books.

Restrictions on Retained Earnings

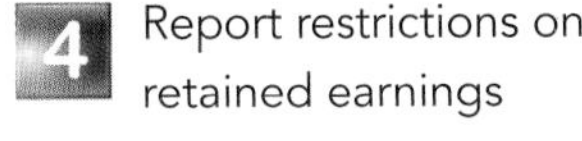

Dividends and treasury stock purchases require a cash payment. These outlays leave fewer resources to pay liabilities. A bank may agree to loan $50,000 only if Jupiter Cable Company limits its payment of dividends and its purchases of treasury stock.

Limits on Dividends and Treasury Stock Purchases

To ensure that a corporation maintains a minimum level of equity, lenders may restrict the amount of treasury stock a corporation may purchase. The restriction often focuses on the balance of retained earnings. Companies usually report their retained earnings restrictions in notes to the financial statements. The following disclosure by Jupiter Cable Company is typical:

NOTES TO THE FINANCIAL STATEMENTS
Note F—Long-Term Debt The . . . Company's loan agreements . . . restrict cash dividends and treasury stock purchases. Under the most restrictive of these provisions, retained earnings of $18,000 were unrestricted at December 31, 2006.

With this restriction, the maximum dividend that Jupiter can pay is $18,000.

Appropriations of Retained Earnings

Appropriations are Retained Earnings restrictions recorded by formal journal entries. A corporation may *appropriate*—that is, segregate in a separate account—a portion of Retained Earnings for a specific use. For example, the board of directors may appropriate part of Retained Earnings for expansion. Appropriated Retained Earnings can be reported as shown near the bottom of Exhibit 12-7.

Variations in Reporting Stockholders' Equity

Companies can report their stockholders' equity in ways that differ from our examples. They assume that investors understand the details. One of the most important skills you will learn in this course is how to read the financial statements of real companies. In Exhibit 12-7, we present a side-by-side comparison of our teaching format and the format you are likely to encounter. Note the following points in the real-world format:

1. The heading Paid-In Capital does not appear. It is commonly understood that Preferred Stock, Common Stock, and Additional Paid-In Capital are elements of paid-in capital.
2. For presentation in the financial statements, all additional paid-in capital accounts are combined and reported as a single amount labeled Additional Paid-In Capital. Additional Paid-In Capital belongs to the common stockholders; therefore, it follows Common Stock in the real-world format.

Retained earnings appropriations are rare. Most companies report retained earnings restrictions in the notes to the financial statements, as shown for Jupiter Cable Company and in the real-world format of Exhibit 12-7.

EXHIBIT 12-7 **Formats for Reporting Stockholders' Equity**

Teaching Format

Stockholders' equity	
Paid-in capital:	
Preferred stock, 8%, $10 par,	
30,000 shares authorized and issued	$ 300,000
Common stock, $1 par,	
100,000 shares authorized,	
60,000 shares issued	60,000
Paid-in capital in excess of par—common	2,150,000
Paid-in capital from treasury stock transactions	20,000
Total paid-in capital	2,530,000
Retained earnings appropriated	
for contingencies	500,000
Retained earnings—unappropriated	1,000,000
Total retained earnings	1,500,000
Subtotal	4,030,000
Less: Treasury stock, common	
(1,000 shares at cost)	(30,000)
Total stockholders' equity	$4,000,000

Real-World Format

Stockholders' equity	
Preferred stock, 8%, $10 par,	
30,0000 shares authorized and issued	$ 300,000
Common stock, $1 par,	
100,000 shares authorized, 60,000 shares issued	60,000
Additional paid-in capital	2,170,000
Retained earnings (Note 7)	1,500,000
Less: Treasury stock, common	
(1,000 shares at cost)	(30,000)
Total stockholders' equity	$4,000,000

Note 7—Restriction on retained earnings.
At December 31, 2009, $500,000 of retained earnings is restricted for contingencies. Accordingly, dividends are limited to a maximum of $1,000,000.

Review the first half of the chapter by studying the Decision Guidelines.

Decision Guidelines

ACCOUNTING FOR RETAINED EARNINGS, DIVIDENDS, AND TREASURY STOCK

Retained earnings, dividends, and treasury stock can affect a corporation's equity. The Decision Guidelines will help you understand their effects.

Decision	Guidelines
How to record:	
• Distribution of a small stock dividend (20% to 25%)?	Retained Earnings .... Market value Common Stock .... Par value Paid-In Capital in Excess of Par .... Excess
• Stock split?	Memorandum only: Split the common stock 2-for-1. Called in the outstanding $10 par common stock and distributed two shares of $5 par for each old share outstanding (amounts assumed).

What are the effects of stock dividends and stock splits on:

	Effects of Stock Dividend	Effects of Stock Split
• Number of shares issued?	Increase	Increase
• Shares outstanding?	Increase	Increase
• Par value per share?	No effect	Decrease
• Total assets, total liabilities, and total equity?	No effect	No effect
• Common Stock?	Increase	No effect
• Retained Earnings?	Decrease	No effect

How to record:

Decision	Account	Debit	Credit
1. Purchase of treasury stock?	1. Treasury Stock	Cost	
Sale of treasury stock?	Cash		Cost
2. At cost? (Amount received = Cost)	2. Cash	Amt.received	
	Treasury Stock		Cost
3. Above cost?	3. Cash	Amt.received	
	Treasury Stock		Cost
	Paid-In Capital from Treasury Stock Transactions		Excess
4. Below cost?	4. Cash	Amt. received	
	Paid-In Capital from Treasury Stock Transactions	Amt. up to prior bal.	
	Retained Earnings	Excess	
	Treasury Stock		Cost

What are the effects of the purchase and sale of treasury stock on:

	Effects of Purchase	Effects of Sale
• Total assets?	Decrease total assets by full amount of payment	Increase total assets by full amount of cash receipt
• Total stockholders' equity?	Decrease total equity by full amount of payment	Increase total equity by full amount of cash receipt

Summary Problem 1

Simplicity Graphics, creator of magazine designs, reported shareholders' equity:

Shareholders' Equity	
Preferred stock, $10.00 par value	
Authorized—10,000 shares; Issued—None	$ —
Common Stock, $1 par value	
Authorized 30,000 shares; Issued 15,000 shares	15,000
Capital in excess of par value	45,000
Retained earnings	90,000
	150,000
Less: Treasury stock, at cost (2,000 common shares)	(16,000)
	$134,000

Requirements

1. What was the average issue price per share of the common stock?
2. Journalize the issuance of 1,000 shares of common stock at $4 per share. Use Simplicity's account titles.
3. How many shares of Simplicity's common stock are outstanding?
4. How many shares of common stock would be outstanding after Simplicity split its common stock 3 for 1?
5. Using Simplicity account titles, journalize the distribution of a 10% stock dividend when the market price of Simplicity common stock is $5 per share. Simplicity distributes the common stock dividend on the shares outstanding, which were computed in requirement 3.
6. Journalize the following treasury stock transactions, which occur in the order given:
   a. Simplicity purchases 500 shares of treasury stock at $8 per share.
   b. Simplicity sells 100 shares of treasury stock for $9 per share.
   c. Simplicity sells 200 shares of treasury stocks for $6 per share.

Solution

1.	Average issue price of common stock was $4 per share [(15,000 + $45,000)/15,000 shares = $4]		
2.	Cash (1,000 × $4)	4,000	
	Common Stock (1,000 × $1)		1,000
	Capital in Excess of Par Value		3,000
	Issued common stock.		
3.	Shares outstanding = 13,000 (15,000 shares issued minus 2,000 shares of treasury stock).		
4.	Shares outstanding after a 3-for-1 stock split = 39,000 (13,000 shares outstanding × 3).		
5.	Retained Earnings (13,000 × 0.10 × $5)	6,500	
	Common Stock (13,000 × 0.10 × $1)		1,300
	Capital in Excess of Par Value		5,200
	Distributed a 10% common stock dividend.		
6.	a. Treasury Stock (500 × $8)	4,000	
	Cash		4,000
	Purchased treasury stock.		
	b. Cash (100 × $9)	900	
	Treasury Stock (100 × $8)		800
	Paid-in Capital from Treasury Stock Transactions		100
	Sold treasury stock.		
	c. Cash (200 × $6)	1,200	
	Paid-in Capital from Treasury Stock Transactions (from entry *b.*)	100	
	Retained Earnings	300	
	Treasury Stock (200 × $8)		1,600
	Sold treasury stock.		

The Corporate Income Statement

5 Analyze a corporate income statement

As we have seen, the stockholders' equity of a corporation is more complex than the capital of a proprietorship or a partnership. Also, a corporation's income statement includes some twists and turns that don't often apply to a smaller business. Most of the income statements you will see belong to corporations. Why not proprietorships or partnerships? Because they are privately held, proprietorships and partnerships don't have to publish their financial statements. But public corporations do, so we turn now to the corporate income statement.

Suppose you are considering investing in the stock of IHOP, Coca-Cola, or Pier 1 Imports. You would examine these companies' income statements. Of particular interest is the amount of net income they can expect to earn year after year. To understand net income, let's examine Exhibit 12-8, the income statement of Allied Electronics Corporation, a small manufacturer of precision instruments. New items are in color for emphasis.

Continuing Operations

In Exhibit 12-8, the topmost section reports continuing operations. This part of the business should continue from period to period. Income from continuing operations, therefore, helps investors make predictions about future earnings. We may use this information to predict that Allied Electronics Corporation will earn approximately \$54,000 next year.

The continuing operations of Allied Electronics include two items needing explanation:

- Allied had a gain on the sale of machinery, which is outside the company's core business of selling electronics products. This is why the gain is reported in the "other" category—separately from Allied's sales revenue, cost of goods sold, and gross profit.
- Income tax expense (\$36,000) is subtracted to arrive at income from continuing operations. Allied Electronics' income tax rate is 40% (\$90,000 × 0.40 = \$36,000).

Special Items

After continuing operations, an income statement may include two distinctly different gains and losses:

- Discontinued operations
- Extraordinary gains and losses

Discontinued Operations

Most corporations engage in several lines of business. For example, IHOP is best known for its restaurants. But at one time IHOP owned Golden Oaks Retirement Homes, United Rent-Alls, and even a business college. Sears, Roebuck & Co. is best known for its retail stores, but Sears also has a real-estate company (Homart) and an insurance company (Allstate).

Each identifiable division of a company is called a **segment of the business.** Allstate is the insurance segment of Sears. A company may sell a segment of its business. For example, IHOP sold its retirement homes, United Rent-Alls, and its business college. These were discontinued operations for IHOP.

EXHIBIT 12-8 Income Statement in Multi-Step Format—Allied Electronics Corporation

ALLIED ELECTRONICS CORPORATION
Income Statement
Year Ended December 31, 2008

Continuing Operations	Net sales revenue	$500,000
	Cost of goods sold	240,000
	Gross profit	260,000
	Operating expenses (detailed)	181,000
	Operating income	79,000
	Other gains (losses):	
	Gain on sale of machinery	11,000
	Income from continuing operations before income tax	90,000
	Income tax expense	36,000
	Income from continuing operations	54,000
Special Items	Discontinued operations, income of $35,000, less income tax of $14,000	21,000
	Income before extraordinary item	75,000
	Extraordinary flood loss, $20,000, less income tax saving of $8,000	(12,000)
	Net income	$ 63,000
Earnings Per Share	Earnings per share of common stock (20,000 shares outstanding):	
	Income from continuing operations	$2.70
	Income from discontinued operations	1.05
	Income before extraordinary item	3.75
	Extraordinary loss	(0.60)
	Net income	$3.15

Financial analysts are always keeping tabs on companies they follow. They predict companies' net income, and most analysts don't include discontinued operations because the discontinued segments won't be around in the future. The income statement reports information on the segments that have been sold under the heading Discontinued operations. Income from discontinued operations ($35,000) is taxed at 40% and reported as shown in Exhibit 12-8. A loss on discontinued operations is reported similarly, but with a subtraction for the income tax *savings* on the loss.

Gains and losses on the sale of plant assets are *not* reported as discontinued operations. Gains and losses on the sale of plant assets are reported as "Other gains (losses)" up among continuing operations because companies dispose of old plant and equipment all the time.

Extraordinary Gains and Losses (Extraordinary Items)

Extraordinary gains and losses, also called **extraordinary items,** are both unusual and infrequent. Losses from natural disasters (floods, earthquakes, and tornadoes) and the taking of company assets by a foreign government (expropriation) are extraordinary items.

Extraordinary items are reported along with their income tax effect. During 2008, Allied Electronics Corporation lost $20,000 of inventory in a flood. This flood loss reduced both Allied's income and its income tax. The tax effect decreases

the net amount of Allied's loss the same way income tax reduces net income. An extraordinary loss can be reported along with its tax effect, as follows:

Extraordinary flood loss	$(20,000)
Less: Income tax saving	8,000
Extraordinary flood loss, net of tax	$(12,000)

Trace this item to the income statement in Exhibit 12-8. An extraordinary gain is reported the same as a loss, net of the income tax.

The following items do *not* qualify as extraordinary:

- Gains and losses on the sale of plant assets
- Losses due to lawsuits
- Losses due to employee labor strikes

These gains and losses fall outside the business's central operations, so they are reported on the income statement as other gains and losses. Examples include the gain on sale of machinery reported up in the Other gains (losses) section of Exhibit 12-8. The two graphics on this page illustrate an extraordinary loss and an "other" gain (loss).

Earnings per Share

The final segment of a corporate income statement reports the company's earnings per share, abbreviated as EPS. EPS is the most widely used of all business statistics.

Earnings per share (EPS) reports the amount of net income for each share of the company's *outstanding common stock*. Recall that:

$$\text{Outstanding stock} = \text{Issued stock} - \text{Treasury stock}$$

For example, Allied Electronics has issued 25,000 shares of its common stock and holds 5,000 shares as treasury stock. Allied, therefore, has 20,000 shares of common stock outstanding, and so we use 20,000 shares to compute EPS.

EPS is a key measure of success in business. EPS is computed as follows:

$$\text{Earnings per share} = \frac{\text{Net income} - \text{Preferred dividends}}{\text{Average number of common shares outstanding}}$$

Corporations report a separate EPS figure for each element of income. Allied Electronics Corporation's EPS calculations follow.

Earnings per share of common stock (20,000 shares outstanding):	
Income from continuing operations ($54,000/20,000)	$2.70
Income from discontinued operations ($21,000/20,000)	1.05
Income before extraordinary item ($75,000/20,000)	3.75
Extraordinary loss ($12,000/20,000)	(0.60)
Net income ($63,000/20,000)	$3.15

The final section of Exhibit 12-8 reports the EPS figures for Allied Electronics.

Effect of Preferred Dividends on Earnings per Share

Preferred dividends also affect EPS. Recall that EPS is earnings per share of *common* stock. Recall also that dividends on preferred stock are paid first. Therefore, preferred dividends must be subtracted from income to compute EPS.

Suppose Allied Electronics had 10,000 shares of preferred stock outstanding, each share paying a $1.00 dividend. The annual preferred dividend would be $10,000 (10,000 × $1.00). The $10,000 is subtracted from each of the income subtotals (lines 1, 3, and 5), resulting in the following EPS computations for Allied:

	Earnings per share of common stock (20,000 shares outstanding):	
1	Income from continuing operations ($54,000 − $10,000)/20,000	$2.20
2	Income from discontinued operations ($21,000/20,000)	1.05
3	Income before extraordinary item ($75,000 − $10,000)/20,000	3.25
4	Extraordinary loss ($12,000/20,000)..	(0.60)
5	Net income ($63,000 − $10,000)/20,000	$2.65

Basic and Diluted Earnings per Share

Some corporations must report two sets of EPS figures, as follows:

- EPS based on outstanding common shares (*basic* EPS).
- EPS based on outstanding common plus the additional shares of common stock that would arise from conversion of the preferred stock into common (*diluted* EPS). Diluted EPS is always lower than basic EPS.

Statement of Retained Earnings

The statement of retained earnings reports how the company moved from its beginning balance of retained earnings to its ending balance during the period. This statement is not altogether new; it's essentially the same as the statement of owner's equity for a proprietorship—but adapted to a corporation.

Exhibit 12-9 shows the statement of retained earnings of Allied Electronics for 2008. Notice that corporate dividends take the place of withdrawals in a proprietorship. Allied's net income comes from the income statement in Exhibit 12-8, page 612. All other data are assumed.

EXHIBIT 12-9 **Statement of Retained Earnings—Allied Electronics Corporation**

ALLIED ELECTRONICS CORPORATION
Statement of Retained Earnings
Year Ended December 31, 2008

Retained earnings, December 31, 2007	$130,000
Add: Net income for 2008	63,000
	193,000
Less: Dividends for 2008	(53,000)
Retained earnings, December 31, 2008	$140,000

Combined Statement of Income and Retained Earnings

Companies can report income and retained earnings on a single statement. Exhibit 12-10 illustrates how Allied Electronics would combine its income statement and its statement of retained earnings.

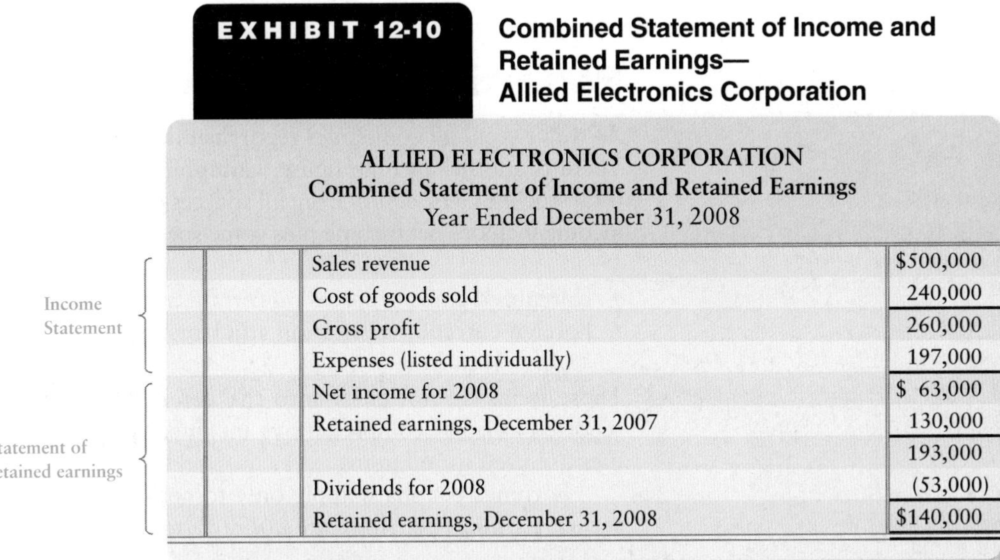

EXHIBIT 12-10 **Combined Statement of Income and Retained Earnings—Allied Electronics Corporation**

ALLIED ELECTRONICS CORPORATION
Combined Statement of Income and Retained Earnings
Year Ended December 31, 2008

Income Statement	Sales revenue	$500,000
	Cost of goods sold	240,000
	Gross profit	260,000
	Expenses (listed individually)	197,000
Statement of retained earnings	Net income for 2008	$ 63,000
	Retained earnings, December 31, 2007	130,000
		193,000
	Dividends for 2008	(53,000)
	Retained earnings, December 31, 2008	$140,000

Prior-Period Adjustments

A company may make an accounting error. After the books are closed, Retained Earnings holds the error, and its balance is wrong until corrected. Corrections to Retained Earnings for errors of an earlier period are called **prior-period adjustments.** The prior-period adjustment either increases or decreases the beginning balance of Retained Earnings and appears on that statement.

In recent years there have been more prior-period adjustments than in the 20 previous years combined. Many companies have restated their net income to correct accounting errors. To illustrate, assume De Graff Corporation recorded $30,000 of income tax expense for 2007. The correct amount of income tax was $40,000. This error:

- Understated income tax expense by $10,000
- Overstated net income by $10,000

In 2008 De Graff paid the extra $10,000 in taxes for the prior year. De Graff's prior-period adjustment will decrease retained earnings as follows (all amounts are assumed).

DE GRAFF CORPORATION
Statement of Retained Earnings
Year Ended December 31, 2008

Retained earnings, December 31, 2007, as originally reported	$390,000
Prior-period adjustment—To correct error in 2007	(10,000)
Retained earnings, December 31, 2007, as adjusted	380,000
Net income for 2008	100,000
	480,000
Dividends for 2008	(40,000)
Retained earnings, December 31, 2008	$440,000

Reporting Comprehensive Income

As we've seen, all companies report net income or net loss on the income statement. There is another income figure. **Comprehensive income** is the company's change in total stockholders' equity from all sources other than from its owners. Comprehensive income includes net income plus some specific gains and losses, as follows:

- Unrealized gains or losses on certain investments
- Foreign-currency translation adjustments

These items do not enter into the determination of net income but instead are reported as other comprehensive income, as shown in Exhibit 12-11. Assumed figures are used for all items.

Earnings per share apply only to net income and its components, as discussed earlier. Earnings per share are *not* reported for other comprehensive income.

EXHIBIT 12-11 **Reporting Comprehensive Income**

NATIONAL EXPRESS COMPANY
Income Statement
Year Ended December 31, 2009

Revenues	$10,000
Expenses (summarized)	6,000
Net income	4,000
Other comprehensive income:	
Unrealized gain on investments	1,000
Comprehensive income	$ 5,000

Decision Guidelines

ANALYZING A CORPORATE INCOME STATEMENT

Three years out of college, you've saved $5,000 and are ready to start investing. Where do you start? You might begin by analyzing the income statements of IHOP, Coca-Cola, and Pier 1 Imports. These Decision Guidelines will help you analyze a corporate income statement.

Decision	Guidelines	
What are the main sections of the income statement? See Exhibit 12-8 for an example.	Continuing operations	• Continuing operations, including other gains and losses and less income tax expense
	Special items	• Discontinued operations—gain or loss—less the income tax effect • Extraordinary gain or loss, less the income tax effect
		• Net income (or net loss) • Other comprehensive income (Exhibit 12-11)
What earnings-per-share (EPS) figures must a corporation report?	Earnings per share	• Earnings per share—applies only to net income (or net loss), not to other comprehensive income Separate EPS figures for: • Income from continuing operations • Discontinued operations • Income before extraordinary item • Extraordinary gain or loss • Net income (or net loss)
How to compute EPS for net income?	$\text{EPS} = \dfrac{\text{Net income} - \text{Preferred dividends}}{\text{Average number of common shares outstanding}}$	

Summary Problem 2

The following information was taken from the ledger of Calenergy Corporation at December 31, 2008.

Common stock, no-par,		Discontinued operations,	
45,000 shares issued	$180,000	income	$20,000
Sales revenue	620,000	Prior-period adjustment—	
Extraordinary gain	26,000	credit to Retained Earnings	5,000
Loss due to lawsuit	11,000	Gain on sale of plant assets	21,000
General expenses	62,000	Income tax expense (saving):	
Preferred stock 8%	50,000	Continuing operations	32,000
Selling expenses	108,000	Discontinued operations	8,000
Retained earnings, beginning,		Extraordinary gain	10,000
as originally reported	103,000	Treasury stock, common	
Dividends	14,000	(5,000 shares)	25,000
Cost of goods sold	380,000		

Requirements

Prepare a single-step income statement and a statement of retained earnings for Calenergy Corporation for the year ended December 31, 2008. Include the EPS presentation and show your computations. Calenergy had no changes in its stock accounts during the year.

Solution

CALENERGY CORPORATION **Income Statement** Year Ended December 31, 2008		
Revenue and gains:		
Sales revenue		$620,000
Gain on sale of plant assets		21,000
Total revenues and gains		641,000
Expenses and losses:		
Cost of goods sold	$380,000	
Selling expenses	108,000	
General expenses	62,000	
Loss due to lawsuit	11,000	
Income tax expense	32,000	
Total expenses and losses		593,000
Income from continuing operations		48,000
Discontinued operations, income of $20,000, less income tax of $8,000		12,000
Income before extraordinary item		60,000
Extraordinary gain, $26,000, less income tax, $10,000		16,000
Net income		$ 76,000
Earnings per share:		
Income from continuing operations [($48,000 – $4,000) / 40,000 shares]		$1.10
Income from discontinued operations ($12,000 / $40,000 shares)		0.30
Income before extraordinary item [($60,000 – $4,000) / 40,000 shares]		1.40
Extraordinary gain ($16,000 / 40,000 shares)		0.40
Net income [($76,000 – $4,000) / 40,000 shares]		$1.80

Computations:

$$\text{EPS} = \frac{\text{Income} - \text{Preferred dividends}}{\text{Common shares outstanding}}$$

Preferred dividends: $\$50{,}000 \times 0.08 = \$4{,}000$

Common shares outstanding:

45,000 shares issued – 5,000 treasury shares = 40,000 shares outstanding

CALENERGY CORPORATION **Statement of Retained Earnings** Year Ended December 31, 2008	
Retained earnings balance, beginning, as originally reported	$103,000
Prior-period adjustment—credit	5,000
Retained earnings balance, beginning, as adjusted	108,000
Net income	76,000
	184,000
Dividends	(14,000)
Retained earnings balance, ending	$170,000

Review Retained Earnings, Treasury Stock, and the Income Statement

Accounting Vocabulary

Appropriation of Retained Earnings
Restriction of retained earnings that is recorded by a formal journal entry.

Comprehensive Income
Company's change in total stockholders' equity from all sources other than from the owners.

Earnings per Share (EPS)
Amount of a company's net income for each share of its outstanding stock.

Extraordinary Gains and Losses
A gain or loss that is both unusual for the company and infrequent. Also called **extraordinary items**.

Extraordinary Item
A gain or loss that is both unusual for the company and infrequent. Also called **extraordinary gains and losses**.

Prior-Period Adjustment
A correction to retained earnings for an error of an earlier period.

Segment of the Business
One of various separate divisions of a company.

Stock Dividend
A distribution by a corporation of its own to stockholders.

Stock Split
An increase in the number of outstanding shares of stock coupled with a proportionate reduction in the value of the stock.

Treasury Stock
A corporation's own stock that it has issued and later reacquired.

Quick Check

1. A company's own stock that it has issued and repurchased is called
   a. Issued stock
   b. Outstanding stock
   c. Treasury stock
   d. Dividend stock

2. A stock dividend
   a. Decreases Common Stock
   b. Increases Retained Earnings
   c. Has no effect on total equity
   d. All of the above

3. In a small stock dividend,
   a. Common stock is debited for the par value of the shares issued.
   b. Retained Earnings is debited for the market value of the shares issued.
   c. Paid-In Capital in Excess of Par is debited for the difference between the debits to Retained Earnings and to Common Stock.
   d. Net income is always decreased.

4. Stock splits
   a. Decrease par value per share
   b. Increase the number of shares of stock issued
   c. Both a and b
   d. None of the above

5. Assume that IHOP paid $10 per share to purchase 1,000 of its $1 par common as treasury stock. The purchase of treasury stock
   a. Decreased total equity by $10,000
   b. Increased total equity by $1,000
   c. Decreased total equity by $1,000
   d. Increased total equity by $10,000

6. Assume that IHOP sold all 1,000 shares of its treasury stock for $15 per share. The sale of treasury stock
   a. Decreased total equity by $15,000
   b. Increased total equity by $5,000
   c. Decreased total equity by $5,000
   d. Increased total equity by $15,000

7. Allied Electronics in Exhibit 12-8, page 612, is most likely to earn net income of $x next year. How much is $x?
   a. $90,000
   b. $79,000
   c. $75,000
   d. $54,000

8. Which of the following events would be an extraordinary loss?
   a. Loss due to an earthquake
   b. Loss on the sale of equipment
   c. Loss on discontinued operations
   d. All of the above are extraordinary items
9. What is the most widely followed statistic in business?
   a. Gross profit
   b. Earnings per share
   c. Retained earnings
   d. Dividends
10. Earnings per share is *not* computed for
   a. Net income
   b. Comprehensive income
   c. Discontinued operations
   d. Extraordinary items

Answers are given after Apply Your Knowledge (p. 639).

Assess Your Progress

Short Exercises

Recording a small stock dividend

S12-1 Crestview Pool Supply has 10,000 shares of $1 par common stock outstanding. Crestview distributes a 10% stock dividend when the market value of its stock is $15 per share.

1. Journalize Crestview's distribution of the stock dividend on September 30. An explanation is not required. (pp. 600–601)
2. What is the overall effect of the stock dividend on Crestview's total assets? On total stockholders' equity? (pp. 600–601)

Comparing and contrasting cash dividends and stock dividends

S12-2 Compare and contrast the accounting for cash dividends and stock dividends. In the space provided, insert either "Cash dividends," "Stock dividends," or "Both cash dividends and stock dividends" to complete each of the following statements:

1. _____ decrease Retained Earnings. (p. 602)
2. _____ have no effect on a liability. (pp. 600–601)
3. _____ increase paid-in capital by the same amount that they decrease Retained Earnings. (p. 602)
4. _____ decrease both total assets and total stockholders' equity, resulting in a decrease in the size of the company. (p. 602)

Accounting for a stock split

2

S12-3 Pier 1 Imports recently reported the following stockholders' equity (adapted and in millions except par value per share):

Paid-in capital:	
Common stock, $1 par, 500 shares authorized 101 shares issued	$101
Paid-in capital in excess of par	142
Total paid-in capital	243
Retained earnings	656
Other equity	(235)
Total stockholders' equity	$664

Suppose Pier 1 split its common stock 2 for 1 in order to decrease the market price of its stock. The company's stock was trading at $20 immediately before the split.

1. Prepare the stockholders' equity section of Pier 1 Imports' balance sheet after the stock split. (p. 602)
2. Which account balances changed after the stock split? Which account balances were unchanged? (p. 602)

Accounting for the purchase and sale of treasury stock (above cost)

3

S12-4 True Discount Furniture, Inc., completed the following treasury stock transactions:

a. Purchased 1,000 shares of the company's $1 par common stock as treasury stock, paying cash of $5 per share. (p. 604)
b. Sold 500 shares of the treasury stock for cash of $8 per share. (p. 604)

continued . . .

Journalize these transactions. Explanations are not required. Show how True Discount will report treasury stock on its December 31, 2008, balance sheet after completing the two transactions. In reporting the treasury stock, report only on the Treasury Stock account. You may ignore all other accounts. (p. 604)

Interpreting a restriction of retained earnings

4

S12-5 MG Corporation reported the following stockholders' equity:

Paid-in capital:	
Preferred stock, $1.50, no par, 10,000 shares authorized; none issued	$ —
Common stock, $1 par, 500,000 shares authorized, 150,000 shares issued	150,000
Paid-in capital in excess of par-common	350,000
Total paid-in capital	500,000
Retained earnings	400,000
Less: Treasury stock, 5,000 shares at cost	(30,000)
Total stockholders' equity	$870,000

1. MG Corporation's agreement with its bank lender restricts MG's dividend payments for the cost of treasury stock the company holds. How much in dividends can MG declare? (pp. 602–607)
2. Why would a bank lender restrict a corporation's dividend payments and treasury stock purchases? (pp. 605–606)

Preparing a corporate income statement

S12-6 List the major parts of a complex corporate income statement for WRS Athletic Clubs, Inc., for the year ended December 31, 2007. Include all the major parts of the income statement, starting with net sales revenue and ending with net income (net loss). You may ignore dollar amounts and earnings per share. (p. 611)

Explaining the items on a corporate income statement

S12-7 Answer these questions about a corporate income statement:

1. How do you measure gross profit? (p. 611)
2. What is the title of those items that are both unusual and infrequent?
3. Which income number is the best predictor of future net income? (pp. 609–611)
4. What's the "bottom line?" (p. 611)
5. What does *EPS* abbreviate? (p. 614)

Preparing a corporate income statement

S12-8 PWC Corp. accounting records include the following items, listed in no particular order, at December 31, 2008:

Other gains (losses)	$ (20,000)	Extraordinary loss	$ (5,000)
Net sales revenue	180,000	Cost of goods sold	70,000
Gain on discontinued operations	15,000	Operating expenses	60,000
Accounts receivable	19,000		

continued . . .

Income tax of 40% applies to all items.

Prepare PWC's income statement for the year ended December 31, 2008. Omit earnings per share. (p. 611)

Reporting earnings per share

S12-9 Return to the PWC Corp. data in Short Exercise 12-8. PWC had 10,000 shares of common stock outstanding during 2008. PWC declared and paid preferred dividends of $4,000 during 2008.

Show how PWC reported EPS data on its 2008 income statement. (p. 614)

Interpreting earnings-per-share data

S12-10 Owens-Illinois, Inc. has preferred stock outstanding.

1. Give the basic equation to compute earnings per share of common stock for net income. (p. 614)
2. List all the income items for which Owens-Illinois must report EPS data. (p. 614)

Reporting comprehensive income

S12-11 Use the PWC Corp. data in Short Exercise 12-8. In addition, PWC had unrealized gains of $4,000 on investments during 2008. Start with PWC's net income from Short Exercise 12-8 and show how the company could report other comprehensive income on its 2008 income statement.

Should PWC Corp. report earnings per share for other comprehensive income? (pp. 615–616)

Reporting a prior-period adjustment

S12-12 Statistical Research Service, Inc. (SRSI) ended 2008 with retained earnings of $75,000. During 2009 SRSI earned net income of $90,000 and declared dividends of $30,000. Also during 2009, SRSI got a $20,000 tax refund from the Internal Revenue Service. A tax audit revealed that SRSI paid too much income tax back in 2007.

Prepare Statistical Research Service, Inc.'s statement of retained earnings for the year ended December 31, 2009, to report the prior-period adjustment. (pp. 615–616)

Exercises

Journalizing a stock dividend and reporting stockholders' equity

1

E12-13 The stockholders' equity of Lakewood Occupational Therapy, Inc., on December 31, 2009, follows.

STOCKHOLDERS' EQUITY	
Paid-in capital:	
Common stock, $1 par, 100,000 shares authorized, 50,000 shares issued	$ 50,000
Paid-in capital in excess of par	200,000
Total paid-in capital	250,000
Retained earnings	120,000
Total stockholders' equity	$370,000

On April 30, 2010, the market price of Lakewood's common stock was $14 per share and the company distributed a 10% stock dividend.

continued . . .

Requirements

1. Journalize the distribution of the stock dividend. (pp. 600–601)
2. Prepare the stockholders' equity section of the balance sheet after the stock dividend. (p. 601)

Journalizing cash and stock dividends

E12-14 Martial Arts Schools, Inc., is authorized to issue 500,000 shares of $1 par common stock. The company issued 80,000 shares at $4 per share. When the market price of common stock was $6 per share, Martial Arts distributed a 10% stock dividend. Later, Martial Arts declared and paid a $0.30 per share cash dividend.

Requirements

1. Journalize the distribution of the stock dividend. (pp. 600–601)
2. Journalize both the declaration and the payment of the cash dividend. (pp. 561–563)

Reporting stockholders' equity after a stock split

E12-15 Cobra Golf Club Corp. had the following stockholders' equity at December 31, 2007:

Paid-in capital:	
Common stock, $1 par, 200,000 shares authorized, 50,000 shares issued	$ 50,000
Paid-in capital in excess of par	100,000
Total paid-in capital	150,000
Retained earnings	200,000
Total stockholders' equity	$350,000

On June 30, 2008, Cobra split its common stock 2 for 1. Make the memorandum entry to record the stock split, and prepare the stockholders' equity section of the balance sheet immediately after the split. (p. 602)

Effects of stock dividends, stock splits, and treasury stock transactions

E12-16 Identify the effects of the following transactions on total stockholders' equity. Each transaction is independent.

a. A 10% stock dividend. Before the dividend, 500,000 shares of $1 par common stock were outstanding; market value was $6 at the time of the dividend. (p. 602)

b. A 2-for-1 stock split. Prior to the split, 60,000 shares of $4 par common were outstanding. (p. 602)

c. Purchase of 1,000 shares of treasury stock (par value $0.50) at $5 per share. (pp. 602–603, 605–606)

d. Sale of 600 shares of $1 par treasury stock for $5 per share. Cost of the treasury stock was $2 per share. (pp. 604, 605–606)

Journalizing treasury stock transactions

E12-17 Journalize the following transactions of Austin Driving School, Inc.:

Feb. 4	Issued 20,000 shares of 1 par common stock at $10 per share. (pp. 554–555)
Apr. 22	Purchased 1,000 shares of treasury stock at $14 per share. (pp. 602–603)
Aug. 22	Sold 600 shares of treasury stock at $20 per share. (p. 604)

Journalizing treasury stock transactions and reporting stockholders' equity
3

E12-18 Mid America Amusements Corporation had the following stockholders' equity on November 30:

STOCKHOLDERS' EQUITY	
Common stock, $5 par, 500,000 shares authorized, 50,000 shares issued	$250,000
Paid-in capital in excess of par	150,000
Retained earnings	490,000
Total stockholders' equity	$890,000

On December 30, Mid America purchased 10,000 shares of treasury stock at $9 per share.

1. Journalize the purchase of the treasury stock, and prepare the stockholders' equity section of the balance sheet at December 31. (pp. 602–603)
2. How many shares of common stock are outstanding after the purchase of treasury stock?

Reporting a retained earnings restriction
4

E12-19 The agreement under which Toshiba Printers issued its long-term debt requires the restriction of $100,000 of the company's retained earnings balance. Total retained earnings is $250,000, and common stock, no-par, has a balance of $50,000.

Requirements

Report stockholders' equity on Toshiba's balance sheet, assuming the following:

a. Toshiba discloses the restriction in a note. Write the note. (pp. 606–608)

b. Toshiba appropriates retained earnings in the amount of the restriction and includes no note in its statements. Follow the Teaching Format on page 607.

Preparing a multistep income statement
5

E12-20 Cannon Photographic Supplies, Inc., accounting records include the following for 2008:

Income tax saving—extraordinary loss	$ 6,000	Sales revenue	$430,000
Income tax saving—loss on discontinued operations	20,000	Operating expenses (including income tax)	120,000
Extraordinary loss	15,000	Cost of goods sold	240,000
		Loss on discontinued operations	50,000

Requirement

Prepare Cannon's multistep income statement for 2008. Omit earnings per share. (p. 611)

Computing earnings per share
5

E12-21 Palestine Corp. earned net income of $108,000 for 2007. Palestine's books include the following figures:

Preferred stock, 6%, $50 par, 1,000 shares issued and outstanding	$ 50,000
Common stock, $10 par, 52,000 shares issued	520,000
Paid-in capital in excess of par	480,000
Treasury stock, common, 2,000 shares at cost	40,000

continued . . .

Requirement
Compute Palestine's EPS for the year. (p. 614)

Computing earnings per share

E12-22 Athens Academy Surplus had 50,000 shares of common stock and 10,000 shares of 5%, $10 par preferred stock outstanding through December 31, 2008. Income from continuing operations of 2008 was $110,000, and loss on discontinued operations (net of income tax saving) was $8,000. Athens also had an extraordinary gain (net of tax) of $20,000.

Requirement
Compute Athens' EPS amounts for 2008, starting with income from continuing operations. (p. 614)

Preparing a combined statement of income and retained earnings

E12-23 Good Times Express Company had retained earnings of $160 million at December 31, 2006. The company reported these figures for 2007:

	($ Millions)
Net income	$140
Cash dividends—preferred	2
common	98

Requirement
Beginning with net income, prepare a combined statement of income and retained earnings for Good Times Express Company for the year ended December 31, 2007. (pp. 614–616)

Preparing a statement of retained earnings with a prior-period adjustment

E12-24 Sarah Lou Bakery, Inc., reported a prior-period adjustment in 2008. An accounting error caused net income of prior years to be overstated by $5,000. Retained earnings at December 31, 2007, as previously reported, stood at $39,000. Net income for 2008 was $70,000, and dividends were $24,000.

Requirement
Prepare the company's statement of retained earnings for the year ended December 31, 2008. (pp. 614–616)

Computing comprehensive income and reporting earnings per share

E12-25 During 2009, Newfoundland Corp. earned income from continuing operations of $135,000. The company also sold a segment of the business (discontinued operations) at a loss of $30,000 and had an extraordinary gain of $10,000. At year-end, Newfoundland had an unrealized loss on investments of $5,000.

1. Compute Newfoundland's net income and comprehensive income for 2009. All amounts are net of income taxes. (pp. 614–616)
2. What final EPS figure should Newfoundland report for 2009? Name the item and show its amount. Newfoundland had 57,500 shares of common stock (and no preferred stock) outstanding. (pp. 614–616)

Problems (Group A)

Journalizing stockholders' equity transactions

1 2 3

P12-26A Dearborn Manufacturing Co. completed the following transactions during 2009.

Jan. 16	Declared a cash dividend on the 4%, $100 par preferred stock (1,000 shares outstanding). Declared a $0.35 per share dividend on the 100,000 shares of common stock outstanding. The date of record is January 31 and the payment date is February 15. (pp. 561–563)
Feb. 15	Paid the cash dividends. (pp. 561–563)
June 10	Split common stock 2 for 1. Before the split, Dearborn had 100,000 shares of $2 par common stock outstanding. (p. 602)
July 30	Distributed a 5% stock dividend on the common stock. The market value of the common stock was $10 per share. (pp. 600–601)
Oct. 26	Purchased 2,000 shares of treasury stock at $11 per share. (pp. 602–603)
Nov. 8	Sold 1,000 shares of treasury stock for $17 per share. (p. 604)

Requirement

Record the transactions in Dearborn's general journal.

Journalizing dividend and treasury stock transactions and reporting stockholders' equity

P12-27A The balance sheet of Lennox Health Foods, at December 31, 2007, reported 100,000 shares of no-par common stock authorized, with 30,000 shares issued and a Common Stock balance of $180,000. Retained Earnings had a balance of $140,000. During 2008, the company completed the following selected transactions:

Mar. 15	Purchased 5,000 shares of treasury stock at $7 per share. (pp. 602–603)
Apr. 30	Distributed a 20% stock dividend on the 25,000 shares of *outstanding* common stock. The market value of Lennox common stock was $9 per share. (pp. 600–601)
Dec. 31	Earned net income of $110,000 during the year. Closed net income to Retained Earnings. (pp. 551–552)

Requirements

1. Record the transactions in the general journal. Explanations are not required.
2. Prepare the stockholders' equity section of Lennox Health Foods' balance sheet at December 31, 2008. (pp. 601–603)

Using dividends to fight off a takeover of the corporation

P12-28A Jennifer Vera, Inc., is the only company with a distribution network for its imported goods. The company does a brisk business with specialty stores such as Neiman Marcus, Saks Fifth Avenue, and Nordstrom. Vera's recent success has made the company a prime target for a

continued . . .

takeover. Against the wishes of Vera's board of directors, an investment group from France is attempting to buy 51% of Vera's outstanding stock. Board members are convinced that the French investors would sell off the most desirable pieces of the business and leave little of value.

At the most recent board meeting, several suggestions were advanced to fight off the hostile takeover bid. One suggestion is to increase the stock outstanding by distributing a 100% stock dividend. The intent is to spread the company's ownership in order to make it harder for the French group to buy a controlling interest.

Requirement

As a significant stockholder of Jennifer Vera, Inc., write a short memo to explain to the board whether distributing the stock dividend would make it difficult for the investor group to take over the company. Include in your memo a discussion of the effect that the stock dividend would have on assets, liabilities, and total stockholders' equity—that is, the dividend's effect on the size of the corporation. (pp. 598–599)

Journalizing dividend and treasury stock transactions; reporting retained earnings and stockholders' equity

P12-29A The balance sheet of Morrisey Management Consulting, Inc., at December 31, 2007, reported the following stockholders' equity:

Paid in capital:	
Common stock, $10 par, 100,000 shares authorized, 20,000 shares issued	$200,000
Paid-in capital in excess of par	300,000
Total paid-in capital	500,000
Retained earnings	160,000
Total stockholders' equity	$660,000

During 2008, Morrisey completed the following selected transactions:

Feb. 6	Distributed a 10% stock dividend on the common stock. The market value of Morrisey's stock was $25 per share. (pp. 600–601)
July 29	Purchased 2,000 shares of treasury stock at $25 per share. (pp. 602–603)
Nov. 27	Declared a $0.30 per share cash dividend on the 20,000 shares of common stock outstanding. The date of record is December 17, and the payment date is January 7, 2009. (pp. 561–563)
Dec. 31	Closed the $86,000 net income to Retained Earnings. (pp. 561–563)

Requirements

1. Record the transactions in the general journal.
2. Prepare a retained earnings statement for the year ended December 31, 2008. (p. 615)
3. Prepare the stockholders' equity section of the balance sheet at December 31, 2008. (pp. 601–603)

Preparing a detailed income statement

P12-30A The following information was taken from the records of Mobile Motorsports, Inc., at September 30, 2008.

General expenses	$133,000	Cost of goods sold	$435,000
Preferred stock, $2, no-par,		Retained earnings, beginning	88,000
5,000 shares issued	200,000	Selling expenses	121,000
Common stock, $10 par, 25,000		Income from discontinued	
shares authorized and issued	250,000	operations	8,000
Net sales revenue	837,000	Income tax expense:	
Treasury stock, common		Continuing operations	72,000
(1,000 shares)	11,000	Income from discontinued	
		operations	2,000

Requirement

Prepare a multistep income statement for Mobile Motorsports, Inc., for the fiscal year ended September 30, 2008. Include earnings per share. (p. 611)

Preparing a corrected combined statement of income and retained earnings

5

P12-31A Lisa Sheraton, accountant for Chase Home Finance, was injured in a boating accident. Another employee prepared the accompanying income statement for the year ended December 31, 2008.

The individual *amounts* listed on the income statement are correct. However, some accounts are reported incorrectly, and two items don't belong on the income statement at all. Also, income tax has *not* been applied to all appropriate figures. The income tax rate on discontinued operations was 40%. Chase Home Finance issued 52,000 shares of common stock in 2006 and held 2,000 shares as treasury stock during 2008. Retained earnings at December 31, 2007 was $167,000.

CHASE HOME FINANCE **Income Statement** Year Ended December 31, 2008		
Revenue and gains:		
Sales		$362,000
Paid-in capital in excess of par—common		90,000
Total revenues and gains		452,000
Expenses and losses:		
Cost of goods sold	$105,000	
Selling expenses	67,000	
General expenses	61,000	
Dividends	17,000	
Sales returns	11,000	
Sales discounts	6,000	
Income tax expense	20,000	
Total expenses and losses		287,000
Income from operations		165,000
Other gains and losses:		
Gain on discontinued operations		5,000
Net income		$170,000
Earnings per share		$ 3.40

continued . . .

Requirement

Prepare a corrected combined statement of income and retained earnings for 2008, including earnings per share. Prepare the income statement in single-step format. (pp. 273–275, 611, 614–616)

Computing earnings per share and reporting a retained earnings restriction

P12-32A The capital structure of Knightsbridge, Inc., at December 31, 2006, included 20,000 shares of $1.25 preferred stock and 40,000 shares of common stock. Common stock outstanding during 2007 totaled 40,000 shares. Income from continuing operations during 2007 was $105,000. The company discontinued a segment of the business at a gain of $20,000, and also had an extraordinary gain of $10,000. The Knightsbridge board of directors restricts $100,000 of retained earnings for contingencies.

Requirement

1. Compute Knightsbridge's earnings per share for 2007. Start with income from continuing operations. All income and loss amounts are net of income tax. (p. 614)
2. Show two ways of reporting Knightsbridge's retained earnings restriction. Retained earnings at December 31, 2006, was $100,000, and the company declared preferred dividends of $25,000 during 2007. (pp. 606–608)

Problems (Group B)

Journalizing stockholders' equity transactions

P12-33B Maxfli Hot Air Balloons, Inc., completed the following selected transactions during 2009:

Feb. 9	Declared a cash dividend on the 10,000 shares of $1.50, no-par preferred stock. Declared a $0.20 per share dividend on the 10,000 shares of common stock outstanding. The date of record is February 16, and the payment date is February 28. (pp. 561–563)
Feb. 28	Paid the cash dividends. (pp. 561–563)
Mar. 21	Split common stock 2 for 1. Before the split, Maxfli had 10,000 shares of $10 par common stock outstanding. (p. 602)
Apr. 18	Distributed a 10% stock dividend on the common stock. The market value of the common stock was $27 per share. (pp. 600–601)
June 18	Purchased 2,000 shares of treasury stock at $25 per share. (pp. 602–603)
Dec. 22	Sold 1,000 shares of treasury stock for $28 per share. (p. 604)

Requirement

Record the transactions in the general journal.

Journalizing dividend and treasury stock transactions and reporting stockholders' equity

P12-34B The balance sheet of Banc One Corp. at December 31, 2007, reported 500,000 shares of $1 par common stock authorized with 100,000 shares issued. Paid-In Capital in Excess of Par had a balance of $300,000. Retained Earnings had a balance of $101,000. During 2008 the company completed the following selected transactions:

Jan. 12	Purchased 10,000 shares of the treasury stock at $4 per share. (pp. 602–603)
Sep. 28	Distributed a 10% stock dividend on the 90,000 shares of *outstanding* common stock. The market value of Banc One's common stock was $5 per share. (pp. 600–601)
Dec. 31	Earned net income of $73,000 during the year. Closed net income to Retained Earnings. (pp. 551–552)

Requirements

1. Record the transactions in the general journal. Explanations are not required.
2. Prepare the stockholders' equity section of the balance sheet at December 31, 2008. (pp. 601–603)

Purchasing treasury stock to fight off a takeover of the corporation

3

P12-35B Guatemalan Imports is the only company with reliable sources for its imported gifts. The company does a brisk business with specialty stores such as Pier 1 Imports. Guatemalan Imports' recent success has made the company a prime target for a takeover. An investment group from Mexico City is attempting to buy 51% of Guatemalan Imports' outstanding stock against the wishes of the company's board of directors. Board members are convinced that the Mexico City investors would sell the most desirable pieces of the business and leave little of value.

At the most recent board meeting, several suggestions were advanced to fight off the hostile takeover bid. The suggestion with the most promise is to purchase a huge quantity of treasury stock. Guatemalan Imports has the cash to carry out this plan.

Requirements

1. As a significant stockholder of Guatemalan Imports, write a memorandum to explain to the board how the purchase of treasury stock would make it difficult for the Mexico City group to take over the company. Include a discussion of the effect that purchasing treasury stock would have on stock outstanding and on the size of the corporation. (pp. 602–603)
2. Suppose Guatemalan Imports is successful in fighting off the takeover bid and later sells the treasury stock at prices greater than the purchase price. Explain what effect these sales will have on assets, stockholders' equity, and net income. (p. 604)

Journalizing dividend and treasury stock transactions; reporting retained earnings and stockholders' equity

P12-36B The balance sheet of Oriental Rug Company at December 31, 2008, included the following stockholders' equity:

Paid-in capital:	
Common stock, $1 par, 250,000 shares authorized, 50,000 shares issued	$ 50,000

continued . . .

Paid-in capital in excess of par	350,000
Total paid-in capital	400,000
Retained earnings	100,000
Total stockholders' equity	$500,000

During 2009, Oriental Rug completed the following selected transactions:

Mar. 29	Distributed a 10% stock dividend on the common stock. The market value of Oriental common stock was $8 per share. (pp. 600–601)
July 13	Purchased 10,000 shares of treasury stock at $8 per share. (pp. 602–603)
Dec. 10	Declared a $0.20 per share cash dividend on the 45,000 shares of common stock outstanding. The date of record is December 17, and the payment date is January 2. (pp. 561–563)
31	Closed the $79,000 net income to Retained Earnings. (pp. 551–552)

Requirements

1. Record the transactions in the general journal.
2. Prepare the retained earnings statement for the year ended December 31, 2009. (p. 615)
3. Prepare the stockholders' equity section of the balance sheet at December 31, 2009. (p. 601)

Preparing a detailed income statement

P12-37B The following information was taken from the records of Underwood Company at June 30, 2007:

Selling expenses	$120,000	Common stock, no-par, 22,000 shares authorized and issued	$350,000
General expenses	75,000	Preferred stock, 6%, $25 par, 4,000 shares issued	100,000
Gain on discontinued operations	5,000	Income tax expense:	
Retained earnings, beginning	63,000	Continuing operations	28,000
Cost of goods sold	275,000	Gain on discontinued operations	2,000
Treasury stock, common (2,000 shares)	28,000		
Net sales revenue	565,000		

Requirement

Prepare a multistep income statement for Underwood Company for the fiscal year ended June 30, 2007. Include earnings per share. (p. 611)

Preparing a corrected combined statement of income and retained earnings

5

P12-38B Jeremy Hawk, accountant for Rainbow International Corp., was injured in an auto accident. Another employee prepared the following income statement for the year ended December 31, 2007:

continued . . .

RAINBOW INTERNATIONAL CORP. Income Statement December 31, 2007		
Revenue and gains:		
Sales		$733,000
Paid-in capital in excess of par—common		111,000
Total revenues and gains		844,000
Expenses and losses:		
Cost of goods sold	$383,000	
Selling expenses	103,000	
General expenses	91,000	
Sales returns	22,000	
Sales discounts	10,000	
Dividends	15,000	
Income tax expense	32,000	
Total expenses and losses		656,000
Income from operations		188,000
Other gains and losses:		
Loss on discontinued operations		(15,000)
Net income		$173,000
Earnings per share		$ 17.30

The individual *amounts* listed on the income statement are correct. However, some accounts are reported incorrectly, and two items don't belong on the income statement at all. Also, income tax has *not* been applied to all appropriate figures. The income tax rate on discontinued operations is 40%. Rainbow issued 14,000 shares of common stock in 2004 and held 4,000 shares as treasury stock during fiscal year 2007. Retained earnings at June 30, 2006, was $117,000.

Requirements

Prepare a corrected combined statement of income and retained earnings for the fiscal year ended December 31, 2007. Prepare the income statement in single-step format, and include earnings per share. (pp. 273–275, 611, 614–616)

Computing earnings per share and reporting a retained earnings restriction

P12-39B The capital structure of Audiology Associates, Inc., at December 31, 2007, included 5,000 shares of $2 preferred stock and 100,000 shares of common stock. Common shares outstanding during 2008 were 100,000. Income from continuing operations during 2008 was $370,000. The company discontinued a segment of the business at a gain of $60,000 and also had an extraordinary gain of $30,000. Audiology Associates' board of directors has restricted $250,000 of retained earnings for expansion of the company's office facilities.

Requirements

1. Compute Audiology Associates' earnings per share for 2008. Start with income from continuing operations. Income and loss amounts are net of income tax. (p. 614)
2. Show two ways of reporting Audiology Associates' retained earnings restriction. Retained Earnings at December 31, 2007, was $160,000, and the company declared cash dividends of $100,000 during 2008. (pp. 606–608)

for 24/7 practice, visit www.MyAccountingLab.com

Apply Your Knowledge

Decision Cases

Analyzing cash dividends and stock dividends

1

Case 1. Valley Mills Construction, Inc., had the following stockholders' equity on June 30, 2008:

Common stock, no-par, 100,000 shares issued	$250,000
Retained earnings	190,000
Total stockholders' equity	$440,000

In the past, Valley Mills has paid an annual cash dividend of $1 per share. Despite the large retained earnings balance, the board of directors wished to conserve cash for expansion. The board delayed the payment of cash dividends and in July distributed a 5% stock dividend. During August, the company's cash position improved. The board then declared and paid a cash dividend of $0.9524 per share in September.

Suppose you owned 1,000 shares of Valley Mills common stock, acquired three years ago, prior to the 50% stock dividend. The market price of the stock was $30 per share before any of these dividends.

Requirements

1. What amount of cash dividends did you receive last year—before the stock dividend? What amount of cash dividends will you receive after the stock dividend?
2. How does the stock dividend affect your proportionate ownership in Valley Mills Construction, Inc.? Explain.
3. Immediately after the stock dividend was distributed, the market value of Valley Mills stock decreased from $30 per share to $28.571 per share. Does this decrease represent a loss to you? Explain.

Reporting special items

3 5

Case 2. The following accounting issues have arisen at T-Shirts Plus, Inc.:

1. Corporations sometimes purchase their own stock. When asked why they do so, T-Shirts Plus management responds that the stock is undervalued. What advantage would T-Shirts Plus gain by buying and selling its own undervalued stock?
2. T-Shirts Plus earned a significant profit in the year ended December 31, 2008, because land that it held was purchased by the State of Nebraska for a new highway. The company proposes to treat the sale of land as operating revenue. Why do you think the company is proposing this plan? Is this disclosure appropriate?
3. The treasurer of T-Shirts Plus wants to report a large loss as an extraordinary item because the company produced too much product and cannot sell it. Why do you think the treasurer wants to report the loss as extraordinary? Would that be acceptable?

Ethical Issue

Bobby's Bagels just landed a contract to open 100 new stores in shopping malls across the country. The new business should triple the company's profits. Prior to

continued . . .

disclosing the new contract to the public, top managers of the company quietly bought most of Bobby's Bagels stock for themselves. After the discovery was announced, Bobby's Bagels stock price shot up from $7 to $52.

Requirements

1. Did Bobby's Bagels managers behave ethically? Explain your answer.
2. Identify the accounting principle relevant to this situation. Review Chapter 6 if necessary.
3. Who was helped and who was harmed by management's action?

Financial Statement Case

Corporate income statement, earnings per share

5

Use the Amazon.com financial statements in Appendix A at the end of this book to answer the following questions.

Requirements

1. Show how Amazon.com computed basic earnings per share of $0.87 for 2005.
2. Prepare a T-account to show the beginning and ending balances and all activity in Retained Earnings (Accumulated Deficit) for 2005.
3. How much in cash dividends did Amazon declare during 2005? Explain your answer.
4. How much treasury stock did Amazon have at December 31, 2005? Explain.

Team Project

Requirements

Obtain the annual reports (or annual report data) of five well-known companies. You can get the reports either from the companies' Web sites, your college library, or by mailing a request directly to the company (allow two weeks for delivery). Or you can visit the Web site for this book (http://www.prenhall.com/horngren) or the SEC EDGAR database, which includes the financial reports of most well-known companies.

1. After selecting five companies, examine their income statements to search for the following items:
   a. Income from continuing operations
   b. Discontinued operations
   c. Extraordinary gains and losses
   d. Net income or net loss
   e. Earnings-per-share data
2. Study the companies' balance sheets to see
   a. What classes of stock each company has issued.
   b. Which item carries a larger balance—the Common Stock account or Paid-In Capital in Excess of Par (also labeled Additional Paid-In Capital).

continued . . .

c. What percentage of each company's total stockholders' equity is made up of retained earnings.

d. Whether the company has treasury stock. If so, how many shares and how much is the cost?

3. Examine each company's statement of stockholders' equity for evidence of

a. Cash dividends

b. Stock dividends (Some companies use the term *stock split* to refer to a large stock dividend.)

c. Treasury stock purchases and sales

4. As directed by your instructor, either write a report or present your findings to your class. You may be unable to understand *everything* you find, but neither can the Wall Street analysts! You will be amazed at how much you have learned.

For Internet exercises, Excel in Practice, and additional online activities, go to the Web site www.prenhall.com/horngren.

Quick Check Answers

1. *c* 2. *c* 3. *b* 4. *c* 5. *a* 6. *d* 7. *d* 8. *a* 9. *b* 10. *b*

13 Long-Term Liabilities

Learning Objectives

1. Account for bonds payable
2. Measure interest expense by the straight-line amortization method
3. Account for retirement and conversion of bonds payable
4. Report liabilities on the balance sheet
5. Show the advantages and disadvantages of borrowing

In earlier chapters of this book you were adventuresome and operated In Motion T-Shirts while in college. You continued with the business after graduation and expanded to several locations. Suppose you grew In Motion to a good-size company and then sold it at a nice profit. What will you do with the cash you received from selling out?

You've noticed that discount airlines Jet Blue and Virgin Airways have done quite well. So you decide to take the plunge and start an airline. You get a charter, issue stock, and raise $5 million. Air West Airlines is up and running.

Needing more cash you must borrow. This will require Air West to issue long-term notes payable or bonds payable. Virtually all companies—both large and small—have borrowed this way.

In this chapter we show how to account for long-term liabilities—notes payable and bonds payable. The chapter appendix 13A includes some related topics that your instructor may or may not wish to cover.

Notes payable and bonds payable are accounted for similarly. Since we covered notes payable back in Chapter 10, we focus on bonds payable here. Before launching into bonds payable, let's compare bonds with stock, which you learned about in Chapters 11 and 12. The following chart shows how stocks and bonds differ.

Stocks	Bonds
1. Stock represents the *ownership* of a corporation. Each stockholder is an *owner.*	1. Bonds represent a *liability* of the corporation. Each bondholder is a *creditor.*
2. The corporation is *not* obligated to repay the stock.	2. The corporation *must* repay the bonds.
3. The corporation *may* or *may not* pay dividends on the stock. Dividends are *not* an expense.	3. The corporation *must* pay interest on the bonds. Interest is an expense.

Bonds: An Introduction

Large companies such as Blockbuster and American Airlines need large amounts of money to finance operations. They may issue bonds payable to the public. **Bonds payable** are groups of notes payable issued to multiple lenders, called bondholders. By issuing bonds payable, Blockbuster can borrow millions of dollars from thousands of investors. Each investor can buy a selected amount of Blockbuster bonds.

Each bondholder gets a bond certificate, which shows the name of the company that borrowed the money, exactly like a note payable. The certificate states the *principal,* which is the amount the company has borrowed. The bonds' principal amount is also called *maturity value,* or *par value.* The company must then pay each bondholder the principal amount at a specific future date, called the maturity date. In Chapter 10 we saw how to account for short-term notes payable. There's a lot of similarity between the accounting for short-term notes payable and long-term notes payable.

People buy bonds to earn interest. The bond certificate states the interest rate that the company will pay and the dates the interest is due (generally twice a year). Exhibit 13-1 shows a bond certificate issued by Air West Airlines, Inc.

Review these bond fundamentals in Exhibit 13-1.

- **Principal amount** (also called **maturity value**, or **par value**) The amount the borrower must pay back to the bondholders.
- **Maturity date** The date on which the borrower must pay the principal amount to the bondholders.
- **Stated interest rate** The annual rate of interest that the borrower pays the bondholders.

Types of Bonds

There are various types of bonds, including the following.

- **Term bonds** all mature at the same time.
- **Serial bonds** mature in installments at regular intervals. For example, a $500,000, 5-year serial bond may mature in $100,000 annual installments over a 5-year period.

Bond Interest Rates

Bonds are sold at their market price, which is the bonds' present value. Two interest rates work together to set the price of a bond:

- The **stated interest rate** determines the amount of cash interest the borrower pays each year. The stated interest rate is printed on the bond and *does not change*. For example, Air West Airlines' 9% bonds payable have a stated interest rate of 9% (Exhibit 13-1). Thus, Air West pays $900 of interest annually on each $10,000 bond.
- The **market interest rate** (also known as the **effective interest rate**) is the interest rate that investors demand to earn for loaning their money. The market interest rate *varies* daily. A company may issue bonds with a stated interest rate that differs from the market interest rate.

Air West Airlines may issue its 9% bonds when the market rate has risen to 10%. Will the Air West bonds attract investors in this market? No, because investors can earn 10% on other bonds. Therefore, investors will purchase Air West bonds only at a price less than maturity value. The difference between the lower price and the bonds' maturity value is a *discount*.

Conversely, if the market interest rate is 8%, Air West's 9% bonds will be so attractive that investors will pay more than maturity value for them. The difference between the higher price and maturity value is a *premium*. Exhibit 13-3 shows how the stated interest rate and the market interest rate work together to determine the price of a bond.

EXHIBIT 13-3 **Interaction of the Stated Interest Rate and the Market Interest Rate to Determine the Price of a Bond**

Example: Bond with a Stated Interest Rate of 9%

Bond's Stated Interest Rate		Market Interest Rate		Issue Price of Bonds Payable
9%	=	9%	→	Maturity value of the bond
9%	<	10%	→	Discount (price below maturity value)
9%	>	8%	→	Premium (price above maturity value)

Issuing Bonds Payable to Borrow Money

The basic journal entry to record the issuance of bonds payable debits Cash and credits Bonds Payable. The company may issue bonds for three different bond prices:

- At *maturity (par)* value
- At a *discount*
- At a *premium*

We begin with the simplest case: issuing bonds payable at maturity (par) value.

Issuing Bonds Payable at Maturity (Par) Value

1 Account for bonds payable

Air West Airlines has $50,000 of 8% bonds payable that mature in 5 years. Air West issued these bonds at maturity (par) value on January 1, 2008. The issuance entry is:

Date	Accounts and Explanation	Debit	Credit
2008			
Jan. 1	Cash	50,000	
	Bonds Payable		50,000
	Issued bonds.		

Air West, the borrower, makes this one-time journal entry to record the receipt of cash and issuance of bonds payable. Interest payments occur each January 1 and July 1. Air West's first semiannual interest payment is journalized as follows:

Date	Accounts and Explanation	Debit	Credit
2008			
Jan. 1	Interest Expense ($50,000 × 0.08 × 6/12)	2,000	
	Cash		2,000
	Paid semiannual interest.		

Each semiannual interest payment follows this same pattern.

At maturity, Air West will record payment of the bonds as follows:

Date	Accounts and Explanation	Debit	Credit
2013			
Jan. 1	Bonds Payable	50,000	
	Cash		50,000
	Paid off bonds at maturity.		

Now let's see how to issue bonds payable at a discount. This is one of the most common situations.

Issuing Bonds Payable at a Discount

We know that market conditions may force a company such as Air West Airlines to accept a discount price for its bonds. Suppose Air West issues $100,000 of its 9%, five-year bonds when the market interest rate is 9 1/2%. The market price of the bonds drops to 98, which means 98% of par value. Air West receives $98,000 ($100,000 × 0.98) at issuance and makes the following journal entry:

Date	Accounts and Explanation	Debit	Credit
2008			
Jan. 1	Cash ($100,000 × 0.98)	98,000	
	Discount on Bonds Payable	2,000	
	Bonds Payable		100,000
	Issued bonds at a discount.		

After posting, the bond accounts have these balances:

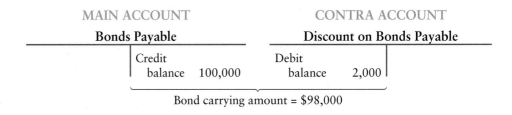

MAIN ACCOUNT **Bonds Payable**		CONTRA ACCOUNT **Discount on Bonds Payable**	
	Credit balance 100,000	Debit balance 2,000	

Bond carrying amount = $98,000

Discount on Bonds Payable is a contra account to Bonds Payable. Bonds Payable *minus* the discount gives the carrying amount of the bonds. Air West would report these bonds payable as follows immediately after issuance.

Long-term liabilities:		
Bonds payable	$100,000	
Less: Discount on bonds payable	(2,000)	$98,000

Interest Expense on Bonds Payable with a Discount

We saw that a bond's stated interest rate may differ from the market interest rate. The market rate was 9 1/2% when Air West issued its 9% bonds. The 1/2% interest-rate difference created the $2,000 discount on the bonds. Investors were willing to pay only $98,000 for a $100,000, 9% bond when they could earn 9 1/2% on other bonds.

Air West borrowed $98,000 but must pay $100,000 when the bonds mature five years later. What happens to the $2,000 discount? The discount is additional interest expense to Air West. The discount raises Air West's interest expense on the bonds to the market interest rate of 9 1/2%. The discount becomes interest expense for Air West through a process called *amortization,* the gradual reduction of an item over time.

Straight-Line Amortization of Bond Discount

2 Measure interest expense by the straight-line amortization method

We can amortize a bond discount by dividing it into equal amounts for each interest period. This method is called *straight-line amortization.* In our example, the initial discount is $2,000, and there are 10 semiannual interest periods during the bonds' 5-year life.

Therefore 1/10 of the $2,000 bond discount ($200) is amortized each interest period. Air West's first semiannual interest entry is:[1]

2008			
July 1	Interest Expense	4,700	
	Cash ($100,000 × 0.09 × 6/12)		4,500
	Discount on Bonds Payable ($2,000/10)		200
	Paid interest and amortized discount.		

Interest expense of $4,700 for each six-month period is the sum of

- The stated interest ($4,500, which is paid in cash)
- *Plus* the amortization of discount ($200).

[1]You can record the payment of interest and the amortization of bond discount in two separate entries, as follows:

2008			
July 1	Interest Expense	4,500	
	Cash ($100,000 × 0.09 × 6/12)		4,500
	Paid semiannual interest.		
July 1	Interest Expense	200	
	Discount on Bonds Payable ($2,000/10)		200
	Amortized discount on bonds payable.		

These two entries record the same amount of interest expense ($4,700) as the single entry shown above.

Discount on Bonds Payable has a debit balance. Therefore we credit the Discount account to amortize its balance. Ten amortization entries will decrease the Discount to zero. Then the carrying amount of the bonds payable will be $100,000 at maturity.

Finally, the entry to pay off the bonds at maturity is:

2013			
Jan. 1	Bonds Payable	100,000	
	Cash		100,000
	Paid off bonds at maturity.		

Decision Guidelines

LONG-TERM LIABILITIES—PART A

Air West Airlines has borrowed some money by issuing bonds payable. What type of bonds did Air West issue? How much cash must Air West pay each interest period? How much cash must Air West pay at maturity? The Decision Guidelines address these and other questions.

Decision	Guidelines
a. When will you pay off the bonds?	Types of bonds:
• At maturity? →	• Term bonds
• In installments? →	• Serial bonds
b. Are the bonds secured?	
• Yes →	• Mortgage (secured) bonds
• No →	• Debenture (unsecured) bonds
How are bond prices	
• Quoted? →	• As a percentage of maturity value (Example: A \$500,000 bond priced at \$510,000 would be quoted at 102 (\$510,000 ÷ \$500,000 = 1.02)
• Determined? →	• Present value of the future principal amount to pay *plus* present value of the future interest payments (see Appendix 13A)
What are the two interest rates used for bonds? →	• The *stated interest rate* determines the amount of cash interest the borrower pays. This interest rate does *not* change. • The *market interest rate* is the rate that investors demand to earn for loaning their money. This interest rate determines the bonds' market price and varies daily.
What causes a bond to be priced at	
• Maturity (par) value? →	• The *stated* interest rate on the bond *equals* the *market* interest rate.
• A discount? →	• The *stated* interest rate on the bond is *less than* the *market* interest rate.
• A premium? →	• The *stated* interest rate on the bond is *greater than* the *market* interest rate.
How to report bonds payable on the balance sheet? →	Maturity (par) value { −Discount on bonds payable or +Premium on bonds payable
What is the relationship between interest expense and interest payments when bonds are issued at	
• Maturity (par) value? →	• Interest expense *equals* the interest payment.
• A discount? →	• Interest expense is *greater than* the interest payment.
• A premium? →	• Interest expense is *less than* the interest payment.

Summary Problem 1

West Virginia Power Company has 8% 10-year bonds payable that mature on June 30, 2018. The bonds are issued on June 30, 2008, and West Virginia Power pays interest each June 30 and December 31.

Requirements

1. Will the bonds be issued at par, at a premium, or at a discount if the market interest rate on the date of issuance is 7%? If the market interest rate is 9%?
2. West Virginia Power issued $100,000 of the bonds at 94.
   a. Record issuance of the bonds on June 30, 2008.
   b. Record the payment of interest and amortization of the discount on December 31, 2008. Use the straight-line amortization method.
   c. Compute the bonds' carrying amount at December 31, 2008.
   d. Record the payment of interest and amortization of discount on June 30, 2009.

Solution

Requirement 1

M Market Interest Rate	Bond Price for an 8% Bond
7%	Premium
9%	Discount

Requirement 2

	2008			
a.	June 30	Cash ($100,000 × 0.94)	94,000	
		Discount on Bonds Payable	6,000	
		Bonds Payable		100,000
		Issued bonds at a discount.		
b.	Dec. 31	Interest Expense	4,300	
		Cash ($100,000 × 0.08 × 6/12)		4,000
		Discount on Bonds Payable ($6,000/20)		300
		Paid interest and amortized discount.		
c.		Bond carrying amount at Dec. 31, 2008: $94,300 [$100,000 – ($6,000 – $300)]		
	2009			
d.	June 30	Interest Expense	4,300	
		Cash ($100,000 × 0.08 × 6/12)		4,000
		Discount on Bonds Payable ($6,000/20)		300
		Paid interest and amortized discount.		

Issuing Bonds Payable at a Premium

The issuance of bonds payable at a premium is rare because a premium occurs only when a bond's stated interest rate exceeds the market rate, and companies don't like to pay a stated interest higher than the market rate.

To illustrate a bond premium, let's change the Air West Airlines example. Assume that the market interest rate is 8% when Air West issues its 9%, five-year bonds. These 9% bonds are attractive in an 8% market, and investors will pay a premium to acquire them. Suppose the bonds are priced at 104 (104% of maturity value). In that case, Air West receives $104,000 cash upon issuance. Air West's entry to borrow money and issue these bonds is:

2008			
Jan. 1	Cash ($100,000 × 1.04)	104,000	
	Bonds Payable		100,000
	Premium on Bonds Payable		4,000
	Issued bonds at a premium.		

After posting, the bond accounts have these balances:

MAIN ACCOUNT		COMPANION ACCOUNT	
Bonds Payable		**Premium on Bonds Payable**	
	Credit balance 100,000		Credit balance 4,000

Bond carrying amount $104,000

Bonds Payable and the Premium account each carries a credit balance. The Premium is a companion account to Bonds Payable. Therefore, we add the Premium to Bonds Payable to determine the bond carrying amount. Air West Airlines would report these bonds payable as follows immediately after issuance:

Long-term liabilities:		
Bonds payable	$100,000	
Plus: Premium on bonds payable	4,000	$104,000

Interest Expense on Bonds Payable with a Premium

The 1% difference between the bonds' 9% stated interest rate and the 8% market rate creates the $4,000 premium. Air West borrows $104,000 but must pay back only $100,000 at maturity. The premium is like a saving of interest expense to Air West. The premium cuts Air West's cost of borrowing and reduces interest expense to 8%, the market rate. The amortization of bond premium decreases interest expense over the life of the bonds.

Straight-Line Amortization of Bond Premium

In our example, the beginning premium is $4,000, and there are 10 semiannual interest periods during the bonds' 5-year life. Therefore, 1/10 of the $4,000 ($400) of bond premium is amortized each interest period. Air West's first semiannual interest entry is:[2]

2008			
July 1	Interest Expense	4,100	
	Premium on Bonds Payable ($4,000/10)	400	
	Cash ($100,000 × 0.09 × 6/12)		4,500
	Paid interest and amortized premium.		

Interest expense of $4,100 is:

- The stated interest ($4,500, which is paid in cash)
- *Minus* the amortization of the premium ($400)

At July 1, 2008, immediately after amortizing the bond premium, the bonds have this carrying amount:

$103,600 [$100,000 + ($4,000 − $400)]

At December 31, 2008, the bonds' carrying amount will be:

$103,200 [$100,000 + ($4,000 − $400 − $400)]

At maturity on January 1, 2013, the bond premium will have been fully amortized, and the bonds' carrying amount will be $100,000.

Now we move on to some additional bond topics.

Additional Bond Topics

3 Account for retirement and conversion of bonds payable

Companies that issue bonds payable face additional issues, such as:

- Adjusting entries for bonds payable
- Issuance of bonds payable between interest dates
- Retirement of bonds payable
- Convertible bonds payable
- Reporting bonds payable on the balance sheet
- Advantages and disadvantages of issuing bonds versus stock

Adjusting Entries for Bonds Payable

Companies issue bonds payable whenever they need cash. The interest payments seldom occur on December 31, so interest expense must be accrued at year end. The accrual entry should also amortize any bond discount or premium.

[2]The payment of interest and the amortization of bond premium can be recorded in separate entries as follows:

2008			
July 1	Interest Expense	4,500	
	Cash ($100,000 × 0.09 × 6/12)		4,500
	Paid semiannual interest.		
July 1	Premium on Bonds Payable ($4,000/10)	400	
	Interest Expense		400
	Amortized premium on bonds payable.		

These two entries record the same amount of interest expense ($4,100) as the single entry shown above.

Suppose Air West Airlines issued $100,000 of 8%, 10-year bonds at a $2,000 discount on October 1, 2009. The interest payments occur on March 31 and September 30 each year. On December 31, Air West accrues interest and amortizes bond discount for three months (October, November, and December) as follows:

2009			
Dec. 31	Interest Expense	2,050	
	Interest Payable ($100,000 × 0.08 × 3/12)		2,000
	Discount on Bonds Payable ($2,000/10 × 3/12)		50
	Accrued interest and amortized discount.		

Interest Payable is credited for three months (October, November, and December). Discount on Bonds Payable must also be amortized for these three months.

The next semiannual interest payment occurs on March 31, 2010, and Air West makes this journal entry:

2010			
Mar. 31	Interest Payable (from Dec. 31)	2,000	
	Interest Expense	2,050	
	Cash ($100,000 × 0.08 × 6/12)		4,000
	Discount on Bonds Payable ($2,000/10 × 3/12)		50
	Paid interest and amortized discount.		

Amortization of a bond premium is similar except that Premium on Bonds Payable is debited.

Issuing Bonds Payable Between Interest Dates

In most of the examples we've seen thus far, Air West Airlines issued bonds payable on an interest date, such as January 1. Corporations can also issue bonds between interest dates. That creates a complication.

Air West Airlines has $100,000 of 8% bonds payable that are dated January 1. That means the interest starts accruing on January 1.

Suppose Air West issues these bonds on April 1. How should we account for the interest for January, February, and March? At issuance on April 1, Air West collects three months' accrued interest from the bondholder and records the issuance of bonds payable as follows:

2008			
April 1	Cash	102,000	
	Bonds Payable		100,000
	Interest Payable ($100,000 × 0.08 × 3/12)		2,000
	Issued bonds two months after the date of the bonds.		

Companies don't split up interest payments. They pay in six-month or annual amounts as stated on the bond certificate.

On the next interest date, Air West will pay six months' interest to whoever owns the bonds at that time. But Air West will have interest expense only for the three months the bonds have been outstanding (April, May, and June). To allocate interest expense to the correct months, Air West makes this entry on July 1 for the customary six-month interest payment:

2008			
July 1	Interest Payable (from April 1)	2,000	
	Interest Expense (for April, May, June)	2,000	
	Cash ($100,000 × 0.08 × 6/12)		4,000
	Paid interest.		

Retirement of Bonds Payable

Normally, companies wait until maturity to pay off, or *retire,* their bonds payable. The basic retirement entry debits Bonds Payable and credits Cash, as we saw earlier. But companies sometimes retire their bonds prior to maturity. The main reason is to relieve the pressure of paying interest.

Some bonds are **callable**, which means the company may *call,* or pay off, the bonds at a specified price. The call price is usually 100 or a few percentage points above par value, perhaps 101 or 102. Callable bonds give the issuer the flexibility to pay off the bonds whenever it is beneficial. An alternative to calling the bonds is to purchase them in the open market at their current market price. Whether the bonds are called or purchased in the open market, the journal entry is the same.

Suppose Air West Airlines has $700,000 of bonds payable outstanding with a remaining discount of $30,000. Lower interest rates have convinced management to pay off these bonds now. These bonds are callable at 100. If the market price of the bonds is 95, will Air West call the bonds at 100 or purchase them in the open market at 95? The market price is lower than the call price, so Air West will pay off the bonds at their market price. Retiring the bonds at 95 results in a gain of $5,000, computed as follows:

Maturity value of bonds being retired	$700,000
Less: Discount	(30,000)
Carrying amount of bonds payable	670,000
Market price ($700,000 × 0.95) paid to retire the bonds	665,000
Gain on retirement of bonds payable	$ 5,000

The following entry records retirement of the bonds, immediately after an interest date:

June 30	Bonds Payable	700,000	
	Discount on Bonds Payable		30,000
	Cash ($700,000 × 0.95)		665,000
	Gain on Retirement of Bonds Payable		5,000
	Retired bonds payable.		

After posting, the bond accounts have zero balances.

Bonds Payable	
Retirement 700,000	Prior balance 700,000

Discount on Bonds Payable	
Prior balance 30,000	Retirement 30,000

The journal entry removes the bonds from the books and records a gain on retirement. Any existing premium would be removed with a debit. If Air West retired only half of these bonds, it would remove only half the discount or premium.

When retiring bonds before maturity, follow these steps:

1. Record partial-period amortization of discount or premium if the retirement date does not fall on an interest date.
2. Write off the portion of Discount or Premium that relates to the bonds being retired.
3. Credit a gain or debit a loss on retirement.

Convertible Bonds Payable

Convertible bonds are popular both with investors and with companies needing to borrow money. **Convertible bonds** may be converted into common stock at the option of the investor. These bonds combine the benefits of interest and principal on the bonds with the opportunity for a gain on the stock. The conversion feature is so attractive that investors accept a lower interest rate than on non-convertible bonds. For example, Amazon.com's convertible bonds payable carry an interest rate of only 4 3/4%. The low interest benefits Amazon.com.

The issuance of convertible bonds payable is recorded like any other debt: Debit Cash and credit Convertible Bonds Payable. Then, if the market price of Amazon's stock rises above the value of the bonds, the bondholders will convert the bonds into stock. The corporation then debits the bond accounts and credits the stock. The carrying amount of the bonds becomes the book value of the newly issued stock. There is no gain or loss.

Assume the Amazon bondholders convert $100,000 of Amazon's bonds payable into 20,000 shares of Amazon's common stock, which has a par value of $0.01 (1 cent) per share. Assume further that the carrying amount of the Amazon bonds is $90,000; thus, there is a bond discount of $10,000. To record the conversion, Amazon would make this journal entry:

May 14	Bonds Payable	100,000	
	Discount on Bonds Payable ($100,000 – $90,000)		10,000
	Common Stock (20,000 × $0.01)		200
	Paid-In Capital in Excess of Par		89,800
	Recorded conversion of bonds payable.		

The entry zeroes out the Bonds Payable account and its related Discount exactly as for a bond retirement. This journal entry transfers the carrying amount of the bonds ($90,000) to stockholders' equity, as follows:

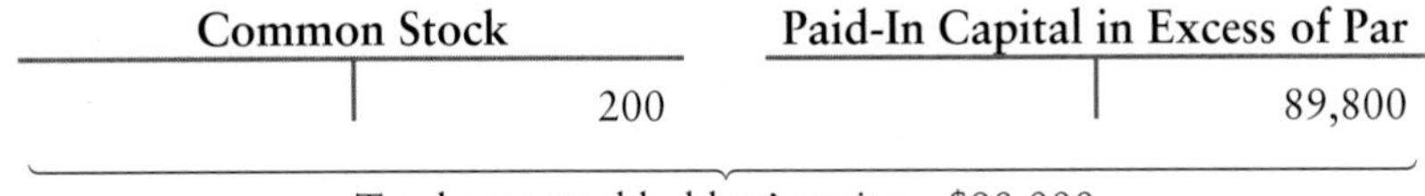

Reporting Liabilities on the Balance Sheet

4 Report liabilities on the balance sheet

Companies report their bonds payable and notes payable among the liabilities on the balance sheet. As we have seen throughout, there are two categories of liabilities, current and long-term.

Serial bonds are payable in installments. The portion payable within one year is a current liability, and the remaining debt is long-term. For example, assume that Toys "Я" Us has $500,000 of bonds payable maturing in $100,000 amounts each year for the next 5 years. The portion payable next year is $100,000. This amount is a current liability, and the remaining $400,000 is a long-term liability. Toys "Я" Us would report the following among its liabilities:

Current liabilities:	
Bonds payable, current	$100,000
Long-term liabilities:	
Bonds payable, long-term	400,000

Notes payable are reported in a similar fashion. We show bonds payable with a discount on page 651 and bonds payable with a premium on page 647.

Advantages and Disadvantages of Issuing Bonds Versus Stock

Borrowing by issuing bonds payable carries a risk: The company may be unable to pay off the bonds. Why then do companies borrow so heavily? Because bonds are a cheaper source of money than stock. Borrowing can help a company increase its earnings per share. Companies thus face this decision: How shall we finance a new project—with bonds or with stock?

Suppose Air West Airlines has net income of $300,000 and 100,000 shares of common stock outstanding before the new project. Air West needs $500,000 for the project and the company is considering two plans:

- Plan 1 is to borrow $500,000 at 10% (issue $500,000 of 10% bonds payable).
- Plan 2 is to issue 50,000 shares of common stock for $500,000.

Air West management believes the new cash can be used to earn income of $200,000 before interest and taxes.

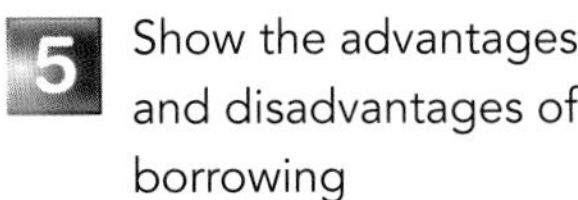

5 Show the advantages and disadvantages of borrowing

Exhibit 13-4 shows the earnings-per-share (EPS) advantage of borrowing.

EXHIBIT 13-4 **Earnings-per-Share Advantage of Borrowing Versus Issuing Stock**

	Plan 1 Issue $500,000 of 10% Bonds Payable		Plan 2 Issue $500,000 of Common Stock	
Net income before new project		$300,000		$300,000
Expected income on the new project before interest and income tax expenses	$200,000		$200,000	
Less: Interest expense ($500,000 × 0.10)	(50,000)		0	
Project income before income tax	150,000		200,000	
Less: Income tax expense (40%)	(60,000)		(80,000)	
Project net income		90,000		120,000
Net income with new project		$390,000		$420,000
Earnings per share with new project:				
Plan 1 ($390,000/100,000 shares)		$3.90		
Plan 2 ($420,000/150,000 shares)				$2.80

EPS is higher if Air West issues bonds. If all goes well, the company can earn more on the new project ($90,000) than the interest it pays on the bonds ($50,000). Earning more income on borrowed money than the related interest expense is called using **leverage**. It is widely used to increase earnings per share of common stock.

Borrowing can increase EPS, but borrowing has its disadvantages. Debts must be paid during bad years as well as good years. Interest expense may be high enough to eliminate net income and even lead to bankruptcy. This happens to lots of ambitious companies.

Now let's wrap up the chapter with some Decision Guidelines.

Decision Guidelines

LONG-TERM LIABILITIES—PART B

Suppose Air West Airlines needs $50 million to purchase airplanes. Air West issues bonds payable to finance the purchase and now must account for the bonds payable.

The Decision Guidelines outline some of the issues Air West must decide.

Decision	Guidelines
What happens to the bonds' carrying amount when bonds payable are issued at	
• Maturity (par) value? →	• Carrying amount *stays* at maturity (par) value.
• A premium? →	• Carrying amount *falls* gradually to maturity value.
• A discount? →	• Carrying amount *rises* gradually to maturity value.

How to account for the retirement of bonds payable?	**At maturity date:**
	Bonds Payable .... Maturity value
	  Cash .... Maturity value
	
	Before maturity date (assume a discount on the bonds and a gain on retirement):
	Bonds Payable .... Maturity value
	  Discount on Bonds Payable .... Balance
	  Cash .... Amount Paid
	  Gain on Retirement of Bonds Payable ... Excess

How to account for the conversion of convertible bonds payable into common stock? (Assume a bond premium.)	Bonds Payable .... Maturity value
	Premium on Bonds Payable .... Balance
	  Common Stock .... Par value
	  Paid-in Capital in Excess of Par .... Excess over par value

What are the advantages of financing operations with	
• Stock? →	• Creates no liability or interest expense. Less risky to the issuing corporation.
• Bonds (or notes) payable? →	• Results in higher earnings per share—under normal conditions.

Summary Problem 2

Trademark, Inc., has outstanding a $100,000 issue of 6% convertible bonds payable that mature in 2026. Suppose the bonds were dated April 1, 2006, and pay interest each April 1 and October 1.

Requirements

Record the following transactions for Trademark:

a. **Issuance of the bonds at 104.8 on April 1, 2006.**

b. **Payment of interest and amortization of premium on October 1, 2006.**

c. **Accrual of interest and amortization of premium on December 31, 2006.**

d. **Payment of interest and amortization of premium on April 1, 2007.**

e. **Conversion of one-half of the bonds payable into no-par common stock on April 1, 2007.**

f. **Retirement of one-half of the bonds payable on April 1, 2007. Purchase price to retire the bonds was 102.**

Solution

	Date	Accounts and Explanation	Debit	Credit
	2006			
a.	April 1	Cash ($100,000 × 1.048)	104,800	
		Bonds Payable		100,000
		Premium on Bonds Payable		4,800
		Issued bonds at a premium.		
b.	Oct. 1	Interest Expense	2,880	
		Premium on Bonds Payable ($4,800/40)	120	
		Cash ($100,000 × 0.06 × 6/12)		3,000
		Paid interest and amortized premium.		
c.	Dec. 31	Interest Expense	1,440	
		Premium on Bonds Payable ($4,800/40 × 1/2)	60	
		Interest Payable ($100,000 × 0.06 × 3/12)		1,500
		Accrued interest and amortized premium.		
	2007			
d.	April 1	Interest Payable (from Dec. 31)	1,500	
		Interest Expense	1,440	
		Premium on Bonds Payable ($4,800/40 × 1/2)	60	
		Cash ($100,000 × 0.06 × 6/12)		3,000
e.	April 1	Bonds Payable ($100,000 × 1/2)	50,000	
		Premium on Bonds Payable		
		[($4,800 – $120 – $60 – $60) × 1/2]	2,280	
		Common Stock		52,280
		Recorded conversion of bonds payable.		
f.	April 1	Bonds Payable ($100,000 × 1/2)	50,000	
		Premium on Bonds Payable		
		[($4,800 – $120 – $60 – $60) × 1/2]	2,280	
		Cash ($50,000 × 1.02)		51,000
		Gain on Retirement of Bonds Payable		1,280
		Retired bonds payable.		

Review Long-Term Liabilities

Accounting Vocabulary

Bond Discount
Excess of a bond's maturity value over its issue price. Also called a **discount (on a bond)**.

Bond Premium
Excess of a bond's issue price over its maturity value. Also called a **premium**.

Bonds Payable
Groups of notes payable issued to multiple lenders called bondholders.

Callable Bonds
Bonds that the issuer may call or pay off at a specified price whenever the issuer wants.

Convertible Bonds
Bonds that may be converted into the common stock of the issuing company at the option of the investor.

Debentures
Unsecured bonds backed only by the good faith of the borrower.

Discount (on a bond)
Excess of a bond's maturity value over its issue price. Also called a **bond discount.**

Effective Interest Rate
Interest rate that investors demand in order to loan their money. Also called the **market interest rate**.

Leverage
Earning more income on borrowed money than the related interest expense, thereby increasing the earnings for the owners of the business.

Market Interest Rate
Interest rate that investors demand in order to loan their money. Also called the **effective interest rate**.

Maturity (par) value
A bond issued at par has no discount on premium.

Mortgage
Borrower's promise to transfer the legal title to certain assets to the lender if the debt is not paid on schedule.

Par Value
Another name for the maturity value of a bond.

Premium
Excess of a bond's issue price over its maturity value. Also called **bond premium.**

Present Value
Amount a person would invest now to receive a greater amount in the future.

Secured Bonds
Bonds that give bondholders the right to take specified assets of the issuer if the issuer fails to pay principal or interest.

Serial Bonds
Bonds that mature in installments over a period of time.

Stated Interest Rate
Interest rate that determines the amount of cash interest the borrower pays and the investor receives each year.

Term Bonds
Bonds that all mature at the same time for a particular lease.

Quick Check

1. Which type of bond is unsecured?
   a. Common bond
   b. Mortgage bond
   c. Serial bond
   d. Debenture bond

2. A $100,000 bond priced at 103.5 can be bought or sold for
   a. $100,000 + interest
   b. $103,500
   c. $3,500
   d. $10,350

3. Which interest rate on a bond determines the amount of the semiannual interest payment?
   a. Market rate
   b. Effective rate
   c. Stated rate
   d. Semiannual rate

4. The final journal entry to record for bonds payable is

a. Bonds Payable	XXX	
Cash		XXX
b. Cash	XXX	
Bonds Payable		XXX
c. Interest Expense	XXX	
Cash		XXX
d. Discount on Bonds Payable	XXX	
Interest Expense		XXX

5. Lafferty Corporation's bonds payable carry a stated interest rate of 7%, and the market rate of interest is 8%. The price of the Lafferty bonds will be at
   a. Par value
   b. Maturity value
   c. Premium
   d. Discount

6. Bonds issued at a premium always have
   a. Interest expense equal to the interest payments
   b. Interest expense greater than the interest payments
   c. Interest expense less than the interest payments
   d. None of the above

7. Galena Park Fitness Gym has $500,000 of 10-year bonds payable outstanding. These bonds had a discount of $40,000 at issuance, which was 5 years ago. The company uses the straight-line amortization method. The carrying amount of these bonds payable is

   a. $480,000
   b. $460,000
   c. $500,000
   d. $540,000

8. Nick Spanos Antiques issued its 8%, 10-year bonds payable at a price of $440,000 (maturity value is $500,000). The company uses the straight-line amortization method for the bonds. Interest expense for each year is

   a. $35,200
   b. $46,000
   c. $44,000
   d. $50,000

9. Spice Inc. issued bonds payable on December 31. Spice's bonds were dated July 31. Which statement is true of Spice's journal entry to record issuance of the bonds payable?

   a. Spice must pay one month's accrued interest.
   b. Spice will collect one month's accrued interest in advance.
   c. Spice will collect five months' accrued interest in advance.
   d. Spice will pay five months' interest in advance.

10. Bull & Bear, Inc., retired $100,000 of its bonds payable, paying cash of $103,000. On the retirement date, the bonds payable had a premium of $2,000. The bond retirement created a

   a. Loss of $1,000
   b. Loss of $3,000
   c. Gain of $5,000
   d. Loss of $5,000

Answers are given after Apply Your Knowledge (p. 678).

Assess Your Progress

Short Exercises

Determining bond prices at par, discount, or premium

S13-1 Determine whether the following bonds payable will be issued at maturity value, at a premium, or at a discount: (pp. 642–643)

a. The market interest rate is 7%. Denver Corp. issues bonds payable with a stated rate of 6 1/2%. (pp. 642–643)

b. Houston, Inc., issued 7% bonds payable when the market rate was 6 3/4%.

c. Cincinnati Corporation issued 8% bonds when the market interest rate was 8%.

d. Miami Company issued bonds payable that pay stated interest of 7%. At issuance, the market interest rate was 8 1/4%.

Pricing bonds

S13-2 Compute the price of the following 7% bonds of Allied Telecom. (pp. 644–645)

a. $100,000 issued at 77.75

b. $100,000 issued at 103.8

c. $100,000 issued at 92.6

d. $100,000 issued at 102.5

Maturity value of a bond

S13-3 For which bond payable in Short Exercise 13-2 will Allied Telecom have to pay the most at maturity? Explain your answer. (pp. 643–644)

Journalizing basic bond payable transactions

S13-4 Hunter Corporation issued a $100,000, 6 1/2%, 10-year bond payable. Journalize the following transactions for Hunter. Include an explanation for each entry.

a. Issuance of the bond payable at par on January 1, 2008. (pp. 645–646)

b. Payment of semiannual cash interest on July 1, 2008. (pp. 645–646)

c. Payment of the bond payable at maturity. (Give the date.) (pp. 645–646)

Determining bonds payable amounts

S13-5 Sonic Drive-Ins borrowed money by issuing $1,000,000 of 6% bonds payable at 96.5.

1. How much cash did Sonic receive when it issued the bonds payable? (pp. 648, 651)
2. How much must Sonic pay back at maturity? (pp. 648, 651)
3. How much cash interest will Sonic pay each six months? (pp. 648, 651)

Bond interest rates

S13-6 A 7%, 10-year bond was issued at a price of 93. Was the market interest rate at the date of issuance closest to 6%, 7%, or 8%? Explain. (pp. 642–643, 646–647)

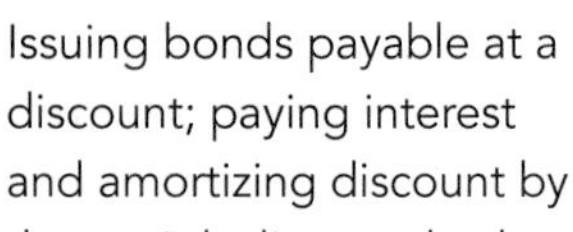

Issuing bonds payable at a discount; paying interest and amortizing discount by the straight-line method

S13-7 Ogden, Inc., issued a $50,000, 8%, 10-year bond payable at a price of 90 on January 1, 2006. Journalize the following transactions for Ogden. Include an explanation for each entry.

a. Issuance of the bond payable on January 1, 2006. (pp. 646–647)

b. Payment of semiannual interest and amortization of bond discount on July 1, 2006. Ogden uses the straight-line method to amortize bond discount. (pp. 648, 651)

Issuing bonds payable at a premium; paying interest and amortizing premium by the straight-line method

S13-8 Washington Mutual Insurance Company issued an $80,000, 7%, 10-year bond payable at a price of 110 on January 1, 2009. Journalize the following transactions for Washington. Include an explanation for each entry.

a. Issuance of the bond payable on January 1, 2009. (pp. 652–653)

b. Payment of semiannual interest and amortization of bond premium on July 1, 2009. Washington uses the straight-line method to amortize the premium. (pp. 652–653)

Issuing bonds payable and accruing interest

S13-9 Onstar Communication issued $100,000 of 6%, 10-year bonds payable on October 1, 2008, at par value. Onstar's accounting year ends on December 31. Journalize the following transactions. Include an explanation for each entry.

a. Issuance of the bonds on October 1, 2008. (pp. 645–646)

b. Accrual of interest expense on December 31, 2008. (pp. 652–653)

c. Payment of the first semiannual interest amount on April 1, 2009. (pp. 652–653)

Issuing bonds payable between interest dates and then paying the interest

S13-10 Simons Realty issued $250,000 of 6%, 10-year bonds payable at par value on May 1, 2006, four months after the bond's original issue date of January 1, 2006. Journalize the following transactions. Include an explanation for each entry.

a. Issuance of the bonds payable on May 1, 2006. (pp. 652–653)

b. Payment of the first semiannual interest amount on July 1, 2006. (p. 654)

Accounting for the retirement of bonds payable
3

S13-11 On January 1, 2007, Pacifica, Inc., issued $100,000 of 9%, 5-year bonds payable at 104. Pacifica has extra cash and wishes to retire the bonds payable on January 1, 2008, immediately after making the second semiannual interest payment. To retire the bonds, Pacifica pays the market price of 98.

1. What is Pacifica's carrying amount of the bonds payable on the retirement date? (p. 654)
2. How much cash must Pacifica pay to retire the bonds payable? (p. 654)
3. Compute Pacifica's gain or loss on the retirement of the bonds payable. (p. 654)

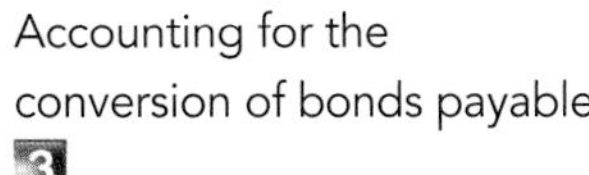

Accounting for the conversion of bonds payable
3

S13-12 Newmarket Corp. has $1,000,000 of convertible bonds payable outstanding, with a bond premium of $20,000 also on the books. The bondholders have notified Newmarket that they wish to convert the bonds into stock. Specifically, the bonds may be converted into 400,000 shares of Newmarket's $1 par common stock.

1. What is Newmarket's carrying amount of its convertible bonds payable prior to the conversion? (p. 655)
2. Journalize Newmarket's conversion of the bonds payable into common stock. No explanation is required. (p. 655)

Reporting liabilities

4

S13-13 Master Suites Hotels includes the following selected accounts in its general ledger at December 31, 2008:

Notes payable, long-term	$100,000	Accounts payable	$32,000
Bonds payable	200,000	Discount on bonds payable	6,000
Interest payable (due next year)	1,000		

Prepare the liabilities section of Master Suites' balance sheet at December 31, 2008, to show how the company would report these items. Report a total for current liabilities. (pp. 518, 656–657)

Earnings-per-share effects of financing with bonds versus stock

S13-14 Speegleville Marina needs to raise $1 million to expand. Speegleville's president is considering two plans:

- Plan A: Issue $1,000,000 of 8% bonds payable to borrow the money
- Plan B: Issue 100,000 shares of common stock at $10 per share

Before any new financing, the company expects to earn net income of $300,000, and the company already has 100,000 shares of common stock outstanding. Speegleville believes the expansion will increase income before interest and income tax by $200,000. The income tax rate is 35%.

Prepare an analysis similar to Exhibit 13-4 to determine which plan is likely to result in higher earnings per share. Which financing plan would you recommend? (p. 656–657)

Exercises

Determining whether the bond price will be at par, at a discount, or at a premium

1

E13-15 Havens Corp. is planning to issue long-term bonds payable to borrow for a major expansion. The chief executive, Richie Havens, asks your advice on some related matters, as follows:

a. At what type of bond price will Havens have total interest expense equal to the cash interest payments? (pp. 645–646)

b. Under which type of bond price will Havens's total interest expense be greater than the cash interest payments? (p. 648)

c. The stated interest rate on the bonds is 7%, and the market interest rate is 8%. What type of bond price can Havens expect for the bonds? (pp. 642–643)

d. Havens could raise the stated interest rate on the bonds to 9% (market rate is 8%). In that case, what type of price can Havens expect for the bonds? (pp. 642–643)

Issuing bonds payable, paying interest, and amortizing discount by the straight-line method

E13-16 On January 1, Deutsch Limited issues 8%, 20-year bonds payable with a maturity value of $100,000. The bonds sell at 97 and pay interest on January 1 and July 1. Deutsch amortizes bond discount by the straight-line method. Record (a) issuance of the bonds on January 1, and (b) the semiannual interest payment and amortization of bond discount on July 1. (pp. 646–651)

Issuing bonds payable, paying and accruing interest

E13-17 Pluto Corporation issued $400,000 of 7%, 20-year bonds payable on March 31, 2006. The bonds were issued at 100 and pay interest on March 31 and September 30. Record (a) issuance of the bonds on March 31, 2006, (b) payment of interest on September 30, (c) accrual of interest on December 31, and (d) payment of interest on March 31, 2007. (pp. 645–646)

Bond transactions at par, at a discount, and at a premium

E13-18 Columbus, Inc., issued $50,000 of 10-year, 6% bonds payable on January 1, 2006. Columbus pays interest each January 1 and July 1 and amortizes discount or premium by the straight-line method. The company can issue its bonds payable under various conditions:

a. Issuance at par (maturity) value (pp. 645–646)

b. Issuance at a price of 95 (pp. 645–648)

c. Issuance at a price of 105 (pp. 652–653)

Requirements

1. Journalize Columbus's issuance of the bonds and first semiannual interest payment for each situation. Explanations are not required.
2. Which bond price results in the most interest expense for Columbus? Explain in detail. (pp. 648, 652–653)

Issuing bonds, accruing interest, and paying interest

E13-19 Fleetwood Homebuilders issued $200,000 of 6%, 10-year bonds at par on August 31. Fleetwood pays semiannual interest on February 28 and August 31. Journalize for Fleetwood:

a. Issuance of the bonds payable on August 31, 2007. (pp. 645–646)

b. Accrual of interest on December 31, 2007. (pp. 652–653)

c. Payment of semiannual interest on February 28, 2008. (pp. 652–653)

Issuing bonds between interest dates

E13-20 Saturn Corporation issued $400,000 of 6% bonds payable on June 30. The bonds were dated April 30, and the semiannual interest dates are April 30 and October 31.

1. How much cash will Saturn receive upon issuance of the bonds on June 30? (pp. 652–653)
2. How much cash interest will Saturn pay on October 31, the first semiannual interest date? (p. 654)

Issuing bonds between interest dates and paying interest

E13-21 Lakewood Co. issues $100,000 of 6%, 20-year bonds payable that are dated April 30. Record (a) issuance of bonds at par on May 31 and (b) the next semiannual interest payment on October 31.

Recording retirement of bonds payable

3

E13-22 Virtuoso Transportation issued $600,000 of 8% bonds payable at 97 on October 1, 2010. These bonds are callable at 100 and mature on October 1, 2018. Virtuoso pays interest each April 1 and October 1. On October 1, 2015, when the bonds' market price is 99, Virtuoso retires the bonds in the most economical way available.

continued . . .

Requirement

Record the payment of the interest and amortization of bond discount at October 1, 2015, and the retirement of the bonds on that date. Virtuoso uses the straight-line amortization method.

Recording conversion of bonds payable

E13-23 Worldview Magazine, Inc., issued $700,000 of 15-year, 8 1/2% convertible bonds payable on July 31, 2006, at a price of 98. Each $1,000 maturity amount of the bonds is convertible into 50 shares of $5 par stock. On July 31, 2009, bondholders converted the bonds into common stock.

Requirements

1. What would cause the bondholders to convert their bonds into common stock?
2. Without making journal entries, compute the carrying amount of the bonds payable at July 31, 2009. The company uses the straight-line method to amortize bond discount.
3. All amortization has been recorded properly. Journalize the conversion transaction at July 31, 2009. No explanation is required.

Recording early retirement and conversion of bonds payable

E13-24 Superhero Industries reported the following at September 30:

Long-term liabilities:		
Convertible bonds payable	$200,000	
Less: Discount on bonds payable	(12,000)	$188,000

Requirements

1. Record retirement of half of the bonds on October 1 at the call price of 101.
2. Record conversion of the remainder of the bonds into 10,000 shares of Superhero Industries $1 par common stock on October 1. What would cause the bondholders to convert their bonds into stock?

Reporting liabilities

E13-25 At December 31, MediShare Precision Instruments owes $50,000 on accounts payable, plus salary payable of $10,000 and income tax payable of $8,000. MediShare also has $200,000 of bonds payable that require payment of a $20,000 installment next year and the remainder in later years. The bonds payable require an annual interest payment of $7,000, and MediShare still owes this interest for the current year.

Report MediShare's liabilities on its classified balance sheet. List the current liabilities in descending order (largest first, and so on), and show the total of current liabilities. (pp. 518, 656–657)

Analyzing alternative plans for raising money

5

E13-26 MC Electronics is considering two plans for raising $1,000,000 to expand operations. Plan A is to issue 9% bonds payable, and plan B is to issue 100,000 shares of common stock. Before any new financing, MC has net income of $300,000 and 100,000 shares of common stock outstanding. Management believes the company can use the new funds to earn additional income of $420,000 before interest and taxes. The income tax rate is 40%.

Requirement

Analyze MC Electronics' situation to determine which plan will result in higher earnings per share. Use Exhibit 13-4 as a guide. (pp. 656–657)

Analyzing bond transactions

E13-27 This (partial and adapted) advertisement appeared in *The Wall Street Journal*.

New Issue

$300,000,000

HEWITT CORPORATION

10.5% Subordinated Debentures due March 31, 2015
interest payable March 31 and September 30

Price 98.50% **March 31, 2005**

A *subordinated* debenture gives rights to the bondholder that are more restricted than the rights of other bondholders.

Requirements

Answer these questions about Hewitt Corporation's debenture bonds payable:

1. Hewitt issued these bonds payable at their offering price on March 31, 2005. Describe the transaction in detail, indicating who received cash, who paid cash, and how much.
2. Why is the stated interest rate on these bonds so high?
3. Compute Hewitt's annual cash interest payment on the bonds.
4. Compute Hewitt's annual interest expense under the straight-line amortization method.

Analyzing bond transactions

1

E13-28 Refer to the bond situation of Hewitt Corporation in Exercise 13-27. Hewitt issued the bonds at the advertised price. The company uses the straight-line amortization method and reports financial statements on a calendar-year basis.

Requirements

1. Journalize the following bond transactions of Hewitt Corporation. Explanations are not required.

2005	
Mar. 31	Issuance of the bonds.
Sep. 30	Payment of interest expense and amortization of discount on bonds payable.

continued . . .

2. What is Hewitt's carrying amount of the bonds payable at
   a. September 30, 2005?
   b. March 31, 2006?

Problems (Group A)

Analyzing bonds, recording bonds at par, and reporting on the financial statements

P13-29A Environmental Concerns Limited (ECL) issued $500,000 of 10-year, 6% bonds payable at maturity (par) value on May 1, 2008. The bonds pay interest each April 30 and October 31, and the company ends its accounting year on December 31.

Requirements

1. Fill in the blanks to complete these statements: (pp. 644–645)
   a. ECL's bonds are priced at (express the price as a percentage) _____. (pp. 644–645)
   b. When ECL issued its bonds, the market interest rate was _____%. (pp. 642–643)
   c. The amount of bond discount or premium for ECL to account for is $ _____ because the bonds were issued at _____. (pp. 645–646)
2. Journalize for ECL
   a. Issuance of the bonds payable on May 1, 2008. (pp. 645–646)
   b. Payment of interest on October 31, 2008. (pp. 645–646)
   c. Accrual of interest at December 31, 2008. (pp. 652–653)
   d. Payment of interest on April 30, 2009. (pp. 645–646)

   Explanations are not required.
3. Show what ECL will report on its income statement for 2008 and on its classified balance sheet at December 31, 2008. (pp. 656–657)

Issuing bonds and amortizing discount by the straight-line method

1 2

P13-30A On March 1, 2007, Educators Credit Union (ECU) issued 6%, 20-year bonds payable with maturity value of $300,000. The bonds pay interest on February 28 and August 31. ECU amortizes bond premium and discount by the straight-line method.

Requirements

1. If the market interest rate is 5% when ECU issues its bonds, will the bonds be priced at maturity (par) value, at a premium, or at a discount? Explain. (p. 647)
2. If the market interest rate is 7% when ECU issues its bonds, will the bonds be priced at par, at a premium, or at a discount? Explain. (p. 644)
3. The issue price of the bonds is 98. Journalize the following bond transactions:
   a. Issuance of the bonds on March 1, 2007. (pp. 652–653)
   b. Payment of interest and amortization of discount on August 31, 2007. (pp. 652–653)
   c. Accrual of interest and amortization of discount on December 31, 2007. (pp. 652–653)
   d. Payment of interest and amortization of discount on February 28, 2008. (pp. 652–653)

Determining bond price, recording bond transactions by the straight-line amortization method

P13-31A El Conquistador, Inc., finances operations with both bonds and stock. Suppose El Conquistador issued $500,000 of 10-year, 8% bonds payable under various market conditions. Match each market interest rate with the appropriate bond price, as follows. The three possible bond prices are $467,000; $500,000; and $536,000.

Market Interest Rate	Bond Price
7%	?
8%	?
9%	?

El Conquistador pays annual interest each December 31.

After determining the respective bond prices, make the following journal entries for the bond discount situation (explanations are not required):

Dec. 31, 2006	Issuance of the bonds at a discount. (pp. 646–647)
Dec. 31, 2007	Payment of interest and amortization of bond discount by the straight-line method. (pp. 648, 651)
Dec. 31, 2016	Payment of interest and amortization of bond discount by the straight-line method. (pp. 648, 651)
Dec. 31, 2016	Final payment of the bonds payable. (pp. 648, 651)

How much total interest expense will El Conquistador have during the 10-year life of these bonds?

Analyzing a company's long-term debt and journalizing its transactions

P13-32A Captain Billy Whizbang Hamburgers, Inc., issued 6%, 10-year bonds payable at 95 on December 31, 2005. At December 31, 2007, Captain Billy reported the bonds payable as follows:

Long-Term Debt:		
Bonds payable..................	$200,000	
Less: Discount..................	(8,000)	192,000

Captain Billy uses the straight-line amortization method and pays semiannual interest each June 30 and December 31.

Requirements

1. Answer the following questions about Captain Billy Whizbang's bonds payable:
   a. What is the maturity value of the bonds? (pp. 646–647)
   b. What is the carrying amount of the bonds at December 31, 2007? (pp. 646–647)
   c. What is the annual cash interest payment on the bonds? (pp. 648, 651)
   d. How much interest expense should the company record each year? (pp. 648, 651)
2. Record the June 30, 2008, semiannual interest payment and amortization of discount. (pp. 648, 651)
3. What will be the carrying amount of the bonds at December 31, 2008? (pp. 648, 651)

Recording bonds (at par) and reporting bonds payable on the balance sheet—bond issued between interest dates

P13-33A The board of directors of Changing Seasons Health Spa authorizes the issuance of $600,000 of 7%, 10-year bonds payable. The semiannual interest dates are May 31 and November 30. The bonds are issued on July 31, 2008, at par plus accrued interest.

Requirements

1. Journalize the following transactions:
   a. Issuance of the bonds on July 31, 2008.
   b. Payment of interest on November 30, 2008.
   c. Accrual of interest on December 31, 2008.
   d. Payment of interest on May 31, 2009.
2. Report interest payable and bonds payable as they would appear on the Changing Seasons balance sheet at December 31, 2008.

Reporting liabilities on the balance sheet

P13-34A The accounting records of Earthlink Wireless include the following:

Mortgage note payable, long-term	$77,000	Salary payable	$ 9,000
Accounts payable	74,000	Bonds payable, long-term	160,000
Bonds payable, current installment	20,000	Premium on bonds payable (all long-term)	13,000
Interest payable	14,000	Unearned service revenue	3,000
		Common stock, no par	100,000

Requirements

Report these liabilities on the Earthlink Wireless balance sheet, including headings and totals for current liabilities and long-term liabilities. (pp. 518, 646–647, 656–657)

Financing operations with debt or with stock

P13-35A Two businesses are considering how to raise $5 million.

Buchanan Corporation is having its best year since it began operations in 1998. For each of the past 10 years, earnings per share have increased by at least 15%. The outlook for the future is equally bright, with new markets opening up and competitors unable to manufacture products of Buchanan's quality. Buchanan Corporation is planning a large-scale expansion.

Garfield Company has fallen on hard times. Net income has been flat for the last 6 years, with this year falling by 10% from last year's level of profits. Top management has experienced turnover, and the company lacks leadership. To become competitive again, Garfield desperately needs $5 million for expansion.

Requirements

1. As an independent consultant, propose a plan for each company to raise the needed cash. Which company should issue bonds payable? Which company should issue stock? Consider the advantages and the disadvantages of raising money by issuing bonds and by issuing stock, and discuss them in your answer. Use the following memorandum headings to report your plans for the two companies. (pp. 656–657)
   - Plan for Buchanan Corporation to raise $5 million
   - Plan for Garfield Company to raise $5 million

continued . . .

Set up your memo as follows:

Date: ____________________

To: Managements of Buchanan Corporation and Garfield Company

From: (Student Name)

Subject: Plan for each company to raise $5 million

- Plan for Buchanan Corporation to raise $5 million
- Plan for Garfield Company to raise $5 million

2. How will what you learned in this problem help you manage a business?

Problems (Group B)

Analyzing bonds, recording bonds at par, and reporting on the financial statements

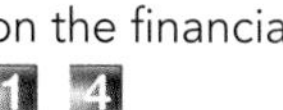

P13-36B Total Placement Service (TPS) issued $600,000 of 20-year, 7% bonds payable at maturity (par) value on February 1, 2008. The bonds pay interest each January 31 and July 31, and the company ends its accounting year on December 31.

1. Fill in the blanks to complete these statements:
   a. TPS's bonds are priced at (express the price as a percentage) _____. (pp. 644–646)
   b. When TPS issued its bonds, the market interest rate was _____ %. (pp. 642–643)
   c. The amount of bond discount or premium for TPS to account for is $_____ because the bonds were issued at _____. (pp. 645–646)
2. Journalize for TPS
   a. Issuance of the bonds payable on February 1, 2008. (pp. 645–646)
   b. Payment of interest on July 31, 2008. (pp. 645–646)
   c. Accrual of interest at December 31, 2008. (pp. 652–653)
   d. Payment of interest on January 31, 2009. (pp. 645–646)
   Explanations are not required.
3. Show what TPS will report on its income statement for the year ended December 31, 2008, and on its classified balance sheet at December 31, 2008. (pp. 656–657)

Issuing notes payable and amortizing premium by the straight-line method

P13-37B On April 1, 2006, US Ultracom issued 7%, 10-year bonds payable with maturity value of $400,000. The bonds pay interest on March 31 and September 30, and US Ultracom amortizes premium and discount by the straight-line method.

continued . . .

Requirements

1. If the market interest rate is 6 1/2% when US Ultracom issues its bonds, will the bonds be priced at maturity (par) value, at a premium, or at a discount? Explain. (pp. 643–644)
2. If the market interest rate is 8% when US Ultracom issues its bonds, will the bonds be priced at par, at a premium, or at a discount? Explain. (pp. 643–644)
3. Assume that the issue price of the bonds is 101. Journalize the following bonds payable transactions:
   a. Issuance of the bonds on April 1, 2006. (pp. 652–653)
   b. Payment of interest and amortization of premium on September 30, 2006. (pp. 652–653)
   c. Accrual of interest and amortization of premium on December 31, 2006. (pp. 652–653)
   d. Payment of interest and amortization of premium on March 31, 2007. (pp. 652–653)

Determining bond price; recording bond transactions by the straight-line amortization method

1 2 3

P13-38B Tristate Recreation Park (TRP) finances operations with both bonds and stock. Suppose TRP issued $200,000 of 10-year, 6% bonds payable under various market conditions. Match each market interest rate with the appropriate bond price, as follows. The three possible bond prices are $216,000; $200,000; and $186,000.

Market Interest Rate	Bond Price
7%	?
6%	?
5%	?

TRP pays annual interest each December 31.

After determining the respective bond prices, make the following journal entries for the bond premium situation (explanations are not required):

Dec. 31, 2008	Issuance of the bonds at a premium. (pp. 652–653)
Dec. 31, 2009	Payment of interest and amortization of bond premium by the straight-line method. (pp. 652–653)
Dec. 31, 2018	Payment of interest and amortization of bond premium by the straight-line method. (pp. 652–653)
Dec. 31, 2018	Final payment of the bonds payable. (pp. 652–653)

How much total interest expense will TRP have during the 10-year life of these bonds?

Analyzing a company's long-term debt and journalizing its transactions

P13-39B Holze Music Co. issued 5%, 10-year bonds payable at 75 on December 31, 2006. At December 31, 2009, Holze reported the bonds payable as follows:

Long-Term Debt:		
Bonds payable..................	$200,000	
Less: Discount..................	(35,000)	$165,000

Holze uses the straight-line amortization method.

continued . . .

Requirements

1. Answer the following questions about Holze's bonds payable:
   a. What is the maturity value of the bonds? (pp. 646–647)
   b. What is the carrying amount of the bonds at December 31, 2009? (pp. 646–647)
   c. What is Holze's annual cash interest payment on the bonds? (pp. 648, 651)
   d. How much interest expense should Holze record each year? (pp. 648, 651)
2. Holze pays annual interest for these bonds each year on December 31. Record the December 31, 2010, annual interest payment and amortization of discount. (pp. 648, 651)
3. What will be the carrying amount of the bonds at December 31, 2010? (pp. 648, 651)

Recording bonds (at par) and reporting bonds payable on the balance sheet—bonds issued between interest dates

P13-40B The board of directors of Beta North America, Inc., authorizes the issuance of $1 million of 9%, 20-year bonds payable. The semiannual interest dates are March 31 and September 30. The bonds are issued on April 30, 2007, at par plus accrued interest.

Requirements

1. Journalize the following transactions:
   a. Issuance of the bonds on April 30, 2007. (pp. 652–653)
   b. Payment of interest on September 30, 2007. (p. 654)
   c. Accrual of interest on December 31, 2007. (pp. 652–653)
   d. Payment of interest on March 31, 2008. (pp. 652–653)
2. Report interest payable and bonds payable as they would appear on the Beta balance sheet at December 31, 2007. (pp. 656–657)

Reporting liabilities on the balance sheet

4

P13-41B The accounting records of Compass Bookstores, Inc., include the following:

Accounts payable	$ 68,000	Salary payable	$32,000
Mortgage note payable—		Bonds payable, current portion	25,000
long-term	110,000	Discount on all bonds payable	
Interest payable	19,000	(all long-term)	10,000
Bonds payable, long-term	300,000	Income tax payable	16,000
Common stock, no par	155,000		

Requirement

Report these liabilities on Compass Bookstores' balance sheet, including headings and totals for current liabilities and long-term liabilities. (pp. 518, 646–647, 656–657)

Financing operations with debt or with stock

5

P13-42B Brigadier Homebuilders is embarking on a massive expansion. Plans call for building 100 homes within the next two years. Management estimates that the expansion will cost $15 million. The board of directors is considering obtaining the $15 million through issuing either bonds payable or common stock.

continued . . .

Requirements

1. Write a memo to company management. Discuss the advantages and disadvantages of issuing bonds and of issuing common stock to raise the needed cash. Use the following format for your memo (pp. 656–657):

Date:	____________________
To:	Management of Brigadier Homebuilders
From:	(Student Name)
Subject:	Advantages and disadvantages of issuing bonds and of issuing stock to raise $15 million for expansion

Advantages and disadvantages of issuing bonds:

Advantages and disadvantages of issuing stock:

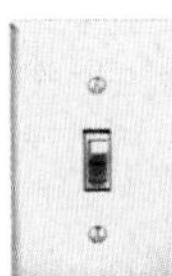

for 24-7 practice, visit www.MyAccountingLab.com

2. How will what you learned in this problem help you manage a business?

Apply Your Knowledge

Decision Cases

Questions about long-term debt

Case 1. The following questions are not related.

1. Duncan Brooks Co. needs to borrow $500,000 to open new stores. Brooks can borrow $500,000 by issuing 5%, 10-year bonds at a price of 96. How much will Brooks actually be borrowing under this arrangement? How much must Brooks pay back at maturity? How will Brooks account for the difference between the amount borrowed and the amount paid back? (pp. 646–647, 648, 651)

2. Brooks prefers to borrow for longer periods when interest rates are low and for shorter periods when interest rates are high. Why is this a good business strategy? (Challenge)

Analyzing alternative ways of raising $4 million

5

Case 2. Business is going well for Email Designers. The board of directors of this family-owned company believes that Email Designers could earn an additional $1,000,000 income before interest and taxes by expanding into new markets. However, the $4,000,000 the business needs for growth cannot be raised within the family. The directors, who strongly wish to retain family control of the company, must issue securities to outsiders. They are considering three financing plans.

Plan A is to borrow at 6%. Plan B is to issue 100,000 shares of common stock. Plan C is to issue 100,000 shares of nonvoting, $2.50 preferred stock ($2.50 is the annual cash dividend for each share of preferred stock). Email Designers currently has net income of $1,200,000 and 400,000 shares of common stock outstanding. The company's income tax rate is 40%.

Requirements

1. Prepare an analysis similar to Exhibit 13-4 to determine which plan will result in the highest earnings per share of common stock. (pp. 656–657)

2. Recommend one plan to the board of directors. Give your reasons.

Ethical Issue

Axiom Sports Co. owes $5 million on notes payable that will come due for payment in $2.5 million annual installments, starting next year. Cash is scarce, and Axiom management doesn't know where next year's note payment will come from. Axiom has prepared its balance sheet as follows:

Liabilities	
Current:	
Accounts payable	$1,900,000
Salary payable and other accrued liabilities	300,000
Unearned revenue collected in advance	500,000
Income tax payable	200,000
Total current liabilities	2,900,000
Long-term:	
Notes payable	5,000,000

What is wrong with the way Axiom reported its liabilities? Why did Axiom report its liabilities this way? What is unethical about this way of reporting *these* liabilities? Who can be harmed as a result?

Financial Statement Case

Analyzing long-term debt

1 2

The Amazon.com balance sheet, income statement (statement of operations), and Note 4 in Appendix A at the end of this book provide details about the company's long-term debt. Use those data to answer the following questions.

Requirements

1. How much did Amazon.com owe on long-term debt at December 31, 2005? How much of this debt was payable in the coming year?
2. Journalize in a single entry Amazon's interest expense for 2005. Amazon paid cash of $105 million for interest.
3. Refer to Note 4 and compute the annual interest on Amazon's 4.75% convertible subordinated notes. Round to the nearest $1 thousand.

Team Project

Each member of the team should select a large corporation and go to its Web site. Surf around until you find the company's balance sheet. Often the appropriate tab is labeled as

- Investor Relations
- About the Company
- Financial Reports
- 10-K Report

From the company's balance sheet scroll down until you find the liabilities.

Requirements

1. List all the company's liabilities—both current and long-term—along with each amount.
2. Read the company's notes to the financial statements and include any details that help you identify the amount of a liability.
3. Compute the company's current ratio and debt ratio. (p. 214)
4. Bring your findings to your team meeting, compare your results with those of your team members, and prepare either a written report or an oral report, as directed by your instructor.

For Internet exercises, Excel in Practice, and additional online activities, go to the Web site www.prenhall.com/horngren.

Quick Check Answers

1. *d* 2. *b* 3. *c* 4. *a* 5. *d* 6. *c* 7. *a* 8. *b* 9. *c* 10. *a*

Appendix 13A

The Time Value of Money: Present Value of a Bond and Effective-Interest Amortization

The term *time value of money* refers to the fact that money earns interest over time. Interest is the cost of using money. To borrowers, interest is the expense of renting money. To lenders, interest is the revenue earned from lending. In this chapter we focus on the borrower, who owes money on the bonds payable.

Present Value

Often a person knows a future amount, such as the maturity value of a bond, and needs to know the bond's present value. The present value of the bond measures its price and tells an investor how much to pay for the bond.

Present Value of 1

Suppose an investment promises you $5,000 at the *end* of one year. How much would you pay *now* to acquire this investment? You would be willing to pay the present value of the $5,000 future amount.

Present value depends on three factors:

1. the amount to be received in the future
2. the time span between your investment and your future receipt
3. the interest rate

Computing a present value is called *discounting* because the present value is *always less* than the future value.

In our example, the future receipt is $5,000. The investment period is one year. Assume that you demand an annual interest rate of 10% on your investment. The following diagram shows that the present value of $5,000 at 10% for one year is $4,545.

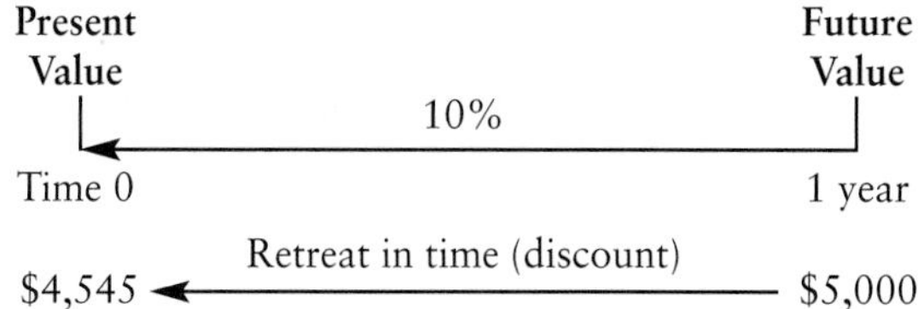

You can compute the present value of $5,000 at 10% for one year, as follows:

$$\frac{\text{Future value}}{(1+\text{Interest rate})} = \frac{\$5,000}{1.10} = \$4,545$$

If the $5,000 is to be received two years from now, you will pay only $4,132 for the investment, as follows:

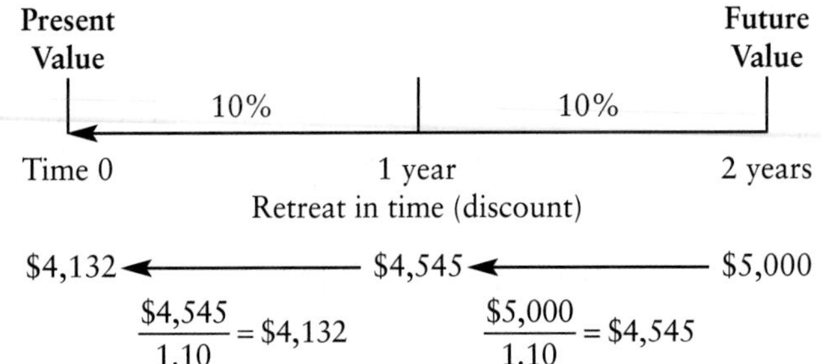

Present-Value Tables

We have shown how to compute a present value. But that computation is burdensome for an investment that spans many years. Present-value tables ease our work. Let's reexamine our examples of present value by using Exhibit 13A-1, Present Value of $1.

EXHIBIT 13A-1 **Present Value of $1**

Present Value of $1

Period	4%	5%	6%	7%	8%	10%	12%	14%	16%
1	0.962	0.952	0.943	0.935	0.926	0.909	0.893	0.877	0.862
2	0.925	0.907	0.890	0.873	0.857	0.826	0.797	0.769	0.743
3	0.889	0.864	0.840	0.816	0.794	0.751	0.712	0.675	0.641
4	0.855	0.823	0.792	0.763	0.735	0.683	0.636	0.592	0.552
5	0.822	0.784	0.747	0.713	0.681	0.621	0.567	0.519	0.476
6	0.790	0.746	0.705	0.666	0.630	0.564	0.507	0.456	0.410
7	0.760	0.711	0.665	0.623	0.583	0.513	0.452	0.400	0.354
8	0.731	0.677	0.627	0.582	0.540	0.467	0.404	0.351	0.305
9	0.703	0.645	0.592	0.544	0.500	0.424	0.361	0.308	0.263
10	0.676	0.614	0.558	0.508	0.463	0.386	0.322	0.270	0.227
11	0.650	0.585	0.527	0.475	0.429	0.350	0.287	0.237	0.195
12	0.625	0.557	0.497	0.444	0.397	0.319	0.257	0.208	0.168
13	0.601	0.530	0.469	0.415	0.368	0.290	0.229	0.182	0.145
14	0.577	0.505	0.442	0.388	0.340	0.263	0.205	0.160	0.125
15	0.555	0.481	0.417	0.362	0.315	0.239	0.183	0.140	0.108
16	0.534	0.458	0.394	0.339	0.292	0.218	0.163	0.123	0.093
17	0.513	0.436	0.371	0.317	0.270	0.198	0.146	0.108	0.080
18	0.494	0.416	0.350	0.296	0.250	0.180	0.130	0.095	0.069
19	0.475	0.396	0.331	0.277	0.232	0.164	0.116	0.083	0.060
20	0.456	0.377	0.312	0.258	0.215	0.149	0.104	0.073	0.051

For the 10% investment for one year, we find the junction in the 10% column and across from 1 in the Period column. The figure 0.909 is computed as follows: 1/1.10 = 0.909. This work has been done for us and all the present values are given in the table. The heading in Exhibit 13A-1 states $1. To figure present value for $5,000, we multiply $5,000 by 0.909. The result is $4,545, which matches the result we obtained by hand.

For the two-year investment, we read down the 10% column and across the Period 2 row. We multiply 0.826 (computed as 0.909/1.10 = 0.826) by $5,000 and get $4,130, which confirms our earlier computation of $4,132 (the difference is due to rounding in the present-value table). Using the table, we can compute the present value of any single future amount.

Present Value of an Annuity

Let's return to the investment example that provided a single future receipt ($5,000 at the end of two years). Annuity investments provide multiple receipts of an equal amount at fixed intervals.

Consider an investment that promises *annual* cash receipts of $10,000 to be received at the end of each of three years. Assume that you demand a 12% return on your investment. What is the investment's present value? The present value determines how much you would pay today to acquire the investment. The investment spans three periods, and you would pay the sum of three present values. The computation follows.

The present value of this annuity is $24,020. By paying $24,020 today, you will receive $10,000 at the end of each of the three years while earning 12% on your investment.

Year	Annual Cash Receipt	×	Present Value of $1 at 12% (Exhibit 13A-1)	=	Present Value of Annual Cash Receipt
1	$10,000	×	0.893	=	$ 8,930
2	10,000	×	0.797	=	7,970
3	10,000	×	0.712	=	7,120
			Total present value of investment	=	$24,020

The example illustrates repetitive computations of the three future amounts. One way to ease the computational burden is to add the three present values of $1 (0.893 + 0.797 + 0.712) and multiply their sum (2.402) by the annual cash receipt ($10,000) to obtain the present value of the annuity ($10,000 × 2.402 = $24,020).

An easier approach is to use a present value of an annuity table. Exhibit 13A-2 on the next page shows the present value of $1 to be received at the end of each period for a given number of periods. The present value of a three-period annuity at 12% is 2.402 (the junction of the Period 3 row and the 12% column). Thus, $10,000 received annually at the end of each of three years, discounted at 12%, is $24,020 ($10,000 × 2.402), which is the present value.

Present Value of Bonds Payable

The present value of a bond—its market price—is the sum of

- the present value of the principal amount to be received at maturity—a single amount (present value of $1) *plus*
- the present value of the future stated interest amounts—an annuity because it occurs periodically (present value of annuity of $1).

EXHIBIT 13A-2 Present Value of Annuity of $1

Present Value of Annuity of $1									
Period	4%	5%	6%	7%	8%	10%	12%	14%	16%
1	0.962	0.952	0.943	0.935	0.926	0.909	0.893	0.877	0.862
2	1.886	1.859	1.833	1.808	1.783	1.736	1.690	1.647	1.605
3	2.775	2.723	2.673	2.624	2.577	2.487	2.402	2.322	2.246
4	3.630	3.546	3.465	3.387	3.312	3.170	3.037	2.914	2.798
5	4.452	4.329	4.212	4.100	3.993	3.791	3.605	3.433	3.274
6	5.242	5.076	4.917	4.767	4.623	4.355	4.111	3.889	3.685
7	6.002	5.786	5.582	5.389	5.206	4.868	4.564	4.288	4.039
8	6.733	6.463	6.210	5.971	5.747	5.335	4.968	4.639	4.344
9	7.435	7.108	6.802	6.515	6.247	5.759	5.328	4.946	4.607
10	8.111	7.722	7.360	7.024	6.710	6.145	5.650	5.216	4.833
11	8.760	8.306	7.887	7.499	7.139	6.495	5.938	5.453	5.029
12	9.385	8.863	8.384	7.943	7.536	6.814	6.194	5.660	5.197
13	9.986	9.394	8.853	8.358	7.904	7.103	6.424	5.842	5.342
14	10.563	9.899	9.295	8.745	8.244	7.367	6.628	6.002	5.468
15	11.118	10.380	9.712	9.108	8.559	7.606	6.811	6.142	5.575
16	11.652	10.838	10.106	9.447	8.851	7.824	6.974	6.265	5.669
17	12.166	11.274	10.477	9.763	9.122	8.022	7.120	6.373	5.749
18	12.659	11.690	10.828	10.059	9.372	8.201	7.250	6.467	5.818
19	13.134	12.085	11.158	10.336	9.604	8.365	7.366	6.550	5.877
20	13.590	12.462	11.470	10.594	9.818	8.514	7.469	6.623	5.929

Discount Price

Let's compute the present value of the 9%, five-year bonds of Air West Airlines. The maturity value of the bonds is $100,000 and they pay 4 1/2% stated interest semiannually. At issuance, the annual market interest rate is 10% (5% semiannually). Therefore, the market interest rate for each of the 10 semiannual periods is 5%. We use 5% to compute the present value (PV) of the maturity and the present value (PV) of the stated interest. The market price of these bonds is $96,149, as follows:

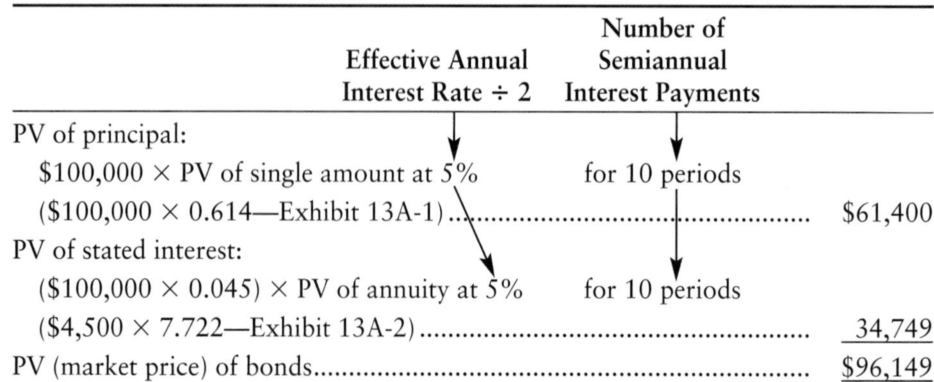

AIR WEST BONDS—DISCOUNT PRICE $96,149

	Effective Annual Interest Rate ÷ 2	Number of Semiannual Interest Payments	
PV of principal:			
$100,000 × PV of single amount at 5%		for 10 periods	
($100,000 × 0.614—Exhibit 13A-1)			$61,400
PV of stated interest:			
($100,000 × 0.045) × PV of annuity at 5%		for 10 periods	
($4,500 × 7.722—Exhibit 13A-2)			34,749
PV (market price) of bonds			$96,149

The market price of the Air West bonds shows a discount because the stated interest rate on the bonds (9%) is less than the market interest rate (10%). We discuss these bonds in more detail in the next section of this appendix.

Premium Price

Let's consider a premium price for the Air West bonds. Now suppose the market interest rate is 8% at issuance (4% for each of the 10 semiannual periods):

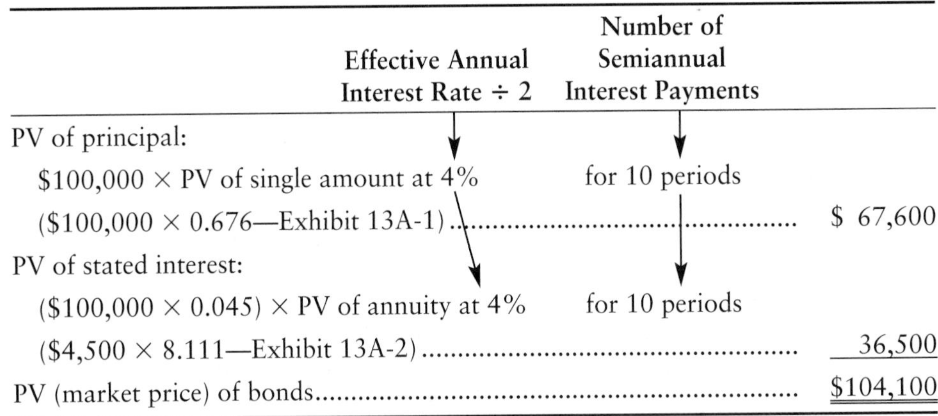

AIR WEST BONDS—PREMIUM PRICE $104,100

	Effective Annual Interest Rate ÷ 2	Number of Semiannual Interest Payments	
PV of principal:	↓	↓	
$100,000 × PV of single amount at	4%	for 10 periods	
($100,000 × 0.676—Exhibit 13A-1)			$ 67,600
PV of stated interest:	↓	↓	
($100,000 × 0.045) × PV of annuity at	4%	for 10 periods	
($4,500 × 8.111—Exhibit 13A-2)			36,500
PV (market price) of bonds			$104,100

We discuss accounting for these bonds in the next section.

Effective-Interest Method of Amortization

We began this chapter with straight-line amortization to introduce the concept of amortizing bonds. A more precise way of amortizing bonds is used in practice, and it's called the **effective-interest method**. That method uses the present-value concepts covered in this appendix.

Generally accepted accounting principles require that interest expense be measured using the *effective-interest method* unless the straight-line amounts are similar. In that case, either method is permitted. Total interest expense over the life of the bonds is the same under both methods. We now show how the effective-interest method works.

Effective-Interest Amortization for a Bond Discount

Assume that Air West Airlines issues $100,000 of 9% bonds at a time when the market rate of interest is 10%. These bonds mature in 5 years and pay interest semiannually, so there are 10 semiannual interest payments. As we just saw, the issue price of the bonds is $96,149,[3] and the discount on these bonds is $3,851 ($100,000 – $96,149). Exhibit 13-A3 shows how to measure interest expense by the effective-interest method. (You will need an amortization table to account for bonds by the effective-interest method.)

EXHIBIT 13A-3 **Effective-Interest Amortization of a Bond Discount**

PANEL A—Bond Data

Maturity value—$100,000
Stated interest rate—9%
Interest paid—4 1/2% semiannually, $4,500 ($100,000 × 0.045)
Market interest rate at time of issue—10% annually, 5% semiannually
Issue price—$96,149 on January 1, 2008

PANEL B—Amortization Table

	A	B	C	D	E
End of Semiannual Interest Period	Interest *Payment* (4 1/2% of maturity value)	Interest *Expense* (5% of preceding bond carrying amount)	Discount Amortization (B – A)	Discount Balance (D – C)	Bond Carrying Amount ($100,000 – D)
Jan. 1, 2008				$3,851	$ 96,149
July 1	$4,500	$4,807	$307	3,544	96,456
Jan. 1, 2009	4,500	4,823	323	3,221	96,779
July 1	4,500	4,839	339	2,882	97,118
Jan. 1, 2010	4,500	4,856	356	2,526	97,474
July 1	4,500	4,874	374	2,152	97,848
Jan. 1, 2011	4,500	4,892	392	1,760	98,240
July 1	4,500	4,912	412	1,348	98,652
Jan. 1, 2012	4,500	4,933	433	915	99,085
July 1	4,500	4,954	454	461	99,539
Jan. 1, 2013	4,500	4,961*	461	0	100,000

*Adjusted for effect of rounding.

Notes
- *Column A* The interest payments are constant.
- *Column B* The interest expense each period is the preceding bond carrying amount multiplied by the market interest rate.
- *Column C* The excess of interest expense (B) over interest payment (A) is the discount amortization.
- *Column D* The discount decreases by the amount of amortization for the period (C).
- *Column E* The bonds' carrying amount increases from $96,149 at issuance to $100,000 at maturity.

The *accounts* debited and credited under the effective-interest method and the straight-line method are the same. Only the *amounts* differ.

[3]We compute this present value on page 682.

Exhibit 13-A3 gives the amounts for all the bond transactions of Air West Airlines. Let's begin with issuance of the bonds payable on January 1, 2008, and the first interest payment on July 1. Entries follow, using amounts from the respective lines of Exhibit 13-A3.

2008			
Jan. 1	Cash (column E)	96,149	
	Discount on Bonds Payable (column D)	3,851	
	Bonds Payable (maturity value)		100,000
	Issued bonds at a discount.		

2008			
July 1	Interest Expense (column B)	4,807	
	Discount on Bonds Payable (column C)		307
	Cash (column A)		4,500
	Paid interest and amortized discount.		

Effective-Interest Amortization of a Bond Premium

Air West Airlines may issue its bonds payable at a premium. Assume that Air West issues $100,000 of 5-year, 9% bonds when the market interest rate is 8%. The bonds' issue price is $104,100,[4] and the premium is $4,100.

Exhibit 13-A4 provides the data for all the bond transactions of Air West Airlines. Let's begin with issuance of the bonds on January 1, 2008, and the first interest payment on July 1. These entries follow.

2008			
Jan. 1	Cash (column E)	104,100	
	Bonds Payable (maturity value)		100,000
	Premium on Bonds Payable (column D)		
	Issued bonds at a premium.		4,100

2008			
July 1	Interest Expense (column B)	4,164	
	Premium on Bonds Payable (column C)	336	
	Cash (column A)		4,500
	Paid interest and amortized premium.		

[4]Again, we compute the present value of the bonds on page 682.

EXHIBIT 13A-4 **Effective-Interest Amortization of a Bond Premium**

PANEL A—Bond Data

Maturity value—$100,000
Stated interest rate—9%
Interest paid—4 1/2% semiannually, $4,500 ($100,000 × 0.045)
Market interest rate at time of issue—8% annually, 4% semiannually
Issue price—$104,100 on January 1, 2008

PANEL B—Amortization Table

	A	B	C	D	E
End of Semiannual Interest Period	Interest *Payment* (4 1/2% of maturity value)	Interest *Expense* (4% of preceding bond carrying amount)	Premium Amortization (B – A)	Premium Balance (D – C)	Bond Carrying Amount ($100,000 + D)
Jan. 1, 2008				$4,100	$104,100
July 1	$4,500	$4,164	$336	3,764	103,764
Jan. 1, 2009	4,500	4,151	349	3,415	103,415
July 1	4,500	4,137	363	3,052	103,052
Jan. 1, 2010	4,500	4,122	378	2,674	102,674
July 1	4,500	4,107	393	2,281	102,281
Jan. 1, 2011	4,500	4,091	409	1,872	101,872
July 1	4,500	4,075	425	1,447	101,447
Jan. 1, 2012	4,500	4,058	442	1,005	101,005
July 1	4,500	4,040	460	545	100,545
Jan. 1, 2013	4,500	3,955*	545	0	100,000

*Adjusted for effect of rounding.

Notes
- *Column A* The interest payments are constant.
- *Column B* The interest expense each period is the preceding bond carrying amount multiplied by the market interest rate.
- *Column C* The excess of interest payment (A) over interest expense (B) is the premium amortization.
- *Column D* The premium balance decreases by the amount of amortization for the period.
- *Column E* The bonds' carrying amount decreases from $104,100 at issuance to $100,000 at maturity.

Appendix 13A Assignments

Problems

Computing present-value amounts

P13A-1 Exxel, Inc., needs new manufacturing equipment. Two companies can provide similar equipment but under different payment plans:

a. General Electric (GE) offers to let Exxel pay $60,000 each year for five years. The payments include interest at 12% per year. What is the present value of the payments? (pp. 681–683)

continued . . .

b. Westinghouse will let Exxel make a single payment of $400,000 at the end of five years. This payment includes both principal and interest at 12%. What is the present value of this payment? (pp. 679–680)

c. Exxel will purchase the equipment that costs the least, as measured by present value. Which equipment should Exxel select? Why? (Challenge)

Computing the present values of bonds

P13A-2 Determine the present value of the following bonds (pp. 652–653):

a. Ten-year bonds payable with maturity value of $88,000 and stated interest rate of 12%, paid semiannually. The market rate of interest is 12% at issuance.

b. Same bonds payable as in a, but the market interest rate is 14%.

c. Same bonds payable as in a, but the market interest rate is 10%.

Recording bond transactions; straight-line amortization

P13A-3 For each bond in Problem 13A-2, journalize issuance of the bond and the first semiannual interest payment. The company amortizes bond premium and discount by the straight-line method. Explanations are not required. (pp. 646–647, 648, 651–653)

Issuing bonds payable and amortizing discount by the effective-interest method

P13A-4 IMAX, Inc., issued $600,000 of 7%, 10-year bonds payable at a price of 90 on March 31, 2008. The market interest rate at the date of issuance was 9%, and the bonds pay interest semiannually.

1. How much cash did IMAX receive upon issuance of the bonds payable? (p. 684)
2. Prepare an effective-interest amortization table for the bond discount, through the first two interest payments. Use Exhibit 13-A3 as a guide, and round amounts to the nearest dollar. (p. 684)
3. Record IMAX's issuance of the bonds on March 31, 2008, and on September 30, 2008, payment of the first semiannual interest amount and amortization of the bond discount. Explanations are not required. (p. 685)

Issuing bonds payable and amortizing premium by the effective-interest method

P13A-5 Jon Spelman Co. issued $200,000 of 8%, 10-year bonds payable at a price of 110 on May 31, 2008. The market interest rate at the date of issuance was 6%, and the Spelman bonds pay interest semiannually.

1. How much cash did Spelman receive upon issuance of the bonds payable? (p. 685)
2. Prepare an effective-interest amortization table for the bond premium, through the first two interest payments. Use Exhibit 13-A4 as a guide, and round amounts to the nearest dollar. (p. 685)
3. Record Spelman's issuance of the bonds on May 31, 2008, and, on November 30, 2008, payment of the first semiannual interest amount and amortization of the bond premium. Explanations are not required. (p. 685)

Effective-interest method for bond discount: recording interest payments and interest expense

P13A-6 Serenity, Inc., is authorized to issue 7%, 10-year bonds payable. On January 2, 2007, when the market interest rate is 8%, the company issues $300,000 of the bonds and receives cash of $279,600. Serenity amortizes bond discount by the effective-interest method. Interest dates are January 2 and July 2.

continued . . .

Requirements

1. Prepare an amortization table for the first two semiannual interest periods. Follow the format of Exhibit 13-A3, page 684.
2. Record issuance of the bonds payable and the first semiannual interest payment on July 2. (p. 684)

Debt payment and discount amortization schedule

P13A-7 Neiderhoffer Corp. issued $500,000 of 8 3/8% (0.08375), five-year bonds payable when the market interest rate was 9 1/2% (0.095). Neiderhoffer pays interest annually at year-end. The issue price of the bonds was $478,402.

Requirement

Create a spreadsheet model to prepare a schedule to measure interest expense on these bonds. Use the effective-interest method of amortization. Round to the nearest dollar, and format your answer as follows. (p. 684)

1	A	B	C	D	E	F
2						Bond
3		Interest	Interest	Discount	Discount	Carrying
4	Date	Payment	Expense	Amortization	Balance	Amount
5	1-1-01				$ ☐	$478,402
6	12-31-01	$ ☐	$ ☐	$ ☐	↓	☐
7	12-31-02	↓	↓	↓	↓	↓
8	12-31-03	↓	↓	↓	↓	↓
9	12-31-04	↓	↓	↓	↓	↓
10	12-31-05	↓	↓	↓	↓	↓
		500000*.08375	+F5*.095	+C6−B6	500000−F5	+F5+D6

Computing a bond's present value, recording its issuance, interest payments, and amortization by the effective-interest method

P13A-8 On December 31, 2008, when the market interest rate is 8%, Willis Realty Co. issues $400,000 of 7.25%, 10-year bonds payable. The bonds pay interest semiannually.

Requirements

1. Determine the present value of the bonds at issuance. (pp. 652–653)
2. Assume that the bonds are issued at the price computed in requirement 1. Prepare an effective-interest method amortization table for the first two semiannual interest periods. (p. 684)
3. Using the amortization table prepared in requirement 2, journalize issuance of the bonds and the first two interest payments. (p. 685)

Comprehensive Problem for Chapters 11 - 13

Apache Motors' Corporate Transactions

Apache Motors' corporate charter authorizes the company to issue 1 million shares of $1 par-value common stock and 200,000 shares of no-par preferred stock. During the first quarter of operations, Apache completed the following selected transactions:

Oct. 1	Issued 50,000 shares of $1-par common stock for cash of $6 per share. (pp. 554–555)
1	Issued $200,000 of 9%, 10-year bonds payable at 90. (pp. 646–647)
5	Issued 2,000 shares of no-par preferred stock, receiving cash of $100,000. (pp. 556–557)
Nov. 2	Purchased 11,000 shares of Apache common stock for the treasury at $5 per share. (pp. 602–603)
19	Experienced a $16,000 extraordinary flood loss of inventory that cost $20,000. Cash received from the insurance company was $4,000. There is no income tax effect from this loss. (pp. 612–613)
Dec. 1	Sold 1,000 shares of the treasury stock for cash of $6.25 per share. (p. 604)
30	Sold merchandise on account, $700,000. Cost of goods sold was $400,000. Operating expenses totaled $170,000, with $160,000 of this amount paid in cash. Apache uses a perpetual inventory system. (pp. 74–75, 211–212)
31	Accrued interest and amortized discount (straight-line method) on the bonds payable issued on October 1. (pp. 652–653)
31	Accrued income tax expense of $35,000. (pp. 569–570)
31	Closed all revenues, expenses, and losses to Income Summary in a single closing entry. (pp. 549–552)
31	Declared a quarterly cash dividend of $1.00 per share on the preferred stock. Record date is January 11, with payment scheduled for January 19. (pp. 561–563)

Requirements

1. Record these transactions in the general journal. Explanations are not required.
2. Prepare a multistep income statement, including earnings per share, for the quarter ended December 31. Apache had 40,000 shares of common stock outstanding. (pp. 611–614)

Appendix A

2 0 0 5

ANNUAL REPORT

REPORT OF ERNST & YOUNG LLP
INDEPENDENT REGISTERED PUBLIC ACCOUNTING FIRM

The Board of Directors and Stockholders
Amazon.com, Inc.

We have audited the accompanying consolidated balance sheets of Amazon.com, Inc. as of December 31, 2005 and 2004, and the related consolidated statements of operations, stockholders' equity (deficit), and cash flows for each of the three years in the period ended December 31, 2005. Our audits also included the financial statement schedule listed in the Index at Item 15(a)(2). These financial statements and schedule are the responsibility of the Company's management. Our responsibility is to express an opinion on these financial statements and schedule based on our audits.

We conducted our audits in accordance with the standards of the Public Company Accounting Oversight Board (United States). Those standards require that we plan and perform the audit to obtain reasonable assurance about whether the financial statements are free of material misstatement. An audit includes examining, on a test basis, evidence supporting the amounts and disclosures in the financial statements. An audit also includes assessing the accounting principles used and significant estimates made by management, as well as evaluating the overall financial statement presentation. We believe that our audits provide a reasonable basis for our opinion.

In our opinion, the financial statements referred to above present fairly, in all material respects, the consolidated financial position of Amazon.com, Inc. at December 31, 2005 and 2004, and the consolidated results of its operations and its cash flows for each of the three years in the period ended December 31, 2005, in conformity with U.S. generally accepted accounting principles. Also, in our opinion, the related financial statement schedule, when considered in relation to the basic financial statements taken as a whole, presents fairly in all material respects the information set forth therein.

As discussed in Note 1 to the consolidated financial statements, the Company adopted Statement of Financial Accounting Standards No. 123 (revised 2004), Share-Based Payment, effective January 1, 2005.

We also have audited, in accordance with the standards of the Public Company Accounting Oversight Board (United States), the effectiveness of Amazon.com, Inc.'s internal control over financial reporting as of December 31, 2005, based on criteria established in Internal Control-Integrated Framework issued by the Committee of Sponsoring Organizations of the Treadway Commission and our report dated February 16, 2006 expressed an unqualified opinion thereon.

/s/ ERNST & YOUNG LLP

Seattle, Washington
February 16, 2006

AMAZON.COM, INC.

CONSOLIDATED STATEMENTS OF CASH FLOWS
(in millions)

	Year Ended December 31,		
	2005	2004	2003
CASH AND CASH EQUIVALENTS, BEGINNING OF PERIOD	$ 1,303	$ 1,102	$ 738
OPERATING ACTIVITIES:			
Net income	359	588	35
Adjustments to reconcile net income to net cash provided by operating activities:			
Depreciation of fixed assets, including internal-use software and website development, and other amortization	121	76	76
Stock-based compensation	87	58	88
Other operating expense (income)	7	(8)	3
Gains on sales of marketable securities, net	(1)	(1)	(10)
Remeasurements and other	(42)	1	130
Non-cash interest expense and other	5	5	13
Deferred income taxes	70	(257)	1
Cumulative effect of change in accounting principle	(26)	—	—
Changes in operating assets and liabilities:			
Inventories	(104)	(169)	(77)
Accounts receivable, net and other current assets	(84)	(2)	2
Accounts payable	274	286	168
Accrued expenses and other current liabilities	60	(14)	(26)
Additions to unearned revenue	156	110	102
Amortization of previously unearned revenue	(149)	(107)	(112)
Net cash provided by operating activities	733	566	393
INVESTING ACTIVITIES:			
Purchases of fixed assets, including internal-use software and website development	(204)	(89)	(46)
Acquisitions, net of cash acquired	(24)	(71)	—
Sales and maturities of marketable securities and other investments	836	1,427	813
Purchases of marketable securities	(1,386)	(1,584)	(536)
Proceeds from sale of subsidiary	—	—	5
Net cash (used in) provided by investing activities	(778)	(317)	236
FINANCING ACTIVITIES:			
Proceeds from exercises of stock options and other	66	60	163
Proceeds from long-term debt and other	11	—	—
Repayments of long-term debt and capital lease obligations	(270)	(157)	(495)
Net cash used in financing activities	(193)	(97)	(332)
Foreign-currency effect on cash and cash equivalents	(52)	49	67
Net (decrease) increase in cash and cash equivalents	(290)	201	364
CASH AND CASH EQUIVALENTS, END OF PERIOD	$ 1,013	$ 1,303	$1,102
SUPPLEMENTAL CASH FLOW INFORMATION:			
Cash paid for interest	$ 105	$ 108	$ 120
Cash paid for income taxes	12	4	2

See accompanying notes to consolidated financial statements.

AMAZON.COM, INC.

CONSOLIDATED STATEMENTS OF OPERATIONS
(in millions, except per share data)

	Year Ended December 31,		
	2005	2004	2003
Net sales	$8,490	$6,921	$5,264
Cost of sales	6,451	5,319	4,007
Gross profit	2,039	1,602	1,257
Operating expenses (1):			
Fulfillment	745	601	495
Marketing	198	162	128
Technology and content	451	283	257
General and administrative	166	124	104
Other operating expense (income)	47	(8)	3
Total operating expenses	1,607	1,162	987
Income from operations	432	440	270
Interest income	44	28	22
Interest expense	(92)	(107)	(130)
Other income (expense), net	2	(5)	7
Remeasurements and other	42	(1)	(130)
Total non-operating expense	(4)	(85)	(231)
Income before income taxes	428	355	39
Provision for income taxes	95	(233)	4
Income before change in accounting principle	333	588	35
Cumulative effect of change in accounting principle	26	—	—
Net income	$ 359	$ 588	$ 35
Basic earnings per share:			
Prior to cumulative effect of change in accounting principle	$ 0.81	$ 1.45	$ 0.09
Cumulative effect of change in accounting principle	0.06	—	—
	$ 0.87	$ 1.45	$ 0.09
Diluted earnings per share:			
Prior to cumulative effect of change in accounting principle	$ 0.78	$ 1.39	$ 0.08
Cumulative effect of change in accounting principle	0.06	—	—
	$ 0.84	$ 1.39	$ 0.08
Weighted average shares used in computation of earnings per share:			
Basic	412	406	395
Diluted	426	425	419

(1) Includes stock-based compensation as follows:

	2005	2004	2003
Fulfillment	$16	$10	$18
Marketing	6	4	5
Technology and content	45	32	50
General and administrative	20	12	15
Total stock-based compensation expense	$87	$58	$88

See accompanying notes to consolidated financial statements.

AMAZON.COM, INC.

CONSOLIDATED BALANCE SHEETS
(in millions, except per share data)

	December 31, 2005	December 31, 2004
ASSETS		
Current assets:		
Cash and cash equivalents	$ 1,013	$ 1,303
Marketable securities	987	476
Cash, cash equivalents, and marketable securities	2,000	1,779
Inventories	566	480
Deferred tax assets, current portion	89	81
Accounts receivable, net and other current assets	274	199
Total current assets	2,929	2,539
Fixed assets, net	348	246
Deferred tax assets, long-term portion	223	282
Goodwill	159	139
Other assets	37	42
Total assets	$ 3,696	$ 3,248
LIABILITIES AND STOCKHOLDERS' EQUITY(DEFICIT)		
Current liabilities:		
Accounts payable	$ 1,366	$ 1,142
Accrued expenses and other current liabilities	563	478
Total current liabilities	1,929	1,620
Long-term debt and other	1,521	1,855
Commitments and contingencies		
Stockholders' equity (deficit):		
Preferred stock, $0.01 par value:		
Authorized shares—500		
Issued and outstanding shares—none	—	—
Common stock, $0.01 par value:		
Authorized shares—5,000		
Issued and outstanding shares—416 and 410 shares	4	4
Additional paid-in capital	2,263	2,123
Accumulated other comprehensive income	6	32
Accumulated deficit	(2,027)	(2,386)
Total stockholders' equity (deficit)	246	(227)
Total liabilities and stockholders' equity (deficit)	$ 3,696	$ 3,248

See accompanying notes to consolidated financial statements.

AMAZON.COM, INC.

CONSOLIDATED STATEMENTS OF STOCKHOLDERS' EQUITY (DEFICIT)
(in millions)

	Common Stock		Additional Paid-In Capital	Accumulated Other Comprehensive Income	Accumulated Deficit	Total Stockholders' Equity (Deficit)
	Shares	Amount				
Balance at December 31, 2002	388	$ 4	$1,643	$ 10	$(3,009)	$(1,352)
Net income	—	—	—	—	35	35
Foreign currency translation gains, net	—	—	—	15	—	15
Increase of net unrealized gains on available-for-sale securities	—	—	—	2	—	2
Net activity of terminated Euro Currency Swap	—	—	—	11	—	11
Comprehensive income	—	—	—	—	—	63
Exercise of common stock options, net and vesting of restricted stock	15	—	163	—	—	163
Income tax benefit on stock awards	—	—	2	—	—	2
Deferred stock-based compensation, net	—	—	4	—	—	4
Issuance of common stock – employee benefit plan	—	—	1	—	—	1
Stock compensation – restricted stock units	—	—	31	—	—	31
Stock compensation – variable accounting	—	—	52	—	—	52
Balance at December 31, 2003	403	4	1,896	38	(2,974)	(1,036)
Net income	—	—	—	—	588	588
Foreign currency translation losses, net	—	—	—	(1)	—	(1)
Decline of unrealized gains on available-for-sale securities, net of tax effect	—	—	—	(11)	—	(11)
Amortization of unrealized loss on terminated Euro Currency Swap, net of tax	—	—	—	6	—	6
Comprehensive income	—	—	—	—	—	582
Exercise of common stock options, net and vesting of restricted stock	6	—	60	—	—	60
Income tax benefit on stock awards	—	—	107	—	—	107
Deferred stock-based compensation, net	—	—	3	—	—	3
Issuance of common stock – employee benefit plan	1	—	3	—	—	3
Stock compensation – restricted stock units	—	—	49	—	—	49
Stock compensation – variable accounting	—	—	5	—	—	5
Balance at December 31, 2004	410	4	2,123	32	(2,386)	(227)
Net income	—	—	—	—	359	359
Foreign currency translation losses, net	—	—	—	(15)	—	(15)
Decline of unrealized gains on available-for-sale securities, net of tax effect	—	—	—	(14)	—	(14)
Amortization of unrealized loss on terminated Euro Currency Swap, net of tax	—	—	—	3	—	3
Comprehensive income	—	—	—	—	—	333
Exercise of common stock options, net and vesting of restricted stock	6	—	58	—	—	58
Change in accounting principle	—	—	(26)	—	—	(26)
Income tax benefit on stock awards	—	—	10	—	—	10
Issuance of common stock – employee benefit plan	—	—	4	—	—	4
Stock-based compensation	—	—	94	—	—	94
Balance at December 31, 2005	416	$ 4	$2,263	$ 6	$(2,027)	$ 246

See accompanying notes to consolidated financial statements.

AMAZON.COM, INC.

NOTES TO CONSOLIDATED FINANCIAL STATEMENTS (Excerpts)

Note 1—DESCRIPTION OF BUSINESS AND ACCOUNTING POLICIES

Description of Business

Amazon.com, Inc., a Fortune 500 company, opened its virtual doors on the World Wide Web in July 1995 and today offers Earth's Biggest Selection. We seek to be Earth's most customer-centric company, where customers can find and discover anything they might want to buy online, and endeavor to offer customers the lowest possible prices.

Amazon.com and its affiliates operate retail websites, including: *www.amazon.com, www.amazon.co.uk, www.amazon.de, www.amazon.co.jp, www.amazon.fr, www.amazon.ca,* and *www.joyo.com.* We have organized our operations into two principal segments: North America and International. The North America segment includes the operating results of *www.amazon.com* and *www.amazon.ca.* The International segment includes the operating results of *www.amazon.co.uk, www.amazon.de, www.amazon.fr, www.amazon.co.jp,* and *www.joyo.com.* In addition, we operate other websites, including *www.a9.com* and *www.alexa.com* that enable search and navigation; *www.imdb.com,* a comprehensive movie database; and Amazon Mechanical Turk at *www.mturk.com* which provides a web service for computers to integrate a network of humans directly into their processes.

Principles of Consolidation

The consolidated financial statements include the accounts of the Company, its wholly-owned subsidiaries, and those entities (relating to *www.joyo.com*) in which we have a variable interest. Intercompany balances and transactions have been eliminated.

Use of Estimates

The preparation of financial statements in conformity with GAAP requires estimates and assumptions that affect the reported amounts of assets and liabilities, revenues and expenses, and related disclosures of contingent liabilities in the consolidated financial statements and accompanying notes. Estimates are used for, but not limited to, valuation of investments, receivables valuation, sales returns, incentive discount offers, inventory valuation, depreciable lives of fixed assets, internally-developed software, valuation of acquired intangibles, deferred tax assets and liabilities, stock-based compensation, restructuring-related liabilities, and contingencies. Actual results could differ materially from those estimates.

Business Acquisitions

We acquired certain companies during 2005 for an aggregate cash purchase price of $29 million. Acquired intangibles totaled $10 million and have estimated useful lives of between one and three years. The excess of purchase price over the fair value of the net assets acquired was $19 million and is classified as "Goodwill" on our consolidated balance sheets. The results of operations of each of the acquired businesses have been included in our consolidated results from each transaction closing date forward. The effect of these acquisitions on consolidated net sales and operating income during 2005 was not significant.

In 2004, we acquired all of the outstanding shares of Joyo.com Limited, a British Virgin Islands company that operates an Internet retail website in the People's Republic of China ("PRC") in cooperation with a PRC subsidiary and PRC affiliates, at a purchase price of $75 million, including a cash payment of $71 million (net of cash acquired), the assumption of employee stock options, and transaction-related costs. Acquired intangibles were $6 million with estimated useful lives of between one and four years. The excess of purchase price over the fair value of the net assets acquired was $70 million and is classified as "Goodwill" on the consolidated balance sheets. The results of operations of Joyo.com have been included in our consolidated results from the acquisition date forward.

AMAZON.COM, INC.

NOTES TO CONSOLIDATED FINANCIAL STATEMENTS—(Continued)

The PRC regulates Joyo.com's business through regulations and license requirements restricting (i) the scope of foreign investment in the Internet, retail and delivery sectors, (ii) Internet content and (iii) the sale of certain media products. In order to meet the PRC local ownership and regulatory licensing requirements, Joyo.com's business is operated through a PRC subsidiary which acts in cooperation with PRC companies owned by nominee shareholders who are PRC nationals.

Joyo.com does not own any capital stock of the PRC affiliates, but is the primary beneficiary of future losses or profits through contractual rights. As a result, we consolidate the results of the PRC affiliates in accordance with FIN 46R, "Consolidation of Variable Interest Entities." The net assets and operating results for the PRC affiliates were not significant.

Accounting Change

As of January 1, 2005, we adopted SFAS No. 123(R) using the modified prospective method, which requires measurement of compensation cost for all stock-based awards at fair value on date of grant and recognition of compensation over the service period for awards expected to vest. The adoption of SFAS 123(R) resulted in a cumulative benefit from accounting change of $26 million, which reflects the net cumulative impact of estimating future forfeitures in the determination of period expense, rather than recording forfeitures when they occur as previously permitted. See "Note 1—Description of Business and Accounting Policies—Stock-based Compensation."

Cash and Cash Equivalents

We classify all highly liquid instruments, including money market funds that comply with Rule 2a-7 of the Investment Company Act of 1940, with a remaining maturity of three months or less at the time of purchase as cash equivalents.

Inventories

Inventories, consisting of products available for sale, are accounted for using the FIFO method, and are valued at the lower of cost or market value. This valuation requires us to make judgments, based on currently-available information, about the likely method of disposition, such as through sales to individual customers, returns to product vendors, or liquidations, and expected recoverable values of each disposition category. Based on this evaluation, we adjust the carrying amount of our inventories to lower of cost or market value.

We provide fulfillment-related services in connection with certain of our third parties and Amazon Enterprise Solutions programs. In those arrangements, as well as all other product sales by third parties, the third party maintains ownership of the related products.

Accounts Receivable, Net and Other Current Assets

Included in "Accounts receivable, net and other current assets" are prepaid expenses of $15 million and $12 million at December 31, 2005 and 2004, representing advance payments for insurance, licenses, and other miscellaneous expenses.

Allowance for Doubtful Accounts

We estimate losses on receivables based on known troubled accounts, if any, and historical experience of losses incurred. The allowance for doubtful accounts receivable was $43 million and $23 million at December 31, 2005 and 2004.

AMAZON.COM, INC.

NOTES TO CONSOLIDATED FINANCIAL STATEMENTS—(Continued)

Internal-use Software and Website Development

Costs incurred to develop software for internal use are required to be capitalized and amortized over the estimated useful life of the software in accordance with Statement of Position (SOP) 98-1, *Accounting for the Costs of Computer Software Developed or Obtained for Internal Use.* Costs related to design or maintenance of internal-use software are expensed as incurred. For the years ended 2005, 2004, and 2003, we capitalized $90 million (including $11 million of stock-based compensation), $44 million, and $30 million of costs associated with internal-use software and website development, which are partially offset by amortization of previously capitalized amounts of $50 million, $30 million, and $24 million.

Depreciation of Fixed Assets

Fixed assets include assets such as furniture and fixtures, heavy equipment, technology infrastructure, internal-use software and website development, and our DVD rental library. Depreciation is recorded on a straight-line basis over the estimated useful lives of the assets (generally two years or less for assets such as internal-use software and our DVD rental library, three years for our technology infrastructure, five years for furniture and fixtures, and ten years for heavy equipment). Depreciation expense is generally classified within the corresponding operating expense categories on the consolidated statements of operations, and certain assets, such as our DVD rental library, are amortized as "Cost of sales."

Leases and Asset Retirement Obligations

We account for our lease agreements pursuant to SFAS No 13, *Accounting for Leases*, which categorizes leases at their inception as either operating or capital leases depending on certain defined criteria. On certain of our lease agreements, we may receive rent holidays and other incentives. We recognize lease costs on a straight-line basis without regard to deferred payment terms, such as rent holidays that defer the commencement date of required payments. Additionally, incentives we receive are treated as a reduction of our costs over the term of the agreement. Leasehold improvements are capitalized at cost and amortized over the lesser of their expected useful life or the life of the lease, without assuming renewal features, if any, are exercised.

In accordance with Statement of Financial Accounting Standards (SFAS) No. 143, *Accounting for Asset Retirement Obligations,* we establish assets and liabilities for the present value of estimated future costs to return certain of our leased facilities to their original condition. Such assets are depreciated over the lease period into operating expense, and the recorded liabilities are accreted to the future value of the estimated restoration costs.

Goodwill

We evaluate goodwill for impairment, at a minimum, on an annual basis and whenever events and changes in circumstances suggest that the carrying amount may not be recoverable. Impairment of goodwill is tested at the reporting unit level by comparing the reporting unit's carrying amount, including goodwill, to the fair value of the reporting unit. The fair values of the reporting units are estimated using discounted projected cash flows. If the carrying amount of the reporting unit exceeds its fair value, goodwill is considered impaired and a second step is performed to measure the amount of impairment loss, if any. We conduct our annual impairment test as of October 1 of each year, and have determined there to be no impairment in 2005 or 2004. There were no events or circumstances from the date of our assessment through December 31, 2005 that would impact this assessment.

At December 31, 2005 and December 31, 2004, approximately 71% and 72% of our acquired goodwill was assigned to our International segment, the majority of which relates to our acquisition of Joyo.com in 2004.

AMAZON.COM, INC.

NOTES TO CONSOLIDATED FINANCIAL STATEMENTS—(Continued)

Unearned Revenue

Unearned revenue is recorded when payments are received in advance of performing our service obligations and is recognized ratably over the service period. Unearned revenue was $48 million and $41 million at December 31, 2005 and 2004. These amounts are included in "Accrued expenses and other current liabilities" on the consolidated balance sheets.

Note 3—FIXED ASSETS(partial)

Fixed assets, at cost, consist of the following (in millions):

	December 31, 2005	December 31, 2004
Gross Fixed Assets (1):		
Fulfillment and customer service (2)	$309	$263
Technology infrastructure	69	38
Internal-use software, content, and website development	138	79
Other corporate assets	55	43
Gross fixed assets	571	423
Accumulated Depreciation (1):		
Fulfillment and customer service	123	106
Technology infrastructure	27	15
Internal-use software, content, and website development	51	32
Other corporate assets	22	24
Total accumulated depreciation	223	177
Total fixed assets, net	$348	$246

Depreciation expense on fixed assets was $113 million [for 2005] and $75 million [for 2004] . . .

Note 4—LONG-TERM DEBT AND OTHER

Our long-term debt and other long-term liabilities are summarized as follows:

	December 31, 2005	December 31, 2004
	(in millions)	
4.75% Convertible Subordinated Notes due February 2009	$ 900	$ 900
6.875% PEACS due February 2010	580	935
Other long-term debt and capital lease obligations	44	22
	1,524	1,857
Less current portion of other long-term debt and capital lease obligations	(3)	(2)
Total long-term debt and other	$1,521	$1,855

Appendix B

Investments and International Operations

Investments in stock can be a few shares or the acquisition of an entire company. In Chapters 11 through 13 we discussed the stocks and bonds that companies issued to finance their operations. Here we examine stocks and bonds for the investor who bought them.

Stock Investments

Some Basics

The owner of the stock in a corporation is the *investor.* The corporation that issued the stock is the *investee*. If you own shares of McDonald's stock, you are the investor and McDonald's is the investee.

Classifying Investments

An investment is an asset to the investor. The investment may be short-term or long-term.

- **Short-term investments**—sometimes called **marketable securities**—are current assets. Short-term investments are liquid (readily convertible to cash), and the investor intends to convert them to cash within one year.
- **Long-term investments** are all investments that are not short-term. Long-term investments include stocks and bonds that the investor expects to hold longer than one year or that are not readily marketable—for instance, real estate held for sale.

Exhibit B-1 shows the positions of short-term and long-term investments on the balance sheet.

EXHIBIT B-1 Reporting Investments on the Balance Sheet

Assets		
Current Assets		
Cash	$X	
Short-term investments	X	
Accounts receivable	X	
Inventories	X	
Prepaid expenses	X	
Total current assets		$X
Long-term investments (or simply Investments)		X
Property, plant, and equipment		X
Intangible assets		X
Other assets		X

The balance sheet reports assets by order of liquidity, starting with cash. Short-term investments are the second-most-liquid asset. Long-term investments are less liquid than current assets but more liquid than property, plant, and equipment.

Trading and Available-for-Sale Investments

We begin stock investments with situations in which the investor owns less than 20% of the investee company. These investments in stock are classified as trading investments or as available-for-sale investments.

- **Trading investments** are to be sold in the very near future—days, weeks, or only a few months—with the intent of generating a profit on a quick sale. Trading investments are short-term.
- **Available-for-sale investments** are all less-than-20% investments other than trading investments. Available-for-sale investments are current assets if the business expects to sell them within the next year or within the operating cycle if longer than a year. All other available-for-sale investments are long-term.

The investor accounts for trading investments and available-for-sale investments separately. Let's begin with trading investments.

Trading Investments

The **market-value method** is used to account for trading investments because they will be sold in the near future at their current market value. Cost is the initial amount for a trading investment. Assume McDonald's Corporation has excess cash to invest. Suppose McDonald's buys 500 shares of Ford Motor Company stock for $50 per share on October 23, 2008. Assume further that McDonald's management plans to sell this stock within three months. This is a trading investment, which McDonald's records as follows:

2008			
Oct. 23	Short-Term Investment (500 × $50)	25,000	
	Cash		25,000
	Purchased investment.		

Short-Term Investment	
25,000	

Ford pays cash dividends, so McDonald's would receive a dividend on the investment. McDonald's entry to record receipt of a $2-per-share cash dividend is

2008			
Nov. 14	Cash (500 × $2.00)	1,000	
	Dividend Revenue		1,000
	Received cash dividend.		

Trading investments are reported on the balance sheet at current market value, not at cost. This requires a year-end adjustment of the trading investment to current market value. Assume that the Ford stock has decreased in value, and at December 31,

2008, McDonald's investment in Ford stock is worth $20,000 ($5,000 less than the purchase price). At year-end, McDonald's would make the following adjustment:

2008			
Dec. 31	Loss on Trading Investment ($25,000 – $20,000)	5,000	
	Short-Term Investment		5,000
	Adjusted trading investment to market value.		

Short-Term Investment	
25,000	5,000
20,000	

Reporting Trading Investments

The T-account shows the $20,000 balance of Short-Term Investment. McDonald's would report its trading investment on the balance sheet at December 31, 2008, and the loss on trading investment on the 2008 income statement, as follows:

Balance Sheet (Partial):	
ASSETS	
Current assets:	
Short-term investments, at market value	$20,000

Income Statement (Partial):	
Other gains and losses:	
Gain (loss) on trading investment	$(5,000)

If the investment's market value had risen above $25,000, McDonald's would have debited Short-Term Investment and credited Gain on Trading Investment.

Selling a Trading Investment

When a company sells a trading investment, the gain or loss on the sale is the difference between the sale proceeds and the last carrying amount. If McDonald's sells the Ford stock for $18,000, McDonald's would record the sale as follows:

2009			
Jan. 19	Cash	18,000	
	Loss on Sale of Investment	2,000	
	Short-Term Investment		20,000
	Sold investment.		

Short-Term Investment	
25,000	5,000
20,000	20,000

For reporting on the income statement, McDonald's could combine all gains and losses ($5,000 loss + $2,000 loss) on short-term investments and report a single net amount under Other gains (losses). . . . $(7,000).

Long-Term Available-for-Sale Investments

The **market-value method** is used to account for available-for-sale investments because the company expects to resell the stock at its market value. Available-for-sale investments therefore are reported on the balance sheet at their *current market value*, just like trading investments.

Suppose Dell Corporation purchases 1,000 shares of Coca-Cola common stock at the market price of $33. Dell plans to hold this stock for longer than a year and classifies it as a long-term available-for-sale investment. Dell's entry to record the investment is

2008			
Feb. 23	Long-Term Available-for-Sale Investment (1,000 × $33)	33,000	
	Cash		33,000
	Purchased investment.		

Assume that Dell receives a $0.60 per share cash dividend on the Coca-Cola stock. Dell's entry for receipt of the dividend is

2008			
July 14	Cash (1,000 × $0.60)	600	
	Dividend Revenue		600
	Received dividend.		

Available-for-sale investments are accounted for at market value. This requires an adjustment to current market value. Assume that the market value of Dell's investment in Coca-Cola stock has risen to $36,000 on December 31, 2008. In this case, Dell makes the following adjustment:

2008			
Dec. 31	Allowance to Adjust Investment to Market ($36,000 – $33,000)	3,000	
	Unrealized Gain on Investment		3,000
	Adjusted investment to market value.		

Allowance to Adjust Investment to Market is a companion account to Long-Term Investment. The Allowance account brings the investment to current market value. Cost ($33,000) plus the Allowance ($3,000) equals the investment carrying amount ($36,000).

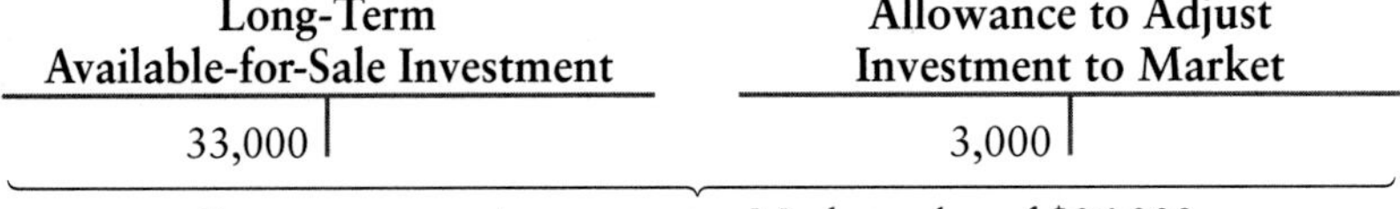

Observe that the Long-Term Available-for-Sale account is carried at cost, not at market value. It takes the allowance account to adjust the investment carrying amount to market value.

Here the Allowance has a debit balance because the investment has increased in value. If the investment's value declines, the Allowance is credited. In that case, the investment carrying amount is cost *minus* the Allowance. The Allowance with a credit balance becomes a contra account.

Reporting Available-for-Sale Investments

The other side of the December 31 adjustment credits Unrealized Gain on Investment. If the investment declines, the company debits an Unrealized Loss. *Unrealized* means that the gain or loss resulted from a change in market value, not from a sale of the investment. A gain or loss on the sale of an investment is said to be *realized* when the company receives cash. For available-for-sale investments, the Unrealized Gain (or Loss) account is reported on the balance sheet as part of stockholders' equity, as shown here.

BALANCE SHEET (PARTIAL)

Assets		Stockholders' Equity	
Total current assets	$ XXX	Common stock	$ XXX
Long-term available-for-sale investments—at market value	36,000	Retained earnings ...	XXX
Property, plant, and equipment, net	XXX	Unrealized gain on investments	3,000

Selling an Available-for-Sale Investment

The sale of an available-for-sale investment usually results in a *realized* gain or loss. Suppose Dell Corporation sells its investment in Coca-Cola stock for $32,000 during 2009. Dell would record the sale as follows:

Date	Accounts	Debit	Credit
2009			
May 19	Cash	32,000	
	Loss on Sale of Investment	1,000	
	Long-Term Available-for-Sale Investment (cost)		33,000
	Sold investment.		

Dell would report the Loss on Sale of Investment as an "Other gain or loss" on the income statement.

Equity-Method Investments

An investor with a stock holding between 20% and 50% of the investee's voting stock can *significantly influence* the investee's decisions. For this reason, investments in the range of 20% to 50% are common. For example, General Motors owns nearly 40% of Isuzu Motors. We use the **equity method** to account for 20% to 50% investments.

Recording the Initial Investment

Investments accounted for by the equity method are recorded initially at cost. Suppose Walgreen Co. pays $400,000 to purchase 20% of the common stock of

Drugstore.com. Walgreen then refers to Drugstore.com as an *affiliated company.* Walgreen's entry to record the purchase of this investment follows.

2008			
Jan. 6	Long-Term Equity-Method Investment	400,000	
	Cash		400,000
	Purchased equity-method investment.		

Adjusting the Investment Account for Investee Net Income

Under the equity method, the investor applies its percentage of ownership to record its share of the investee's net income. The investor debits the Investment account and credits Investment Revenue when the investee reports income. As the investee's equity increases, so does the Investment account on the investor's books.

Suppose Drugstore.com reported net income of $250,000 for the year. Walgreen would record 20% of this amount as an increase in the investment account, as follows:

2008			
Dec. 31	Long-Term Equity-Method Investment ($250,000 × 0.20)	50,000	
	Equity-Method Investment Revenue		50,000
	Recorded investment revenue.		

Receiving Dividends on an Equity-Method Investment

Walgreen records its proportionate part of cash dividends received from Drugstore.com. Suppose Drugstore.com declares and pays a cash dividend of $100,000. Walgreen receives 20% of this dividend and makes the following journal entry:

2009			
Jan. 17	Cash ($100,000 × 0.20)	20,000	
	Long-Term Equity-Method Investment		20,000
	Received dividend on equity-method investment.		

The Investment account is credited for the receipt of a dividend on an equity-method investment. Why? Because the dividend *decreases* the investee's equity. It also decreases the investor's investment.

Reporting Equity-Method Investments

After the preceding entries are posted, Walgreen's Investment account shows its equity in the net assets of Drugstore.com:

Long-Term Equity-Method Investment

2008			2009		
Jan. 6	Purchase	400,000	Jan. 17	Dividends received	20,000
Dec. 31	Net income	50,000			
2009					
Jan. 17	Balance	430,000			

Walgreen can report the long-term investment on the balance sheet and the revenue on the income statement as follows:

Balance Sheet (Partial):	
ASSETS	
Total current assets	$ XXX
Long-term equity-method investments	430,000
Property, plant, and equipment, net	XXX

Income Statement (Partial):	
Income from operations	$ XXX
Other revenue:	
Equity-method investment revenue	50,000
Net income.........................	$ XXX

Selling an Equity-Method Investment

There is usually a gain or a loss on the sale of an equity-method investment. The gain or loss is the difference between the sale proceeds and the investment carrying amount. Suppose Walgreen sells one-tenth of the Drugstore.com common stock for $40,000. The sale is recorded as follows:

Feb. 13	Cash	40,000	
	Loss on Sale of Investment	3,000	
	Long-Term Equity-Method Investment		
	($430,000 × 1/10)		43,000
	Sold investment.		

The following T-account summarizes the accounting for equity-method investments:

Long-Term Equity-Method Investment	
Cost	Share of losses
Share of income	Share of dividend received

Joint Ventures

A *joint venture* is a separate entity owned by a group of companies. Joint ventures are common in international business. Companies such as ExxonMobil, British Telecom, and Toyota partner with companies in other countries. A participant in a joint venture accounts for its investment by the equity method.

Consolidated Subsidiaries

Most large corporations own controlling interests in other companies. A **controlling** (or **majority**) **interest** is more than 50% of the investee's voting stock. A greater-than-50% investment enables the investor to elect a majority of the board of directors and thereby control the investee. The corporation that controls the other company is called the **parent company**, and the company that is controlled by another corporation is called the **subsidiary**. A well-known example is Saturn Corporation, which is a subsidiary of General Motors, the parent company. Because GM owns Saturn Corporation, the stockholders of GM control Saturn. Exhibit B-2 shows some of the subsidiaries of three large automakers.

EXHIBIT B-2 **Selected Subsidiaries of Three Large Automobile Manufacturers**

Parent Company	Selected Subsidiaries
General Motors Corporation	Saturn Corporation Hughes Aircraft Company
Ford Motor Company	Ford Aerospace Corporation Jaguar, Ltd.
DaimlerChrysler Corporation	Jeep/Eagle Corporation DaimlerChrysler Rail Systems

Consolidation Accounting

Consolidation accounting is the way to combine the financial statements of two or more companies that have the same owners. Most published financial reports include consolidated statements. **Consolidated statements** combine the balance sheets, income statements, and cash-flow statements of the parent company plus those of its majority-owned subsidiaries. The final outcome is a single set of statements as if the parent and its subsidiaries were the same entity.

In consolidation accounting, the assets, liabilities, revenues, and expenses of each subsidiary are added to the parent's accounts. For example, Saturn's cash balance is added to the cash balance of General Motors, and the overall sum is reported on GM's balance sheet. The consolidated financial statements bear only the name of the parent company, in this case General Motors Corporation.

Exhibit B-3 summarizes the accounting for investments in stock by showing which accounting method is used for each type of investment.

EXHIBIT B-3

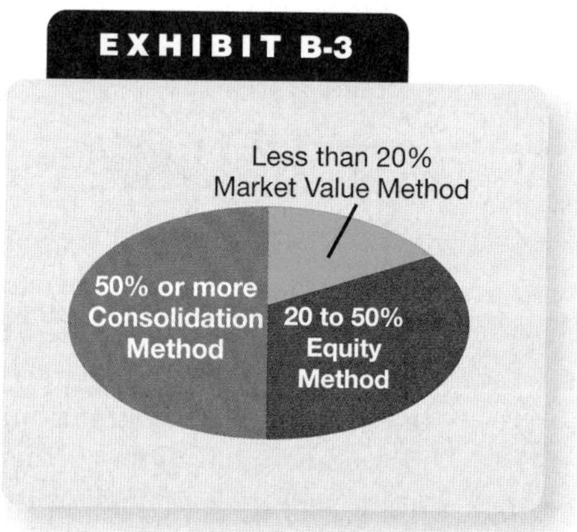

Accounting Methods for Stock Investments by Percentage of Ownership

Goodwill and Minority Interest

Goodwill is an intangible asset that is recorded in the consolidation process. Goodwill is reported on the parent company's consolidated balance sheet. As we saw in Chapter 9, **goodwill** is the excess of the cost to acquire another company over the sum of the market value of its net assets.

A parent company may purchase less than 100% of a subsidiary company. For example, Nokia, the cellular telephone company, has a minority interest in (owns less than 100% of) several other companies. **Minority interest** is the portion (less than 50%) of a subsidiary's stock owned by outside stockholders. Nokia Corporation, the parent company, therefore reports on its consolidated balance sheet an account titled Minority Interest.

Bond Investments

The relationship between the issuing corporation (the debtor that borrowed money) and the bondholders (investors who own the bonds) may be diagrammed as follows:

Issuing Corporation Has		Bondholder Has
Bonds payable	←——→	Investment in bonds
Interest expense	←——→	Interest revenue

The dollar amount of a bond transaction is the same for both the issuing corporation and the bondholder because money passes from one to the other. However, the accounts debited and credited differ. For example, the corporation has bonds payable; the bondholder has an investment. The corporation has interest expense, and the bondholder has interest revenue. Chapter 13 covers bonds payable.

Virtually all investments in bonds are long-term. These are called **held-to-maturity investments.** Bond investments are recorded at cost. At maturity, the bondholders will receive the bonds' full face value. We must amortize any discount or premium, as we did for bonds payable in Chapter 13. Held-to-maturity investments are reported at their *amortized cost.*

Suppose an investor purchases $10,000 of 6% CBS bonds at a price of 94 (94% of maturity value) on July 1, 2008. The investor intends to hold the bonds as a long-term investment until their maturity. Interest dates are June 30 and December 31. These bonds mature on July 1, 2010, so they will be outstanding for 60 months. Let's amortize the discount by the straight-line method. The bondholder's entries for this investment follow.

2008			
July 1	Long-Term Investment in Bonds ($10,000 × 0.94)	9,400	
	Cash		9,400
	Purchased bond investment.		

At December 31, the year-end entries are

Dec. 31	Cash ($10,000 × 0.06 × 6/12)	300	
	Interest Revenue		300
	Received interest.		
Dec. 31	Long-Term Investment in Bonds		
	[($10,000 – $9,400)/5 × 6/12]	60	
	Interest Revenue		60
	Amortized discount on bond investment.		

Reporting Bond Investments

The financial statements at December 31, 2008, report the following for this investment in bonds:

Balance sheet at December 31, 2008:	
Long-term investments in bonds ($9,400 + $ 60)......................	$9,460

Income statement for 2008:	
Other revenues:	
Interest revenue ($300 + $60).......	$ 360

Decision Guidelines

ACCOUNTING FOR LONG-TERM INVESTMENTS

Suppose you work for Bank of America. Your duties include accounting for the bank's investments. The following Decision Guidelines can serve as your checklist for using the appropriate method to account for each type of investment.

Decision	Guidelines
INVESTMENT TYPE	**ACCOUNTING METHOD**
Short-Term Investment	
Trading investment	Market value—report all gains (losses) on the income statement
Long-Term Investment	
Investor owns less than 20% of investee stock (available-for-sale investment)	Market value—report *unrealized* gains (losses) on the balance sheet —report *realized* gains (losses) from sale of the investment on the income statement
Investor owns between 20% and 50% of investee stock	Equity
Investor owns more than 50% of investee stock	Consolidation
Long-term investment in bonds (held-to-maturity investment)	Amortized cost

Summary Problem 1

Requirements

1. Identify the appropriate accounting method for each of the following situations:
   a. Investment in 25% of investee company's stock.
   b. Available-for-sale investment in stock.
   c. Investment in more than 50% of investee company's stock.
2. At what amount should the following available-for-sale investment portfolio be reported on the December 31 balance sheet? All the investments are less than 5% of the investee's stock.

Stock	Investment Cost	Current Market Value
Amazon.com	$ 5,000	$ 5,500
Intelysis	61,200	53,000
Procter & Gamble	3,680	6,230

   Journalize any adjusting entry required by these data.

3. Investor paid $67,900 to acquire a 40% equity-method investment in the common stock of Investee. At the end of the first year, Investee's net income was $80,000, and Investee declared and paid cash dividends of $55,000. Journalize Investor's (a) purchase of the investment, (b) share of Investee's net income, (c) receipt of dividends from Investee, and (d) sale of Investee stock for $80,100.

Solutions

1. (a) Equity (b) Market value (c) Consolidation
2. Report the investments at market value, $64,730, as follows:

Stock	Investment Cost	Current Market Value
Amazon.com	$ 5,000	$ 5,500
Intelysis	61,200	53,000
Procter & Gamble	3,680	6,230
Totals	$69,880	$64,730

Adjusting entry:

	Unrealized Loss on Investments ($69,880 – $64,730)	5,150	
	Allowance to Adjust Investment to Market		5,150
	To adjust investments to current market value.		

3. a.	Long-Term Equity-Method Investment	67,900	
	Cash		67,900
	Purchased equity-method investment.		
b.	Long-Term Equity-Method Investment ($80,000 × 0.40)	32,000	
	Equity-Method Investment Revenue		32,000
	Recorded investment revenue.		
c.	Cash ($55,000 × 0.40)	22,000	
	Long-Term Equity-Method Investment		22,000
	Received dividend on equity-method investment.		
d.	Cash	80,100	
	Long-Term Equity-Method Investment		
	($67,900 + $32,000 – $22,000)		77,900
	Gain on Sale of Investment		2,200
	Sold investment.		

Accounting for International Operations

Accounting across national boundaries is called *international accounting*. Did you know that Coca-Cola, IBM, and Bank of America earn most of their revenue outside the United States? It is common for U.S. companies to do a large part of their business abroad. McDonald's and AMR (American Airlines) are also very active in other countries. Exhibit B-4 shows the percentages of international sales for three leading companies.

EXHIBIT B-4 **Extent of International Business**

Company	Percentage of International Sales
McDonald's	65%
IBM	63%
AMR (American Airlines)	35%

Foreign Currencies and Foreign-Currency Exchange Rates

If Boeing, a U.S. company, sells a 747 jet to Air France, will Boeing receive U.S. dollars or euros? If the transaction is stated in dollars, Air France must buy dollars to pay Boeing in U.S. currency. If the transaction is in euros, Boeing will collect euros. To get dollars, Boeing must sell euros. In either case, a step has been added to the transaction: One company must convert domestic currency into foreign currency, or vice versa.

One nation's currency can be stated in terms of another's monetary unit. The price of a foreign currency is called the **foreign-currency exchange rate.** In Exhibit B-5, the U.S. dollar value of a European euro is $1.28. This means that one euro can be bought for $1.28. Other currencies are also listed in Exhibit B-5.

EXHIBIT B-5 **Foreign-Currency Exchange Rates**

Country	Monetary Unit	U.S Dollar Value	Country	Monetary Unit	U.S Dollar Value
Canada	Dollar	$0.90	Japan	Yen	$0.009
European Common Market	European currency unit	1.28	Mexico	Peso	0.090
Great Britain	Pound	1.90	Russia	Ruble	0.037

Source: The Wall Street Journal, Sept. 26, 2006, p. C11.

We use the exchange rate to *translate* the price of an item stated in one currency to its price in a second currency. Suppose an item costs 200 Canadian dollars. To compute its cost in U.S. dollars, we multiply the amount in Canadian dollars by the translation rate: 200 Canadian dollars × $0.90 = $180.

Currencies are described as "strong" or "weak." The exchange rate of a **strong currency** is rising relative to other nations' currencies. The exchange rate of a **weak currency** is falling relative to other currencies.

Foreign-Currency Transactions

Many companies conduct transactions in foreign currencies. D. E. Shipp Belting of Waco, Texas, provides an example. Shipp makes conveyor belts for several industries, including M&M Mars, which makes Snickers candy bars. Farmers along the Texas–Mexico border use Shipp conveyor belts to process vegetables. Shipp Belting conducts some of its business in pesos, the Mexican monetary unit.

Collecting Cash in a Foreign Currency

Consider Shipp Belting's sale of conveyor belts to Artes de Mexico, a vegetable grower in Matamoros. Suppose Artes orders conveyor belts valued at 1,000 pesos (approximately $90), and Artes will pay in pesos. Shipp will need to convert the pesos to dollars. Let's see how to account for this transaction.

Shipp Belting sells goods to Artes de Mexico for a price of 1,000 pesos on June 2. On that date, a peso was worth $0.090. One month later, on July 2, the peso has strengthened against the dollar and a peso is worth $0.100. Shipp still receives 1,000 pesos from Artes because that was the agreed price. Now the dollar value of Shipp's cash receipt is $10 more than the original amount, so Shipp ends up earning $10 more than expected. The following journal entries account for these transactions of Shipp Belting:

June 2	Accounts Receivable—Artes (1,000 pesos × $0.090)	90	
	Sales Revenue		90
	Sale on account.		

July 2	Cash (1,000 pesos × $0.100)	100	
	Accounts Receivable—Artes		90
	Foreign-Currency Gain		10
	Collection on account.		

Paying Cash in a Foreign Currency

Shipp Belting buys inventory from Gesellschaft Ltd., a Swiss company. The two companies decide on a price of 10,000 Swiss francs. On August 10, when Shipp receives the goods, the Swiss franc is priced at $0.72. When Shipp pays two weeks later, the Swiss franc has strengthened against the dollar and is now worth $0.78. This works to Shipp's disadvantage. Shipp would record the purchase and payment as follows:

Aug. 10	Inventory (10,000 Swiss francs × $0.72)	7,200	
	Accounts Payable—Gesellschaft Ltd.		7,200
	Purchase on account.		
Aug. 24	Accounts Payable—Gesellschaft Ltd.	7,200	
	Foreign-Currency Loss	600	
	Cash (10,000 Swiss francs × $0.78)		7,800
	Payment on account.		

In this case, the strengthening of the Swiss franc gave Shipp a foreign-currency loss.

Reporting Foreign-Currency Gains and Losses on the Income Statement

The Foreign-Currency Gain (Loss) account reports gains and losses on foreign-currency transactions. The company reports the *net amount* of these two accounts on the income statement as Other gains (losses). For example, Shipp Belting would combine the $600 foreign-currency loss and the $10 gain and report the net loss of $590 on the income statement, as follows:

Other gains (losses):	
Foreign-currency gain (loss), net ($600 − $10)	$(590)

These gains and losses fall into the "Other" category because they arise from outside activities. Buying and selling foreign currencies are not Shipp Belting's main business.

International Accounting Standards

In this text, we focus on generally accepted accounting principles in the United States. Most accounting methods are consistent throughout the world. Double-entry, the accrual system, and the basic financial statements (balance sheet, income statement, and so on) are used worldwide. But some differences exist among countries, as shown in Exhibit B-6.

EXHIBIT B-6 Some International Accounting Differences

Country	Inventories	Goodwill	Research and Development Costs
United States	Specific unit cost, FIFO, LIFO, weighted-average.	Written down when current value decreases.	Expensed as incurred.
Germany	LIFO is unacceptable for tax purposes and is not widely used.	Amortized over 5 years.	Expensed as incurred.
Japan	Similar to U.S.	Amortized over 5 years.	May be capitalized and amortized over 5 years.
United Kingdom (Great Britain)	LIFO is unacceptable for tax purposes and is not widely used.	Amortized over useful life or not amortized if life is indefinite.	Expense research costs. Some development costs may be capitalized.

The International Accounting Standards Committee (IASC), headquartered in London, operates much as the Financial Accounting Standards Board in the United States. It has the support of the accounting professions in many countries. However, the IASC has no authority to require compliance and must rely on cooperation by the various national accounting professions.

Decision Guidelines

Foreign-Currency Transactions

You've just opened a boutique to import clothing manufactured in China. Should you transact business in Chinese *renminbi* (the official currency unit), or in U.S. dollars? What foreign-currency gains or losses might occur? The Decision Guidelines will help you address these questions.

Decision	Guidelines
When to record a	
• Foreign-currency gain?	• When you receive foreign currency worth *more* U.S. dollars than the receivable on your books • When you pay foreign currency that costs *fewer* U.S. dollars than the payable on your books
• Foreign-currency loss?	• When you receive foreign currency worth *fewer* U.S. dollars than the receivable on your books • When you pay foreign currency that costs *more* U.S. dollars than the payable on your books

Summary Problem 2

Requirement

Journalize the following transactions of American Corp. Explanations are not required.

2008	
Nov. 16	Purchased equipment on account for 40,000 Swiss francs when the exchange rate was $0.73 per Swiss franc.
27	Sold merchandise on account to a Belgian company for 7,000 euros. Each euro is worth $1.10.
Dec. 22	Paid the Swiss company when the franc's exchange rate was $0.725.
31	Adjusted for the change in the exchange rate of the euro. Its current exchange rate is $1.08.
2009	
Jan. 4	Collected from the Belgian company. The euro exchange rate is $1.12.

Solution

Entries for transactions stated in foreign currencies:

2008			
Nov. 16	Equipment (40,000 × $0.73)	29,200	
	Accounts Payable		29,200
27	Accounts Receivable (7,000 × $1.10)	7,700	
	Sales Revenue		7,700
Dec. 22	Accounts Payable	29,200	
	Cash (40,000 × $0.725)		29,000
	Foreign-Currency Gain		200
31	Foreign-Currency Loss		
	[7,000 × ($1.10 – $1.08)]	140	
	Accounts Receivable		140
2009			
Jan. 4	Cash (7,000 × $1.12)	7,840	
	Accounts Receivable ($7,700 – $140)		7,560
	Foreign-Currency Gain		280

Exercises

Accounting for a trading investment

EB-1 Boston Today Publishers completed the following trading-investment transactions during 2007 and 2008:

2007	
Dec. 6	Purchased 1,000 shares of Subaru stock at a price of $52.25 per share, intending to sell the investment next month.
23	Received a cash dividend of $1.10 per share on the Subaru stock.
31	Adjusted the investment to its market value of $50 per share.
2008	
Jan. 27	Sold the Subaru stock for $48 per share.

Journalize Boston Today Publishers' investment transactions. Explanations are not required. (pp. B-2–B-3)

Accounting for an available-for-sale investment

EB-2 Raider Investments completed these long-term available-for-sale investment transactions during 2007:

2007	
Jan. 14	Purchased 300 shares of Fossil stock, paying $44 per share. Raider intends to hold the investment for the indefinite future.
Aug. 22	Received a cash dividend of $0.60 per share on the Fossil stock.
Dec. 31	Adjusted the Fossil investment to its current market value of $12,000.

1. Journalize Raider's investment transactions. Explanations are not required. (pp. B-4–B-5)
2. Show how to report the investment and any unrealized gain or loss on Raider's balance sheet at December 31, 2007. (p. B-5)

Accounting for the sale of an available-for-sale investment

EB-3 Use the data given in Exercise EB-2. On August 4, 2008, Raider Investments sold its investment in Fossil stock for $45 per share.

1. Journalize the sale. No explanation is required. (p. B-5)
2. How does the gain or loss that you recorded differ from the gain or loss that was recorded at December 31, 2007 (in Exercise EB-2)? (p. B-5)

Accounting for a 40% investment in another company

EB-4 Suppose on January 6, 2008, General Motors paid $500 million for its 40% investment in Isuzu. Assume Isuzu earned net income of $60 million and paid cash dividends of $50 million during 2008.

1. What method should General Motors use to account for the investment in Isuzu? Give your reason. (p. B-5)
2. Journalize these three transactions on the books of General Motors. Show all amounts in millions of dollars and include an explanation for each entry. (pp. B-5–B-6)
3. Post to the Long-Term Equity-Method Investment T-account. What is its balance after all the transactions are posted? (pp. B-5–B-6)

Working with a bond investment

EB-5 Smith Barney & Co. owns vast amounts of corporate bonds. Suppose Smith Barney buys $1,000,000 of Primo Corp. bonds at a price of 98. The Primo bonds pay stated interest at the annual rate of 8% and mature within five years.

1. How much did Smith Barney pay to purchase the bond investment? How much will Smith Barney collect when the bond investment matures? (pp. B-9–B-10)
2. How much cash interest will Smith Barney receive each year from Primo? (pp. B-9–B-10)
3. Compute Smith Barney's annual interest revenue on this bond investment. Use the straight-line method to amortize the discount on the investment. (pp. B-9–B-10)

Recording bond investment transactions

EB-6 Return to Exercise EB-5, the Smith Barney investment in Primo Corp. bonds. Journalize on Smith Barney's books, along with an explanation for each entry:

a. Purchase of the bond investment on January 2, 2007. Smith Barney expects to hold the investment to maturity. (pp. B-9–B-10)
b. Receipt of annual cash interest on December 31, 2007. (pp. B-9–B-10)
c. Amortization of discount on December 31, 2007. (pp. B-9–B-10)
d. Collection of the investment's face value at its maturity date on January 2, 2012. (Challenge) (Interest and amortization of discount for 2011 have already been recorded, so you may ignore these entries.)

Accounting for foreign-currency transactions

EB-7 Suppose Wilson & Co. sells athletic shoes to a Russian company on March 14. Wilson agrees to accept 2,000,000 Russian rubles. On the date of sale, the ruble is quoted at $0.030. Wilson collects half the receivable on April 19, when the ruble is worth $0.028. Then, on May 10, when the price of the ruble is $0.036, Wilson collects the final amount.

Journalize these three transactions for Wilson; include an explanation. Overall, how well did Wilson come out in terms of a net foreign-currency gain or loss? (pp. B-5–B-7)

Problems

Accounting for trading investments

PB-8 Jetway Corporation generated excess cash and invested in securities, as follows:

July 2	Purchased 3,500 shares of common stock as a trading investment, paying $12 per share.
Aug. 21	Received cash dividend of $0.40 per share on the trading investment.
Sep. 16	Sold the trading investment for $13.50 per share.
Oct. 8	Purchased trading investments for $136,000.
Dec. 31	Adjusted the trading securities to market value of $133,000.

continued . . .

Requirements

1. Record the transactions in the journal of Jetway Corporation. Explanations are not required. (pp. B-2–B-3)
2. Post to the Short-Term Investments account, and show how to report the short-term investments on Jetway's balance sheet at December 31, 2007. (p. B-3)

Accounting for available-for-sale and equity-method investments

PB-9 The beginning balance sheet of Media Source Co. included the following:

Long-Term Equity-Method Investments	$600,000

During the year Media Source completed these investment transactions:

Mar. 3	Purchased 5,000 shares of Flothru Software common stock as a long-term available-for-sale investment, paying $9 per share.
May 14	Received cash dividend of $0.80 per share on the Flothru investment.
Dec. 15	Received cash dividend of $80,000 from equity-method investments.
31	Received annual reports from equity-method investee companies. Their total net income for the year was $600,000. Of this amount, Media Source's proportion is 25%.
31	Adjusted the available-for-sale investment to market value of $44,000.

Requirements

1. Record the transactions in the journal of Media Source Co. (pp. B-4–B-7)
2. Post entries to T-accounts for Long-Term Available-for-Sale Investments and Allowance to Adjust Investment to Market. Then determine their balances at December 31.

   Post to a T-account for Long-Term Equity-Method Investment, and determine its December 31 balance. (pp. B-5–B-6)
3. Show how to report the Long-Term Available-for-Sale Investment and the Long-Term Equity-Method Investments on Media Source's balance sheet at December 31. (pp. B-5–B-7)

Accounting for a bond investment; amortizing discount by the straight-line method

PB-10 Financial institutions hold large quantities of bond investments. Suppose Solomon Brothers purchases $800,000 of 6% bonds of Buster Brown Corporation for 92 on January 1, 2004. These bonds pay interest on June 30 and December 31 each year. They mature on January 1, 2009.

Requirements

1. Journalize Solomon Brothers' purchase of the bonds as a long-term investment on January 1, 2004 (to be held to maturity). Then record the receipt of cash interest and amortization of discount on June 30 and December 31, 2004. The straight-line method is appropriate for amortizing discount. (pp. B-9–B-10)
2. Show how to report this long-term bond investment on Solomon Brothers' balance sheet at December 31, 2004. (pp. B-9–B-10)

Recording foreign-currency transactions and reporting the foreign-currency gain or loss

PB-11 Suppose Tommy Hilfiger completed the following transactions:

May 4	Sold clothing on account to a Mexican department store for $70,000. The customer agrees to pay in dollars.
13	Purchased inventory on account from a Canadian company at a price of Canadian $60,000. The exchange rate of the Canadian dollar is $0.85, and payment will be in Canadian dollars.
20	Sold goods on account to an English firm for 80,000 British pounds. Collection will be in pounds, and the exchange rate of the pound is $1.80.
27	Collected from the Mexican company.
June 21	Paid the Canadian company. The exchange rate of the Canadian dollar is $0.82.
July 17	Collected from the English firm. The exchange rate of the British pound is $1.77.

Requirements

1. Record these transactions in Tommy Hilfiger's journal, and show how to report the net foreign-currency gain or loss on the income statement. Explanations are not required. (pp. B-5–B-7)
2. How will what you learned in this problem help you structure international transactions? (Challenge)

Appendix C

Present Value Tables

This appendix provides present value tables and future value tables (more complete than those in the Chapter 13).

EXHIBIT C-1 Present Value of $1

	Present Value										
Periods	1%	2%	3%	4%	5%	6%	7%	8%	9%	10%	12%
1	0.990	0.980	0.971	0.962	0.952	0.943	0.935	0.926	0.917	0.909	0.893
2	0.980	0.961	0.943	0.925	0.907	0.890	0.873	0.857	0.842	0.826	0.797
3	0.971	0.942	0.915	0.889	0.864	0.840	0.816	0.794	0.772	0.751	0.712
4	0.961	0.924	0.888	0.855	0.823	0.792	0.763	0.735	0.708	0.683	0.636
5	0.951	0.906	0.883	0.822	0.784	0.747	0.713	0.681	0.650	0.621	0.567
6	0.942	0.888	0.837	0.790	0.746	0.705	0.666	0.630	0.596	0.564	0.507
7	0.933	0.871	0.813	0.760	0.711	0.665	0.623	0.583	0.547	0.513	0.452
8	0.923	0.853	0.789	0.731	0.677	0.627	0.582	0.540	0.502	0.467	0.404
9	0.914	0.837	0.766	0.703	0.645	0.592	0.544	0.500	0.460	0.424	0.361
10	0.905	0.820	0.744	0.676	0.614	0.558	0.508	0.463	0.422	0.386	0.322
11	0.896	0.804	0.722	0.650	0.585	0.527	0.475	0.429	0.388	0.350	0.287
12	0.887	0.788	0.701	0.625	0.557	0.497	0.444	0.397	0.356	0.319	0.257
13	0.879	0.773	0.681	0.601	0.530	0.469	0.415	0.368	0.326	0.290	0.229
14	0.870	0.758	0.661	0.577	0.505	0.442	0.388	0.340	0.299	0.263	0.205
15	0.861	0.743	0.642	0.555	0.481	0.417	0.362	0.315	0.275	0.239	0.183
16	0.853	0.728	0.623	0.534	0.458	0.394	0.339	0.292	0.252	0.218	0.163
17	0.844	0.714	0.605	0.513	0.436	0.371	0.317	0.270	0.231	0.198	0.146
18	0.836	0.700	0.587	0.494	0.416	0.350	0.296	0.250	0.212	0.180	0.130
19	0.828	0.686	0.570	0.475	0.396	0.331	0.277	0.232	0.194	0.164	0.116
20	0.820	0.673	0.554	0.456	0.377	0.312	0.258	0.215	0.178	0.149	0.104
21	0.811	0.660	0.538	0.439	0.359	0.294	0.242	0.199	0.164	0.135	0.093
22	0.803	0.647	0.522	0.422	0.342	0.278	0.226	0.184	0.150	0.123	0.083
23	0.795	0.634	0.507	0.406	0.326	0.262	0.211	0.170	0.138	0.112	0.074
24	0.788	0.622	0.492	0.390	0.310	0.247	0.197	0.158	0.126	0.102	0.066
25	0.780	0.610	0.478	0.375	0.295	0.233	0.184	0.146	0.116	0.092	0.059
26	0.772	0.598	0.464	0.361	0.281	0.220	0.172	0.135	0.106	0.084	0.053
27	0.764	0.586	0.450	0.347	0.268	0.207	0.161	0.125	0.098	0.076	0.047
28	0.757	0.574	0.437	0.333	0.255	0.196	0.150	0.116	0.090	0.069	0.042
29	0.749	0.563	0.424	0.321	0.243	0.185	0.141	0.107	0.082	0.063	0.037
30	0.742	0.552	0.412	0.308	0.231	0.174	0.131	0.099	0.075	0.057	0.033
40	0.672	0.453	0.307	0.208	0.142	0.097	0.067	0.046	0.032	0.022	0.011
50	0.608	0.372	0.228	0.141	0.087	0.054	0.034	0.021	0.013	0.009	0.003

EXHIBIT C-1 Present Value of $1 (con't)

Present Value

14%	15%	16%	18%	20%	25%	30%	35%	40%	45%	50%	Periods
0.877	0.870	0.862	0.847	0.833	0.800	0.769	0.741	0.714	0.690	0.667	1
0.769	0.756	0.743	0.718	0.694	0.640	0.592	0.549	0.510	0.476	0.444	2
0.675	0.658	0.641	0.609	0.579	0.512	0.455	0.406	0.364	0.328	0.296	3
0.592	0.572	0.552	0.516	0.482	0.410	0.350	0.301	0.260	0.226	0.198	4
0.519	0.497	0.476	0.437	0.402	0.328	0.269	0.223	0.186	0.156	0.132	5
0.456	0.432	0.410	0.370	0.335	0.262	0.207	0.165	0.133	0.108	0.088	6
0.400	0.376	0.354	0.314	0.279	0.210	0.159	0.122	0.095	0.074	0.059	7
0.351	0.327	0.305	0.266	0.233	0.168	0.123	0.091	0.068	0.051	0.039	8
0.308	0.284	0.263	0.225	0.194	0.134	0.094	0.067	0.048	0.035	0.026	9
0.270	0.247	0.227	0.191	0.162	0.107	0.073	0.050	0.035	0.024	0.017	10
0.237	0.215	0.195	0.162	0.135	0.086	0.056	0.037	0.025	0.017	0.012	11
0.208	0.187	0.168	0.137	0.112	0.069	0.043	0.027	0.018	0.012	0.008	12
0.182	0.163	0.145	0.116	0.093	0.055	0.033	0.020	0.013	0.008	0.005	13
0.160	0.141	0.125	0.099	0.078	0.044	0.025	0.015	0.009	0.006	0.003	14
0.140	0.123	0.108	0.084	0.065	0.035	0.020	0.011	0.006	0.004	0.002	15
0.123	0.107	0.093	0.071	0.054	0.028	0.015	0.008	0.005	0.003	0.002	16
0.108	0.093	0.080	0.060	0.045	0.023	0.012	0.006	0.003	0.002	0.001	17
0.095	0.081	0.069	0.051	0.038	0.018	0.009	0.005	0.002	0.001	0.001	18
0.083	0.070	0.060	0.043	0.031	0.014	0.007	0.003	0.002	0.001		19
0.073	0.061	0.051	0.037	0.026	0.012	0.005	0.002	0.001	0.001		20
0.064	0.053	0.044	0.031	0.022	0.009	0.004	0.002	0.001			21
0.056	0.046	0.038	0.026	0.018	0.007	0.003	0.001	0.001			22
0.049	0.040	0.033	0.022	0.015	0.006	0.002	0.001				23
0.043	0.035	0.028	0.019	0.013	0.005	0.002	0.001				24
0.038	0.030	0.024	0.016	0.010	0.004	0.001	0.001				25
0.033	0.026	0.021	0.014	0.009	0.003	0.001					26
0.029	0.023	0.018	0.011	0.007	0.002	0.001					27
0.026	0.020	0.016	0.010	0.006	0.002	0.001					28
0.022	0.017	0.014	0.008	0.005	0.002						29
0.020	0.015	0.012	0.007	0.004	0.001						30
0.005	0.004	0.003	0.001	0.001							40
0.001	0.001	0.001									50

EXHIBIT C-2 Present Value of Annuity of $1

	Present Value										
Periods	1%	2%	3%	4%	5%	6%	7%	8%	9%	10%	12%
1	0.990	0.980	0.971	0.962	0.952	0.943	0.935	0.926	0.917	0.909	0.893
2	1.970	1.942	1.913	1.886	1.859	1.833	1.808	1.783	1.759	1.736	1.690
3	2.941	2.884	2.829	2.775	2.723	2.673	2.624	2.577	2.531	2.487	2.402
4	3.902	3.808	3.717	3.630	3.546	3.465	3.387	3.312	3.240	3.170	3.037
5	4.853	4.713	4.580	4.452	4.329	4.212	4.100	3.993	3.890	3.791	3.605
6	5.795	5.601	5.417	5.242	5.076	4.917	4.767	4.623	4.486	4.355	4.111
7	6.728	6.472	6.230	6.002	5.786	5.582	5.389	5.206	5.033	4.868	4.564
8	7.652	7.325	7.020	6.733	6.463	6.210	5.971	5.747	5.535	5.335	4.968
9	8.566	8.162	7.786	7.435	7.108	6.802	6.515	6.247	5.995	5.759	5.328
10	9.471	8.983	8.530	8.111	7.722	7.360	7.024	6.710	6.418	6.145	5.650
11	10.368	9.787	9.253	8.760	8.306	7.887	7.499	7.139	6.805	6.495	5.938
12	11.255	10.575	9.954	9.385	8.863	8.384	7.943	7.536	7.161	6.814	6.194
13	12.134	11.348	10.635	9.986	9.394	8.853	8.358	7.904	7.487	7.103	6.424
14	13.004	12.106	11.296	10.563	9.899	9.295	8.745	8.244	7.786	7.367	6.628
15	13.865	12.849	11.938	11.118	10.380	9.712	9.108	8.559	8.061	7.606	6.811
16	14.718	13.578	12.561	11.652	10.838	10.106	9.447	8.851	8.313	7.824	6.974
17	15.562	14.292	13.166	12.166	11.274	10.477	9.763	9.122	8.544	8.022	7.120
18	16.398	14.992	13.754	12.659	11.690	10.828	10.059	9.372	8.756	8.201	7.250
19	17.226	15.678	14.324	13.134	12.085	11.158	10.336	9.604	8.950	8.365	7.366
20	18.046	16.351	14.878	13.590	12.462	11.470	10.594	9.818	9.129	8.514	7.469
21	18.857	17.011	15.415	14.029	12.821	11.764	10.836	10.017	9.292	8.649	7.562
22	19.660	17.658	15.937	14.451	13.163	12.042	11.061	10.201	9.442	8.772	7.645
23	20.456	18.292	16.444	14.857	13.489	12.303	11.272	10.371	9.580	8.883	7.718
24	21.243	18.914	16.936	15.247	13.799	12.550	11.469	10.529	9.707	8.985	7.784
25	22.023	19.523	17.413	15.622	14.094	12.783	11.654	10.675	9.823	9.077	7.843
26	22.795	20.121	17.877	15.983	14.375	13.003	11.826	10.810	9.929	9.161	7.896
27	23.560	20.707	18.327	16.330	14.643	13.211	11.987	10.935	10.027	9.237	7.943
28	24.316	21.281	18.764	16.663	14.898	13.406	12.137	11.051	10.116	9.307	7.984
29	25.066	21.844	19.189	16.984	15.141	13.591	12.278	11.158	10.198	9.370	8.022
30	25.808	22.396	19.600	17.292	15.373	13.765	12.409	11.258	10.274	9.427	8.055
40	32.835	27.355	23.115	19.793	17.159	15.046	13.332	11.925	10.757	9.779	8.244
50	39.196	31.424	25.730	21.482	18.256	15.762	13.801	12.234	10.962	9.915	8.305

EXHIBIT C-2 Present Value of Annuity of $1 (con't)

Present Value											
14%	15%	16%	18%	20%	25%	30%	35%	40%	45%	50%	Periods
0.877	0.870	0.862	0.847	0.833	0.800	0.769	0.741	0.714	0.690	0.667	1
1.647	1.626	1.605	1.566	1.528	1.440	1.361	1.289	1.224	1.165	1.111	2
2.322	2.283	2.246	2.174	2.106	1.952	1.816	1.696	1.589	1.493	1.407	3
2.914	2.855	2.798	2.690	2.589	2.362	2.166	1.997	1.849	1.720	1.605	4
3.433	3.352	3.274	3.127	2.991	2.689	2.436	2.220	2.035	1.876	1.737	5
3.889	3.784	3.685	3.498	3.326	2.951	2.643	2.385	2.168	1.983	1.824	6
4.288	4.160	4.039	3.812	3.605	3.161	2.802	2.508	2.263	2.057	1.883	7
4.639	4.487	4.344	4.078	3.837	3.329	2.925	2.598	2.331	2.109	1.922	8
4.946	4.772	4.607	4.303	4.031	3.463	3.019	2.665	2.379	2.144	1.948	9
5.216	5.019	4.833	4.494	4.192	3.571	3.092	2.715	2.414	2.168	1.965	10
5.553	5.234	5.029	4.656	4.327	3.656	3.147	2.752	2.438	2.185	1.977	11
5.660	5.421	5.197	4.793	4.439	3.725	3.190	2.779	2.456	2.197	1.985	12
5.842	5.583	5.342	4.910	4.533	3.780	3.223	2.799	2.469	2.204	1.990	13
6.002	5.724	5.468	5.008	4.611	3.824	3.249	2.814	2.478	2.210	1.993	14
6.142	5.847	5.575	5.092	4.675	3.859	3.268	2.825	2.484	2.214	1.995	15
6.265	5.954	5.669	5.162	4.730	3.887	3.283	2.834	2.489	2.216	1.997	16
6.373	6.047	5.749	5.222	4.775	3.910	3.295	2.840	2.492	2.218	1.998	17
6.467	6.128	5.818	5.273	4.812	3.928	3.304	2.844	2.494	2.219	1.999	18
6.550	6.198	5.877	5.316	4.844	3.942	3.311	2.848	2.496	2.220	1.999	19
6.623	6.259	5.929	5.353	4.870	3.954	3.316	2.850	2.497	2.221	1.999	20
6.687	6.312	5.973	5.384	4.891	3.963	3.320	2.852	2.498	2.221	2.000	21
6.743	6.359	6.011	5.410	4.909	3.970	3.323	2.853	2.498	2.222	2.000	22
6.792	6.399	6.044	5.432	4.925	3.976	3.325	2.854	2.499	2.222	2.000	23
6.835	6.434	6.073	5.451	4.937	3.981	3.327	2.855	2.499	2.222	2.000	24
6.873	6.464	6.097	5.467	4.948	3.985	3.329	2.856	2.499	2.222	2.000	25
6.906	6.491	6.118	5.480	4.956	3.988	3.330	2.856	2.500	2.222	2.000	26
6.935	6.514	6.136	5.492	4.964	3.990	3.331	2.856	2.500	2.222	2.000	27
6.961	6.534	6.152	5.502	4.970	3.992	3.331	2.857	2.500	2.222	2.000	28
6.983	6.551	6.166	5.510	4.975	3.994	3.332	2.857	2.500	2.222	2.000	29
7.003	6.566	6.177	5.517	4.979	3.995	3.332	2.857	2.500	2.222	2.000	30
7.105	6.642	6.234	5.548	4.997	3.999	3.333	2.857	2.500	2.222	2.000	40
7.133	6.661	6.246	5.554	4.999	4.000	3.333	2.857	2.500	2.222	2.000	50

EXHIBIT C-3 Future Value of $1

	Future Value												
Periods	1%	2%	3%	4%	5%	6%	7%	8%	9%	10%	12%	14%	15%
1	1.010	1.020	1.030	1.040	1.050	1.060	1.070	1.080	1.090	1.100	1.120	1.140	1.150
2	1.020	1.040	1.061	1.082	1.103	1.124	1.145	1.166	1.188	1.210	1.254	1.300	1.323
3	1.030	1.061	1.093	1.125	1.158	1.191	1.225	1.260	1.295	1.331	1.405	1.482	1.521
4	1.041	1.082	1.126	1.170	1.216	1.262	1.311	1.360	1.412	1.464	1.574	1.689	1.749
5	1.051	1.104	1.159	1.217	1.276	1.338	1.403	1.469	1.539	1.611	1.762	1.925	2.011
6	1.062	1.126	1.194	1.265	1.340	1.419	1.501	1.587	1.677	1.772	1.974	2.195	2.313
7	1.072	1.149	1.230	1.316	1.407	1.504	1.606	1.714	1.828	1.949	2.211	2.502	2.660
8	1.083	1.172	1.267	1.369	1.477	1.594	1.718	1.851	1.993	2.144	2.476	2.853	3.059
9	1.094	1.195	1.305	1.423	1.551	1.689	1.838	1.999	2.172	2.358	2.773	3.252	3.518
10	1.105	1.219	1.344	1.480	1.629	1.791	1.967	2.159	2.367	2.594	3.106	3.707	4.046
11	1.116	1.243	1.384	1.539	1.710	1.898	2.105	2.332	2.580	2.853	3.479	4.226	4.652
12	1.127	1.268	1.426	1.601	1.796	2.012	2.252	2.518	2.813	3.138	3.896	4.818	5.350
13	1.138	1.294	1.469	1.665	1.886	2.133	2.410	2.720	3.066	3.452	4.363	5.492	6.153
14	1.149	1.319	1.513	1.732	1.980	2.261	2.579	2.937	3.342	3.798	4.887	6.261	7.076
15	1.161	1.346	1.558	1.801	2.079	2.397	2.759	3.172	3.642	4.177	5.474	7.138	8.137
16	1.173	1.373	1.605	1.873	2.183	2.540	2.952	3.426	3.970	4.595	6.130	8.137	9.358
17	1.184	1.400	1.653	1.948	2.292	2.693	3.159	3.700	4.328	5.054	6.866	9.276	10.76
18	1.196	1.428	1.702	2.026	2.407	2.854	3.380	3.996	4.717	5.560	7.690	10.58	12.38
19	1.208	1.457	1.754	2.107	2.527	3.026	3.617	4.316	5.142	6.116	8.613	12.06	14.23
20	1.220	1.486	1.806	2.191	2.653	3.207	3.870	4.661	5.604	6.728	9.646	13.74	16.37
21	1.232	1.516	1.860	2.279	2.786	3.400	4.141	5.034	6.109	7.400	10.80	15.67	18.82
22	1.245	1.546	1.916	2.370	2.925	3.604	4.430	5.437	6.659	8.140	12.10	17.86	21.64
23	1.257	1.577	1.974	2.465	3.072	3.820	4.741	5.871	7.258	8.954	13.55	20.36	24.89
24	1.270	1.608	2.033	2.563	3.225	4.049	5.072	6.341	7.911	9.850	15.18	23.21	28.63
25	1.282	1.641	2.094	2.666	3.386	4.292	5.427	6.848	8.623	10.83	17.00	26.46	32.92
26	1.295	1.673	2.157	2.772	3.556	4.549	5.807	7.396	9.399	11.92	19.04	30.17	37.86
27	1.308	1.707	2.221	2.883	3.733	4.822	6.214	7.988	10.25	13.11	21.32	34.39	43.54
28	1.321	1.741	2.288	2.999	3.920	5.112	6.649	8.627	11.17	14.42	23.88	39.20	50.07
29	1.335	1.776	2.357	3.119	4.116	5.418	7.114	9.317	12.17	15.86	26.75	44.69	57.58
30	1.348	1.811	2.427	3.243	4.322	5.743	7.612	10.06	13.27	17.45	29.96	50.95	66.21
40	1.489	2.208	3.262	4.801	7.040	10.29	14.97	21.72	31.41	45.26	93.05	188.9	267.9
50	1.645	2.692	4.384	7.107	11.47	18.42	29.46	46.90	74.36	117.4	289.0	700.2	1,084

EXHIBIT C-4 Future Value of Annuity $1

	Future Value												
Periods	1%	2%	3%	4%	5%	6%	7%	8%	9%	10%	12%	14%	15%
1	1.000	1.000	1.000	1.000	1.000	1.000	1.000	1.000	1.000	1.000	1.000	1.000	1.000
2	2.010	2.020	2.030	2.040	2.050	2.060	2.070	2.080	2.090	2.100	2.120	2.140	2.150
3	3.030	3.060	3.091	3.122	3.153	3.184	3.215	3.246	3.278	3.310	3.374	3.440	3.473
4	4.060	4.122	4.184	4.246	4.310	4.375	4.440	4.506	4.573	4.641	4.779	4.921	4.993
5	5.101	5.204	5.309	5.416	5.526	5.637	5.751	5.867	5.985	6.105	6.353	6.610	6.742
6	6.152	6.308	6.468	6.633	6.802	6.975	7.153	7.336	7.523	7.716	8.115	8.536	8.754
7	7.214	7.434	7.662	7.898	8.142	8.394	8.654	8.923	9.200	9.487	10.09	10.73	11.07
8	8.286	8.583	8.892	9.214	9.549	9.897	10.26	10.64	11.03	11.44	12.30	13.23	13.73
9	9.369	9.755	10.16	10.58	11.03	11.49	11.98	12.49	13.02	13.58	14.78	16.09	16.79
10	10.46	10.95	11.46	12.01	12.58	13.18	13.82	14.49	15.19	15.94	17.55	19.34	20.30
11	11.57	12.17	12.81	13.49	14.21	14.97	15.78	16.65	17.56	18.53	20.65	23.04	24.35
12	12.68	13.41	14.19	15.03	15.92	16.87	17.89	18.98	20.14	21.38	24.13	27.27	29.00
13	13.81	14.68	15.62	16.63	17.71	18.88	20.14	21.50	22.95	24.52	28.03	32.09	34.35
14	14.95	15.97	17.09	18.29	19.60	21.02	22.55	24.21	26.02	27.98	32.39	37.58	40.50
15	16.10	17.29	18.60	20.02	21.58	23.28	25.13	27.15	29.36	31.77	37.28	43.84	47.58
16	17.26	18.64	20.16	21.82	23.66	25.67	27.89	30.32	33.00	35.95	42.75	50.98	55.72
17	18.43	20.01	21.76	23.70	25.84	28.21	30.84	33.75	36.97	40.54	48.88	59.12	65.08
18	19.61	21.41	23.41	25.65	28.13	30.91	34.00	37.45	41.30	45.60	55.75	68.39	75.84
19	20.81	22.84	25.12	27.67	30.54	33.76	37.38	41.45	46.02	51.16	63.44	78.97	88.21
20	22.02	24.30	26.87	29.78	33.07	36.79	41.00	45.76	51.16	57.28	72.05	91.02	102.4
21	23.24	25.78	28.68	31.97	35.72	39.99	44.87	50.42	56.76	64.00	81.70	104.8	118.8
22	24.47	27.30	30.54	34.25	38.51	43.39	49.01	55.46	62.87	71.40	92.50	120.4	137.6
23	25.72	28.85	32.45	36.62	41.43	47.00	53.44	60.89	69.53	79.54	104.6	138.3	159.3
24	26.97	30.42	34.43	39.08	44.50	50.82	58.18	66.76	76.79	88.50	118.2	158.7	184.2
25	28.24	32.03	36.46	41.65	47.73	54.86	63.25	73.11	84.70	98.35	133.3	181.9	212.8
26	29.53	33.67	38.55	44.31	51.11	59.16	68.68	79.95	93.32	109.2	150.3	208.3	245.7
27	30.82	35.34	40.71	47.08	54.67	63.71	74.48	87.35	102.7	121.1	169.4	238.5	283.6
28	32.13	37.05	42.93	49.97	58.40	68.53	80.70	95.34	113.0	134.2	190.7	272.9	327.1
29	33.45	38.79	45.22	52.97	62.32	73.64	87.35	104.0	124.1	148.6	214.6	312.1	377.2
30	34.78	40.57	47.58	56.08	66.44	79.06	94.46	113.3	136.3	164.5	241.3	356.8	434.7
40	48.89	60.40	75.40	95.03	120.8	154.8	199.6	259.1	337.9	442.6	767.1	1,342	1,779
50	64.46	84.58	112.8	152.7	209.3	290.3	406.5	573.8	815.1	1,164	2,400	4,995	7,218

Photo Credits

Chapter 1, *Pages 2–3,* Courtesy of www.istockphoto.com. iStock Photo International/Royalty Free.

Chapter 2, *Pages 60–61,* © Gary Houlder/CORBIS. All Rights Reserved.

Chapter 3, *Pages 126–127,* Courtesy of PhotoEdit Inc.

Chapter 4, *Pages 198–199,* Courtesy of Howard Koby Photography.

Chapter 5, *Pages 256–257,* Courtesy of Getty Images–Stockbyte.

Chapter 6, *Pages 314–315,* Courtesy of Corbis Royalty Free.

Chapter 7, *Pages 356–357,* Courtesy of Corbis Royalty Free.

Chapter 8, *Pages 404–405,* Courtesy of Getty Images–Stockbyte.

Chapter 9, *Pages 454–455,* Courtesy of The Image Works.

Chapter 10, *Pages 498–499,* Courtesy of Getty Images–Stockbyte.

Chapter 11, *Pages 544–545,* Courtesy of PhotoEdit Inc.

Chapter 12, *Pages 596–597,* Courtesy of Joel Gordon Photography.

Chapter 13, *Pages 640–641,* Courtesy of www.istockphoto.com. iStock Photo International/Royalty Free.

Chapter 14, *Pages 690–691,* Courtesy of Getty Images, Inc.

Chapter 15, *Pages 754–755,* Courtesy of Alamy Images.

Chapter 16, *Pages 806–807,* Courtesy of www.istockphoto.com. iStock Photo International/Royalty Free.

Chapter 17, *Pages 850–851,* Courtesy of Corbis Royalty Free.

Chapter 18, *Pages 900–901,* Courtesy of Corbis Royalty Free.

Chapter 19, *Pages 958–959,* Courtesy of Getty Images–Stockbyte.

Chapter 20, *Pages 1006–1007,* Courtesy of PhotoEdit Inc.

Chapter 21, *Pages 1056–1057,* Courtesy of Tim Boyle, Getty Images, Inc.

Chapter 22, *Pages 1110–1111,* Courtesy of Karl Weatherly, © Karl Weatherly/CORBIS, all rights reserved.

Chapter 23, *Pages 1168–1169,* Courtesy of Amazon.com®.

Chapter 24, *Pages 1220–1221,* Courtesy of Corbis Royalty Free.

Chapter 25, *Pages 1266–1267,* Courtesy of Myrleen Ferguson Cate, FotoEdit Inc.

Glindex

A Combined Glossary/Subject Index

A

Absorption costing *The costing method that assigns both variable and fixed manufacturing costs to products,* 1049
- and manager incentives, 1052
- and variable costing, differences between, 1049, 1049E20A-1
- applying, *vs.* variable costing, 1050–1051, 1051E20A-2
- exercises, 1052–1053
- problems, 1053–1054
- team project, 1054–1055

Accelerated depreciation method *A depreciation method that writes off more of the asset's cost near the start of its useful life than the straight-line method does,* 463

Account *The detailed record of the changes in a particular asset, liability, or owner's equity during a period. The basic summary device of accounting,* 62
- balance of, normal, 64–65, 71, 71E2-9
- numbers, 64–65

Account form, 212

Accounting *The information system that measures business activities, processes that information into reports, and communicates the results to decision makers,* 4
- concepts and principles of, 11–12
- financial *vs.* management, 5, 5E1-2
- users of, 4–5, 4E1-1

Accounting concepts and principles
- in the adjusting process, 128–132
- in the business environment, 11–12

Accounting cycle *Process by which companies produce their financial statements for a specific period,* 199, 200, 200E4-1

Accounting cycle, completing, 206E4-7
- accounting ratios, 214
- accounting vocabulary, 220
- adjusting entries, recording, 207, 207E4-8
- applying your knowledge
  - decision case, 240
  - ethical issue, 240–241
  - financial statement case, 241
  - team project, 241–242
- assessing your progress
  - exercises, 223–229
  - problems, 229–239
- assets and liabilities, classifying, 211–212
- balance sheet
  - classified, 212
  - forms, 212, 213E4-12–13
- closing the accounts, 208, 208E4-9
  - net income, 209–210, 209E4-10
  - net loss, 210
- decision guidelines, 215
- financial statements, preparing, 207
- postclosing trial balance, 210–211, 211E4-11
- review questions (quick check), 221–222
- summary problems, 204–205, 216–219

Accounting data, flow of, 71–72, 72E2-10

Accounting equation *The basic tool of accounting, measuring the resources of the business and the claims to those resources: Assets = Liabilities + Owner's Equity,* 13, 13E1-6
- assets and liabilities, 13
- debit and credit, rules of, 67, 67E2-3, 68E2-4
- owners' equity, 13–14
- retained earnings, components of, 14, 14E1-7
- revenues and expenses, 70E2-7

Accounting period, 129–130

Accounting profession
- ethics in, 6–7
- governing organizations, 6, 7E1-3
- professional conduct, standards of, 7

Accounting rate of return *A measure of profitability computed by dividing the average annual operating income from an asset by the average amount invested in the asset,* 1117E25-14
- decision rule for, 1119
- investments with no residual value and, 1117–1118, 1118E22-4
- investments with residual value and, 1118–1119
- net book value of B2B and Z80 portals, 1118E22-4

Accounting ratios, 214

Accounting records, 358

Accounting, and the business environment
- accounting vocabulary, 28–29
- applying your knowledge
  - decision cases, 47–48
  - ethical issues, 48–49
  - financial statement case, 49
  - team projects, 49–50
- assessing your progress
  - exercises, 32–37
  - problems, 38–46
- business organizations, types of, 8–9, 9E1-4
- concepts and principles of, 11–12
- language of, 4–5
- major business decisions, guidelines for, 25
- profession of, 6–7
- review questions (quick check), 30–31
- summary problem, 26–27
- transactions in, 15–19
  - analysis (demo docs), 51–59
  - and financial statements used, 21–24, 22E1-9
  - evaluating, user perspective of, 19–21, 20E1-8

Accounts payable *A liability backed by the general reputation and credit standing of the debtor,* 63, 500

Accounts receivable *A promise to receive cash from customers to whom the business has sold goods or for whom the business has performed services,* 62–63, 406
- computers and, 24

Accounts receivable turnover *Measure a company's ability to collect cash from credit customers. To computer accounts receivable turnover, divide net credit sales by average net accounts receivable,* 770

Accrual accounting *Accounting that records the impact of a business event as it occurs regardless of whether the transaction affected cash,* 128
- ethical issues in, 148
- *vs.* cash-basis accounting, 128–129, 129E3-1

Accrued expense *An expense that the business has incurred but not yet paid. Also called accrued liability,* 138, 503
- accounting for, 243–244
- accruing interest income, 139
- accruing salary expense, 138–139
- adjustments, 142E3-7

Accrued liability *An expense that the business has not yet paid. Also called accrued expense,* 63, 503

Accrued revenue *A revenue that has been earned but not yet collected in cash,* 140

Accumulated depreciation *The cumulative sum of all depreciation expense recorded for an asset,* 136

Acid-test ratio *Ratio of the sum of cash plus short-term investments plus net current receivables, to total current liabilities. Tells whether the entity could pay all its current liabilities if they came due immediately. Also called the quick ratio,* 426, 767

Activity-based costing (ABC) *Focuses on activities as the fundamental cost objects. The costs of those activities become building blocks for compiling the indirect costs of products, services, and customers,* 961
- accounting vocabulary, 982
- activity-based management, using ABC for decision making, 966
  - for cutting costs, 967–969, 969E19-11
  - for pricing and product mix, 965E19-8, 966–967, 966E19-9
- applying your knowledge
  - decision cases, 1002–1003
  - ethical issue, 1003
  - team project, 1003–1005
- assessing your progress
  - exercises, 985–994
  - problems, 994–1001
- cost drivers, E19-3
- decision guidelines, 970
- refining cost systems, 960–961, 960E19-1, 961E19-2
- review questions (quick check), 983–984
- summary problems, 971–972, 981
- system of, 964–965, 965E19-7–8
  - *vs.* traditional cost system, 962–964, 963E19-5, 964E42-6
  - developing, 961, 962E19-3–4
- *see also* Just-in-time (JIT)

Activity-based management (ABM) *Using activity-based cost information to make decisions that increase profits while satisfying customers' needs,* 966
- cutting costs, 967–969, 967E19-10, 969E19-11
- pricing and product mix decisions, 966–967, 966E19-9
- *see also* Activity-based costing

Additional paid-in capital *The paid-in capital in excess of par, common plus other accounts combined for reporting on the balance sheet,* 555, 557

Adjusted trial balance *A list of all the accounts with their adjusted balances,* 145
- preparing, 145E3-10
  - demo doc, 185–195

B

J

N

O

Company Index

T

U

V

W

X

Y

Z